Bloomsbury Rooms

Bloomsbury Rooms

Modernism, Subculture, and Domesticity

Christopher Reed

Published for
The Bard Graduate Center
for Studies in the Decorative Arts,
Design, and Culture, New York
by Yale University Press
New Haven and London

Copyright © 2004 by Yale University
Art by Vanessa Bell © 1961 Estate of Vanessa Bell
Art by Duncan Grant © 1978 Estate of Duncan Grant
reproduced courtesy of Henrietta Garnett

Library of Congress Cataloging-in-Publication Data

Reed, Christopher, 1961-
Bloomsbury interiors : modernism, subculture, and the reimagination of
domesticity / by Christopher Reed.
p. cm.
(Bard studies in the decorative arts)
Includes bibliographical references and index.
ISBN 0-300-10248-8 (cl : alk. paper)
1. Bloomsbury group. 2. Arts, English--20th century. 3.
Artists--Homes and haunts--England. 4. Interior
decoration--England--History--20th century. 5. Modernism
(Aesthetics)--England. 6. Interpersonal relations--England. I. Title.
NX543 .R44 2004
747'.09421'09041--dc22

2003024676

Typeset in Ehrhardt
Designed by Kate Gallimore
Printed in Singapore

Contents

Acknowledgments

I sometimes feel that more nonsense has been said and written about Bloomsbury than any other avant-garde contingent in the history of art. Certainly a great deal of discouraging nonsense was read by and said to me during the course of this project (some of these sources meet a just reward in my notes).

All the more heartfelt, therefore, are my acknowledgments to those who helped and encouraged me. First, to Robert L. Herbert, who allowed himself to be convinced about, and then never wavered in his support for, first a dissertation on Bloomsbury art, and then for two very different books drawn from that project. I want also thank my dissertation committee, Duncan Robinson, Susan Casteras, and Lisa Tickner for their help and support.

Tickner is also prominent among those whose work has inspired me and sustained me in the belief that Bloomsbury art, and British modernism in general, reward careful, sympathetic scholarly attention. Simon Watney, too, in both his writings and his tremendous personal kindness to me at the beginning stages of this project and throughout, offered a model of intellectual acumen and warm collegiality.

Other colleagues who, over the years, have earned my sincere thanks with their suggestions and encouragement include: Mark Antliff, Becky Conekin, David Getsy, Craufurd Goodwin, Martin Hammer, Tanya Harrod, Jongwoo Kim, Christina Lodder, Robert K. Martin, Patricia McColl, Christine Poggi, Gillian Robinson, Richard Shiff, Richard Shone, Frances Spalding, Nancy Troy, and Douglas Turnbaugh. Many of those just named also helped with the enormous logistical project of gathering illustrative material for this book. Others who have earned my deep gratitude in that project are: Tony Bradshaw, Susan Cloud, David Cottington, Lynda Morris, Patricia Phagan, and Richard Morphet. I am also grateful to Annabel Cole and Henrietta Garnett for permissions to reproduce images and hitherto unpublished quotations by Roger Fry, Vanessa Bell, and Duncan Grant.

I am also thankful to the staffs of all the libraries I consulted in researching this book, but I want especially to acknowledge the extraordinary helpfulness of everyone at the Tate Gallery Archives; Jaqueline Cox, formerly of the Modern Archive Centre at King's College; and Russell Maylone of Northwestern University. I want also to thank my generous and patient collaborators at Yale University Press, Sally Salvesen, Emily Winter, and Kate Gallimore. For help preparing the manuscript, I am also grateful to Becca Shrier and Deborah Cox. I expect readers will share my gratitude toward the Bard Graduate Center for Studies in the Decorative Arts, Design, and Culture, for its generous support of this project as part of its publication programme.

Much needed time to concentrate on this project was provided by generous grants in the forms of a University of Pennsylvania Mellon Fellowship in the Humanities, a J. Paul Getty Postdoctoral Fellowship, a sabbatical and research subvention from Lake Forest College, and the Dorothy K. Hohenberg Chair of Excellence in Art History at the University of Memphis. I want also to thank, for creating and sustaining an ideal work environment, my truly collegial colleagues in the Art Department at Lake Forest: Amy Cuthbert, Tom Denlinger, Rebecaa Goldberg, Karen Lebergott, Fran Pacheco, and Ann Roberts.

My deepest debts intellectually and emotionally are to my family: my parents, Gervais and Mary Katherine Reed, and the one with whom I have re-imagined domesticity, Chris Castiglia. This book is dedicated to them.

Introduction

Heroism and Housework
Competing Ideas of the Modern

Making Modernism

In 1929, Dorothy Todd, recent editor of English *Vogue* and future translator of Le Corbusier, collaborated with Raymond Mortimer, friend and patron of the Bloomsbury artists, on a book that brought the latest in interior design before the English public.[1] Their collaboration was more additive than synthetic, however, for although *The New Interior Decoration* presents itself as a single text, it speaks with two distinct voices. One praises the high-tech look of International Style design, quoting Le Corbusier to locate the inspiration for an appropriately modern style in the new machines of the twentieth century, while the other observes that Corbusian rooms "seem intended for Robots, rather than human beings." The first voice celebrates mass-production and standardized housing, insisting "uniformity is not only an economy but a beauty," while the second posits domestic design as a refuge from mass-production and standardization, promoting the home as the "last refuge" of "that individuality which modern conditions are suppressing in our public life." The first voice, asserting that "the only vital architecture . . . should clearly result from a scientific approach," prescribes big windows and flat surfaces because "the extreme importance of light for the preservation of health has been discovered by scientists" and "our increased knowledge of the dangers of dust has resulted in an ever-increasing distaste for unnecessary objects which collect it." The second voice favors designs that "depend for their success to a far larger extent upon individual taste than upon any logical principles." Where the first voice defines gracefulness as "an elimination of the unnecessary" and suggests that the householder begin redecoration by covering or removing "every touch of existing ornament," including moldings, mantels, railings, and window frames; the second voice praises eclectic decorating schemes that combine "modern French pictures, eighteenth-century French furniture, a Georgian mantelpiece and decorations by contemporary English painters."[2]

The schizophrenia of *The New Interior Decoration* can be attributed to its dual authorship. Todd articulates what became modernism's standard rationales and her illustrations cover the canon of modernist design, from Le Corbusier's Maison Laroche to the Breuer chair. Mortimer proposes a less familiar version of modernism, and prominent among his illustrations are carpets, curtains, ceramics, furniture, and murals designed by the artists of the Bloomsbury group: Vanessa Bell, Roger Fry, and Duncan Grant. Although Todd and Mortimer, in their claim to present *the* new interior decoration, ignore the schism dividing Corbusian from Bloomsbury domestic design, what is most striking about this book today is how different Bloomsbury's interiors are from the aesthetic that, as *The New Interior Decoration* went to press, was poised to become the definitive look of the modern. When, in 1932, the Museum of Modern Art's exhibition, *The International Style*, charted the boundaries of modernist design, the fanciful eclecticism of the Bloomsbury artists was cast beyond the pale.[3] It was an exile that would last half a century.

Bloomsbury's exclusion from the modernist mainstream was part of broader trends as, around 1930, the multiplicity of self-styled modernist movements was narrowed to the few that could be sequenced to culminate in the International Style.[4] This process included both fine and decorative art: the famous flow-chart that the Museum of Modern Art published in 1936 to explain modernism showed its diverse sources funneling into two movements of abstract art, "geometrical" and "non-geometrical," and just one design style, called simply "modern."[5] Though contested at every step, by the boom years after World War II this logic emerged victorious: high-tech design and abstract art became the look of modernity. Ironically, it has been noted, this idea of modernism was finally cemented by the emergence of "postmodernism," which ceded the rubric of modernism to this canon by claiming alternatives as part of a new movement, even though this meant citing some modern artists like Marcel Duchamp, rather awkwardly, as pre-postmodernists.[6] A study of Bloomsbury's artists, too, might emphasize—especially in their work of the 1920s and '30s—their parallels with postmodernism's play with historical pastiche, as they seem to anticipate postmodernist architect Robert Venturi's famous rejection of "heroic and original" design in favor of the "decorated shed."[7] But to accept the anachronism of inviting Bloomsbury's artists into a movement that post-dates them sacrifices the more radically revisionary project of challenging accepted definitions of modernism and constructions of its history with evidence of the wide range of people and practices that once had a claim to be considered "modern." Such revisionary histories reveal modernism's development, not as an inevitable evolution, but as a sequence of choices within what has been evocatively described as "a cascade of oppositions," including functional/ornamental, pictorial/decorative, "engineer/leisure class, reality principle/pleasure principle, production/consumption, active/passive, masculine/feminine, machine/body, west/east."[8] To this list of overlapping dyads, I would add heroism/housework.

Domesticity and Modernism

A definitive feature of modernism, it has been argued, is the invention of the "avant-garde," a term drawn from military theory that asserts ideals of art as onslaught and of the artist as hero.[9] Exploiting the Odyssean contrast of heroic mission with domestic stasis, the modernist avant-garde positioned itself in opposition to the home. The anti-domestic tendency of mainstream modernism is encapsulated in the writings of Le Corbusier, whose influential *Towards a New Architecture* inveighs against the "sentimental hysteria" surrounding the old-fashioned "cult of the house." Le Corbusier conjures the heroic figures of the "healthy and virile" engineer and the "big business men, bankers, and merchants" for whom "economic law reigns supreme, and mathematical exactness is joined to daring and imagination." The virility of these latter-day heroes is endangered by "unworthy houses," however, which, Le Corbusier says, "ruin our health and our *morale*":

> One can see these same business men, bankers and merchants away from their businesses in their own homes, where everything seems to contradict their real existence—rooms too small, a conglomeration of useless and disparate objects. . . styles of all sorts and absurd bric-à-brac. Our industrial friends seem sheepish and shrivelled like tigers in a cage.

With the rallying cry, "We claim in the name of the steamship, of the airplane, and of the motor-car, the right to health, logic, daring, harmony, perfection," Le Corbusier stakes his claims for modernity on the rejection of domesticity. These words were matched by a stylistic rhetoric that enacts the hero's victory over the home by replacing the signifiers of traditional domesticity with a mechanical aesthetic expressive of his now-famous dictum, "the house is a machine for living in." Even the "Modulor," the basic unit of Le Corbusier's ideal proportions, is "the height of a man" standardized at 1.83 meters (6 feet).[10] The figure of the hero—the engineer, the ideal man—is thus materialized in the style and proportions of the modernist dwelling, which becomes a kind of anti-home.

A heroic ideal, guaranteed through the suppression of domesticity, defined not just design but also avant-garde art at mid-century. In 1939, Clement Greenberg famously contrasted the avant-garde to "kitsch," a term he identified with the decoration of middle-class homes, and throughout his influential writings imputations of domesticity are signs of failure.[11] Greenberg complains, for instance, that some of Robert Motherwell's paintings achieved an "archness like that of the interior decorator who stakes everything on a happy placing," and dismisses de Chirico's late work with the phrase, "It was not even easel painting; it was elementary interior decoration."[12] A well-known essay on Cézanne ends in anxiety over the domestic comforts enjoyed by the progenitor of cubism, finally concluding that his "was a more heroic artist's life than Gauguin's or Van Gogh's, for all its material ease."[13] Greenberg worried, too, about artists who experimented with the methods and materials of home decoration. Attempting to prove "[h]ow little a decorator Matisse is by instinct," Greenberg insists: "His paper cut-outs, his ventures into applied art, and most of what I have seen of his tapestry designs, book decorations, and even murals seem to me the feeblest of the things he has done. He is an easel painter from first to last."[14]

Like Greenberg, avant-garde artists seized on the opposition between heroism and housework to promote their art. The Abstract Expressionists repeatedly invoked the heroic in the titling and iconography of their work: Barnett Newman's massive painting, *Vir Heroicus Sublimus*, is just the most obvious example.[15] And again, heroic achievement was constituted through the suppression of the domestic. Adolph Gottlieb and Mark Rothko announced in the *New York Times* in 1943 that their art "must insult anyone who is spiritually attuned to interior decoration; pictures for the home; pictures for over the mantel. . . ."[16] Motherwell, perhaps compensating for Greenberg's strictures, dismissed the influence of the critic's theories, to create his own narrative of a post-war American art led by painters ("artists don't respond to critics, critics respond to artists") pushing the size of their canvases: "The large format, at one blow, destroyed the century-long tendency of the French to domesticize modern painting, to make it intimate," Motherwell asserted in one interview, emphasizing the heroism implied in this claim with, "Brother! What a gesture! Perhaps, someday, when we no longer threaten our contemporaries, someone will write our Iliad with empathy. One of the great images, like Achilles' shield, should be the house-painter's brush."[17]

Such rhetoric in post-war American modernism perpetuated the binary of heroic progress versus domestic stasis that had animated Le Corbusier's writings of the 1920s. But these ideas were formulated earlier. Like so much in modernism, the anti-domestic definition of the avant-garde arose in the turbulent years before World War I, when various would-be avant-garde contingents competed to define the look of the modern. In France, the status of domesticity may be measured in the declining fortunes of the term *décoratif*, which was embraced by Impressionists like Monet and Nabis like Gauguin, only to be rejected by the cubists.[18] Gauguin's art, for instance, was praised for its "decorative deformations" by the painter and critic Maurice Denis, who in 1909 asserted:

Here we are dealing with a decorator . . . ! He who at Pouldu decorated the hall of his inn as well as his gourd and clogs! He who, in Tahiti, despite anxieties, sickness, and misery, cared above all for the decoration of his hut.[19]

By 1912, Albert Gleizes and Jean Metzinger's *Du Cubisme* announced, "we ought to regard a preoccupation for decoration, if we find it in a painter, as an anachronistic artifice, useful only to conceal impotence."[20] Likewise, in Germany, influential critics such as Julius Meier-Graefe and Karl Scheffler during the first decade of the twentieth century switched from celebrating the links between abstract art and applied decoration to policing the border between them.[21] In England, the chief competitors for avant-garde status were the Bloomsbury artists and the Vorticists, led by the painter Wyndham Lewis, and their struggle, too, played out over the issue of domesticity.

Modernism in England

Domesticity was a potent issue in England in the first decades of the twentieth century, for the previous generation of artists had made the home the central arena of aesthetic and social reform. While Europe looked to France for new movements in painting at the turn of the century, England was the primary source of new ideas about design. And both Aestheticism and the Arts and Crafts movement, twin strands of the Victorian avant-garde, focused on the look of daily life. Where the Arts-and-Craftsers proposed a return to the guild-like production of handcrafted objects, the Aesthetes cultivated complementary notions of careful consumption of fewer, better things.[22] Writings by influential English critics, from John Ruskin and William Morris to Oscar Wilde, along with illustrations of interiors exemplifying their ideas, flooded art and design journals around the world, inspiring designers and influencing the deployment of terms like "decorative." Roger Fry, who was older than his Bloomsbury colleagues, was deeply enmeshed in the late-Victorian avant-garde, and Bloomsbury's rhetoric—both verbal and visual—draws heavily on that precedent.[23] When Wyndham Lewis tarred his rivals with accusations of domesticity, therefore, his implication was that they were both provincial and old-fashioned in contrast to the Vorticists with their ties to the Italian Futurists.[24]

Lewis's manifestos of 1913–14 trade heavily on the opposition between heroism and housework (along with several other of modernism's constitutive binaries, especially masculine/feminine).[25] His public letter severing connections to Bloomsbury complained of the group: "The Idol is still Prettiness, with its mid-Victorian languish of the neck, and its skin is 'greenery-yallery.'" Attempting to justify his brief association with his rivals, Lewis claimed, "This party of strayed and Dissenting Aesthetes were compelled to call in as much modern talent as they could find, to do the rough and masculine work without which they knew their efforts would not rise above the level of a pleasant tea party."[26] Publicizing his short-lived Rebel Artists Centre a few months later, Lewis anticipated Le Corbusier in appealing to the "modern city man," who "in his office . . . is probably a very fine fellow—very alert, combative, and capable of straight, hard thinking," but in his "villa in the suburbs" is reduced to "an invalid bag of mediocre nerves, a silly child." To promote his hard-edged abstract paintings, Lewis insisted, "The best type of artist would rather give expression to the more energetic part of that City man's life—do pictures to put in his office, where he is most alive—than manufacture sentimental and lazy images . . . for his wretched vegetable home existence."[27]

Bloomsbury's Domestic Modernism

Promoting his own practice over that of his rivals, Lewis correctly identified the essence of Bloomsbury's art in its relation to domesticity. For this group—named for the London neighborhood where its members lived—modernism was not conceived as heroic quest. On the contrary, skepticism about heroic ideology is explicit in the writings of Virginia Woolf, Bloomsbury's best known figure, whose early memoirs argue that she and her sister, Vanessa Bell, were vulnerable to the sexual predations of their older half-brother because their upbringing prompted them "to impose our conventional heroic shape upon the tumult of his character." Woolf's last memoir returns to the insidious effects of cultural norms that rationalize and even celebrate male aggression as a talisman of creativity, analyzing the ways her father imbibed "the convention . . . that men of genius were naturally uncontrolled." "Ill to live with" is the domestically oriented phrase she chooses to characterize his behavior:

It never struck my father, I believe, that there was any harm in being ill to live with. I think he said unconsciously as he worked himself up into one of those violent outbursts, "This is a sign of my genius," and he . . . let himself fly. It was part of the convention that after these outbursts, the man of genius became "touchingly apologetic"; but he took it for granted that his wife or sister would accept his apology.[28]

In contrast to this description of her father, Woolf, in a 1931 speech to a women's group, praised the men in her circle, "who have triumphed over all the difficulties of their very lopsided education . . . men of generous and wide humanity . . . men with whom a woman can live in perfect freedom, without any fear." Extending her antagonism to heroism from life to art, Woolf asserted, "I doubt that a writer can be a hero. I doubt that a hero can be writer. . . . the moment I become heroic, I become shrill and hard and positive."[29] A quarter-century earlier, Vanessa Bell had proposed a similar anti-heroic standard in a letter analyzing her sister's character. Speculating about "the domestic strain in you," Bell concluded, "Perhaps it's the sign of real genius. If you were only very clever you wouldn't care for such things."[30] By inverting the assumption that modern art and design should accommodate the home to new conditions generated by science and technology, Bloomsbury made the conditions of domesticity its standard for modernity, projecting the values of home life outward onto the public realm in both its aesthetic and socio-political initiatives.

This book focuses on the aesthetic, tracing the development of Bloomsbury's artwork and interiors from projects created by the artists before the coalescence of the group, through their establishment of the Omega Workshops (an atelier for the production of household goods) to their collaborative decorative works of the 1920s and 1930s. This approach reverses the usual priorities of art history, which have made the notion of avant-garde domesticity an oxymoron, in the process removing Bloomsbury's paintings from the canon of modernism and refusing to consider the murals, ceramics, textiles, and wallpapers as art at all. In proffering the full range of Bloomsbury's visual output as a subject of study, I am, of necessity, challenging some prevailing assumptions of art history and engaging a debate with ramifications far beyond the specifics of Bloomsbury, for anti-domestic rhetorics continue to function to enforce definitions of artistic accomplishment. In 1983, for example, when a reviewer complained that a London exhibition on cubism included too much work by artists other than Picasso and Braque—thus challenging his vision of this movement as the product of two isolated, heroic pioneers—he blamed the influence of Roger Fry and Bloomsbury fifty years before:

> Fry's enthusiasm, shared by many of his Bloomsbury friends, was largely reserved for the more decorative aspects of Cubism. These he eagerly adopted as design elements in the furniture and textiles produced by the Omega Workshops he organized in 1913. Yet far from advancing any real understanding of the Cubist aesthetic, this cozy, decorative use of its more superficial devices only served to blur its artistic importance. The Omega style—so typically Bloomsbury in the way it diluted and distorted modernism in the interests of aesthetic sociability—made Cubism look homey and insipid.[31]

The persistence of an anti-domestic critical standard is clear here, as the cozy and decorative are equated with the superficial and unimportant, the homey is necessarily insipid, and modernism is seen as incompatible with sociability. It is hard work breaking through this ideology, which through constant reassertion has come to seem self-evident. It is necessary work, however, if we are to understand Bloomsbury in anything like its own terms—necessary, that is, if we are to understand the group's rejection of heroism and its adherence to the domestic ideals I characterize with the term "housework." This is the primary purpose of this book: to present an analysis of the Bloomsbury artists responsive to their own values.

Domesticity and Bloomsbury's Group Identity

Even with this new critical stance, however, my account of the Bloomsbury artists is not a simple story of goals set and achieved in a movement outside mainstream modernism. On the contrary, the history of the Bloomsbury artists exemplifies the complexity of counter-hegemonic movements, which are never completely outside the mainstream cultural forms they challenge, but co-exist in a more complicated—less heroic—dynamic strongly inflected by the dominant culture's efforts to neutralize challenges to its authority. Two basic strategies of that neutralizing force can be described as alienation and co-option, and the effects of both continue, in crucial ways, to condition perceptions of Bloomsbury. Alienation has the effect of reifying the identity of deviant groups (a process Michel Foucault has analyzed in relation to criminality, madness, and sexuality[32]), while co-option distorts the past in order to incorporate the group into consensus-driven historical narratives. Bloomsbury might be a case study in the result: a powerful minority identity that is widely misunderstood.

One of the most remarkable characteristics of Bloomsbury was the strength of its identity as a group. Where other avant-garde coalitions rapidly formed and dissolved, Bloomsbury stuck together, its members collaborating on books and artwork, corresponding, traveling and cohabiting from around 1910 for the rest of their often very long lives (Duncan Grant, the last of the group's original members, lived until 1978). This cohesion has subsequently been both vilified as an insidious plot to dominate British culture and romanticized as an escapist fantasy of leisure and comfort. Both these myths, however, ignore the origins of Bloomsbury's cohesiveness in its members' alienation from the culture into which they were born, an alienation they often described as a sense of exclusion from a suitable form of domesticity.

This yearning for an appropriate home is registered in Bloomsbury's ideal of "a room of one's own." The phrase, of course, is the title of Virginia Woolf's well-known essay of 1929, which described women's oppression under patriarchy in terms of denied private space. It also echoes a passage from a letter Lytton Strachey wrote to Duncan Grant in 1909:

> Good God! to have a room of one's own with a real fire and books and tea and company, and no dinner bells and distractions, and a little time for doing something! It's a wonderful vision, and surely worth some risks.[33]

Four years earlier, Strachey had expressed his sense of alienation with the cry, "I feel desperately homesick—but for what home?"[34] E. M. Forster claimed that a crucial source of his personality was the fact, as he put it, "that I have been deprived of a house." In a talk prepared for his Bloomsbury friends, Forster described how he and his mother were evicted from their home when he was fourteen, concluding, "If I had been allowed to stop on there I should have become a different person, married, and fought in the war."[35] Here Forster attributes the attitudes that allied him with Bloomsbury to his exclusion from the childhood home that appears in his 1910 novel, *Howards End*, where it mystically confers on its inhabitants the ability to resist patriarchal norms and the violence used to enforce them. Far from simply nostalgic, *Howards End* roots a utopian vision of "a new life, obscure, yet gilded with tranquility" in the values of domesticity.[36] Investing the home with the power to connote—and even to create—new ways of life, Forster encapsulates Bloomsbury's ideal. Forster's vision of utopia—a rural idyll that allows for intellectual and sensual fulfillment indifferent to patriarchal norms (and is less successful in resolving class disparities)—uncannily predicts the most definitive aspects of Bloomsbury's lifestyle.

Like the group's writers, Bloomsbury's painters imagined an alternative domesticity in response to a condition of homelessness, though they arrived at this shared attitude by different routes. Roger Fry was turned from the mold of domestic normality by his wife's illness, which by 1910 left her mentally incapacitated and made him the single parent of two children, desiring female companionship yet ineligible for remarriage. Vanessa Bell rejected notions of home and family that required her professional aspirations to be subordinated—and her sexual experience limited—to her husband. And Duncan Grant found that the prevailing norms of domesticity had no place for the fulfillment of his homoerotic desire.[37] Deprived of that prerequisite of the heroic paradigm—a home to leave behind—Bloomsbury's artists dedicated themselves, individually and collectively, to creating the conditions of domesticity outside mainstream definitions of home and family. This emphasis on domesticity was more than a gambit in the rhetorics of avant-garde one-upmanship.[38] The following chapters trace these artists' efforts to create domestic environments appropriate to their aspirations for new ways of life. Here it is enough simply to emphasize the roots of Bloomsbury's group identity in a shared sense of exclusion from traditional domesticity, and to suggest the extent to which that alienation grounded a collective identity strong enough to sustain its members' participation in activist initiatives—sexual, aesthetic, and political—bitterly resisted by the dominant culture.

Aesthetics and Activism in Bloomsbury

To acknowledge this record of activism is to challenge misrepresentations of Bloomsbury as isolated and apolitical by recalling, for instance, that the book Clive Bell wrote after his well known *Art* of 1914 was the almost unknown *Peace at Once* of 1915, which was deemed so subversive that the authorities had it confiscated and destroyed (as discussed in Chapter 10). Amid the idyllic pictures of the restored Charleston farmhouse that today appear in travel and design magazines, it is easy to forget that when Bloomsbury's members took over this dilapidated rural outpost it was without electricity, running water, or heating, and they were under threat of imprisonment for refusing military service. Running as a counterpoint in the careers of those in Bloomsbury whose primary professional commitment was to the arts is a record of engagement in political activities: organizations joined, meetings attended, posters designed, envelopes stuffed, appeals answered, contributions made.[39]

Beyond such evidence of political consciousness among Bloomsbury's artists and art critics is the constitution of the group as a whole. Far from being just an artists' colony, Bloomsbury was a center of political activism. All of the group's creative artists, in fact, shared homes with political activists: Virginia Woolf, herself the author of several important feminist tracts, lived with Leonard, a director of the *New Statesman* and an official of the Labour Party. Grant and the Bells shared Charleston with John Maynard Keynes, who wrote *The Economic Consequences of the Peace* there, and with the Bells' son, Julian, who was deeply committed to left-wing politics and died driving an ambulance for the anti-Fascist volunteers in Spain. Roger Fry shared his home with his sister, Margery, a prominent penal reformer and advocate for women's education.[40] In short, if there is any truth to the stereotype of Bloomsbury aesthetes painting and writing behind high walls, it is that in the rooms next door political articles were being written, speeches rehearsed, and meetings held.

Bloomsbury's politics were not just concurrent with the group's art, but animated by the same values. Leonard Woolf's angry and activist *Barbarians at the Gate* and Clive Bell's complacent rumination over the conditions of an aesthete's life, *Civilization*—to take examples from opposite ends of Bloomsbury's political spectrum—both propose social ideals conceived in terms of values the group associated with domesticity: leisure, comfort, the privacy that protects diversity, and the pleasures of intellectual conversation and artistic creativity. In *Civilization* Bell describes his social ideal as:

> a taste for truth and beauty, tolerance, intellectual honesty, fastidiousness, a sense of humour, good manners, curiosity, a dislike of vulgarity, brutality, and over-emphasis, freedom from superstition and prudery, a fearless acceptance of the good things in life.

Here even values not usually associated with home life are given a domestic cast, as Bell defines "tolerance" with a quotation from Pericles that presents difference in terms of the daily life of neighbors: "we tolerate peculiarities of all sorts in each other's daily lives: we have no objection to our neighbor following the bent of his humour."[41] Woolf's 1939 *Barbarians at the Gate* is in many ways a riposte from within Bloomsbury to *Civilization*, challenging Bell's complacency over the exclusion of the less privileged classes from his ideal and worrying over the threat of Fascism. But when Woolf enumerates his conditions of civilization, the list, though not identical, registers many of the same values: "freedom, democracy, equality, justice, liberty, tolerance"—which he defines with the same quotation from Pericles—"and a love of truth, beauty, art, and intellect."[42] In his political writings of the 1930s, Woolf juxtaposed this ideal against not only the violent megalomania of Hitler and Stalin but also the authoritarian tendencies in modern thought he believed lent credence to Fascism, a heritage he traced from Kant through Hegel to Carlyle and Nietzsche, and then to Spengler and Bergson.[43] He might well have added Wyndham Lewis, whose writings of the Thirties celebrated Fascism in general and Hitler in particular.[44] Even in an era that styles itself as postmodern and is accustomed to critiques of modernism, the scope of Woolf's attack on the pillars of modernist philosophy is a testament to Bloomsbury's distance from the dominant culture of its day. For art historians today to dismiss Bloomsbury for not keeping up with the modernist mainstream is to ignore both the causes and the implications of the alienation that was central to the group's identity. Attention to Bloomsbury's commonly misunderstood social and political ideals, moreover, opens up fundamental flaws in mainstream modernism's construction of its own history.

Bloomsbury Aesthetics and Mainstream Modernism

Despite Bloomsbury's alienation from mainstream modernism, the group was hardly without influence on the canon. Ironically, it seems that the farther Bloomsbury's actual practice of art and design deviated from the accepted look of the modern, the more the theories grounding that practice were cited as central to modernist aesthetics. Just as the flow-chart model of modernism misreads Ruskin and Morris to present Bauhaus design and International Style architecture as fulfilling their ideals, Clive Bell and Roger Fry are widely cited to justify the American formalism in the second half of the century, which was inimical to their values.[45] Like Duchamp, then, Bloomsbury's aestheticians are in a historically anomalous position: important actors in some of modernism's defining episodes, yet at odds with the ideologies that came to define the modernist standard.[46] Mainstream modernism took two important ideas from Bloomsbury aesthetics: first, the doctrine of "Significant Form" (that abstract form has significance independent of subject matter); and second, the related belief in the autonomy of art (the proposition that, as Fry put it in a famous essay, "Art and Life," "the usual assumption of a direct and decisive connection between art and life is by no means correct. . . . [W]e find the rhythmic sequences of change determined much more by [art's] own internal forces—and by the readjustment within it, of its own elements—than by external forces").[47] To return to the original articulation of these ideas is to find that both have been misunderstood.

To begin with the autonomy of art, what Fry called the separation of art from life: this was interpreted by later modernists to mean that art—and its study—are distinct from the cultural forces that structure its creation, dissemination, and reception. Virginia Woolf may have been the first to challenge this reading, noting that Fry's argument in this 1917 lecture explicitly addresses its wartime context, as he scrambled to refute claims that a "great" art would necessarily arise out of the experience of the Great War and to salvage some hope for his own, less bombastic, modernist ideals. This essay "helps to explain how it was that he survived the war," Woolf explains, pointing out that the tenor of Fry's argument is contradicted, not only by his other writings, but most strikingly by his own life, in which he struggled to achieve the same kind of objective "detachment" he aspired to in the contemplation of art. For Fry, Woolf argues:

It seems as if the aesthetic theory were brought to bear upon the problems of private life. Detachment, as he insisted over and over again, is the supreme necessity for the artist. Was it not equally necessary if the private life were to continue? That rhythm could only grow and expand if it were detached from the deformation which is possession. To live fully . . . could only be done by asking nothing for oneself. It was difficult to put that teaching into practice. Yet in his private life he had during those difficult years forced himself to learn that lesson.[48]

An aesthetic ideal of selfless objectivity, renouncing impulses to possess or control, was what Fry meant by his constant exhortations to "disinterested" or "detached" vision; this he distinguished explicitly from the consumer's possessive gaze that registers, for instance, "the minute visual characteristics that distinguish margarine from butter."[49] In a socio-political order structured around aggression and acquisition, this insistence on the aesthetic as a separate realm is not apolitical. On the contrary, it may be seen as another form of wartime "conscientious objection," deployed not just in response to military conscription but also against capitalist imperatives to commercialize all aspects of experience. Bloomsbury's consistent valorization of the "amateur"—a term often turned against the group by its critics—is another way of articulating this ideal.[50]

Similarly, Bloomsbury's doctrine of significant form later acquired very different connotations than those it held for its originators. As Clive Bell explained the term in *Art*, "lines and colours combined in a particular way, certain forms and relations of forms, stir our aesthetic emotions."[51] In the flow-chart model of modernism, what is important about this claim is that it justifies abstract art, an implication Bloomsbury found of only slight and passing interest (see Chapter 9). What was important for Bloomsbury in this idea was that it rooted aesthetics in individual experience, overriding authoritative hierarchies of artistic technique (time-consuming and expensive) and subject matter (morally uplifting), which reinforced dominant cultural values. Formalism let Bloomsbury supplant such criteria of quality generated in the public sphere with standards that trumped appeals to morality or tradition by claiming as their proof and justification the viewer's emotions before the work of art. "The starting point for all systems of aesthetics must be the personal experience of a peculiar emotion," Bell insisted in *Art*, and he made this "aesthetic emotion" the guarantor of significant form.[52]

Fry's review of *Art* records his excitement over the way ideas of significant form allowed Bell to "walk into the holy of holies of culture in knickerbockers with a big walking-stick in his hand, and just knock one head off after another."[53] Emphasizing these implications of Bloomsbury's aesthetic theory, a war-time exhibition catalog written by Fry instructs viewers of modern art to "allow your sense to have full play, dwell as long as possible in the contemplation of colour and form . . . and discover by this process what happens to you. If no pleasure or emotional excitement follows from this process, the picture is a failure, for you at all events."[54] This relativism in relation to modern art Fry extended to art history, writing:

> Qua object the picture or statue is so much matter of no particular consequence or value. To become a work of art it requires to react upon someone's sensibility in such a way as to produce a particular kind of spiritual experience. For it to have any value a work of art must produce this effect on some person. . . . If that transaction does not take place the work of art is for the time being dead matter. . . . Each generation has to remake the old masters or they too die until someone comes along who can renew the transaction.[55]

Perhaps the most striking deployment of formalist criteria to override conventional systems of judgements may be found in Bloomsbury's private correspondence, however. Writing to Grant about a visit she and Clive paid to his former lover, Vanessa Bell reported that when the two women were alone together:

> she wanted to go to the po [chamber pot] . . . and her skirt was too tight to do it in the ordinary way and she got into the most extraordinary attitude, something like this [here a sketch is provided]. . . . It would have been a very good thing to paint,

as her legs somehow made a very good design and her blouse was bright yellow, carried out by the other yellow touches.[56]

The determination evident here to use individual experience of formal pleasure to validate what conventional social and aesthetic standards would deplore exemplifies Bloomsbury's connection of modern art and modern life.

In Defense of Individualism

In privileging individual experience over dominant cultural values, Bloomsbury's aesthetics are contiguous with its politics. Clive Bell, for instance, invoked individual experience to counter authoritative rationales for war. "I want to reduce such phrases as 'National Honour,' 'National Existence,' 'National Interests,' 'National Independence,' to terms of men, women, and children," Bell wrote in his suppressed *Peace at Once*:

> Instead of talking about English "interests" and "prestige," "balance of power," "international obligations," "German hegemony," "natural frontiers," "national aspirations," "eternal disgrace," let us try to think about something quite real, James Smith, a gardener, his wife and three children. . . . Let us think, if we can, of Smith—his life and death, hunger and thirst, health and sickness, wants, appetites, and amusements, of his prestige too, and his eternal disgrace.

Demanding that readers weigh the risks of war against the risks of foreign domination for the average person, Bell asks:

> Does the ordinary artisan willingly sacrifice all hope of a finer, freer, and more spacious life lest he should be compelled to pay rent and taxes in marks instead of shillings? Would he rather kill and die than have his children taught in German? Is it so grand a satisfaction that the hooter which hoots him to work hoots for the benefit of Sir Josiah Fleshman instead of that of Herr Julius Fleishmann?[57]

Cast in terms of individual lives, such questions have the potential to undermine all manner of political abstractions.

Deploying an analogous standard of individual experience, Bell's aesthetic theory dismissed canons based on sanctioned subject matter, ruling the moralizing narratives of Royal Academy painters outside the topic of *Art*—and thus the realm of art—altogether. Instead, anti-authoritarianism grounded in individual subjectivity emerges as Bell's definition of modernism. Explaining how twentieth-century painting differs from that of the aristocrat-sponsored academies of the preceding two centuries, Bell distinguished between "order", which arises from the individual, and a coercive exterior "authority":

> order imposed by the artist's inmost sense of what a work of art should be, is something altogether different from the order obtained by submission to a theory of painting. One springs from a personal conviction; the other is enjoined by authority. Modern artists tend to feel strongly the necessity for the former.

Tying this distinction to the art most prototypically modern, Bell defined cubism as "nothing but the extreme manifestation of the passion for order."[58] This passage reiterates the claim of Bell's catalog essay introducing his selection of English painters for the Second Post-Impressionist Exhibition: "These artists are of the movement because, in choice of subject, they recognize no authority but the truth that is in them; in choice of form, none but the need of expressing it. That is Post-Impressionism."[59]

For Bell, the triumph of individual order over conventional authority is evidenced in an iconographic shift away from traditional heroic subjects—his example is an execution scene—in favor of an art that begins by looking "at objects (the contents of a room, for instance)."[60] This argument was taken up by Fry in an unpublished lecture that describes a "tendency of the human spirit" to evolve from concern with "the exceptional" to fascination with "the familiar, normal, commonplace things of life," a progression that culminates with modernism. Fry traces this trajectory in literature, beginning with the transition "from the myth to the heroic story":

> Then comes the stage when [the protagonist] is more probable but still has very unusual and exciting circumstances, and finally the so-called hero (for the name still sticks) becomes a very credible, perhaps not altogether creditable or praiseworthy individual, he is just a man or woman like Pendennis in Thackeray or Madame Bovary in Flaubert.[61]

Fry concludes his history with Proust, who "begins his great series of novels with ten pages of description of waking up in the morning, an everyday experience which no one had ever before examined with a view to finding out what extraordinary possibilities of imaginative beauty it might conceal." Citing Proust may be seen as Fry's way of invoking a novelist nearer at hand, however. Bloomsbury was well aware of its own pre-eminent novelist's Proustian qualities, and a similar equation of domesticity with individuality is implied in Virginia Woolf's own essays on modern fiction.[62] Condemning those who betray "the form of the novel" by using it "to preach doctrines, sing songs, or celebrate the glories of the British Empire," Woolf urges the modern novelist to turn to the quotidian. "Examine for a moment an ordinary mind on an ordinary day," she writes, invoking for the first time "the life of Monday or Tuesday," a phrase that would reappear as the title of her first book of short stories.[63]

Woolf's new art of individual experience was linked to a broad range of initiatives that, taken together with the beginning of a new century, defined modernism for Bloomsbury both politically and aesthetically. Leonard Woolf's memoirs recall "the profound revolution of Cézanne, Matisse, and Picasso" as part of his sense—in retrospect, he realized, naive—that in the years before World War I, "it looked for a moment as if militarism, imperialism, and antisemitism were on the run."[64] In 1917, Roger Fry, lecturing on "Applied Art and the New Movement," allied modernist aesthetics to egalitarian class politics. Fry attributed "the violent opposition to all creative ideas of the cultured classes" to the fact that:

> the cultured have had leisure and time to acquire a knowledge of and familiarity with the art of all periods, and this knowledge is a social asset. So that to *know* the difference between Louis XV and Louis XVI furniture is one of the easily distinguished marks of a lady or gentleman—even more so in America than here.

In contrast to knowledge premised on class status, Fry argued, sensibility to abstract form was innate and, therefore, created its own meritocracy: "though it can be cultivated [it] is a grace—a grace that one's sculley [slang for scullery maid] may have in greater degree than oneself."[65] Like Leonard Woolf, Fry later saw such beliefs as naive; when he revised this passage for his first anthology, he admitted that "Matisse has become a safe investment for persons of taste."[66] But the desire to ground modernism in anti-authoritarian individualism was fundamental to Bloomsbury. Woolf's memoirs describe the group's philosophy as "refusing to swallow anything or anyone on the mere 'authority' of anyone."[67] John Maynard Keynes's autobiographical essay "My Early Beliefs" fleshed out the group's ethos, which he said was "for the outer world . . . our most obvious and dangerous characteristic":

> We repudiated entirely customary morals, conventions, and traditional wisdoms. We were, that is to say, in the strict sense of the term immoralists . . . we recognized no moral obligation on us, no inner sanction, to conform or obey. Before heaven we claimed to be our own judge in our own case.[68]

Keynes's conclusion, "I remain, and always will remain, an immoralist," is only slightly less strident than Forster's famous assertion of individual prerogative over authoritative abstractions: "If I had to choose between betraying my country and betraying my friend, I hope I should have the guts to betray my country."[69] The coherence of Bloomsbury's aesthetic and social values may be clearest in Virginia Woolf's angry rebuttal of the assumption that Fry's aesthetics were apolitical: "Didn't he spend half his life, not in a tower, but traveling about England addressing masses of people, who'd never looked at a picture and making them see what he saw. And wasn't that the best way of checking Nazism?" she demanded.[70]

For Bloomsbury, to be modern was to challenge the authoritative institutions of the old order, an attitude it shared with other avant-garde contingents. But the nature of Bloomsbury's resistance was different and lies at the heart of the group's contested place in the history of modernism. A fundamental belief in individuality led Bloomsbury to reject modernist ideologies that subordinate individual subjectivity to deterministic systems—those, for example, Keynes airily dismissed as "Freud cum Marx," and those of Le Corbusier, who proclaimed as the basis of his design:

> All men have the same organism, the same functions.
> All men have the same needs.[71]

Like Bloomsbury, these rival schools of modernist thought integrated aesthetics and politics. The standardized look of International Style architecture, for example, was promoted as the image of revolutionary repudiation of bourgeois individualism by critics like Walter Benjamin, who identified the home as a manifestation of bourgeois notions of the individual "private citizen." Analyzing the nature of "The interior [that] was not only the private citizen's universe, it was also his casing," Benjamin saw "the resident's own traces" [*Spur*] left in every spot [*Fleck*] in the middle-class home. The German nouns here evoke physical tracks or stains, an implication that—echoing Adolf Loos's earlier comparison of decoration with graffiti and tattooing—corrupts the catalog of furnishings onto which middle-class residents project their identity: "the knick-knacks on the shelves, the antimacassars on the armchairs, the filmy curtains at the windows, the screen before the fireplace." Exactly inverting Bloomsbury's values, Benjamin condemned this domestic expression of individuality, heralding as a corrective to bourgeois interiors the modernist "glass houses" proposed by Le Corbusier and the Bauhaus, which "'will completely transform people'" because this "hard and flat material" resists the imprint of the individual: "they have made rooms in which it is difficult to leave a trace."[72]

What proved the easy adaptability of Corbusian architecture to both authoritarian governments and global capitalist enterprise reveals Benjamin's assumptions to have been as naive as Fry's belief that the rich could not accept Matisse's aesthetic of intuitive subjectivity.[73] Though neither ideology can be credited with much predictive value, together they reveal what was at stake in early-twentieth-century debates over the look of modernity. Fry's arguments against the International Style mirror the terms of Benjamin's logic, reversing—as mirrors will—the priorities. For Fry, the anti-individualism of Corbusian design is a "startling contradiction" to modern art's embrace of individual "sensibility, with its tremulous, vital, rhythmic irregularity." The "paintings which seem most expressive of the modern idea are the result of pushing sensibility to its utmost limits," Fry asserts, while in modern design, conversely, "sensibility is rigorously proscribed" by an ideology in which "love of the motor car and the machine" and a passion for "hygiene and sport," "converging on the home, have swept and ungarnished it to a bare clean efficiency." The "strangely paradoxical result" is that "the last word in luxury and comfort wears the air of an almost monastic asceticism." With the self-deprecatory disclaimer that "my wish is likely enough to be father to my thought," Fry predicted that "before very long there will be a reaction against the bleak austerity of the modern home."[74]

Bloomsbury's commitment to an individualism closely identified with domesticity set the group at odds with both the political right and left. While the group's anti-authoritarian stance attracted hostility from the barely post-Victorian establishment of its era—as from the neo-Victorian right-wing today—left-wing critics at the time and since condemned Bloomsbury for what they perceived as its retrograde attachment to notions of individualism associated with bourgeois culture.[75] More thoughtful leftists have criticized this tendency, with Raymond Williams arguing:

> The paradox of many retrospective judgements of Bloomsbury is that the group lived and worked this position with a now embarrassing wholeheartedness: embarrassing, that is to say, to those many for whom "civilised individualism" is a

mere flag to fly over a capitalist, imperialist and militarist social order; embarrassing, also, to those many others for whom "civilised individualism" is a summary phrase for a process of privileged consumption.

Williams warns historians to attend to "the difference between the fruit and its rotting, or between the hopefully planted seed and its monstrously distorted tree." Yet Williams, too, faults Bloomsbury for failing to articulate "any alternative idea of a whole society."[76]

Utopia vs. Subculture

Underlying Williams's disappointment in Bloomsbury is a fundamental difference in models of social reform, a difference I would characterize as *utopia* versus *subculture*. Where utopians from Thomas More on imagine total social overhaul—Ruskin and Morris, for example, designed their benevolent new hegemonies down to the dress of their happy inhabitants—subcultures sustain opposition to dominant norms without the promise of eventually becoming, themselves, normative. Through most of the twentieth century, leftist theory, following Marx's analysis of class-based revolution, concentrated on utopias. More recently, however, this homogenizing ideal has been challenged by models responsive to networks of identity beyond economic class.[77] This has occasioned a renewed interest in subculture, a concept whose pre-eminent nineteenth-century theorist was Oscar Wilde.[78]

This is not the place to debate the relative merits of utopia and subculture as activist strategies or scholarly ideologies; I want simply to insist on the latter as an alternative to—not an incomplete version of—the former. Wilde did not aspire to accede to a position of authority. "All authority is quite degrading," he said; "It degrades those who exercise it, and degrades those over whom it is exercised." Wilde's argument is clearest in his 1890 *Soul of Man Under Socialism*, which endorses the redistribution of wealth while critiquing the assumptions of utopian reformers who assumed Marxist revolution to be coincident with freedom. "Many of the socialistic views that I have come across seem to me to be tainted with ideas of authority, if not actual compulsion," Wilde warns; "If the Socialism is Authoritarian, if there are Governments armed with economic power as they are now with political power . . . then the last state of man will be worse than the first." Wilde's doubts about the benevolence of hegemonies, even—or especially—those that claimed to embody the will of the masses, underlies his analysis of the "three kinds of despots":

> There is the despot who tyrannizes over the body. There is the despot who tyrannizes over the soul. There is the despot who tyrannizes over soul and body alike. The first is called the Prince. The second is called the Pope. The third is called the People.[79]

When Fry addressed the topic of "Art and Socialism" in an essay that is virtually a paraphrase of Wilde's *Soul of Man*, he distinguished between a "Bureaucratic Socialism" that "would carefully organise the complete suppression of original creative power" and a "Great State [that] aims at human freedom."[80] Describing Wilde as "infinitely nearer to some kind of truth than all the noble rhetoricians, the Carlyles, Ruskins, etc., of the day," Fry said, "He has a way of being right, which is astonishing at that time, or any for that matter."[81]

Wilde's skepticism was tied to his identity as a member of a sexual minority, a concept that gained currency in his generation.[82] The same anxiety can be found in the writings of Edward Carpenter, another Victorian sex activist, who in 1889, after helping Ruskin extricate himself financially from a failed utopian community, speculated about such endeavors:

> I think one reason why all these little communal schemes fail is their narrowness. . . . Personally, I would not like to belong to a community of under a million people! I think with that number one might feel safe, but with less there would be a great danger of being *watched*.[83]

Many in Bloomsbury could identify with Wilde's and Carpenter's concerns. As homosexuals, feminists, pacifists, or members of religious minorities, Bloomsbury's members had reasons to distrust majority culture, reasons the course of the twentieth century did nothing to mitigate. Against the tyranny of conformity and the threat of totalitarianism, Bloomsbury followed Wilde in upholding individualism. Virginia Woolf wrote that for Fry after World War I:

> The herd [took] the place of the adversary; the herd is the adversary, swollen immensely in size and increased in brute power. The herd on one side, the individual on the other—hatred of one, belief in the other—that is the rhythm, to use his favorite word, that vibrates beneath the surface.[84]

Despair over "the immense suggestibility of the crowd" peppers Fry's political commentary at this era; in 1933, he observed, "humanity in any collective group accepts a great deal that would be recognized as madness in the individual. I suppose very few people to-day would not repudiate most of the *idées reçues* of say the *Times* if he came to them using his ordinary sense of what is credible or probable."[85] The alternative to group-think, for Fry, was self-conscious individualism. Like Wilde, Fry acknowledged the correlation of criminality and individualism, but—also like Wilde—his ultimate locus of individualism was art.[86] "Art is the most intense mode of individualism that the world has known," Wilde insisted: "I am inclined to say that it is the only real mode of individualism that the world has known."[87] A quarter century later, Fry wrote, "in a world where the individual is squeezed and moulded and polished by the pressure of his fellow-men the artist remains irreclaimably individual."[88]

At least in its own eyes, this was Bloomsbury: a collocation of individuals, many of them artists, all of them with claims to interest in the arts. Whether in art or literature, politics or economics, however, Bloomsbury's members claimed to speak (or write, or paint) as individuals outside—and often in opposition to—institutional authority. Clive Bell insisted that Bloomsbury's members "differed widely . . . in opinions, tastes and preoccupations," and asked, "Can a dozen individuals so loosely connected be called a group?"[89] Leonard Woolf argued, "Maynard's crusade for Keynesian economics against the orthodoxy of the Banks and academic economists, and Roger's crusade for post-impressionism and 'significant form' against the orthodoxy of academic 'representational' painters and aestheticians were just as purely individual as Virginia's writing of *The Waves*—they had nothing to do with any group."[90] Hence the problem Raymond Williams addresses: Bloomsbury's denial of what many observers saw as its most prominent characteristic, its "groupiness." As Williams shows, Bloomsbury was undoubtedly a "specific social formation," but one that made a belief in individualistic dissent a principle for collaboration.[91] Although it has been argued that Wilde personified "a genuine sub-culture" in late-nineteenth-century England, this claim—something of an oxymoron in that a genuine subculture could not be embodied in a single person—overstates Wilde's own motives and commitments.[92] It was Bloomsbury's accomplishment to make Wilde's values the basis of community.

Subculture and Domesticity

Despite the claims of Clive Bell and Leonard Woolf, the subculture of Bloomsbury undoubtedly had a house style. Certain modes of thought, habits of conduct, and even tones of speech have been identified with the group. More to the point of this study, Bloomsbury had a literal house style. The look of its dwellings set them apart from both conventional domestic spaces and from the high-tech minimalism that supplanted connotations of domesticity in mainstream modernist design. For Bloomsbury, modern houses were not the machines of a standardized utopia, but the outcome of an individualism hard-won in the face of repression. Todd's and Mortimer's *The New Interior Decoration* compares Corbusian French and Bloomsbury English modernism on this issue of utopian aspiration, ceding utopian ambitions to the modernist architects of continental Europe. The book's first voice acknowledges rather grumpily that British design "does not presuppose the possibility of pulling down all ugly houses and rebuilding them in a style appropriate to our civilization. . . . It is a palliation, not a dream." The second voice, however, proposes what we now recognize as Bloomsbury's ideal, celebrating English houses as the "last refuge" of "that individuality which modern conditions are suppressing in our public life."[93]

Always willing to launch another sally in the ongoing rivalry among the arts in Bloomsbury, Virginia Woolf claimed that it was actually writers whose homes were most individual:

> It would seem to be a fact that writers stamp themselves upon their possessions more indelibly than other people. Of artistic taste they may have none; but they seem always to possess a much rarer and more interesting gift—a faculty for housing themselves appropriately, for making the table, the chair, the curtain, the carpet into their own image.[94]

Despite this assertion, when it came to Woolf's own tables, chairs, cushions, and carpets, she, like others in Bloomsbury, summoned the group's artists—those embodiments of individualism—to materialize the ambition to create new forms of domesticity. This book describes this effort to make domesticity the basis of a new social and aesthetic order, and to give visual expression to that order through the look of the home.

Sections I and II, each in three chapters, trace the development of Bloomsbury's domestic modernism before World War I. Section I investigates each of the artist's earliest efforts to reconceive the home, initiated before the coalescence of the group. In introducing early domestic projects by Bell, Fry, and Grant, these chapters challenge common perceptions of Bloomsbury's relation to its late-Victorian forerunners, to feminism, and to emerging notions of sexual identity. Chapter 1 describes Bell's decorations at 46 Gordon Square, looking in particular at the gendered aspect of her responses to the models of avant-garde practice offered by Augustus John and Walter Sickert. Chapter 2, on Fry's Durbins, explores his roots in the Arts and Crafts Movement, developing the comparison between this English legacy of modernist design and Le Corbusier. Chapter 3, on Grant's first domestic mural done for Keynes's lodgings in King's College, Cambridge, examines Bloomsbury's reception of nascent concepts of sexual identity inherited from the Victorians. Following these studies of Bloomsbury's artists apart, Section II examines the group's first collaborations, during 1911–12, on decorative projects for schools and houses. Themes introduced in Section I—Bloomsbury's relation to feminism, sexual identity, and other aspects of the legacy of Victorian radicalism—re-emerge in these chapters in relation to the group's understanding of primitivism, which allowed them to forge a modern language from allusions to Byzantium and the Near East.

Section III takes up what is today the best-known aspect of Bloomsbury domestic design, the collaborative Omega Workshops founded by Bell, Fry, and Grant. Although its chronology and output have been well documented, the Omega's relationship to both British precedents and French contemporaries is poorly understood. The first chapter in this section offers new answers to these questions of context. It is followed by two chapters analyzing specific aspects of the Omega's practice: its use of Edenic imagery and the relationship of domestic design to the Bloomsbury artists' abstract paintings. Throughout these chapters, issues of gendered and sexual identity continue to be central to the development of Bloomsbury's aesthetics, even when—as in the case of the group's abstract paintings—the art seems closest to the mainstream of avant-garde practice.

The Bloomsbury artists' divergence from this mainstream after 1915 is traced through Sections IV and V. Section IV deals with interiors decorated by Bell and Grant during and just after World War I, comparing the group's rapidly shifting aesthetic priorities with its engagement with anti-war politics. My argument that the look of Bloomsbury's domestic spaces during this period constitutes a visualization of the political concept of "conscientious objection" to the war contests the common claims that the group's post-war aesthetic represented a retreat from modern issues and concerns. The first two chapters of Section IV examine the aesthetic developed by Bell and Grant as they decorated the sequence of rural houses they shared during the war, while the last explores the post-war development of this style in the urban context of the London homes of John Maynard Keynes and Mary Hutchinson.

Section V, like the others divided into three chapters, examines Bloomsbury's domestic decorations during the 1920s and 1930s, the era when the artists were best known and most reviewed in their own lifetimes, but which is least studied today. This period coincides with the emergence into the public eye of others in Bloomsbury, shifting popular perceptions of the group away from an art-world contingent toward a broader subculture. The first chapter in this section deals with the design and publication of interiors Bell and Grant created for Bloomsbury's most celebrated members: Keynes's new Cambridge rooms and the Woolfs' London flat. Overlooked links between the artists' decorative work and Bloomsbury's fiction here support my contestation of Bloomsbury's exclusion from heroes-only versions of modernism that, even in revisionist social histories, continue to be limited to conventional standards of masculine accomplishment. Turning to Bloomsbury's role in the development of modern identities organized around sexuality and promulgated through the mass media, the second chapter in this section also challenges conventional histories of Bloomsbury, which remain limited to the group's pre-war members. Though Bloomsbury's "fringe" of younger members is little studied today, my focus on the artists' domestic designs reveals their importance to Bloomsbury in the Twenties, and Bloomsbury's importance to the history of sexual subculture in Britain in that decade. The concluding chapter of this section returns to the arguments of this introduction, looking at the moment, around 1930, when a rising culture of "experts," responding to what they framed as a "crisis" in British national identity, seized upon the rhetorics of Le Corbusier to help reassert an authoritative masculinity over the promiscuous pleasures of jazz and the "Amusing Style" of interior design associated with Bloomsbury.

Where, in the 1930s as today, partisans of a heroic version of modernism would consign Bloomsbury domesticity to oblivion, this study finds much of interest in the histories of dissent—individual, collaborative, and subcultural—embodied in the efforts of Roger Fry, Vanessa Bell, and Duncan Grant to design environments appropriate to their ideals of modern life. Focused on this intellectual and cultural history, this study is not a complete catalog of these artists' domestic designs. Certain domestic projects are passed over, while some easel paintings and non-domestic designs are analyzed for what they reveal about the relationship between Bloomsbury's social and aesthetic ideals. Throughout, my aim is to present Bloomsbury's art in the context of the group's aspirations and ideologies, and to place those aspirations and ideologies in the broader context of the history of modernism. Because the group is so often misrepresented, I have tried as much as possible to allow its members to speak for themselves through extensive quotations from letters and other texts, some previously published, others presented here for the first time.

Some may object that by emphasizing the social and historical context of Bloomsbury's modernism, this study betrays its subjects by bringing a non-formalist approach to the progenitors of formalism. In defense, I wish to be explicit in describing my project as what Roger Fry would call—and sanction as—art history, rather than aesthetic criticism.[95] To justify this approach in Bloomsbury's own words, I might cite Clive Bell, who echoed Fry in insisting that although "just at present it is the thing to laugh at biographical and historical critics," actually "few things do more to disseminate a taste for art and letters and, I will add, for all things of the spirit, than biographical and historical criticism and the discussion of tendencies and ideas."[96] I prefer, however, to claim as my sanction Virginia Woolf's charge "to the students of those famous colleges that they should re-write history

. . . so that women might figure there without impropriety."[97] This task I extend to include not just women, but everything that patriarchy has dismissed as negligible by its association with the feminine. Stepping outside the traditional priorities of art history, this study acknowledges a community of men and women who worked to imagine new forms of domesticity and who embodied their ideas in the look of the home.

Rooms of One's Own
Three Early Domestic Environments

The influence of houses on their inhabitants might well be the subject of a scientific investigation.

Lytton Strachey

This, the opening line of an autobiographical essay Strachey read to other members of the Bloomsbury group in 1922, posits the childhood home as a silent protagonist in the history of author and auditors alike. He continues, "Those curious contraptions of stones or bricks, with all their peculiar adjuncts, trimmings, and furniture, their specific immutable shapes, their intense and inspissated atmospheres, in which our lives are entangled as completely as our souls in our bodies—what powers do they not wield over us . . . ?"[1] Strachey's assertion of the power of domestic space to condition and express the life it contains echoes the convictions of other Bloomsbury men, from E. M. Forster's earnest assertions of the beneficent effects of Howards End in the novel where that house earns the title role to John Maynard Keynes's witty (and unpublished) essay on "The influence of furniture on Love," which asked, "Who could commit sodomy in a boudoir or sapphism in Neville's Court [at Cambridge]?"[2]

In structuring his memoir around his childhood home, Strachey allied himself most closely, however, with Virginia Woolf, who, just a few months before, had read to her friends an autobiographical essay that began with a description of the black folding doors that divided her parents' drawing-room, separating scenes of tea-table superficiality from the economic and sexual realities of their domestic life: "a servant dismissed, a lover rejected."[3] Woolf's and Strachey's descriptions of their parents' houses are remarkably similar: stories tower rickety floor upon floor; windows are veiled by drapery, frosted glass, and hanging vines; rooms are small, dark, and awkwardly shaped, with the only private space allotted to the father. "Strangest of all," Strachey reported, anticipating a central point of Woolf's later writings, "my mother had no room of her own."[4]

Bloomsbury sought forms of domesticity to replace this standard. Strachey identified his generation by its new sensitivity to its surroundings: "We find satisfaction in curves and colours, and windows fascinate us, we are agitated by staircases, inspired by doors, disgusted by cornices, depressed by chairs, made wanton by ceilings, entranced by passages, and exacerbated by a rug," he proclaimed. In contrast, he cited "our fathers, . . . who would have laughed at such speculation. . . . [T]he notion that the proportions of a bedroom, for instance, might be significant would have appeared absurd to them; and so they were able to create, and to inhabit, South Kensington."[5] Strachey's claim to belong to a generation that rejected its father's houses exemplifies the values that united a group under the name of the neighborhood it claimed as its own territory: Bloomsbury.[6] The following three chapters explore Bloomsbury's formation through an analysis of dwellings created by its artists before they coalesced as a group. At first independently, then collaboratively, Vanessa Bell, Roger Fry, and Duncan Grant sought to redefine life on modern terms by reconfiguring the rooms where it was lived.

Facing page:
Detail of fig. 50.

Vanessa Bell and 46 Gordon Square (1904–12)

A little too symbolically, Bloomsbury was born from the death of a patriarch, when, on February 22, 1904, the eminent scholar Leslie Stephen died of cancer. A widower for nine years, Stephen had long relied on the eldest daughter from his second marriage to manage his household. On his death, however, Vanessa, now almost twenty-five, uprooted her siblings, Thoby, Adrian, and Virginia, abandoning the family home in Hyde Park Gate, South Kensington, in order to set up housekeeping at 46 Gordon Square in London's Bloomsbury district. This address would remain for forty years the geograpical heart of Vanessa's circle, which took its name from its neighborhood of bookshops, museums, concert halls, art schools and students' lodgings. Vanessa was amused to discover, through a newspaper photograph, that one neighbor in Gordon Square sold programs at football matches, and in a memoir recounted how, "we resisted strong pressure put upon us by family and old friends to live as they did in one of the recognized districts and insisted on inspecting houses in Bloomsbury."[1] More pointedly, Virginia recalled that "Vanessa—looking at a map of London and seeing how far apart they were— had decided that we should leave Kensington and start life afresh in Bloomsbury."[2] The Bloomsbury group's re-imagination of domesticity began with the look of 46 Gordon Square.

Though the Kensington house proved impossible to let, the need to symbolize a new way of life justified the expense of leaving it empty while renting quarters across town. This profligacy was, itself, part of a daughters' rebellion, a rejection of the obsessive thrift that, according to Virginia, had been manifest in Leslie Stephen's weekly fury over the household accounts:

> [D]own came his fist on the account book. His veins filled; his face flushed. Then there was an inarticulate roar. The he shouted . . . "I am ruined." Then he beat his breast. Then he went through an extraordinary dramatisation of self pity, horror, anger. Vanessa stood by his side silent. . . . Never have I felt such rage and such frustration. For not a word of what I felt—that unbounded contempt for him and of pity for Nessa—could be expressed.[3]

This history suggests why his children refused to worry, as Vanessa put it, about "how much we had" but just to live "gaily as long as we could" in their new house in Bloomsbury.[4] "46 Gordon Square could never have meant what it did had not 22 Hyde Park Gate preceded it," Virginia Woolf later wrote, explaining how she and her sister threw off domestic convention:

We were full of experiments and reforms. We were going to do without table napkins, we were to have large supplies of Bromo instead; we were going to paint; to
write; to have coffee after dinner instead of tea at nine o'clock.

Woolf's catalog of reforms associates middle-class domestic customs—napkins and
evening tea—with constraints on women's professional aspirations. Another essay
makes this connection explicit, explaining how the domestic arrangements of their
father's house limited his daughters' ability to pursue their careers: at Hyde Park
Gate, "for three hours we lived in the world which we still inhabit. For at this
moment she is painting . . . and I am writing," Woolf wrote, but then "Victorian
society began to exert its pressure" and "father must be given his tea."[5]

This language of domestic rebellion was not just Woolf's retrospective gloss on
the years at Gordon Square. "Phyllis and Rosamond," a short story Woolf wrote at
Gordon Square, showed the incompatibility of conventional domesticity and
women's achievement. Beginning by asserting documentary "veracity" as an expli-
cation of the female condition "at this moment (the 20th June, 1906)," the story
compares two sets of sisters, one living in their parents' "great ugly house" in
Kensington, the other—a writer and "an artist of great promise"—living in "the
great tranquil squares" of Bloomsbury. When the Kensington sisters, "educated for
marriage," are pressed by their Bloomsbury counterparts who demand "what's your
trade?" they can only reply, "we are brought up just to come out in the evening and
make pretty speeches, and well, marry I suppose." Asked why they do not change,
the Kensington sisters answer, "We haven't a room, for one thing: and then we
should never be allowed to do it. We are daughters, until we become married
women." Because they will not escape their parents' home, will not "burn, shoot,
jump out a window, at least do something," as their Bloomsbury counterparts suggest, they will never achieve "the life we should like to lead," and the narrator's
sympathy for them is exhausted.[6] The same values animate Vanessa's letters to her
sister during this time. One remarks, "I really think families are wicked institutions
. . . many vices seem inevitable, at any rate in the commanding members." Another
letter about "the drawbacks to family life" details the domestic formalities Woolf
later railed against: "long meals and aimless sitting afterwards and all the small tiresome conventions." Especially after Bell's marriage in 1907 and the birth of her first
child the following year, these observations are accompanied by promises to create a
domestic situation different from "that awful atmosphere of Sunday and best
clothes" in which she and her sister had been raised.[7]

More than any of the other advantages that made Gordon Square seem, as Woolf
put it, "in October 1904 . . . the most beautiful, the most exciting, the most romantic place in the world," was that it offered its female inhabitants that most precious
of Bloomsbury commodities, rooms of their own.[8] This idea returns again and
again in the sisters' memoirs of this period. Woolf recalled how, years before their
father's death, the sisters schemed over "painting and writing and how to arrange
social life and domestic life better," often concluding with the idea of "changing a
room, so as to have somewhere to see our own friends."[9] Describing their new life in
Bloomsbury, she recalled:

> What was . . . exhilarating was the extraordinary increase of space. At Hyde Park
> Gate one had only a bedroom in which to read or see one's friends. Here Vanessa
> and I each had a sitting room . . . .[10]

Vanessa corroborated her sister's account, recalling that: "all that seemed to matter
was that at last we were free, had rooms of our own and space in which to be alone
or to work or to see our friends."[11]

The friends who came with increasing regularity to 46 Gordon Square—among
them Clive Bell, Lytton Strachey, and Leonard Woolf—were, with the Stephen sisters' brother Thoby, completing their university studies at Cambridge. University
life represented for these men an ideal made all the more powerful after the brutal
rites of masculine socialization that constituted British secondary education. Just as
Virginia Woolf saw the socialization of girls in the Victorian home as impeding the
development of a mature female creativity, a conversation between Leonard Woolf

and E. M. Forster links the limitations of English literature to the training of its male authors in preparatory schools:

> [Forster begins:] They are repressed in school. . . . Beaten by the masters. And they turn into bullies. They despise self expression. . . . [Leonard Woolf responds:] In our Public Schools they breed sadists like Kipling who talk of "lesser breeds beyond the law". . . . His young characters are cruel because he never matured. He remained the schoolboy too long.[12]

In contrast, the warm intellectual community of Cambridge undergraduate colleges was a revelation: "everything changed and almost for the first time one felt that to be young was very heaven," Leonard Woolf recalled; "I found to my astonishment that there were a number of people near and about me with whom I could enjoy the exciting and at the same time profound happiness of friendship." This friendship ripened into a confederation opposed to the ideologies their secondary education had sought to instill. Woolf describes how his Cambridge friends came to feel that they "were mortally involved in revolt against a social system and code of conduct and morality which, for convenience sake, may be referred to as bourgeois Victorianism."[13]

Thoby Stephen's enthusiasm for undergraduate life sparked in his sisters, who were kept at home, a yearning for its social and intellectual freedoms. Virginia complained to her brother, "I have to delve from books, painfully and all alone, what you get every evening sitting over your fire and smoking your pipe with Strachey etc."[14] When the sisters set up their new residence in Gordon Square, they tried to emulate college life: "Vanessa and I got probably much the same pleasure that undergraduates get when they meet friends of their own for the first time," Woolf recalled. The gatherings at Gordon Square were not elegant. Refreshments generally consisted of buns, cocoa, and whiskey—and Strachey complained privately about the abstemious portions of the last. But it was exactly this flouting of domestic conventions that, in Virginia's words, "meant that things could go on . . . in abstract argument, without dressing for dinner, and never revert to the ways, which I had come to think so distasteful, at Hyde Park Gate."[15]

For the men, who "had no 'manners' in the Hyde Park Gate sense," Gordon Square also became a refuge.[16] Leonard Woolf recalled how the "sweeping away of formalities and barriers" that took place at Gordon Square between 1904 and 1911 created a "sense of intimacy which was both emotional and intellectual. It carried back, and carried me back, to the Cambridge of my youth."[17] Numerous Bloomsbury memoirs record the liberating effect of 46 Gordon Square as it became the site of a social life modeled on a collegiate ideal that combined free-wheeling intellectual discourse with an atmosphere of intimate community. "We did not hesitate to talk about anything," remembered Vanessa; "you could say what you liked about art, sex, or religion, you could also talk freely and very likely dully about the ordinary doings of daily life."[18] The rooms at Gordon Square became the setting for now-familiar Bloomsbury anecdotes of abstract philosophical debate spiced with bawdy language and gossip. A 1909 letter from Vanessa to Clive Bell reports that at dinner they "discussed whether there was such a thing as a right to anything. We also discussed copulation with Virgins which was much more interesting."[19] It was at Gordon Square that, after their marriage, Vanessa and Clive Bell were said—with some exaggeration—to have made love on a bed in the drawing room, and here that Vanessa invited her new friend Duncan Grant to shave in the bathroom while she bathed.[20]

As the headquarters of what Vanessa Bell described as "a company of the young, all free, all beginning life in new surroundings," 46 Gordon Square visually proclaimed a domestic ideology opposite to that represented by the dark woodwork and heavy red velvet of Hyde Park Gate. No known images remain from the early years at Gordon Square. Bell, however, later recalled, "It seemed as if in every way we were making a new beginning in the tall clean rather frigid rooms," and other textual sources record how she worked to retain this visual promise of a fresh start.[21] Shortly after moving in, Vanessa wrote to her sister, describing how the "Indian shawls of brilliant colours" she put over the chairs "look rather fine and barbaric against our white walls."[22] To replace the delicate writing table that their dead half-sister had embellished with ladylike care in a leaf pattern—"at that time staining and enamelling and amateur furniture decorating were much the rage" Woolf explained—Vanessa bought her sister a new worktable, "much more what you want than the other one was—very solid and steady and nice to look at."[23] And instead of the "mounds of plush" of Hyde Park Gate, Gordon Square had light chintz uphol-stery and drapes.[24] That the extraordinary look of the house betokened an icono-clastic life within was clear to regulars like Strachey, who took obvious delight in setting the scene for an anecdote of Bloomsbury impropriety by describing how "the drawing room has no carpet or wall paper, curtains some blue and some white, [and] a Louis XV bed (on which they lie side by side)."[25] A half-century later, the Bells' son, Quentin, recalled: "We were odd and, as I knew, disreputable. Our door was bright vermillion, while every other door on Gordon Square was dark blue or dark grey or black."[26]

The spirit of informality and improvisation set the decoration of 46 Gordon Square apart from the fussy permanence of Hyde Park Gate and became a hallmark of Bloomsbury's domestic style. Although it has been disparaged as incompetent by adherents of high-finish modern aesthetics from the Arts and Crafts to Art Deco and the International Style (more on this in Chapter 7), Bloomsbury's domestic aes-thetic makes its own claims to modernity, articulated, for instance, in Woolf's man-ifesto for women's colleges—which, in some ways, 46 Gordon Square was. Imagining an institution opposed to patriarchal rigidity and permanence, Woolf in *Three Guineas* exhorts women's schools to

> be built not of carved stone and stained glass, but of some cheap, easily com-bustible material which does not hoard dust and perpetrate traditions. Let the pictures and the books be new and always changing. Let it be decorated afresh by each generation with their own hands cheaply.

Only in such an environment, Woolf says, can colleges abandon traditions of instruction in "the arts of dominating other people . . . of ruling, of killing, of acquiring land and capital," and devote themselves instead to "the arts that can be taught cheaply and practised by poor people, such as medicine, mathematics, music, painting and literature," to which Woolf adds the rather domestic catalog of "the arts of human intercourse; the art of understanding other people's lives and minds, and the little arts of talk, of dress, of cookery that are allied with them."[27]

The most intriguing evidence of gendered self-consciousness in the look of the Gordon Square house is the display of portraits Vanessa hung in the front hall in 1904. Describing them in a letter to Virginia, she wrote:

> On the right hand side as you come in I have put a row of celebrities: 1. Herschel—Aunt Julia's photograph. 2. Lowell. 3. Darwin. 4. father. 5. Tennyson. 6. Browning. 7. Meredith—Watts' portrait. Then on the opposite side I have put five of the best Aunt Julia photographs of Mother. They look very beautiful all together.[28]

Visitors to Gordon Square, then, found themselves between the masculine moral and intellectual tradition Woolf in *Three Guineas* characterized as "a procession of educated men" and, confronting it across the passage, an alternative legacy of female beauty and artistry, which came to the Stephen siblings through their mother.[29] It is worth examining the ambivalent implications of that legacy.

The Stephen sisters' "Aunt Julia" was Julia Margaret Pattle Cameron (actually a great-aunt), the pioneering photographer whose "gift of ardent speech and pictur-esque behavior," in Woolf's words, "impressed itself upon the calm pages of Victorian biography."[30] With her sisters, Cameron created an artistic circle that included the poet Alfred Tennyson, the painter G. F. Watts, and the actress Ellen Terry. For the Stephens, the Pattle sisters, who were of Italian and French descent, represented an alternative to their paternal Scots heritage. Vanessa wrote to her sis-ter, "I hope we come from the Patelli and de l'Etang. I often feel far more akin to them than to the Stephens of Aberdeen, who would be as much horrified by us . . . as by the Patelli."[31] What intrigued the Stephen sisters was their Pattle ancestors' success in fashioning unconventional domestic lives. Woolf wrote that they had "the art of making round them . . . a society of their own ('Pattledom' it was christened by Sir Henry Taylor), where they could drape and arrange, pull down and build up, and carry on life in a high-handed and adventurous way."[32] Nevertheless, Woolf also recognized in this milieu the origins of her mother's tendency to sacrifice herself for men in her role as the "Angel in the House." It was among her aunts, Woolf wrote, that "she was taught to take such part as girls did then in the lives of distinguished men; to pour out tea; to hand them their strawberries and cream; to listen devoutly, reverently to their wisdom; to accept the fact that Watts was the great painter; Tennyson the great poet."[33] That Julia Stephen might be said to have only once rivaled her husband's masculine vocation as the man of letters behind the *Dictionary of National Biography*, when she wrote the entry on Julia Margaret Cameron from "personal knowledge," only complicates the fraught relationship between the restrictive and liberating elements in the Stephen sisters' maternal legacy.[34]

Among the Pattle sisters, it was Julia—known for neither beauty nor charm, but for her skill as a photographer and her extreme eccentricity—who captured the imagination of her great-nieces. As early as 1919, Woolf, while exploring issues of a daughter's relation to her artistic heritage in the novel *Night and Day*, left herself a "note for future use" about the potential of Cameron's milieu as the basis for comedy.[35] She completed a script for a comic play based on her aunt's circle in 1923, revising it in 1935, when it was staged in Vanessa Bell's London studio, starring Bell as Cameron. The first draft offers the clearest insight into the Stephen sisters' ambivalent fascination with "Pattledom." In its last act, Ellen Terry, the youngest woman of the Pattle circle, escapes the conflicting demands of her high-powered colleagues by running off with a young man after proclaiming, "We're going to Bloomsbury—number 46 Gordon Square." The final words, however, are given to Julia Margaret Cameron: "Take my lens. I bequeath it to my descendents. See that it is always slightly out of focus."[36] Both Woolf and Bell, at various points in their careers, struggled with the implications of this legacy, at once absurd and empowering.

When, in 1926, Woolf, who was notorious for her self-doubt, co-authored with Roger Fry a book on Cameron's photographs, she emphasized her great-aunt's megalomaniacal confidence, quoting from her great-aunt's writings:

> "I longed to arrest all beauty that came before me, and at length the longing has been realized." . . . She herself blazed up at length into satisfaction with her own creations. "It is a sacred blessing which has attended my photography," she wrote. "It gives pleasure to millions."[37]

For Woolf—though she may have imagined her sister had inherited this self-confidence—Cameron's exaggerated self-regard, unnuanced by creative doubt, undermined the usefulness of her precedent. Cameron interested Woolf most in conjunction with her frequent model: her beautiful niece and namesake, the Julia who was Virginia's and Vanessa's mother and whom they both resembled. Fascination with a conflicted maternal heritage of female artistic agency and passive feminine beauty is suggested by the fact that when Woolf—who claimed she had to slaughter the maternal "Angel in the House" in order to write, and who killed off the character based on her mother in *To The Lighthouse* so that the artist in the text could realize her vision—began to achieve celebrity, she presented herself to the world as her mother. When in 1924, *Vogue* featured Woolf in its "Hall of Fame" as "the most brilliant novelist of the younger generation," she posed for the accompanying photograph as a Cameron model: a Victorian maiden, sitting sedately, her hands clasped before her and hair pulled back, actually wearing one of her mother's dresses (fig. 1).[38] At the moment she acceded to a position of prominence in her father's masculine profession—an accomplishment she herself associated with matricide—Woolf's public self-presentation asserted her maternal heritage in the artistic and eccentric circle of the Pattles, suggesting the continuing power of the

1. Virginia Woolf, photographed for *Vogue* by Beck and MacGregor, 1924, published in late May 1924.

2. Vanessa Bell, *The Red Dress*, c. 1929. Oil on canvas, 73.3 × 60.5 cm. Brighton Art Gallery and Museum.

twinned legacies her sister had visualized at the entrance to their new home twenty years before.

Like her sister, Vanessa Bell was fascinated by the troublesome but compelling heritage of female creativity that descended to the Stephens through their mother. In the 1920s and again around 1950, Bell based paintings on Cameron photographs, focusing on portraits of her mother. Bell began exhibiting these works in 1926, just as Woolf was creating her troubled portrait of her mother in relation to a female artist in *To the Lighthouse*.[39] Best known of these paintings is a portrait titled *The Red Dress* (fig. 2), based on a photograph reproduced in Woolf's and Fry's book on Cameron (fig. 3).[40] Bell's copy, as its title suggests, transforms the monochrome original to a study in hue, the brilliant expanse of the red gown set off by the light blue of the shawl and icier white-blue highlights of the cuff, collar, and belt buckle. Where Cameron's portrait documents the appearance of her sitter, Bell emphasizes the play of color. This shift away from the subject and toward its depiction is underlined by Bell's slight alterations of the figure, making her cheeks, neck, and lips slightly plumper than in the photographic original, bringing the image closer to the look of the generic females in Bell's contemporary decorative work. Bell, in this way, incorporates both Cameron and her mother into her own signature style.

Bell's incorporation of her maternal legacy may be clearest in her still life, *Flowers in a Jug*, which depicts two photographs (fig. 4). Here Bell again subordinates the photograph's documentary value to its abstract form by orienting the most visible image sideways, divorced from its mimetic orientation, and by providing only a sketchy rendering of its female subject. This frustration of representation in favor of form reaches an extreme in the juxtaposition of the photograph with a rolled-up sheet that seems to be a second photo or an embroidery canvas, its image completely obscured so that it functions simply as a cylindrical mass. The visual importance of the V-shape generated by the intersection of the two is emphasized

3. Julia Margaret Cameron, photograph of Julia Jackson Duckworth, from Virginia Woolf and Roger Fry, *Victorian Photographs of Famous Men and Fair Women*, Hogarth Press, 1926.

4. Vanessa Bell, *Flowers in a Jug*, 1948–50. Oil on canvas, 50.8 × 40.6 cm. Private collection.

by its echo in the abstract backdrop behind the still life, just as the round, dark photographic image of the woman is tied to the form of the vase, confusing conventional distinctions between two- and three-dimensional space, abstract pattern and mimetic rendering, in a way that is characteristic of Bell's art at this period. The casual assortment of spring flowers, arranged for their color and form, might even be read as Bell's flouting of Cameron's elaborate Pre-Raphaelite system of horticultural symbolism. At the same time that Bell undermines Cameron's authority by her modernist emphasis on abstraction, she nevertheless presents her painting in relation to her maternal heritage in Cameron's art of "fair women." Placing Cameron's photograph at the bottom of her still life, Bell makes these samples of women's work the foundation of her image, the generators of the forms—light angles and dark circles—from which her composition is built.[41] Although Bell's paintings, like Woolf's invocations of Pattledom, date from after their inhabitation of 46 Gordon Square, they suggest some of the connotations implied by Bell's display of portraits in her new front hall. Escaping from a house that was too much their father's, the Stephen sisters envisioned their new home as a place where a masculine tradition of intellectual debate and scholarship might be balanced by a maternal legacy of female artistic accomplishment and social daring.

The links between domesticity and art are encapuslated in Woolf's citations of painters' names to schematize the early history of 46 Gordon Square. Describing the shift from Hyde Park Gate to Bloomsbury, Woolf wrote, "the Watts–Venetian tradition of red-plush and black paint had been reversed; we had entered the Sargent–Furse era."[42] Personifying the old era was G. F. Watts, whose style, Vanessa noted as a young art student, drew from Titian and other Venetians.[43] Literally the artist of the fathers, Watts had painted portraits of Leslie Stephen and his first wife; it was probably this image of her father that hung in the front hall alongside Watts's portrait of Meredith. Though Bell during her father's lifetime had been encouraged to emulate Watts, Woolf's term, "the Sargent–Furse era," invokes her sister's interest in less traditional role models. The fashionable portraitist John Singer Sargent taught Bell at the Royal Academy schools in 1903–4, and she was delighted to be remembered when she visited his studio a year later.[44] Bell enjoyed a much closer acquaintance with the painter Charles Wellington Furse, an enthusiastic follower of both Sargent and London's other famous expatriate American, J. A. M. Whistler.[45] Furse in 1900 had married Katharine Symonds in a ceremony at which Vanessa was bridesmaid, and he painted a full length portrait of her shortly thereafter.[46] Bell admired not only Furse's art but also his home, where he followed Whistler in replacing Victorian patterned papers and textiles with light fabrics and plain walls washed with a single carefully chosen color. For Bell, the look of Furse's house was inspirational. In contrast to Hyde Park Gate, where "in the evening faces loomed out of the surrounding shade like Rembrandt portraits," Bell said, "one of the chief excitements" of a visit to the Furses "was the bare plaster walls and faces seen against them."[47] A letter written a few months after the move to Gordon Square conveys Bell's admiration for the twin stars of Charles Furse's firmament. In it she describes the visit to Sargent, "the great man," at his studio, then asks about her brother and sister's appreciation of the views on their trip to Spain, "Didn't you long to be Whistler?"[48] Though together Furse, Sargent, and Whistler represented for Vanessa all that was modern in life and art, by the end of 1904 Furse and Whistler were dead, and Sargent's status was rapidly waning. If, as has been argued, "the liberties that the Miss Stephens now sought were, even by the standards of their own age, modest," the same is true of their aesthetic ambitions.[49] The point in both cases, however, is not the Stephen sisters' tardy arrival to a position well behind the lines of the avant-garde, but their self-conscious bid to reconfigure their lives—socially and aesthetically—on terms that seemed to them modern.

This bid for modernity was no one-shot effort. The "Sargent–Furse era" was followed a few years later by what Woolf called "Chapter Two" in Bloomsbury's history, in which the precedents of Sargent and Whistler gave way to the more up-to-date models of Walter Sickert and Augustus John, while the group's social and sexual adventurousness evolved to a point that seems—by the standards of their age or even ours—far from modest. Woolf characterized this second phase of Bloomsbury's history as "the age of Augustus John," invoking a painting by that artist purchased by Vanessa and Clive in 1908, which dominated the drawing room at 46 Gordon Square.[50] Again, visual records of the house's decoration are lacking, but evidence of the aesthetic issues at play in this period may be found in Vanessa Bell's paintings. These reveal their author's determined push for modernity, charting a progression from the brushy elegance of Sargent and the misty aestheticism of Whistler to—and quickly beyond—the more avant-garde examples of Sickert and John.[51] Ultimately neither Sickert nor John, though they represented opposite poles of the Edwardian modernism, proved satisfactory models, for, despite their differences, both presented biases inimical to Bell's experiences and aspirations. Her struggle to adapt the modernist paradigms represented by Sickert and John reveals, by contrast, her determination to imagine a modernism grounded in domesticity and conducive to female creativity.

By 1907, when the Bells married and "Chapter Two" in the history of 46 Gordon Square began, the leader of London's artistic avant-garde was widely recognized to be Walter Sickert, who had recently returned from a seven-year residence in France with ambitions to foster the development of modern British art along the principles laid out by his teacher, Edgar Degas. Despite his leadership of the "Camden Town Group," Sickert's headquarters was a studio in Fitzroy Street, Bloomsbury, just around the corner from the house Virginia and Adrian Stephen moved into when the Bells took over 46 Gordon Square. There Sickert exhibited and sold his own paintings as well as work by his followers, establishing what was, until the first Post-Impressionist exhibition in late 1910, London's closest link to Parisian modernism. Inspired by Degas, Sickert and his circle created their own variations on both his style—carefully stippled application of paint, quirky off-center compositions, color schemes of bright highlights against an overall dull field—and subject matter: nightclubs, cafés, train stations, theaters, race tracks, brothels, and tenements. It was their focus on these aspects of modern urban life that associated this group with Camden Town, an industrial district around the railroad terminals and canals just north of Bloomsbury. For Sickert, following Degas, this combination of style and subject was part of a vision of the modernist artist, rooted in the literary ideals of the dandy or *flâneur* as dispassionate, aestheticizing reporters of the spectacle of modern life. The off-center viewpoint suggestive of casual observation rather than the studied pose, dull tones redolent of urban banality but suddenly infused with flashes of brilliant color, the tiny brush strokes at once fussily precise and, in contrast to the polished surfaces of academy art, evocative of first-hand observation of transient phenomena—all of these combine to express in visual terms the *flâneur*'s ideal.[52]

Vanessa Bell's interest in Sickert's style is nowhere more apparent than in her *Apples: 46 Gordon Square* of 1908 (fig. 5), with its tightly stippled technique, off-center viewpoint emphasized by the slanting grid of the window frame and railing, and background tones of brown and dull green set off by colorful highlights from the porcelain bowl and fruit.[53] While Bell assumed elements of Sickert's style, however, it was not so easy to adopt its essential complement: the subject matter of the urban working class. When, in 1911, Sickert's informal Fitzroy Street salon solidified into a formal organization that called itself the Camden Town Group, his manifestos exhorted painters to explore modern life by following their models as they "leave the studio and climb the first dirty little staircase in the first shabby little house. . . . Follow her into her kitchen, or better still . . . into her bedroom."[54] Like Degas, Sickert's treatment of modern sexual subjects both signified the *flâneur*'s access to the city's most intimate secrets and proclaimed an avant-garde opposition to older rules of art. Trumpeting his rejection of "puritan standards of propriety," Sickert insisted on the artist's right to "treat pictorially the ways of men and women, and their resultant babies;" otherwise, he says, "we must affect to be . . . seduced by oranges."[55]

In the terms laid out in the introduction, the aesthetic of the *flâneur*, with its emphasis on individual quest into foreign territory, partakes in the heroic mode of modernism. Charles Baudelaire, the pre-eminent theorist of the artist as *flâneur*, was explicit in his anti-domestic bias, describing "The Painter of Modern Life" as "a man of the crowd," who curses the hours he must spend inside instead of outdoors recording "the landscapes of the great city."[56] Not coincidentally, the role of the *flâneur* was problematic for women.[57] Like "Shakespeare's sister," who, Virginia Woolf pointed out, could not "seek her dinner in a tavern or roam the streets at midnight," Bell could not explore the boarding houses, brothels, and pubs of Camden Town, which Sickert made the defining locus of modernism.[58] The masculine bias of Sickert's practice was institutionalized when, forming the Camden Town Group, he excluded Nan Hudson and Ethel Sands, who had earlier exhibited and sold in the Fitzroy Street studio, telling them: "The Camden Town Group is a male club, and women are not eligible. There are lots of 2 sex clubs, and several one sex clubs, and this is one of them."[59] Bell, therefore, found little in Sickert's example of modern artist as *flâneur* to support her creation of a domestic modernism. Sickert was highly critical of any hint of domesticity in art, reprimanding Hudson and Sands for depicting each other and their shared home:

> I stick to it that it gives a want of variety to your *œuvre* and something amateurish as if your *art* were subordinate to your *establishment*. . . . *"Parler de soi c'est ce qu'il y a de moins fort"* Flaubert says.[60]

5. Vanessa Bell, *Apples: 46 Gordon Square*, 1908. Oil on canvas, 71 × 50.8 cm. Charleston Trust.

Similarly, Duncan Grant recalled "Sickert coming to see Vanessa in Gordon Square once, when we had painted the end of the wall, and he was *furious*. 'You might be painting pictures!' " he complained.[61]

Bell's *Apples: 46 Gordon Square*, though an exercise in the Sickertian technique she admired, may be seen as a riposte to his accompanying insistence that "The plastic arts are gross arts, dealing joyfully with gross material facts . . . and while they flourish in the scullery, kitchen, or on the dunghill, they fade at a breath from the drawing-room."[62] Bell's subject, clearly set in the upper-story drawing room of her town house with Gordon Square visible outside, flouts these strictures, while the brilliant tones of the fruit that are the focus of her composition proclaim her willingness to be, in Sickert's disparaging phrase, "seduced by oranges"—or at least by apples. Like Woolf, who countered the dramatic and didactic social realism of Victorian novels with a domestic aesthetic rooted in the experience of "the ordinary

6. Augustus John, *The Childhood of Pyramus*, c. 1908. Oil on canvas, 120.6 × 150.5 cm. Johannesburg Art Gallery.

mind on an ordinary day," so Bell turns the stylistic devices of Sickert's modernism to the service of the drawing-room domesticity that enabled her own—and her sister's—creativity.[63] A passage from Woolf's memoirs shows just how closely Bell's picture matches her sister's verbal profession of faith in the domestic ideal Gordon Square represented. Recalling the new house's difference from Hyde Park Gate, Woolf wrote:

> It was astonishing to stand at the drawing room window and look into all those trees . . . instead of looking at old Mrs Redgrave washing her neck across the way. The light and the air after the rich red gloom of Hyde Park Gate were a revelation. Things one had never seen in the darkness there—Watts pictures, Dutch cabinets, blue china—shone out for the first time in the drawing room of Gordon Square.[64]

Here the view of the trees, the porcelain bowl, the shine of the furniture, and especially the brilliant light of *Apples* are revealed as the image of a new way of life.

If *Apples: 46 Gordon Square* is evidence that for Vanessa Bell "Chapter Two" in Bloomsbury's history opened with Sickert, her sister was, nevertheless, astute in labeling the years between 1907 and 1910 "the age of Augustus John." During the summer of 1908, Clive and Vanessa first visited the studio of John, whose bohemian lifestyle and artistic facility had propelled him to the forefront of London's avant-garde. There they purchased John's *Childhood of Pyramus* (fig. 6), a gesture that both asserted their participation in the avant-garde and celebrated the birth of their son, Julian, the February before. John's massive idyll of women rejoicing over a blond toddler spoke to the Bells' identity as both modernists and parents in a way that Sickert's *flâneur* aesthetic could not. In the succeeding two years, Bell kept pace with John as he experimented with increasingly abstract blocks of brilliant color to depict his lovers and children in gypsy garb.

Although, at first, John's iconography seemed to allow a place within modernism for women—and specifically for mothers—closer inspection revealed gender dynamics at least as pernicious as Sickert's, however. John's avant-garde reputation was inextricably linked to an iconography of gypsy life, which he celebrated for its primitive simplicity and natural dignity. John modeled his own persona on that of a gypsy king, becoming well known in London's artistic circles for his looks (flowing black cape, bushy beard, and earrings), for his stories of exploits among the gypsies, and for his rag-tag entourage of lovers and children, all of which created an air of exoticism that made him the most sought-after painter of his day. Like the modernism of the *flâneur*, John's gypsy stance ill suited Bell's aspirations, for its primitivism—though in theory exalting a maternal ideal—indulged the values of heroic masculine quest predicated on the subordination of women and the home. There was no place for a woman artist in the image John self-mockingly advanced as his aesthetic ideal: "Earth-Mother and Child . . . installed in a covered waggon . . . drawn by oxen and attended by dancing corybantes."[65] For the women in John's circle, life was a constant round of pregnancies, miscarriages, sickness, and child-rearing on the run. The abortive careers of a generation of Bell's contemporaries among the women art students at the Slade who followed John testifies to the incompatibility of his bohemian artistic community and female professional accomplishment.[66] John's long-time lover, Dorelia McNeill, best fulfilled his ideal; having few intellectual aspirations, she is remembered for her silence. John's wife, Ida Nettleship, on the other hand, abandoned an artistic career to follow him, and died alone in 1907 in the wake of her fifth pregnancy in five years. John's sister, Gwen, emigrated from London at least in part to escape her brother's powerful influence.[67]

As Bloomsbury came to know John between 1908 and 1910, they became increasingly aware of these implications of his gypsy persona. Ottoline Morrell, among Bell's closest friends at this period, knew that Dorelia felt her unmarried status obliged her to decline invitations to participate in avant-garde gatherings or meet people like the Bells.[68] More dramatic were Duncan Grant's accounts of John's bohemia, as seen through the eyes of Euphemia Lamb, a Slade-trained painter who had married John's follower, Henry Lamb, and moved with his circle to Paris, where

7. Vanessa Bell,
*Julian Bell and
Nanny*, 1909–10.
Oil on board,
28 × 52.2 cm.
Private collection.

Grant was also studying. Dismayed by the sexual politics in John's entourage, she made Grant her confidant, prompting him to conclude in a letter to Strachey: "That man John, I'm convinced now he's a bad lot."[69] Informed by Grant's stories, Keynes acerbically reported in letters from Cambridge in 1909, "John is encamped with two wives and ten naked children . . . he spends most of his time in Cambridge public houses, and has had a drunken brawl in the streets smashing the face of his opponent."[70] Clive Bell's later disparagement of "fashionable portrait painters . . . wrapping up in the cloak of genius and fronting the world mysteriously," like Fry's condemnation of "a very minor artist . . . the Bohemian . . . who is always kicking over the traces and yet gets toleration and even consideration from the world by reason of a purely magic gift called genius," reflect the ultimate verdict of Bloomsbury's members who were once most enthusiastic about John.[71]

Bloomsbury's difference from John's circle remained important enough for Grant to cite in a memoir of his accession to the group:

They were not Bohemians. The people I had come across before who had cut themselves off from respectable existence had been mainly painters and Bohemians. If the Stephens defied the conventions of their particular class, it was from being intellectually honest. They had suffered much, had struggled and finally arrived at an attitude of mind which I think had great influence on their friends.[72]

Vanessa Bell's distance from John's bohemianism is visible in her adaptation of his avant-garde style to her own ends. Just as she had turned Sickert's modernism to the expression of her own domestic ideal, Bell turned the brusque confidence of John's simple blocky style to her own vision of maternity in paintings like the 1909–10 *Julian Bell and Nanny* (fig. 7). Echoing the techniques John used to represent his gypsy family, Bell's portrait, nevertheless, contrasts sharply with his iconography of "Earth-Mother and Child." Where John proposes an apparently timeless mythology of maternity, Bell focuses on the nanny and pram as signifiers of a modern middle-class motherhood compatible with female artistic agency.

With *Julian Bell and Nanny*, Bell inaugurated a series of paintings that challenge conventional depictions of mothers and children. Rejecting isolated images of mother and child, Bell multiplies her figures to reflect the social complexity of child-rearing, as she structures her compositions to reject the conventional gaze of the (implied male) viewer-artist. In *Bathers* (1911), *Studland Beach* (1911–12), and *Nursery Tea* (1912), Bell's figures refuse to acknowledge a viewer, turning their backs and looking at one another to create systems of visual relationships complete within themselves.[73] The four figures in *Nursery Tea* (fig. 8), for example, correspond to the sides of the rectangular table, while the open space at the corner through which the viewer sees the group is echoed by the opposite corner, which is left very obviously vacant. In *Studland Beach*, the overpowering diagonals—strengthened between the preliminary sketch and the final canvas—sweep the viewer's gaze up the empty beach between the figures that in a traditional composition would be the painting's focus, leaving the reciprocal groupings of bathers to

8. Vanessa Bell, *Nursery Tea*, 1912.
Oil on canvas, 76.2 × 105.4 cm.
Private collection.

balance each other without reference to any third term (fig. 9). In *Bathers*, the viewer's focus is fragmented by a solid frieze of foreground figures, which form a barrier to the scenes of intimacy and nudity beyond (fig. 10). The self-sufficiency of Bell's figures is reinforced by poses that, together or singly, create pyramids, the most stable of geometric forms, each complete in itself. A comparison between a sketch for *Studland Beach* (fig. 11) and the final version emphasizes this tendency, especially in the central standing figure, who evolves from a sensually twisting form with her hands to her hair, into a static triangle, her back to the viewer. In what seems an explicit reworking of the conventions of traditional bathing scenes, Bell's nudes do not display themselves, but turn away or cover their bodies with their hands, while in *Studland Beach* the tent where women disrobe out of sight becomes a prominent compositional element.

Analyzing *Studland Beach*, Bell's biographer has compared the children clustered at the base of the tent to the way Piero della Francesca's madonnas enfold clusters of children and worshippers in their robes, and links this to Bell's identity as a mother.[74] This reference is supported by Bell's explicit efforts to re-imagine mother-and-child iconography at this period, most notably in two six-foot-square nativity scenes.[75] The first of these, now lost without visual record, was based on Roger Fry's drawings of her with her own children (fig. 12). In the second, Bell, pushing beyond John's visions of primitive maternity, drew from Paul Gauguin's *L'Esprit veille*, which Fry had included in the first Post-Impressionist exhibition (fig. 13). Just as Bell evaded the masculinist assumptions in John's images of mothers and children, she also reworked Gauguin's precedent, substituting for his eerie fetish the nurturing form of a seated woman and inverting the infantilizing (almost thumb-sucking) gesture of Gauguin's nude so that the woman's crooked elbow becomes a cradle for her child. Such changes replace Gauguin's erotic fantasy of masculine escape from bourgeois domesticity, with a feminized and domesticized version of primal themes.[76] Childbirth in what is clearly a modern bourgeois milieu is here pictured as an occasion of solemn female community. "None but a woman . . . could have so perfectly expressed, with a new sympathy, all the pathos and bewilderment of this time-worn theme," wrote one reviewer.[77] Bell's presentation of modern women in the pictorial langage of Gauguin locates the modernist primitive in the home and in women's experience.

11. Vanessa Bell, sketch for *Studland Beach*, 1911. Oil on board, 25.4 × 34.5 cm. Private collection.

9. Vanessa Bell, *Studland Beach*, 1911–12. Oil on canvas, 76.2 × 101.2 cm. Tate Britain.

Bell's images of women and children may be understood in contrast to her assessment in 1911 of an exhibition of John's recent work as "the same rather sentimental drawings badly put together with no feeling for the whole, and the child is beastly."[78] Bell's own paintings reject the crowd-pleasing appeal of John's images, not only by her thematic emphasis on communities of women and children, but also compositionally. Fry's injunctions to formal unity—what Bell praised as a "feeling for the whole"—are manifested visually in her work by the inherent completeness in the arrangement of the figures, no longer dependent on their relationship to the

10. Vanessa Bell, *Bathers*, 1911. Oil on canvas, 76.2 × 101.2 cm. Private collection.

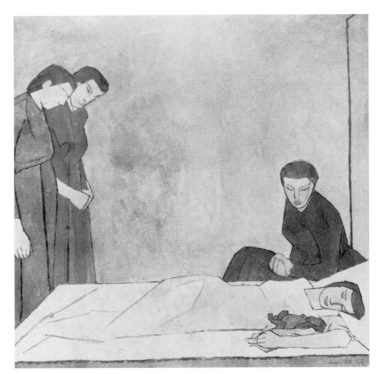

12. Vanessa Bell, *A Nativity* (also known as *Women and Baby*), 1911–12. No longer extant, illustration from *Vogue*, early February 1926.

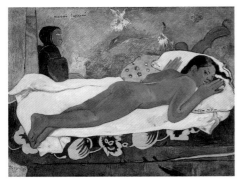

13. Paul Gauguin, *L'Esprit veille* (also known as *Spirit of the Dead Watching*), 1892. Oil on burlap mounted on canvas, 72.4 × 92.4 cm. Albright Knox Art Gallery, A. Conger Goodyear Collection.

viewer. The end of "the age of Augustus John" was signaled at Gordon Square in 1912, when Vanessa decided to sell his *Childhood of Pyramus*. Marking her new aesthetic and social allegiances, she wrote to Clive, "I would rather possess a Cézanne or some modern French painting."[79] John's age, like Sickert's before it, was characterized by a concerted attempt on the part of a woman artist to imagine modernist styles loosed from the masculine imperative to heroism, and instead adapted to the realm of the domestic. Making modernism the sign of her break with her Victorian upbringing, Bell refused to submit to the equally constrictive avant-garde ideologies of either the *flâneur* or the gypsy king. In Roger Fry, Bell would find an ally in her endeavor to forge a domestic modernism. The following chapter takes up the development of his aesthetic in the years before their collaboration.

Roger Fry and Durbins (1909–19)

My claim that Bloomsbury was united by an alienation from the traditional home and a concomitant interest in alternative forms of domesticity is, like all history, a verdict of hindsight, in this case informed by a post-1960s awareness of the importance of gender and sexuality to identity formation in middle-class culture. The idea that, around 1910, feminist women and gay men might have bonded over their exclusion from conventional domesticity—though it contradicts the separatist impulses that have sometimes marked subsequent notions of gay and feminist identity—will likely strike readers as intuitively plausible. But Bloomsbury in general, and the case of Roger Fry in particular, challenge assumptions, present in much feminist and gay theory, that alienation from domestic norms is specific to these identities, while heterosexual men accede easily to positions of privilege within patriarchy. In fact, like Lytton Strachey and Virginia Woolf, Roger Fry's alienation from the values of his parents' generation also found expression first in the ideal of a private room and ultimately in the creation of a new kind of home. This chapter begins by tracing the roots—both personal and cultural—of Roger Fry's efforts to re-imagine domesticity, and then analyzes the house that was their outcome.

Long before Strachey and Woolf, the young Roger Fry challenged his parents' values by criticizing their home. In the late 1880s at Cambridge, Fry was part of a circle of students who, critical of their parents' political and religious certainties, earnestly applied themselves to social and aesthetic reform. Among Fry's closest friends was Charles Robert Ashbee, who left Cambridge to train craftsmen in the slums of east London. Writing to Ashbee during a weekend visit to his family in 1888, Fry contrasted his friend's workshops to the style of his parents' new house in upper-crust Bayswater. Mocking it as an emanation of the "arch-genius of ugliness," Fry reported:

> It is huge and palatial, the outside being covered with blackish yellow-grey stucco which is moulded into the form of gigantic worm casts which are divided up in the shape and semblance of stones. . . . [T]he inside . . . is a consummate conception carried out at enormous cost in sham marble stucco ormulu and gilt. . . . I went home for Sunday to this place and was very wretched all day thinking of what might be going on further east.[1]

Within a year, Fry was teaching drawing classes for Ashbee, and, over his parents' objections, starting formal training as an artist. On the day of his first painting class, he wrote to another college friend, "I'm going to have a room with a fire in it where I shall work my own wicked will and have Socialists all unbeknown to the rest of the family."[2] Though phrased with typical self-mockery, Fry's early link between his rejection of his family's professional and political expectations and his accession to his own space manifests what would become one of Bloomsbury's central ideas.

Fry's penchant for domesticity makes the failures of his home life especially tragic. His marriage, which began in 1896, was cut short after a few years of happiness—attested to by an enormous record of affectionate correspondence—by his wife's mental health, which deteriorated until in 1910 she was permanently confined to an asylum.[3] Roger wrote to his mother at this time, "The great sorrow of Helen's loss and worse than loss. . . . has destroyed my own particular kind of home," and later described to Vanessa Bell his frustration in trying to recreate "the kind of intimate companionship in little things which my domestic nature longs for."[4] Raising two children and desiring sexual and emotional intimacy with a woman, yet legally unable to remarry, Fry found himself excluded from conventions of home and family as surely as Bloomsbury's other members. It is no coincidence that the collapse of Fry's domestic life in 1910 coincided with both his first efforts to promote modernist art in England and his accession to the Bloomsbury group.

Though Fry's outsider status contributed to his participation in Bloomsbury's development of a modernist domesticity, his "domestic nature" had deeper roots among the Victorian activists for whom aesthetic and social reform began with the home. The domestic origins of British radicalism—and Fry's epistolary style—are clear in Ruskin's writings. Presaging Fry's account of his parents' house, a famous passage in Ruskin's *Stones of Venice* contrasted the elaborate aspect of the bourgeois home—"all those accurate mouldings, and perfect polishings, and unerring adjustments of the seasoned wood and tempered steel"—to the miserable conditions in which such luxuries were produced: "Alas! if read rightly these perfectnesses are signs of slavery in our England a thousand times more bitter and more degrading than that of the scourged African, or helot Greek."[5] Ruskin's emphasis on the look of the home was matched by the moral weight he accorded domesticity itself. To describe the genius of the middle ages as exemplified in the art of Giotto, Ruskin wrote, "I must lean . . . distinctly on the word 'domestic.'" Contrasting this quality with the militarism, pompous religiosity, "rationalism and commercial competition" of his own era, Ruskin defined it as a kind of "household wisdom" evident in the "incidents of gentle actual life." Giotto, Ruskin says, "makes the simplest household duties sacred; and the highest religious passions servic-eable and just."[6]

In the 1870s, Ruskin attempted to enact this domestic ideal by founding a rural commune modeled on a gothic village. Saint George's Guild, as it was called, failed—it was this venture that prompted Edward Carpenter's speculations (quoted in the Introduction) on the narrowness of utopian villages.[7] By the time Fry reached adulthood in the late 1880s, however, the Arts and Crafts movement had translated Ruskin's ideals into a wide array of reform-minded workshops and guilds. Fry, in his own words, "worshipped" the "Ruskin idol" in his youth, participating in a number of these, including Arthur H. Mackmurdo's Century Guild, a small federation of artists founded in 1882, and the much larger and looser Art-Workers' Guild, formed in 1884 to sponsor artists' lectures and discussions.[8] Fry was most closely invloved, however, with the Guild and School of Handicraft, founded in 1888 by his friend, Ashbee, who at the age of twenty-five transformed a class on Ruskin for workers into a guild so successful that in 1902 it moved—with its 150 participants—to a village in the Cotswolds where William Morris had earlier dreamed of locating his firm in the abandoned silk mills.

While founding his guild, Ashbee wrote to Fry at Cambridge, urging him to join the cause: "I believe that as soon as you take the great leap on to the stern mountain of reality we shall inevitably climb hand in hand."[9] When, in January 1889, Fry came to London to study painting, he became a drawing instructor in Ashbee's program. Fry stopped teaching for Ashbee during the 1890s, when, under the influence of the connoisseur Bernard Berenson, his aesthetic ideals drew him to Mackmurdo, who eschewed the cozy-cottage anglocentricism of Ashbee and other Arts and Crafts movement designers in favor of Italian precedents. Despite Fry's differences with

14. Roger Fry, mural in C. R. Ashbee's house, 37 Cheyne Walk, *c.*1894.

Ashbee, however, they remained friends and collaborators. In 1894, Fry contributed a mural to a house in Chelsea that Ashbee designed as a showcase for his guild's work (fig. 14). Ashbee's 37 Cheyne Walk was widely publicized for its innovative decorations in wood, metal, and leather. The main public space, an upstairs drawing room, was dominated by Fry's floor-to-ceiling mural depicting a formal garden. A feature on the house in the Arts and Crafts journal *The Studio* praised Fry's work as a "most notable innovation," "happily imagined," and "cleverly planned" to match the room's blue and green color scheme, "so that it grows out of the walls as part of them, and does not detach itself as a painting is apt to do."[10]

Fry's success with Ashbee's domestic decoration prompted a spate of commissions. The following spring, he was asked to decorate another Cheyne Walk house for the writers Hubert Crackenthorpe and Leila Macdonald, who had taken Whistler's former rooms. He gave them white walls and black dadoes, and registered tongue-in-cheek Whistlerian horror when his clients "proceeded to furnish it and therewith destroy all my schemes of colour. . . . Oh the pity of it."[11] In this period, Fry also contributed a mural and three sets of wrought-iron gates to his parents' country house, and designed curtains for Alys Russell and furniture for the university rooms of his friend John McTaggart.[12] While he was engaged on the Cheyne Walk projects, Fry shared a nearby house with the poet Robert Trevelyan, who four years later asked Fry to decorate his new home near Dorking. Fry's stenciled frieze of figures mingling under trees in Trevelyan's drawing room echoed the decorations Ashbee and his sister executed in the dining room at 37 Cheyne Walk.[13] As late as 1910, Fry's was still involved with this kind of decoration, painting Apollo in his chariot for the ceiling of a house in Scotland.[14]

Roger Fry and Durbins

Fry's background in this late-Victorian culture of ideal homes and aesthetic interiors makes it unsurprising that when in 1908 his wife's doctors recommended that the family leave the city, he rejected conventional suburban houses in favor of his own design. Neither is it surprising, given the enthusiasm with which Fry throughout his life tackled new projects, that he had the confidence to act as his own architect. What is surprising is the originality with which Fry was able to add himself to the lineage of aesthetic activists in England who made their homes the expression of new domestic ideals. A half-century after it was built, the historian of modern architecture, Nikolaus Pevsner, characterized Fry's imaginative deployment of the Arts and Crafts style as "one of the landmarks in the evolution of an independent contemporary style in English architecture," and it has since been compared to both Adolf Loos's contemporary Austrian villas and Le Corbusier's first houses of a decade later.[15] Fry's design exemplifies his early engagement with many of the issues that came to characterize Bloomsbury's aesthetic, and it was in this house that the Bloomsbury artists produced their first collaborative domestic decorations. Fry's own enthusiasm for his design is evident in a letter he wrote to the painter Will Rothenstein shortly after moving in in 1910: "I do so want you to see this house. I think you will like it as an attempt to make a house very economical and yet expressive of the needs of our sort of life."[16] Fry remained pleased enough with his design to write an account of it for *Vogue* in 1918 and to include this essay in his first anthology, the 1920 *Vision and Design*. This article, like the letter, presents the house as the embodiment of the domestic life it was designed to contain. Fry opens his analysis with the question: "What if people were just to let their houses be the direct outcome of their actual needs, and of their actual way of life?"[17]

The way of life for which Fry designed his house was—like that of 46 Gordon Square—emphatically opposed to Victorian norms: "It was characteristic of my purse that I could not afford to keep up a gentleman's establishment and of my tastes that I could not endure to," Fry wrote for *Vogue*. In passages seized on by Virginia Woolf in her biography of Fry, he gleefully reported that his house was "regarded as a monstrous eyesore" by his "snobbish" neighbors in wealthy Guildford, and contrasted the "gentlemanly picturesqueness" of their houses, "from which tiny gables with window slits jut out at any unexpected angle," to the huge symmetrical windows of his own boxy design. Against the Romanesque, Gothic, Jacobean, and Queen Anne "architectural 'features' which have been duly copied by modern machinery, and carefully glued on to the houses," Fry upheld the functional simplicity of his own design.[18]

Fry's language reflects his background in the Arts and Crafts movement, echoing not only Ruskin but typical passages from *The Studio*, which, for example, in 1897 described how the architect C. F. A. Voysey, "in order to prevent the builder from displaying the usual 'ovolo mouldings', 'stop chamfers', fillets, and the like, [had] to prepare eighteen sheets of contact drawings to show where his beloved ornamentation *was to be omitted*."[19] Fry's allegiance to this broad movement of aesthetic reform also expressed more personal dynamics. His assertion in *Vogue* that the design of a gentleman's house "is generally terribly conscious of its social aspect, of how the house will look, not to those who live in it so much as to those who come to visit," invokes his own upbringing, when even at his parents' country retreat family members were required to use the back staircase to preserve the appearance of the formal carpet at the front.[20]

Like Virginia Woolf, however, Fry's attitude toward his parents' values was ambivalent. Woolf—perhaps drawing from her own experience—recognized how Fry from childhood felt "the contrast between the father who, when he gave way for once to his passion for skating, was all laughter and high spirits; and the father whose large bright eyes suddenly clouded; and whose voice became one of awful severity as he accused him of sins which he could not understand."[21] Fry worked to maintain a level of intimacy with his parents, emphasizing their political common ground in Quaker pacifism and encouraging areas of mutual interest, especially his father's love of nature. When Fry named his anti-Victorian house "Durbins," it was after "Durbins Batch," a field on his parents' property that was a particular favorite of his very Victorian father.

Though its name recalled family memories, the design of Durbins looked forward from even the advanced domestic architecture of Arts and Crafts practioners like Voysey and Ashbee. It is not just Fry's vanguard adoption of technologies like a central steam heating system and concrete raft foundation that mark Durbins as among the most modern of Edwardian homes. While the north facade is quite typical of cottagey Arts and Crafts domestic design, the south facade applies the movement's claims to serviceability and simplicity with unprecedented rigor (fig. 15).[22] With its boxy massing and industrial-scale windows, this aspect of Durbins finds its nearest English equivalent in contemporary institutional architecture: schools, libraries, apartment blocks, and factories.[23] Inside, Durbins's most striking feature is its split-level floor plan and two-story central room. Both the scale and the interior detailing, from the simple unpainted woodwork to the row of three barrel vaults in the foyer, reflect Fry's Arts and Crafts influences.[24] Designers like M. H. Baillie Scott, who wrote frequently for *The Studio*, advocated a central hall as "a place where the family may assemble round the fire in the evening." Making an historical case for the revival of such a space, Baillie Scott argued, "In seeking for a basis for the plan of a small house it may be well to follow the evolution of the complex modern house; and in tracing this back to its source it will be found that it originally comprised but one apartment—the hall or house-place."[25] That Fry habitually refered to the main room at Durbins as the "house-place" confirms his Arts and Crafts sources.[26]

The look of Fry's house-place (figs. 20, 21), however, had little in common with the dark, low, heavily beamed rusticity and intricate detailing of Baillie Scott's interiors. Two stories high, with blank walls painted gray, and flooded with light from the columnar windows, Fry's house-place proclaimed his difference from some basic tenets of the Arts and Crafts aesthetic. The language of Fry's *Vogue* article underlines his distance from the Victorian reformers. Where Voysey in 1901 condemned "the modern craze for high rooms (originating in foreign travel)," Fry announced as the rationale for his house-place: "I hate Elizabethan rooms with their low ceilings . . . I love the interiors of the baroque palaces of Italy."[27] Where Baillie Scott described the "low snug effect which is so characteristic of the old English house, and which always seems desirable and appropriate in the country," Fry insisted, "I was a town dweller, and I wanted a town house . . . in the country," matching his words with a resolutely vertical facade. Both Voysey and Baillie Scott, following Morris, insisted on tiny leaded windows as part of a rhetoric in which darkness and coolness connoted "shelter and retreat." Fry, on the subject of windows, said, "There is need of a certain amount of light, and my own taste is to have as much as possible."[28] The huge columns of glass on Durbins's south facade are the most striking evidence of Fry's departure from an Arts and Crafts domestic aesthetic.

Fry was not alone in challenging the nationalistic and quaintly bucolic aspects of Arts and Crafts design. The Aestheticism associated with Whistler offered late Victorians an alternative both simpler and more exotic. Whistler's importance for Vanessa Bell's first efforts to signify a modernist domesticity has already been noted. His precedent informs Fry's claims in *Vogue* that the slight projection of the house-place from the flanking walls in his design was necessitated by local ordinances that prohibited a completely flat facade—this echoes well known stories of the Chelsea Board of Works's requirement that decorative detailing be added to Whistler's White House in 1878. Inside, too, the simplicity of Fry's decoration drew on Whistler's example, so that, with only a change of wall color (from terracotta and white to gray and brown), a description of White House could apply equally well to Durbins:

> entering one found oneself at once midway upon a flight of stairs,—I was directed to descend, and found myself in a large terracotta coloured room with white woodwork—very plainly furnished and very unusual. There were two long windows about sixteen feet high on one side of the room, looking upon a little bit of garden. They had small square panes about a foot square.[29]

15. Durbins, south facade, photographed for *Vogue* by A. C. Cooper, 1917, published in late March 1918.

As in Whistler's house (and in contrast to conventional houses, where the floor below the entrance was given over to servants), visitors to Durbins descended a half-flight of stairs into a strikingly plain, brilliantly lit room opening on to a garden. Here the plain walls set off what *Vogue* described as a "wonderful fifteenth-century Korean screen representing a red Phoenix on a very faded gold background" evocative of Whistler's sensational "Peacock Room," which, when it was finished in 1877, made exotic birds and Oriental bibelots staples in the repertoire of Aesthetic decoration.[30]

Combining elements of both Aesthetic and Arts and Crafts precedents, Fry's roots in the reform movements of the Victorian age reveal the artificiality of the division historians have imposed between these two movements. Their overlap is clear in Mackmurdo's Arts and Crafts guild in Aesthetic style, and this circle had profound influence on Fry, not least because he met his wife in Mackmurdo's guild when she sought his help as an expert in Italian art who could help her decorate a harpsichord.[31] At the time he was designing Durbins, another of Fry's primary commitments was to the editorial board of the *Burlington Magazine*, where he was colleagues with Herbert Horne, Mackmurdo's protégé and co-editor of the Century Guild's journal, *The Hobby Horse*.[32] The *Burlington*, which was modeled on the look and tone of the *Hobby Horse*, also charted a path between Aestheticism and the Arts and Crafts. An anonymous review of Baillie Scott's architecture, which appeared in 1907—when Fry was one of the most active members on the magazine's managing committee—praised the Arts and Crafts movement for improving popular taste in decoration even as it assessed Baillie Scott's houses as unsuitable for its own readers with their interest in the fine arts. Too dark and over-decorated to display paintings, Baillie Scott's rooms, designed down to the last candlestick, were judged appropriate for "patrons of the crafts," but the "Arts and Crafts movement, with the architecture corresponding to it," made "the collection of pictures ridiculous, if not impossible."[33]

As a connoisseur of early Renaissance painting, Fry's un-Arts and Crafts design for Durbins signifies, in this context, his identification as an active participant in the arts. His house finds its nearest precedents in the architecture of Mackmurdo and the Century Guild. A townhouse Mackmurdo designed in 1899 for the Japanese art collection of Whistler's friend, Mortimer Menpes, features a mansard roof and columnar window-recesses that anticipate Durbins's basic massing.[34] Even closer to

Durbins is the suburban London house Mackmurdo built for his brother around 1883 (fig. 16). Its boxiness, simple tripartite facade, and plain stucco finish foreshadow Fry's even greater simplification, while the urns that surmount Durbins's prominent pilasters correspond in placement to the terracotta statuettes in Mackmurdo's Italianate facade, reinforcing the anti–Arts and Crafts classicism common to the two designs. The visual parallels between Mackmurdo's and Fry's designs are emphasized by their writings. A text published in the *Hobby Horse* with renderings of Mackmurdo's design for his brother's house anticipates Fry's arguments in *Vogue*. Both begin by condemning overdecorated houses built for commercial speculation, proposing instead an aesthetic based on the straightforward use of construction materials modulated by what Mackmurdo called "proportions . . . made artistically valuable," and what Fry characterized as "a nice sense of proportion and feeling for values of plastic relief."[35]

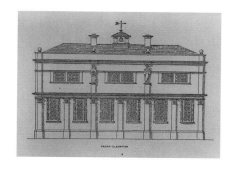

16. A. H. Mackmurdo house, illustrated as "Century Guild Design," *The Hobby Horse*, 1887.

Fry's visual and verbal echoes of Mackmurdo pinpoint his origins along the spectrum of the Victorian avant-garde on a scholarly middle ground between the Aesthetes and the Arts and Crafts. Mackmurdo's influence on Durbins's design, however, may have been augmented by Fry's most personal hopes for his new home. It is known that Fry later tried to help his wife recover memories of their shared past by painting for her a scene from their honeymoon near Avignon, so a reference in the design of the house to their shared appreciation of Mackmurdo's aesthetic is not out of the question.[36] From this perspective, Fry's architectural evocation of "the interiors of the Baroque palaces of Italy" may also be more than the personal preference he described; a trip to Italy in 1897 had earlier cured his wife of pleurisy, and many of their happiest days were spent there. By the same token, the curious checkerboard panel of bricks over Durbins's garden door may be a reference to the similar ornamental string-courses on the house overlooking Hampstead Heath where the Frys lived before Helen's breakdown.[37] Such checkerboard ornamentation is common in Arts and Crafts designs, as well as in the older buildings that inspired them, but its use in a panel, excerpted and framed as Fry has done, is idiosyncratic, and suggests a visual quotation.

Fry's design for Durbins is not, however, explained by its Victorian antecedents or an iconography of personal reference, for its effect is not nostalgic. Far from seeking to recreate the past, Durbins reflects its author's stated determination to make his house express the "actual way of life" of its modern inhabitants, a mode of living that anticipates important aspects of what came to characterize Bloomsbury's domestic ideal. Fry's own description of Durbins focuses on the economic advantages of its boxy plan and hipped roof. Fry matched Durbins's practical exterior with equally functional interior finishing. His daughter later recalled:

> The woodwork was all to be treated with creosote, which had just been introduced for interior decoration as the final answer to both cost and maintenance. The fireplaces were all to be constructed of plain fire-resistant bricks, with no grates or other concessions to custom.[38]

Even Vanessa Bell found the "bareness and austerity" of Durbins something "to which one had to get accustomed."[39]

Against the prevailing ideal of the suburb-dweller as an ersatz country squire, Fry proposed a less formal, more convivial domestic ideal, pointing proudly to Durbins's labor-saving devices, from the dumbwaiter to the central heating system, which eliminated the rituals of the fully staffed "gentlemen's establishments, with lodge, stabling, and greenhouses" that typified the towns around London.[40] The emphasis on domestic sociability in Fry's design is epitomized by the central "house-place," off which opened the front hall, the children's playroom, and studies for Fry and his wife—rooms of one's own all around. But the most striking aspect of Fry's design—and the feature most evocative of Bloomsbury's later domestic aesthetic—is the interpenetration of inside and outside in this central social space.

For visitors arriving at the front door, the first impression of the house is as a conduit to the garden. From the entrance hall, the wide, short stairway following the contour of the sloping plot creates a central axis from the front door down into the light-filled main room and out on to the terrace through a door that, casual photographs reveal, stood open on fine days. All the rooms in the house below the attic feature oversized windows, which reach their largest proportions in the columnar panes of the house-place. Filling the central room with light, the big windows also allow vistas out into the garden. Vanessa Bell later remembered that the house "faced south and seems to me in memory to have been nearly always filled with blazing sunshine."[41] The tall windows not only illuminate the room from above as if it were open to the sky, but also allow people passing along the interior balcony leading to Fry's upper-story study to look out over the living space on to the garden and beyond, a view that stretched in Fry's day as far as the river Wey. Fry's large combination study and studio boasted windows that opened panoramically to the north, south, and west; landscape sketching from this room was an aspect of visits to Durbins mentioned by both Vanessa Bell and Duncan Grant.[42]

While oversized windows brought the outside world into Durbins, the design of the garden made it an extension of the house's interior space. Like his architecture, Fry's garden revealed his ideological roots in the Arts and Crafts movement, which linked the look of houses and gardens, measuring both as indices of health and happiness. Ruskin's *Sesame and Lilies*, for example, allegorized the immorality of war with a dream of squabbling children who wreck the paradisaical house and garden their host gives them to enjoy; his autobiography personalizes this metaphor, recalling early memories of his family's garden as "the little domain [that] answered every purpose of Paradise to me," and regretting their move to a grander establishment where they were "Never any more 'at home'."[43] Echoing Ruskin, an autobiographical fragment by Fry begins with a description of his childhood garden, which he describes as both "the scene of . . . my first passion and my first disillusion" and his imagination's vision of the primal garden: "The serpent still bends down to Eve from the fork of a peculiarly withered and soot begrimed old apple tree which stuck out of the lawn."[44]

17. Roger Fry, *The Artist's Garden at Durbins*, *c.*1917. Oil on canvas, 46.6 × 75.9 cm. Yale Center for British Art.

Rooms of One's Own

Putting principle into practice, Arts and Crafts designers placed great emphasis on gardens. Following their lead, Fry set his house far back on the north end of its narrow lot to maximize the sunny expanse to the south, and consulted with Gertrude Jekyll, one of the most prominent Arts and Crafts landscape designers, to plan his garden. Like the house itself, however, Durbins's garden reflected Fry's particular values, for, unlike the gardens Jekyll usually designed, it eschewed the studied informality associated with English tradition in favor of the symmetrical plantings that characterized continental Europe. Extending the central axis of the house down the hill, the garden stepped down through a sequence of room-like rectangular terraces, each given over to a different kind of planting, while centrally placed elements—circular stairs and two reflecting pools, one rectangular and one round—punctuated the axis linking the various levels. Nearest the house was a wide, gravel terrace; from there steps led down to a sandy area planted with flanking rectangular beds of yucca; below that a lawn surrounded the rectangular pool; beneath that the circular pool was flanked by beds of strawberries, gooseberries, and currants; on the lowest levels were a tennis court and vegetable garden.[45] A painting Fry made from the sand terrace emphasizes the tidy rectilinearity of each level and reinforces the effect of the garden's enclosure by presenting the distant hills and trees, not as an expansive vista, but as an enclosing wall (fig. 17).[46]

As soon as Fry took up residence at Durbins, he began to furnish his garden "rooms" with sculptures by young artists. He was among the first to appreciate the erotically charged sculpture of Eric Gill, who in 1910 had just begun to carve in the round. Fry's friendship with Gill is significant for the way it anticipates his attraction to Bloomsbury as his identity shifted from married man to single father, from historian of Renaissance painting to promoter of contemporary art, and from participant in the waning Victorian guilds to spokesman for an aesthetic that claimed to embody the look of modernity. From Durbins Fry wrote late in 1910:

> It is very strange that just as my inner life which was all bound up in Helen seems definitely crumbling to pieces the general life seems to have suddenly become so immensely more worthwhile. . . . Gill is here and we talked til one this morning. He's given me the first conviction of middle age—not because I don't follow him because I do, but because he moves so easily among all the new and growing ideas and I have moments of giddiness.[47]

Refusing to remain in befuddled middle age, Fry encouraged Gill's new work, commissioning a Cupid as well as an over-life-size standing nude, Gill's largest work to date.[48] The latter provoked objections from Joan Fry, Roger's sister, who had joined the household to help care for the children, and worried that Gill's sculpture would offend visitors to her philanthropic meetings, so another version—equally nude, but striding with elbows and face raised to the sky—replaced it in the summer of 1912 (fig. 18).[49] Fry borrowed this sculpture from its place on the border of the rectangular pool at Durbins for the second Post-Impressionist exhibition, where it occupied a prominent position at the end of the largest gallery in front of Matisse's *Dance*. Another young sculptor Fry commissioned was Henri Gaudier-Brzeska, who around 1913 designed for Durbins a birdbath or fountain in the form of two figures—male and female—supporting a broad dish. Only a maquette for this, Gaudier's largest sculpture, was finished when the artist was repatriated to France to fight in World War I (fig. 19).

The angular style of Gaudier's maquette, evocative of African carving, exemplifies the primitivism that was crucial to Fry's appreciation of both Gaudier and Gill.[50] Praising Gill's "simple, sincere, and deeply-felt images" in *The Nation* in 1911, Fry described him as "a sculptor . . . to whom the language of plastic imagery is instinctive and natural," citing as comparisons "the Pacific islanders," "the workmen of Benin," "the native of the Congo today," and "the great school of medieval sculpture."[51] Likewise, in an elegiac essay on Gaudier's brief career, Fry compared his work to "certain phases of early sculpture—Greek, for instance . . . but still more early Chinese" and noted "traces of an interest in negro sculpture."[52] Bringing such work into his domestic environment, Fry marked his home as both

18. Eric Gill, *The Virgin*, 1911–12, photographed with Pamela Fry at Durbins by Vanessa Bell.

19. Henri Gaudier-Brzeska, maquette for bird bath, *c.*1914. Painted plaster, 28 × 28 × 26.3 cm Macmaster University.

20. Durbins interior, house-place, photographed for *Vogue* by A. C. Cooper, 1917, published in late March 1918.

modern and primitive—or more specifically, modern because of its embrace of primal sensations and experiences. Like Vanessa Bell's re-working of Gauguin's anti-domestic primitivism in her painting, *A Nativity*, which hung at Durbins (as discussed in Chapter 1), Fry's sculpture commissions challenged associations of primitivism with flight from the middle-class home, positioning the primitive as, not just compatible with, but expressive of aspirations for a new kind of domesticity. No less than the "ungentlemanly" appearance of his house, the sculpture Fry commissioned for his garden proclaimed his dissent from conventional domesticity, asserting access to realms of primal pleasure far beyond the nostalgic simplicity of the Arts and Crafts style. Fry's conception of the house as a garden, at once modern and primitive, was to strike a responsive chord in the younger members of the Bloomsbury group.

As Fry's importance for Bloomsbury grew, the house he designed helped shape the group's domestic ideal. For Vanessa Bell, Durbins was "one of Roger's most successful works" and embodied all that she admired about him.[53] After one of her first visits, she wrote:

> What an extraordinary person you are. When I see you in your own home I understand that even better. I do like seeing you among the things you have chosen yourself. They all seem like you full of quite peculiar charm and rightness.[54]

Bell's enthusiasm was shared by Virginia Woolf, whose descriptions of the house emphasize the ideology behind its appearance in words that link it to many subsequent Bloomsbury establishments (figs. 20, 21):

> There were paintings and carvings, Italian cabinets and Chippendale chairs, blue Persian plates, delicately glazed, and rough yellow peasant pottery bought for farthings at fairs. Every sort of style and object seemed to be mixed, but harmoniously. It was a stored, but not a congested, house, a place to live in, not a museum.[55]

At the same time, Durbins's eclectic appearance came to reflect the influence of some of those on whom it had made such a strong impression. By 1917, the fireplace on the east wall of the house-place was flanked by a quattrocento Madonna and Child and Vanessa Bell's monumental *Nativity*, a pairing that exemplified the links Fry posited between the Italian "primitives" and modern artists.[56] Bracketing the

21. Durbins interior, house-place, photographed for *Vogue* by A. C. Cooper, 1917, published in late March 1918.

22. Roger Fry, *Nina Hamnett*, 1917, oil on canvas, 136 × 90.1 cm. University of Leeds Art Collection.

Roger Fry and Durbins

wide central doorway leading from the front hall were a sixth-century Chinese bodhisattva and a Brancusi bronze, this juxtaposition anticipating Clive Bell's comparison of Brancusi to Wei and T'ang dynasty sculpture.[57] On either side of these sentinels were portraits of seated women in nearly identical poses: Grant's 1913 image of Ka Cox, and Fry's 1917 portrait of the painter Nina Hamnett (fig. 22).[58] Painted at Durbins, Fry's portrait of Hamnett—one of the women with whom, after his wife's institutionalization, he tried to re-establish an "intimate companionship in little things"—can be read as a catalog of his hopes for a Post-Impressionist domesticity. It presents its vivacious sitter leaning casually on a chair with paintings propped behind her. Worked at the time when Fry was first applying his aesthetic theories to literature, the portrait proposes a congruence between these arts, matching a French novel, in its characteristic yellow jacket, with the similarly brilliant cubistic pattern of a cushion covered in one of the textiles designed and marketed by the Omega Workshops; the sitter's dress, too, is an Omega design. The modern colors and design of the book and cushion contrast with the fussy flowers in subdued tones on the old-fashioned upholstery of the chair where Hamnett perches on one arm, so that both the form and function of this conventional piece of furniture are adapted to a newer, more casual domestic life. The contrast between old and new—both artefacts and attitudes—is the implicit subject of this portrait of life at Durbins.

As with Fry's earlier connections to Arts and Crafts institutions, his allegiance to the Omega was both broadly ideological and deeply personal. The two identifiable Omega products in this portrait—the dress and the cushion—were designed by the workshop's co-founder, Vanessa Bell, with whom Fry fell deeply in love.[59] From 1911 on, Bell occupied a central place in Fry's ideal of modern domesticity, modeling the integration of what he called "your extraordinary performances in both life and art."[60] Though their sexual liaison was short-lived, the ensuing friendship lasted the rest of their lives and was rooted in domestic intimacy, having been sparked during the winter of 1910–11 by Fry's empathy with Bell's anxiety over the illness of her new-born son. "He knew exactly what it felt like to have one's baby ill. There couldn't be any question that here was sympathy far more intimate than anyone had had before," Bell later recalled.[61] Their love deepened the following spring, when Fry nursed her through a miscarriage during a trip to Turkey (discussed in Chapter 4), and was sustained by their shared focus on parenting and family life. Responding to one of her first letters, Fry wrote, "it was a good one and I loved its being so domestic and all about the children."[62] Fry's desire to set up house with Bell is a recurrent theme of this letters. Long after their sexual liaison ended, a letter from Fry exclaimed, "Wasn't your visit a success?—the best time we've had for years and years. You see we seemed as though we'd been married so long that the effervescence was over."[63]

Bell's influence on Durbins was most concretely embodied in a mural in the entrance hall and an unfinished mosaic in the garden, both dating from April of 1914, when she and Grant joined Fry at the house for a holiday (fig. 23). In good weather they worked on a mosaic to decorate the back wall of a small pavilion off the terrace, while on damp days they painted murals in the foyer. A combination of factors—a preponderance of rainy days, inadequate supplies of the glass tesserae, and, perhaps, the realization that they had begun the mosaic at a scale too large to finish it without raising the roof—resulted in the outdoor project remaining unfinished. A preliminary sketch and the existing fragment, however, reveal its subject was a doubles match at badminton, a theme that would have reinforced the idea of the garden as a space of modern leisure (figs. 24, 25).

While the unfinished mosaic only hints at its intended effect, the completed murals inside Durbins—thanks to Fry's foresight in shielding them behind plasterboard when he sold the house—still exist as they were painted (excepting only portions of the background pattern that originally extended up on to the roof vaults, which were effaced) (fig. 26). Filling the niches under two of the three arches opposite the front door, the murals depict three nude figures against an abstract background. Under the central arch above the wide flight of stairs leading to the living

23. Roger Fry and Duncan Grant working on mosaic at Durbins, 1914.

24. Existing
fragment of mosaic
at Durbins, 1914.

room and garden are two male figures painted by Grant and Bell. Grant's man, in
deep red, leans with arms folded against the right side of the niche, while Bell's yellow man walks away to the left. Between them, a shaft of mottled orange seems to
emerge from a rent in the otherwise dark background in an echo of the light bursting
through the curtained doorway from the sunny room beneath the figures. This beam
of light extends from the central panel to the niche on the left, where it illuminates
the feet of Fry's blue-haired female, who holds another wedge of orange light in her
hands. Fry's figure, springing from this light, reaches over the door that opens onto

25. Attributed to
Roger Fry, sketch for
mosaic at Durbins,
1914. Pencil,
19 × 29.2 cm. Private
collection.

26. Vanessa Bell, Roger Fry, and Duncan Grant, murals in entry hall at Durbins, 1914, as photographed for *Vogue* by A. C. Cooper, 1917, published in late March 1918 (*right*), and as extant (*above*).

the gallery running above the house-place, the energy of her pose inviting visitors to enter the light-filled room. Combining the stylistic exuberance of crude outline and broad patches of daubing with the thematic sensuality of nudes and sunlight, the murals in Durbins's foyer initiate the visitor to the environment of primitivist pleasure created by the design and decoration of the house-place and garden beyond. That Fry planned to extend this aesthetic throughout the house is suggested by a letter to Bell, which refers to "my wall" that she had promised to paint, and one of Bell's designs for an overmantel has been identified as this project for Durbins (fig. 27). Like the foyer murals, it features large standing nudes, roughly colored between dark outlines.[64] Had Fry remained at Durbins, his house might eventually have manifested the same abundance of decoration now found only at Charleston.

Fry was not to experience the domestic ideal Durbins was designed and decorated to contain, however. Like other projects optimistically begun in 1914, Durbins's decoration was cut short by the war. Military conscription and limits on travel reduced his visitors, and by 1916 Fry found himself "sitting alone in my study at Durbins—no one else is here. . . . God it's lonely."[65] Concluding that he could no longer afford to maintain both Durbins and the Omega, Fry rented the house to the Strachey family, who remained in residence through the end of the war; it was there that Lytton completed *Eminent Victorians*.[66] In 1917, coal shortages shut down the heating system, freezing the water pipes. Two years later, Fry, strapped by the financial collapse of the Omega and unable to find tenants to replace the Stracheys, was forced to sell the house he had designed.

Despite these disappointments, Fry remained convinced of Durbins's importance as a model for the design and organization of modernist domesticity. His 1918 *Vogue* essay records his continuing pride in language that blends his old Arts and Crafts vocabulary with newer, formalist criteria. Rejecting the imitation of historical styles in architecture, Fry invoked the formalist claim that forms present on the canvas are more "real" than mimesis. Having defended the Post-Impressionist painters by asserting, "They do not seek to imitate form, but to create form. . . . they aim not

27. Vanessa Bell, design for overmantel, 1912–13. Oil on paper, 76.2 × 56.3 cm. Private collection.

at illusion but at reality," Fry now argued that modern houses, rather than imitating historical models, should be the "direct outcome" of their inhabitants' domestic life: "Instead of looking like something, they would then *be* something." When Fry asserted that in architecture "it is through the artist's sense of proportion and his feeling for plastic relief" that "a work of mere utility may become a work of art," both the term "plastic" and the idea that successful formal manipulation is what distinguishes art from non-art echo his defenses of Post-Impressionism.[67]

Fry's rhetoric in his 1918 *Vogue* article, as well as a lecture he delivered in 1921 to the Royal Institute of British Architects, is striking for its anticipation of ideas often attributed to Le Corbusier's 1923 *Vers une architecture*, which was translated into English in 1927 by one of the original Omega artists, Frederick Etchells. Both Le Corbusier and Fry invoked what the former called "the Engineer's Aesthetic" and the latter termed "engineering beauty" as the basis for a new architecture, to be inflected by the visual imagination of the artist. The "beauty" Fry urged architects to achieve he defined as "the evident sign of an inward spiritual state" and "the expression of a plastic idea." On the same point Le Corbusier said, "The Architect, by his arrangement of forms, realizes an order which is a pure creation of his spirit; by forms and shapes he . . . provokes plastic emotions; . . . it is then that we experience the sense of beauty."[68] To achieve this new beauty, both Fry and Le Corbusier called for an end to ornamentation in historical styles in favor of greater attention to the clear expression of basic masses and the play of light upon surfaces. This rhetorical compatibility provides a theoretical background for the rarely recognized fact that the Bloomsbury critics were among the first in England to appreciate modernist commercial architecture.[69]

Despite these points of compatibility (and their visual manifestation, which prompted historians of modernism to compare Durbins to Le Corbusier's early villas), the differences between Bloomsbury's modernism and mainstream modernism are clear in Fry's essays on architecture. Never claiming the functionalist standard that later came to justify International Style design, Fry's *Vogue* essay emphasizes the aesthetic basis of modern design. After the basic elements are "determined by need," Fry says, "there is still a wide margin for choice" in the design.[70] Other differences between Fry's article on Durbins and Le Corbusier's *Vers une architecture* reinforce the distinctions proposed in my Introduction between Bloomsbury's domestic ideals and the heroic ideology of mainstream modernism. Even the slight difference between the similar phrases "engineering beauty" and "the Engineer's Aesthetic" reflects Le Corbusier's emphasis on the heroic figure he conjured behind the new architecture. This figure of the authoritative hero-engineer animates Le Corbusier's enthusiasm for standardization and "the state of mind for living in mass-production houses." "All men," he proclaimed in one-sentence paragraphs, "have the same organism, the same functions. All men have the same needs."[71] In contrast, Fry described modern domestic architecture as an expression of individuality. "If people were just to let their houses be the direct outcome of . . . their actual way of life, and allow other people to think what they like," he asked, "Wouldn't such houses have really a great deal more character, and therefore interest for others"?[72] And where Le Corbusier upheld the "virile atmosphere" of "the world of industry and business" as the inspiration for a new architecture, Fry urged the largely female readers of *Vogue* to follow his example, assuring them, "it does not require genius or even any extraordinary talent to make a genuine and honest piece of domestic architecture."[73] This modest reassurance marks the full measure of Fry's distance from Le Corbusier's heroic modernism. Retaining one of the most productive aspects of the Victorian legacy of domestic reform, Fry's ideal, represented in both the house he designed and the architectural theories he propounded, draws its strength from a vision of a new world ordered around values generated from—rather than imposed upon—the home.

3

Duncan Grant and King's College, Cambridge (1910)

Vanessa Bell's 46 Gordon Square and Roger Fry's Durbins offer two early independent examples of the Bloomsbury artists' re-imagination of domestic environments to express the new ways of life they contained. In 1910, however, neither Bell's nor Fry's homes manifested what would become the look of Bloomsbury's domestic modernism. The Gordon Square house remained in what Woolf called the "age of Augustus John," while the just-finished Durbins, though an imaginative blend of Aesthetic and Arts-and-Crafts design, was, nevertheless, a variation on late-nineteenth-century conventions. It was not until the winter of 1910–11 that the first of the modernist murals that came to epitomize Bloomsbury's house-style appeared in a home associated with the group. The artist was Duncan Grant, the newest initiate to Bloomsbury, and his first experiment at domestic design took place in the sitting room of John Maynard Keynes at King's College, Cambridge (fig. 28).

Though the work of Grant alone, the Keynes mural might be seen as the group's first collaboration. Powerfully informed by the ideological background of Bloomsbury—including Post-Impressionism, Cambridge, and sexual nonconformity—its interweaving of new ideas of aesthetics and erotics anticipates much of what would become most characteristic in Bloomsbury's domestic design. Stylistically, the mural's uneasy combination of proto-Renaissance precedents and French modernist styles reveals both the origins and the future of Bloomsbury's aesthetics. Analogously, the mural reveals the Victorian roots of Bloomsbury's sexual ideology, even as it proposes a self-consciously modern revision of that precedent. Now clearly a marker of important transitions in the histories of both art and sexuality in England, the Keynes mural began—like Bell's and Fry's experiments in domestic design—as the embellishment of private space. It, too, re-imagined a domestic room to set a modern stage for a new way of life, in this case the life of a young economist who was Grant's lover and friend.

This first definitive Bloomsbury interior was created by an artist anomalous within Bloomsbury. Five years younger than the generation of men who first congregated with Thoby Stephen's sisters at Gordon Square in 1905, Grant, alone among Bloomsbury's men, did not attend Cambridge. And, like Fry, Grant came late to the group. Although Grant, who was a cousin of Lytton Strachey's, first met Vanessa in the winter of 1905–6 and re-encountered the Bells on their honeymoon in Paris in 1907, he did not join their circle of friends until late in 1909, when, with Keynes, he rented a two-room ground-floor flat at 21 Fitzroy Square, a townhouse that had been broken up into small flats. By this time, Bell's siblings, Virginia and Adrian, were living at 29 Fitzroy Square, having left the nearby Gordon Square

28. Duncan Grant, mural for John Maynard Keynes, King's College Cambridge, 1910, now obscured.

house to Vanessa and her new husband. Bloomsbury's regular Thursday evening parties moved with them from Gordon Square to Fitzroy Square, and Grant, as an acquaintance and neighbor, began to attend.

Grant's introduction to Bloomsbury coincided with a change in the group's character that Virginia Woolf, with facetious overprecision, dated anecdotally to the moment when Strachey, she said, pointed to a stain on Vanessa's dress and uttered the one-word question, "Semen?":

> With that all barriers of reticence and reserve went down. A flood of the sacred fluid seemed to overwhelm us. Sex permeated our conversation. The word bugger was never far from our lips. We discussed copulation with the same excitement and openness that we had discussed the nature of good.[1]

Behind Woolf's witty pinpointing of Strachey's role in revolutionizing Bloomsbury's sexual attitudes lies a more sober story of the affection that developed between Vanessa and Lytton after Thoby Stephen's death in 1906: "I have loved him ever since the time when Thoby died and he came and was such an inexpressible help and made one think of the things most worth thinking of," Bell later recalled; "[O]ne could talk to Lytton and he seemed to see further into things than anyone else could."[2] Strachey, who had long used sexual language to create an atmosphere of intimacy and freedom among his friends at Cambridge, brought the same liberating spirit to Bloomsbury's women, and Bell revelled in what she called "my native bawdiness."[3] During the winter of 1907–8, the Bells began a play-reading club with their friends, starting with a seventeenth-century drama, because, Strachey reported, "Vanessa said that we'd better begin with the most indecent thing we could, so as to get it settled."[4] By 1914 Bell could be found writing in a note after a visit to Keynes:

> Did you have a pleasant afternoon buggering one or more of the young men we left for you? It must have been delicious out on the downs in the afternoon sun—a thing I have always wanted to do but one never gets the opportunity and the desire at the right moment. I imagine you, however, with your bare limbs entwined with his and all the ecstatic preliminaries of sucking sodomy—it sounds like the name of a station. . . . Perhaps all this is imaginary however and it really

took place in a bedroom. I wonder whose? Not Gerald's at any rate for one really couldn't have the heart to disarrange his exquisitely tight trousers.

Her speculation concludes that her visit made her feel "singularly happy and free tongued."[5] The Bloomsbury women's enthusiasm for their male friends' homoerotic adventures has perplexed—even angered—observers, but what Bell called "bawdy" talk was a crucial signifier of the group's rejection of conventions of sexuality and gender. Virginia Woolf asserted that it was because of her friendship with "buggers" that "the old sentimental views of marriage in which we were brought up were revolutionized," while Bell, recalling the freedom of Gordon Square, concluded:

> This freedom was I believe largely owing to Lytton Strachey. . . . Only those just getting to know him well in those days when complete freedom of mind and expression were almost unknown, at least among men and women, can understand what an exciting world of explorations of thought and feeling he seemed to reveal. . . . [He] showed a world in which one need no longer be afraid of saying what one thought.[6]

It was into this sexually radicalized Bloomsbury that Keynes and Grant were made welcome. Encouraged by Strachey, who was their elder, in a forthright acceptance of their homosexual desires, they fell easily—Grant especially—into his circle of friends.[7] Also linking Grant and Keynes to Bloomsbury was a common delight in domesticity. When they moved together to Fitzroy Square, Grant took charge of outfitting their rooms, writing to Keynes at Cambridge to describe how he ordered wallpaper of "cuckoo green" for his studio in the front room and installed, with the bravado of a would-be Oscar Wilde, "the most exquisite pot of chrysanthemums of a pale purplish hue . . . which in themselves completely furnish the room."[8] The domestic nature of their relationship was recognized by Vanessa Bell, who observed in 1914, when the Brunswick Square household that included Grant and Keynes was breaking up, that although the men had not been lovers for years, "Maynard seems to be fearfully lonely in his rooms. He talked a great deal about Duncan . . . they had lived together now for six years off and on."[9] Though their London quarters took on greater importance in later years, in 1909 the kitchenless two-room flat Grant and Keynes shared was little more than a sleeping annex to their friends' houses down the block in Fitzroy Square and in nearby Gordon Square. In contrast, Keynes's rooms at King's College followed Bell's 46 Gordon Square and Fry's Durbins in becoming a symbol of the life it contained. Anticipating one of the Omega's most characteristic products, Grant designed needlepoint upholstery for Keynes's chairs in this room, but these were to complement his major project: the mural that first manifested Bloomsbury's domestic aesthetic.[10]

Grant's decorations for Keynes were conceived from the start as an expression of sexual identity—an identity rooted in the legacy of Aestheticism as it was manifest at King's College. Aestheticism, personified most publicly by Oscar Wilde and Walter Pater, was represented among the influential faculty of King's by the philosopher G. E. Moore and the historians G. L. Dickinson and Oscar Browning. Though their public reputations were limited in comparison to Wilde and Pater, their influence on Bloomsbury's generation of students would be hard to overstate.[11] The flamboyant Browning, known as "the O.B.," was especially important. A proponent of "Greek love" as the passion of master and (male) student, Browning pursued a pedagogical career based on erotically charged relationships with young men of varying class backgrounds, whom he tutored, took on trips, and established in careers. Browning's Sunday night open-house parties were a university institution, according to Dickinson, "the centre of all that was most sociable, genial, and stimulating in Cambridge."[12] Desmond MacCarthy recalled how at these parties one would be introduced to the young men who were " 'O.B.'s' numerous beneficiaries. With an affectionate hand on the shoulder of each of us, and bringing us almost nose to nose, he seemed to be performing a sort of marriage ceremony."[13] It was largely due to his influence on student life at King's that by 1908, the college historian records, visitors to the college were shocked by "the openness of the display of affection between [male] couples."[14] As early as 1886, C. R. Ashbee's journals record his idealized passion for Roger Fry: "Fry is sacred, loved and loving to me as ever, a transfigured world when I look into his eyes and a calm confidence in the future when hand in hand we are together in the moonlight on the bridge."[15] By 1909, Keynes effused to Grant about the culture of homosexuality at King's: "the thing is absolutely universal . . . nothing else is talked about and everybody considers himself one."[16] Comic exaggeration is a hallmark of Bloomsbury correspondence, and Browning, like other Aesthetes, vehemently denied imputations of eroticism attached to his defenses of masculine love. Nevertheless, Keynes's comment reflects how the social atmosphere at King's offered Bloomsbury a model of subculture: a community where certain mores of bourgeois British life gave way to a set of conventions that accorded homoerotic impulses a privileged place. So much a part of this legacy were Browning's rooms that Keynes tried unsuccessfully to get them for himself. "I am very disappointed that you have not got the O.B.'s rooms after all. . . . It would be rather nice to draw up a scheme for their decoration," Grant wrote to him in October of 1910.[17]

Overcoming this disappointment, Grant quickly started work in the suite Keynes was assigned, re-imagining the rather formal room as a fanciful vineyard where a grape harvest offered the occasion for a Dionysian revel of naked dancers. Grant's imagery links the abundance of nature with the sensual pleasures of wine, music, and the body, so that nature is figured as sensual and sensuality is asserted as natural. These themes anticipate the subsequent half-century of Bloomsbury's domestic iconography, and, in broadest terms, express the group's determination to implement a domestic existence in opposition to the conventional Victorian equation of civilization with dominion over nature and discipline over the body. In this first manifestation as a setting for Keynes's university life, allusions to a classicized golden age in the lands bordering the Mediterranean are more specific to the legacy of Aestheticism at King's. No student among Keynes's Cambridge contemporaries, raised in the Pre-Raphaelite era and drilled in classical literature, would have approached Grant's imagery unaware of the conventions of pastoral poetry and art from Virgil's *Eclogues* to Botticelli's *Primavera*, which the circle of dancing figures in the mural evokes. The pastoral was more than a category in critical theory, for, from the sixteenth century onward, English poets had invoked pastoral language to describe homosexual love.[18] By the late nineteenth century, Bloomsbury's Cambridge predecessors—Browning and Dickinson, along with John Addington Symonds—had solidified notions of a classical Arcadia into the ideal of "Greek love," as an affirmative outlet for homoerotic desire.

Symonds, a graduate of King's, was especially attentive to what he saw as modern manifestations of this ancient ideal. His 1873 *The Greek Poets* describes the Athenians' male-oriented "sense of beauty," concluding, that to find "some living echo" of Greek sculpture, "we must visit the fields where boys bathe in early morning, or the playgrounds of our public schools in summer, or the banks of the Isis when the eights are on the water, or the riding schools of young soldiers." Symonds's investment in this lovingly detailed list of modern equivalents to Greek institutions becomes explicit in a footnote (omitted from later editions) that connects a contemporary minority to this historical ideal: "Some will always be found . . . to whom Greece is a lost fatherland, and who, passing through youth with the *mal du pays* [homesickness] of that irrecoverable land upon them, may be compared to visionaries." Seizing this role for himself, Symonds, in the main text, explained how "the convent or the prison life of early Catholicity," had sundered "the animal unity of man with nature," a rift that such Renaissance artists as Michelangelo had partially healed. Now, however, Symonds identified "at least a hope of future reconciliation" in the era of Science, "which teaches man to know himself and explains his real relation to Nature," teaching "a healthy acceptance of the physical laws" and proving "that there is no antagonism between our physical and spiritual constitution." Again the footnote makes the implications explicit: asking how "modern man" might again make "the Hellenic tradition vital," Symonds answers, "There is indeed this one way only—to be natural. We must imitate the Greeks . . . by approximating to their free and fearless attitude of mind." "To do this in the midst of our conventionalities and prejudices," Symonds acknowledges, "is no doubt hard," but one modern writer shows the way:

> Strange as it may seem, Walt Whitman is more truly Greek than any man of modern times. Hopeful and fearless, accepting the world as he finds it, recognizing the value of each human impulse . . . he, in the midst of a chaotic age, emerges clear and distinct, at one with nature, and therefore Greek. . . . It is that which the Greeks had of eternal, indestructible, separable from local customs and transient conventionalities.[19]

Symonds's fusion of "nature" (justified by "Science") with a homoeroticism founded in ancient Greece, revived by the Italian Renaissance, and brought explicitly up to date in the writings of Whitman and the cavorting of soldiers and schoolboys, offered late-Victorian readers a powerful and influential model of homosexual identity. Dickinson's 1896 *The Greek View of Life* drew heavily on Symonds's idea of Greek ethics: "Moral virtue they conceived not as obedience to an external law, a sacrifice of the natural man to a power that is in a sense alien to himself, but rather as the tempering into due proportion of the elements of which human nature is composed."[20] Dickinson's scholarly books have been described as "part of the working library of liberation" for educated gay men in England through the 1930s.[21] His most forthright text, by far, however, was an autobiography unpublished until 1973. Here Dickinson relates how, as an undergraduate, he first realized his homosexuality when he, like Ashbee, fell in love with Roger Fry:

> One evening, in a talk with a student of Classics, I discovered that the Greek love, as I had read of it in Plato, was a continuous and still existing fact. . . . This I suppose, set free a current of feeling that was natural to me. And the next thing I remember is going one night into Roger's bedroom to say good night, and stooping down to kiss his forehead. This was a decisive moment. I went back to my lodgings strangely excited, lay awake reading . . . and said to myself "I must be in love."[22]

This passage linking Dickinson's homoerotic desires with the example of ancient Greece explains what is implied in *The Greek View of Life*. His autobiography offers the clearest record of what Bloomsbury's men imbibed from their personal relationship with this teacher and friend: a confidence that Greek precedent sanctioned homoerotic impulses in the present.

Dickinson's *Autobiography* also asserts a link between modern Italy and the classical past. Describing his first trip to Rome with Ashbee in 1887, he wrote, "Then, as often before and later, the illusion possessed me that somehow life might, and could, be something far more pleasurable and passionate than it ever seemed to be to modern men, as it had been (I thought) to Virgil or Horace."[23] This ideal was not unique to Dickinson. Italy figured for many in England as a site of pleasures and passions forbidden at home; Vanessa Bell's letters rehearse, half-ironically, ideas of Italy as a place where "we would all loaf and have love affairs by the dozen and become creatures of the senses alone."[24] More concretely, homosexual acts were not criminalized in France, Italy, and other territories once governed by the Napoleonic Code—a doctor explains this to the hero of E. M. Forster's *Maurice*, observing that, in contrast, "England has always been disinclined to accept human nature."[25] Well-known communities of English Aesthetes emerged in many Italian cities, inspired both by current law and by a belief that Mediterranean culture still manifested the lingering values of ancient Greece, where homoeroticism was not merely tolerated but celebrated as the highest manifestation of sensual and intellectual bonding between men.

This idea, evident in British literature from Byron to Forster, had a powerful impact on Bloomsbury's men.[26] Keynes and Grant traveled together to Greece and Turkey in 1910 and to Sicily and Tunis in 1911. On these trips, Keynes photographed Grant naked in such classical settings as the temple at Bassae, enacting

Duncan Grant and King's College, Cambridge

29. Piero della Francesca, detail from *Exultation of the Cross*, from the cycles of frescos, *The Legend of the True Cross*, c.1460, Arezzo.

30. Attributed to Michelangelo, *Entombment*, Oil on wood, 161.7 × 149.9 cm. National Gallery, London.

the links they perceived between ancient and modern homoeroticism. Back in England, Grant wrote to Keynes about the photographs, "You must say that it was a shepherd or something and that no one wears clothes in Arcadia."[27] How completely Grant adopted this idea of southern Europe as a modern Arcadia, free of the repressive strictures of his own culture, is suggested by his account of a trip to Florence when he was twenty-two. Writing to Strachey, Grant reveals his absorption of the pastoral fantasy propounded by the champions of "Greek love," his strong identification with its challenge to middle-class English mores, and his belief in the power of art to express and promulgate this alternative ethic:

> I often in my journey by the sea longed to get out and live the rest of my life unbeknownst and lost among the beautiful youths I saw playing about in and out of the mirror-like sea with roses trailing on the sands and nothing to do but pick up a few olives when they fall to the ground. . . . I suppose you won't believe me when I tell you nearly all the youths here are miraculously lovely and that very often they bathe and look for frogs with nothing on just outside the drawing room window. ("Oh! Look!" said Mrs. Ewbank in her vague way, "those men have taken all their clothes off!" "Really!!" says I, showing I'm afraid too much eagerness to see. "Do you think it ought to be allowed, Duncan?") In the cool of the evening the whole town turns out to see the gilded youth[s]. . . . As each tremblingly steps out of the water a murmur of admiration or the reverse ascends from the bridge. My neighbor turned to me and said (after a burst of derisive laughter at some rather fat legs), "that young man's grace is entirely in his torso—his legs are much too gross, which is never beautiful." Wasn't it rather wonderful? I suppose they've been educated by Michel Angelo.[28]

These are the themes Grant brought together in his mural for Keynes's Cambridge rooms: a pastoral myth of natural abundance and sensual indulgence made manifest in contemporary social practices of rural Italy through the influence of Renaissance art and Michelangelo in particular. The precedent of Italian art is clear in the two end panels of Grant's mural, which depict nude men and semi-nude women bearing baskets of fruit from the trellises above. The static solidity of the women recalls Piero della Francesca, whose murals in the church of San Francesco in Arezzo Grant visited in 1904 and again in 1907 (fig. 29).[29] The active muscularity of the male nudes, shown reaching for and lifting the fruit, evokes both Piero and Michelangelo—whose mural-scale *Entombment* (fig. 30), with its central naked figure of Christ, Grant was copying at the National Gallery at this time—suggesting his ambition to offer Cambridge an education in the aesthetics of the male body like that Italians received from their art.[30] These stylistic allusions to Italy's classical heritage complement the iconography of the canephoroe (classicized figures holding baskets of fruit on their heads), which returns repeatedly in Grant's work to suggest links between Arcadian abundance and contemporary Italian life.[31] His first known use of this device in the 1910 *Lemon Gatherers* (fig. 31) was inspired by a performance of a troupe of Italian actors known as the Sicilian Players, whose effect on Bloomsbury may be gauged by Lytton Strachey's review of their performance in *the Spectator*. Strachey praised the Italian spectacle in language like that of Grant's letter from Italy as "totally dissimilar to the refined self-consciousness of the civilised society today," concluding, "no English actor or actress, however gifted, could hope to rival in intensity of physical expressiveness, these hot-blooded children of the south."[32] Writing to Grant, Strachey was more explicit in his appreciation of the male lead: "I was transported by him . . . —that dance!—like a stag in the rutting season."[33]

The image of canephoroe—evocative of Mediterranean art from ancient statuary to the headdresses in Piero's frescos and at the same time consistent with spectacles of labor in Italy's farms and harbors—was ideally suited to blend pastoral myth with the mores of modern Italy. And Grant was not the first to discover it. Victorian associations of Italy with eroticized classicism are nowhere clearer than in the photographs of Wilhelm von Gloeden, an expatriate German living in Sicily, where he photographed local youths, naked or loosely draped in togas and posed in classical

31. Duncan Grant, *The Lemon Gatherers*, 1910. Oil on canvas, 57 × 80 cm. Tate Britain.

attitudes and settings (fig. 32). Von Gloeden's photographs circulated widely in ethnographic journals, such as *The National Geographic*, and, billed as artists' substitutes for live models, in magazines like *The Studio*, and as postcards. These images reflect the same conflation of contemporary Mediterranean culture with classical and pastoral allusions that animated the champions of Greek love, and they were collected by interested amateurs, including Browning, Symonds, and Oscar Wilde—in fact, Grant claimed that one of his own von Gloeden photographs had been Wilde's.[34] A comparison of one of von Gloeden's photographs with Grant's *Two Nudes on a Beach*, a painting contemporary with the Keynes mural, shows a similar fusion of contemporary life and ancient art (fig. 33). In both the stylized nudity and classicized poses of the central figure(s) is juxtaposed with background character(s) who set the scene in modern Italy. Whether Grant's image drew directly on homoerotic photographs circulated at Cambridge (as some of his later work was based on photographs from muscle magazines) is a matter for speculation. The similarities between Grant's paintings and such pictures, however, demonstrate a shared belief in Italy as a modern Arcadia, where ancient custom, the heritage of the Renaissance, and even the beneficence of nature seem to combine to sanction homoerotic impulses condemned in England.

Where the Cambridge men of Browning's generation kept their homoerotic photographic collections discreetly in albums, however, Grant realized his sensual vision in brilliant color and nearly life-size scale on the wall of Keynes's sitting room. Although Bloomsbury's men had absorbed their teachers' idealized vision of ancient Greece and modern Italy, the group rejected what it perceived as the hypocrisy attending the earlier generation's rhetoric of Platonic love, which they mocked with the phrase "the higher sodomy." Subsequent commentators have misrepresented

Duncan Grant and King's College, Cambridge

32. Wilhelm von Gloeden, photograph.

this term as Bloomsbury's self-congratulatory characterization of its own sexual ethic, but the group's use of the phrase to condemn what Strachey called "a sort of ideological homosexuality which manifested itself more in words than in deeds" is clear in his correspondence with Keynes and Grant.[35] Describing another student he encountered on a trip through Italy in 1906, Keynes wrote Strachey:

> Scott is dreadfully Oxford—a sort of aesthetic person. . . . Even in his sodomy, which he takes more solidly than anything else, he seems to want to worship an idealised vision in which he has clothed some good-looking absurdity rather than to come to close quarters.[36]

Summarizing Keynes's account in a letter to Grant, Strachey commented:

> Scott would drive me to an asylum. . . . He's what I call a "higher" sodomite of the most virulent type, besides being hopelessly cultured. He's mild—in love, Keynes says, with an impossibly flimsy ideal, with impossibly flimsy balls (added by me).[37]

33. Duncan Grant
Two Nudes on a Beach, c.1910.
Oil on board,
106.7 × 68.6 cm.
Yale Center for
British Art.

Strachey, in a related letter to Grant, also satirized the poetry of "the flabby old sodomite John Addington Symonds" penned under the inspiration of photographs like Van Gloeden's, mocking their studied gender-neutrality and pedantically classical obfuscation of the author's sexual interest. His creative paraphrase runs:

> No longer are the hills divine
> As in the days of yore;
> Deserted is Athene's shrine,
> Boy Bacchus laughs no more

And so on, the gist of it being that, in spite of these changes, a great many things go on just the same. The last verse is as follows—

> In spite of Time and Change and Fate,
> The sun still clasps the shore,
> And youths and maidens copulate
> As in the days of yore.

Or words to that effect. . . . He of course thought of youths copulating with youths. . . .[38]

Thus Bloomsbury gleefully rejected what it saw as the Aesthetes' repression in the name of refinement, asserting a forthright acceptance of homosexual desire more appropriate to what Strachey characterized as "These days of motors, sodomy, and general advance."[39] Keynes could, therefore, photograph his lover nude in poses reminiscent of voan Gloeden's pictures of Sicilian youths, forgoing the distance implied by the older generation's claims to detached observation of homoeroticism, with Grant now presenting himself as the self-conscious—hence modern—primitive. In a self-portrait contemporary with the Keynes mural Grant shows himself bare-shouldered, bearing a basket on his head, as if to become one of his cane-phoroe.[40] Similarly, his inclusion of slim and sinuous men in the ring of dancers in the center panels of Keynes's mural revises conventions—consistent from Botticelli through Matisse—that made women the exclusive embodiment of sensual ecstasy. Grant's determination to push beyond the Aesthetes' "higher sodomy" toward franker and more pleasurable expressions of homoeroticism distinguished Keynes's mural not only from the traditional book-and-portrait-lined university residences the economist had previously inhabited, but even from the "*art-nouveau* symphony in green and white" that had seemed so advanced when Lytton Strachey commissioned it for his brother James's Cambridge rooms in 1905.[41] By comparison, Grant's mural was unmistakably modern, not only in the sensuality of its imagery, but also in its exuberant style, evocative of the most recent developments in French art.

To understand how Parisian modernism helped Grant resolve the ambivalence inherent in the earlier generation's "higher sodomy," it helps to recall the context in which modern art—especially Matisse—was introduced to English audiences. No event was more crucial to the definition of modernism in England than the exhibition that opened in November of 1910 under the title *Manet and the Post-Impressionists*. Organized by Roger Fry, with help from Clive Bell, in order to bring contemporary French art to the insular London art world, the exhibition was both popular and controversial; one measure of its impact was the general acceptance of the term Post-Impressionism, which Fry had hastily coined. Grant, typically laconic, recalled, "We were wildly enthusiastic about the exhibition."[42] Vanessa Bell's more detailed account suggests how Bloomsbury linked the show to a broad ethos of rebellion against authoritative convention:

> It is impossible I think that any other single exhibition can ever have had so much effect as did that on the rising generation . . . here was a sudden pointing to a possible path, a sudden liberation and encouragement to feel for oneself which were absolutely overwhelming. . . . [I]t was as if one might say things one had always felt instead of trying to say things that people told one to feel.[43]

Bell's memoir echoes the terms in which the catalog for *Manet and the Post-Impressionists* presented the new art. The catalog essay, written by the exhibition's secretary from Fry's notes, asserts as the distinguishing characteristic of French modernism "the resolve of each artist to express his own temperament, and never to permit contemporary ideals to dictate to him what was beautiful, significant, and worthy to be painted." Even in this company of nonconformists, the catalog asserts, one artist stands out among all those who were "pushing their ideas further and further":

> In the work of Matisse, especially, this search for an abstract harmony of line, for rhythm, has been carried to lengths which often deprive the figure of all appearance of nature. The general effect of his pictures is that of a return to primitive, even perhaps of a return to barbaric, art.[44]

The defenses of Post-Impressionism that Fry published in *The Nation* concurrently with the exhibition expanded on the argument of the catalog, making clear that by "primitive" he referred to the Italian painters of the quattrocento. Fry's advocacy of modernist painting drew heavily on his authority as an expert on these "Italian primitives," whom he praised as more expressive than their better-known successors. "When you can draw like Tintoretto, you can no longer draw like Giotto, or even like Piero della Francesca. You have lost the power of expression which the bare recital of elementary facts of mass, gesture, and movement gave," Fry said. This presentation of modernism as a return to the uninhibited expressiveness of Italian primitives, able to "give to the rendering of nature its response in human passion and human need," was ideally suited to capture the imagination of an artist like Grant by appealing simultaneously to notions of Italy as an Arcadia of unfettered sensuality and to claims for the most advanced modernity. Likewise, when Fry exhorted his reader to "look without preconception as to what a picture ought to be and do [and] allow his senses to speak to him instead of his common sense," his rhetoric matched Grant's belief in the possibility of a modern return to primal sensuality from the repressiveness of recent convention.[45]

For Grant, the influence of the first Post-Impressionist exhibition was intensified by simultaneous overtures of friendship from its organizer. The day after the opening, Fry wrote to Grant, asking him to submit work for an exhibition by the New English Art Club and inviting him to visit Durbins.[46] "I thought Roger Fry extremely nice but rather exhausting," Grant reported to Keynes after this visit; "he makes up his mind so extraordinarily quickly."[47] In the first flush of Fry's energetic influence, Grant began work on his Cambridge mural, and the speed with which, over the winter of 1910–11, he pushed to develop his own avant-garde sensibility is marked in the difference between the middle panels and their flanking sections. Grant's visual citations of Piero and Michelangelo in the end panels contrasts strongly with the center section, where the circle of naked dancers is rendered with the broad, loose brushstrokes of Post-Impressionism.

This stylistic incoherence may account for reports that Grant was dissatisfied with the mural and considered it unfinished (ten years later, working with Vanessa Bell, Grant replaced it with a different scheme, discussed in Chapter 13).[48] Grant's frustration might also be, at least in part, ascribed to a disjuncture between the rhetorical claims made for Post-Impressionism by the organizers of the Grafton show and the examples of Post-Impressionist art they were able to bring to London. None of the paintings in the catalog to the exhibition offers a visual model for Grant's mural, which seems clearly indebted to Matisse—this link is especially clear in the extant preliminary studies, where the motif of dancers is combined with Matisse's characteristic heavy outlines and broad scrubbing brush work (fig. 34).[49] Fry acknowledged that Matisse was "quite inadequately represented" in the exhibition, with only two landscapes and a Fauvist portrait on display. It would not be until Fry's second Post-Impressionist exhibition in 1912 that Matisse's most obvious precedents, his mural-scale dance paintings, would be shown in London (see fig. 60).[50]

Matisse's skimpy representation in the Post-Impressionist exhibition does not negate the influence of this artist and this show on Grant's mural, however. Although Fry's claims for Matisse's primitivism were weakly supported by the

34. Duncan Grant, sketch for Keynes mural, 1910. Private collection.

paintings in London, this was not Grant's first exposure to the artist. Grant later recalled that while studying in Paris in the spring of 1909, he toured Gertrude Stein's collection, which included Matisse's *Bonheur de vivre* with its central motif of whirling naked figures, and also visited Matisse's studio, where he could have seen preliminary versions of the *Dance* mural and the sculpture *Le dos*, both of which Fry would bring to London for the second Post-Impressionist show.[51] Grant's most recent biographer assigns these visits later dates, however.[52] If so, his knowledge of Matisse derived from just two small still-lifes Grant noted in an exhibition of recent French art in Brighton during the summer of 1910, undoubtedly augmented by Fry's accounts of the 1910 Paris *Salon d'automne*. In a review published shortly before the opening of the first Post-Impressionist exhibition, Fry praised Matisse's "quite original linear rhythm, which comes out finely in the ring of dancing figures" in *Dance*.[53] The gap between Grant's superficial knowledge of Matisse's art and the extraordinarily Matissian dancers he produced for Keynes

35. Henri Matisse, painted vase, 1907. Musée d'Art Moderne de la Ville de Paris.

36. Duncan Grant, painted Tunisian vase, 1911, 35 cm high. Charleston Trust.

remains mysterious, however, only as long as scholars continue to overlook one display in *Manet and the Post-Impressionists*: a selection of seven ceramic vases painted by modern artists, including one by Matisse, which had been made for the 1907 *Salon d'automne* (fig. 35).[54] Fry concluded his articles defending the exhibition by urging "special attention" to these works in which "there is scarcely any appeal made through representation . . . and yet they will arouse a definite feeling."[55] Although it is not now known exactly which of Matisse's vases was exhibited in London, it is likely to have been one of several—another was purchased by the Steins—that featured a ring of spinning dancers drawn with the same kind of black outline that Fry praised in Matisse's *Dance* and that reappears in the center panel of Grant's mural for Keynes.[56] Additional evidence of the influence of Matisse's ceramics is provided by Grant's own decoration of a Tunisian vase with calligraphic nudes during the summer after the first Post-Impressionist show (fig. 36).

Whatever Grant's immediate visual sources, Fry's descriptions of the Post-Impressionists—Matisse in particular—as effecting a modern return to the passionate primitivism of Italy offered Grant the tools he needed to mark Keynes's Cambridge rooms as the site of a sensual Italiante modernity. Grant's perception of Post-Impressionism as subverting conventional values was encouraged by critical reactions to *Manet and the Post-Impressionists*, which associated the new art with any number of challenges to authority, from the violence of the Ulster Unionists to the militancy of the suffragettes, whose first major clash with the police coincided with the opening of the show.[57] Post-Impressionism was repeatedly described as a form of anarchy, with *the Athenaeum* warning that the exhibition could undermine the "many generations of sustained thought on long-established premises [that] have given a certain concrete reality to standards of truth, morals, and aesthetics."[58] At the same time, radicals of all sorts embraced analogies with the Post-Impressionists. The left-wing *Daily Herald*, for instance, reported, "The Post-Impressionists are in the company of the Great Rebels of the World. In politics the only movements worth considering are Woman Suffrage and Socialism. They are both Post-Impressionist in their desire to scrap old decaying forms and find for themselves a new working ideal."[59] This rhetoric was picked up by the art critic Frank Rutter, whose defense of modern painting, published shortly after the exhibition under the title *Revolution in Art*, was dedicated "to the rebels of either sex all the world over who in any way are fighting for freedom of any kind."

Specifically sexual connotations to the rebellion proposed by the Post-Impressionists were registered in accusations of vice and degeneracy—the same terms applied by the dominant culture to homosexual desire—lodged against the new art by hostile critics who replayed the charges of effeminacy and insanity that had earlier been leveled against Wilde and the Aesthetes. The *Art Chronicle* complained that the Post-Impressionist pictures, all of which were by men, constituted "girlish, hysterical impatience in paint."[60] A letter in the conservative *Morning Post* piously hoped that "the youth of England, being healthy in mind and body, is far too virile to be moved save in resentment at the providers of this unmanly show."[61] The diary of the diplomat Wilfred Blunt demonstrates that journalists were not alone in associating the exhibition with affronts to sexual propriety. "Nothing but the gross puerility which scrawls indecencies on the walls of a privy . . . a pornographic show," Blunt concluded, despite the fact that Desmond MacCarthy, the exhibition's secretary, had excluded any nude he thought might arouse controversy.[62] Grant's new status as a Bloomsbury insider would have included him in conversations recounting—and probably exaggerating—the accusations of pornography and indecency voiced by visitors to the gallery after the *Morning Post* characterized a Maillol sculpture as "alien to the spirit of all ancient art not deliberately pornographic."[63] The pleasure Grant took in Mrs. Ewbank's discomfort at the nudity of the bathing youths in Italy is echoed in MacCarthy's enthusiastic recounting of gallery-goers shaking their umbrellas at the offending images.[64]

Among Virginia Woolf's most often quoted remarks is her observation that, "in or about December 1910, human character changed."[65] As facetiously overprecise as her pinpointing the moment of Bloomsbury's sexual awakening by Strachey, Woolf's claim nevertheless identifies an important period of transition within Bloomsbury and in the group's relation to English culture at large. With debates raging around its Post-Impressionist show, Bloomsbury found itself at the forefront of the English avant-garde. For Grant, this transition is marked by the mural in Keynes's Cambridge rooms. His first domestic decoration, it is also his first experiment in a Post-Impressionist idiom, and the first manifestation of what became Bloomsbury's domestic aesthetic. Quite literally, the Keynes mural originated the Bloomsbury artists' collaborative careers, for its reputation prompted Grant's commission for both the Borough Polytechnic and Newnham College murals, discussed in the following chapters. More significantly, however, in Grant's Cambridge mural, two related ideas—one aesthetic and one social—converged powerfully enough to remain an operative force behind Bloomsbury's domestic design: a vision of modern art as a return to primal expressiveness, and the aspiration to supplant middle-class social norms with a more natural indulgence in sensual pleasure. With this conjunction, the Bloomsbury artists, who independently had been fashioning their domestic environments as self-conscious expressions of the lives they contained, discovered a model that, with variations, they would manipulate for the subsequent half-century.

Sailing to Byzantium
Post-Impressionist Primitivism

And therefore I have sailed the seas and come
To the holy city of Byzantium.
William Butler Yeats, "Sailing to Byzantium"

The previous chapter concluded by describing how important the winter of 1910–11 was in defining the character of the group just beginning to call itself "Bloomsbury." Today, when Bloomsbury is associated primarily with literature and Post-Impressionism is taken for granted, it is worth emphasizing that the group's first public identity was as an avant-garde art contingent. The controversy over the first Post-Impressionist exhibition propelled Bloomsbury to the head of the British avant-garde, displacing John Singer Sargent and Walter Sickert, whose denunciations of the show now allied them with their former antagonists in the Royal Academy. Sargent wrote to *The Nation* denying any endorsement of the Post-Impressionist paintings: "I am absolutely sceptical as to their having any claim whatever to being works of art."[1] Sickert concluded his condescending review of the exhibition with the claim that, despite the merits of some of the exhibited works, Fry and his colleagues had been duped by Parisian dealers:

If the innocent and none too discriminating enthusiasm of an English committee proposes exhibitions of this kind, it is the French dealer and the state of his stock which disposes. But not all the remainder biscuit of Manet's great studio can induce us to swallow Matisse as next-of-kin.[2]

Younger English artists also sought to distance themselves from the notoriety of the Post-Impressionists. Augustus John remained publicly silent and privately hostile throughout the exhibition, despite reviews linking a concurrent exhibition of his work to Post-Impressionism.[3] Fry's erstwhile friend Eric Gill joined John, claiming, "If you are like me and John . . . feeling yourself beyond the reaction and beyond the transition [represented by the exhibition], you have a right to feel superior to Mr Henri Matisse . . . and can say you don't like it."[4] This remark came in a letter to the painter William Rothenstein, another of Fry's friends (the one he had so enthusiastically invited to witness the embodiment of "our sort of life" at Durbins a year before). Rothenstein, too, came out against the show, telling Fry that the furore it created was merely an "affair of social excitement." For artists, he said, the spectacle of the Post-Impressionists was like the "charge of the light brigade—a glorious episode, but leaving things very much where they were before."[5]

Virginia Woolf's biography of Fry reports that he was "amazed and amused" at the general uproar and personal notoriety aroused by his exhibition. In letters to his parents, Fry reported, "I have been the centre of a wild hurricane of newspaper abuse from all quarters over this show," comparing himself to the pre-eminent outcast artist of their generation: "There has been nothing like this outbreak of militant Philistinism since Whistler's day."[6] Although not all reviewers panned *Manet and*

Facing page:
Detail of fig. 54.

the Post-Impressionists, the daily papers attacked Fry by name.[7] *The Times* scolded him for misusing his authority as a "distinguished scholar and critic" to promote artists like Matisse whose sole aim was to "*Epater le bourgeois*," while the *Morning Post*'s critic "regret[ted] to say" that Fry had organized the exhibition and professed "a certain feeling of sadness that distinguished critics whose profound knowledge and connoisseurship are beyond question should be found to welcome pretension and imposture."[8] The latter rebuke was especially personal, for the *Post*'s critic was Robert Ross, Fry's first dealer.[9] In a lecture to close the exhibition, Fry alluded to his former colleagues at the Art Workers' Guild, which had sponsored a lecture by the director of a mental asylum who interpreted the new art as evidence of insanity. Other critics, Fry remarked, implied "that all the pictures . . . should be burned, and that I myself should be offered up upon the holocaust as a propitiation of the outraged feelings of the British public."[10]

How much amusement alternated with amazement for Fry during the winter of 1910–11 can only be guessed. While he had been, in his own words, "preparing for a huge campaign of outraged British Philistinism," he was unprepared for the derision of those he had counted as friends and colleagues.[11] Writing a decade later, Fry dated to the controversy over the first Post-Impressionist show his alienation from "the cultured public" with whom, as an art historian, he had previously identified.[12] In the months preceding the exhibition, moreover, Fry lost his position as an acquisitions advisor for the Metropolitan Museum in New York, was passed over for the new Slade Professorship of Fine Art at Oxford, and had to commit his wife to an asylum. This last event rendered critical imputations of insanity all the more painful and, as he later explained to his mother, "made me feel a great indifference to most of the things men work for . . . and with that a kind of recklessness perhaps which has enabled me to say what I think about art without considering the consequences."[13] By the spring of 1911, Fry realized the extent to which he had separated himself from his former colleagues. Trying to follow *Manet and the Post-Impressionists* with an exhibition of recent English art, Fry found his overtures rejected by Sickert, John, and Rothenstein. The latter concluded his refusal by firmly severing their links: "As my work is really more academic than revolutionary . . . my absence . . . will allow you a freer and less troubled path."[14] By this point, Fry had been stripped of much that had hitherto constituted his personal and public identity. Virginia Woolf recalled Fry remarking at this period that "at the age of forty-four he found himself where most people find themselves twenty years earlier—at the beginning of life, not in the middle, and nowhere within sight of the end."[15] As he embarked on his new ventures, Fry's allies became a community of intellectuals fifteen years his juniors.

The same "recklessness" that alienated Fry from his former associates strengthened his alliance with Bloomsbury. For Clive Bell, Fry's plans "to show the British public the work of the newest French painters" seemed part of a widespread "excitement in the air" in 1910, when a new age was dawning and "miracles seemed likely enough to happen."[16] Bell, whose studies in Paris afforded him a background in modern French art, energetically supported the Post-Impressionist exhibition, traveling with Fry to select many of the works and recommending his friend, Desmond MacCarthy, as the exhibition's secretary. A few weeks after a chance meeting at the Cambridge train station when Fry announced his proposed exhibition to the Bells, Vanessa invited him to 46 Gordon Square to lecture on "Representation as a Means of Expression" for an audience of young artists, among them Duncan Grant, who reported to Keynes, "It was rather an interesting discussion and a very successful party."[17]

Bloomsbury's incorporation of Fry was not accomplished without anxieties on both sides, as documented in letters of the period. His worries about his age in relation to this band of young rebels are suggested by Bell's reassuring response in a letter from the summer of 1911: "You know it's utter nonsense for you to talk of having done everything at the wrong time of life. Really intelligent people . . . always are old and sedate when they're young."[18] At the same time, the younger members of Bloomsbury were relieved that Fry's roots among the adherents of

"Greek love" at Cambridge enabled him to accept their sexual mores. Wryly casting doubt on the myth of Fry's propriety before his inauguration into Bloomsbury, Vanessa Bell reported in another letter from the summer after the first Post-Impressionist show: "I am supposed to have educated you to hear free talk."[19]

This, then, was the background for Bloomsbury's collaborative decorative projects of 1911–12, which are discussed in this section. United under the banner of Post-Impressionism, Bloomsbury combined Fry's erudition and status with its younger members' energy and iconoclasm, while the scorn of what Fry called the "cultured public" helped solidify the group's self-image as a coalition of outsiders and confirm its association of modern art with social and sexual rebellion. These forces first came together just a few months after the first Post-Impressionist show in a plan to test Fry's hypothesis that compelling precedents for Post-Impressionism could be found earlier than the Italian "primitives," in the art of ancient Byzantium. The following three chapters trace the development of Bloomsbury's collaborative construction of a modernist aesthetic, in which aspirations for new styles of art and life are expressed in relation to the precedent of Byzantium.

Greek Loves

Mediterranean Modernism and the Borough Polytechnic Murals (1911)

Defending the Post-Impressionists in 1910, Fry praised these artists' use of "flat colour in frank opposition," citing what he called the "decorative unity" of paintings that keep their formal elements in the same plane:

> This fact has always been more or less present to the minds of artists when the decoration of a given space of wall has been demanded of them; in such cases they have always tended to feel the need for keeping the relations upon a flat surface, and have excused the want of illusion, which was supposed to be necessary for a painting, by making a distinction between decorative painting and painting a picture, a distinction which I believe to be entirely fallacious.[1]

Fry's bid to merge easel and mural painting was not idle rhetoric. Soon after the close of the show he began planning the first public project of Post-Impressionist decoration, choosing a setting that matched his challenge to distinctions between "high" and "low" art with a concomitant challenge to social divisions. By early March, Fry could announce a commission "to supervise a series of wall paintings at the Borough Polytechnic," a vocational school in a working-class district of south London.[2]

Like other Bloomsbury initiatives, this project was a modernist variation on a Victorian idea, for the Arts and Crafts movement had left a rich legacy of murals in schools. Ruskin had argued that collaborative work on "the permanent decoration of public buildings" was ideal training for young artists, and cited schools as the "most important kind of public buildings" for such work.[3] Morris made the first major project of his Pre-Raphaelite brotherhood the murals for the new Union Debating Hall at Oxford, while Ashbee laid the groundwork for his Guild of Handicraft by organizing the students in his Ruskin course to decorate the refectory at Toynbee Hall.[4] Where the Arts and Crafts Movement expressed its educational ideals in the reanimation of gothic architecture and early Renaissance painting, however, Bloomsbury looked farther into the past to envision the future, drawing from Byzantium to create the look of the modern.

Although not unique among modernists, Bloomsbury's fascination with the Byzantine "primitive" is unusual.[5] Fry's first published comment on the painters he later called the Post-Impressionists, however, defended these avant-garde French artists against charges of ineptitude by citing recent scholarship on the mosaics at Santa Maria Maggiore in Rome, which, he said, showed it was "a mistake to suppose . . . that Byzantinism was due to a loss of the technical ability to be realistic." Fry in this 1908 letter to *The Burlington* proposed an argument Clive Bell would make famous in his 1914 *Art*, asserting that Byzantine art was "a necessary and inevitable reaction" to a realism so exact that "there is left no power to express the personal attitude and emotional conviction." Comparing Impressionism to the realistic art of the late Roman empire, Fry made an analogy with the modern movement—"We may call it for convenience Byzantinism." He insisted that Cézanne and Gauguin "are not really Impressionists at all. They are proto-Byzantines."[6] Two years later, when, laying the groundwork for the first Post-Impressionist show, Fry translated for *The Burlington* Maurice Denis's influential essay on Cézanne, his brief introduction challenged Denis just once. Where Denis linked Cézanne to El Greco, Fry speculated:

> Was it not rather El Greco's earliest training in the lingering Byzantine tradition that suggested to him his mode of escape into an art of direct decorative expression? And is not Cézanne after all these centuries the first to take up the hint El Greco threw out?[7]

When, therefore, in the letter announcing the commission to decorate the Borough Polytechnic, Fry also said he had long wanted "a nearer insight into Byzantine art," the two ideas were not unrelated. Byzantine precedent played a vital role in his conception of the new art. Fry's letter went on to explain his plan to spend the month of April in Turkey.

The plan was for a foursome—Fry, Clive and Vanessa Bell, and their Cambridge friend, the mathematician H. T. "Harry" Norton—to start in Constantinople and travel to Greece, passing by way of the first Ottoman capital, Bursa. This itinerary reversed the path taken by Keynes and Grant on their Mediterranean voyage the year before, suggesting the influence of their enthusiastic accounts. Grant's descriptions prepared his friends to admire the Hagia Sophia and the mosaics of the Kariye Djami in Constantinople. After a week of painting and sightseeing there, the group moved to Bursa. The stop at this out-of-the-way city was also prompted by Grant's enthusiasm, which Fry quickly came to share: "I think it's the most beautiful place I was ever in. Up above is Olympus all snow covered with red and purple sides, then this town of mosques and muddle scrambling down into a plain which is all dotted with pale golden and silver poplars and below seas of almond blossom."[8]

Fry's enthusiasm for Turkey found visual expression in large-scale easel paintings worked on his return to England from sketches made in Bursa. In these paintings, careful rendering of the cityscape in tiny rectilinear chips of color combines Cézanne's technique with evocations of the tesserae of ancient mosaics, exemplifying Fry's belief in a "proto-Byzantine" modernism. Like the Byzantine mosaics, where passages of flat pattern coexist with images of three-dimensional space, Fry's paintings juxtapose the flatness of the color chips with an illusion of planes receding in space. This tension is clearest in the view of Bursa known as *Turkish Landscape* (fig. 37), where the foreground trees divide the cityscape behind them into narrow panels, alternating flattened with sharply receding vignettes: the city in the leftmost panel is a flat band of mottled white and brown, the next panel emphasizes the recession of the buildings angled along the cliffs, followed by a glimpse of structures frontally presented, while the rightmost panel with its winding path and disappearing street is once again strongly recessive. Fry emphasized his reference to Byzantine mosaic by setting his canvas in a hand-painted frame decorated in squares of brown and gold that simulate the effect of the decorative borders around the scenes depicted in the Kariye Djami. Critics quickly noticed the Byzantinism in Fry's new work. Robert Ross, mitigating his condemnation of the Post-Impressionist exhibition, wrote in a review of Fry's one-man show in January of 1912, "Alone, probably of all the Post-Impressionists, French or English, Mr. Fry has actually been to Constantinople in order to obtain a new Mosaic dispensation for Art."[9]

Ross, of course, underestimated Bloomsbury's other artists. In the spring of 1911, while Fry was in Turkey with the Bells, Grant and Keynes were also in the Mediterranean basin, exploring the relics of Byzantium in Tunis—sites almost unknown to English travelers, but visited by the Frys on their honeymoon.[10] These overlapping voyages by the artists just cohering as the Bloomsbury group reveal a

37. Roger Fry, *Turkish Landscape*,
1911. Oil on canvas, 60.4 × 91.1 cm.
Tatham Art Gallery,
Pietermaritzburg, South Africa.

shared investment in the primitive precedent offered by Mediterranean cultures, though the nature of that investment varied. For Grant and Keynes, the lure of the Mediterranean was charged with sexual, as well as aesthetic, discovery. Like Italy and Greece (as discussed in the previous chapter), the Islamic countries around the Mediterranean were perceived by many Englishmen as places where customs rooted in classical tradition overrode Protestant strictures against homosexuality.[11] Edward Carpenter's 1902 *Ioläus*, a sourcebook of affirmative references to homoeroticism in history and literature, devoted a section to poetry and travelers' accounts from the Arab world, while so many episodes in Richard Burton's 1885 *Book of the Thousand Nights and a Night* concerned such passions that he included a "Terminal Note" on homosexual practices in what he called the "Sotadic Zone," which encircled the world at the latitude of the Mediterranean.[12] Prompted by such literature, Grant and Keynes in 1910 had discovered among the attractions of Turkey what Grant called (using an archaic spelling for the town), "the indecency of the Broussa baths."[13] Writing from Tunis in 1911, Keynes reported to Strachey, "The Arabs are wonderful—very beautiful and the first race of buggers I've seen."[14] Both in Turkey and in Tunis, Grant's and Keynes' perceptions of homoeroticism were associated with the legacy of Byzantine art. Although very little of the decoration of the Bursa baths is now dated to their original Byzantine construction, Keynes's letters show that he and Grant saw the elaborately tiled baths as an ancient environment. In Tunis the following year, they studied ancient mosaics at the Bardo Museum, then travelled to Sicily to see the cycles of Byzantine mosaics at Palermo and Monreale. Keynes's letters from this trip move seamlessly from erotic admiration of the Arabs to awe at the churches "entirely clothed with pictures and mosaic."[15] For Grant, this experience confirmed Fry's version of modernism as a return to the primitive sensuality of

Sailing to Byzantium

the Mediterranean, now made specific to the Byzantine. Following his 1911 trip, visual and verbal references to Byzantine mosaic infused Grant's modernism.

The Mediterranean's appeal to other members of Bloomsbury, though less erotic, rested on similar perceptions of an alternative to the restrictions of middle-class English life. As early as 1897, writing to his parents from his honeymoon, Fry had contrasted the English with the Tunisians, whom he described as "a people who can't be vulgar or really bad mannered and who have complete *social* equality—in fact a sheik talks on terms of absolute equality with the man who serves his coffee at a few pence a day."[16] Here Fry was reiterating impressions of Mediterranean culture formed in Italy six years before:

> Somehow I think it would be easier to be friends with "the people" here than in England. Class distinctions are not really deeply implanted, and there is always a substructure of latent culture; civilisation has had so long to sink in and has penetrated the people so that they have all sorts of fine and delicate perceptions even when they can't read or write.[17]

Fry's contrast of the propriety of the British ruling class with the simpler culture of the Mediterranean spread from his private correspondence to his published writings in the weeks following his return from Bursa in 1912. He opened a contemptuous survey of London's art scene with a comparison between England and Turkey, "where the Turks, for all their alleged cruelty, have never applied the torture of the picture gallery, and where the people show in all the interests of daily life a vital sense of beauty in colour and design." Inverting nationalistic rhetorics of the advance of British civilization over countries like Turkey, Fry exploded in exasperation:

> To return to England to find people engaged in unveiling statues eighty feet high, in discovering geniuses eighty years old, and to find the country cousins gloating over the sticky slabs of sentimentality which the keepers of our artistic conscience have just been handing round at the annual feeding time, all this is a trying experience, and it requires some weeks to recover the innocent belief that any good can come of talking and writing about art in a country which seems so well adapted for other activities.[18]

Positioning the Mediterranean as an antidote to what ailed Britain aesthetically, socially, and sexually, Bloomsbury imagined modernism as a form of Byzantinism. The Borough Polytechnic decorations were the first public demonstration of this ethos. Fry began by scrapping the commission's specification of a didactic idealization of the labor of food production, replacing this program with "The Amusements of London," a theme suggestive of the spontaneous, sensual pleasures of modern life. The amusements depicted were conceived to reflect the experiences of a working-class audience, and included the zoo, a Punch and Judy show, a football match, as well as scenes of swimming and sailing toy boats in city parks (fig. 38). Long before Fry committed to print his description of modernism as an art for housemaids rather than their employers (quoted in the Introduction), the Borough Polytechnic murals proclaimed his belief in Post-Impressionism as an art that could transcend class boundaries by appealing to the untutored senses.

Fry assembled for the project a group of young painters. Bernard Adeney worked a ten-foot-long panel showing toy boats on the Round Pond at Kensington Gardens. Frederick Etchells, a recent graduate of the Royal College of Art, was given the largest panel, a twenty-foot-long space on which to illustrate a fair at Hampstead Heath. Fry himself took on an irregular space around a side door for his zoo scene. Grant, on the strength of his Cambridge mural, was asked to contribute two panels, the first, six feet long, depicting a football match (fig. 39), and the second, at ten feet, representing swimmers in the Serpentine (fig. 40). The remaining areas, including the walls of a passage into the dining room, were painted in blocks of light blue, orange, white, and pink. When it became clear that Fry's team was too small to finish the job by the end of the summer recess, he hurriedly enlisted two more workers, both younger brothers of more prominent artists. Macdonald Gill, brother of Eric

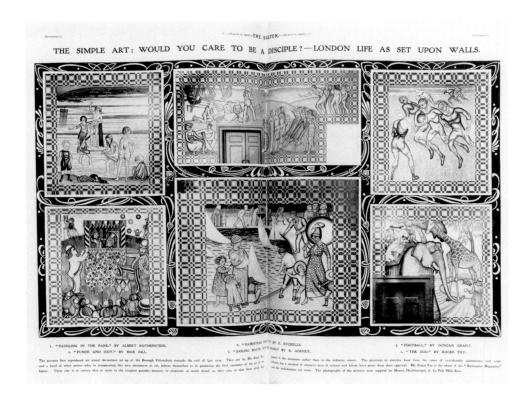

38. Photo–collage of the Borough Polytechnic murals, *The Sketch*, supplement, 6 March 1912.

Gill, completed a six-foot panel representing a Punch and Judy show; Albert Rothenstein, William's brother, depicted children playing around a pond.[19]

The look of the Polytechnic murals was deeply affected by Fry's experience of Turkey. Adeney recalled that, under Fry's direction, the artists adopted a common "technique of graduating the color tones to a dark contour to increase the rhythm of the design—as in Byzantine mosaics."[20] And the various scenes were linked together by borders reminiscent of the patterned bands between the mosaics at the Kariye Djami. The most striking references to Byzantine precedent, however, came, not in Fry's panel, which—like those painted by Gill and Rothenstein—was rather conventionally realistic. In contrast, the critics were quick to note the Byzantinism of the three panels contributed by Grant and Etchells, who became close friends and collaborators over the course of the project.

Grant's smaller panel is dominated by a trinity of footballers tumbling in stylized repetition like a detail from a Byzantine crowd scene—their furrowed locks and rounded musculature echo closely the treatment of hair and drapery in the figures at the cathedral of Monreale, for example (fig. 41). The action takes place against a ground of tiny sinuous lines that simultaneously stand for the grass of the playing field and suggest the shimmering effect of tesserae. This football scene, the last of three panels along the side of the refectory, abutted Etchells's mammoth fair scene, which filled the rear wall. Like Grant's work, Etchells's panel, with its similar shallow ranks of identically posed figures, was seen as invoking Byzantine prototypes, though *The Spectator*'s reference to Etchells's "Assyrian coster lads" dancing with "Egyptian coster girls" shows how the English combined Mediterranean cultures into a unitary signifier of the ancient and exotic.[21] *The Times* was content to characterize the holiday activities Etchells depicted as simply "crowded together in a primitive manner."[22] Etchells accentuated the archaic jumbling of disparate picture planes by using patches of parallel lines to define areas of foreground and background. Especially in their awkward overlap, these lines conspicuously flout the rules of Renaissance perspective as they replicate the visual effect of old mosaics, where masonry rows are revealed as the tesserae fall away.

Of all the panels in the Borough Polytechnic dining hall, however, Grant's swimmers pushed reference to Byzantine art the furthest. Today, Grant's panel seems

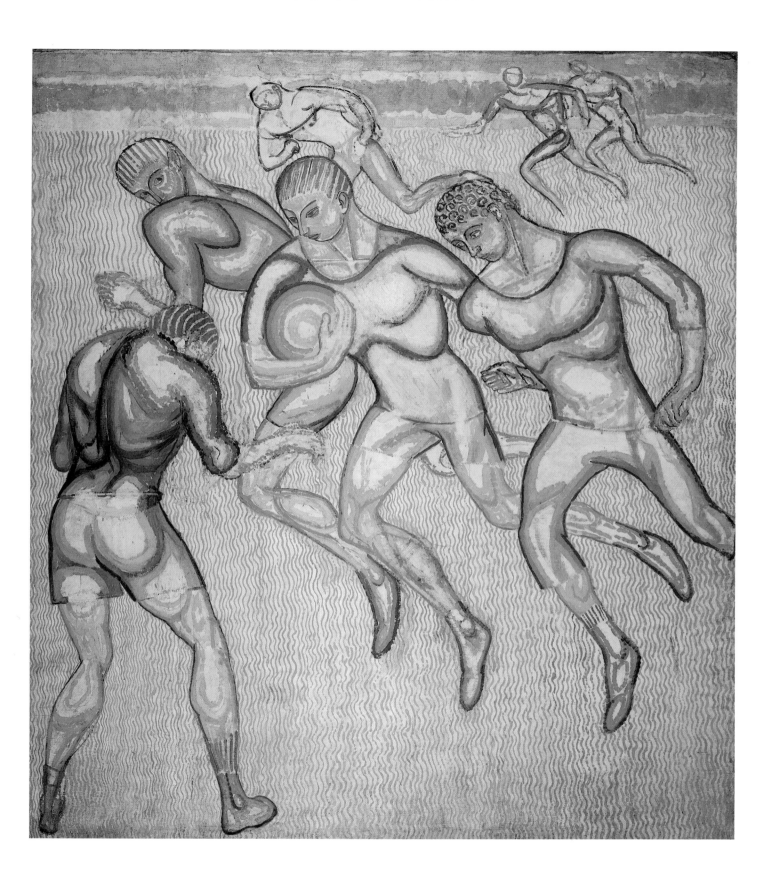

39. Duncan Grant, Borough Polytechnic mural: football match, 1911. Oil on casein on canvas, 228 × 197 cm. Tate Britain.

40. Duncan Grant, Borough
Polytechnic mural: swimmers in the
Serpentine, 1911. Oil on casein on
canvas, 228.6 × 306.1 cm. Tate
Britain.

most striking in its similarity to the stop-action dynamism of Italian Futurist paint-
ing. But in 1911 the mural was universally seen as a return to the aesthetics of
Byzantium. The *Morning Post*'s Robert Ross reversed his call to burn the pictures
in the first Post-Impressionist exhibition, praising Grant's panel by comparing its
rendering of water to what "you see in Christian fifth-century mosaic."[23] *The
Spectator* reported, "It makes one want to swim—even in waters like an early
Christian mosaic."[24] *The Times* described the scene as seeming, "rather than
Cockney bathers in the Serpentine, to be primitive Mediterraneans in the morning
of the world."[25] It is the water in Grant's panel—undulating ribbons of color
quoted from mosaics Grant had seen at Monreale and the Baptistry in Florence—
that most stridently assert Byzantine precedent (fig. 42). Like the parallel lines in
Etchells's panel and the tiny squiggles behind Grant's footballers, the regular patterning of the water contrasts with the energetic contours of the human forms for
an effect quite different from Byzantine prototype, however. The result is modern
in the way Bloomsbury understood that term: a self-consciously erudite return to
sensual, primal pleasures.

The ambition evident in the style of Grant's swimmers was well suited to the subject. The image of men boating and swimming, at one with nature and each other,
drew from late-Victorian rhetorics of reform and renewal. In William Morris's 1890
novel *News from Nowhere*, for instance, the hero's response to awakening in a utopian
future is to swim in the Thames with an oarsman whose appearance—"dark-haired

and berry brown of skin, well-knit and strong, and obviously used to exercising his muscles, but with nothing rough or coarse about him, and clean as might be"—embodies the social virtues of the new age.[26] At the opposite end of the spectrum of Victorian reformers from Morris's hearty Arts and Crafts idealism, Aesthetic poetry of journals like *The Artist* also extolled the sight of "dull" working-class boys:

> When sudden in the midst of all their play
> They strip and plunge into the stream below;
> Changed by a miracle, they rise as though
> The youth of Greece burst on this later day.[27]

Grant's mural, identified as "Bathing in the Serpentine," places his bathers in modern London, but, like Aesthetic poetry, invests the scene with connotations of the Mediterranean past. Betraying the same habits of thought that inspired his delight in the "gilded youths" of Florence bathing before an audience steeped in a Michelangelesque ideal of male beauty (quoted in the previous chapter), Grant pictured his London swimmers in the strenuous poses of Renaissance studies of the male nude. Grant's topmost bather—buttocks raised and legs open provocatively over the gunwale as he climbs into the rowboat—is quoted directly from Michelangelo's well known contribution to this genre, the *Battle of Cascina* (fig. 43). With this overt reference to Michelangelo, it is hard to ignore the way Grant's sprawling foreground swimmer aspires to match the simultaneous power and passivity that Walter Pater had noted in Michelangelo's definitive male nude, the Sistine Chapel Adam.[28] Grant's bather—legs pulled up, neck thrown back, and fingers loosely outstretched in a gesture unrelated to any known swimming stroke—echoes the sensuous monumentality of the first man in Michelangelo's version of the "morning of the world."

If Grant's combination of Michelangelesque swimmers and water evocative of the blue and green tiled baths at Bursa seems to fuse Byzantine and Renaissance sources into a homoerotic fantasy of Mediterranean sensuality unrelated to modernism—or downright inappropriate to a workers' college—this is a sign of how thoroughly stereotypes of Aestheticism as apolitical and nostalgic have permeated conventional histories, obscuring the links between erotics, politics, and aesthetics that the generation of late-Victorian activists taught Bloomsbury to see. The proponents of "Greek love" challenged both the sexual restrictions and the class barriers that defined the British middle class. It is no coincidence that Fry's impressions of the egalitarianism of Mediterranean culture were formed under the influence of John Addington Symonds, whom he met in Venice in 1891, "sitting boozing with a lot of Italian workmen."[29] The same letter in which Fry ruminated over how "it would be easier to be friends with 'the people' here than in England," because "class distinctions are not really deeply implanted" in Italy, begins:

41 and 42. Details of mosaics at the cathedral of Monreale.

43. Aristotle da Sangallo, detail of a copy of Michelangelo's *Battle of Cascina*. Earl of Leicester and Trustees of the Holkham Estate.

> Symonds has been awfully good to me—taking me out in his gondola and so on. He is the most pornographic person I ever saw, but not in the least nasty. He also delighted greatly in discussing paederastia, which is almost a special subject with him and he has become most confidential to me over certain passages in his life.[30]

By the same token, when Virginia Woolf encapsulated her first impression of E. M. Forster she recalled him as if in one breath "talk[ing] of Italy and the Working Men's College."[31] Many of the advocates of "Greek love" channeled at least some of their passion into a zeal for education that reached beyond the upper classes. Symonds and Browning took on the personal mentorship of working-class youths, but no one was more influential in connecting social and sexual radicalism than the break-away Cambridge teacher, Edward Carpenter.[32]

Inspired by Walt Whitman's hymns to the democracy of class-transcending erotic "comradeship," Carpenter's copious publications focused on the links between sexual and political reform. His 1894 pamphlet, "Homogenic Love: and its Place in a Free Society," for instance, cites Whitman's vision of "inseparable cities with their arms about each others necks, by the love of comrades" to argue that even in England, "below the stolid surface and reserve of British manners," a "homogenic passion" could "by the most passionate and lasting compulsion draw members of the different classes together."[33] Putting his principles into the kind of small-scale practice that befitted his anarchist convictions, Carpenter in 1883 established a rural commune with a working-class couple, and later created a domestic partnership with George Merrill, a man from the Sheffield slums. Throughout this period, Carpenter's unconventional household, where he farmed, made sandals, and kept up a prodigious outpouring of writing, became a point of pilgrimage for reformers of all sorts, but especially for young men from King's College, among them in 1887 Roger Fry, who reported in a letter to his parents that Carpenter was "quite one of the best men I have ever met."[34] In his enthusiasm Fry acquired a pair of Carpenter's handmade sandals, a badge of leftist intellectuals at the period, and even urged his jurist father to buy some. Picking up on Carpenter's primitivizing vocabulary, Fry wrote home, "A Lord Justice in sandals will be a landmark in the progress of civil . . . I mean decivilisation."[35]

If Carpenter's ideas attracted Fry, they inspired others close to Bloomsbury. Fry's college friends, C. R. Ashbee and G. L. Dickinson, welcomed Carpenter's political conception of homoerotic attraction, and each made several visits to his home. Under Carpenter's influence, Dickinson volunteered as an itinerant lecturer for working-class university extension students, then, on his return to the Cambridge faculty, turned his scholarly expertise in the classics to two causes: documenting Greek attitudes toward homosexuality and promoting a system of world government he christened the "League of Nations."[36] Ashbee (as discussed in Chapter 2), founded a guild to train and employ working-class craftsmen, which he promoted by citing "the experience of my friend Edward Carpenter," who "attacked the problem [of industrialization] from a simple, direct, and human point of view."[37] Carpenter was also important for Forster, who, in his own words, came to Carpenter in 1913 "as one approaches a savior." Carpenter's "Love of Comrades . . . attracted me in my loneliness. For a short time he seemed to hold the key to every trouble," Forster wrote, pinpointing the moment that inspired him to write *Maurice*, his posthumously published novel dealing with homosexuality:

> It must have been on my second or third visit to the shrine that the spark was kindled and he and his comrade George Merrill combined to make a profound impression on me and to touch a creative spring. George Merrill also touched my backside—gently and just above the buttocks. I believe he touched most people's. The sensation was unusual and I still remember it, as I remember the position of a long vanished tooth. It was as much psychological as physical. It seemed to go straight through the small of my back into my ideas, without involving my thoughts.[38]

The impact of Merrill's gesture—a touch that was intimate without being sexual—attests to the poverty of homoerotic expression available to Forster, whose time at Cambridge shortly predated Bloomsbury's. That it came from an uneducated worker—there is some doubt that Merrill was literate—confirmed a primitivist faith that the intuitive physicality of the working class might indicate a way beyond the restrictive morality of the bourgeoisie. Significantly, *Maurice* concludes with its protagonist forsaking his middle-class life for a rural idyll with a gamekeeper.

Grant shared such beliefs in the value of cross-class homoerotic bonding. His letters with Keynes from this period record the course of their long-term relationship with a Cockney pantomime performer, who introduced them to, in Keynes's words, "low comedians—whose chief characteristic seems to be their extraordinary kindness," and to football matches, "exactly what we ought to have in Cambridge."[39] Grant's record of his pleasure in a letter from this man as "very typical of the wonderful way he is ready to take whatever comes along" reveals his investment in Carpenter's vision of the virtues of working-class men.[40] Grant's Borough Polytechnic murals, therefore, take their place with Forster's *Maurice*, written two years later, as manifestations of Bloomsbury's efforts to imagine a modernism infused with the ideals of a sexually charged, class-transcendent comradeship formulated by the previous generation.

Viewed from this perspective, the iconography of Grant's footballers and swimmers evoke the aspirations for comradeship proposed by Whitman and his English allies. Whitman's "Song of Myself," for instance, compares the fraternity and physicality of athletics to his poetic mission: "I am the teacher of athletes,/ He that by me spreads a wider breast than my own proves the width of my own." Bathing in Whitman's poetry signifies the uninhibited sensuality of the new man, which is contrasted to the old world where "the talkers were talking":

> while they dis-
> cuss I am silent, and go bathe and admire myself.
>   Welcome is every organ and attribute of men, and of
> any man hearty and clean.
> Not an inch nor a particle of an inch is vile, and
> none shall be less familiar than the rest.
>
> I am satisfied—I see, dance, laugh, sing:
> As the hugging and loving bed-fellow sleeps at my
> side through the night. . . .[41]

The influence of such ideas on Edwardian reformers is apparent in Ashbee's journals, which are full of enthusiastic accounts of swimming trips and athletic matches. A entry from 1907 records a visit from a former Guild apprentice named Sammy, who had continued Ashbee's social work in east London by founding a "sports club" for working men:

> "The Apollos" he had called them. Quite a nice name wasn't it? For if they did not sing to the lyre, they enjoyed their naked bodies in the sun, and if they could not get the sun Victorian Park way—they took to the Whitechapel baths instead.

To show Ashbee the success of his club, Sammy took him to the Guild-built pond, saying, "*you* first taught me to swim." There he "stripped, took a long breath, drew up his arms," and showed off his back muscles. "Then he sprang to the board and took a beautiful dive taking care as he did it that I should observe his form, for part of the joy of athletics—'*pure* athletics'—is a healthy self-consciousness in the eye of those we care for."[42] Grant's careful description of the stages of the dive in his Borough Polytechnic panel offers a visual counterpart to Ashbee's enthusiasm for the "healthy self-consciousness" of "*pure* athletics," while both echo Whitman's passion, expressed in *Leaves of Grass*, for "The swimmer naked in the swimming-bath, seen as he swims through the transparent green shine." By the same token, Grant's stylized footballers, running forward shoulder to shoulder, their muscles bulging through the translucent sheaths of their uniforms, seem archetypes of athletic comradeship. Uniting the eroticized politics (or politicized eroticism) of the late-Victorian radicals with an aesthetic at once modern and grounded in the ancient precedent of Mediterranean culture, Grant's Borough Polytechnic figures seem to answer Carpenter's call for a new art to effect "the redemption and acknowledgment of the Body—that body which Luxury and Puritanism between them have so soiled and desecrated." The artist who achieves "the redemption of Sex," Carpenter said, "will have achieved a work which can scarcely be said to have been attempted since the time of Michel Angelo."[43]

Critical reactions—both favorable and not—to the Borough Polytechnic designs show how the project was seen as responding, if not to Carpenter in particular, then to this climate of challenges to social and aesthetic norms. Sympathetic critics praised the murals' resistance to urban industrialism. C. Lewis Hind in the *Daily Chronicle* wrote that Grant's bathing panel "calls you to the open air," while Desmond MacCarthy described the "Post-Impressionist frescoes" in *The Eye-Witness* as a "protest against fog, smears, and grime."[44] *The Athenaeum* adopted more overtly political language to warn that "the decorators of the Borough Polytechnic must prepare to be howled at as anarchists and charlatans."[45] But the social implications of debates over aesthetics at this moment are most clearly revealed in the *National Review*'s rambling attack, which concluded by demanding

Greek Loves

the murals' removal. Casting himself as a *flâneur* in the Impressionist tradition of Whistler and Sickert, the anonymous critic opened with an account of his stroll to the Borough Polytechnic through the atmosphere "of pale copper and silver, and a strange purple one sees only in London." This aesthetic endorsement of air pollution is followed by a contrast between Grant's Post-Impressionist bathers and the more seemly use of Impressionist conventions to keep the depicted working class at a picturesque distance:

> The scene on a summer evening might inspire a Japanese painter . . . ; the tawny lake, diamond-besprinkled, responding to boyish merriment, splashing and iridescent, abundant in light, half-concealing spray. Most delicious the gaiety of boys in the element of purity. Their perhaps meagre bodies, half revealed as a radiant mystery, and their garments, perchance rags, scattered in groups on the grass edging, made a note in various dark tints that a great painter would see and arrest.

The Borough Polytechnic bathers, in contrast—their bodies neither meager nor semi-concealed, their element not obviously one of purity, their rags not under properly aesthetic arrest—according to this reviewer are, along with the whole project, "related to London hooligans," and—paradoxically—also too sophisticated for working-class viewers. A related paradox is the reviewer's assertion of the innate "strength" of the working class—"this is why the industrial class is the backbone of England"—and simultaneous warning of the murals' power to "deteriorate young and sensitive minds," leading them toward "inefficiency and ugliness." Educational institutions supported by tax money, he complains, are charged to teach

> sons and daughters of the working class. . . . that they may know the difference between good and evil. . . . [and] their outlook on life may become purified and elevated. Hence advance. Hence progress may be maintained and degeneracy defeated. . . . Let them be degenerated by bad examples and false ideals and their pith and fibre will dissolve like butter.[46]

For this critic, the Post-Impressionist mural contained the seeds of social disarray.

The *National Review* notwithstanding, critical reaction to the Borough Polytechnic project was far less hostile than that aroused by the first Post-Impressionist exhibition. Two factors combined to temper assessments of the murals, the first being the Post-Impressionist show itself. Reviews of the murals demonstrate the speed with which Fry's vocabulary gained currency in discussions of contemporary art.[47] A second factor in the general reaction of benign amusement was the subordinate status of decorative art, which allowed critics a greater tolerance for experimentation. Fry's site in London's working-class South Bank—not even the slums of Whitechapel, where philanthropy had become chic[48]—also mitigated any affront to the art world. The *National Review* described the area the Polytechnic served as an "almost foreign district," while *The Spectator* styled it a "drab, partly charted region." The sympathetic *Athenaeum* insisted on the murals' ultimate irrelevance to the usual audiences for art:

> Critics and connoisseurs . . . will be glad to admire, but the decorations are not made for them, still less for archaeologists and historians. They are made for a common-room where men will talk and eat and think and feel and live, and what they express is the significance of the commonplace amusements of these common men.[49]

What "common men" made of this uncommon art is impossible to know, for their reactions are filtered through middle-class observers whose differing accounts reveal their own preconceptions. Press reports of the murals' unveiling describe the neighborhood's initial reaction as bafflement. The *National Review* purported to transcribe viewers' reactions in Cockney dialect, mocking their garbled grasp of such modernist buzzwords as "'Sin' something" and "'Prim' something" (the fact that "Synthetic" and "Primitive" were spelled out in footnotes suggests the editors' anxieties over the sophistication of their own readers). *The Spectator* was equally contemptuous. Claiming the locals preferred Rothenstein's panel, the reviewer compared "the attitude of the Borough" to "that of the horrible child on the bus who, after glaring hideously at the people on the opposite side, pointed his dirty finger at one passenger with these words, 'I hate that one least.'"[50] For his part, MacCarthy in the *Eye-Witness* recorded a mix of reactions that accorded with Bloomsbury's prejudices: "grins and giggles" from many in the audience offset only by "indignation, natural in some cultured student who had recently acquired, say, a photograph of Watts' *Love and Life*." MacCarthy expressed the hope, however, that "Long after the frescoes have grown familiar, someone, looking up from dinner or a game of chess, his standard that art should represent objects as closely as possible . . . for the moment forgotten, may find himself interested, and absent-mindedly understanding the intention of some willfully clumsy figure."

Whatever the murals' initial effect on their South Bank viewers, the installation ceremony became an opportunity for education: "They had a great debate upon it the other night which I was asked to open. It was a very amusing occasion, with much freedom of speech, but on the whole they seemed inclined to be converted to my view," Fry reported.[51] The most specific anecdote that survives from this debate concerns the comment of a young mechanic: "I know nothing about art, but I do know that this sort of thing makes me want to whistle." "That," responded Fry, "is just the mood I wanted to create."[52] His confidence in the suitability of the Borough Polytechnic murals to their audience was registered a year later when he sent photographs of the project to an exhibition of school murals where they appeared with the credit line "lent by Roger Fry for the workers."[53]

For Fry, the Borough Polytechnic project confirmed his hopes for a modern art that could transcend class-based educational boundaries by its appeal to the senses, and unite young artists in a venture of mutual cooperation. The success of this collaboration was crucial to his decision, a year later, to found the Omega Workshops. Fry's letter soliciting funds for the Workshops told potential benefactors, "The group of young artists who decorated the Borough Polytechnic . . . have already formed the habit of working together with mutual assistance instead of each insisting on the singularity of his personal gifts."[54] Ultimately, the status of the Borough Polytechnic murals as the embodiment of Fry's aspirations for modern art seems most assured in his own mind, however. It is doubtful that the working-class audience enjoyed the level of unmediated access to the murals that he assumed. It is certain that Fry overestimated the selfless cooperation of the contributing artists when in 1913 he told the *Pall Mall Gazette* that they "worked together, taking their ideas from one another, developing them along their own lines, and feeling so thoroughly all the time that the work was a common effort that they refused to sign the pictures, saying, 'No, these we did together; let there be no individual signature.'"[55] While the personal and artistic bonds that developed between Grant and Etchells during the project suggests that Fry's ideal of collaborative aesthetic production was largely realized, nevertheless both Grant and Rothenstein signed their panels.[56]

Fry's over-optimistic gloss on the Borough Polytechnic decorations should not be allowed to discount their importance, however. Even the terms of Fry's exaggeration of the Borough Polytechnic's achievement reiterate Bloomsbury's association of modernist aesthetics with a broad range of challenges to convention. The complexity of Bloomsbury's roots in the overlapping Arts and Crafts and Aesthetic movements of the late-Victorian era is evident in the Borough Polytechnic murals' synthesis of reforms directed at pedagogy, class, and sexuality. The murals might also be described as synthesizing important elements of the earlier decorations by the Bloomsbury artists for private houses: Bell's determination to look modern, Fry's earnest simple-life reforms, and Grant's assertion of Mediterranean sensuality. More important than the roots of the Borough Polytechnic project, however, are its implications. Although invocations of Byzantine mosaic grew subtler in Bloomsbury's art after the summer of 1911, visual allusions to Byzantium continued to define the group's work both in style and subject, as will be seen in the following two chapters. More fundamentally, the vision of modernism as a return to the "morning of the world" remained fundamental to Bloomsbury's creation of modern environments throughout its artists' careers. With the Borough Polytechnic murals, moreover, the Bloomsbury artists, just months after bursting into the public eye with the Post-Impressionist exhibition, moved to involve other young painters in an initiative to bring a decorative aesthetic developed in the home to a wide audience and to address the social implications of modernism. In this respect, this project both anticipates the key elements of the far better known Omega Workshops and demonstrates once again the strength of Bloomsbury's association of modern forms of art with new ways of life.

Forging a Feminist Primitivism
Byzantine Women by Duncan Grant and Vanessa Bell
(1912)

Like Grant's panels for the Borough Polytechnic, which evoked Byzantinism to express the modern ideal of homoerotic democracy proposed by Whitman's English disciples, his next decorative commission—also for an educational institution—used Byzantium to address a second preoccupation of Victorian reformers: education for women. Grant's involvement in this project may be surprising today, for recent commentary on Bloomsbury's feminism has focused on Vanessa Bell and Virginia Woolf in relation to other female reformers. This perspective imposes a separatist cast on Bloomsbury, inimical to the group's own values, in the process disregarding the significance of Bell's and Woolf's commitment to Bloomsbury over the women's institutions of their era and ignoring the participation of the group's men in feminist causes. Grant's upbringing among his progressive Strachey cousins, for instance, involved him with feminist campaigns for the vote and for education reforms, so that by 1907, at the behest of Philippa Strachey, he was designing posters for women's suffrage.[1] In 1912, another of the Strachey sisters involved Grant in a project to paint murals for Newnham College, a pioneering institution for women's education at Cambridge (fig. 44).

Newnham's energetic dons, Pernel Strachey and Jane Harrison, initiated their scheme for "wall decorations" by contacting John Maynard Keynes, at King's College: "Miss Strachey tells me Mr Duncan Grant has frescoed a bit of your walls," Harrison wrote to Keynes, asking if she could visit his rooms. Harrison admitted she had not seen the Borough Polytechnic, but Grant's participation in the project directed by Fry, with his Cambridge ties, must have impressed her, for she told Keynes, "I am inclined to hope Mr Grant is the coming genius."[2] Ultimately— and for reasons unknown—the Newnham commission was not realized, but Grant executed for it a four-foot-square panel depicting Solomon and the Queen of Sheba.[3]

As the Bible tells it, "when the queen of Sheba heard of the fame of Solomon . . . she came to prove him with hard questions."[4] This story of a wise queen who tests the knowledge of a masculine authority—"there was not any thing hid from the king, which he told her not"—suited the walls of a pioneering institution of women's education, and Grant made his version specific to Cambridge with a hint of biographical reference in the figures: the queen, with her high forehead and pursed lips, has been compared to both Pernel and Philippa Strachey, while Solomon's long nose, huge hands, and great red beard exaggerate Lytton's most characteristic features.[5] The theatrical Arab costumes of his figures, moreover, recalled, for anyone familiar with Bloomsbury, the much-publicized "Dreadnaught

44. Duncan Grant, *Queen of Sheba*, 1912. Oil on board, 120 × 120 cm. Tate Britain.

45. Piero della Francesca, *The Queen of Sheba Received by Solomon*, from the cycle of frescos, *The Legend of the True Cross*, *c.* 1460. Arezzo.

Hoax" of 1910, in which Grant, with Virginia and Adrian Stephen, impersonated Abyssinian royalty to tour the navy's most sophisticated battleship, unrecognized by its commander, their own cousin. This episode confirmed Bloomsbury in its contempt for masculine military rituals, which Woolf in *Three Guineas* contrasted to the less grandiose but more valuable mission of women's colleges.[6]

Viewers needed no acquaintance with Bloomsbury or its attitudes, however, to see in Grant's *Queen of Sheba* a challenge to conventional versions of the tale. In Grant's image, Solomon, far from winning the queen with his inspired wisdom, listens passively to the animated figure of his interlocutor. This revision of the story is clear in relationship to a prototype well known to Grant, Piero della Francesca's cycle of frescoes in Arezzo, in which the queen, hardly distinguishable from her ladies in waiting, bows before the sumptuously dressed figure of Solomon (fig. 45). In Grant's version, the two figures meet as equals, literally embodying opposing points of view. As they gaze at one another, Solomon, heavy, dark, and listless, pulls away into the corner and the queen, bright and active, leans forward to press her point. The contrast between the two figures is summarized in the counterpoint of their gestures: though their right hands assume similar positions, Solomon's static gesture supports his heavy head, while the queen's hand, caught in action, emphasizes her rhetorical power. Grant's version of the story omits—even reverses—both the queen's awed submission to Solomon and her conversion to his patriarchal religion, undoing the validation of traditional authority asserted by the biblical source.

To tell old tales in new ways: this strategy is not unique to modern art, but the case has been made that women artists and poets in the twentieth century subjected the fundamental myths of European culture to unprecedented levels of critical revision as they worked to supplant patriarchal authority with new systems of value.[7] In Bloomsbury, however, this revision of myth was not the province of women alone.

Six years after Grant's *Queen of Sheba*, Lytton Strachey's *Eminent Victorians* would retell the stories of four emblematic figures of Victorian authority. But Strachey, in letters and essays circulated among his friends, had long twisted religious narratives to new purposes. A 1906 letter to Grant castigates "womanizer[s] and believer[s] in God," then concludes, "You observe nearly the whole of the human race comes under the range of my condemnation. Well, at any rate Christ escapes, and the O. B."[8] Claiming Christ as a gay atheist, Strachey prepares the way for Grant's iconoclastic reinterpretation of the Bible, not only in his *Queen of Sheba*, but in his subsequent treatment of Adam and Eve (discussed in Chapter 8).

To retell the story of Solomon and the Queen of Sheba, Grant drew heavily on ideas of the exotic East. The power of the queen is associated with the landscape behind her, a mystical purplish desert filled with milling camels painted from photographs and sketches from Grant's trip with Keynes to Tunis.[9] Grant links the queen visually to this vista of desert and camels, which crowds Solomon's comparatively barren, dark corner just as she leans forward against his retreating posture. Her red coat and brown turban blend with the sill that frames the desert scene, emphasizing her status as a representative of Arab culture. Emphatically not one of the black-veiled women of the purdah whom Grant would have seen in Turkey and Tunisia, his queen wears trousers and turban, evoking the romantic fantasies of the East from *The Arabian Nights*—or *Book of the Thousand Nights and a Night*, as it was called in Richard Burton's famous translation—where Shahrazade recounts her myriad tales to outwit the sultan. "Many readers of these volumes have remarked to me with much astonishment," wrote Burton, "that they find the female characters more remarkable for decision, action and manliness than the male; and are wonderstruck by their masterful attitude and by the supreme influence they exercise upon public and private life."

Like the theme, Grant's technique in *The Queen of Sheba* develops the Byzantinism of the Borough Polytechnic panels. The broad, choppy brush strokes that define the background of Grant's Borough Polytechnic bathers have spread all over *The Queen of Sheba*, imbuing figures and ground with the uniform texture for an effect "more as of a mosaic than of an oil painting," as one critic noted when Grant's panel was displayed in London.[10] Style and theme here combined to question, not just the ancient queen's submission to Solomon, but the broader subordination of Byzantium to Europe. Retelling the biblical story in a new way, Grant's decoration asks, "what if?" What if the Arabian queen converted the Judaic king to her ways? Would women be educated at Cambridge? Would Protestant sexual strictures give way to Mediterranean sensuality? Would Byzantine mosaic spawn the new art of a new age?

Though it never reached its intended home at Newnham College, Grant's *Queen of Sheba* came to fill a perhaps more public function as an exemplar of Bloomsbury's decorative aesthetic. Purchased by Roger Fry, it was exhibited at the second Post-Impressionist exhibition later in 1912 and acquired for the Tate Gallery in 1917, attracting along the way a record of favorable comment. The one voice of dissent, however, was Vanessa Bell's. She complained to Fry that the "usual English sweetness" was "coming in and spoiling" Grant's art: "I thought . . . that *The Queen of Sheba* was not only a failure because he had gone on and spoilt it, but that the whole conception was really sweet and too pretty and small."[11] Bell's own paintings from this period show her striving after greater strength and monumentality in the deployment of Byzantine reference than Grant demonstrated in the light-hearted *Queen of Sheba*. "I flatter myself that I am painting in an entirely new way (for me)," Bell wrote about her *Nursery Tea* in June of 1912 (fig. 8). "I am trying to paint as if I were mosaicing," she explained, "not by painting in spots, but by considering the picture as patches each of which has to be filled by the definite space of colours as one has to do with mosaic or woolwork, not allowing myself to brush the patches into each other."[12] If the subject and composition of *Nursery Tea* can be read as asserting a feminine vision against Augustus John's highly masculine modernism (as suggested in Chapter 1), Bell's technique can be seen as a similarly feminist claim on the methods of modernism asserted by Grant.

46. Empress Theodora, from mosaics at Ravenna, sixth century, detail of illustration in Clive Bell, *Art*, 1914.

This dynamic is evident in both Bell's writings and her paintings. A letter from January of 1912 records her experimenting in a portrait of Fry with what she called "Duncan's leopard manner," but this is the contrast with the "entirely new way" of painting she soon announced in *Nursery Tea*.[13] The visual terms of Bell's challenge to Grant's Byzantine modernism are clearest in head-to-head comparisons of portraits painted at the same time of the same sitters. Among these, the contest over the meaning of Byzantium for modernism is literally personified in a pair of portraits of a model dressed as the Empress Theodora from the mosaics at San Vitale at Ravenna. The Theodora mosaic was something of a paradigm in Bloomsbury's vision of a Byzantine-inflected modernism (fig. 46). It illustrates the chapter in *Art* where Clive Bell, recapitulating (in typically extreme terms) Fry's argument that Byzantine art redeemed decadent Roman realism, describes the aesthetic degeneration from the Byzantines' "great primitive morning, when men create art because they must," to the Renaissance: "that darkest hour when men confound imitation with art." Here, Bell contrasted the San Vitale mosaics to the "coarsely classical" decorations in the nearby fifth-century Galla Placida, where "there is a nasty, woolly realism about the sheep, and about the good shepherd more than a suspicion of the stodgy, Graeco-Roman, Apollo." The purely Byzantine sixth-century mosaics of San Vitale, on the other hand, constitute "the primitive and supreme summit" of Christian art, Bell said, going on to explicate their relevance for Post-Impressionism:

> Go to Ravenna, and you will see the masterpieces of Christian art, the primitives of the slope: go to the Tate Gallery or the Luxembourg, and you will see the end of that slope—Christian art at its last gasp. These *memento mori* are salutary when looking at the pictures of Cézanne, we feel, not inexcusably, that we are high above the mud. . . . Are we in the period of a new incubation? Or is the new age born? . . . This alone seems sure: since the Byzantine primitives set their mosaics at Ravenna no artist in Europe has created forms of greater significance unless it be Cézanne.[14]

Given the centrality of Byzantine precedent in Bloomsbury's conception of modernism, Vanessa Bell's claim to create her own "mosaicing" technique was a powerful assertion of her own identity among her artist colleagues—but one that matched other expressions of autonomy: "Don't give anyone too many ideas beforehand as to what I'm like," she warned Fry; "I want to make a favorable impression for myself."[15] Historians have been slow to notice Bell's distinctive qualities, at first relegating her to what she deplored as "the usual female fate" by presuming her stylistic submission to her male colleagues, then, after the acceptance of Bloomsbury as a critical category, stressing the artists' collaboration.[16] The differences between Bell's *Byzantine Lady* (fig. 47) and Grant's *The Countess* (fig. 48), however, suggest the nature of the separate identity she was determined to forge. Grant's version complements the casual asymmetry of the figure's tilted head with the dynamism of his scrubby rendering against areas of bare canvas. In contrast, Bell's static profile view evokes the solemnity of Byzantine icons in its careful construction from large blocks of flat color. For Grant, it was the intuitive, sensual spontaneity of "that great primitive morning" represented by Byzantium that was most compelling in its legacy for modernism. For Bell, the monumentality of the ancient mosaics offered a model for a modern idiom of power and permanence.[17]

Bell continued to refine her brand of Byzantine modernism throughout the summer of 1912. A series of pictures of painters painting, including *The Studio: Duncan Grant and Henri Doucet at Asheham* and *Frederick and Jessie Etchells in the Studio* (both illustrated in Chapter 6), subordinates images of her colleagues to her own powerful style.[18] Bell's portraits of artists painting together, of course, also suggest the importance she attached to artistic community, but her ideal was a community of equals, not a school with a leader surrounded by followers. Bell's determination to distinguish herself from her own nearest colleague is confirmed in her letters. She reported in September 1912:

47. Vanessa Bell, *Byzantine Lady*, 1912. Oil on canvas, 72 × 51.5 cm. United Kingdom Government Art Collection.

48. Duncan Grant, *The Countess*, 1912. Current location unknown, reproduced from Roger Fry, *Duncan Grant*, London Hogarth Press, 1923.

I find that I am not now much impeded by working with Duncan, although of course I always think why didn't I see it like that? But as I have come to the conclusion that I didn't see it like that I no longer try to think I did.[19]

Bell's assertions of power and permanence in her modernist style did not—as so often in avant-garde rivalries—sacrifice the traditionally feminine domestic attributes to these conventionally masculine values. On the contrary, by comparing her mosaic-like technique to "woolwork" and "patches," Bell fused attributes of monumentality and domesticity at the same time as she condemned what she called the "fatal prettiness" of English art, demanding: "It isn't what we want even for the minor arts, is it?"[20] In this context, it is significant that Bell's first bid for a new monumentality in her painting came in an image of her children at tea in their nursery. And she sustained a domestic setting for her portraits of painters rendered in her blocky new style. Bell's *Self-Portrait at the Easel* might be seen as a companion piece for her other images of painters in her circle (fig. 49). Though it is set in a sitting-room with books, a fireplace, and sofa, Bell's emphasis on the sheer size of the hearth, matched only by the artist's towering easel, belies any implication of domestic fragility. Likewise, the strong black stroke of Bell's neck aligns with the edge of the fireplace, the pointed "V" of the dress, and the edge of the sofa to organize the canvas as powerfully as the famous mark that completes the painting of Woolf's Post-Impressionist woman artist in *To the Lighthouse*.[21] As an index of painterly gesture, Bell's straight black line claims an equal measure of strength for the woman who made it and for the woman she depicts—who are, of course, one and the same. Bell's application of her new modernist style to this depiction of her

49. Vanessa Bell, *Self-Portrait at the Easel*, 1912. Oil. Private collection.

own home-based artistic practice encapsulates her aspirations for Post-Impressionism. Her figure, seated but nevertheless decisive and active, animates the composition, claiming simultaneously the strength of ancient Byzantine mosaics and the domestic associations of woolwork.

Bell's revision of Grant's Byzantine modernism follows his own rewriting of patriarchal myth in *The Queen of Sheba*. Neither hostile nor dismissive, Bell's differences from Grant mark her determination to develop an independent vision from a shared perspective. For both artists, however, it was not enough to invent new styles of easel painting. Both were immediately concerned to apply the lessons of Post-Impressionism to the home. The application of their individual styles to their domestic environments in 1912 is the topic of the following chapter.

6

Country and City
Asheham and Brunswick Square (1911–12)

The previous two chapters, organized around decorative schemes for schools, bear somewhat tangentially on domesticity, though the themes they develop—Bloomsbury's use of a primitivism centered on the Near East to create modern spaces for modern enactments of sex and gender—undergird my analysis of the group's domestic aesthetic. This chapter focuses on the first domestic interiors to be called "Post-Impressionist," one created for a shared country retreat, the other for a communal house in Bloomsbury. This juxtaposition of city and country reflects the prejudices of the British intelligentsia, which disdained the in-between of the suburbs, an attitude that helps explain why, though the group took its name from a central London neighborhood, it is at least as identified with the Sussex countryside near Lewes. More importantly, this division is reflected in the ideology of Post-Impressionism. Bloomsbury's interest in the French avant-garde focused on artists like Cézanne and Matisse, who used pastoral iconography to appeal to an urban avant-garde.[1] An analogous dualism animates Bloomsbury's aesthetic theory. Phrases like Fry's "the science of expressive design" present modernism as an erudite and logical route to primitive spontaneity. Defending the Post-Impressionists, Fry claimed: "We must begin at the beginning, and learn once more the ABC of abstract form. And it is just this that these French artists have set about, with that clear, logical intensity of purpose . . . which has nobly distinguished the French genius."[2] At once primitive and sophisticated, emotional and erudite, Bloomsbury's aspirations for modernism seem at face value counter-productive (though it should be noted that this tension characterizes many paradigmatic modernist forms from Frank Lloyd Wright's architecture and cubist painting to psychoanalysis). In the case of Bloomsbury's domestic designs, these currents branched into two streams: rural homes enlivened with an iconography of primal, natural abundance filtered through sophisticated references to continental art (Wissett, Charleston, and Penns-in-the-Rocks, all the topics of subsequent chapters); and urban homes in which the primal spontaneity of the Post-Impressionist style enlivens an iconography of modern pursuits, such as athletics and travel (decorations for Arthur Ruck, for Keynes at 46 Gordon Square, and for the Woolfs at Tavistock Square). Both streams have their origin in 1911–12, when Bloomsbury, now conscious of itself as a group, set up shared houses in the country and the city.

Bloomsbury's move to Sussex was initiated by Virginia Woolf. Her famous claim that, "In or about December 1910, human character changed," is often quoted by historians (as it was in Chapter 3) in reference to the furor over the first Post-Impressionist show, but that exhibition opened early in November and ran until the following January. What was new in December of 1910 was her decision to lease what she described as a "hideous suburban villa" in the otherwise unspoiled Sussex village of Firle.[3] In an echo of Fry's decision to name Durbins for a field at his parents' country house (see Chapter 2), Woolf called her rural retreat Little Talland House in honor of Talland House, the Stephen family's summer house in Cornwall that became the setting of *To the Lighthouse*, suggesting a similarly ambivalent relationship to parental legacies. Despite her bid to invest her "suburban villa" with the permanence of childhood memories, however, Woolf inhabited Little Talland House only briefly, and her residence there has been noted chiefly for inaugurating Bloomsbury's connection with the countryside around Lewes. But Little Talland House is also significant as the site of Vanessa Bell's first Post-Impressionist domestic decorations. By February 1911, Bell reported from Firle, "We have been putting up violet-orange curtains as fast as we could. They are rather sketchy in consequence but full of emotion."[4] Only a few months earlier, Fry had introduced London to Post-Impressionism with claims that the new style enabled "art . . . to regain its power to express emotional ideas."[5] Now, when Woolf invited Desmond MacCarthy—secretary for the exhibition—and his wife to stay at Little Talland House, she described it as "done up in patches of post-Impressionist colour."[6] The rapidity of this domestic application of Post-Impressionism highlights the Stephen sisters' eagerness to use the new aesthetics to define a new kind of home life.

Bloomsbury's project to invent a Post-Impressionist domesticity in rural Sussex continued over the next half century through a series of houses culminating with Charleston. The first Sussex house with claims to a sustained place in this history was described by Leonard Woolf as "an extra-ordinarily romantic-looking house . . . in one of those lovely folds or hollows in the down," which he and Virginia discovered on a walk from Little Talland House.[7] Asheham quickly became Bloomsbury's rural headquarters, and, as at Little Talland House, Vanessa embarked on a project of modernist decoration. "I am very busy inside the house, putting up curtains, etc.," Bell wrote her sister; "I have just been getting a bright reddish orange stuff for curtains for the sitting room, to be lined and bordered with mauve."[8] Such exuberant colors cast the house as the realization of a Post-Impressionist painting, an effect

50. Vanessa Bell,
*Virginia Woolf at
Asheham*, 1912.
Oil on canvas,
40 × 34 cm.
National Portrait
Gallery, London.

Sailing to Byzantium

52. Vanessa Bell, *Frederick and Jessie Etchells in the Studio*, 1912. Oil on board, 51 × 53 cm. Tate Britain.

51. Vanessa Bell, *The Studio: Duncan Grant and Henri Doucet at Asheham*, 1912. Oil on board, 57.2 × 44.5 cm. Private collection.

Bell, completing the cycle of reference, delighted in documenting in her art. Her 1912 portrait, *Virginia Woolf at Asheham*, for example, depicts its sitter, engaged in the domestic ritual of needlework, cradled between the sinuous wings of a fiery-orange armchair (fig. 50).[9]

Significantly for the connections of domesticity and modernism, Bell's depictions of artists at work—discussed in the previous chapter as evidence of her ambition to forge a personal style that allied woolwork and mosaic—were painted at Asheham, marking the Post-Impressionist home as a site of female creativity. The ambiguous patch of brilliant red (perhaps a paint rag perched on part of the easel) that protrudes unexpectedly from the right edge of the canvas in *The Studio: Duncan Grant and Henri Doucet at Asheham* (fig. 51) evolved in *Frederick and Jessie Etchells in the Studio* (fig. 52), painted in the same room just a few weeks later, into a complex relationship of highlights. The red-stockinged leg of the woman artist is picked up by the brilliant red-orange curtain (probably one Bell made); the warm tones of the curtain are echoed in the lighter orange patches of the tiled walkway and wall seen through the open door. That this sequence of warm tones was self-conscious is clear from close examination of the painting, which reveals that the strong orange bands of the garden view replaced closed French doors (their central vertical shows through the overpainting just to the left of the standing figure).[10] These widening ripples of color suggest the conceptual links between the figure of the female artist, Bell's colorful blocky style of painting, and this Post-Impressionist domestic environment.

Such visual suggestions of Asheham's importance as a locus for a lifestyle associated with Post-Impressionism are explicit in Bell's letters. In 1915, she wrote to Woolf from another rented house on the Sussex coast, describing it as "all the very opposite from Asheham":

The garden is on the road so all that goes on in it must be irreproachably respectable—no posing naked as at Asheham. Inside the house, the walls are drab and grey . . . A few works by me and Duncan have now been stuck over them in places in the hope of introducing a little colour. It's incredible how these people dread colour . . . .[11]

The connection of modernist aesthetics and new ways of life is here quite clear, and it is in this context that Woolf's comment about human character changing in December of 1910 might be read. Describing the change, Woolf moves seamlessly from its manifestation in the arts to "the character of one's cook": "The Victorian cook lived like a leviathan in the lower depths, formidable, silent, obscure, inscrutable; the Georgian cook is a creature of sunshine and fresh air; in and out of the drawing-room, now to borrow the *Daily Herald*, now to ask advice about a hat." In discussing Bloomsbury, it is no non-sequitur to speak of a Post-Impressionist lifestyle in which challenges to artistic convention go hand in hand with challenges to the norms of middle-class domesticity.

Links between Post-Impressionist domesticity and the creativity of Asheham's female inhabitants are suggested by the house's re-appearance at critical moments in the evolution of the art of both Virginia Woolf and Vanessa Bell. When in 1919 Woolf began in short stories to experiment with self-consciously modernist prose, one of her first stories made the house its subject. Drawing on local legends of ghosts and buried treasure at Asheham, Woolf's "A Haunted House" describes a ghostly couple whose memories of "sleeping, in the garden reading, laughing, rolling apples in the loft" make "the pulse of the house" beat softly, gladly, proudly, then wildly, "Safe! safe! safe!" In Woolf's story, it is memory of domestic pleasure that creates the powerful atmosphere of comfort and tranquility, which becomes the house's "buried treasure."[12]

Though Woolf's story functioned as an elegy for Asheham after the landlord dispossessed her, the house's deployment as a subject for stylistic experimentation recalled its role in the development of Bell's landscape painting during 1912, the first summer of their tenancy.[13] The house's role in expanding Bell's domestic iconography beyond interiors and figures should not be underestimated, for Bloomsbury's perception of Asheham's continuity with its setting in the downs ideally matched the homogenizing aesthetic of her new "mosaicing" style. Bell's compositions emphasize this continuity. In *Landscape with Haystack, Asheham*, for instance, the house-like shape of the foreground haystack is linked to the house behind it and echoes the forms of the outbuildings (fig. 53). The importance of this motif is evidenced by Bell's completion of at least two versions of this composition and her defense of it against Fry's critique; she insisted, "it rather interests me and I want to work it out."[14] Three other paintings showing Asheham, moreover, return to the idea of the house as a microcosm of its natural setting. Viewed from the front, the flat crest of the hill behind the house, bracketed within the higher projections of the middle-ground trees, repeats the shape of the roof and chimneys, forming a natural room in which the house sits (fig. 54). A view of the back of the house relates the way its enclosed garden opens off one side to the landscape, which trails off from a solid mass of trees to a flat vista, a resonance emphasized by a wispy tree that parallels the sloping line of the roof and the edges of the chunky, angular clouds (fig. 55). A second back view positions the house against the woods to the side, emphasizing the visual echoes between its tall chimneys and the trees, which are no longer an undifferentiated mass but a series of clearly delineated vertical forms (fig. 56). Taken together, Bell's 1912 landscapes claim for Asheham's domesticity all the solidity and permanence of its setting; at the same time, they present the natural world as a reverberation of the home. As in Woolf's experimental short story, where sudden shifts in temporal setting and in the references of pronouns like "you" and "I" blur boundaries between house and setting, and between seer and seen, the formal reverberations of Post-Impressionism allowed Bell to imbue this domestic site with emotional significance.

While the rural ideal represented by Asheham initiated one enduring aspect of Bloomsbury's domestic aesthetic, Bell's decorative work in the Sussex countryside

had its counterpart at an urban house also discovered by her sister: 38 Brunswick Square in the London neighborhood that gave the group its name. Leonard Woolf dated the formation of Bloomsbury to the moment Duncan Grant, John Maynard Keynes, Adrian Stephen, and the as-yet-unmarried Woolfs moved together to Brunswick Square.[15] Without debating when Bloomsbury began, it is undeniable that this transformation of friendship into residence in a communal house solidified the group's identity through a new kind of domesticity. The way of life represented by 38 Brunswick Square marked Bloomsbury's final rejection of conventional organizations of home life around the nuclear family. The unmarried Stephen siblings, Adrian and Virginia, growing increasingly antagonistic in their shared quarters in Fitzroy Square, rejected the more predictable responses of separation or sublimation and determined instead to inaugurate a different kind of household, expanded to include their friends.[16]

53. Vanessa Bell, *Landscape with Haystack, Asheham*, 1912. Oil on board, 60.3 × 65.7 cm. Smith College Museum of Art, Northampton, Mass.

54. Vanessa Bell, *Asheham House*, 1912. Oil on board, 47 × 53.5 cm. Private collection.

That 38 Brunswick Square continued the process of domestic reformulation the Stephen sisters began when they moved to Gordon Square in 1904 is suggested by the language Woolf used to describe both moves. Looking back on Gordon Square, Woolf recalled their "experiments and reforms"; in 1911, she announced her move to Brunswick Square by explaining, "We are going to try all kinds of experiments. . . . We have spent a month discussing how to live."[17] And as when the Stephen sisters left Kensington for Bloomsbury, part of the attraction of the move to Brunswick Square was the opposition it aroused from relatives and friends from the Hyde Park Gate days. Woolf recalled:

> My mother's ghost was invoked once more—by Violet Dickinson—to deplore the fact that I had taken a house in Brunswick Square and had asked young men to share it. George Duckworth came all the way from Charles Street to beg Vanessa to make me give up the idea and was not comforted perhaps when she replied that after all the Foundling Hospital was handy.[18]

The antagonism of George Duckworth, Woolf's half-brother, could only have confirmed her determination to imagine new forms of domestic life. One of her first expressions of desire for a communal house comes in an account of a conversation with her former Greek tutor, Janet Case, in which an outline of her new living arrangement follows seamlessly from the acknowledgment that the now-upstanding and disapproving Duckworth molested her as a child.[19]

The experimental organization of the Brunswick Square house was codified in a notice distributed to the inhabitants. Expenses were shared equally, with meals and cleaning provided by a cook and maid retained from Hyde Park Gate. Meals were left on trays in the hall so residents could eat either alone or together in their rooms, and the routine of the household was organized to promote creative work. Leonard and Virginia, for instance, held each other to an agreement to work uninterruptedly in the mornings, writing 500 words a day on their novels.[20] The sense of community afforded by this new living arrangement is celebrated in a painting executed in

55. Vanessa Bell, *Asheham House*, 1912. Oil on board, 47 × 53.5 cm (verso of fig. 54).

56. Vanessa Bell, *Asheham*, 1912. 47 × 53.5 cm. Current location unknown.

57. Duncan Grant, *On the Roof, 38 Brunswick Square*, 1912. Oil on panel, 96.5 × 118.7 cm. Private collection.

Grant's equally novel "leopard manner." *On the Roof: 38 Brunswick Square* shows Leonard reading, perhaps aloud, while Adrian and Virginia relax in the sun; Grant's presence, of course, is registered by his distinctive style of rendering (fig. 57). The unconventional setting of this scene emphasizes the new kind of domestic life accommodated at Brunswick Square, where friends were as likely to congregate on the roof as in the drawing room.

Despite the air of privacy suggested by Grant's image of the group protected behind their parapet, the Brunswick Square house became a center of Bloomsbury's activities. "There are so many people to attract callers that callers come in rather a thick stream," Keynes reported.[21] Vanessa Bell analyzed the importance of the Brunswick Square house to Bloomsbury's development, noting that:

> Brunswick Square was a little nearer Gordon Square than was Fitzroy Square, and all sorts of parties at all hours of the day or night happened constantly. Rooms were decorated, people made to sit for their portraits . . . all seemed a sizzle of excitement. Brunswick would come round to Gordon Square when tired of the tray system of meals, and in those easy days the larder always held enough for two or three unexpected guests. . . . So it was natural to say "stay to dinner" and to sit and talk as of old till all hours, either in the familiar room at No. 46 or in the Square garden.[22]

Leonard Woolf's account of his deepening relationship with Virginia during the spring of 1912 also cites the importance of her circle and its shared pastimes: "We often lunched or dined together, we went together to Gordon Square to see Vanessa or have a meal there . . . we went to the theatre or to the Russian Ballet."[23] Ultimately their compatibility in the unconventional domestic arrangement of a communal house seemed to Virginia among the strongest arguments for marriage, and she accepted his proposal on May 29, 1912. Writing to a friend, Virginia explained, "He has been living at Brunswick Square since December—we know each other as I imagine few people do before marriage."[24] Intimated in the contrast Woolf drew between conventional courtship and her own relationship to her future husband is pride in her radically refashioned home.

In what was quickly becoming a Bloomsbury characteristic, the new ways of living at Brunswick Square found visual expression in redecoration. Although the house was destroyed by bombs in World War II, photographs and memoirs offer partial documentation of the most ambitious of Bloomsbury's domestic decorations to date, while letters and memoirs attest to the house's extraordinary effect on both visitors and inhabitants. All that is known about Grant's ground-floor studio at the back of the house is that it was decorated with abstract designs.[25] The adjacent sitting-room, which Grant shared with Keynes when the latter was down from Cambridge, is remembered for its riot of Post-Impressionist imagery. On one wall hung Frederick Etchells's large (five by three foot) painting, *The Dead Mole* (fig. 58), which Keynes had purchased from the artist, Grant's friend since the Borough

58. Frederick Etchells, *The Dead Mole*, 1912. Oil on canvas, 167 × 106 cm. Fitzwilliam Museum, Cambridge University.

Polytechnic project. Thematically, this painting seemed to test the formalist principle that any subject could yield aesthetically significant art, for it shows a towering man and a small boy dancing around the body of a dead rodent. The bright colors of Etchells's painting matched the brilliant yellows and greens of the furnishings, contributing to an environment of Post-Impressionist domesticity. The most striking aspect of this room, however, was a mural that began on the side wall next to the fireplace and ran around the curved back wall, filling the expanse between wainscot and ceiling for a distance of about thirty feet.[26] Worked in Grant's mosaic-like patches in May and June of 1912, the mural in the sitting room he shared with Keynes is distinguished from Bloomsbury's other domestic designs to date by its urban subject: an accident between two horse-drawn cabs. The mural was Grant's gift to Keynes, and suggests its recipient's relationship to the Brunswick Square establishment, which was his London base ("I am getting, through this house, a complete London life," Keynes explained to his mother in Cambridge[27]). Grant's shift to an urban, public imagery, in contrast to the pastoral sensuality of his first mural for Keynes, may also reflect the change in their relationship, which cooled from sexual involvement to close friendship in the period between the two projects.

More significant than the biographical motivations for this mural, however, is the insight it offers into the relationship between Bloomsbury and Walter Sickert's Camden Town painters, which was far more ambivalent and fluid than later polemics would suggest.[28] Just as Vanessa Bell looked to Sickert's example to fashion her own modernist style (discussed in Chapter 1), when Grant wanted to evoke urban modernity, he looked to the Camden Town artists. Grant's iconography of horses and hansoms echoes Robert Bevan's cab-yard paintings, which were so admired in the Camden Town painters' first exhibition in June of 1911 that they have been credited with inspiring this group to commit itself to urban imagery.[29] Although Grant's interest in Camden Town painting was reciprocated to the extent that he was invited to show in the second Camden Town exhibition in December of 1911, Sickert's positioning Camden Town's ideology in opposition to the values of domesticity left it to Bloomsbury to apply this aesthetic to the home.[30] Grant's Street Accident mural at Brunswick Square (fig. 59) and the Omega's 1916 mural for Arthur Ruck (discussed in the introduction to Section IV; see fig. 122) offer provocative evidence of both the connections between Bloomsbury and Sickert and the potential—largely unrealized—for expansion of the Camden Town aesthetic beyond easel painting.

Like the Borough Polytechnic project completed the year before, this Brunswick Square mural also challenges the myth of Bloomsbury's rigid clubbiness. Grant

59. Duncan Grant and Frederick Etchells, *Street Accident*, mural at 38 Brunswick Square, 1912, no longer extant.

enlisted two other artists to contribute to this decoration: Frederick Etchells and an art-school friend, Vera Waddington. Little is known about Waddington's contribution, except that Grant was alone in admiring it and her section of the mural was ultimately whitewashed over as incompatible with the rest.[31] Etchells, on the other hand, was an ideal collaborator. Grant later recalled, "Etchells and I both liked to experiment at that stage, and were very much in sympathy with each other."[32] Etchells's Borough Polytechnic panel, the scene of a fair at Hampstead Heath, anticipated the busy mood of the Brunswick Square mural, while his concurrent paintings aesthetically updating the popular imagery of hunting prints and religious artefacts may inform the mural's evocation of newspaper illustrations.[33] For Vanessa Bell, the collaborative aspect of the Brunswick Square mural was what made it interesting. Writing to Fry in June of 1912, she reported, "I saw D[uncan]'s and Etchells' decoration . . . it's extraordinary how indistinguishable they become." Visually, the uniform patterning of Grant's "leopard manner" pointillism was given new depth by the overlapping contours of Etchells's linear rendering. The effect, combining the tesserae-like patches of paint with a consistent dark outline, brings the Brunswick Square mural closer to the Byzantinism of the Borough Polytechnic project than any of Grant's intervening work. Bell admired the result, saying, "I think [it] very good," though she was quick to add, "no one else does."[34]

Bell did not explain why others disliked the Street Accident mural. Since its modernist style was well on the way to becoming a definitive feature of Bloomsbury painting, however, reservations may have centered on the urban subject matter that was anachronistic in its Bloomsbury context. This inference is buttressed by the fact that a second mural at Brunswick Square, though far more stylistically daring, was roundly applauded. If Bloomsbury was reluctant to welcome Grant's domestic fusion of the Byzantine modernism of the Borough Polytechnic panels and the cosmopolitan imagery of Camden Town, he found greater approval with another kind of modernism that combined contemporary themes with suggestions of a primitive sensuality.

Grant's second Brunswick Square mural is remarkable, not only in the context of the British avant-garde, but in the wider field of European modernism, where it finds its closest comparison in Matisse's murals of the 1930s. Matisse's later murals, of course, developed from his earlier work, including the dancers that, to one degree or another, informed Grant's mural for Keynes's Cambridge apartment in 1910 (as discussed in Chapter 3; see fig. 52). Since 1910, Grant's knowledge of Matisse's work had deepened. By the time he came to decorate the first-floor sitting room at Brunswick Square, Grant had had the opportunity to study Matisse's work more closely in the second Post-Impressionist show, which ran from October through December of 1912. Matisse was the undisputed star of this exhibition, represented by six sculptures along with thirty-four drawings and paintings. The centerpiece of the show was Matisse's mural-scale Dance I, described in the catalog as a "design for a decoration in Prince Tschoukine's Palace at Moscow" (fig. 60). Writing to Keynes in September of 1912, a month before the exhibition opened, Grant reported, "A great many of the French pictures have already come. The Matisses are radiantly beautiful."[35] Grant was encouraged to conceive himself as part of this Matissian movement by the organization of this exhibition, which included examples of British and Russian Post-Impressionism, among them his The Queen of Sheba and The Countess (discussed in Chapter 5; see figs 44 and 48).[36] Like his panels for Keynes's Cambridge rooms two years before, the upstairs mural at Brunswick Square—painted for the sitting room of Adrian Stephen, who had replaced Keynes as Grant's lover—seems inspired by a desire to imagine a domestic environment redolent of the uninhibited sensuality he saw in Matisse's art. In the process, Grant discovered potentials of this aesthetic Matisse himself realized decades later.

If Dance I was a model for the Brunswick Square mural, Grant transformed it in two important ways. Matisse's pale pink figures were altered in Grant's version to red; Matisse made the same change in revising his design for its domestic installation in Moscow, which Grant may have known.[37] More originally, Grant transformed Matisse's dancers into tennis players (fig. 61). This motif was appropriate to

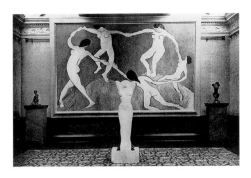

60. Henri Matisse, *Dance I*, photographed at the Second Post-Impressionist Exhibition behind Eric Gill's *The Virgin* (fig. 18), reproduced from the catalog to the Second Post-Impressionist Exhibition, London: Ballentyne & Company, 1912.

the room, which looked out over the tennis courts in Brunswick Square. But tennis had greater significance as an image of modern life. Historians have described tennis as one of the middle-class challenges to aristocratic social norms, with the game supplanting formal dances as a forum for the mingling of the sexes, and Bloomsbury memoirs confirm these associations.[38] Both Stephen sisters expressed anxiety and discomfort over ballroom dances, while tennis—and its counterpart, badminton—were favorite Bloomsbury sports.[39] Like the badminton mosaic Grant, Fry, and Bell began at Durbins, the tennis-player mural documents Bloomsbury's association of racquet sports with the uninhibited physical pleasures of modern life. The tennis game depicted by Grant presents itself as particularly modern. The subdued physicality of the game's usual execution at this period cedes, in Grant's version, to an exuberant athleticism, especially on the part of the woman with her bare legs spread wide apart. The mere hint of her yellow triangular skirt seems to mock current debates over the length of attire necessary to ensure the decent—which was to say total—concealment of female legs during play.[40] Perhaps the only thing more shocking than the tiny patch of tennis skirt on Grant's female player is the total nudity implied by his monochrome male figures, who outnumber her two to one. Grant's energetic tennis players emphasize the game's association with both modern athleticism and primitive sexuality. In this, they are close cousins to the dancers

61. Duncan Grant, tennis player mural at 38 Brunswick Square, 1912–13, no longer extant.

in Matisse's decoration, who have long been seen as claiming for modern art a primal sensuality.

The idea of tennis as a kind of dance, at once modern and sensual, might seem far-fetched, but this was exactly the theme of a better-known project contemporary with—and related to—Grant's mural: the Ballets Russes's 1913 production of *Jeux* (translated as *Playtime* for the London season) (fig. 62). Conceived in London during the summer of 1912 as a response to calls for a modern form of dance, *Jeux* premiered in Paris in the spring of 1913. Set to music by Claude Debussy, *Jeux* was choreographed and danced by Vazlov Nijinsky, who used the term "cubist" to describe its stylized, angular gestures. *Jeux* was the first work by the Ballets Russes to be performed in modern dress, and the program emphasized its modernity by setting the scene ahead to 1930. The original idea, according to Jacques-Emile Blanche, who was present when Nijinsky proposed it, combined two signifiers of the modern: "the game of tennis (with licentious motifs) was to be interrupted by the crashing of an aeroplane."[41] This juxtaposition of tennis with a violent accident involving modern machines replicates the effect of the two murals at Brunswick Square. As performed, however, the ballet abandoned the airplane crash, leaving the licentious tennis match to carry the full signification of modernity. *Jeux* followed Nijinsky's *L'Après-midi d'un faune*, which notoriously concluded with the dancer simulating orgasm over a scarf dropped by a fleeing nymph, and the erotic implications of the new ballet are clear in the scenario published with the piano score in 1912. The dance begins with a tennis ball rolling across the stage. Then three figures—two women and a man—in tennis costume enact a drama of jealousy, the man dancing first with one, then with the other. It concludes:

62. Publicity photograph of Vaslav Nijinski for Ballets Russes production of *Jeux*, 1913.

> They dance together in a crescendo of movement; and then, with a passionate gesture, the young man brings their three heads together, and a triple kiss drowns them in ecstacy.
> From nowhere a tennis ball falls at their feet . . . Surprised and frightened they flee into the nocturnal depths of the park.[42]

Romola Nijinsky's biography of her husband explains the modernity of this scenario as a release from Victorian sexual inhibitions:

> [I]n *Jeux* the feeling is modern. . . . Love becomes, not the fundamental driving force of life, but merely a game, as it is in the twentieth century. The object (here the excuse of finding the ball) is easily abandoned and flirtation begins, but this also is quite as easily given up when the idea of the former activity is recalled. He sees here love as nothing more than an emotion, a pastime, which doesn't even require consummation, which can be found among three as well as among the same sex.[43]

This final point is emphaszied in Vazlov Nijinsky's diary, which explains how the version of *Jeux* that reached the stage was modified from his first idea: "The story of this ballet is about three young men making love to each other," he said; "I changed the characters, as love between three men could not be represented on the stage."[44]

Nijinsky's ballet is linked to Grant's Brunswick Square mural by more than a coincidence of themes and imagery. The society hostess Ottoline Morrell claimed that *Jeux* was inspired during a party in front of her house in Bedford Square, where Nijinsky and the Ballets Russes set designer Léon Bakst watched Grant playing tennis in the twilight; "*Quel décor*!" the Russians are said to have exclaimed.[45] In fact, *Jeux* was already under way during the summer of 1912 when this party took place, but Morrell's anecdote suggests the shared preoccupations of London's prewar avant-garde, in which Bloomsbury and the Ballets Russes both held an important place. Bloomsbury saw the Russians as allies who had realized in dance a shared aspiration for new forms of artistic expression appropriate to the modern age. Leonard Woolf's memoirs embed the Ballet in the context of all the manifestations of modernity that made it "exciting to be alive in London in 1911":

> It looked for the moment as if militarism, imperialism, and antisemitism were on the run. . . . The revolution of the motor car and the aeroplane had begun; Freud

63. Boris Anrep, *Allegorical Composition, c.* 1912, as illustrated in the catalog to the Second Post-Impressionist Exhibition, London: Ballentyne & Company, 1912.

and Rutherford and Einstein were at work beginning to revolutionize our knowledge of our own minds and the universe. Equally exciting things were happening in the arts. . . . we were in the middle of the profound revolution of Cézanne, Matisse, and Picasso. . . . And to crown all, night after night we flocked to Covent Garden, entranced by a new art, a revelation to us benighted British, the Russian Ballet in the greatest days of Diaghilev and Nijinsky.[46]

The unprecedented combination of athleticism and eroticism in the dancing of the Ballets Russes reflected the exuberant sensuality that Bloomsbury ascribed to modernism, while the technical expertise of the dancers revealed their grounding in a powerful classical tradition. Leonard Woolf describes the "element of classicism" that made the Ballets Russes "so entrancing," confirming the assessment of more recent historians who have argued that the Russians were seen as "both barbaric and civilized. . . . both 'ultra natural' (wild, untamed, passionate, chaotic, animal) and 'ultra-artificial' (fantastic, androgynous, bejewelled, decorative, decadent)."[47] This combination appealed strongly to Bloomsbury's primitivist ideals, and the fact that the dancers who created this spectacle came from Russia confirmed the group's belief in a modernism rooted in Eastern tradition.

For Bloomsbury, Russia was a crucial source of modernist culture, second only to Paris in its influence. As early as 1909, Fry—rather improbably—credited Tolstoy as a source of his theories of aesthetics, while in the 1920s the Woolfs' Hogarth Press committed itself strongly to the English-language dissemination of Russian literature that Virginia studied Russian in order to be able to assess the translations.[48] Evidence of Russia's centrality to Bloomsbury's vision of modernism is nowhere clearer than in the second Post-Impressionist exhibition, which upheld Russian art, along with French and English, as the only vital "Post-Impressionist schools." Post-Impressionism, Fry announced in the catalog, had "liberated and revived an old native tradition" in Russian art.[49] Claims for a Russian Post-Impressionism were developed in the catalog by the curator of the Russian section, the expatriate artist Boris Anrep. Although later well known for his mosaics, Anrep at this time was painting stylistically updated versions of vernacular Russian religious images, and he included a selection of popular religious prints in the exhibition (fig. 63). This fusion of the primitive with the modern accorded closely with Bloomsbury's ideals, and Anrep's catalog essay (with his stilted English left unedited) emphasized the primitive—specifically Byzantine—roots of Russian art:

> Russian spiritual culture has formed itself on the basis of a mixture of its original Slavonic character with Byzantine culture and with the cultures of various Asiatic nations. In later times European influence has impressed itself on Russian life, but does not take hold of the Russian heart, that continues to stream the Eastern blood through the flesh of the Slavonic people.

Anrep went on to characterize the Russian modernists in the show as the "new Byzantine group," emphasizing their "decorative interpretation of their feelings." His description of Nicolas Roerich—a painter who also designed for the Ballets Russes—exemplifies his Russian-inflected primitivism:

> [T]hough he does not appropriate entirely the forms of the [Byzantine] ikones, he succeeds, may be, more than others, to translate in his own manner the essence of the Russian religious and fantastical spirit. His imagination carries him further to the dawn of the Russian life, and he gives an emotional feeling of the prehistoric Slavonic Pagans."[50]

Bloomsbury's belief in the existence of a widespread movement of Russian modernism rooted in Eastern tradition was encouraged by exposure to the Ballets Russes. Two of the most popular works in the troupe's first London season (June–July of 1911), *Cléopatre* and *Schéhérazade*, appealed directly to Bloomsbury's aspirations for a modern art growing from Mediterranean roots, while the well-received dance sequences from the ballet–opera *Prince Igor* featured Russian folk dancers and a troupe of Persian women on a strikingly minimal set designed by

Sailing to Byzantium

Roerich. In the 1912 London season, *Thamar*, with its Caucasian folk dancing, and Stravinsky's *L'Oiseau de feu* [*The Firebird*], based on a Russian folk-tale, continued to stress the troupe's Eastern origins, while *Le Dieu Bleu*, a ballet starring Nijinsky and based on Siamese dance, developed the Oriental exoticism of *Schéhérazade*.[51] These associations were emphasized in the second Post-Impressionist show, where Roerich's eight paintings were displayed with now-unidentified designs for costumes.

Bloomsbury was inspired by the Ballets Russes's success in winning audiences for a version of modernism so similar to its own. Leonard Woolf recalled that:

> Night after night one could go to Covent Garden and find all round one one's friends, the people whom one liked best in the world, moved and excited as one was oneself. In all my long life in London this is the only instance in which I can remember the intellectuals going night after night to a theatre.[52]

As one recent historian puts it, the Ballets Russes "brought Society and the arts into contact in a way which Post-Impressionism had not, and in this Bloomsbury, naively no doubt, saw a great hope: the governing class was being civilized at last. . . . the arts, 'progressive' politics, economic improvement seemed to be marching hand in hand."[53] This analysis is borne out by the example of Edward Marsh, a civil servant who was then Winston Churchill's assistant. Describing *Jeux*, which opened a few months after the second Post-Impressionist show closed, Marsh reported to the poet, Rupert Brooke, "It's a Post-Impressionist picture put in motion . . . it has almost brought me around to Matisse's pictures!"[54]

What was especially exciting about the Russians' success in converting audiences for its new aesthetic was that they did so without sacrificing the transgressive eroticism so central to Bloomsbury's investment in modernism. In *Cléopatre*, for example, the queen, costumed as a belly-dancer, infatuates a noble youth, compelling him to forsake his dutiful lover and sacrifice his own life for a single night of passion. When the lovers retreat to the queen's bed, their lovemaking, which is the choreographic focus of the ballet, is evoked by a series of dances, beginning in the London production with Nijinsky and Tamara Karsavina performing what was billed as a "Turkish" dance with a billowing scarf (the same theme and device characterized the 1912 *Thamar*). Also in the 1911 season, Nijinsky, in a costume of rose petals, danced the title role in *Le Spectre de la rose*, a more gently erotic evocation of a girl's romantic reverie after her first night at a ball. Reviewing the Paris production in the same season, Jean Cocteau wrote of Nijinsky:

> In his costume of curling petals, behind which perhaps the Girl perceives the image of her recent dancing-partner, he comes through the blue cretonne curtains out of the warm June night. . . . Exulting in his rosy ecstasy he seems to impregnate the muslin curtains and take possession of the dreaming Girl.[55]

The eroticism of Nijinsky's performances grew legendary in the Ballets's 1912 season, when he danced the title role of *Narcisse*. Like *L'Après-midi d'un faune*, which had created such a scandal in Paris that it was not scheduled for the London season, *Narcisse* exploited the eroticism of classical myth. The artist Charles Ricketts reported of Nijinsky's Narcissus: "He leaps like a faun, with such rare clothing on that Duchesses had to be led out of the audience, blinded with emotion, and with their diamond tiaras all awry."[56]

The eroticism associated with Nijinsky's performance was remarkable not only in degree but in kind. The simple fact of a male lead in a ballet was remarkable. Male roles—often actually danced by women—were conventionally written to support famous ballerinas in productions that were, as the *Daily News* recognized in its awed review of the Ballets Russes's opening, "merely a frivolous excuse for showing pretty girls and dresses behind the footlights."[57] Nijinsky's challenge to choreographic conventions, therefore, put him in the spotlight reserved for ballerinas, presenting himself to the public as a willing object of desire. This die was cast in the Ballets Russes's first London season with *Schéhérazade*, an orgy between harem women and male slaves that ends in the death of all involved. Nijinsky played the

Golden Slave, the favorite wife's caged plaything. Nijinsky's provocative inversion of conventions of masculine display is clear in accounts of his performance as "half-cat, half-snake, fiendishly agile, feminine and yet wholly terrifying."[58] Such praise shaded easily into sexual aspersion. Michel Fokine, who choreographed *Schéhérazade* but was replaced by Nijinsky, explained that "the lack of masculinity which was peculiar to him and which made him unfit for certain roles . . . suited very well the role of the Negro Slave."[59] Critics hostile to modern dance derided Nijinsky as effeminate—this term was also attached to Nijinsky's costume for *Le Spectre de la rose*, which the *New York Times* described as "fashioned about the shoulders exactly like a woman's *décolleté*." *The Times* went on to censure Nijinsky's "super-refinement of gesture and posture," including his practice of "dancing on the toes, which is not ordinarily indulged in by male dancers."[60] In fact, this inversion of ballet's gendered conventions originated with Nijinsky's first ideas for *Jeux*, which he proposed to perform in the pointe shoes reserved for ballerinas.[61]

For those who knew the Russians offstage as well as on—as Bloomsbury did—the exotic and androgynous sensuality of the Ballets's productions was connected to the homosexuality of its leading personalities. Even early histories of the Ballets Russes, like that published in 1936 by Prince Peter Lieven, dealt openly with the "homosexualism" of Sergei Diaghilev, the Russians' manager, and his longstanding relationship with Nijinsky, which "was in its time almost public." Lieven explained, "He had the choice either to hide it and not live with Nijinsky, or to live with him and thereby admit his inclinations before the public eye. He chose the second course."[62] What fascinated Bloomsbury was that the Ballets Russes could adopt this position without sacrificing public acclaim. The Russians' first London season caused a sensation, and performances continued to sell out through the second. Despite the *Pall-Mall Gazette*'s condemnation of "the endlessness of this orgy of perverted desire" in *Thamar* and *The Times*'s observation that there was "something irritating in the insensibility of Narcissus to the charms of the Nymphs," most reviews were ecstatic. By 1913 the *Daily Mail* seemed more titillated than disapproving when—evoking the precedent of Oscar Wilde's notorious *Salome*, well known for the edition published with salacious woodcuts by Aubrey Beardsley—it described the Russians' 1913 production of *La Tragédie de Salome*: "Eying the extravagant production with delicate approval, the spirit of Aubrey Beardsley was, one felt assured, haunting the house last night."[63]

For Bloomsbury, the Ballets Russes, with its charismatic male lead, seemed to realize aspirations for a modernism that challenged the authority of convention with a legacy of primitive sensuality—and specifically the expressions of female desire and male homoeroticism associated with the Near East. Keynes, Strachey, and Grant became avid followers of the Ballets Russes, regularly attending its performances and mingling with the performers backstage. In 1911, Keynes wrote of trips to London "to see Mr. Nijinsky's legs." Fourteen years later, he married Lydia Lopokova, one of the Russians' leading ballerinas, whom he met while pursuing Nijinsky's successor.[64] Strachey admired Nijinsky's beauty and was thrilled to see flowers he had sent presented to the dancer on stage.[65] Grant, too, was fascinated by Nijinsky; he later recalled that his presence on the tennis courts the day that he made such an impression on Nijinsky was motivated by a desire to see the dancer leap the net.[66] Six decades after the Ballets Russes premiered in London, Grant could still be found reworking Nijinsky's image in a painting composed around a photograph of the dancer in costume for *Les Orientales* (fig. 64). This painting aligns Nijinsky's leg, with its massive calf muscle (descriptions of Nijinsky often mention the tremendous size of his leg muscles), and the leg of one of the fleshy male nudes Grant painted on either side of the fireplace in his studio at Charleston (discussed in Chapter 14). Such allusions are the subtle side of erotic fantasies made blatant in some of Grant's late sketches, which combine the positions of classical dance with acts of sexual penetration.[67]

Grant's late paintings and sketches may be seen as a distant reverberation of the effect created in the upstairs drawing-room at Brunswick Square, where he and Adrian Stephen augmented the tennis mural with other decorations. Stephen's

64. Duncan Grant, *Still Life with Portrait of Nijinsky*, *c.* 1972. Private collection.

Following pages:

65. Duncan Grant, female nude: design for shutter decoration at 38 Brunswick Square, 1912–13. Oil and pencil on paper, 34.8 × 22.6 cm. Courtauld Institute Galleries.

66. Duncan Grant, male nude: design for shutter decoration at 38 Brunswick Square, 1912–13. Oil and pencil on paper, 23.6 × 31.6 cm. Courtauld Institute Galleries.

designs—female nudes painted in the panels of a cabinet door—have been lost without visual record.[68] More is known about Grant's small nudes painted on the woodwork around the windows (figs 65, 66). Long documented only by preliminary sketches preserved in the design files of the Omega Workshops, Grant's figures were assumed, in part because of their blue background, to be horizontal swimmers. Recently discovered photographs of the decorations *in situ*, however, reveal their vertical orientation on panels of the interior shutters, making the nudes not swimmers but dancers, whose athletic poses and ballooning thigh muscles evoke the most characteristic features of Nijinsky and others in the corps of the Ballets Russes (fig. 67).[69] Another design, linked to the nudes by its vertical format and the figure's pose and musculature, shows a tennis player in a stance strikingly like the gestures of Nijinsky's "cubist" dance in *Jeux*; the theatricality of this design is emphasized by Grant's treatment of the court, which rises like a backdrop to enclose the figure in its frame (fig. 68).

Taken together, these decorations made the living quarters at Brunswick Square a walk-in version of the modernist fantasy created by the Ballets Russes. The effect of fantasy was emphasized by the play with scale between the huge figures on the

67. Photographs of shutters *in situ* 38 Brunswick Square, photograph from Tate Gallery Archive.

wall and the tiny figures around the windows, in relation to which viewers would have found themselves alternately dwarfed or magnified. By the same token, the gestures of dance and tennis—both figured as metaphors for erotic abandon—echoed one another in the nude figures, mediated by the dancer in tennis costume, so that experience of the decorations unfolded as a series of allusions to sex and art. This effect is echoed in the late painting of the Nijinsky photograph, made when Grant was almost ninety, which plays in a similar—albeit subtler—way with scale and reference: the tiny figure in the photograph alludes to a specific historical figure who embodied the sensuality associated with a Mediterranean legacy of male nudes, here present only as a fleshy leg, jarringly over-scale, from the painted decorations. In both cases, Grant turns domestic space into a site where modernist aesthetics evoke primitive sensuality.

In his memoirs, Osbert Sitwell recalled that in pre-war London, "Every chair cover, every lampshade, every cushion, reflected the Russian Ballet."[70] If this is true, Bloomsbury was largely responsible, for by the time Grant was painting dancers on the shutters at Brunswick Square, the group's artists had hatched plans for a workshop to market modernist domestic design to the public that flocked to the ballet. The Bloomsbury artists were not alone among the English in drawing inspiration from the Ballets Russes,[71] but it was they who applied the aesthetics associated with the Russian dancers to the home. Whether in the country or the city, Bloomsbury turned its houses into stages for a domestic life that, like the Ballets Russes, would incorporate the primitive, sensual freedom associated with the Near East into something entirely modern.

Facing page:
68. Duncan Grant, tennis player: design for shutter decoration at 38 Brunswick Square, 1912–13. Oil, gouache and pencil on paper, 24.8 × 15.9 cm. Courtauld Institute Galleries.

Sailing to Byzantium

The usual things, turned round to extremes.
Duncan Grant, describing Omega Christmas decorations[1]

Looking for a historical moment to represent the peak of Bloomsbury's artistic activity and influence, one could do no better than the autumn of 1912, the time of the Second Post-Impressionist Exhibition and a moment when many of the currents traced through the previous chapters combined with powerful momentum. Vanessa Bell was just back from her first summer of Post-Impressionist domesticity at Asheham, and Duncan Grant was painting his exuberant tennis-player murals at Brunswick Square. Bell's letters convey their shared delight in domestic extravagance:

I was interrupted yesterday by Duncan who came in and lay on the floor and talked in a desultory way of . . . how we are to turn my studio into a tropical forest with great red figures on the walls, a blue ceiling with birds of paradise floating from it (my idea), and curtains, each one different.

Bell's summation of this project—"This is all to cheer us through London winters"—encapsulates Bloomsbury's belief in the potential of modernist domesticity to transcend everything repressive in British culture, including the climate. Even her rejection of Grant's idea to sink a bath into the floor underscores her determination to escape any taint of Victorian convention. Referring to the house-museum of former Royal Academy president Frederic Leighton, Bell said, "I told him that was *à la Leighton House*, which made him rather cross."[2]

When they weren't spinning remodeling fantasies, Grant and Bell in the autumn of 1912 were caught up in the Second Post-Impressionist Exhibition, which Fry asserted was necessary, since "the British public has dozed off again since the last show and needs another electric shock."[3] Both artists contributed work to the show and Leonard Woolf, recently returned from his post as a colonial administrator, acted as secretary. "Nine out of ten" visitors, he recalled,

either roared with laughter at the pictures or were enraged by them. . . . I used to think, as I sat there, how much nicer were the Tamil or Sinhalese villagers who crowded into the veranda of my Ceylon kachcheri than these smug, well dressed, ill-mannered, well-to-do Londoners.[4]

In publications occasioned by the exhibition, Roger Fry and Clive Bell manifested a similar alienation from their countrymen. Bell, who curated the British section of the show, asserted in his catalog essay the primacy of French modernism, praising the British artists for overcoming the handicaps that "for two centuries have made our art the laughing stock of Europe."[5] Fry's commentary also took on the "British Philistinism [that] is as strong and self-confident and as unwilling to learn by past

Facing page:
Detail of fig. 90.

experience as ever it was."[6] Like Bell, Fry rooted Post-Impressionism in France, "its native place," linking it to a legacy of classicism "common to the best French work of all periods from the twelfth century onwards." For Fry, "Classic art . . . records a positive and disinterestedly passionate state of mind," an attitude he contrasted with the British:

> [T]he intensity and singleness of aim with which these [French] artists yield themselves to certain experiences in the face of nature may make their work appear odd to those who have not the habit of contemplative vision, but it would be rash for us, who as a nation are in the habit of treating our emotions, especially our aesthetic emotions, with a certain levity, to accuse them of caprice or insincerity.[7]

Through these remarks by various members of Bloomsbury runs the primitivism the previous section argued was central to the group's aesthetic. Against what they experienced as the rigid insularity of British culture, Bloomsbury's members upheld a modernism rooted, with varying degrees of specificity, elsewhere. For Vanessa Bell, it was enough to imagine a fantastical jungle. Leonard Woolf invoked his experiences in Ceylon. Clive Bell and Roger Fry described a classical Mediterranean heritage channeled through France. Though geographically disparate, the fundamental characteristics of Bloomsbury's primitivist ideal remain constant: an intellectual, emotional, and sensual freedom at odds with what they perceived as British closed-mindedness, conformity, and coldness. And this ideology had implications beyond the arts. Fry defined Post-Impressionism sweepingly as the work of "modern men trying to find a pictorial language appropriate to the sensibilities of the modern outlook." In short—and in contrast to frequent presentations of Bloomsbury aesthetics as apolitical—while the formalist theory the group developed and propagated at this period asserted that intuitive emotional experiences of art suffered from any encumbrance of social purpose, this principle did not itself lack social implications. As part of a "modern outlook," it was part of Bloomsbury's challenge to a wide range of barely post-Victorian values.

A recognition of the social implications of Bloomsbury's modernism helps explain what has perplexed—and even angered—so many commentators: that the group's first response to modern French paintings was to imagine them realized as places to inhabit. At "the first sight of a room of Matisse's work," Fry later recalled, "I thought how splendid this would be if translated into mosaic."[8] Far from trivializing modernist aesthetics through interior decoration, Bloomsbury's aspired to make modernism the look of modern life. Ironically, in view of Bloomsbury's alienation from Victorian values, the group's domestic focus (as I argued in the Introduction) places it firmly within the legacy of Victorian radicalism manifested in the writings of Ruskin, the workshops of the Arts and Crafts Movement, the interior designs of Aesthetes like Whistler—and even the eccentric domestic fantasy world of Leighton House. All these factions of the Victorian avant-garde used the look of the home to signify new ways of life. Nothing in the Bloomsbury artists' careers more dramatically demonstrates their inheritance of this British legacy that their collaborative creation of the Omega Workshops. Dedicated to the application of modernist aesthetics to domestic design, the Omega, more broadly, aimed to revolutionize the look—and thus the values—of the British home.

The Origins of the Omega

Looking back in 1924, Roger Fry described how, after the Post-Impressionist exhibitions "let the continental cat out of the bag," some English artists adopted the new style:

[W]e had an idea which was natural enough to Englishmen. The only considerable art movement in England had been that of the pre-Raphaelites and that movement had attempted to use the artist's gifts for practical life in the direction of the applied arts. Morris had started and to some extent . . . impressed a style of furniture and household fittings. We saw that the new movement once more allowed the artist the possibility of utilizing his gifts in applied design and we started the ill-fated Omega workshops. It was a failure. I think it would have failed apart from the war, but I think it would have succeeded in any other European country but England.[1]

This analysis astutely summarizes the history of the Omega, which was initially enabled, but ultimately doomed, by its position between its English heritage and its continental European models.

Indeed, the Omega may be said to have failed twice: first to sustain itself financially in its own era, and then to signify as a meaningful episode in the history of British design. Although the Omega remained virtually the only center of avant-garde design in London during World War I, it was quickly forgotten thereafter. When in the early thirties a campaign to revitalize the British design industry began with a spate of books and articles asserting the historical legacy of English design, the Omega was ignored, leading Fry to complain that "people who now buy degraded and meaningless imitations of what we did twenty years ago feel that they are on the crest of the wave of the new movement."[2] As it happens, Fry was just the first to observe that his workshops were "too far ahead of our time." A decade after Fry's observation, Nikolaus Pevsner argued, "the style called 'Teutonic Expressionism' or 'Paris 1925,' as the case may be, was in fact created as early as 1913 by the Omega."[3] Pevsner's 1941 essay marks the first round of a cycle in which the Omega was forgotten and rediscovered at twenty-year intervals. A small Omega exhibition at the Victoria and Albert Museum in the mid-1960s prompted polite interest among some critics, but this was overwhelmed by the vehemence with which others insisted that, because the workshops "never succeeded in developing a viable modern style," its "William Morrisy furniture" had no place on the "straight line" between the continental design movements of Art Nouveau and the Bauhaus.[4] By 1984, when the Crafts Council rediscovered the Omega in a major exhibition, critiques of such linear historical schemas and a revival of interest in early twentieth-century Scottish and English offshoots of Morris and the Arts and Crafts movement precluded damnation in these terms. Critics responded by excluding the Omega from this rehabilitated history of British design. Insisting that the Omega "was no descendant of the Arts and Crafts Movement," the *Guardian*'s review claimed that Fry "acquired his own cheap taste for flashy brushstrokes and gaudy colors" from "Tuscany, or the South of France," and concluded that Omega products are "as out of place in the English winter as a lemon yellow frock."[5] Such claims that the Omega was fundamentally un-English coexisted with assertions that the workshops were unrelated to contemporary developments in continental design, a paradox that resulted in the exclusion of the Omega from any historical tradition at all.[6] This chapter counters this campaign to loose the Omega from its temporal and geographic moorings by describing the workshops' actual connections with both the lingering Arts and Crafts institutions in London and the contingents of the pre-war Parisian avant-garde most involved with the decorative arts.

To re-attach the Omega to its English and French contexts is, by implication, also to challenge conventional constructions of the history of modern design. For the French, this will mean focusing on individuals and institutions that, like the Omega, have slipped from historical view. For the English, the situation is more complicated. The Arts and Crafts movement, personified by John Ruskin and William Morris, remained throughout the twentieth century a crucial reference point in debates over both art and politics. The exigencies of these debates, however, warped perceptions of these figures, exaggerating certain tendencies in their thought and obscuring others. In the second half of the twentieth century, Ruskin and Morris were so regularly invoked in defense of two causes in particular—design appropriate to industrial production and state-administered social welfare initiatives—that their legacy came to seem coincident with these projects. While it is true that the Omega was largely irrelevant to these histories, it does not follow that Bloomsbury's workshops were unconnected to Ruskin and Morris. Quite the contrary, the Omega may be closer to Ruskin's and Morris's ideals than the aesthetic and social enterprises later justified in their names. Neither Morris nor Ruskin can be reasonably read as endorsing either industrialization or the welfare state. The heroic ambitions of later utopians, moreover, are deeply at odds with Morris's description of his political and artistic career as the accidental result of his inablity to find suitable furniture.[7] Proposing this etiology as a general principle, he argued that "those who begin to consider carefully how to make the best of the chambers in which they eat and sleep and study, and hold converse with their friends, will breed in their minds a wholesome and fruitful discontent with the sordidness that even when they have done their best will surround their island of comfort." The goal of the Arts and Crafts movement, Morris said, was to "make [people] think about their homes, to take the trouble to turn them into dwellings fit for people free in mind and body."[8] This chapter's situation of the Omega in this domestic-centered Arts and Crafts legacy is part of the project, outlined in the Introduction, to reclaim the history of domesticity from the obscurity imposed on it by modernists enamored of heroic scale in industry and government.

Fry, citing Morris's precedent, invoked the Arts and Crafts connection of domestic design and social reform in his prospectus for the Omega, which dedicated the workshops to attacking "the lamentable condition of the applied arts which affects our well-being at almost every moment of our lives."[9] As a small-scale effort to sustain a small group of artists-turned-artisans in the production of handmade domestic objects displaying a strongly anti-industrial aesthetic, the Omega was very much the heir to Morris's Pre-Raphaelite atelier, and Fry echoed Morris in citing as precedent for his workshops the studios of medieval Florence before the division of art from craft.[10]

As it evolved into a haven for refugees and pacifists during World War I, the Omega also exemplified the broader moral tradition of Ruskin, who urged his readers to act so that "we may enter a period of our world's history in which domestic life, aided by the arts of peace, will slowly, but at last entirely, supersede public life and the arts of war."[11] The Omega's founding documents reveal Ruskins' influence most clearly in the preface to the workshops' first catalog, issued in 1914. Fry here closely paraphrased Ruskin's famous essay on "The Nature of the Gothic," with the significant substitution of African artisans for Ruskin's medieval craftsmen as the embodiment of the primitivist ideal. Where Ruskin urges his readers to "go forth again and gaze upon the old cathedral front where you have smiled so often at the fantastic ignorance of the old sculptors," Fry begins from the observation that, "If you look at a pot or a woven cloth made by a negro savage of the Congo . . . you may begin by despising it for its want of finish." Just as Ruskin then turns the tables on his English audience's disdain for the rough grotesqueries of gothic carvings, warning, "do not mock at them, for they are signs of the life and liberty of every workman who struck the stone," Fry proceeds, "if you will allow the poor savage's handiwork longer contemplation . . . it will become apparent that the negro enjoyed making his pot or cloth, that he pondered delightedly over the possibilities of his craft and that his enjoyment finds expression in many ways." Then as Ruskin goes on to condemn the capitalist economy where workers "have no pleasure in the work by which they make their bread, and therefore look to wealth as the only means of pleasure," so too Fry explains that "modern factory products were made almost entirely for gain, no other joy than that of money making entered into their creation." As an antidote, Ruskin orders his readers: "Rather choose rough work than smooth work . . . and never imagine there is reason to be proud of anything that may be accomplished by patience and sandpaper." According to Fry, the Omega artists "refuse to spoil the expressive quality of their work by sand-papering it down to a shop finish."[12] Nowhere is it clearer how Fry fused the exhortative rhetoric of the English Arts and Crafts Movement with the visual vocabulary of the Parisian avant-garde, which had recently made African art a privileged signifier of the primitive.

69. Roger Fry, Omega chair, c.1913. Cane and painted wood, 130.2 × 50.8 × 54.6 cm.

Where Fry's language—both explicit citations and implicit rhetorical echoes—invokes Ruskin, Morris, and the Pre-Raphaelites generally, his personal links to the Arts and Crafts Movement are evident in the look of his Omega designs. The red dining chairs that were marketed as a visual signature for the workshops—some models were even topped with a wooden omega—evoked Morris's firm's association with the "Morris chair," but Fry's designs eschew Morris's cozy medieval aesthetic (fig. 69). With their highly simplified rectilinear profile, Fry's chairs recall the classicizing products of the Century Guild, run by Ruskin's protégé, A. H. Mackmurdo, whose influence on Durbins is discussed in Chapter 2 (fig. 70). Just as Fry's house echoed Mackmurdo's architecture, the chairs he designed for the Omega's inaugural display at the 1913 Ideal Home Show recall those Mackmurdo designed for his guild's stand at the Liverpool International Exhibition of 1886. As a self-described alliance of artists—as opposed to craftworkers—the Century Guild anticipated the rationale for the Omega, an ideological connection with its geographic analog in the fact that, after the guild dissolved as a formal organization around 1890, its founding members maintained a meeting place for artists and writers in Fitzroy Street, just around the corner from where Fry later established the Omega. Long before Bloomsbury made the name of the adjacent neighborhood synonymous with a new style of literature and art, Mackmurdo's headquarters, according to the poet Victor Plarr, was "a sacred house. . . . referred to as 'Fitzroy'," and " 'Fitzroy' was a movement, an influence, a glory."[13] Fry's relationship to another Arts and Crafts institution, C. R. Ashbee's Guild of Handicraft (discussed in Chapter 2), is, likewise, visible in his Omega work. One of Fry's designs, for instance, features a pair of peacocks in a composition that echoes Ashbee's design for a silver tray (fig. 71). Omega practice was for all designs to be filed at the workshops for common use, and Fry's peacocks found their way, with some variation, onto an inlaid wooden table and a silk scarf (fig. 72). With the lily that Duncan Grant painted for the workshops' signboard, the repertoire of Omega motifs sustained the preoccupations of Victorian designers who followed Ruskin's directive that "the most beautiful things in the world are the most useless, peacocks and lilies for instance."[14]

Historians who discount the Omega's place in the legacy of Ruskin and Morris seize upon a distinction articulated by Fry in the workshops' prospectus: "Less

70. Arthur Mackmurdo, mahogany chair with carved and inlaid decoration, made by E. Goodhall for the Century Guild, 1886, Victoria and Albert Museum.

71. C. R. Ashbee, tray with peacock motif, silver, 1896–97. Victoria and Albert Museum.

ambitious than William Morris," he said, the Omega artists "do not hope to solve the social problems of production at the same time as the artistic."[15] This statement has been read as proof of Bloomsbury's complacent élitism, but that ignores Fry's clear sympathy with Arts and Crafts challenges to conventional social hierarchies. Writing in *The Burlington* in 1910, for instance, Fry echoed the Arts and Crafts critique of the still-prevailing idea that "Among professional artists there is a certain social class-feeling . . . , a vague idea that a man can still remain a gentleman if he paints bad pictures, but must forfeit the conventional right to his Esquire if he makes good pots or serviceable furniture."[16] Fry's assertion that the Omega would limit itself to "artistic" problems does not endorse these social hierarchies. In the context of a document soliciting investors for a new workshop, Fry's limitations on the Omega's ambitions reflect lessons learned from the histories of the earlier guild-like enterprises of which he was a part.

In this regard, it is important to recall that, Morris's stated ambitions notwithstanding, his own firm was no workers' cooperative, but began as a small consortium

72. Attributed to Roger Fry, peacock design, 1913. Oil and pencil on paper, 33.3 × 50.8 cm. Courtauld Institute Galleries.

On to Omega

of what its prospectus described as "Artists of reputation" turning their hands to decorative work. Even when financial success allowed the firm's expansion to a large rural workshop with many employees, the traditional division of labor and profit remained unchallenged. Morris acknowledged that his workshops "could not do anything (or at least but little) to give this pleasure [of artistic creation] to the workman," for "it is impossible to work in that manner in this profit-grinding society."[17] By the first decade of the twentieth century, Morris & Co. was thriving as a conventional commercial decorating firm in which artists' designs were carried out by salaried artisans. Meanwhile, any association between the look of its medieval-revival furnishings and new ways of life had been, as Fry put it, "drowned in the commercial flood of machine made imitation Morris," reduced not just to one of many historical-revival styles, but one with more conservative nationalist associations than most.[18]

Today, when academics have revived Morris's reputation as a socialist revolutionary, it is easy to forget that Bloomsbury's generation had seen his design legacy assimilated into a Ye-Olde-English style that became the look of the establishment. At the 1908 Franco-British Exhibition, Morris & Co. products, promoted as "as perfect as anything turned out by Sheraton and Chippendale," represented "modern" design in the display "The History of British Furniture."[19] Official endorsement of Morris's aesthetic was matched by disenchantment with his politics among radicals like the sculptor Eric Gill, who in 1909—just the time he and Fry were closest (see Chapter 2)—published an essay on "The Failure of the Arts and Crafts Movement" in *The Socialist Review*. Gill attacked Morris and his followers for "putting the world on a false track" by ignoring large economic trends so that its goals, "to raise the conditions of ordinary workers and the quality of ordinary workmanship," remained farther out of reach than ever, while the Arts and Crafts style became "a fashion to be exploited by Liberty and Waring and hosts of firms producing similar looking things at less cost." Gill concluded that the best means to economic reform were not guilds and workshops but trade unions and the Labour Party.[20] Such doubts about the efficacy of guild-based initiatives toward economic reform were combined by 1913 with the realization that, in contrast to the prosperity of Morris's company and other large firms, more idealistic workshops were not self-sustaining. The strongest of these was Ashbee's Guild of Handicraft, but even this had collapsed in 1907, with its founder acknowledging it "ruined itself" in attempting "to show . . . that standard of workmanship and standard of life must be taken together and that the one is dependent on the other."[21] By the era of the Omega, the only Arts and Crafts institutions still viable were the businesslike enterprises like Morris's firm, the even more commercial manufacturers supplying major retailers like Liberty, and the associations of moneyed amateurs who abjured economic self-sufficiency and made no claims to improve the lot of the worker.[22] Seen in this light, Fry's assurance to potential investors of his workshops' scaled-back aims reads not as a repudiation of Arts and Crafts values, but as an attempt to situate his workshops in the movement's latest phase, with lessons learned from his forerunners.

The Omega's distance from the Arts and Crafts movement as it existed in 1913 can be measured, then, less in terms of ideology or organization than of aesthetics. Analogous in its goals of promoting a modern aesthetic through the design of domestic interiors, the look associated with the Omega differed radically from even its closest Arts and Crafts forerunners. Thus Ashbee supported the idea of the Omega—until he saw its work. After a conversation with Fry, Ashbee praised the plan for the Omega as "excellent in its way," writing in his journal, "It was curious and interesting to see him apparently treading the same ground with his venture that we had been over twenty years before with the Guild shops and the 'Arts and Crafts' exhibitions."[23] A month later, when his wife visited the Omega, however, she reported, "Roger's things are TOO AWFUL, simply a *crime* against truth and beauty . . . *wool-work* mats and bags, ghastly cushions and curtains looking as if they had fallen by mistake into several dye vats . . . I am sure you would loathe it all."[24] That her reaction was not atypical is suggested by the Omega's ongoing struggle to get its products shown in Arts and Crafts exhibitions.[25]

The antipathy, of course, was mutual. Fry's attitude toward the still-functioning Arts and Crafts educational institutions of the era is evident in an anecdote recounted by the Omega's manager. Facing difficulties with batik, she recalled, Fry joked that "one of us ought to offer themselves up" as a sacrifice to the Central School of Arts and Crafts in order to learn the technique.[26] Given Fry's commitment to art education for children of all classes, his jibe was aimed at the particular nature of the Central School, where the director, W. R. Lethaby, promoted an exacting standard of craft work as a means to instill middle-class values in a largely lower-class student body. Upholding an idea of art in which "order, construction, beauty, and efficiency are one," Lethaby compared his aesthetic to the British Navy, "tea in the garden, Boy Scouting, and tennis in flannels."[27] Nothing could be further from Bloomsbury's ideals for a spontaneous, intuitive, and sensual modernism.

If Bloomsbury's aesthetic ideals distanced the Omega from its closest British counterparts, however, they linked the workshops with the avant-garde across the Channel. Surrounded by the furniture, fabrics, murals, and knick-knacks on sale when the Omega officially opened in July 1913, shoppers might imagine they had stepped into a painting by Matisse or Picasso (fig. 73). Comparisons with Matisse are clearest, for many of the props depicted in his interiors of 1911–12 turn up in Omega products: the simple red furniture, the goldfish, the nude figures dancing or reclining, the sketchy rugs, the abundance of flowers. It is possible to overemphasize Bloomsbury's debt to Matisse, however. As with Grant's tennis mural at Brunswick Square, the Omega artists seemed able to seize the visual logic of Matisse's aesthetic to achieve effects he did not realize until years—even decades—later. A model nursery installed by Vanessa Bell in the Omega showrooms late in 1913, for instance, used paper cut-outs to strew colorful silhouettes of trees, animals, and clouds around the walls, anticipating Matisse's decorations of the 1930s and after (fig. 74; this project is discussed further in Chapters 8 and 9).

Although the Omega designs drew most intensely from the Fauves, cubism, too, contributed significantly to its aesthetic. Omega fans display cubist faces (fig. 75), while a design for an apparently unexecuted tray closely echoes Picasso's collages (fig. 76). Traces of Picasso's cubist still lifes—such as the 1908 *Pots et citron* (fig. 77) owned by the Bells[28]—are evident in the jagged planes and sharp ellipses of Vanessa Bell's Omega mosaic for a house in Hyde Park Gardens (fig. 78) and the related murals the workshops carried out for the Cadena Café (fig. 79). Cubist influence may be most apparent in Fry's 1918 decoration of a harpsichord, which makes the irregular shape of the case the basic element in its angular decoration (fig. 80). This harpsichord is emblematic of Fry's historical position *between* the British and French avant-gardes, however, for under its French-modernist exterior it is an Arts and Crafts product, made by Arnold Dolmetsch, a pioneer in the revival of medieval music who twenty years earlier had built the harpsichord that Fry and his future wife decorated for Mackmurdo's Arts and Crafts Exhibition Society display (discussed in Chapter 2).[29]

Cubism's collage technique also left its mark on Omega designs, which are often patched together out of different materials—a practice carried over to Bloomsbury painting at this time (discussed in Chapter 9). Especially influential in this regard were Picasso's "assemblages": three-dimensional combinations of various materials. Fry owned a painted fragment from one of Picasso's assemblages—the face from the 1913 *Assemblage with Guitar Player* (fig. 81)—and Bell admired similar works in Picasso's studio the following spring, describing in a letter his "amazing arrangement of coloured papers and bits of wood which do somehow give me great satisfaction."[30] Picasso's assemblages have been seen as a source for a number of Grant's paintings of 1914–15, which featured, for example, a necklace draped around the neck of one portrait, fabric from the dress worn by a sitter attached to another portrait, and abstract compositions that were roundly panned by London critics as "bits of firewood glued on to a dirty canvas, with here and there a few vertical stripes of colour."[31]

It is unsurprising that reviewers in the Teens failed to connect Omega products to what were, at the time, little-known works by Picasso. The continuing critical

73. Omega Workshops, Ideal Home Room, 1913, no longer extant.

74. Vanessa Bell, model nursery for the Omega, 1913, no longer extant.

75. Omega fan and boxes attributed to Duncan Grant, *c.* 1913. Victoria and Albert Museum. Photograph by Howard Grey.

obliviousness to Bloomsbury's interest in the *ad hoc* techniques of cubism, however, is one consequence of the failure to locate the workshops between the aesthetics of avant-garde French art and the principles of Arts and Crafts design, which privileged careful workmanship in traditional modes. Today, Picasso's use of newspaper clippings and other commercial detritus in his collages and assemblages is celebrated for its creative challenge to the conventions of oil painting. Yet commentary on Bloomsbury continues to apply the same assumptions about craftsmanship and finish that in 1914, when Fry exhibited his fragment from Picasso's *Assemblage with*

76. Unattributed Omega design for a tray, *c.* 1913, Graphite, watercolour, bodycolour on paper, 28.2 × 20.2 cm. Courtauld Institute Galleries.

On to Omega

Guitar Player (fig. 82) along with photographs of the assemblages in Picasso's studio, led English critics to conclude that Picasso was "ponderously making game of the public," as evidenced by "the fact that this 'sculpture' could not be trusted to cross the Channel without falling to pieces [which] seems to point to a deficiency in technique. We suggest screws instead of nails and glue, as more monumental."[32]

The Omega's reliance on French precedent was recognized by at least one sophisticated—if unsympathetic—observer. A satirical watercolor by Henry Tonks shows a skeptical high-society shopper (said to be Nancy Cunard) in the Omega showroom, poking with her walking stick at a painted table so rickety that one leg is propped up by two books; in the background Fry hovers anxiously, while Clive Bell dusts shelves of gaudy, misshapen pottery (fig. 83). The imputation that Omega wares are serviceable only when supported by the substantial mass of Bloomsbury's critical theory is reiterated in another of Tonks's satires, this one showing Fry instructing an unconvinced audience on the aesthetic significance of a dead cat, while Bell chants, "CEZANNAH, CEZANNAH" (fig. 84). As a member of the Impressionist-inspired New English Art Club displaced from London's avant-garde by Post-Impressionism, Tonks was well aware of the theoretical context for the Omega's work. Confronting Bloomsbury on this ground, he campaigned against recent French art, dismissing Cézanne's paintings as "follies" and urging his drawing students at the Slade School, where Fry also taught, that, though he would not prohibit them seeing the first Post-Impressionist show, "he would only warn us and say how very much better pleased he would be if we did not risk contamination but stayed away."[33]

Laughable as Tonks's plea seems now, he might be pleased to note that, though his compatriots did not resist looking at Post-Impressionism, almost a century of English commentary on the Omega suggests they remained largely uncontaminated by the principles behind avant-garde French art. Now as then, the Omega's

77. Pablo Picasso, *Pots et citron*, 1907, as illustrated in Clive Bell, *Art*, 1914.

78. Vanessa Bell, Omega mosaic for house at 1 Hyde Park Gardens, 1914, now obscured.

79. Omega murals for Cadena Café, 1914, destroyed.

80. Roger Fry, design for harpsichord lid, 1918. Oil and pencil on board, 25 × 36.2 cm. Courtauld Institute Galleries.

81. Pablo Picasso, *Assemblage with Guitar Player*, 1913, no longer extant.

82. Pablo Picasso, *Tête d'homme*, 1913. Oil, charcoal, ink, crayon on paper, 62 × 46.5 cm. Richard S. Zeisler Collection, New York.

detractors invoke a guildlike standard of fine craftsmanship to condemn its products as shoddy, while apologists respond by defending the skill of the artists, the "rocklike strength" of their tables, the sturdiness of their ceramics, and the durability of other Omega wares.[34] Overlooked in this debate is that it was Bloomsbury that first—and with great relish—drew attention to the haphazard craftsmanship of the workshops' products. In her biography of Fry, Virginia Woolf reported, "Cracks appeared. Legs came off. Varnish ran."[35] Fry himself emphasized the speed of the Omega's painters, promoting the workshops' murals by telling a reporter, "If people get tired of one landscape, they can easily have another. It can be done in a very short time."[36] Vanessa Bell responded to the owner of a garden bench whose paint had cracked off in the frost by suggesting that the Omega simply "send her a pot of the right color with directions how to paint it again."[37] The Omega showrooms confronted customers with wares that, far from upholding an Arts and Crafts standard of expert training, were the intuitive work of non-experts—not only artists, but children and Africans.

This flouting of craft standards proclaimed the Omega's rejection of the professionalism espoused by Lethaby in favor of the ideals behind the modern French art and critical theory Bloomsbury most admired. When Matisse's "Notes of a Painter" was published in 1908, for instance, it carried an introduction by Georges Desvallières, who rooted the artist's accomplishment in the "instinctive serendipities [*trouvailles instinctives*] of medieval artists, Hindus, and Oriental decorators."[38] In the essay, Matisse mocks the idea that artists could learn "rules" of art, insisting instead on "expressions" that are "honest" because "purely instinctive." Visually, Matisse's art—like that of his Fauve colleagues—had since 1906 combined a rough, expressive style with allusions to African themes, characteristics extended in Picasso's cubism.[39] All of these developments were well known to Bloomsbury through the Post-Impressionist shows, which included African-inspired sculptures by Matisse (in both exhibitions) and drawings by Picasso (in 1912).

Fry's rejection of craftsmanship in favor of an ideal of spontaneous expressiveness originated in his defenses of the Post-Impressionists: "that they have abandoned the advantage which that professional skill affords is surely rather a sign of the sincerity of their efforts," he argued during the first Post-Impressionist show.[40] Twenty years after the Omega, Fry's Slade lectures at Cambridge returned to this point, defining "the ideal work of art" as "the outcome of a free spiritual activity," in contrast to both "the craftsman's pride in his skill" and "the luxury effect" that provokes consumers to covet highly crafted objects. Fry explains, "If the craftsman happens to be also an artist he may recognize that the expression of his own sensi-

83. Henry Tonks, *The Omega Shop*, c. 1914. Watercolor. Current location unknown.

84. Henry Tonks, *The Unknown God (Roger Fry Preaching the New Faith and Clive Bell Ringing the Bell)*, c. 1923. Oil on canvas, 40.6 × 54.6 cm. Private collection.

bility is significant and may even be content to pass as a clumsy craftsman rather than obliterate it. But the pride of the craftsman as such will always urge the suppression of sensibility in an art-object."[41] The subtler among Bloomsbury's hostile critics recognized that the Omega did not fail to attain a desired standard of craftsmanship. As John Rothenstein described the Omega in the 1950s, Fry "persuade[d] his artist friends to exaggerate the irregularities which characterize the handmade object," to the point of "wilful clumsiness."[42] Rothenstein attributed these tendencies to the whims of Fry's personality, however, rather than recognizing their origins in the French modernism Bloomsbury was striving to bring to England.

For Fry and his colleagues, the starting point of the Omega was the modernist aesthetic they discovered in avant-garde French painting, but the artists Bloomsbury most admired offered few models for experimentation in the decorative arts. Fry later explained, "In France very little was done before the war except that a few artists did some admirable decorations of pottery," a reference, probably, to the vases decorated by Fauve painters in 1907, which were exhibited in the first Post-Impressionist exhibition.[43] Nevertheless, Bloombury sought out what Parisian precedents it could find. Soliciting investors for the Omega, Fry cited the precedent of Paul Poiret's Ecole Martine and promised, "my workshop would be carried on on similar lines and might probably work in conjunction with the Ecole Martine, by mutual exchange of ideas and products."[44] This reference in the earliest advertisement for the Omega suggests how, from their inception, the workshops were presented as a London outpost of French modernism.

Fry's citation of the Ecole Martine registers Bloomsbury's high ambitions for its workshops, since Poiret was at the forefront of Parisian fashion. But Poiret presented a somewhat problematic model, since he was not an artist but a *couturier* who allied his clothing and perfume with the fine arts. Poiret employed the painter Raoul Dufy to design textiles, collaborated with other artists in designs for the theater using his fabrics, and leased part of his expansive showrooms as an art gallery. It was this last enterprise that brought Bloomsbury into contact with Poiret when, in July 1912, Fry organized an exhibition of recent English art for this space. Poiret's primary focus, however, remained high fashion. If the structure of Poiret's enterprise related only tangentially to the Omega, his aesthetic was equally problematic as precedent. His interiors—like his clothes—combined elements of Orientalist fantasy congenial to Bloomsbury with echoes of the severe but sumptuous late eighteenth-century Directoire style, which was strongly associated with French nationalism. In practice, this meant velvet hangings; fanciful doorways shaped like entrances to Etruscan tombs; and cushions of gold, silver, or fur on highly finished furniture made "modern" by colorful upholstery. Poiret's products find a place in design history between the high-finish styles of Art Nouveau and Art Deco, but have little in common with the "primitive" expressiveness of the Omega, where the artists painted directly on roughly finished wood. Even in textile design, the Omega owed little visually to Poiret and Dufy, who at this period were putting modernist twists (large scale, bright colors, blocky printing) on relatively conventional floral motifs—Dufy's famous cubistic textiles were created after World War I, and hence were anticipated by similar Omega designs.[45] The distance between Poiret and the Omega aesthetic is indicated by the fact that, despite Fry's claims to institutional affiliation, Poiret chose as his London distributor, not the Omega, but an expatriate French designer who mocked cubism in cartoons for London magazines and stressed that his interiors were "not at all aggressively modern," but boasted such Art Nouveau details as amethyst doorknobs and lights disguised as baskets of glass fruit.[46]

What attracted Fry to Poiret was less his products than his process. It is significant that Fry did not cite the Maison Martine, the showroom that sold Poiret's furnishings, but the Ecole Martine, where many of the designs originated. Founded in 1911, Poiret's "school" employed adolescent girls from working-class families, who were paid a daily wage for textile and wallpaper designs inspired by trips to zoos, parks, and botanical gardens. The girls were trained to paint on porcelain and glass so that they could decorate Poiret's perfume bottles. They received instruction in carpet-making as well, and their hand-knotted rugs and tapestries became the best known of the Martine's products.[47] At first glance, Poiret's employment of working-class children might seem to link his school to such reform-minded Arts and Crafts establishments as Ashbee's Guild of Handicraft or Lethaby's Central School.[48] But Poiret's aims ran opposite to those of his English counterparts. Where Lethaby and Ashbee trained workers in careful craftsmanship and middle-class values, Poiret, like Fry, emphasized the untutored expressiveness of his workers. "These children, left to their own devices, quickly forgot the false empirical precepts they had been taught in school and rediscovered all the spontaneity and freshness of their natures," he claimed.[49] Echoing Poiret, critics for journals such as L'Art Décoratif effused over the work—"charming, vivid, a bit crude"—of girls who "threw themselves with great spirit into the decorative fantasies of their fresh imaginations."[50] The differences between the English and French models is less in the technique—the Martine girls' hand-knotted carpets represent labor as meticulous as that of any English guild—than in the ideology of the two styles. Where the subtle tones and fine detail in Arts and Crafts fabrics and metalwork proclaim the value of artisanal training as an imposition of discipline on unruly natures, the Martine's jumbles of over-sized blossoms in brilliant colors assert the power of primitive expressiveness. Poiret's claims to have released the primal spontaneity of his workers accorded with Bloomsbury's ambitions for modernism. Clive Bell's *Art* praised the workers of the Ecole Martine in primitivist terms, saying, "They have borrowed quite unconsciously with the quality of their bodies and their minds from the history and traditional culture of their race. Their art differs from savage art as a French *midinette* [working girl] differs from a squaw, but it is as original and vital as the work of savages." Bell, who resisted his Bloomsbury colleagues' enthusiasm for the decorative arts in general and the Omega in particular, did not accept the Martine girls as artists, but concluded, "I rate the artisans of the *Ecole Martine* with the best contemporary painters, not as artists, but as manifestations of the movement."[51]

The Omega, of course, did not rely on working-class girls to bring primitive authenticity to modernism. Unlike the Martine, which dealt with the conflicting valences of "primitive" and "modern" by separating them into different bodies and different stages of the design process—Poiret used his "modern" taste to choose the best designs from the girls' "primitive" output—the Omega artists sought to embody both qualities themselves. As the Omega catalog explained, the workshops' artists "try to keep the spontaneous freshness of primitive or peasant work while satisfying the needs and expressing the feelings of the modern cultivated man."[52] This determination to become primitive is evident not only in the sketchy decoration and rough finish of much Omega work, but also in the workshops' requirement of cooperative anonymity from its artists. Like the girls of the Ecole Martine—and unlike the way Poiret commissioned Dufy to produce signature work in his own studio with assistants—Omega artists were paid a daily wage for designs that became common property to be applied to products marketed under the corporate name. This commitment to cooperative, anonymous production was a fundamental principle of the Omega. From Fry's earliest discussions of the workshops, he emphasized the artists' willingness to subsume their individuality in the creation of a cooperative aesthetic, and years later he listed "anonymity" first among the Omega's principles.[53] Promoting the Omega in 1913, Fry was quoted in the press explaining that the artists would "work together, freely criticizing one another and using one another's ideas without stint. I think it is very important that they should work together in this way, and that we should cease to insist upon the extreme individuality of artists."[54] The first London exhibition of paintings by artists associated with the workshops extended the principle of anonymity even to the display of fine art (as discussed in the following chapter). The Omega's fusion of primitivism and anonymity exemplifies its position between the French and British art worlds, which resulted in the workshops' exclusion from both traditions.

Anonymity was among the founding ideals of the Arts and Crafts movement. Though the first Arts and Crafts guilds fostered anonymous production, however, the movement quickly drifted from this principle. Despite Morris's frequent praise for works of "collective genius," when his first company—a collaboration of seven partners inspired by the collective Pre-Raphaelite Brotherhood of artists known as "The Firm"—was reorganized in 1875 as Morris & Co., it institutionalized the name recognition that was already present in references to "Morris papers" and "Morris chairs."[55] Historians have traced the tendency within the Arts and Crafts movement "to centre all claims of quality, authenticity and rank around the person of the invidual designer," a trend that by 1886 resulted in a faction breaking from the Art Workers' Guild because of its commitment to anonymity, in order to form the competing Arts and Crafts Exhibition Society, which provided a venue for the display and sale of signed work.[56] Because of the lag between the development of the Arts and Crafts movement in Britain and its influence on the continent, European workshops, drawing primarily from the later stages of the British movement as they were publicized in art magazines that emphasized particular makers, eschewed anonymity in order to structure themselves around the reputation of individual designers.[57] Even when the cooperative ideals of British Arts and Crafts pioneers were acknowledged, these were—ironically—treated as manifestations of their quirky individualism.[58] Historians now cite this period of European design as the origin of the twentieth-century vogue for "designer" lines of clothing, perfumes, and accessories—a phenomenon centered in Paris and first fully embodied by Paul Poiret.[59]

Although the French avant-garde rejected anonymity for its own artists and designers, however, it embraced primitivist claims to the values associated with anonymity. During the 1880s, Parisian modernists looked to the French peasantry—the women and children of Brittany especially—as living primitives who embodied, spontaneously and collectively, modernist values. Most famous among the Breton primitivists, Paul Gauguin in 1888 proclaimed, "I love Brittany," explaining, "there I find the savage and the primitive. When my wooden shoes resound on that granite ground, I hear the muffled, flat and powerful tone that I am seeking in painting."[60] In this formulation, the very soil of the countryside, struck by the artist who acts the peasant (he is wearing peasant shoes), yields modern art. Gauguin—like Emile Bernard, Maurice Denis, Paul Sérusier, and scores of other artists who traveled to Brittany—made names for themselves as modernists by borrowing from Breton folk art, with its stiff poses and flat areas of bright color between black outlines. Their paintings were characterized by sympathetic critics as "decorative," and the style called "cloisonnism," in reference to the Byzantine and medieval *cloisonné* enamels it resembled. This version of modernism, which straddled the boundary between art and decoration, was central to Bloomsbury's perception of the French avant-garde. All the artists just cited were included in the first Post-Impressionist show, which included many cloisonnist Breton scenes.[61] Looking to Poiret returned the Omega directly to this precedent, for the girls of the Ecole Martine were selected and trained by Marguerite Gabriel-Claude, a student and the fiancée of Sérusier, who was among the artists most committed to Breton primitivism.[62] The Ecole Martine may be the ultimate manifestation of this primitivist interest in the French peasantry. Here, lower-class girls were urged to forget their education and be inspired instead by excursions to such microcosms of natural wildness as zoos and botanical gardens, with summer vacations spent in Brittany. Their resulting designs were seen as having regained a state of natural, primitive expressiveness. This primitive modernism, however, was marketed under Poiret's name, while he claimed his workers as his progeny: the Ecole Martine was named for Poiret's daughter, born the year he opened the school.

By the era of the Omega, the French modernists' grounding of individual accomplishment in primitive culture had expanded beyond Brittany to the south of France, the South Seas, and Africa. What Bloomsbury found in Paris around 1910 was the now familiar modernist concept of the "primitive," a single category of a collective and anonymous aesthetic that lumped together European folk art with indigenous crafts of Africa, the South Seas, Asia, and the Americas, the appreciation and application of which marked certain educated European men as modern.[63]

Picasso, for instance, concurrently with his discovery of African art, championed the work of the untrained Parisian painter whose nickname, "*Le Douanier*" [the customs agent] Rousseau, signaled his working-class status.[64] For Poiret, who compared the sketches of the Martine girls to "the prettiest paintings of the douanier Rousseau," the aesthetic of these modern primitives blended so smoothly with the Orientalism for which the Maison Poiret was famous that wags in Paris joked that his working girls "must have had Russian nursemaids—among them Nijinski."[65] In London, his representative sold "specimens of negro art" alongside Poiret's products.[66] Fry was among the first in England to adopt this expanded notion of the primitive. By 1910, his articles asserted the relevance of "primitive" drawing to modern art, pulling examples from African, Australian, and Oriental art to imagery by children and the insane in ways that echoed his French sources and laid the groundwork for his promotion of Post-Impressionism.[67] Fry's references to the "negro savage of the Congo" in the Omega catalog and Bell's invocation of "squaws" in his praise for the "savage" Martine girls reflect Bloomsbury's absorption of ideas current in Paris. This amalgamation of diverse aesthetics into the category of the primitive was asserted visually for visitors to the Omega, where the modernist objects created by contributing artists were marketed with, at various times, Asian and North African textiles and ceramics, displays of children's drawings, reproductions of the Byzantine mosaics at Ravenna, and contemporary Italian folk art.[68]

Such primitivist ideas grew so central to the development of modernism—for good and ill—that it is easy to overlook their novelty in England around 1910.[69] In 1908, while African-inspired art by cubists and Fauves was circulating through Paris galleries, London's most avant-garde artists, Augustus John and his colleagues, responded to the Franco–British Exhibition by sending newspapers what *The Times* called "a protest couched in somewhat extravagant terms" about the subordination of Impressionist to Pre-Raphaelite painting in the modern art displays, completely ignoring the way the African mock-villages were presented as, again quoting *The Times*, evidence "that the mental and artistic capacities of the Africans are far less highly developed than those of the Asiatics," let alone of Europeans— this two years into the French avant-garde's debate over whether African sculpture rivaled, or even surpassed, the beauty of the Venus de Milo.[70] The only challenge to the London exhibition's disparaging presentation of African artefacts came from missionary societies, which argued that the "artisanal" skill of the Africans made them ideal candidates for improvement through the kind of "expert training" in good craftsmanship that Arts and Crafts reformers had applied to the British working classes.[71] The English avant-garde's obliviousness to the ideas of its French counterparts is demonstrated, once again, by Tonks. In a letter to Robert Ross reacting to Fry's first article on primitive drawing, Tonks exploded in baffled exasperation at his former colleague: "I say, don't you think Fry might find something more interesting to write about than Bushmen. Bushmen!"[72]

The differences between the avant-gardes of London and Paris in the era of the Omega meant that Fry's hybrid notions of primitive anonymity failed to register with either the French or the British. On one hand, the Omega followed the Victorian precedent of Arts and Crafts practitioners who trained in the techniques of anonymous medieval craft work—Morris, for instance, picked apart old embroideries to see how they were made. But though the British could conceive of artists retrieving the skills of anonymous craftsmen, they were unprepared to value the qualities of intuitive spontaneity and expressiveness—visualized as awkwardness and roughness—that the Parisians associated with the primitive. The French, on the other hand, though they pioneered modernist associations of anonymity with the primitivist appeal of folk and African art, had no tradition of fine artists making themselves anonymous. From Gauguin to Picasso, the artists of the Parisian avant-garde borrowed eagerly from artistic genres they associated with the aesthetics of collective anonymity, but they did so in their own names. This helps account for the comparative lack of interest by French artists in the decorative arts at any level but that of signed editions and commissions.

In the long run, the French emphasis on the authorizing signature became—like so much about the Parisian avant-garde—definitive of the modernist mainstream.[73] And by the time the Omega opened in 1913, this long run had almost arrived. The signature's centrality to modernism was pronounced enough that by the end of the decade Marcel Duchamp and his Dada colleagues could wittily exploit its authorizing power in his Readymades (including *Fountain*, the signed urinal of 1917), and his 1919 *Dada Drawing: Tzanck Cheque*, a hand-made check for his dentist where the meticulous draftsmanship imitating the bank's security printing is contrasted to the scrawled signature that actually conferred value on the slip of paper.[74] In this context, the Omega's commitment to anonymity contributed to its failures both to make money and to register in the annals of art history. On a purely practical level, as early as October 1913, just three months after the Omega opened, resentment over the requirement of anonymous collaborative production led some of the participating artists to desert the workshops, with their leader, Wyndham Lewis, condemning Bloomsbury's allegiance to "mid-Victorian" artistic attitudes.[75] More damaging was Fry's discovery in 1917 that one of the Omega's customers had commissioned Grant and Bell, the workshops' best known artists, to decorate two rooms of her house under their own names. This, according to Virginia Woolf, was "a source of unmitigated disillusion" for Fry, which prompted him to threaten to close the workshops at this time.[76] If the commitment to collectivity and anonymity could not be sustained by the Omega's artists and clients, it is small wonder that it failed to arouse the interest of the avant-garde elsewhere or since. The Omega's bid to market the primitivist products of its artists anonymously stranded the workshops between the rapidly expiring Arts and Crafts circles of England and the newly powerful modernist avant-garde of Paris. It is no coincidence that the recent renewal of interest in the Omega has occasioned the further undoing of the workshops' commitment to anonymity, as scholars have deployed a range of connoisseurial skills in order to attribute each of its objects and designs to a particular hand.[77]

Although Bloomsbury failed to accommodate its practices to the French in the matter of anonymity, the Omega was linked to the Parisian avant-garde in other ways. Fry wooed potential investors, not only with comparisons to Poiret, but with claims to have "the promise of assistance from several young French artists who have had experience of such work."[78] His reference was to the circle of painters around Charles Vildrac, a poet and art dealer whom Fry befriended around 1911.[79] Vildrac, in 1906, had co-founded the Abbaye de Créteil, a French version of a British rural-utopian guild; both the name—the archaic "Abbaye"—and the motto that Vildrac took from Rabelais's *Abbaye de Thélème* echo the medievalism of the Arts and Crafts. Although the Abbaye, like many of its English counterparts, failed to sustain itself financially and closed after fifteen months, its attempt to guarantee a subsistence wage for its artists anticipated Fry's ideas for the Omega. Each member of the Abbaye pledged four or five hours a day to work on a small press that was supposed to provide revenue to support the group's other artistic projects.[80] Fry similarly justified the Omega as a place where, if "for two or three days a week the artist can earn a living wage he will be able to devote the rest of this time to painting."[81] Omega salaries varied, but the plan was for member designers to be guaranteed a living wage (five shillings per half-day, which was approximately the pay of a clerk) for a maximum of three full days' labor each week, freeing the rest of their time for their own art.[82]

The legacy of the Abbaye was manifest at the Omega in more than just financial structure. Fulfilling the promises of his prospectus, Fry recruited for the Omega the French painter, Henri Doucet, who had exhibited at the Abbaye and, under the auspices of Vildrac's gallery, at the second Post-Impressionist show. Doucet, who ran an artists' housing cooperative in Paris, may have been especially sympathetic to Fry's schemes to generate income for impecunious members of the avant-garde.[83] Doucet came to London to help prepare for the Omega's opening, designing pottery, stenciling violet ferns onto the puce walls, and painting a set of curtains with figures of Adam and Eve (discussed in Chapter 8).[84] Bloomsbury's excitement over the presence of this bona fide French modernist is suggested by the number of portraits of him. He appears in three Vanessa Bell paintings of 1912, including—pictured with Duncan Grant—*The Studio* (discussed in Chapter 6). Grant painted Doucet at least twice, like Bell including him in the Bloomsbury context in *Group at Asheham*.[85] Though Doucet seems to be the only "young French artist" actually to work at the Omega, its links to Vildrac's French circle were reinforced when the workshops took up printing in 1915. Like the Abbaye, the Omega produced books of poetry, and its second offering was Fry's translation of one of the Abbaye's poets, Pierre Jean Jouve.[86] Under Fry's direction, the Omega also followed the Abbaye in expanding beyond the production of decorative arts, becoming a venue for exhibitions, readings, plays, and discussion groups, often with a distinctly francophile emphasis. In 1915, productions of Racine's play *Bérénice* and a dance set to Debussy's *Boîte à joujoux* were staged at the Omega using puppets made by its artists.[87]

By 1912, some of those involved in the Abbaye had forged connections to another group that offers a revealing French comparison with the Omega: the artists André Mare assembled to create modernist rooms for the annual *Salons d'automne*. For the 1912 salon, Mare's group created an installation—a façade and entryway leading to a furnished sitting room and bedroom—that came to be called the Maison Cubiste (fig. 85). Among the better-known artists participating in this project, Jacques Villon painted a tea service, while Roger de la Fresnaye contributed fireplaces, painted moldings, and a clock, which was purchased by Poiret. This 1912 display differed in both ideology and aesthetic from the Omega. Ideologically, Mare's group retained the conventional distinctions between artists and designers: their promotional brochure lists the artists' work first, in large type, and organized by name; following this, and in smaller type, the provenance of the other furnishings is listed, led by those who lent pieces, with the names (and addresses) of commercial designers and craftsmen bringing up the rear. Visually, too, the Maison Cubiste separated art from craft. Unlike, for example, the Omega display in the 1913 Ideal Home exhibition, with its murals and hand-painted wallpapers (see fig. 73), the Maison Cubiste defaulted to framed paintings in conventional genres—landscapes and portraits—to decorate the walls, making no effort to tie the art to the furnishings. Also unlike the cubistic patterns of the Omega textiles, the decorations of the Maison Cubiste—like the products of the Martine, which were displayed nearby in the same exhibition—relied on brilliant colors to claim their status as modern.[88]

Although the single room Mare displayed in the 1913 *Salon d'automne* widened the distinction between art and craft with a brochure that reduced the names of the designers who were not also artists to tiny footnotes, one aspect of this project offers striking visual confirmation of the Omega's links to the French avant-garde. For this project, only Raymond Duchamp-Villon's architectural decoration straddled the boundary between art and craft, but his four cubist tondos, depicting a cat (fig. 86), a dog, a parrot, and two doves, each curled into the circular format, are very like the animal motifs on a circular ground that Grant designed, also in 1913, for the embroidered cushions that were among the Omega's most popular products. One of Grant's designs, light-heartedly described by Fry as "a cat lying on a cabbage playing with a butterfly," encircled the animal in prismatic cubist forms (fig. 87), anticipating Duchamp-Villon's tondo down to the protruding paw and wrap-around tail.[89] Direct influence is unlikely, but not impossible, for Grant's cat design was one of two "in the very new style" illustrated in the popular magazine *Sketch* in March of 1913, when examples of Omega embroidery were included in an exhibition mounted as advance publicity for the Omega (fig. 88). Speculation over possible influence, however, is ultimately less important than the point that the similarity between these designs produced in London and in Paris in 1913 exemplifies the Omega's immersion in the most up-to-date aesthetics of the French avant-garde.

This allegiance did not win the Omega much credit on its own side of the Channel. Supportive reviewers dismissed continental connections, with *The Times* assuring readers that "anyone who goes to [the Omega] and forgets all about words such as post-impressionist and futurist and their horrid associations will find many things that are simply pleasant to the eye."[90] A hostile review in the *Pall-Mall Gazette*, apparently still confident that Aestheticism's muted tones constituted

85. Salon bourgeois from Maison Cubiste, Salon d'automne, Paris, 1912.

86. Boudoir from the *Salon d'automne*, Paris, 1913, showing Raymond Duchamp-Villon's tondo of a cat at top center.

87. Duncan Grant, "Cat on a Cabbage" design. Gouache and pencil on paper, 62.4 × 72.3 cm. Courtauld Institute Galleries.

88. Illustration from *Sketch* 2 April 1913 showing "Cat on a Cabbage".

IN THE VERY NEW STYLE: EMBROIDERED CHAIR "BACKS"
SHOWN BY MEMBERS OF THE GRAFTON GROUP.

modernity, dismissed Omega work sarcastically as "gay and subtle in colouring and design as an Early Victorian beadwork bag."[91] What this reviewer intended as condemnation, however, Fry used to promote the Omega, boasting to interviewers about the workshops' revival of Victorian embroidery materials and techniques in products like Grant's cushions. Describing one of Grant's designs, Fry coined a phrase that sums up the Omega's relationship to its British heritage: "It was a mid-Victorian idea, but it was not treated in a mid-Victorian manner."[92]

From the Victorians, Bloomsbury drew, first and foremost, its belief in the home as the primary arena for aesthetic renewal. This legacy of the Arts and Crafts movement is most evident in the speed with which the group sought to turn the lessons of French modernism to domestic decoration. Sometimes, the application was quite literal. One of Cézanne's favorite motifs, a mountain framed by trees, became a stained glass window (fig. 89), while the cubistic pattern of "Amenophis" (fig. 90)— among the Omega's most strikingly modernist fabrics (available both in linen and as stair carpet)—was excerpted from one of Fry's recent paintings, *Still Life: Jug and Eggs* (fig. 91).[93] Other paintings by Grant and Bell formed the basis of designs for table tops, folding screens, and cushions.[94] But though the impulse was Victorian, British critics saw nothing traditional in the Omega's aesthetic. "The walls of the Post-Impressionist home will not be as the walls of ordinary homes," reported the *Daily News and Leader*.[95] More sensationally, the *Mirror* headlined an article on the Omega, "A POST-IMPRESSIONIST FLAT: WHAT WOULD THE LANDLORD THINK?" Captions under the accompanying illustrations described "the kind of room in which you would live, that is if your nerves could stand it," and "Mr. Fry thinking out some new futurist nightmare, something that will eclipse even the room above."[96] *The Bystander* took the same tone, captioning a photograph of a bed in the Omega showroom with "This is the sort of decoration that brings healthy sleep to the tired Futurist, but we fear that to us, the uninitiated, it rather suggests a nightmare!"[97]

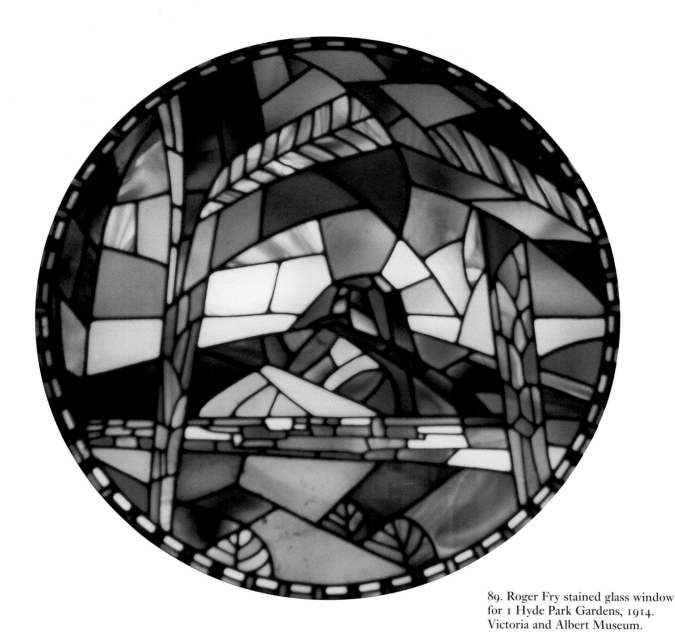

89. Roger Fry stained glass window for 1 Hyde Park Gardens, 1914. Victoria and Albert Museum.

Even signage for the Omega caused offence. Critics complained vociferously about a signboard depicting "an emaciated Byzantine youth" flanked by two large paintings (over six feet high) by Bell and Grant, each depicting dancing couples in evening dress, which were set into rectangular recesses outside the house leased by the Omega (fig. 92). Subjected to the weather, these elements have been lost, but extant sketches for Bell's "Post-Impressionist Titans," as Virginia Woolf called them, reveal an energetic Futurist style with the figures subordinated to a pattern of arcs suggestive of the rhythms of dance.[98] One reviewer, who had dismissed the French paintings in the first Post-Impressionist show with the remark, "Germany is welcome to them," equally xenophobically—but more aptly—decried the Omega's "flirting decorations," which "gay, giddy and slight—might hold their places on some sunbaked wall within the equatorial belt, but . . . affront the grave decorum of Fitzroy Square."[99] Critics were right to see this work as a challenge to its surroundings. Bell told Fry that she and Grant tried to make their paintings "rather bright

90. Roger Fry, "Amenophis" fabric, produced for the Omega 1912.

91. Roger Fry, *Still Life with Jug and Eggs*, 1911–12. Oil on panel, 30.5 × 35.3 cm. Art Gallery of South Australia, Adelaide.

92. Vanessa Bell, design for Omega sign, 1912. Gouache and oil on paper, 76.2 × 37.5 cm. Victoria and Albert Museum.

and full of accent as I think with London greyness all around that's necessary."[100] Although hardly shocking by continental standards—indeed, rather elegant, and, Bell feared, "too boring for words"—the panels were condemned as "hideous" by Marjorie Strachey, who warned Bell somewhat facetiously that the police might prevent their display.[101] George Bernard Shaw, too, disapproved, writing to Fry: "That noble facade which is the glory of the square may not be in your line; but why insult it?"[102]

Post-Impressionist signs on a Georgian building in a London square: these encapsulated the Omega's ambition to meld continental modernism with British tradition. And the criticism encapsulated the reaction. What the Omega artists saw as a brilliant antidote to "London greyness" seemed to their countrymen, if not a crime, at least an insult to the nobility and "grave decorum" of the setting.

Ironically, what Bloomsbury shared with its British critics was a frame of reference that made the antipathy between them more pronounced. The assumption that changes in what Omega publicity called "objects of common life" implied changes in the forms of the life lived among those objects animated both Bloomsbury's aesthetic innovation and its critics' reactions. The critics' condemnation hinted at transgressions both eroticized ("flirting") and gendered feminine ("gay, giddy and slight"), while, for its part, Bloomsbury delighted in anecdotes about customers hoping to see the "immoral" furniture they had been warned about in the papers.[103] It may be that the Omega could only have arisen in Britain, with its legacy of aesthetic and social reform focused on the home. But the nature—both visual and social—of the reforms Bloomsbury proposed prevented observers, at the time and since, from granting the Omega a place in histories constructed around presumptions of an essential English sensibility distinguished by restraint and propriety and defined against the sensual indulgence associated with Mediterranean culture in general and France in particular.

This chapter has argued for the Omega's ideological connections to both French and British modernists. The following chapter extends these arguments in more visual terms, looking specifically at the iconography of Eden in a group of related objects—some Omega products, some easel paintings by Omega artists—produced in 1913, the year the Omega was founded. Edenic imagery offered a powerful symbol of the primitivist ideal of return to uncorrupted origins; the specifics of its deployment by the artists associated with the Omega offers a useful case study in Bloomsbury's social and aesthetic aspirations.

A Modern Eden (1913–14)

W hat can we conceive of that first Eden which we might not yet win back, if we chose?" Ruskin's question, it has been argued, motivated his life's work to realize "dreams of an English Eden."[1] Certainly, Edenic allusions permeate the rhetoric of Ruskin and his Victorian followers, who responded to the poverty and pollution attending industrialization by imaging a return to harmony with nature. The re-establishment of gardens on overrun and exploited land became, in Ruskin's writings, a powerful symbol of his aesthetic and social aspirations.[2] His followers realized this vision, establishing as a hallmark of Arts and Crafts design the informal "English" garden, where the lost countryside could be recreated in idealized microcosm, with indigenous herbs and flowers instead of the hybrid roses and other fragile hot-house flora of mid-Victorian fashion. This conception of reform as the restoration of paradise lost made images of Eden a common motif in Arts and Crafts design, especially for objects intended to represent the movement's fundamental aspirations. An image of Adam and Eve, for instance, was among the scenes Dante Gabriel Rossetti painted in 1859 to decorate Morris's Red House, a showplace of Pre-Raphelite design. Morris himself designed painted tiles on the theme of Adam and Eve for the International Exhibition of Art and Industry, at which his firm made its first display in 1862.[3]

This was the legacy Bloomsbury inherited. Like Ruskin and Morris, Fry's promotion of modernism relied on appeals to a simpler, more natural past. As discussed in the preceding chapters, this primitivism was reflected in Bloomsbury's earliest domestic decorations in both an iconography (Arcadian invocations of nature as a timeless repository of abundance and sensual pleasure) and a style (rough brushwork, bold colors, heavy outlines, awkward drawing) that proposed a return to primal simplicity of expression and sensation. Both iconography and style persisted when Bloomsbury, through the Omega, expanded beyond its own walls to design modern rooms for the public. Flowers and leaves form the basis of most Omega designs not purely abstract, though the distinction between these two categories was not always precise. Among the Omega's most popular patterns for painted furniture, for instance, was one called "Lilypond," which began as a straightforward—if Post-Impressionistic—representation of the rectangular pool in Fry's garden at Durbins as seen from above (fig. 93). As it was applied to tables and screens, however, the paint was poured in puddles and drips directly onto the surface, retaining the original design's colors of brilliant orange fish amid green and brown lilypads, but sacrificing the specific iconography for more gestural allusions to natural spontaneity in the free forms of flowing paint (fig. 94).[4]

Visitors to the Omega showrooms found themselves invited not so much to view as to inhabit an environment at once modern and Edenic. The first newspaper

93. Duncan Grant, "Lilypond" design. Oil on paper, 47.5 × 61.6 cm. Private collection.

94. "Lilypond" table, 1913–14. Oil on wood, 125.5 × 72.5 × 80.5 cm. Art Gallery of South Australia, Adelaide.

95. Photograph of Omega showrooms featuring landscape mural, from *Daily Mirror*, 8 November 1913.

reports of the Omega describe the showroom dominated by a mural on the rear wall, which depicted "a wonderful landscape in aesthetic tones, pale purple skies, a shining moon, and blue mountains."[5] Press photographs of the mural, which remained in place from the summer of 1913 through the six years of the Omega's operation, show an array of brushy, larger-than-life flowers strewn across the foreground to create a screen through which is glimpsed the mountainscape beyond (fig. 95 and 96). The effect is to blend the Omega furnishings, which were decorated with floral colors and patterns in an exuberantly brushy style, with the mural's foreground flowers, so that chairs, chests, and bed seem to sprout as part of the fantastical garden depicted on the wall. This room-as-garden effect was sustained by the model nursery displayed upstairs. Here viewers standing on a floor of sandy yellow felt were encircled by a collaged landscape featuring an elephant and a pond of cavorting fish; above, the ceiling was speckled with birds, clouds, and, according to one dubious reviewer, "what one takes to be a sunset" on the cornice.[6] Omega toys, in the form of painted wooden animals—camels, rhinoceri, elephants, and tigers—with jointed legs, extended the theme of exotic fauna into three dimensions. The primitivist style, at once childlike and modern, of Vanessa Bell's cut-outs—prescient of Matisse's famous collages—was, thus, conjoined with the theme of the primal garden. Describing this room, one journalist captured the prelapsarian overtones of the Omega's modernist primitivism, speculating that, "Here, long

A FUTURIST BEDROOM
At the Omega Workshops, in Fitzroy Square, W., where Mr. Roger Fry and his Post Impressionist friends have a Christmas show of their works. Here are to be seen the latest Futurist designs in rugs, lampshades, boxes, crockery,—and the bedroom seen above. This is the sort of decoration that brings heathy sleep to the tired Futurist, but we fear that to us, the uninitiated, it rather suggests a nightmare!

96. Photograph of Omega showrooms featuring landscape mural, from *Bystander*, 31 December 1913.

A Modern Eden

97. Photograph of Omega room from Omega catalog, 1914.

before evil habits have been formed, the prattling infant is to be led, all unconsciously, into the gay groves of Post-Impressionism."[7] If Post-Impressionism was a joyful garden ("gay groves"), Omega interiors offered a return for those modern enough to be uncorrupted by Victorianism.

Like the showroom displays, the earliest Omega decorating schemes transformed conventional rooms into fantasy gardens. In a painted antechamber illustrated in the Omega's 1914 catalogue, larger-than-life scale propels an iconography of fruit and flowers into the realm of the fantastic (fig. 97). Huge pots of flowers towered over viewers' heads and a bowl of fruit above the fireplace stretched as wide as the mantel itself. Though documented only in black-and-white photographs, these decorations' magnitude of scale was matched by their brilliance of color, if the pictured firescreen is any indication. Extant versions of Grant's design (both embroidered and drawn) set off yellow flowers against a ground of variegated greens and blues. One well preserved embroidered version, worked by Ottoline Morrell, displays remarkable combinations of pinks, purples, and oranges in the birds and flowers.[8] Even if the room matched the golds and dusky purples of the more subdued sketches, such colors, extrapolated to the scale of the murals and combined with the free handling of the wall-paintings evident in the photograph, would have created a room indubitably—even overwhelmingly—modern, in exactly the ways that Bloomsbury understood that concept: an exuberant return to modes of natural spontaneity and instinctive pleasure associated with the idea of paradise.

The general paradaisical allusions present in the mural's imagery of fruit and flowers take on more specific reference to Bloomsbury primitivism in their similarity to the floral motifs in the mosaics of the Galla Placidia in Ravenna.[9] Despite Clive's condemnation of "nasty, woolly realism about the sheep" in the Galla Placidia, which he visited with the other Bloomsbury artists in the spring of 1913, Duncan and Vanessa perceived the Ravenna murals as proof of an Italian heritage of spontaneous and sensual aesthetic sensitivity.[10] Grant sent a postcard of the mosaics to Keynes with the message: "This is a much better place than Venice. It is full of things like this."[11] It was not just the look of the Byzantine mosaics preserved at Ravenna that enthralled Bloomsbury, but their context in what seemed a living paradise. Bell wrote her sister, "The best place we have been to was Ravenna, where I could have stayed happily for some time." She reported that they had "bought large quantities of crockery, stuffs, etc." to sell at the Omega, and that they had "discovered a genius, a young man of exquisite beauty and a charming smile, called Dante Paradiso, from whom Duncan bought two painted caryatids, and Clive a large painting. Roger has commissioned him to do another and boxes for the shop too!"[12] The combination of ancient aesthetic heritage, popular artistic sensibility, and erotic sensuality, which Bloomsbury was delighted to discover in modern Italy and to project as modernism's ideal, is encapsulated in this letter, with its quick shifts from Italian peasant crafts to the discovery of a handsome "genius" named Paradiso and his commission to provide stock for the Omega.[13] Fry's letters recording his impressions of their trip make explicit Bloomsbury's comparison of its modernist aspirations with the precedent of the Ravenna mosaics. The Byzantines, he explained, "were in a hopeless muddle; the old stupid Roman attitude (dully materialistic and fatuous like that of modern popular art) still persisting, and yet this new ferment working . . . a new excitement." "We're so like that now," he continued, "somehow all the people in this new movement are alive and whatever they do has life and that's new."[14] This claim to a renewal of primal vitality is clear in the Omega antechamber murals, with their imagery of overwhelming natural abundance couched in ancient Italian precedent but rendered in the energetic modernist style. Fry's only worry, expressed in the next sentence of this letter, is that the new modernism will "fizzle out like the Pre-Raphaelites," a remark that reflects all Bloomsbury's ambivalence about its relationship to its Victorian predecessors.

It would be surprising if, in their effort to imagine domestic spaces as returns to primitive gardens, Bloomsbury's artists did not, like their forerunners, turn to the iconography of Eden.[15] The primal garden of Genesis became a leitmotif in the work of the Omega artists during the first months of the workshops' existence. This subject was not, of course, unproblematic for Bloomsbury's purposes. As a foundational myth justifying the subordination of women and the necessity of pain and labor, the story of the Fall was deeply implicated in the Victorian moral conventions the group rebelled against. Exactly because conventional understandings of the biblical narrative were at odds with Bloomsbury's aspirations for modernism, however, the artists' reworking of the story offers a clear example of the ideological connections between the group's social and aesthetic vision. If the look of Bloomsbury's earlier decorations—the revised Queen of Sheba story no less than the updated Byzantinism of the Borough Polytechnic decorations—had implications for their intended setting in schools, the treatment of humanity's first family by the Omega seems likewise significant in the context of furnishings designed for the modern home.

From the opening of the Omega showrooms, Eden was evoked, not just implicitly in murals suggestive of prelapsarian abundance, but, more specifically, in the figures of Adam and Eve. Reporting on the "curiously exhilarating effect" of the Omega's opening display, the *Daily News and Leader* described and illustrated floor-to-ceiling curtains that hung between two downstairs showrooms (fig. 98). "The pattern at first sight seems little more than a confused medley of lines—purple, green, blue, crimson, and yellow," the paper reported, "but as one regards it one finds that there is method in the madness. It is a pictorial presentment of Adam and Eve in the Garden of Eden," suggestive, the reporter noted, of "sunshine, dawn, high noon, light and laughter—everything that is gay and living, nothing that is dull or dead," the look of the curtains, attributed to Henri Doucet and Duncan Grant, rejected the grim tenor of the canonic Eden story.[16] More than the exuberant style, however, the composition of the curtains flouts conventional morals attached to Adam and Eve. Where the Biblical characters, through awareness of their sexuality, were expelled from the garden by an angry god who transformed their blissful unity into unending toil on sex-specific tasks, the Omega's version involved the viewer in a playful sundering of the sexes. With the curtains drawn apart, the rather androgynous Adam and Eve gaze at each other across the divide. With the curtains pulled together, the breach is repaired, as Adam's recumbent figure (difficult to see in the photograph, but described as lying on his stomach with his upright head supported by his elbows) glides into Eve's arms. Where sexuality in the Bible results in shame and isolation, when these draperies close—with all the ideas of privacy and intimacy drawn curtains imply—humanity is returned to a state of primal bliss. For Bloomsbury's cheerful atheists, God is banished from the modernist garden, where Adam and Eve live happily ever after.

This visual claim to biblical revision accords with texts from and about Bloomsbury. As early as 1902, Lytton Strachey, in a paper read for a Cambridge

98. Photograph of Omega showrooms featuring Adam and Eve curtains, from *Daily News and Leader*, 7 August 1913.

literary society, claimed allegiance with Caliban—emblem of primitive freedom—over Christ, asserting his willingness "to put myself back into one or other of those more violent ages where railways and fig leaves were equally unknown."[17] As late as 1967, Leonard Woolf ridiculed the "inveterate political conservatism" of "the ruling castes and classes," which "has produced an unending series of unnecessary horrors and disasters, ever since the Lord began it by trying to prevent Adam and Eve from learning the truth about the badly devised universe and world which He ill-advisedly had just created."[18] That Bloomsbury's coupling of this kind of iconoclasm with Post-Impressionist décor was registered by contemporaries is suggested by Arnold Bennett's novel *The Pretty Lady*, which is set in London during the war. When the rooms of the most fashionable character are described, not only are the walls, carpet, upholstery, and cushions "irregularly covered with rhombuses, rhomboids, lozenges, diamonds, triangles, and parallelograms" all colored with "excessive brightness, crudity and variety," but also:

> Every piece of furniture was painted with primitive sketches of human figures, or of flowers, or of vessels, or of animals. On the front of the mantelpiece were perversely but brilliantly depicted, with a high degree of finish, two nude, crouching women who gazed longingly at each other across the impassable semicircular abyss of the fireplace; and just above their heads, on a scroll, ran these words:
> "The Ways of God are Strange."[19]

Although Bennett transforms the lovers into lesbians and the curtains into a vaginal "abyss" (changes that accord with the novel's focus on the inscrutability of female sexuality), his allusion to the Omega style is obvious. In the novel, this scene is set in 1916, the year when, Bennett's journals record, he visited the Omega and was so impressed by Fry's "very persuasive and reasonable" theorizing that he made two purchases.[20]

The witty iconoclasm of the showroom curtains set a tone for the Omega, repeated—on a smaller scale—in other pieces produced by the workshops. Two of Vanessa Bell's designs from this period depict Adam and Eve, both reiterating the ambition to have Eden without the Expulsion. The first, probably intended for a screen, sets animated nude figures—one male and one female—against a backdrop where a flat pattern of leaves and branches stretches over a lozenge-shaped pool of yellow light (fig. 99). On the left the female braces herself with legs wide apart as she pulls down a branch, as if to shake from it the fruit the male eagerly bends to retrieve. These energetic nudes dance their way through a narrative that promises to end, not with shame and banishment, but in the enveloping warmth of the yellow light they reach into. In another design, this one for a bedstead, Bell unites the forms of man, woman, and snake into a single sinuous pattern that cheerfully denies the moral distinctions created by conventional biblical hermeneutics (fig. 100). Adam, Eve, and the baby-blue snake reach together to hold the pale green apple that forms the center of the design, a collaborative gesture that erases the blame usually reserved for the woman and serpent, while it insists there is nothing forbidden about the fruit. Particularly considered as a motif to decorate a bed, Bell's design seems calculated to counteract repressive sexual codes that claimed their authority from the story of humanity's corruption in the garden. Bell's design reasserts a prelapsarian indulgence in the sensuality of vibrant color, active gesture, and unabashed eroticism.

As designs for curtains, screens, and furniture, Omega renderings of Adam and Eve domesticate the sensual pleasures of life in the garden, turning the home into a paradise both primitive and modern. This effect parallels aspects of the Pre-Raphaelites' aspirations to design comprehensive environments for new ways of life, but runs counter to the goals of Bloomsbury's nearest French contemporaries, André Mare and his circle, who (as discussed in Chapter 7) disciplined brilliant modernist color to the conventional subjects, forms, and finishes of what Mare's promotional catalog called the "salon bourgeois." Where the French designed "Cubiste" furnishings and paintings to add a stylish accent to middle-class parlors without disrupting their ambiance, Omega wares were acknowledged—both in principle and in practice—to demand an entirely new environment.[21] Even before the Omega opened, its artists, exhibiting in March 1913 under the name the "Grafton Group" (a reference to the Grafton Gallery, where the two Post-Impressionist shows had been held), combined furnishings and paintings in a show that, reviewers noted, offered "a foretaste of the post-impressionist shop that is soon to be established in London" in the form of "firescreens, bed-screens, woolwork chair-covers and table-covers, all in the most approved of modernist designs."[22] C. Lewis Hind's sympathetic review evoked the spirit of Post-Impressionism as having "all the charm of... a house refurnished from cellar to garret by somebody who has cast away or sold all his old belongings and started afresh with a light heart and without any encumbrances."[23] Defending the Omega's work against a critical press notice later that year, Fry wrote, "I do not think it will be doubted by those who have seen a whole room in which everything has been designed by these artists working in conjunction that they have created a quite new and distinct decorative style, a style which we believe to be expressive of the needs and aspirations of modern life."[24] More colloquially, after May Dickinson (elder sister of Fry's Cambridge friend, Goldsworthy Lowes Dickinson) visited Fry's home in 1920, she reported to the Omega skeptic Janet Ashbee, "the whole decoration scheme is delightful—I always said that you must be *all* Omega and start fresh—and this proves it."[25]

This ambition to re-imagine the look of the home was linked to the Omega's determination to break down conventional distinctions—maintained at the Maison Cubiste—between art and design. In addition to mixing paintings and sculptures with decorative work in its exhibitions of this period, Fry and his colleagues suppressed the names of the makers of both kinds of objects, encouraging viewers to apply to fine art habits of vision normally reserved for anonymous craft work. The catalog to the 1913 Grafton Group exhibition opened with the explanation, "It has been thought interesting to try the experiment of exhibiting the pictures anonymously in order to invite the spectator to gain at least a first impression of the several works without the slight and almost unconscious predilection which a name generally arouses."[26] This statement has been explicated by reference to a passage from Clive Bell's *Art*, which was being written at this time, where he argues that the "visual shallowness of most civilised adults" is rooted in "the habit of recognizing the label and overlooking the thing, of seeing intellectually instead of seeing emotionally."[27] Although Bell does not refer to labels in exhibitions here, what is relevant is his formalist aspiration to forsake "civilised" ways of "seeing intellectually"—among which must be assessing the reputation of an artist—in favor of emotional reactions to form that, paradoxically, are the province of the most and least sophisticated: "Only artists and educated people of extraordinary sensibility and some savages and children feel the significance of form so acutely that they know how things

look," Bell claimed.[28] The aspiration to make modernism a return to innocence—to ways of seeing prior to knowledge but deeply felt—links the Edenic iconography in Omega products to Bloomsbury's broader theoretical ambitions to define new, and specifically modern, modes of experience.

The most striking evidence of the Grafton Group's ambition to supplant—rather than simply augment—a conventional domestic aesthetic was the sheer size of the work on display: tri-fold screens (Grant's extant *Blue Sheep* screen is 6½ feet long) competed with paintings reviewers struggled to categorize. "Huge mural posters" was one phrase applied to Wyndham Lewis's (now lost) *Three Women*, which the papers described as a "composition of life-size figures" that stymied the usual distinctions between fine and decorative art by being "not a picture, hardly, indeed a work of art at all, [but] a very powerful design."[29] Even larger was a painting by Grant titled, according to different reviewers, *Construction* or *Work* (also lost). Because of its size (approximately 8 by 4 feet) and placement over the central fireplace, Grant's piece became "the centre of attraction of all the enthusiasts of the New Art," the *Star* reported.[30] Again reviewers struggled for nomenclature: the *Pall-Mall Gazette* called it a "large 'decorative' design," while *The Times* registered the ambitious scale of the work with the cautious suggestion that "it might be beautiful if it were one of a series placed in some large building where it could be seen at a distance."[31] Even skeptical reviews noted the "tremendous expressiveness" and "impression of great strength and absorbed energy" in Grant's painting.[32] Under the headline "Picture Shocks," the *Star* reported:

> It represents the huge figure of a hasheesh-soaked gorilla stark naked, heaving and straining at some herculean labour. The enormous strength of the beast is suggested in staggering slabs of paint.
> Gradually it dawns upon the observer that the beast is not a gorilla at all, but a man. . . . And he is engaged in building a little blue church—a tottering edifice less than one-third the size of himself.

Suggestions of a return to primitive human—or even anthropoid—domination over religious authority were not lost on this reviewer, who accounted for the "futurist flesh-tint" of the giant with the facetious explanation, "in his struggle with this tiny, lopsided ecclesiastical monument he has become bruised from head to foot—dreadful blue, purple, and red smudges. The poor church, angry at being messed about so much, has evidently lost its head, and got up and smote him!"[33]

Notwithstanding this imaginative scenario of divine wrath, Grant's *Construction*, for most viewers, read as a manifesto in the spirit—if not exactly the form—of the Pre-Raphaelites. Like their predecessors, the Omega artists asserted their claims to modernity with a new style that harked back to the past, expressed in Grant's image by the remodeling of the kind of ecclesiastical structure Arts and Crafts activists used to symbolize a squandered legacy of British design. Writing about a reworked version of this painting, David Garnett recalled it as a portrait of the "spiritual form of Sir Christopher Wren . . . overshadowing St. Paul's Cathedral."[34] If this is true, Grant's iconography sprang from Bloomsbury's roots among such second-generation Arts and Crafts activists as C. R. Ashbee and A. H. Mackmurdo, who echoed Ruskinian rhetorics promoting a return to a lost paradise of social and aesthetic harmony, but dated England's fall from grace long after the Middle Ages. Ashbee argued that "the English middle class . . . and in great measure also the mass of the people" enjoyed a "humanistic regard for the values of life . . . through the seventeenth and eighteenth centuries. But all this was changed by the Industrial Revolution," and he posited Wren as the last great figure in what he called the original "Arts and Crafts" era.[35] Enumerating the attractions of London's East End slums, where he first established his Guild of Handicraft, Ashbee cited "the beautiful Trinity Hospital of Wren and Evelyn that we . . . have saved from destruction."[36] As part of his campaign in 1896 to preserve the two-hundred-year-old structure, Ashbee authored a book about the hospital, and in 1903 his Essex House Press published a volume on Wren. Ashbee's publications followed Mackmurdo's well known book on Wren's city churches, which, though now famous primarily for

Facing page:
99. Vanessa Bell, design for screen: Adam and Eve, 1913–14. Oil and pencil on paper, 35.6 × 50.8 cm. Courtauld Institute Galleries.

Facing page:
100. Vanessa Bell, design for bedstead: Adam and Eve. Pencil, gouache, oil on paper, 24.8 × 66.7 cm. Private collection.

A Modern Eden

its Art Nouveau title page, when it appeared in 1883 sparked widespread admiration for Wren within Fry's generation of Arts and Crafts practitioners.[37]

No one proposed such specific references to Arts and Crafts hagiography in Grant's *Construction* in 1913, but more general claims to Ruskinian forms of aesthetic redemption were clearly registered by reviewers. The *Evening Standard*, for instance, concluded from the Grafton Group show, "We are at the beginning of a genuine revival in folk art." Citing Lewis's and Grant's large-scale works, it effused, "the painters responsible know their trade, and address themselves to the communal mind." This Ruskinian appeal to ideas of artists as craftsmen with communal values became explicitly Pre-Raphaelite as the reviewer continued, claiming that the large-scale Post-Impressionist designs demonstrated that "painting is once more a man's job; as when the Italian—or Early English, for the matter of that—fresco painters said: 'Hullo! What larks! There's a wall. Chuck us a bit of ochre and let's make a picture on it.'"[38]

To perceive Post-Impressionist primitivism through the lense of the Pre-Raphaelite romance with medieval craft—especially in this absurdly chatty rendition—may strike readers today as eccentric. But our attitudes reflect later tendencies, outlined in the previous chapter, to divorce the Arts and Crafts movement from subsequent developments in modern art in Britain. When Fry and his colleagues sought to apply a modernist aesthetic to the creation of domestic environments, however, the parallels with their Arts and Crafts forebears were clear to friend and foe alike. The *Daily Chronicle* concluded its sympathetic review of the first Grafton Group show with the announcement that, "Fry and his friends are wayfaring out on just such another gallant adventure as that on which William Morris and his friends voyaged forth years ago."[39] Ten months later, the *New Age*'s unsympathetic review of the second Grafton Group show made the same point, describing the work as "a new disguise of aestheticism":

> At first appearance the pictures seem to have no resemblance to pre-Raphaelitism. But when the spectator has overcome his first mild shock and is familiarised with them, he will perceive the fundamental likeness . . . .[E]ssentially the same English aesthetic is behind both, and essentially the same cultured reminiscent pleasure is given to the spectator.[40]

The combination of Post-Impressionist style with the prelapsarian iconography of the Pre-Raphaelites was probably clearest at the second Grafton show in January 1914, for which Grant created another mural-scale canvas, this one depicting Adam and Eve. Like the first Grafton Group exhibition, the second mixed paintings and sculpture with domestic furnishings—two screens and designs for a screen and for needlework provided by the Omega. Also like the first show, the work of the British modernists was contextualized by examples of continental art, including paintings Fry owned by André Derain and Picasso, and work by Doucet, André Lhote, Othon Friesz, Jean Marchand and others, on loan from Charles Vildrac's Paris gallery.[41] Writing to Vildrac, Fry boasted, "I note this time, for the first time, that the French pictures do not explode our canvases. That is to say, I think we have profited so much from your collaboration that now we are starting to construct real pictures. I am very proud of them."[42]

Fry's pride in the show must have encompassed Grant's large (approximately 7 by 11 feet) *Adam and Eve*, which rivaled the Omega screens as a monument to the new aesthetic (fig. 101). Fourteen years later, when it was exhibited again, Fry still found Grant's work a "great sensation. . . . lovely colour and exquisitely subtle in line and I think very grand in its general disposition."[43] Now lost, Grant's *Adam and Eve* is revealed by photographs to have proclaimed its author's allegiance to recent French art. Eve's head—also documented in the oil study known as *Head of Eve* (fig. 102)—echoes Picasso's borrowing from tribal masks in its stylized contours and patterns of hatch marks. This Cubist head, however, rests on a body that, rather than evoking the sharp planes of Cubism, exaggerates the sinuous curves characteristic of Matisse.[44] Grant's enthusiastic embrace of avant-garde styles was condemned by the critics, especially in comparison to what they perceived as a stylistic retreat in the work of other Omega artists and a trend even among the French painters to

101. Duncan Grant, *Adam and Eve*, 1913. Oil on canvas, no longer extant.

102. Duncan Grant, *Head of Eve*, 1913. Oil on board, 75.6 × 63.5 cm, Tate Britain.

retrace their "steps from the frontiers of cubism."[45] Under the headline "The Normal and the Abnormal," the *Morning Post* praised the realism of the other artists in the show, saying, "the best work there is really a confession of failure in new and of faith in old methods," but complained that the "revolutionary" Grant

> abjectly humiliates himself in his mistaken belief. We are glad of it. . . . [I]n his "Adam and Eve" his contentions fail and he has not the good manners to be grateful to the symbols without which neither he nor anyone else can be audible.[46]

Likewise, the *Pall-Mall Gazette*, invoking the biblical parable of the prodigal son, was "inclined to kill the fatted calf" over Fry's return from the stylistic excesses of "the West African blood-and-bamboo school" among other influences, but complained that Grant's *Adam and Eve* was "spoken in a language not only unintelligible but discordant in its suggestion."[47] That two reviews five days apart should treat painting as a form of speech in order to attack the style of *Adam and Eve* as inaudible or unintelligible is not surprising. Reviewers read one another and the same critics often wrote for several journals, so repetition was common. The charge is striking, however, in that, in fact, *Adam and Eve* was not incomprehensible at all, as is shown by the very next sentence of the *Gazette*'s review, which complains that the subject of the picture marked "the callous destruction of a cherished idea which derives its true significance from the beauty of primitive faith."[48] The reviewer here read the artist's iconoclastic intent exactly. Grant described his image in a letter as "a surreptitious attack on the subject picture . . . it has a rather pretentious subject and the design obviously doesn't treat it seriously."[49]

Grant—literally and on a lifesize scale—upended conventions of morally uplifting subject paintings by turning them upside-down. Retaining the traditional frontal pairing of Adam and Eve, he presents the couple side by side, but with Adam posed as if mid-handstand. This was registered as iconoclastic by virtually every review. "Does he really think the somersault is a primal pose?" demanded one; "Sheer naughtiness," complained another, adding that "it cannot be sufficiently deplored that this piece of buffoonery has been acquired by the Contemporary Art Society."[50] The reviewer for the *New Statesman* registered Grant's attack on tradition more facetiously:

> It is to some extent mournful to see our cherished ideas toppled over, and in this instance we take leave of tradition with a more than usually bitter pang, as we wave our moist handkerchief in a sad but forever farewell to Dürer and Titian. However far back the modern painters have to go for their inspiration we did feel, somehow, that Adam and Eve were safe.

He consoled himself, however, by deciding Grant's picture "may be called *The Fall of Man*, and be regarded as the impression of an incident rather than as ancestral portraiture."[51] As this critic recognized, the imminent "fall" of Grant's wiry Adam will be, not the portentous issue of corrupting knowledge, but an inconsequential incident of excessive playfulness. Grant may have intended a sweeping condemnation of "subject pictures" of all kinds, but it is significant that he aimed his attack on the biblical story that justified a human legacy of toil, pain, and shame associated with sexuality. All of this—along with the Bible's emphasis on the corrupting agency of women—is here undone by a light-hearted Adam who, if he falls as a result of his own antics, seems ready to pick himself up and frolic on.

Grant's obvious subversion of biblical authority, however, seems to have blinded critics—at the time and since—to his equally iconoclastic approach to more recent inscriptions of patriarchal authority in the avant-garde French art to which he was so clearly responding. The aura of masculine anxiety—if not outright misogyny—in Picasso's masked and angular cubist nudes and in Matisse's impersonal and passive odalisques is punctured by Grant's cheerful pastiche of their most characteristic mannerisms.[52] The idea of pastiche—a witty jumbling of thematic and stylistic quotations—is crucial to any reading of *Adam and Eve*: clearly, the two figures are rendered in different styles and the much-condemned exaggeration of Eve's limbs reads as a comment on the mannerisms of the Matissean avant-garde. In this sense, the critics—or critic—who treated *Adam and Eve* as a collision of sign-systems were astute in their intuition, though their prejudices prevented them from appreciating what they saw: the disruption of the patriarchal presumptions behind established religion and avant-garde painting alike. Patched together from Fauve and cubist gestures that seem to contradict each other—or at least to reveal each other as signs—Grant's Eve is neither a terrifying specter of female power nor a luscious object of masculine desire. Escaping the weight of patriarchal projection, no wonder she appears so cheerful as she lumbers along in her stylized dance, hands upraised in amazement at the male who, for a change, shows off for her visual pleasure.

Grant's Eden—stylized palm trees set against (if the extant study is indicative) a background of pastel pinks and blues—is not undone by sexuality.[53] It is, rather, a place where nudity is joyfully integrated in a general celebration of sensual exuberance. Recently it has been suggested the couple inhabiting this paradise should be read as Grant and Vanessa Bell themselves, "imagined as the originating parents in a new Edenic world of Post Impressionist art in England."[54] If so, this painting sums up the ambitions of the Omega artists to inhabit, in their own garden-rooms, an Eden redeemed by modernist aesthetics—with all their associations of uninhibited spontaneity and primal energy—from restrictions rooted in the biblical story of the Fall. In any case, critics who hoped to distance Vanessa Bell from Grant's painterly excesses would have been distressed to hear her assessment of their opinions. Forwarding him some clippings, she remarked, "of course your Adam and Eve is a good deal objected to, simply on account of the distortion and Adam's standing on his head. . . . I believe distortion is like Sodomy. People are simply blindly prejudiced against it because they think it abnormal."[55] Nowhere is Bloomsbury's connection of aesthetic and sexual rebellion more pithily stated.

To create rooms where Victorian moralism and propriety could be abandoned for a return to primal pleasures: this is the ambition of Omega design, as evidenced in both the energetic modernist style and the Edenic iconography of its showroom displays and related art exhibitions. Such ambitions are clear, as well, in the way the

Omega artists discussed the making and marketing of their work. To a reporter, Fry explained that the Omega was trying to bring "the spirit of fun . . . to furniture and into fabrics. We have suffered too long from the dull and the stupidly serious."[56] When another paper allowed him to respond to an unsympathetic review of the Omega's work, he explained, "We are more anxious to be frank and spontaneous than to be precious and correct."[57] The importance of this spirit in the production of Omega work was asserted in the workshops' 1914 catalog, which describes the participating artists as "allowing free play to the delight in creation in the making of objects for common life." That this was imagined as a return to a primal state of creativity is evident in this text's primitivist comparison (analyzed in Chapter 7 for its echoes of Ruskin) of the Omega artist to "a negro savage of the Congo."[58]

The idea, rehearsed in Fry's promotion of the Omega, that decorative art properly conveys "joy" or "fun" betrays, despite his ambitions toward reform, the lingering prejudices that subordinate craft to art. Where Fry found in easel paintings sophisticated ranges of emotion—including the grotesque and the tragic—his assessments of the decorative arts seem locked in a simple idyll of perpetual pleasure.[59] In this sense, the Omega, as a workshop dedicated to the decorative arts, became for Bloomsbury itself a site of primitivism, allowing retreat to a realm of simple, uninhibited joy. This is clear in the glee with which the Omega founders experimented with craft techniques, refusing (as detailed in the previous chapter) to "civilize" themselves with the knowledge of the established Arts and Crafts schools. This sensuality becomes explicitly sexual in discussions of craft processes in the letters of the Omega artists, with Fry, for instance, describing for Grant an early effort to make pottery. Their teacher did not arrive, Fry reported, so they experimented with the potter's wheel on their own. At first,

> the clay was too stiff and V[anessa] very nearly burst with the effort to control its wobbliness—and in vain. Then we got softer clay and both of us turned out some quite nice things. . . . It's fearfully exciting when you do get it centred and the stuff begins to come up between your fingers. V. never would make her penises long enough, which I thought very odd. Don't you?[60]

Bell's account of the same episode concludes, "the feeling of the clay rising between one's fingers is like the keenest sexual joy!"[61] That such epistolary descriptions—so similar they must reflect the conversation in the studio that day—gloss over the hard work of the Omega goes almost without saying: Fry's other letters complain about managing the finances while Bell's note her and Grant's boredom producing repeated patterns.[62] This aspect of the Omega disappears, however, in its founding artists' perception of craft work as a return to a realm of instinctual pleasures, uninhibited by knowledge or shame. The ideals behind the production of Omega work animated its marketing as well. The Bells devised an advertising scheme to induce buyers into the Omega's spirit of uninhibited pleasure, self-consciously staged as a "Bohemian dinner" in Fry's honor, "given by all the grateful young artists":

> We should get all your disreputable and some of your aristocratic friends to come, and after dinner we should repair to Fitzroy Sq[uare], where would be seen decorated furniture, painted walls, etc. There we should all get drunk and dance and kiss. Orders would flow in and the aristocrats would feel sure they were really in the thick of things.[63]

Here associations of art and eroticism are self-consciously exploited to lure customers into the Omega, which they would experience as a modernist paradise that, in effect, projects its visitors into a realm of prelapsarian sensual pleasure.

The Omega's advocacy of a return to Eden may be clearest in the rhetoric of its critics, who condemned the workshops' aesthetic by invoking all the values conventionally found in the moral of the Fall. The injunction to useful toil underlies the *Observer*'s review of the workshops' opening in 1913, which complained that Omega furnishings were

> to be looked at, not to be used. Pink chairs are there to be pink and not to be sat upon; tables are heavily laden with formless wriggles of paint which disturb the

eye and serve no useful purpose; carpets and rugs cry out from the floor to rebuke the foot that would tread upon them.[64]

That such reactions should appear in conservative papers in Bloomsbury's barely post-Victorian era is, perhaps, less surprising than their perpetuation—and even exaggeration—at the end of the twentieth century. Exemplifying Fry's critique of a "stupidly serious" standard in domestic decoration, the *Financial Times* reviewed the Crafts Council's 1984 Omega exhibition by condemning the "deadly lack of seriousness" in the work, and arguing that any revival of interest was inappropriate to the eighties, "an era far more serious that has no time for such personal indulgence."[65] Other critics deployed the injunction to humility, chastizing the Omega artists who "failed to discipline their instinctive exuberance and act on the realization that their ideal of visual delight should be subtly expressed rather than brandished at the onlooker in such a relentless manner."[66] The *Studio International* managed to combine demands for form-follows-function usefulness with the imperative to sexual modesty by explaining that Omega design was "not conceived in terms of the surface to which it would be applied, but rather picked up at random and arbitrarily used. Such a degree of wilfulness reflects the selfish motivations that seem to have permeated the social and sexual life of the group."[67]

To be free of such standards was exactly Bloomsbury's goal. Art—especially decorative art—they conceived as a realm for the free play of the senses, uninhibited by utilitarian concerns or moralistic conventions. To this end, as letters between Bell and Fry show, Bloomsbury sought consciously to divorce the aesthetic logic of their designs from the purpose of the objects embellished. Contrasting some of her designs to Grant's "gay and lovely" work, Bell characterized hers as "rather dull and stupid" because "I am hampered by thinking how they really will look in life and how badly they'll make anything out of the way and how things will will have to be cut, so the result is very tame."[68] Critics at both ends of the twentieth century who sought a domestic aesthetic expressive of practicality and restraint were left bewildered or outraged by the Omega's claims to return both craftspeople and consumers to a primitive paradise of natural abundance and sensual pleasure. For the Omega artists, like the Pre-Raphaelites a generation before, the image of Eden symbolized this aspiration for aesthetic and social renewal enacted on and in the home. The Omega was Bloomsbury's attempt to expand its aesthetic beyond its own subcultural enclave, and, though its success in this respect was limited, in other ways the workshops were an unparalleled success. Describing the excitement of the Omega as "tremendously encouraging," Grant recalled it as "the best period of my life."[69] For Bloomsbury's artists, sustained immersion in the "free play" and "delight" of the "creation in the making of objects for common life," as the Omega catalog put it, profoundly influenced both their art and design, bringing them briefly, but truly, into the vanguard of European modernism, as the following chapter will show.

Abstraction and Design (1914–15)

In a lecture on abstract art written in the Twenties, Roger Fry cited the Omega as an example of abstract painting's influence on design. The Omega artists, he said, "tried to confine ourselves to the simplest forms, banishing for the time being the too long misused vegetable kingdom, or if we used plant forms choosing those of the simplest and most abstract kind, all based on proportion and relative qualities of masses of colour."[1] Though the Edenic iconography analyzed in the previous chapter reveals a certain selectivity in Fry's memory, it is, nevertheless, true that much Omega decoration relied for its effect on abstract compositions of line and color. Far from proving, as Fry claimed, that this work was inspired by easel painting, however, the influence seems to have flowed the other way. By working under the rubric of the decorative arts, the Bloomsbury artists were able to abandon conventions of figuration in easel painting. The abstract paintings that constitute the Bloomsbury painters' strongest claim for inclusion in mainstream histories of the avant-garde, therefore, may be seen as a direct result of their engagement with domesticity.

In some ways this is surprising. The formalist aesthetics developed by Roger Fry and Clive Bell have long been valued for their justification of abstract art. As was noted in the introduction, however, this implication was not a priority for Bloomsbury. As early as the second Post-Impressionist exhibition, reviewers perceived a gap between the group's aesthetic theory and its artistic practice. Rejecting Fry's defenses of Picasso's cubist abstraction, the *Pall-Mall Gazette*'s review of the show observed smugly, "The odd thing is that some of the painters like Mr. Roger Fry are not loyal to their own theories. Mr. Fry's contributions are all based most punctiliously on nature, and on rather unimaginative accumulations of descriptive facts."[2]

In fact, the ambivalence registered in Fry's paintings is clearly reflected in his writings. Fry's essays leading up to and including his defenses of the first Post-Impressionist exhibition assume figurative reference in painting, as distinguished from "abstract and meaningless" or "merely decorative" patterns.[3] Even in his catalog essay for the second Post-Impressionist show, Fry only proposed a theoretical justification for "the attempt to give up all resemblance to natural form." Picasso's actual explorations of this possibility, Fry concluded, "may or may not be successful. . . . It is too early to be dogmatic on the point, which can only be decided when our sensibilities to such abstract forms have been more practised than they are at present," and he turned with relief to Matisse, whose art, he noted, was marked by "no such extreme abstraction."[4] Not until 1913, when his enthusiasm was seized by three of Wassily Kandinsky's "fascinating experiments into a new world of expressive form," did Fry embrace abstraction. Comparing a Kandinsky landscape to two of his "pure improvisations," Fry reported that though "it is easier to find one's way about" in the first, the other two ultimately "seemed to me the most complete pictures in the exhibition. . . . They are pure visual music, but I cannot any longer doubt the possibility of emotional expression by such abstract visual signs."[5]

Fry's doubts about abstract art—doubts shared by Kandinsky's primary English patrons[6]—help explain why neither he nor his Bloomsbury colleagues investigated pure abstraction before 1913. Even after Fry's discovery of Kandinsky, Bloomsbury's painting continued to deploy color and line to inflect—but not to replace—depicted subjects in the way Fry described in his defenses of the first Post-Impressionist show back in 1910. This is true even of Grant, who among Bloomsbury's artists was most attracted to Kandinsky's abstract calligraphy. A number of Grant's still lifes of 1914–15 at first glance resemble Kandinsky's fanciful blending of representational and abstract forms. On closer inspection, however, the colorful swirls resolve into spatially coherent images. Many of these works depict bouquets of the artificial flowers made at the Omega from brightly colored fabrics trimmed with details in wool, picturing them against the multicolored walls Bloomsbury favored for its domestic interiors. Further allusion to the Omega is made in Grant's still life known as *On the Mantelpiece*, where an Omega box paint- ed with swimmers like those he painted on the shutters at 38 Brunswick Square appears among the patches of color, its brilliant hues and organic forms blending with the flowers (fig. 103).[7] What may look at first glance like pure abstractions, then, are revealed as depictions of the modernist garden-rooms of the Omega.

When, during the winter of 1913–14, Fry, Grant, and Bell became the first British artists to forego figuration in favor of purely abstract painting, they did not extrapolate from Kandinsky's free-flowing compositions, but turned instead to a more geometrical style. Lacking models among artists exhibiting in London, their impetus for geometrical abstraction was the methods and materials of design at the Omega, where the commercial production of rugs, fabrics, and inlaid furniture required designs to be worked out on gridded paper. Significantly, these products were the first to be decorated with abstract forms, in contrast to the figurative designs on Omega wares that were simply painted. Marquetry lent itself to the juxtaposition of flat, hard-edged shapes, while the rugs were designed by shading in squares of gridded paper to indicate the colors of the knots, both effects that characterize Bloomsbury's abstract paintings with their flat arrangements of colored shapes. An illustration of the Omega's commercially manufactured products from the 1914 catalog demonstrates the workshops' hard-edged abstraction, evident in the inlaid desk and tray, as well as in a rug (fig. 104). The tray, in particular, with its angled accents against a field of vertical rectangles, parallels the most distinctive features of Bloomsbury's abstract art.[7] Studies for these paintings blend with drawings for rugs, so that sketches that have been cataloged as designs for rugs can, in fact, be matched to passages in abstract paintings, suggesting how closely these two bodies of work were allied.[9]

Another route to Bloomsbury's style of abstraction also runs by way of the domestic. As early as Bell's 1912 pictures of artists working at Asheham (discussed in Chapter 6), domestic settings had been represented as rectilinear patches of flat color, an effect even more pronounced in Bell's *The Bedroom, Gordon Square*, also from this period, which shows a nude seated on the edge of the bed in an environment of geometrical forms (fig. 105). This painting has been sensitively analyzed on stylistic grounds as Bell's response to Sickert's well known images of female nudes backlit on beds in lonely rooms. Where Sickert emphasized the squalid urban settings he made the signifier of his anti-domestic modernism (discussed in Chapter 1)—in his "Camden Town Murder" series, these sites are explicitly linked to news accounts of violent rape—Bell's image proposes modernist domestic environments as a place for a woman alone and at ease with her own sexuality.[10]

In another of Bloomsbury's fascinating realizations of modernist aesthetics in their own dwelling spaces, Bell's rendering of the female figure with black outlines

103. Duncan Grant, *On the Mantelpiece, 46 Gordon Square*, 1914. Oil and collage on board, 45.5 × 39.2 cm. Tate Britain.

104. Omega furnishings, ceramics, and rug from Omega catalog, 1914.

105. Vanessa Bell, *The Bedroom, Gordon Square*, 1912. Oil on canvas, 56.3 × 46.2 cm. Art Gallery of South Australia, Adelaide.

106. Vanessa Bell, design for fireplace mural, 46 Gordon Square, 1912. Oil on paper, 76.2 × 55.9.

delineating the large shapes of the body and no detailing of the facial features relates this painting to decorations she was adding to the Gordon Square house at this era. The same kind of anonymous, solidly voluptuous women appeared over the fire-place in her studio (fig. 106), where one depicted figure sat casually on the mantel, her body related to the rectilinear forms of the fireplace in a pose that repeats that of the nude perched on the bed in *The Bedroom, Gordon Square*. Remarkable photographs of Bell posing nude with Molly MacCarthy in front of this mural, their upswept hair echoing that of the painted figures, assert an ambition to be at home the way the figures in modernist paintings inhabit their environments: sensuously, instinctively, free of conventional inhibitions, integrated harmoniously with settings perceived in terms of abstract color and form (fig. 107).

107. Photograph taken by Duncan Grant of Vanessa Bell and Molly MacCarthy in Bell's studio, 46 Gordon Square, 1913.

Bell's 1912 domestic images and decorations are closely linked to her portraits of women from her circle—Iris Tree, Mary Hutchinson, Bell herself—painted in 1915–16. These works are often grouped together because of the way Bell surrounds her sitters with rectilinear patterns evocative of her abstract compositions (fig. 108). Especially in two very similar portraits of Mary Hutchinson, the sitter blends coloristically with her environment, lending her flesh tones to the central ground but picking up accents for her green eyebrows and blue eyes from the rectangular elements at the edges (fig. 109). Recent commentary on these works has fallen back on conventional standards of realism in painting, beauty in women, and possessiveness in marriage to analyze Bell's portraits of Hutchinson as "unflattering" expressions of her jealousy toward the sitter, who was Clive Bell's paramour. But this misrepresents Bloomsbury's sexual mores in general, these two women's relationship in particular, and the links connecting these paintings to Bell's depictions of both Tree and her own visage.[11] In all of these works, the female figure is

108. Vanessa Bell, *Abstract*, 1915. Gouache and oil on canvas, 44.2 × 38.8 cm. Tate Britain.

109. Vanessa Bell, *Portrait of Mary Hutchinson*, 1915. Oil on board, 73.7 × 57.8 cm. Tate Britain.

visually unified with the modernist environment represented as an abstract background. Although in some cases, Grant's simultaneous renditions of same sitter and setting reveal certain elements of the background to be parts of an Omega-style décor, Bell's flatter compositions resist such realistic readings.[12] Forsaking specific settings, Bell proposes modernism itself as a congenial environment for modern women. Her works are not so much illustrations as equivalents to Omega rooms in their effect of giving visual form to the desire to create environments where life—and especially women's life—can be lived in a modern way.[13]

If Omega design informed the compositional structure and ideological significance of Bloomsbury's abstract paintings, a third connection was forged in the realm of technique. Marbling and collage were common in Omega designs, for which the artists often attached scraps of colored paper to indicate areas of color, or simply pasted over unsatisfactory parts of designs in order to rework them without having to redraw the whole piece. This collaged look became an aesthetic in itself as the Omega evolved a style of installing hand-painted wallpapers in rectilinear configurations similar to Bloomsbury's abstract art. By 1917, Fry described for *Colour* magazine, which illustrated an Omega interior, how the artists mottled sheets of wallpaper—some in dark blue, others dark red—to create giant collages of rectangular forms (fig. 110). Their visual suggestion of a series of large paintings was enhanced by framing sections of the blue and red wall with papers hand-painted in a yellow tone and block-printed in rough evocation of wood grain (this technique is discussed further in Chapter 11). Though these collaged mural decorations echoed the look of paintings, the first use of collage in Bloomsbury's art followed Bell's use of paper cut-outs for the nursery she installed at the Omega in December of 1913 (discussed in the previous two chapters; see fig. 74). This display recreated the effect of a nursery Bell had decorated for her own children at 46 Gordon Square earlier that summer, but her references to "painting" that jungle scene, which would accord with other decorations for Gordon Square planned or executed around this time, suggest that it was not a collage.[14] The translation of this painted motif to collage—perhaps initially conceived as a time-saving strategy—seems to have provoked Bell's experiments with collage in her abstract art. In one early piece—it is tempting to imagine it leading to the others—black vertical elements reach up to a dark green canopy against a light green ground punctuated with a grey and a blue square in a composition that seems to recall the trees, lake, and, perhaps, the elephant of the Omega nursery (fig. 111).[15]

110. Roger Fry or Nina Hamnett, illustration of an Omega interior for *Colour*, April 1917. Original in oil on card, 46.9 × 30.8 cm. Courtauld Institute Galleries.

111. Vanessa Bell, *Composition*, c.1914. Oil and gouache on collaged paper, 55.1 × 43.7 cm. Museum of Modern Art, New York.

Whatever the details of the reciprocal relationship between Omega design and Bloomsbury's abstraction, Bell and her colleagues were encouraged in their exploration of collage by Picasso's example. Fry had returned from Paris in October of 1913 with the collage-inspired *Tête d'homme* (see Chapter 7, fig. 82), and the following February Grant befriended Picasso at Gertrude Stein's parties by giving him rolls of old wallpaper from his Paris hotel room to use for collage.[16] Fry's collages respond most directly to Picasso's precedent. His *Essay in Abstract Design* (fig. 112), centered on two bus tickets from the route to the pottery where the Omega ceramics were made, mirrors the composition of *Tête d'homme*, with its central angled elements imposed over a vertical structure.[17] This connection was noted derisively by Sickert, who found it "surprising that a painter who has the double advantage of power and erudition should continue to treat seriously *fumisteries à la Picasso* (framed posies of tram tickets, etc.)."[17]

As Sickert's parenthesis implies, Fry's abstraction remained suggestive of conventional genres of easel painting—in this case, the floral still life before a curtained backdrop—in a way the art of his Bloomsbury colleagues did not. This is true also of Fry's only other extant abstract work, in which forms typical of Bell's and Grant's much flatter compositions (her big squares and dark verticals, his "L" shapes) float in a deep three-dimensional environment, superimposed over dun-colored converging triangles and trapezoids and a light blue arch that, if they do not actually depict a road leading through a gateway, at least imply the one-point perspective structure he favored in landscape painting (fig. 113).[19]

If Fry remained more grounded in figurative conventions than his Bloomsbury colleagues, Grant went furthest in exploring abstraction's potential. Most innovative is his *Abstract Kinetic Collage Painting with Sound*, created in the late summer of 1914 (fig. 114). This fifteen-foot scroll displays a sequence of seventeen compositions, each based on the same orange, blue-grey, and green rectangles, which gradually evolve from painted forms to collage (or vice versa) against a marbled ground. Intended to be seen as it scrolled vertically through an illuminated box to musical accompaniment, Grant's piece takes its place with the most experimental work of continental artists at this period.[20] Comparisons are most direct with Guillaume Apollinaire's circle in Paris, which was fascinated by efforts to achieve a visual form of music. One of Grant's sketches for part of the scroll is actually on an issue of Apollinaire's journal *Les Soirées de Paris* that includes an essay by Gabrielle Buffet promoting the projection of literary texts on to a screen with musical accompaniment.[21] Grant much later denied any knowledge of French precedent, however, and analogies between painting and music could be found closer to hand, from Walter Pater's famous dictum that "all art constantly aspires towards the condition of music" to Fry's defenses of Post-Impressionism.[22] If Grant's interest in visual expressions of music had British origins, the scale of his scroll also relates it to Bloomsbury's emphasis on domestic design. The marbled background of the scroll compares quite directly to Grant's recent treatment of the dado in the Omega room painted with over-scale fruit and flowers (discussed in Chapter 8, see fig. 97).[23]

112. Roger Fry, *Essay in Abstract Design*, 1915, oil and collaged bus tickets, Tate Britain.

113. Roger Fry, study for abstract painting, 1914–15, oil and pencil on board, 25 × 36.2 cm, Courtauld Institute Galleries.

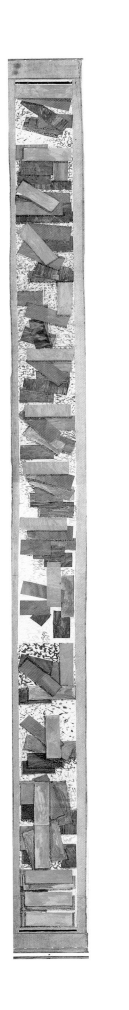

Although the form-flattening "marbling" of Grant's paintings at this period is usually connected to the semi-pointillist style of work like the *Queen of Sheba* panel (discussed in Chapter 5; fig. 44), his early Omega designs offer a far more direct source, suggesting how important his experience as a designer of domestic objects was to his style as a painter. Grant invented the distinctive version of modernist marbling that characterized the Omega's early hand-painted furnishings. These free-form squiggles eschew serious claims to the illusion of either marble or so-called marbled papers, relying for their effect on the calligraphic energy of the line. At the same time, Grant began collaging bits of marbled paper into both his figurative and his abstract paintings. An irregular lozenge of marbled paper floats in the center of *On the Mantelpiece* (fig. 103), for example, drawing attention to other areas of painted mottling and stressing the swirling surface textures of this illusionistic scene. A very different effect is created by the neat rectangle of dark marbled paper in an untitled abstraction (fig. 115) that follows the basic color scheme of the *Abstract Kinetic Collage*. Here, the marbled rectangle offers a tidy contrast to the hand-mottled, irregularly cut patches of painted paper in the surrounding collage. An adjacent piece of commercially printed material displays a pattern that reflects the formal tensions of the piece as a whole: dark vertical and horizontal patches over irregular squiggles of orange on a yellow ground that evoke the effect of marbling. What seems explicitly at issue in this work is the relationship among these different forms of surface patterning, some the direct result of the painter's mark, those of the marbled paper indexing a craft that mixes handwork with the randomness of the water carrying the ink, those of the commercial fabric alluding to these effects through a totally mechanized repetition of random-looking lines. The only relief within the patchwork of horizontals and verticals in this abstract painting is the triangular form that dominates the upper left of the canvas, its striped edge competing with the lines on the printed sheet to create the primary point of visual drama in the composition. The same shape dominates many of Grant's abstractions from this period, including the one he titled *In Memoriam: Rupert Brooke* (fig. 116).[24] It may be too easy to see the themes of this section neatly embodied in the way a house-shape dominates these abstractions, their domestic origins in Omega decorations marked by this ghostly isotype. A more complicated visual case can be made for the connection between domestic imagery and abstraction by comparing *In Memoriam* with a pair of images—one a collage and the other a painting of the same scene—which were completed just a few months before and took as their subject Bloomsbury's domestic headquarters at 46 Gordon Square (figs. 117 and 118).

If Bell's decorations at Gordon Square made the house a walk-in Post-Impressionist painting, Grant's depictions of this environment seem to assert the power of modernism to render inhabitable space as flat abstraction. What is barely recognizable as a view through a doorway into a room stacked with canvases creates the same structure of rectilinear forms framed within vertical borders that characterizes Bloomsbury's abstractions generally and *In Memoriam* in particular. A cushion on the couch and what appear to be shadows provide the analogous—though somewhat weaker—diagonal accents. Even the palette is the same: red and brown rectangles perched on a foundation of black and gray, accented with smaller blue and green patches, as if *In Memoriam* set out to push the domestic depiction in *Interior at Gordon Square* into pure abstraction.

The ideals that drove Bloomsbury to evolve this abstract style of painting may be clearest in *In Memoriam*, which, as its title implies, was a memorial, to the poet Rupert Brooke, who died in military service in April 1915.[25] Grant's title proposes his work as neither a purely aesthetic escape from social issues nor—as in the visually similar paintings by his Continental contemporary Frantisek Kupka—an expression of metaphysical theory.[26] Instead, *In Memoriam* is proposed as a modern alternative to conventional memorials, and, in this sense, might be seen as part of Bloomsbury's project to visualize new art for new social forms. Grant's modern commemoration contrasts radically with the widespread eulogizing of Brooke as a symbol of British patriotism. For Bloomsbury, this nationalistic beatification of Brooke was an infuriating instance of the dominant culture's corruption of a promising modernist, who before the war had moved on Bloomsbury's periphery (Brooke

Facing page:
114. Duncan Grant, *Abstract Kinetic Collage Painting with Sound*, 1914. Gouache, watercolor, and collage on paper, 27.9 × 450.2 cm. Complete work and detail. Tate Britain.

Abstraction and Design

115. Duncan Grant, *Abstract*, 1914–15. Paint, fabric and collaged paper on board, 63 × 45 cm. Hoffmann Collection, Berlin.

116. Duncan Grant, *In Memoriam: Rupert Brooke*, 1915. Oil and collaged paper on panel, 55 × 30.5 cm. Yale Center for British Art.

attended school with Grant, visited Strachey and Keynes, and wrote a thoughtful review of the second Post-Impressionist exhibition). Beautiful and charismatic, Brooke had been the center of his own avant-garde circle, which Virginia Woolf christened the "Neo-Pagans" in an allusion to what seemed their happiness in nature—this was manifest primarily in the co-ed camping trips and swimming parties that seemed very adventurous to the somewhat older members of Bloomsbury. One of Vanessa Bell's painted Omega screens—a Matissian composition of languorous nudes among triangular forms suggesting tents—was inspired by her experience of a Neo-Pagan camping expedition (during which she arranged to sleep at a nearby farmhouse) (fig. 119). Bell wrote to her sister about "the great fun in the camp," and said of the Neo-Pagans: "They are very young and crude, but also very nice. . . . and I found it possible to adopt a pleasant grandmotherly attitude toward them. . . . I lectured them on life and morals, and I only hope it did them good," she went on, concluding, "Well, it is interesting to see what the new generation is like."[27] This sense of avant-garde allegiance made Bloomsbury all the more dismayed when, as soon as war was declared in 1914, Brooke threw himself and his poetry behind what Bloomsbury saw as a pointlessly destructive performance of competing national hubris inimical to the values of both art and life. While Bloomsbury organized, in the face of popular opinion, against the war (as discussed in Chapter 10), Brooke rocketed to fame with his poem *The Soldier*, the opening lines (at least) of which were reprinted in papers and repeated in pulpits throughout England:

> If I should die, think only this of me:
>> That there's some corner of a foreign field
> That is forever England.

The fact that Brooke, like so many others, was not killed in battle but died from inadequate medical attention—in his case, horrifically enough, to infected insect bites—did not dim the patriotic fervor of the mourners.

Bloomsbury's attitude toward the eulogizing of Brooke may be gauged from Virginia Woolf's reaction to the authorized edition of his poems published with a memoir of the poet by Edward Marsh in 1918. "One of the most repulsive biographies I have ever read," she wrote to a friend who had been close to Brooke.[27] In her published review, Woolf argues that the memoir was an older man's fantasy projected onto a young poet. To make her case, she quotes a passage in which Marsh invoked a monument of conventional art—Benozzo Gozzoli's chapel frescoes at the Medici palace—to describe Brooke's "radiant youthful figure in gold and vivid red and blue, like a page in the Riccardi chapel." In contrast, Woolf imagined what she called a "contemporary version" of Brooke's biography: "There would have been less of the vivid red and blue and gold, more that was mixed, parti-coloured, and matter for serious debate"; she might here be describing *In Memoriam*. Woolf's verbal rendition of her memorial begins from the assertion that her memories were "very little related to the Rupert Brooke of legend" and concludes by declaring that, had he lived, Brooke would "have framed a speech that came very close to the

117. Duncan Grant, *Interior at 46 Gordon Square*, 1914–15. Oil on panel, 40 × 32.1 cm. Tate Britain.

118. Duncan Grant, *Interior at 46 Gordon Square*, 1914–15. Collaged paper on board, 60 × 72 cm. Private collection.

119. Vanessa Bell, *Tents*, 1913. Pencil and gouache on paper mounted on canvas as four-panel screen, 178 × 208 cm. Victoria and Albert Museum.

modern point of view . . . , full of intellect, and full of his keen unsentimental curiosity." In between, Woolf says that Brooke was "consciously and defiantly pagan" and "as well versed in the complications of social questions as in the obscurities of the poetry of Donne," quoting with approval one of the female Neo-Pagans: "I can't imagine him using a word of that emotional jargon in which people usually talk or write of poetry. He made it feel more like carpentering."[29] Woolf's essay strives to replace the clergymen's and politicians' Brooke "of legend" with a poet claimed, instead, for a modernist sensibility at odds with conventional expectations for art and concerned with the social world. In the end, Woolf seizes upon the metaphor of the poet as carpenter—again, the connection of art-making with house-building—to describe her ideal.

In Memoriam is Grant's attempt to rescue Brooke's memory from the grand—and grandly self-serving—representations of the establishment. At just twenty-two inches high, the painting's scale suggests a private, not public, memorial, and Grant kept this work in his studio for the rest of his life. By dedicating to Brooke a geometrical abstraction structured around the black scaffolding that is at once house-like and evocative of classical Greek funeral monuments appropriate to a "pagan" who died in the Eastern Mediterranean, Grant, like Woolf, claims the poet for a modernist avant-garde opposed to the religious and patriotic pieties asserted in monuments like the Riccardi frescoes and their conventional derivatives.[30] The single collaged element in Grant's abstraction—a piece of reflective foil from a cigarette pack liner attached at the foundation of the house-like structure—echoes Bell's paintings that situate a female figure or domestic object in environments hovering between abstract compositions and depictions of interior space. If Bell's paintings assert modernism's potential to create new and congenial settings for modern ways of life, the absent, reflective center of *In Memoriam* documents the absence of a figure who once was part of this world. The collaged foil also finds an echo in Woolf's essay, which concludes with the words, "One turns from the thought of him not with a sense of completeness and finality, but rather to wonder and to question still: what would he have been, what would he have done?" A visual equivalent to this intrusion of uncertainty in the way it invites interpretation, the foil has been described as "a source of continual reflected light, almost like a votive candle, within the picture itself."[31] It might equally well be seen as a mirror (symbol of vanity or hubris), or as a reflecting pool (allusion to Narcissus), all readings appropriate to an elegy over the pointless demise of a beautiful, over-confident young man. The ultimate effect of the reflective foil, however, is to propel the painting out of the realm of such symbolism and into the realm of realities like cigarette packs. The reflective foil offered the viewer, instead of a symbol, a distorted image of one's own face, peering anxiously, unable to find definitive meaning, unable to answer Woolf's question, "what would he have been, what would he have done?"

These are questions that, as the war wore on, Bloomsbury was forced to ask about more and more individual modernists, and ultimately about the course of modernism as a whole. By the summer of 1915, the two continental artists who worked for the Omega, Doucet and Gaudier-Brzeska, had been repatriated and killed in action.[32] The diminished Omega staff shifted its focus away from furniture and interiors to concentrate instead, Fry reported to his mother, on "hats and dresses now as being things which people must have *quand même* tho' I confess I am surprised that people are still willing to spend money on things which one can't call necessaries, tho' I'm glad enough for the sake of those who depend on the Omega."[33] It was also at this period that Fry turned the Omega to the production of books—choosing texts that dealt with war and death—and pottery, which, like clothes, were inexpensive and portable, and, thus, better suited to the war-time market. Fry also attempted to apply the lessons of Omega production to assist the war's victims. Travelling in April to France, where his sister Margery was heading a Quaker delegation, Fry brought with him a selection of brightly colored wools and reproductions of Byzantine mosaics to engage refugees in the therapeutic production of modernist crafts. The resulting disjunction of means and ends led Fry to conclude, "I'm no good at philanthropy, it demoralizes me completely."[34]

Back in London, where the Omega showrooms were threatened by air raids, the war found its way into what had been a more idyllic iconography. In November 1915, the workshops contributed to an exhibition of dolls at the Grafton Gallery, sending hand-carved caricatures of the leaders on all sides of the conflict. Similar images turned up in Bloomsbury's art, with Fry turning his collage technique to depictions of the British bulldog, Queen Victoria, and a mural-scale rendition of the Kaiser with two military officers (fig. 120). Like the dolls, Fry's collages cast an irreverent eye on these leaders. The newspaper photograph from which Fry copied the Germans obscured their feet and he displayed the resulting image with a

120. Roger Fry, *German General Staff*, 1915. Oil and collaged paper, current location unknown.

quotation from Nietzsche: "I cannot tolerate the neighbourhood of this race . . . which has no sense of its feet and doesn't even know how to walk. . . . All things considered, the Germans have not got feet at all, they have only legs."[35] Bloomsbury's attitude toward nationalist icons may be judged from Vanessa Bell's tone when she reported to Fry, "I am imitating you and copying a photograph of Queen Victoria. It's too amazing—she's just the sort of middle class woman I am always wanting to paint entirely dressed in furniture ornaments."[36]

For Bloomsbury, as for other avant-garde groups in Britain and on the Continent, the press of current events overwhelmed the impulse to abstraction. The conservative nationalism of war-time politics rapidly infected discourses on aesthetics in London, as throughout Europe, as critics and patrons linked conventional modes of representation to the integrity of national tradition and condemned abstraction as a foreign influence.[37] Having already allied itself with foreign movements and courted the opprobrium of London critics, Bloomsbury was less affected by this trend than some avant-garde contingents, but other effects of the war were more debilitating. On a basic level, there was less time for art making. Duncan Grant reported, a year into the war, on the group's work for anti-conscription organizations, "It is very unusual to see Bloomsbury at work in an office. . . . Bob Trevi, Vanessa, I and Norton sit in a row doing innumerable jobs from morning to night and sticking on stamps when all else fails."[37] The economic and social upheavals of the war also destroyed the infrastructure of inter-related dwellings that had sustained Bloomsbury's collaboration. Just a few weeks into the war, the fantastically decorated Brunswick Square house was let go. The married couples established more conventional households; Keynes moved to his own flat, where Bell found him disconsolate and lonely; and Grant retreated to a room at 46 Gordon Square, though that house, too, became too expensive to support and the Bells began casting about for tenants.[39] Grant reported glumly after a short trip back to London from the country in May 1915, "there is nowhere now for everyone to meet so I saw no one much."[40]

The results of this upheaval for Bloomsbury's domestic aesthetic are taken up in the following section. Here, it is enough to focus on the implications of the war for the painters' attitudes toward abstraction. Like others in the avant-garde, the Bloomsbury artists reacted to the war by falling back on earlier styles, though unlike those who promoted this shift as a return to national traditions, Bloomsbury saw its retreat as recouping personal identities forged in peacetime. An exchange of letters between Fry and Bell in 1916 shows them both channeling their frustration—Fry's anger at Bell for abandoning London, the Omega, and him; Bell's anxiety to keep Fry as a friend—into claims to have abandoned experimental styles to retrieve older identities. "I'm at last throwing off the impressionism you infected me with and I'm getting back to a sort of idea of construction I've always had when I've been myself," Fry begins.[41] "I'm very glad you're beginning to get back to your own ideas more," Bell responded; "that still life of yours did seem to me more definitely your own than most of the things you had done a little time ago. . . . owing to you I have been trying to paint much more solidly."[42] A year later, Fry reported to her on a still life that turned out "fearfully exact and literal though it began by a quite abstract scheme. . . . I think it has design although it could be accepted from the point of view of literal representation."[43] By 1919, the rejection was complete, and Fry wrote to Bell, "The only picture of yours that has gone thin on my hands is the big abstract business which I have in my studio and which doesn't mean anything to me now. All the rest have got better and better."[44] About this time, Fry destroyed his own abstract works that remained in his possession.

Even Grant's more concerted explorations of abstraction ended abruptly at this time. Grant later said he gave up abstraction because "no one was very interested."[45] Although commentators have seized on this as an example of the Bloomsbury artists' supposedly debilitating over-reliance on one another, it was not just Grant's nearest colleagues who were unsupportive.[46] Reviewers were unanimously dismissive when he showed his abstract collages in the 1915 Vorticist exhibition, characterizing them as *"fumisterie"*—not just a joke, but a foreign joke.[47] The

On to Omega

most extensive record of critical disapproval, however, concerns a visit to Grant's studio by E. M. Forster and D. H. Lawrence. After examining his recent paintings and the *Abstract Kinetic Scroll*, Forster remained silent while Lawrence expounded on the worthlessness of his work. "It was not simply that the pictures themselves were bad—hopelessly bad—but they were worthless because Duncan was full of the wrong ideas. He . . . would have to learn to approach his subjects in a completely different frame of mind if he ever wanted to become an artist." Grant offered no defense, but "sat with his hands on his knees, rocking himself gently in his chair," according to one witness.[47] Writing later to Ottoline Morrell, Lawrence reiterated his advice, urging her to "tell him not to make silly experiments in the futuristic line with bits of colour on moving paper."[49]

Grant's abandonment of abstraction may be most dramatically demonstrated in a painting known as *The White Jug*, which began as an abstraction in 1915 (fig. 121). When he reworked the painting in 1918, however, Grant reduced the free-floating rectilinear planes to a small-scale patterned background by imposing over them two still-life elements, a white vase and a lemon. This kind of white vase, significantly, came around 1918 to serve as a signature for Grant (as discussed in Chapter 13). His choice of the lemon has been analyzed as an echo of Picasso's 1907 *Pots et Citron* (fig. 77), an important work in that artist's breakthrough to abstraction and a painting that was iconic for Bloomsbury, for it was owned by the Bells and reproduced to illustrate the culmination of the progression toward "significant form" in Clive Bell's *Art*.[50] The two symbols together, therefore, make *The White Jug* a kind of manifesto for the end of abstraction, not only literally obscuring an abstract composition behind representational elements that supplant its status as abstract, but identifying Grant with a reversal of the avant-garde's evolution away from mimesis by returning to a moment in cubism when figuration was still at issue.

What came to an end when the Bloomsbury artists abandoned their experiments with abstraction was not simply a particular form of the group's visual practice. Bloomsbury's abstract painting had embodied the artists' coherence as an avant-garde alliance united by its efforts to develop new forms of art based on the design and decoration of modernist furnishings. The war brought an end to that coherence, scattering Bloomsbury's members from the neighborhood whose name they had taken as their own, absorbing their attention with more immediate struggles, and dashing their aspirations for the modern age. The war did not end Bloomsbury's production of art and domestic design—far from it—and the following section takes up the changes in their practice. But Bloomsbury's ambition to lead British households in an enthusiastic embrace of modernism, which characterized the first years of the Omega, was among the casualties of World War I.

121. Duncan Grant, *The White Jug*, 1914–15, reworked 1917–18. Oil on panel, 103.5 × 42 cm. Southampton City Art Gallery.

An Aesthetic of Conscientious Objection
Bloomsbury's Wartime Environments

> That a break must be made in every life when August 1914 is reached seems
> inevitable.
>
> Virginia Woolf, *Roger Fry*

Bloomsbury's members were united in the conviction that the First World War
marked a terrible turning-point in modern history.[1] Leonard Woolf, after he
lived through World War II as a Jew under the threat of Nazi occupation of
England, and endured his wife's suicide during that time, nevertheless asserted
without qualification, "The four years of the 1914 war were the most horrible
period of my life."[2] For her part, Virginia Woolf, in one of her last essays, argued
that writers who matured before 1914 differed fundamentally from their more anxious followers.[3] Concurring with her sister, Vanessa Bell described how before the
war, "a great new freedom seemed about to come and perhaps would have come, if it
had not been for motives and ambitions of which we knew nothing. But surely such
awareness can never come again and it is difficult to explain it to those who cannot
hope to feel it." Because of the war, Bell explained:

> The excitement and the joy had gone. The hostility of the general public was real
> now, no longer a ridiculous and even stimulating joke. . . . All the world was hos-
> tile close round one [*sic*] and Bloomsbury had no changing atmosphere in which
> to move and expand and grow.

After the Armistice, Bell said, she realized that "nothing happens twice and
Bloomsbury had had its day."[4]

Despite Bell's reiterated assertions that Bloomsbury fell victim to the war, the
group sustained itself long after 1918, and many of its best known products—most
of Virginia Woolf's writings, in particular—were produced during the 1920s and
1930s. Nevertheless, Bell was not wrong. World War I left Bloomsbury fundamentally changed, ending an era of what Clive Bell called "Utopia-building" among the
group's artists and art critics, whose optimistic sense of public mission turned into
an embattled determination to protect—again quoting Clive Bell—"our little patch
of civility" against forces of violence and intolerance.[5] In her biography of Fry,
Woolf described him as "oppressed by the conviction that art after the war must be
esoteric and hidden like science in the middle ages: 'we can have no public art, only
private ones, like writing and painting, and even painting is almost too public,' he
wrote."[6]

For Fry, the discouraging political situation, to which he responded with imagination and energy, coincided with more personal disappointments less susceptible
to his ingenuity. A few days into the war, he wrote about the Omega, "I cannot dismiss all those who subsist by it just now (they would be destitute owing to the general crisis). So I shall try to carry on for a few months in the hope of a rapid end to
the war." He admitted, however, "It is over with all our ideas and all the really

Facing page:
Detail of fig. 146.

important things for many years."[7] Overcoming this initial bout of pessimism, however, Fry expanded the Omega's activities in response to the war, instituting a series of concerts, readings, and puppet performances, which employed Belgian refugees as musicians and raised funds to help those displaced by the fighting. Accounts of these performances vary, but letters and memoirs refer to an erotic dance between a nymph and satyr—echoes of the Ballets Russes's *Aprés-midi d'un faune*—set to what was apparently the first orchestrated performance of Claude Debussy's *Boîte à joujoux* and to a staging of the preface to G. L. Dickinson's pacifist verse play, *War and Peace*.[8] Justifying the Omega's simultaneous foray into book production in 1915, Fry acknowledged, "It seems an odd time to do this sort of thing, but I think it is as necessary as ever to keep certain things going."[9]

As the war wore on, however, Fry worked more and more without his Bloomsbury colleagues. Vanessa Bell's recollection that the Omega "struggle[d] on only for another year or so" after the start of the war reflects her own participation. In fact, the Omega outlasted the war, finally closing in July 1919, but by then it was a different institution.[10] By 1915, the war had driven Vanessa Bell and Duncan Grant—two of the Omega's three co-directors—from London, where, Bell complained, everyone seemed "rather wretched," leading her to "feel more than ever how nice it would be to live in the country."[11] During this period, Bell also drew away from Fry emotionally as she fell more deeply in love with Grant. By 1916, when Grant took up farmwork to avoid conscription into the military, Bell's primary allegiance was to him. Their abandonment of the Omega meant for Fry, not only the loss of his professional collaborators, but the estrangement of the woman who had been his lover and a man he had counted as a close friend.

Although Bell continued to supervise the dressmaking at the Omega, the absence of its founding members allowed new personalities to shape the workshops' aesthetic. Winifred Gill, a daughter of Fry's Guildford neighbors, took over the workshops' daily management, while Bell and Grant were to some extent replaced by the artists Nina Hamnett and her husband, Edgar de Bergen (who adopted the name Roald Kristian to evade anti-German harassment), both recent refugees from Paris. Hamnett, by her own account, was "never very good at decorative work," but found motivation in the small income the Omega offered: "I made two or three pounds a week and felt like a millionaire." Her work seems to have consisted primarily of dying batiks and painting candlesticks.[12] De Bergen's more substantial contributions—before he was arrested and deported as an enemy alien—included both puppets for the fund-raising concerts and woodcuts for the Omega's first two books: witty illustrations for the satirical poem *Simpson's Choice* and abstract designs for the more serious war poem *Men of Europe*. Another artist who joined the Omega at this period was Dolores "Moucha" Courtney, a friend of Hamnett's who had also been repatriated from Paris, where she had been studying painting. Although they could not completely replace Grant and Bell in either the Omega's work or Fry's affections, these three refugees, who were compatible enough to exhibit together under the rubric of the Independent Artists, offered him another community of francophiles with whom he could "talk art" in London and on weekend trips to Durbins.[13]

Fry turned to this trio when, in the spring of 1916, Grant and Bell could not help with a major decorative commission for the art dealer Arthur Ruck's new quarters on Berkeley Street. Rather than creating a fantastical garden or an "interior with figures," as Vanessa Bell proposed before bowing out of the project, the new Omega artists turned Ruck's room into an urban exterior (fig. 122).[14] De Bergen and Hamnett's murals were destroyed without visual record, but are recalled as representing industrial scenes in dark shades of brown.[15] Fry's and Courtney's murals, which were illustrated in *Colour* magazine, presented a high-keyed, angular composition in which fashionable ladies—not unlike the flattened figures in de Bergen's *Simpson's Choice* woodcuts (fig. 123)—jostle along sidewalks, through parks, and up the stairs of a Tube stop.[16] To go with the murals, Fry designed a rug in matching tones of orange and yellow, and an inlaid table with "a design of a dog which turned out to be another kind of dog when you turned it upside down, the tail being the

Facing page:
122. Roger Fry and Dolores Courtney, murals for Arthur Ruck, 4 Berkeley Street, London, destroyed, as illustrated in *Colour*, June 1916.

An Aesthetic of Conscientious Objection

123. Edgar de Bergen, illustration from Omega Workshops, *Simpson's Choice*, 1915. Woodcut, 17.8 × 15.2.

head, both equally realistic."[17] The ceiling was described by one journal as "like a rainbow chopped in many pieces."[18] This project's crisp countours and witty urbanity contrasts sharply with the Edenic iconography of earlier Omega interiors.

Although the Ruck murals broke with both the styles and themes of pre-war Omega design, Fry seems to have adapted easily to his new collaborators' aesthetic. His openness resulted at least in part from relief at finding artists willing to help him execute such a large commission in a relatively unified style, but his enthusiasm may also be a response to Bell's anti-urbanism. "I feel such a savage here," Bell wrote from the country; "In fact I believe I am getting quite unfitted for town life."[19] Fry, smarting over his abandonment, responded, "It's all very well for you and D[uncan] to talk of how good the country is. Of course if one's got the only happiness in life one likes to go off with it into the country like a dog with his bone to the kitchen garden, but if you've missed it you must come to town to cheat and stifle your hunger."[20] Their differences played out in arguments over the Omega, as Fry complained about Bell's absence from directorial meetings and she responded by advising him to close the workshops.[21] A year later, antagonism continued to fester, with Fry protesting, "Please don't say you couldn't work at Berkeley St. I was most anxious you should only you seemed at that moment to wish to underline the differences in our points of view."[22]

By the time of this exchange in 1917, Bell and Grant had settled at Charleston, the farmhouse that would remain their home for the rest of their lives. The celebrated look of this house—now preserved as a museum—evolved from their decoration of a number of other country houses where Bell and Grant in 1915 and 1916 sought, at first, simply to escape the conditions of wartime London, and then to avoid Grant's imprisonment under the terms of the military conscription act. Those houses and related commissions are the subject of this section, which analyzes the striking shifts in Bloomsbury's domestic aesthetic at this time as expressions of the artists' efforts to re-ground modernism in principled opposition to the values that had destroyed the avant-garde they had hitherto imagined themselves to be leading.

An Aesthetic of Conscientious Objection

Outposts of Peace
Eleanor and Wissett (1915–16)

Peace at Once, Clive Bell's 1915 booklet urging Britain's military withdrawal from the conflict in Europe, described the consequences of the war this way:

> Life will be harder and more joyless. There will be less money to buy food and drink for the ordinary man and woman, less to buy milk for babies and warm clothes for children, less for scientific experiments and social improvements, less for pleasure, less for leisure. Life will become less amusing and less healthy, old age more cheerless, death more masterful. Worst of all there will be less hope.[1]

Vanessa Bell endorsed her husband's manifesto, but doubted its efficacy, telling him, "I'm glad your pamphlet will be published, but evidently the whole world is so mad that no one will take it seriously."[2] As it turned out, even this bitter prediction was optimistic, for the authorities confiscated and destroyed the print run of *Peace at Once*.[3] Though Bloomsbury's public challenge to militarism was squelched, however, the group's private actions more effectively mitigated the effects of war that *Peace at Once* described. Vanessa Bell coordinated this initiative, implementing on a domestic scale her husband's exhortation to retreat from violence that destroyed what it claimed to protect. Remaking her domestic life outside London, Bell established rural outposts where Bloomsbury could protect its values and preserve its hope.

This episode in Bloomsbury's history is often misunderstood. Gender stereotypes underlie common assumptions that Vanessa Bell followed the initiative of Bloomsbury's men who worked to promote pacifist public policy and avoid conscription. Bell's correspondence, however, reveals her agency in turning Bloomsbury against the war. From the day war was declared, Bell's letters repeatedly articulate her anger, not just at the masses who "seem to be so hopelessly stupid and ignorant—even more than I am—that it's most depressing," but also at those in the middle class who "have so little imagination that they simply can't understand what it would all mean."[4] Bell's alienation increased as she recognized that "terrific pressure is being put on everyone to enlist" and that many erstwhile friends supported the war; "I see more and more that we are completely isolated from our kind," she concluded.[5] Bell found even her brother Adrian "half thinks of volunteering. I told him I thought it was very foolish." Bell's role in turning Bloomsbury's men against the war is equally evident in another letter, which reports, "Duncan is afraid of being made to [enlist] by moral pressure" from his family, but "I think it's most necessary to make some sort of stand against this idea of a huge army being sent abroad."[6]

124. Vanessa Bell, *Triple Alliance*, 1914. Oil, pastel, collaged paper on board, 81.9 × 60.3 cm. University of Leeds Art Collection.

From the first, Bell's opposition to the war abroad was matched by a determination to resist its effects at home. Just days after the declaration of hostilities she wrote to Fry, "One can do no good by thinking of the horrors going on and, though you know I don't ignore them, it seems to me now the only thing we can do is to go on keeping some kind of decent existence going."[7] A few weeks later, she despaired: "One thinks that even the sort of thing one vaguely hoped for the children may be spoilt. However it's no good—one must simply work and try to find what is permanent."[8] Bell's determination to resist the climate of violent militarism eventually found form in the rural houses discussed in this and the following chapter. An earlier expression of her beliefs has been recognized in a collage known by the title *Triple Alliance* (fig. 124), which was created at Asheham at this period.[9] The only work in Bell's large oeuvre to comment, even tangentially, on political events, its background is a collage of newspaper clippings, one dated 1 September 1914. These include maps and articles about the war, but all are cut to prevent coherent reading

An Aesthetic of Conscientious Objection

and obscured behind a pale gauze of paint-strokes and the central image of lamp, siphon, and bottle—three objects in alliance—collaged from cancelled cheques and old tickets. The effect is to subordinate news of war to an image of domestic comfort, "as though," one recent historian aptly says, Bell "determined to preserve her life as a painter at a time when everything was under threat."[10]

Despite her efforts, by the spring of 1915, Bell found her London life irreparably disrupted. She observed:

> Everyone is now in such a state of depression that nothing seems to make much difference. I have never known anything like the state of general gloom. The war seems to have destroyed the social world as we knew it and no one can now lead their normal lives. . . . How damnable it is that people with ideas utterly different from one's own should have so much power over one's life.[11]

As it became clear that the war would not end quickly, Bell translated her alienation into a physical remove to the country, spending spring and summer in—and later at a cottage near—a small house called Eleanor on the Sussex coast near West Wittering, which she let from Mary and St John Hutchinson. From Eleanor, Bell wrote a letter prescient of her ultimate strategy. Following her reiterated complaint, "I dread going back [to London]. It is especially bad now on account of the war," she announced; "I have been seriously considering a plan by which we should give up Gordon Sq[uare] and take a house in the country."[12] The following spring, Bell moved to Wissett Lodge, near Halesworth in Suffolk.

Bell's letters describe both houses as outposts of resistance against the emotional and physical effects of the war. From Eleanor, she wrote, "Here we live without newspapers, at least they come at moments when I at any rate can ignore them," warning one correspondent who had volunteered for the Navy Reserve, "You've come to the right person if you don't want to hear anything about the war . . . and that may be the supreme virtue in a letter writer nowadays."[13] Bell's determination to stave off the war is clear in her report about one set of visitors: "Until I made myself rather unpleasant about it we had a good deal of talk about the war. It's too depressing and I feel as if talk about it puts a stop to other thoughts in one's mind now and it's very important they shouldn't be killed."[14] Having made her house an oasis from the ideological effects of the war, she demanded shortly after Rupert Brooke's death (discussed in the previous chapter), "Why shouldn't we spend May here? How idiotic to go home and listen to talk about the War and Rupert?"[15]

The "other thoughts" Bell was determined to preserve included the commitment to the erotic and aesthetic exploration that Bloomsbury associated with modernism. As to the former, Bell shared Eleanor with the object of her love, Duncan Grant, while Grant invited his paramour, David (known as "Bunny") Garnett, for long visits; Garnett, for his part, flirted with a variety of women. In May, when the Hutchinsons took over Eleanor, Clive Bell rented rooms in the nearby village in order to be near his lover, Mary. This situation might seem the stuff of tragedy, but the participants—Vanessa especially—approached it with pleasure. She reported to her husband that she slept alone—"no little Grant has yet had a chance to come into existence"—while to Garnett she wrote that, during one of his absences, "we talked of your looks and decided that we liked looking at you and after all what more can one say of anyone?"[16] Later, again to Garnett, she reported, "In spite of wars and conscription and all horrors and disappointments, I must tell you . . . that I have been extraordinarily selfishly happy lately. One of the advantages of being old is that one isn't happy without knowing it—I have known it often lately."[17] Negotiating the pleasures and frustrations of loving a man who was erotically attracted to other men, she confided to Fry, "it's impossible not to mind some things sometimes," but followed this immediately with, "but I think I am very lucky really. . . . Duncan is simply amazingly good to me and puts up with a great deal I think without ever losing patience. I wish very often that I had such a nice character as his."[18]

What strife was occasioned by Bell's retreat from London came from Fry, who complained to Clive: "I think you and Nessa have managed to make the only breathable atmosphere in England, at least for me. I can't quite put up with any other—

125. Vanessa Bell, *Self-portrait*, 1915. Oil on canvas laid on panel, 63.5 × 45.7 cm. Yale Center for British Art.

only I feel a good deal less in the centre of things than I did."[19] His letters to Vanessa mix anxiety over her absence from the Omega with heartbreak over her abandonment of him. Her responses are reassuring but firm. "It is simply absurd to say that you have counted for so little. You must see if you can think calmly, that you have been and are one of the most important people in the lives of any people who know you well."[20] Dismissing Fry's imputation of her motives in leaving letters unanswered, Bell wrote, "Even if I should be angry or indifferent—and I never am and never have been—that would not be my way of showing it. I am not so cruel. If I am angry I shall at any rate write and say so."[21] Bell's clear determination to remake her life on her own terms—taking Grant as a domestic partner while keeping Fry as a friend—belie later presentations of her as a pawn in Bloomsbury's romantic machinations.

Bell's determination to push beyond the bounds of romantic convention was matched by her artistic ambition. During the first months of the war, she and Grant experimented with purely abstract painting (as discussed in Chapter 9), and a drive for innovation marks her self-portraits of this period as well. A self-portrait painted at Eleanor, presents Bell in an environment of rectilinear and angled forms resembling her abstractions (fig. 125). Against this insistently modernist background, Bell exaggerates her body's bulk, making no effort to hide the seam where she added to her left shoulder so that it looms out of proportion with the right, crowding the canvas edge as if to push into the viewer's space. Her neck Bell represents as a thick trunk supporting a face rendered in blotchy patches of color, with a darkened and twisted nose. The effect is an aggressive flouting of portrait conventions, especially conventional attributes of passive and elegant feminine beauty.

Bell's powerful self-image is all the more remarkable in comparison to a portrait Grant painted of her, also at Eleanor (fig. 126). Though Grant represents her wide-

An Aesthetic of Conscientious Objection

126. Duncan Grant, *At Eleanor: Vanessa Bell*, 1915. Oil on canvas, 76.2 × 56 cm. Yale Center for British Art.

eyed, Bell reported that she dozed through the sittings, which helps explain the posture of languorous passivity in the image. Grant shows Bell sinking back into an armchair with her long hands lying loosely in her lap and face upturned to emphasize her bone structure and what Fry, in an earlier love letter, described as "your throat that swells like a great wave when you throw back your head."[22] There is some irony in the similarity between the written encomium by the man whose love Bell rejected and the visual depiction by the man whose love she sought. Despite their differences—Fry, the older, articulate intellectual in passionate pursuit *versus* Grant, the younger, intuitive painter who was affectionate but elusive—both men's perceptions of Bell remained tied to conventions of femininity that her self-presentation actively disputes. Although Bell seems to have sought in Grant a less assertive partner, the evidence of these verbal and visual portraits suggests that, even for the unconventional men of Bloomsbury, a woman's claims to power could be obscured by conventional perceptions of beauty.

This perspective is not unique to observers within Bloomsbury. Many commentators have allowed clichés of feminine passivity and leisured country life to mask the harsh realities of Bell's wartime retreat from London. Bell reported from Eleanor how hard she worked to make the house livable: "When we first came, the oven wouldn't bake and the water was so incredibly nasty it nearly made one sick... and it's fearfully cold and draughty."[23] Overriding these challenges, however, was a determination to substitute this home for settings lost to the war. Writing to Mary Hutchinson about the property, Grant claimed, "The lapping of the waves might have been the Mediterranean's," while Bell told Fry, "you would like this country I think for often it is much more like Italy than England. . . . The estuary here looks extraordinarily like the lagoons at Venice."[24] The similarity of these remarks must reflect Bell and Grant's conversations at Eleanor as they refashioned this rural retreat into a Mediterranean alternative to the hardships of England during the war.

In the house itself, Grant and Bell could not resist adding Post-Impressionist touches to what Bell described as the Hutchinsons' "New English Art Club style of decoration with spots and stripes and bright colours everywhere—very pretty for the most part with only some lapses."[25] "Tell Mary we are now at work on the lower panels of the dining room doors," Vanessa wrote to Clive; "Duncan has now started a mosaic with stones and glass etc. from the beach. It is lovely. He gets amazing color from all the bits."[26] Against this Post-Impressionist background, by mid-summer much of the life associated with the modernism of the Omega was transferred to Eleanor. Once the Hutchinsons and Clive arrived, Eleanor became a setting for costume parties with masks made by the artists and a sex farce entitled *Euphrosine ou les mystères de la sexe*, in which Vanessa's character transformed into a man.[27]

Amid such high-spirited recreations of pre-war London culture, Bell used the summer of 1915 to think seriously about moving to the country. "I have been trying to find out how I should like to live in the country and be alone a good deal," she wrote to her sister; "Of course my country estate would be much nicer than this and I should have a large studio to work in. On the other hand, I should have much more solitude and it would often be winter."[28] Bell did return to London during the autumn of 1915, but the situation for pacifists was worsening. On the street, women forced white feathers as symbols of cowardice on men not in military uniform; in West Wittering, both Grant and Clive Bell were interrogated by the police, who were empowered by the sweeping language of new laws to imprison anyone who might potentially prejudice public safety.[29] In October Grant was arrested at the French border and prevented from traveling to Paris to execute a commission to design a ballet for Jacques Copeau. At the same time, Bloomsbury's opposition to the war solidified. Adrian Stephen started working for the anti-conscription National Council for Civil Liberties, while Lytton Strachey wrote an anti-conscription pamphlet that was suppressed by its publisher, though not before being denounced by the *Morning Post*.[30]

Despite such efforts, the Military Service Bill was passed in January 1916, for the first time in English history requiring men to join the military.[31] Bloomsbury's attention turned to supporting men who refused conscription. Clive Bell, who was exempt from service due to injury, served on a government committee to set the terms under which Conscientious Objector status would be granted, while Vanessa helped organize "watchers" to ensure fair hearings for resisters in the notoriously hostile tribunals throughout London. "We are now working hard at getting watchers for the tribunals and giving advice to people who want exemption. I go up and down very much sometimes hope and sometimes fear," she reported.[32] On New Year's Day, Bell wrote, "Duncan and Bunny and Lytton have all agreed that they would sooner go to prison than be forced to become soldiers," concluding this letter with yet another expression of alienation phrased—as was now becoming typical—as an ideal of escape to the Mediterranean:

> It's all horrible and I see more and more clearly that after the war life in England will be impossible. I think one will have to leave it and go perhaps to Spain. Not having conscription was the one thing which made it better than other countries, in spite of all, but if that goes, I don't see any reason for bringing up one's children to be English.[33]

In the event, Bell's escape was more immediate and more local, for by April she was again living with Grant and Garnett in the country. Their strategy, suggested by Keynes who was now an official at the Treasury, was to show the military tribunal that the men were engaged in non-combatant service as farmers. Their opportunity was provided by the death of Grant's aunt, which left his father responsible for her orchards and six-acre farm in Suffolk. The opportunity forced Grant to confront his father, a retired army officer, over his refusal of military service. Garnett's memoirs record, "Duncan took the line that he belonged to a tiny minority and that his views differed *in toto* from the majority on almost every subject. His opinions would never be attended to, and he would never fight for those of the majority."[34] Grant's own explanation comes in a letter to his father, which asserts his membership in a minority transcending nationalist distinctions:

> I began to see that one's enemies were not vague masses of foreign people, but the mass of people in one's own country and the mass of people in the enemy country, and that one's friends were people of true ideas that one might and did meet in every country one visited. I still think this and I still think the war utter madness and folly.[35]

The vagueness of this passage offers, ironically, the clearest documentation of the forces that at this era tightened the bonds holding Bloomsbury together as a group. Grant's assertion of allegiance to a minority identity like, but stronger than, nationalism describes what we might call a subculture, though Grant lacked that term and was prevented by both law and propriety from avowing its connection to sexuality. Despite his father's disapproval—manifest in his consistent misarticulation of Garnett's name as "Garbage"—the Grants allowed their son and his friend to manage the farm and orchard, while Vanessa Bell looked after the house, though only on the condition that Keynes guarantee their rent.

Bell's joy—"What seems like a providential fruit farm has fallen from the clouds!" she exulted—masked the difficulties of life at Wissett.[36] With no training or farming experience, Grant and Garnett struggled to revive neglected orchards, plant fields, and care for chickens and bees. With the men working, Bell reported, "I always spend the whole morning, afternoon, and after tea alone, except for perhaps half an hour or so after lunch or after tea."[37] The gleeful impropriety that had informed Bell's earlier domestic endeavors, however, quickly came to characterize her farm life. She wrote to Keynes, "You'll find us flourishing, only one of the . . . rabbits who was said to be a doe and with young has been found to have what is thought to be a penis, but no balls, and no young, and she or he buggers its mate, and one of the hens has a pale comb and the puppy has nits and Bunny has a skin disease."[38] In spite of these contretemps, Wissett, like Eleanor, was a refuge: "It's amazingly remote from the war and all horrors," Bell reported; "How absurd it seems that people shouldn't be allowed to live this kind of life in peace."[39]

The strength of Bell's determination to define Wissett as a refuge for values under siege may be measured by her efforts to transform the house into a setting for a new kind of life. "I find there are some things one *does* object to live with. Especially imitation Morris and early Victorian chintzes," Bell complained after her arrival in April; "We are trying by degrees to get rid of some of the worst covers and curtains."[40] Shortly thereafter she reported, "This house is really very nice. By turning out all the ornaments and a good many small tables, the rooms can be made charming."[41] Wissett's transformation did not end with the elimination of such talismans of convention. Though their tenancy at the farm was temporary—the senior Grants had promised permanent tenants possession in October and the upcoming military tribunal posed a very real threat that Grant and Garnett would be jailed before then—Bell announced, "we are behaving as if we were settled here forever, painting the rooms and making curtains and covers."[42] Letters describe painting the rooms a brilliant blue-green, covering the dark brown trim with white, washing doors with Omega dyes, and applying the marbled Omega wallpapers. Quentin Bell later recalled "my mother and Duncan throwing paint at a wall and letting it dribble down, a process which they described quite inaccurately as 'marbling'. I had to wait nearly half a century to hear it called action painting."[43] Even the chickens at Wissett proclaimed a colorful allegiance to Post-Impressionism: to distinguish their most productive hens from the rest, Grant dipped them in the blue dye Bell had procured for slipcovers. According to Garnett, "the effect was lovely. With their big bright scarlet combs, white bodies, and blue tails they looked like French tricolour flags as they sped about on the green paddock." His enthusiasm was not widely shared, however. According to Garnett:

Every Sunday, groups of village people strolled up to Wissett Lodge and looked for a long time over the paddock gate to see what new folly we had committed. Our tricolour fowls turned out to be the last straw. . . . They thought it was a joke, but as they could not see the point of it became convinced it was a joke at their expense. We were making fun of them, of the birds, of serious poultry keeping.[44]

These projects at Wissett sustained the qualities of exuberant, intuitive, even irreverent experimentation, that had characterized Bloomsbury's earlier efforts to create domestic settings for modern life. Like Eleanor the year before, Wissett in the spring of 1916 briefly recaptured something of the atmosphere of pre-war Bloomsbury. After a visit from Lytton Strachey, Bell reported to Fry, "we have had long discussions in the old style about art and about literature especially," though this pleasure heightened her longing for what the war kept from her: "I hope you'll see some pictures by Matisse and Picasso. It would be such a mercy to see some exciting pictures again."[45] On another occasion, writing to Strachey from Wissett, Bell described a beautiful spring day, concluding, "If only there weren't a war and tribunals in the background it would be perfect. . . . Anyhow, it seems the only thing to enjoy at the present, and the only way of cheating one's fate."

Though Wissett could—briefly and locally—mitigate the war's baneful influence, Bell also recognized a permanent change in her attitudes. Her letter to Strachey continues, "I feel that all our ways are changing. We are so much overcome by the country as compared with London that I doubt if I shall ever return to Gordon Square."[46] To Fry, she asserted, "I feel such a savage here, as if I could never go to a tea party again. In fact I believe I'm getting unfitted for town life."[47] For his part, Grant, on a trip to London, where he lunched with Keynes at a club where "everything was sumptuous and civilized," reported back to Bell, "I saw one must either have that sort of thing and War or Wissett and Peace."[48] These professions of alienation from London coincided with profound changes in the practice of the artists who had previously considered Bloomsbury their home. Grant, writing to Fry from Wissett, explained that farm work prevented him from painting but then said he had been thinking about his art and reported, "I think I shall paint less and less from life and more and more from drawings. . . . I want to paint unrealistic realistic works." This ambition to distance art from reality leads in the letter directly to the assertion, "Anyhow I am never going to live in town again. I can't think why anyone does."[49]

Though links between an artistic withdrawal from "life" and a refusal to live in London are clear in these letters, the small number of works datable to Bell's and Grant's time at Wissett forbids definitive analysis of this idea. Two paintings, however, suggest the practice occasioned by these new principles. Both, significantly, depict female figures in a domestic environment. In Bell's *Interior at Wissett Lodge*, a woman in a light shift stands before a washstand and domestic implements—pitcher, basin, wastebasket, and so forth—all rendered in the same white as the figure (fig. 127). These white forms play across a vibrant blue background that (in addition to confirming a wall color mentioned in Bell's letters) boasts a floral still life, which might be a wall painting or a bouquet in the vase on the washstand. The effect is to meld figure and decoration, so that they are pulled into the same plane: the stuff of the house and its inmates become, in this vision, one. Grant's *By the Fire*, likewise, turns away from the abstractions of the year before, retrieving in its brushy application of rich colors the sensuous delineation of domestic objects of his earlier still lifes (fig. 128). A multiplicity of viewpoints that flattens certain elements (the tabletop and plate of figs) while letting others float in indeterminate space (the glass and carafe), however, sustains the formal freedoms associated with abstract art, while conveying the effect Grant described of composing from—almost collaging— sketches to create a new reality not subject to conventional laws of gravity or perspective. The figure, identified as Vanessa Bell, huddling before the arch of the fireplace hovers as a compositional element allied in scale and shape to the plate of figs below her. The warm colors and emblems of domestic comfort—made specific to Wissett by the figs, which grew on a tree near the house—affirm descriptions of the house as a haven from the war.[50]

127. Vanessa Bell, *Interior at Wissett Lodge*, 1916. Private collection. Photograph courtesy of Anthony d'Offay Galleries.

In their bid to escape the crises of contemporary reality, however, Grant and Bell began to look farther back than these echoes of their pre-war styles, inaugurating at Wissett aesthetic strategies that would characterize Bloomsbury's art and design of the following decades. Just a few days after the local tribunal denied Grant's and Garnett's petitions for conscientious objector status, Bell reported, "Duncan and I have . . . begun copying minute reproductions of Fra Angelico about 10 times as big on the walls of my bedroom in watercolour."[51] This marked, as Fry observed, a significant shift in attitude: "I'm glad you've taken to the Old Masters," he wrote to Bell; "so often I've longed to share that with you, and you always grew impatient and said you really only cared for modern things."[52] It is not hard to discern in Bell's and Grant's new attitudes their rejection of an increasingly hostile and dangerous present in favor of an ideal distant in both time and place. Since

128. Duncan Grant,
By the Fire, 1916.
Oil on canvas,
53.2 × 35.5 cm.
Charleston Trust.

Mediterranean culture in general and "primitive" Italian art in particular had been posited by Bloomsbury as the historical basis of Post-Impressionism (see especially Chapter 3), its invocation at this time seems an attempt to retain the values associated with Post-Impressionism while replacing the unpredictable flux of the avant-garde with the stable timelessness of the art-historical classic. This connection is suggested by Bell's letters, which move in a few paragraphs from outbursts of despair over the ongoing uncertainty caused by the military tribunals—"All these months of never being able to look ahead at all so make one long for some settlement"—to discussions of her copies, in this case of a Giotto: "I enjoy doing it so much. For some reason I feel nearly as free as if I were painting on my own account. I have quite changed the colour scheme."[53]

If Bloomsbury's earlier Post-Impressionist interiors suggested the effect of living in a Fauve painting, with all the associations of avant-garde daring that implied, now Fra Angelico frescoes in Bell's bedroom and her free translations of Giotto proposed an experience much more like dwelling in an early-Renaissance chapel. Undoubtedly an attempt to claim a measure of stability for a life rendered difficult and unpredictable by the war, Bell's first domestic invocation of the early Renaissance may also be seen as an effort to come to terms with the increasingly tense emotional dynamics in her new household. A romance that had seemed a daring exploration of her own desires a year earlier was degenerating for Bell, who acknowledged—though she resolved to squelch—increasing jealousy and irritation

An Aesthetic of Conscientious Objection

over Garnett's presence. In this context, her selection of Fra Angelico's *Visitation* seems—consciously or not—to reflect her emotional status (fig. 129). "The original is a most lovely design," Bell reported, "with the two figures meeting by a doorway and a girl looking on and a man waiting nearby."[54] The fresco nominally depicts a bond between women and a celebration of pregnancy, both themes that reinforce Bell's sense of herself as the powerful female and maternal center of Bloomsbury. But Fra Angelico's embracing figures—one clearly female, the other with a more androgynous tight helmet of hair—being scrutinized by a woman and man, reflect the ambiguity of Bell's situation in a household where expressions of intimacy were constantly shadowed. Whether she identified with the sturdy female observer inspecting the couple as she trudges along in the course of her chores, or with the embracing figures being spied on by the man peering around the edge of the door, the air of claustrophobic solemnity in this image is very different from the exuberance of Bloomsbury's earlier images of sensual embrace.

129. Fra Angelico, *The Visitation*, *c.*1439, predella of the Cortona Annunciation. Museo Diocesano.

Whatever Bell's personal investment in this mural, its retreat from avant-garde to proto-Renaissance reference signaled a crucial shift for Bloomsbury. Like most artists at the period, Bloomsbury's painters had trained by copying the old masters, but the abstractions they exhibited in 1915 seemed—to the artists and the viewing public—to renounce this legacy. Now responding to Bell's revived interest in art history, Fry began sending the artists at Wissett photographs from his scholarly collection. Within a year of Bell's and Grant's quotations of Fra Angelico in her bedroom, Fry was able to mount an entire show of such work under the title *An Exhibition of Omega Copies and Translations*, which opened at the Omega in May of 1917, following an exhibition of children's drawings. On a purely practical level, both shows demonstrate Fry's resourcefulness in maintaining the Omega as a venue for modern art exhibitions despite the near impossibility of getting new work from either the continent or his dispersed colleagues.[55] Taken together, however, Fry's shows also suggest a fundamental shift in strategy as he attempted to locate the basic principles of modernism—the realization of formal pleasure through individual self-expression—in places other than avant-garde art.

The impulse to widen formalism's scope beyond avant-garde art is clear in Fry's writings about the two exhibitions. Upholding children's art over "the Academy painter of anecdotes" in an article accompanying the first show, Fry described how the child's "wonder and delight" leads to representation that "takes inevitably rhythmical form, becomes beautiful . . . due simply to the directness and unconsciousness with which he expresses his emotion." This intuitive formalism of children is suppressed, he argued, by conventional instruction in mimetic art that "destroyed completely the children's particular gifts of representation and design."[56] This argument—both the formalism and the alienation from dominant cultural values—finds franker expression in a letter to Bell written during the exhibition, in which Fry extolled the art of children not taught in conventional classes:

> They're simply marvelous. . . . a kind of cross between early miniatures and Seurat, but all are absolutely individual and original. . . . here's an inexhaustible supply of real primitive art and real vision which the government suppresses at a cost of hundreds of thousands of pounds. If the world weren't the most crazily topsy turvy place one would never believe it possible.[57]

Similar attitudes animate Fry's writings on the *Copies and Translations* show. In the catalog, Fry reclaims the "old masters" from conventional modes of interpretation, arguing, "If we did not go on continually revaluing and remaking them they would not be merely old but dead." Emphasizing that "such copies as those in the present exhibition . . . show what are those elements in the work of various periods which have a special meaning for the modern conception of design," Fry asserts, "the artist, in copying, tends to single out those qualities of design which have still a special applicability to his own work and to discard or slur over those qualities whether of design, or more probably, of illustrative purpose, which the old master was obliged to introduce either because of personal idiosyncracy or through pressure on him of the sentiment of his day." This work of "translation," he concludes, might even "reveal certain qualities more clearly than the original."[58] Again Fry's letters are more direct. Describing his copy of a Sassoferrato *Madonna*, he said, "I've taken the bones of the design, which are, I think, very good, and have tried to leave out a lot of the flummery which he put in."[59] For the most part, however, Fry was pleased to find the principles of Post-Impressionism already present in proto-Renaissance painting. About an Assisi fresco illustrating the healing of the wounded man of Lerida, Fry exclaimed, "the more I study it, the more amazed I am at it. . . . It goes one further than Seurat."[60] Copying a detail of St. Francis from Cimabue's Assisi frescoes, he reported:

> I had never really studied that . . . with enlightened eyes, and find what I thought before were weaknesses of early incapacity are really the results of a sensitivity one had never understood. The whole composition is marvelous. . . . what's so wonderful—when one begins to study the forms in detail one finds just the kind of purposeful distortion and pulling of planes you get in Greco and Cézanne and the same kind of sequence in the contours.[61]

Fry's "discovery that Cimabue is the same thing practically as El Greco and Cézanne" leads in his letters directly to the observation, "I'm very busy in my scandalously individualistic way and fear that I shall go on being impenitently so until death or Lloyd George intervenes to suppress me."[62] Here a return to the art of the past both justifies Cézannian modernism and reaffirms Fry's sense of himself pursuing an individualism inimical to political authority.

Bloomsbury's perception of the old masters as a repository of principles more congenial than the fugitive values of the contemporary avant-garde required a selective view of art history, one that privileges the static solemnity of the Tuscan proto-Renaissance, and even within this limited field overlooks images of violence and absolute authority. No pictures of battle, plague, torture, crucifixion, or enthroned deities intrude on Bloomsbury's ideal of Italian precedent. Instead Bloomsbury emphasized the peaceful anti-authoritarianism enacted by Saint Francis and the nurturing domesticity of nativities and madonnas.[63] This selectivity underscores the ideology that motivated Bloomsbury's turn to the past as a refuge from an uncongenial present and a model for values the group hoped to preserve for the future.

As events transpired, Bloomsbury's turn to the past only deepened its alienation from contemporary culture. Although Fry tried to enlist artists beyond Bloomsbury to participate in the *Copies and Translations* show, and both Walter Sickert and Nina Hamnett agreed to contribute, neither fulfilled this promise. Delores Courtney, who was working at the Omega, lent a copy of a Derain and Mark Gertler added a copy of a Cézanne after the show opened, but neither of these contributed to the theme of reinvestigating old masters.[64] The frustration and isolation Fry experienced in organizing the show were deepened by its reception. Confounding his expectation that less avant-garde paintings would sell easily, only Keynes bought work—two of Grant's pieces—and *Copies and Translations* became the first Omega exhibition to be ignored by reviewers.

The "almost complete fiasco" of the *Copies and Translations* show contributed to Fry's conclusion that "even the most intelligent speak another language to what we do about pictures."[65] Although he continued to promote modern art, it was with an increasing sense of futility. Writing a few weeks after *Copies and Translations* closed, Fry described his efforts to organize an exhibition of modern art in Birmingham— "I shall go down there and hang and give a lecture, so something may come of it,— oh Lord don't I know nothing will and yet I go on." In the same letter, he reacted to the publication of Bell's article "Before the War": "I hope it'll make people sit up, but I believe nothing will disturb the profound self-complacency [*sic*] of the English."[66] Fry's preface to the Birmingham exhibition catalog provoked his hosts with references to English backwardness: "the modern movement has found far less favour in this country than in any other part of Europe," being "regarded as extravagant and absurd . . . by those who uphold the grotesque provincialism of our Royal Academic painting" and even by those—the implication here is artists like Sickert and Tonks—outside the academies, Fry said.[67]

Fry's bitterness pales before Bell's "Before the War," a diatribe against former allies who had shirked his calls to pacifism. Bell here dismissed the avant-garde as snobs and mocked social reformers for failing to recognize how the privations of war would preclude all of their schemes. Casting back to the Napoleonic betrayal of an earlier era's high ideals, Bell complained, "And if one cannot forget the stragglers from the Age of Reason, the old, pre-Revolutionary people who, in the reign of Louis XVIII, cackled obsolete liberalism, blasphemed, and span wrinkled intrigues beneath the scandalized brows of neo-Catholic grandchildren, one becomes exceedingly sorry for oneself."[68]

Clive Bell can be relied on to represent the extreme of Bloomsbury's tendencies at any given moment, but this vivid self-caricature from a man in his mid-thirties imagining himself as a remainder of a lost generation only slightly exaggerates Bloomsbury's war-induced alienation. To return to the artists at Wissett in the summer of 1916 gives some idea of the causes of this attitude. The local tribunal refused to recognize Grant and Garnett as conscientious objectors; Vanessa Bell wrote to Fry, "my only real hope is that it may be possible to get them out of prison before very long."[69] Though two appeals by July finally procured their C.O. status, another hearing in August deferred to the local board's refusal to certify their self-employed farm work as alternative service. "You musn't be upset about this news," Duncan wrote to Vanessa; "I don't want to leave Wissett otherwise I don't care much."[70] So, after the anxious labors of spring and summer, the autumn saw Bloomsbury turned out from Wissett. "Here all is confusion and horror," Garnett reported from Wissett, for "Duncan's parents insist that every particle of paint shall be scraped and washed off."[71]

With Grant planning to seek employment and housing with a local farmer—a plan that would have broken up the household that shared Wissett—it was once again Vanessa Bell whose energies turned a crisis that threatened to fragment Bloomsbury into an occasion to strengthen the group. But her ideal was no longer to contribute to an urban avant-garde. Under Bell's influence, Bloomsbury's artists turned away from an avant-garde model of progressive leadership and toward an ideal of stubborn dissent from a culture gone awry. Though the Woolfs' Hogarth Press, begun in 1917, revived Bloomsbury's avant-garde status in relationship to literature in the post-war years, Bloomsbury's art followed a different trajectory, which will be traced in the following chapters. The end of Bloomsbury's period at Wissett marked the beginning of this new phase. Though Bloomsbury's physical traces at Wissett were obliterated in the fall of 1916, the routines established and the art created there set the terms for the next stage in Bloomsbury's development, which would be worked out at Charleston farmhouse.

Making Charleston (1916–17)

It was Leonard Woolf who found Charleston. Like the other Bloomsbury men who claimed conscientious objector status against military conscription, Woolf and his brother-in-law, Adrian Stephen, hoped to avoid prison by working as farm laborers. To this end Woolf, in the spring of 1916, began inquiring around Asheham for farmers and landlords willing to buck popular opprobrium by hiring and housing conscientious objectors. By May, he had identified Charleston as a possible residence for C.O.s, though, as events transpired, Virginia's doctor procured a medical exemption from service for Leonard to nurse her, and Adrian found agricultural work elsewhere.[1] Virginia wrote to her sister, "I wish you'd leave Wissett and take Charleston. Leonard went over it and says it's a most delightful house. . . . It has a charming garden with a pond, and fruit trees, and vegetables, all now rather run wild, but you could make it lovely."[2] Bell, still struggling to keep the Wissett household together, did not take up her sister's suggestion at the time. In September, however, when Grant and Garnett were denied permission to continue farming at Wissett, Bell decided to capitalize on the Woolfs' more congenial relations with their neighbors near Asheham. By canvassing the marketplace at nearby Lewes, Bell found a farmer willing to employ Grant and Garnett near the house her sister had alerted her to in May. At this point, Bell first visited Charleston, where she was dismayed to find the previous tenants had stabled animals in many of the rooms. She returned a few days later with the farmer who held the lease, however, after which she wrote to Grant at Wissett:

> This time to my surprise I saw something quite different. A large lake, an orchard, trees all round the back of the house and farm buildings, an old house— two hundred years old Mr. Stacey said and he may be right for all I know—a walled garden quite as big or bigger than the Asheham one and a wall nearly as high, fruit trees trained against it all round—a bee hive!—everything much bigger and completely changed—on the whole improved. We went over all of it. The rooms (according to today's impressions) are very large and light and numerous—there are huge cupboards, innumerable larders—a dairy cellar—all sorts of outhouses—lots of rooms for hens. . . .There is also a tennis lawn! It has been so neglected that it's more like a bit of field.

Only the leaseholder's wife was a problem: "Mrs. Stacey and I hated each other instinctively," Bell wrote in a passage indicative of her bitter alienation; "she revealed to me the present state of mind of the British nation and why we want to go on with the war and why mothers like their sons to be killed."[3] Nevertheless, Bell arranged to move into Charleston in October.

The facts of Charleston's discovery are worth rehearsing as a corrective to both journalistic fantasies that Bell, inspired by her sister's "weekend retreat," was just "looking for her own quiet place in the country to paint," and more purposeful misrepresentations of Bloomsbury whiling away the war in the comfort of its country seat.[4] Facing legal persecution and popular prejudice, Bell moved her children and companions to a dilapidated farmhouse, where the men worked six days a week as manual laborers on food rations so insufficient that Grant grew thin and rheumatic.[5] Charleston was unfurnished and Garnett and Grant initially slept on the floor. Even after furniture arrived, the house lacked electricity, central heating, and hot water, while cold water had to be pumped by hand—except when the pump froze altogether during the winter. Visitors were asked to bring their own blankets and hot water bottles. Adding to the logistical complications, Bell, in order to school her children in such an isolated locale, accepted two little girls as boarders and, with her housemaid, taught classes. Leonard Woolf's memoirs stress the rigors of rural living during the war: "our daily life was probably nearer that of Chaucer's than of the modern man," he explained, describing how to reach Asheham from the train station, "more often than not, wet or dry, we walked the four miles along the river bank and across the fields with knapsacks on our backs. All the water we used in the house we had to pump from the well. Sanitation consisted of an earth closet."[6] Virginia's promotion of Charleston to her sister reveals what would be taken today as the extraordinary isolation Bell faced: "it only takes half an hour to walk to Glynde Station . . . and you have Firle, with its telephone, quite near."[7] First reactions to Charleston from others in Bloomsbury tempered appreciation of its beauty with dismay at the work it entailed. "Because the bloody government has made slaves of Duncan and Bunny, need it make one of you?" Clive demanded of Vanessa, offering to sell some of their art so she could hire help.[8] Walking to Charleston on a rainy day, a visiting Molly MacCarthy claimed the prospect of the lonely house and fields looked so much like Wuthering Heights that she burst into tears.[9]

Despite Charleston's drawbacks, the new residents approached it optimistically. Garnett, who preceded Grant from Wissett, reported with delight on Charleston's spaciousness: "I am fond of Wissett—but it is so cramped. . . .Charleston is splended. Easy, roomy. I am quite sure my temper will be infinitely better."[10] Bell's letters about Charleston invoke Bloomsbury houses freely chosen before the war: the walled garden compares to Asheham's; there is a tennis court like those in Bloomsbury squares or the badminton green at Durbins. Describing the interior, Bell emphasized its suitability to her aesthetic and social ideals. "The rooms are very light and good proportions," she told Grant, while to Fry she made the best of the sparseness, writing, "I hope to carry out the idea I have always had of bedrooms with the minimum of furniture."[11] As at Wissett, Bell and Grant immediately began to remake the look of the house. By December, Woolf reported that Charleston was "covered with various bright shades of Distemper" (recent discoveries of old layers of vibrant blue and green paint, often applied directly over the existing wallpapers, bear out this claim).[12] The decorations created at and for Charleston during the war years offer a remarkable record of its artists' determination to create a place where Bloomsbury's social and aesthetic ideals could be preserved.

Probably the first decoration that, in Quentin Bell's words, "brought Charleston into the Post-Impressionist world," was his mother's painted window embrasure (fig. 130) in the sitting room where the household gathered during that first cold winter to eat around a makeshift hearth constructed from firebricks following Fry's instructions.[13] Bell borrowed from her earlier abstract paintings to decorate the narrow panels flanking the window with rectilinear compositions in mottled ochers with blue accents. Another rectilinear decoration, this one in red and mottled shades of gray, also dating to the first months of Bloomsbury's inhabitation, filled one wall of an upstairs room Bell first used as her studio (and which doubled as her sons' bedroom).[14] These early abstract decorations linked Charleston to the decorating schemes being promoted by the Omega at this period (discussed in Chapter 9). By 1917 the Omega was promoting wall decorations based on "the contrast of two or three pure colours applied in simple rectangular shapes, to transform a room

130. Vanessa Bell, painted window embrasure, 1916–17. Charleston Trust.

completely, giving it a new feeling of space or dignity or richness," as Fry described them in *Colour* magazine. Despite their simplicity, Fry insisted, these decorations revealed the sensibility of their artist-creators, because of their "peculiar moiré effect" realized by applying fast-drying paint with small brushes: "only the artist has the necessary free elegance of handling which will render such a transparent quality agreeable." Such marks were not the signature of just any artists, of course, but of modernists. Fry explained, "it is only of late years, and among the more modern artists, that all this interest in the decorative possibilities of paint and of architectural design has grown up. It is all part of the reaction against the photographic vision of the academic schools and of the new interest in pure design."[15] Although she was no longer participating in Omega commissions herself, Bell's first decorations at Charleston reveal her continuing allegiance to the workshops' changing aesthetic. Arrangements of color and texture deployed as expressions of individual sensibility began the work of claiming Charleston for modernism.

Over the subsequent months, as with the arrival of pieces of Omega furniture and pottery, Charleston came increasingly to embody Bloomsbury's ideals for modern domesticity. Fry's semi-rural Durbins (discussed in Chapter 2) was a particularly important model and source. Fry sent flowers and artichokes from Durbins's garden. The latter, which were not commonly grown in England, were particularly significant emblems of Bloomsbury's francophile modernism, both for their culinary uses and for their cubistic appearance, which, Fry claimed, made them ideal ornamental plantings—the patterns of overlapping chevrons in several of his Omega designs have been seen as allusions to artichokes.[16] The closest echo of Durbins in Charleston's garden, however, was what Bell described as a "small cemented place to sit out in," which she proposed to decorate with "a small inlaid piece of mosaic of odd bits of china, glass, etc. in the centre and also a narrow border round the edge," soliciting from Fry the left-over tesserae from his unfinished badminton mosaic.[17]

Through the years, as many commentators have noted, Charleston's interior and exterior were depicted in pictures that blur the boundaries between art and decoration, image and reality, in a cycle where domestic existence and aesthetic creativity reinforce one another in a complex but coherent whole.[18] This reflexivity began in the downstairs room the family used most. Across from Bell's rectilinear designs on the window frame, Grant, during their first year in the house, painted the upper panel of the door with an image that is both a still life—a genre of easel painting with claims to the status of fine art—and a depiction of the window the door faces (including since-removed wallpaper inherited from previous tenants) (fig. 131). This fusion of art and decoration is emphasized by the existence of an oil-on-canvas version of the same composition (minus the wallpaper) that Grant exhibited at the London Association of Artists in 1927, where—in yet another demonstration of reflexivity—it was purchased by Keynes, a part-time resident of Charleston.[19] Both versions of the motif link interior with exterior and art with nature: the flowers (possibly the artificial blooms produced at the Omega) and pot on the inside window sill blend with the forms and colors of the trees seen through the panes, while the flanking columnar forms may be seen equally well as representations of curtains—brilliant orange in the version on the door—or as decorative frame for the image.[20]

A similar analysis applies to Bell's decorations on the upper panels of two doors in Grant's bedroom (figs 132 and 133). Bell reported that she began decorating this room because it was the only one upstairs with a hearth and hovering over the fire allowed her to stay warm.[21] Perhaps inhibited by the cold, she said, "I'm not doing anything very startling—only pots of flowers and marbled circles."[22] Despite this self-deprecation, Bell's bouquets—given the season, these are almost certainly the Omega's dramatic fabric flowers that Vanessa pronounced "more beautiful than God's attempts"—swirl in complicated patterns within frames of bright red, purple, and orange.[23] The stippled and sponged panels of the "marbled" rectangles and circles contrast the free play of modernist mark-making to the neat symmetry of the geometrical forms, with both playing against the swirling brush strokes of the flowers. The brilliant shades of these decorations would have glowed against the dark

An Aesthetic of Conscientious Objection

131. Painted door, upper panel by Duncan Grant, 1917; lower panel later. Charleston Trust.

green paint the artists originally used to obliterate the busy wallpaper, turning this room in the cold farmhouse into a Post-Impressionist environment, where rooms look like paintings, and nature and artifice fuse in an exuberant expression of a modern sensibility.

As these bouquets on doors suggest, much of the decoration at Charleston returned to the garden imagery of early Omega interiors and before. In Bell's bedroom, Grant, apparently reciprocating for her decorations in his bedroom, painted the four-paneled door with a catalog of his favorite symbols of sensuality and abundance. The two narrow upper panels depict the same kind of nearly-nude figures bearing funnel-shaped baskets on their heads that Grant had put in his first Post-Impressionist decorations for Keynes's Cambridge rooms seven years earlier. Each of the smaller lower panels presents another of these distinctive baskets, brimming with multi-colored fruit. Grant updated these allusions to earlier Bloomsbury dwellings by bracketing Bell's window with images of their dog and a farm-yard bird, he recalled, "to guard her at night and wake her up in the morning."[24] The iconography of Grant's decorations in this room, ranging from the family dog to Mediterranean fantasies, reflects an aspiration—consistent since Eleanor and Wissett—to redeem rural exile in England by recasting it in terms of the pleasures associated with Post-Impressionism, now conceived not simply as a modern style of aesthetic self-expression, but also as the stuff of recent memory. This redemptive fantasy is reflected in Garnett's language describing the early years at Charleston, where, he reports, "one after another the rooms were decorated and altered almost out of recognition as the bodies of the saved are said to be glorified after the resurrection."[25]

Furniture painted by Bell and Grant amplifies tendencies evident in their treatment of walls and woodwork. Cupboards painted by Bell during her first year at the house enliven symmetrical arrangements of circles and curves with the occasional floral still life, with all these elements deployed—as in her decorations for the door

and mantel in Grant's room—to emphasize the panels and moldings of the carpentry, exaggerating the forms of conventional design (fig. 134). Grant, on the other hand, embellished carpentered surfaces with fanciful imagery. The chair-shaped ends of a wooden bench, for instance, he filled with figures of naked, kneeling angels, one male and one female, their wings sticking up onto the back support.[26] Similarly, each of the four sides of a simple logbox (fig. 135) displays a naked male angel dancing or making music in a style that alludes equally to Piero della Francesca and to Grant's own painted shutters at Brunswick Square (discussed in Chapter 6).

That these differences were self-conscious is suggested by a bed that Grant painted for Bell, which wittily blends their two styles (figs 136 and 137). Bell's characteristic centralized "marbled" circle dominates the back of the headboard, embellished with her initials but illusionistically tied to the panel's corners by red ribbons, so that her impulse toward pure geometry is turned into a modernist version of a rococo medallion. On the front of the headboard, overlooking the pillow, Grant painted a mask backed by iridescent wings, a figure he identified as Morpheus, the god of sleep and dreaming. Flaunting Bloomsbury's preference for intuitive expressiveness over laborious craftsmanship, Grant roughly nailed two unpainted scraps of wood to the face to create a three-dimensional headdress and nose for an effect that has been compared to both Romanesque stone carvings and Brancusi's sculpture, but that also summons the spirit of Picasso's avant-garde assemblages.[27]

This play with characteristic style, with form and figuration, as well as with allusions to art histories recent and otherwise, characterizes another well-preserved

134. Vanessa Bell, painted cabinet, 1917. Charleston Trust.

example of painted furniture from this era: a simple wooden chest (fig. 138). This piece, too, uses Bell's marbled circles in rectilinear panels, one on a short side, and three lined up along the back. On close inspection, however, the marbling on the central circle on the back resolves into a Post-Impressionist still life in Grant's style, while on the other short end of the trunk a similar still life expands to fill more fully the square panel—though small rounded wedges of marbling intruding on the corners recall the abstract circular format. The long front panel of the trunk, in contrast, is treated as a picture plane with an image of a languorous male swimmer reminiscent of Grant's Borough Polytechnic mural filling the space from corner to corner. The trunk's play with figuration and form combines with iconographic allusions to the tradition of the *cassone* (Italian proto-Renaissance painted trunks, which often juxtapose personal heraldic emblems with a sprawling nude Venus), though the *cassone*'s usual depictions of travel and adventure in landscape are pointedly replaced by the still lifes of domestic objects. This fusion of the mundane and local with the Italianate and erotic is clearest in an image revealed only by opening the lid of trunk. Here Grant's version of the classical nude Leda, instead of being forcibly impregnated by Zeus in his guise as a magnificent swan, welcomes into her curving arms a homely duck of the kind that lived on Charleston's pond. Framed under a proscenium curtain, this Leda reads as a larger-than-life theatrical figure, or, perhaps, as a backdrop to a play in which the duck is the actor. In either case, the image links farm life at Charleston with a fantastical access to the legacy of Italian culture and modern art. Grant's satisfaction with this image is evidenced by its repetition as a more finished painting, which was coveted by several visitors to Charleston (fig. 139).[28]

Facing page:
132 and 133. Vanessa Bell, painted mantel and doors, with detail, 1917. Charleston Trust.

135. Duncan Grant, painted logbox, 1916–17, 34.3 × 34.3 × 31.8 cm. Charleston Trust.

The self-conscious pastiche of historical and modern in—or, rather, on—Charleston's painted furniture undoubtedly reflects the influence of the *Copies and Translations* show at the Omega (discussed in the previous chapter), for which Bell and Grant were busily preparing during their first months at Charleston. More is at stake, however, in Bell's and Grant's habit of decorating ordinary furniture with allusions to classical themes and modernist styles. By mid-century, these objects provoked derision even from viewers sympathetic to Grant's and Bell's art. David Garnett, writing in the 1950s, mocked the "strange blend of hideous objects of

136 and 137. Duncan Grant, painted bed (front and back), 1917. Charleston Trust.

An Aesthetic of Conscientious Objection

138. Duncan Grant, painted chest, *c.* 1917. Charleston Trust.

furniture, painted with delightful works of art" at Charleston, complaining that, "Both Duncan and Vanessa appeared to believe that the inherent horror of any badly designed and constructed piece of furniture could be banished forever by decoration."[29] This critique reflects the mid–century modernist ideology that divided art sharply from design, restricting the latter to an aesthetic of simple, carefully proportioned forms that revealed the qualities of their materials. To appreciate Charleston's interiors, it helps to return to the distinction proposed in my Introduction between the aesthetics of utopia and subculture. From this perspective, Charleston clearly

139. Duncan Grant, *Leda and the Duck*, 1917. Oil on board, 29 × 86.5 cm. Private collection.

140 and 141. Photographs of Green Room (left) and Red Room (right) at Garsington Manor, from Ottoline Morrell, *Memoirs of Lady Ottoline Morrell*, 1964.

embodies a subcultural aesthetic premised on the subversion of dominant norms, rather than on their wholesale re-invention. The conventional forms of the furnishings under the unconventional decoration are, therefore, important to the effect, for they provide a normative context for the subversive play of paint. This is not to deny the practical origins of this aesthetic in the war-time conditions that forced Grant and Bell into this rundown farmhouse, reduced their income, and made new furniture hard to find, so that they were thrown back on second-hand pieces. Rather than chafe at these constraints, however, the artists developed a look that includes and overcomes them, creating an aesthetic of pleasure hard won from privation.

That this subcultural aesthetic was more than a make-shift expedient is evidenced by the fact that Grant and Bell continued to develop it—and preserved their earliest work in this genre—long after the excuse of wartime shortages. Even during the war, moreover, their purposeful development of Charleston's impromptu aesthetic is clear in their dismissive attitude toward Garsington, the estate where Ottoline and Philip Morrell sheltered conscientious objectors and other pacifists, including Clive Bell, in pampered luxury as in-name-only farmers. Larger and grander than Charleston, Garsington might be expected to attract the artists' admiration for its lavish garden, modern paintings, and extravagant décor. Vanessa Bell, however, belittled her husband's contentment at Garsington as "an odd taste," and characterized Strachey's plan to live there as "rather disastrous."[30] Grant, more lightheartedly, mocked Garsington's pretensions in a letter to Virginia Woolf. Reporting that he and Bell had read in a magazine on country estates "a letter from an old gentleman" saying "his flamingoes had weathered the severe winter without shelter, and were admirable birds to keep in England on small ponds," Grant facetiously claimed that Bell was writing for details; he concluded, "if we could only get them going on the pond I feel Charleston would be much more than a match for Garsington with all its peacocks."[31]

Charleston's difference from Garsington was expressed primarily, however, in aesthetic terms. Charleston's inhabitants derided the Morrells' *fin-de-siècle* Aestheticism, delighting in stories of how the lacquered gray foyer walls were said to reflect the red curtains in imitation of a winter sunset and the blue-green paint desecrating the oak paneling in one drawing room supposedly matched Ottoline's eyes (figs 140, 141). Garnett's memoirs suggest Charleston's disapproval of the way "the bare and somber dignity of Elizabethan wood and stone had been overwhelmed with an almost oriental magnificence: the luxuries of silk curtains and Persian carpets, cushions, and pouffes." The house, he claimed, "reeked of bowls of potpourri and orris-root which stood on every mantelpiece, side table, and window sill." Garnett follows this with a description of Philip Morrell, "in riding breeches and rat-catcher coat with a glassy geniality gleaming in his eye and his head thrown so far back that the high bridge of his nose was level with his forehead." "Posing as a farmer," he

An Aesthetic of Conscientious Objection

"exhibited precisely the kind of humbug which the Victorian novelists . . . loved to make the subject of their good-tempered fun."[32] Garsington's excessive aesthetic of "people strewn about in a sealing-wax colored room," as Virginia Woolf put it, implied inimical social values.[33] The same distinction, articulated from Garsington's perspective, is clear in Ottoline Morrell's reaction to Bell's and Grant's self-created domestic aesthetic: "It is difficult to get one's eye used to untidiness if it has been trained to care for order, but with practice I expect one could probably do it."[34]

Letters and memoirs chart the Charleston artists' growing sense that Garsington's carefully planned décor represented values at odds with their own. In 1915, on his first visit to the Morrells' newly acquired estate, Grant was happy to find himself, with the other guests, dragooned into gilding the paneling in the dining room.[35] The following year, during a visit to inspect some pigs for the farm at Wissett, he remained initially delighted at what seemed the spontaneous entertainment of the guests together painting scenes of rural life on the attic walls of an outbuilding one rainy afternoon. A letter written that night to Bell happily describes the "madness" of the project, praising the contributions of the other artists, including the children, and citing Dora Carrington's "amazing one."[36] Grant's pleasure turned to anger the following day, however, when, despite fine weather, he found himself alone coerced into finishing his decoration. Morrell later had the others white-washed over so that "only the masterpiece by Grant dominated the room," also to Carrington's annoyance.[37]

Morrell's determination to acquire a finished product from an individual artist directly opposed the Charleston artists' ethos of spontaneous pleasure in creativity enjoyed for its own sake. This difference went to the core of Bloomsbury's beliefs about what distinguished modernism from conventional aesthetics. Fry's essays from this era extend his identification of Post-Impressionism with the "expression of emotions regarded as ends in themselves" to include a distinction between what he called "the artist's vision" and the "practical vision" cast by the consumer on potential purchases.[38] This opposition between a spontaneous expression of creative emotion and the calculated acquisition of possessions underlies Bell's vehemence in a report to Fry of an argument with Lytton Strachey about Morrell:

> We debated over whether she had any creative gift or not. Norton, Duncan and I took the line that she was a terrifically energetic and vigorous character with a definite, rather bad, taste, which she put into practice but that it was different from having any creative power. . . . To me it seems simply a collection of objects she likes put together with enormous energy but not made into anything.[39]

Bell's and Grant's insistence that Morrell's collector's aesthetic lacked "creative power" was fundamental to their sense of what defined them as modernists. Bell's letter describes the debate about Morrell evolving from an argument in which she defended formalism's premises against Strachey's doubts. The contrast is also clear in Bell's assessment of Charleston on her return after a long absence: "I am rather astonished on coming here again to find how much energy we spent on this place, how many tables and chairs and doors we painted and how many colour schemes we invented. Considering what a struggle it was to exist here at all, I can't think how we had so much surplus energy."[40] Here her delight comes from rediscovering an environment she sees, not as the successful realization of a project to acquire, but as a spontaneous outpouring of creative energy.

This was Bloomsbury's vision of Charleston at its best: an embodiment of modernism conceived as an escape from conventional imperatives of canny consumption in favor of intuitive, spontaneous pleasures enjoyed as ends in themselves. Bloomsbury's belief that this modernism represented a return to primitive states of mind that had been corrupted by the norms of middle-class "civilisation" (discussed in Chapters 7 and 8) is sustained in the group's idealistic descriptions of Charleston. By the spring of 1917, Virginia Woolf described her sister's existence to an old family friend with the claim, "Nessa seems to have slipped civilization off her back, and splashes about entirely nude, without shame, and enormous spirit. Indeed Clive now takes up the line that she has ceased to be a presentable lady—I think it all works admirably." A few days later, to another old friend, she reported: "Nessa is . . . living like an old hen wife among ducks, chickens and children. She never wants to put on proper clothes again—even a bath seems to distress her. Her children are for ever asking her questions and she invents all sorts of answers, having never known very accurately about facts."[41] Woolf's exaggerations highlight the ambition to define Charleston as a place where imperatives concerning everything from etiquette to education could be forsaken in favor of "spirit" and invention.

For Bloomsbury, Charleston achieved something of the return to Eden—a secular, somewhat awkward Eden—that had been proposed in the iconography of early Omega decorations. The associations of Charleston with nature and nudity in Woolf's letters return in Garnett's memoirs, explicitly linked with the production of an art that describes a kind of modern, secular sainthood:

> In summer Julian and Quentin often went naked, adding their beauty to the Charleston flowers and orchard. They would scramble over Maynard [Keynes], ride each other horseback and fall into the pond. Vanessa sometimes followed them about stealthily, a Kodak in her hand. Duncan painted them. One summer I had to pose naked, close to the footpath leading to Firle, kneedeep in the old sheep-dip as an unhaloed St Christopher with Quentin riding astride upon my shoulders.[42]

This sense of secular beatitude is linked specifically to Eden in the memories of Bell's daughter, born in 1918, who recalled Charleston as "a world that was, or tried to be, self-sufficient; an earthly paradise," and noted her family's delight in anecdotes of social solecisms and near-disasters around the house, which reinforced their "marvelously buoyant capacity to fall from grace without reaping the usual consequences."[43]

None of this is to claim that Charleston was—or was believed to be—free from care. Quite the contrary: assertions of Charleston's edenic qualities in letters and memoirs gain force from a context of increasing privation and alienation brought on by the war. Charleston was, as Bell's daughter notes, "an idyll snatched from the horror that surrounded them."[44] The energy of the verb aptly captures the determination that went into creating and sustaining this modernist domestic ideal in the face of all logistical difficulties and ideological opposition. From this perspective, the fanciful exaggerations of Woolf's letters describing Charleston, as well as what is often characterized as the residents' obsessive urge to decorate the house, are revealed as valiant efforts to preserve modernism from the conditions that, since the outbreak of fighting in 1914, increasingly threatened its existence. In this sense, the frequent trivialization of Charleston as a carefree holiday home parallels the misreading of Fry's 1917 essay "Art and Life," in which (as my Introduction argues) the argument for the separation of "great art" from the politics of the "Great War" has been consistently misrepresented as evidence of Bloomsbury's apolitical complacency. Both should instead be recognized for what they were: manifestations, in the realms of aesthetic theory and practice, of a principled "conscientious objection" to values from which Bloomsbury was deeply alienated.

Nor does this chapter claim that, even in its own terms, the community at Charleston during the war completely achieved the prelapsarian ideals described in letters to outsiders and published memoirs. "I haven't answered your letter," Bell wrote in January of 1917, "not because I've been ill, but rather overwhelmed by domestic difficulties and visitors, which made it impossible to get the necessary quiet to consider—or at least to write about—love and friendship." She goes on, describing the challenges of Charleston, culminating with her worry "lest I shouldn't provide all the necessary hot water, etc., which Clive's passion demands for his love." Bell's conflation here of the logistical and emotional demands occasioned by her commitment to Bloomsbury's principles is as crucial an aspect of Charleston as the idealized images of a modernist Eden. But just as Bell accepted the problems of rural housekeeping as the cost of her self-exile from the dominant culture, so too this letter goes on to reassert her commitment to the social mores of her unconventional community. "It seems to me that being in love is never what other people have described," she explained, asserting a very Bloomsbury determination to reason from her own experience; "It's always so conditioned by the person one's in love with." What follows might be claimed as her manifesto:

> Yes, it is very extraordinary when two people care for each other in the right way, but perhaps there's something even more wonderful in just caring without getting the exact return. One can get back and look at the other person in a way that perhaps one can't when they're feeling that about you, at least so one thinks sometimes.[45]

This statement stands beside Virginia Woolf's analysis (quoted in the Introduction) of Fry's determination to apply the unacquisitive, objective detachment of modernist aesthetics to what she called—in a veiled reference to his unrequited love for Bell—"the problems of private life." Here Bell, equally committed to a modern sensibility in emotional life, urges on her correspondent, who was struggling to make sense of an unconventional romance, this ideal of aesthetic distance as a corrective to feelings of selfish frustration.

The importance of the links Bloomsbury saw between modernist aesthetics and modern emotions—and the centrality of domesticity to both—are reflected in major paintings created by Grant and Bell during their first year at Charleston. Bell's mural-scale (5 ½ by 6 feet) canvas now called *The Tub* was conceived as a decoration for the house, intended for a wall beside French doors leading outside from a room that doubled as a storage area for bee-keeping equipment and a second sitting-room (fig. 142). Though her letters attest to her excitement over what she called "my big bath picture," *The Tub* was, for unknown reasons, never installed.[46] Discovered after Bell's death stored away in her studio, it was acquired by the Tate Gallery in 1975, since when it has become among the best-known—and most debated—of her works.

Bell's *Tub* returns to the theme of a painting from her previous rural retreat, the image of a woman and bathing implements now known as *Interior at Wissett Lodge* (discussed in the previous chapter). A water-color sketch for the Charleston painting depicts the domestic situation Bell described in her letter: her husband's paramour, Mary Hutchinson, preparing to bathe in what appears—by the latticed window with the pond beyond—to be the primary sitting-room at Charleston, the warmest spot in the house, and therefore its schoolroom and social center, so its appropriation as a bathroom would disrupt everyone's routines (fig. 143). The standing figure in a light chemise, the pitcher, and the metal tub are, despite their various sizes, evenly arrayed across the center of the image, with the figure glancing toward them as if unsure how to bring them into any kind of useful relationship. Bell's painting transforms these awkward elements into a composition emphasizing her control over its formal elements. Her first description of the image stresses its qualities of color and space. "There's very little in the picture and it's mostly one colour or two—yellow ochre and a greenish grey. The subject is principally floor," she explains, before going on to add that the image also includes "a bath and a semi-nude female rather too like Mary and the pond seen through the window."[47] Perhaps in an effort to distance the figure from Hutchinson, a subsequent letter reports, "I've taken out the woman's chemise and in consequence she is quite nude and much more decent."[48] The impulse, evident in these letters, to subject the scene to a formal order satisfactory to the artistically detached eye governs the composition, facture, and style of the final version of *The Tub*. The primary compositional elements of the woman and bathing implements are united by the sweeping curve of the pond above the lavender window sill on which is centered a red vase of flowers bent to echo the curve of the pond's banks and reminiscent of the burst of flowers that advances from the decoration over the water jug in *Interior at Wissett Lodge*. The same revision of *The Tub* that removed the figure's clothes also eliminated the pitcher, further abstracting the composition to a simple juxtaposition of a circular and a vertical form. Attention to these elements, whether as iconography or as form, however, vies with that claimed by both the physical assertiveness of the paint—the varying shades of ocher and green applied in scrubby patches of thick strokes with

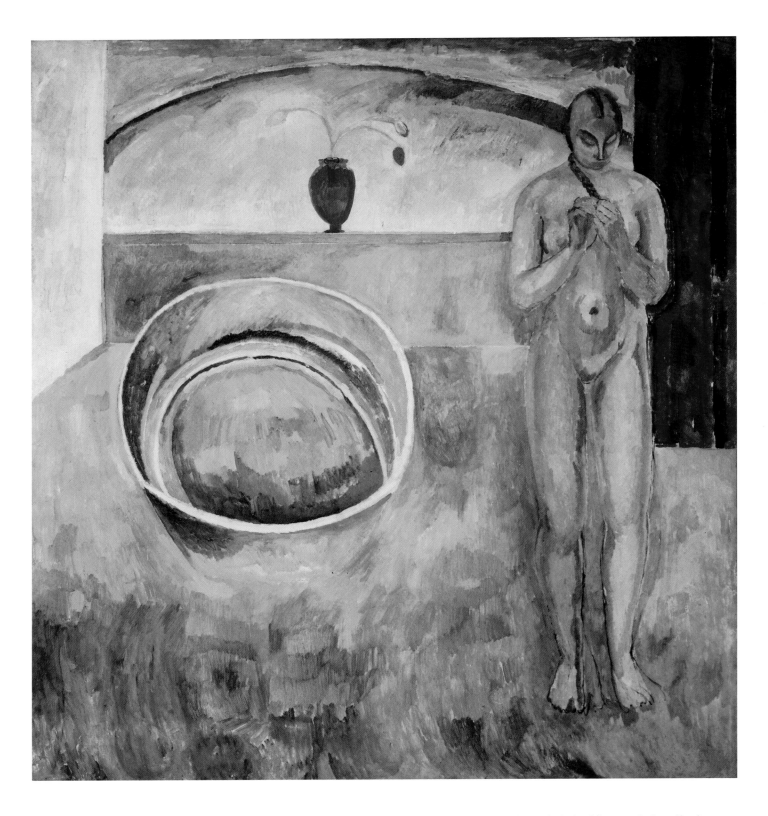

142. Vanessa Bell, *The Tub*, 1917–18.
Oil and gouache on canvas,
167 × 108.3 cm. Tate Britain.

barely concealed pentimenti shadowing the figure's left side—and the allusions to Matisse in the figure's pose and face.[49] The combined effect is to propel all reference to Clive's mistress, Charleston, or hot water, from the aggravating realm of the immediate and practical into the abstract harmonies of Post-Impressionism, where each element can be dispassionately appreciated for its own sake. A photograph of *The Tub* at its first stage (with pitcher and chemise) emphasizes its relationship to Mary Hutchinson, who poses, fully dressed and seated, before the canvas (fig. 144). This photograph, as much as the painting itself, documents the distance between

An Aesthetic of Conscientious Objection

143. Vanessa Bell, *Study for the Tub*, 1917. Watercolor on paper, 44.5 × 40.3 cm. Salford Museum and Art Gallery.

the messy human situation—"Mary has confided her troubles to me," Vanessa wrote while she was at work on *The Tub*, reporting St John Hutchinson's anger over his wife's relationship with Clive—and the image's calm ordering of its elements into a formal equilibrium associated with modernist aesthetics.[50]

Bell's *Tub* is often analyzed in relationship to Grant's paintings of women bathing. Comparisons have been drawn with both Grant's more animated pre-war painting of the same title, with its figure related to his quasi-cubist Eves (discussed in Chapter 8), and—more relevantly—to a lost work, painted in 1916 (fig. 145). Although photographs of the lost painting clearly show holes for hinges or some similar hardware along the top edge of the image, this work seems to have been painted on a discarded panel rather than intended as applied art, for it was mounted in the kind of hand-painted frame the Bloomsbury artists favored at this era. The even distribution of its elements—pitcher and soap, bather in tub, towel on rack—across the horizontal image, however, may have provided a starting point for the even more simplified composition of Bell's domestic decoration.[51]

A more telling comparison with Bell's mural-scale *Tub*, however, is offered by Grant's only slightly smaller (3½ by 4½ feet) painting known as *The Kitchen* (fig. 146). Originally painted around 1914, this work was revised during Grant's first months at Charleston, primarily by the addition of a nude youth on the right side of the busy domestic scene.[52] In contrast to the stillness of Bell's *Tub*, with its concentration on the standing female nude, Grant's image camouflages his nude—presumably bathing in the kitchen—on the edge of a composition crowded with women, children, and domestic implements. When it was first painted in the cooperative household at Brunswick Square (described in Chapter 6), *The Kitchen* might have evoked the vibrant domesticity of that living arrangement, though it is certainly not a literal transcription of the situation in that childless house where the ratio of men to women, staff included, favored the masculine. But Charleston was different. Grant and Garnett, the only adult men, returned from the fields to a house run by Vanessa Bell with the help of a shifting array of women and girls, and organized around the needs of her children and the girls who were taken in as boarders to subsidize the salary of a female teacher. This context has tempted viewers to identify

144. Photograph of Mary Hutchinson at Charleston, seated before first version of *The Tub*, 1917.

145. Duncan Grant, *The Tub*, 1916. Oil on panel, dimensions unknown, destroyed. Reproduced from Roger Fry, *Duncan Grant*, London: Hogarth Press, 1923.

the black-haired woman as Vanessa Bell and the newly added nude as, alternatively, Grant himself or Bell's oldest son, who turned nine in 1917.[53]

Just as with Bell's *Tub*, however, such readings are at odds with the artists' Post-Impressionist commitment to transcend the imitation of life and use form to arouse emotion. Where Bell created a harmonious equilibrium in the manner of Matisse, Grant's *Kitchen* offers the viewer a sensual tapestry of line and color, food and flesh, more suggestive of Pierre Bonnard.[54] Dividing the composition neatly down the center is one of the fairground "caryatids" Grant had purchased from the evocatively named Dante Paradiso in 1913 (see Chapter 8). Anchored by the vertical force—and stylistic precedent—of the Italian "primitive," Grant's composition ripples across patchy surfaces, the swoops and squiggles of his brush-strokes flowing promiscuously around forms from the shoulders of his women to the tiny details on the dishware in a composition that reminded one early reviewer of "some Sienese painting."[55] Just as the style and placement of the Italian element create the formal basis for the work, the female figure on this piece of folk art seems to survey the array of reassuring feminine archetypes multiplied across the surface of the image: the mother tenderly cuddling her child at the center flanked by the busy house-keeper working in a pantry and the buxom maid presiding over the tea table. The marginal figure of the naked boy, rendered in the pastel facets characteristic of Grant's work around 1917, makes no attempt in either style or placement to integrate himself into the composition. This effect has been provocatively analyzed as Grant "straying as if guiltily into a fantasy of his own creation."[56] Though the elements of fantasy seem clear, however, it is hard to read guilt in the figure's coyly conspiratorial glance toward the viewer. The image seems instead to express a tentative delight in its unexpected integration of themes: unveiled masculine eroticism and familial domesticity associated with the feminine.

Though Grant's *Kitchen* was not—any more than Bell's *Tub*—a self-portrait or a depiction of Charleston, both works, through their composition and style as much as through their iconography, evoke their makers' role in the household. Memoirs and letters describe Grant as having "more childish enjoyment of life than anyone I know," and possessed with an intuitive charm and a fanciful wit that enlivened those around him.[57] Bell, on the other hand, appears as an almost super-human force of calm and order. Leonard Woolf, in a description endorsed by Grant, recalled Bell's "magnificent and monumental simplicity" and her "strange combination of great beauty and feminine charm with a kind of lapidification of character" that led to "something adamantine in the content and expression of her judgments."[58] This combination of qualities—a joyful unworldliness and stern determination unshaken by adversity—was, perhaps, ideally suited to create a haven from the cataclysm of the war.

This was Charleston in its early years: a bold and stubborn project to create an environment where the spontaneous pleasures of modernism could be sustained despite the war. What its residents conceived as a temporary and defensive refuge, of

An Aesthetic of Conscientious Objection

146. Duncan Grant, *The Kitchen*, 1914, reworked 1916–17. Oil on canvas, 106.7 × 135.9 cm. King's College Cambridge.

course, became central to Bloomsbury's history. Bell and Grant continued to live off and on (but, as they aged, increasingly on) at Charleston, and the house, as both a setting for their relationship and an expression of their values, helped define and preserve their aesthetic and social ideals. The repeated embellishment of Charleston's rooms and almost endless depictions of the house and its surroundings in paintings from throughout Bell's and Grant's careers (discussed in Chapter 14) attest to Charleston's importance for its inhabitants; today, Charleston offers the most complete record of Bloomsbury's domestic aesthetic. If in later years this living world of Post-Impressionism came to seem sometimes too solipsistic and self-satisfied—Virginia Woolf in the thirties complained of Grant and Bell at Charleston, "There they sit, looking at pinks and yellows, and when Europe blazes all they do is screw up their eyes and complain of a temporary glare in the foreground"—it is important to recognize that this respite was hard-won during the difficult last years of the First World War.[59] It is important to remember, also, that until the return of the wartime conditions that prompted its establishment in the first place, Charleston was not a full-time residence for Grant and Bell, who maintained lodgings in London. The house's almost hermetic reflexivity was part of its function as a retreat.

As a retreat—whether from war or, later, from urban life—Charleston exemplified the possibility of expressing subcultural values through the construction of domestic space. A fascination with Charleston as a world apart, an alternative to conventional ways of life, is evident in the comments of the thousands of visitors and growing piles of coffee-table books about the house and gardens. At its most superficial, this may be simply escapist fantasy. More profoundly, however, the ability to imagine new forms of domestic life is fundamental to any project to re-imagine social values. The enthusiasm of visitors to Charleston today echoes the responses of those who discovered the house immediately after the years covered in this chapter. John Lehmann, a college friend of Julian Bell and visitor to Charleston in the twenties, recorded his sense of the links between the look of the house and the ideology it suggested:

> The doors and fireplaces of the old farmhouse transformed by decorations of fruit and flowers and opulent nudes . . . , the low square tables made of tiles fired at Roger Fry's Omega workshops, and the harmony created all through the house by the free, brightly colored post-impressionist style that one encountered in everything from the huge breakfast cup one drank one's coffee from to the bedroom curtains that were drawn in the morning, not by a silent-footed valet or housemaid but by one's own hand to let in the Sussex sunshine . . . seemed to suggest how easily life could be restored to a paradise of the senses if one simply ignored the conventions that still gripped one in the most absurd ways, clinging from a past that had been superseded in the minds of people of clear intelligence and unspoilt imagination.[60]

The rejection of convention in favor of sensuality, intelligence, and imagination: this was the ideal imagined and embodied at Charleston.

Urban Outposts
River House and 46 Gordon Square (1916–19)

The preceding two chapters examined the impact of World War I on Bloomsbury by tracing Vanessa Bell's and Duncan Grant's retreat to a series of increasingly isolated rural houses culminating in Charleston. This retreat was both physical and ideological, for by leaving London the artists also abandoned the Omega Workshops, and with it the twin projects of fostering larger communities of avant-garde artists and encouraging the public's acceptance of modern art. When the Omega opened, its directors had imagined themselves at the center of expanding circles of modernist colleagues and patrons. After 1914, however, they found themselves increasingly alienated from the art world and society at large, both of which, from Bloomsbury's perspective, were rapidly regressing into attitudes inimical to modernism. "Heaven may delude those whom it wills to destroy," Clive Bell remarked in a 1917 essay on the war's destruction of avant-garde projects for aesthetic and social renewal. Now, he complained, "one foresees the hard, unimaginative view of life regaining the ascendancy, laborious insensibility re-crowned the queen of virtues . . . and the grand biological discovery that the fittest do survive adduced again as an argument against income-tax." "The war has ruined our little patch of civility as thoroughly as a revolution could have done; but, so far as I can see, the war offers nothing in exchange," is his bitter conclusion.[1] By 1917, Vanessa Bell was advocating closing down the Omega completely, and Fry had abandoned the forward-looking term "Post-Impressionism," telling a reporter that the rubric had "died out after a short vogue."[2]

Although the war shifted Grant's and Bell's art away from expansive public initiatives, their domestic projects were not limited to Charleston or the country. On the contrary, between 1916 and 1919, the sense of alliance with "people of true ideas" that Grant asserted as the obverse of his alienation from his countrymen found expression in major decorative schemes he and Bell carried out for the London houses of some of their nearest associates.[3] These projects turned away from the provocative modernism of Bloomsbury's pre-war interiors, however. Even where entire rooms were conceived as a piece, the small scale of the decoration marked a retreat from the ambitious murals of the Omega's early years. Even more significant was the abandonment of the abstract idiom and modern subjects of, for example, Bell's cubist mosaic still life at Hyde Park Gate or Grant's tennis player mural at Brunswick Square (figs. 78, 61). Bloomsbury's new designs looked backward in style and inward in iconography. This chapter examines two commissioned interiors executed in London during the last years of the war and its immediate aftermath, the first for St John and Mary Hutchinson, the second for John Maynard Keynes.

That Vanessa Bell's relationship with Mary Hutchinson was far more complex than accounts saturated in conventional assumptions of rivalrous jealousy would allow (as argued through Chapters 9–11) is further evidenced by the fact that, during the last years of the war, her house was second only to Charleston as a locus for Grant's and Bell's decorative work. When, in September of 1916, the Hutchinsons moved to River House in the London borough of Hammersmith, the site was already associated with the recent history of the English avant-garde. Kelmscott House, William Morris's residence and the namesake of the Kelmscott Press, was nearby in the terrace of eighteenth-century houses that had been a center of the Arts and Crafts Movement in the 1890s. Morris's famous *News from Nowhere* begins in this riverside house in Hammersmith, which becomes the first site in the book's lovingly described vignettes of life in a future restored to the beauty of the past. In the first decade of the twentieth century, the neighborhood had attracted a new generation of artists, including the sculptor and designer Eric Gill (whose relationship to Fry is discussed in Chapter 2). River House itself had been the home and workshop of the Arts and Crafts bookbinder and printer T. J. Cobden-Sanderson, a pacifist who, in despair over the war, in 1917 sank his type in the Thames and gave up his craft. The Hutchinsons emphasized their house's Arts and Crafts legacy, muddling this history so that an article on their decorating in *Vogue* in 1919 misidentified River House as the site of the Kelmscott Press.[4]

Such associations with the late-Victorian avant-garde may have influenced Bell's first decoration for the Hutchinsons (figs. 147 and 148). Writing from Wissett in August 1916, she reported:

> I have been painting Mary's bed. . . . One side is a woman asleep, rather like "Flaming June" by Lord Leighton with poppies and waves (I think) all deeply symbolical. On the other is the remains of a dessert she has been eating and down below flowers tied in a true lover's knot of white satin ribbon. You see what I can do on occasion.[5]

Bell's comparison of her work with Leighton's "deeply symbolical" painting—a characterization augmented in a letter to the Hutchinsons describing the design as a "nude figure of the most romantic description"—clearly challenges the precepts of Post-Impressionism, allying the decorated bed with the historical quotations in her paintings and decorations at this time for Wissett and the *Copies and Translations* show (discussed in Chapter 10).[6] Despite Bell's claims for the old-fashionedness of her design, however, its look remained indubitably Post-Impressionist. A simple composition, brilliantly colored in energetic brush strokes, the nude on Bell's bedstead—like her nursery for the Omega (fig. 24)—finds its closest visual comparison in Matisse's work decades later.[7] Bell's presentation of her design as an experiment in historical reference, however, reflects Bloomsbury's changing ideas about modernism's relationship to the past.

This shift is also clear in Fry's contemporary work for the Omega. Executing a commission for Lalla Vandervelde—the wife of the Belgian ambassador and, like Mary Hutchinson, a cosmopolitan socialite who was both a friend and a patron—Fry in October 1916 produced another painted bedstead that took as its theme the relationship of traditional forms of representation to modernist abstraction (figs 149, 150 and 151).[8] Following Bell, Fry juxtaposed images of a reclining nude and a still life of food (though his featured fruit, rather than Bell's "remains of a dessert"). Unlike Bell, however, Fry provided both a headboard and footboard, affording him four surfaces to paint. Exploiting this format to compare modernist effects on conventional genres of imagery, Fry rendered in contrasting styles the same still life on each side of the footboard, and the same nude on each side of the headboard. The contrast is especially striking for the nude. On the side of the headboard facing the pillow, the figure is softly modeled. The opposite side of the board shows the same figure flattened and abstracted, demonstrating the procedure of "translation" Fry would promote the following spring in the *Copies and Translations* exhibition. Fry's claim that the show demonstrated how "Cimabue is the same thing practically as El Greco and Cézanne" both reiterated his claims that Post-Impressionism was rooted in older art and reauthorized historical modes of representation as part of the legitimate vocabulary of modern artists.

An Aesthetic of Conscientious Objection

147. Mary Hutchinson's bedroom at River House, Hammersmith, as illustrated in *Vogue*, early February 1919, featuring bed painted by Vanessa Bell, 1916.

The principle of modernism's compatibility with earlier aesthetics became the basis for the decoration of River House, carried out in stages between 1917 and 1919. "A Harmony of the Furnishing of Two Centuries" ran the headline when the house was featured in *Vogue* in 1919 (fig. 152). The text described the interior as a "happy example of how an old-fashioned house may be harmonized with a modern scheme of decoration arranged by Duncan Grant and Vanessa Bell." Painted furniture and pottery from the Omega, along with examples of Post-Impressionist painting, combined with the Hutchinsons' eighteenth-century portraits and Georgian furniture to "strike an amusing note of contrast" against walls colored "warm apricot" with "broad upright bands of cobalt blue" separated by "a line of

148. Vanessa Bell, *Nude with Poppies* (study for bedstead for Mary Hutchinson), 1916. Oil on canvas, 23.5 × 42.5 cm. Swindon Museum and Art Gallery.

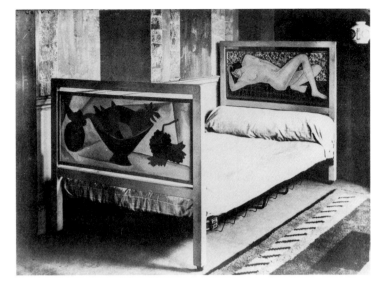

149. Lalla Vandervelde's bedroom, furnished and decorated by the Omega, 1916.

150 and 151. Roger Fry, painted bed for Lalla Vandervelde, 1916, each panel 45.7 × 76.2 cm. Victoria and Albert Museum.

greenish yellow."[9] A 1924 *Vogue* feature, noting the Hutchinsons' collection of modern art by Matisse, Derain, Dufy, and Laurencin, asserted that "holding these together, framing them, and keeping them on terms, are the decorations arranged by Duncan Grant and Vanessa Bell."[10] Such claims for the harmonizing effects of Grant's and Bell's designs—here accorded the power to create continuities both among modernists and between modernism and the past—are a far cry from the headlines just a few years before, when Omega rooms were seen by advocates and antagonists alike as uncompromising announcements of a new era: a "futurist

An Aesthetic of Conscientious Objection

152. Duncan Grant and Vanessa Bell, decorations in drawing room of River House, Hammersmith, 1918–19, as illustrated in *Vogue*, early February 1919.

nightmare" according to journalists, or "the usual things turned round to extremes" in Grant's phrase.[11]

Paradoxically, the aspect of the River House décor that most closely anticipates later modernist art was, at the time, cited as evidence of the new, more historically conciliatory, aesthetic. For the wall over the drawing-room fireplace, Grant made wallpaper by splattering paint in rhythmic gestures prescient of 1950s Action Painting (fig. 153).[12] Far from heralding the future, however, Grant's drip-work settled in among other modernist variations on earlier design practices: sponged *faux-*

153. Duncan Grant and Vanessa Bell, painted mantel and wall paper in drawing room of River House, 1918–19, as illustrated in *Vogue*, early January 1925.

154. Vanessa Bell, painted door in study of River House, 1919, as illustrated in *Vogue*, early November 1924.

marbre under the mantel and old woodwork painted in contrasting colors to high-light its patterns. Contextualized in this way, Grant's design was seen by *Vogue* in 1925 as simply a background "'écriture' of soft browns and yellows."[13] This assessment is reflected in photographs of the room. Pictures taken shortly after the decoration in 1918 show the dripped panel left bare and juxtaposed with a painting by Grant of almost equal size, creating a visual suggestion of its equivalence with his work of art. Photographs of the same room in the mid-1920s, however, show a Matisse painting (acquired by the Hutchinsons in 1920) hung over the painted papers, and now balanced by another small painting on the adjacent wall where the larger canvas had been, reducing the drip-work panel to a decorative background. A growing emphasis on the continuities between old and new is also clear in Grant's and Bell's ongoing decorations at River House. In 1919, while Grant painted fruit over the mantel in the study, Bell decorated a door to the room with a still life of fruit and flowers in the upper panel and a fanciful vase evocative of eighteenth-century ornamental porcelain in the lower panel (fig. 154).[14] Eschewing the brushy energy of similar motifs painted a few years earlier at Charleston, these decorations mediate between the Hutchinsons' Post-Impressionist paintings and their more traditional eighteenth- and nineteenth-century furniture and bibelots.

The extent to which the Hutchinsons' furnishings and attitudes may have determined the decoration of River House is impossible to gauge. That Grant's and Bell's retreat from a forward-looking modernism reflected their own ideas as well, however, is shown by a concurrent project of decoration they carried out closer to home. The significance to Bloomsbury of 46 Gordon Square—the house that, more than any other, gave the group its name—would be hard to overstate. When, during Vanessa Bell's move from Wissett to Charleston in 1916, she and Clive realized they could no longer afford the lease on their London house, Clive jestingly borrowed a phrase from French tourist guides to wonder if, "our friends would like to save 46 Gordon Square as a 'monument historique.'"[15] Ultimately, that is just what happened. Keynes, with two Cambridge friends now working in London, took over the house, sharing its expenses and reserving rooms for the Bells' visits to town.[16] This reorganization of Bloomsbury's London headquarters called for new decoration. Bell's and Grant's decorations for the reconfigured 46 Gordon Square marked the changes in the group's constituency and ideology.

A crucial aspect of Bloomsbury's changed constituency was the dissolution of its triumvirate of artists. During the war, Grant and Bell drifted away from Fry and toward others—Keynes and the Woolfs especially—who had been peripheral to the group's first appearances in the public eye during the controversies over the Post-Impressionist exhibitions and the Omega. Keynes, in addition to sharing 46 Gordon Square with the Bells, became a weekend resident at Charleston, sharing expenses and gardening. Keynes's integration into the Charleston household is at first glance surprising, for it united the Bloomsbury figure who was most involved in the war

An Aesthetic of Conscientious Objection

with those most determined to escape the effects of the conflict. But it was the Charleston artists' determination to ignore the war that made their house Keynes's refuge from both government colleagues and those in Bloomsbury who were more active in pacifist politics and critical of his career.[17] To Grant he could confess, "I pray for the most absolute financial crash (and yet strive to prevent it—so that all I do is in contradiction with all I feel)."[18] When, in 1919, Keynes angrily resigned from the Treasury, he retreated to Charleston, where he wrote most of *The Economic Consequences of the Peace*, the bitter indictment of the signatories to the Treaty of Versailles that made him a best-selling author.

No less important was the Charleston artists' deepening connection with the Woolfs, who maintained dwellings near Charleston—Asheham throughout the war, then, after their eviction in 1919, Monk's House in the village of Rodmell—allowing for regular contact between Virginia and Vanessa. Their relationship was strengthened when in 1917 the Woolfs founded the Hogarth Press, which supplanted the Omega as a producer of illustrated books and created opportunities for professional collaboration between the sisters. The Hogarth Press's 1919 *Kew Gardens* bracketed Woolf's latest experiments in modernist prose between a woodcut frontispiece and endpiece by Bell. An enthusiastic review of this collaboration in the *Times Literary Supplement* made this booklet the Press's first success, and was credited by Leonard Woolf with turning their hobby into a business.[19]

The Charleston artists' new links with Keynes and the Woolfs coincided with a loosening of their bonds to Fry and the Omega. For Fry, this was deeply frustrating. "It can't help being rather full of moments of pain coming and seeing how completely satisfied and absorbed you are, however much I may be glad for you that it is so," Fry confessed after an early visit to Charleston. Several weeks later, he complained to Bell, "It's dreadful how much I want to be something in your life quite real and definite—how I feel that to stop out of it is a kind of death."[20] For her part, Bell firmly delineated new boundaries in her relationship with Fry: "what I want is not exactly what you want, for I sometimes think you do want more than you yourself are quite aware of," she wrote; "it's not true to say that our going on depends upon me simply—it also depends upon your being able to believe both that I know what I want and am honest about it. . . . It depends much more upon your caring to have what I can give."[21]

Fry's loss was both personal and professional. As his co-directors absorbed themselves in rural life, the financial and managerial responsibilities of the Omega fell increasingly to him. Ignoring Bell's advice to close the Omega, Fry rented Durbins to the Stracheys to pay for the workshops.[22] The River House commission deepened the breach. For his colleagues to contract for design work outside the Omega, Fry believed, established them as "a rival firm." Begging Grant and Bell, "as directors and original members of the Omega," to refuse independent decorative commissions, Fry wrote: "it would avoid a thing that gives me great and I daresay unreasonable pain; it dots the i's so very much of you and D[uncan]'s secession from the Omega in the eyes of the world; and, after all, I have done a good deal in the past to give both you and D. your present position."[23] Having lost this argument, Fry later in 1917 accepted a personal commission for design work from Lalla Vandervelde, effectively ending the Omega's status as a collaborative design firm and reducing it to a shop. It was in this context of realignment and retrenchment that the decorations for both River House and Gordon Square were conceived and executed during the last months of the war.

Although the renovations at Gordon Square were less comprehensively documented than River House, what records remain suggest that Keynes's London décor evoked the refuge he found on weekends at Charleston. Most of the work was in the shared sitting room, which had been Bell's studio, and, on the evidence of paintings depicting this space, had walls of a rich red. Grant exulted, "I'm looking forward to doing this room, it will be great fun I think, the walls are really a wonderful color." Bell and Grant planned decorations for the doors, mantel, and shutters of this room, though only the set of double doors are documented (fig. 155).[24] The upper panel of one door depicts a woman fixing her hair in a pose echoing

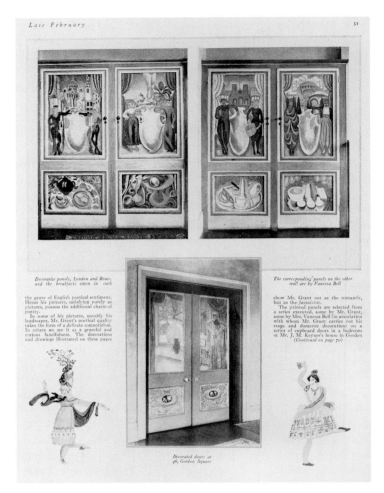

155. Page from *Vogue*, late February 1923, showing Vanessa Bell and Duncan Grant, painted cupboard doors (top) and painted double doors (bottom) at 46 Gordon Square, 1918.

Grant's depictions of Bell.[25] Beside her, expanding on to the other panel, was another quotation from a painting, this one by Bell, showing a window at Charleston embellished with an Omega vase on the sill and open to a vista of the pond (fig. 156).[26] Closing the doors to the sitting room at Gordon Square, therefore, revealed an image of Charleston that unified its interior and exterior, as well as its two primary inhabitants. Under this scene, the lower panels of the doors displayed, against a stippled background, the same kind of antique vases Bell painted for the door at River House.

As the stage for Keynes's London life, the sitting room proclaimed his modernity. "My drawing room is . . . going to be, when finished, the flashiest room in London," Keynes announced to his mother while the work was underway.[27] The decorations' contribution to Keynes's mystique is recorded in Roy Harrod's recollection of his first meeting with Keynes in 1922 in the drawing room at Gordon Square: "The room itself made a strong impression. It seemed empty, devoid of the usual ornaments and appendages, in a style that was rapidly to come into fashion, but was strange to me. . . . This environment, with its assertion of modernity, itself provided a slightly exciting background" for Keynes himself.[28] This version of modernity—novel as it may have been for Harrod—contrasted strongly with Bloomsbury's pre-war interiors, including the nursery murals upstairs at Gordon Square (discussed in Chapters 8 and 9), which were apparently destroyed at this time. The drawing room that constituted the most public space in the London house of the most public member of Bloomsbury turned away from both the ambitious scale and forward-looking style of Omega-era designs, proposing a version of modernism that narrowed the scope of reference from Edenic allusions to a shared paradise to the specific iconography of Charleston and the art produced there. This

An Aesthetic of Conscientious Objection

effect, of course, was only evident to the extent that viewers could contrast the style of the decoration with earlier projects and recognize visual references to Charleston. Gordon Square, Keynes, and even modernism itself were here claimed for Charleston in a language best understood by Bloomsbury insiders.

This inward turn in Grant's and Bell's domestic aesthetic is reflected, as well, in the only still extant component of the redecoration at 46 Gordon Square: two double sets of painted cupboard doors for Keynes's bedroom, which present across their four upper panels emblematic vignettes of cities important to Bloomsbury's history of residence and travel: London, Rome, Paris, and Constantinople (figs. 155, 157–60).[29] These nostalgic images are humorously enlivened with the suggestion of domestic intimacy by the still lifes in the smaller lower panels of the doors, each of which juxtaposes to the heraldic urban scene above a depiction of the breakfast eaten in each city. Both the city scenes and the breakfasts (except London's) are framed by curtains, pulled back as if to reveal a stage, while the two figures in each of the upper panels present blank escutcheons, suggesting theatrical tableaux.

Following pages:
157–60. Vanessa Bell and Duncan Grant, painted cupboard doors for 46 Gordon Square, 1918. Gouache on wood: London, 183.5 × 74.3 cm; Rome 183.8 × 74 cm; Paris 183.2 68.3 cm; Constantinople 182.9 × 68.3 cm. King's College, Cambridge University.

156. Vanessa Bell, *Charleston Pond*, c.1919. Oil on canvas, 63.5 × 67.3 cm. City Art Galleries, Sheffield.

The formality of these designs is offset by such witty details as the abruptly truncated sculpture in the picture of Rome, a hatbox as an attribute of the emblematic female figure of Paris, and the presentation of the spirit of London in the form of two lissome youths in uniform, hinting at Keynes's sexual adventures in his home city. Far from any call to a forward-looking modernism, these decorations suggest a sensibility attuned nostalgically—if ironically—to the fantasies and delights of pre-war European travel to historic sites of artistic accomplishment; even London is represented by the spires and domes of Christopher Wren's churches rather than by a modern structure.

Behind the light-hearted fantasy evoked by these decorations lies a serious point. Like the more public decorations in the sitting-room at Gordon Square, these panels assert a modernism without ambitions to ground-breaking novelty or overwhelming scale. On the contrary, this modernism defines itself through a loving incorporation of history and human scale. The relationship to the past expressed here is eclectic, pastichy, even overtly touristy in its choice of emblematic sites and meals. Rather than dismissing these qualities as banal or bourgeois, however, it would be well to contrast them with the violent jingoism of an art world grown increasingly enamored of propagandistic imagery and claims to have retrieved national styles from the polyglot influences of the pre-war avant-garde.[30] In this context, these images' delight in spectacles of foreignness, and the presentation of London as equivalent to other capitols, are revealed as part of Bloomsbury's determination to resist the ideological effects of the war.

This assessment is buttressed by Bloomsbury's writings of this era, which show the group's sense of its identity as modern shifting away from association with vanguard explorations of the new and toward claims to protect certain fundamental values at risk because of the war. This is the argument of Clive Bell's wartime essays. His 1915 "Art and War" argues, "The state of mind which art provokes and which comprehends and reacts to art is one in which nationality has ceased to exist," and that art creates "a world in which patriotism has become meaningless," while his 1917 "Before the War" mourns the lost "open-mindedness" of the pre-war years.[31] Bell republished both these essays in 1918. Similar ideas animate Fry's 1917 dismissal of people who "promised themselves a great new art as a result of the present war," and underlie Grant's 1916 claim (referred to at the opening of this chapter) to find comradeship among "people of true ideas that one might and did meet in every country."[32] More to the point, these are the ideas behind Keynes's *Economic Consequences of the Peace*, which begins by describing how the unprecedented economic growth and social mobility before the war swelled the ranks of "the middle and upper classes, for whom life offered, at a low cost and with the least trouble, conveniences, comfort, and amenities beyond the compass of the richest and most powerful monarchs of other ages." Among the opportunities enjoyed by the pre-war middle class, Keynes noted, "the inhabitant of London could order by telephone, sipping his morning tea in bed," services including "cheap and comfortable means of transit to any country or climate without passport or other formality . . . and could then proceed abroad to foreign quarters, without knowledge of their religion, language, or customs." "Most important of all," Keynes said, the middle classes "regarded this state of affairs as normal, certain, and permanent." Their confidence was misguided, of course, for it ignored the agents that would "play the serpent to this paradise," primary among them "projects and politics of militarism and imperialism, of racial and cultural rivalries." The idyll "came to an end in August 1914," Keynes wrote, and would not be restored by the peace settlements because of nationalism, the belief, as he put it, that "Nations are real things, of whom you love one and feel for the rest indifference—or hatred." It was nationalism that provoked the burdening of the defeated nations with war reparations bills so high that their starving children must "pay tribute until they are forty or fifty years of age in relief of the British taxpayer." Keynes's bitterness is summarized in this tragically prescient passage:

> If we take the view that . . . while all our recent Allies are angels of light, all our recent enemies, Germans, Austrians, Hungarians, and the rest, are children of

An Aesthetic of Conscientious Objection

the devil, that year by year Germany must be kept impoverished and her children starved and crippled. . . . heaven help us all. If we aim deliberately at the impoverishment of Central Europe, vengeance, I dare predict, will not limp. Nothing can then delay for very long the final [European] civil war . . . before which the horrors of the German war fade into nothing. . . .[33]

Keynes's anger was shared by his Bloomsbury colleagues, who, persecuted for opposing the war from the start, now found themselves powerless to prevent the perpetuation of many of its worst effects. Keynes, of course, differed from his friends at Charleston who retreated in the face of such disillusionment, but his sympathy with them is clear in one of the most poignant and personal passages of *The Economic Consequences of the Peace*: "No one can feel more intensely than the writer how natural it is to retort to the folly and impracticability of the European statesmen,—Rot, then, in your own malice, and we will go our way." This comment is addressed specifically to Americans, on whose treasury the European recovery depended. Keynes's response, however, reveals his own rationale against alienation as he urges America to recall as motivation "what Europe has meant to her and still means to her, what Europe, the mother of art and of knowledge, in spite of everything, still is and still will be."[34] Despite Grant's and Bell's willingness to succumb to the impulse to retreat, it is tempting to see their decorative evocations of great European cities in Keynes's bedroom as an effort to sustain him in his work for the common weal.

The Bloomsbury of the post-war period was very different from the one that flourished before 1914. Having made its name as a contingent of the avant-garde art world, the group emerged from the war associated with new voices in politics and literature. Keynes's 1919 *Economic Consequences of the Peace* followed Lytton Strachey's 1918 *Eminent Victorians* in challenging political authority, while Virginia Woolf's experimental fiction, which began appearing in 1917, undermined literary convention. The dissolution of the group of artists who had been Bloomsbury's public face coincided with a shift in Fry's interests first noted by Woolf in 1916 when she predicted "the complete rout of post impressionism, chiefly because Roger, who has been staying with us, is now turning to literature, and says pictures only do 'to look at about 4 times.'"[35] The results of this realignment included not only Fry's translation of the poems of Stephane Mallarmé and Woolf's exploration of the links between painting and writing in her 1927 *To the Lighthouse*, but a fundamental re-thinking of aesthetic theory to make a place for representation alongside the role claimed for form.[36]

The final section of this book traces Bloomsbury's shifting conceptions of the meaning of the modern through the rooms created by Grant and Bell for themselves and their friends after the war. (It is significant of the changes in Bloomsbury that, after the Omega closed in 1919, Fry abandoned large-scale domestic decorations.[37]) Bloomsbury's interiors of the Twenties are probably the least examined of its artists' work, dismissed out of hand by histories of modern design still responsive to the heroic values the group associated with the war and steeled itself to oppose. Many of the qualities of Bloomsbury's post-war design—especially its humor and aura of nostalgic fantasy—find their origins in the interiors the chapters in this section have analyzed as an aesthetic of conscientious objection. Where this section has grounded this emerging aesthetic in Bloomsbury's subcultural social values, the following two chapters are concerned with the ways Grant's and Bell's post-war design were—and remain—a legitimate form of modernism.

Section V

Re-Imagining Modernism

In fifty years, when peace outshines
Remembrance of the battle lines
. . .
Some ancient man with silver locks
Will lift his weary face to say:
  "War is the fiend who stopped our clocks."

Siegfried Sassoon
"Song-Books of the War," 1917

The previous section proposed the phrase "aesthetic of conscientious objection" to stress the often-overlooked continuities between Bloomsbury's political and aesthetic resistance to a war that threatened what the group saw as modernism's fundamental principles. Though the changes in Bloomsbury's domestic aesthetic began as acts of isolated resistance, however, their new ideals conformed to broad trends in European art at this period. The avant-garde's widespread abandonment of experiments in abstraction and concomitant reassertions of various historical precedents are often glossed with the phrase "*le rappel à l'ordre*" [the recall to order], which was coined in 1919 by the painter and critic André Lhote, an influential voice in the post-war French art press.[1] An "aesthetic of conscientious objection" versus a "return to order": the differing emphases of these two phrases suggests how Bloomsbury's participation in the reconfigured of avant-garde of the post-war era differed from that of its French counterparts, despite the visual parallels that have prompted some historians to dismiss Bloomsbury as an English derivative of French sources.

On a basic factual level, the first experiments in historical quotation that Bell and Grant executed early in 1916 seem to have taken place in ignorance of comparable developments in the French avant-garde. More importantly, although the motivations for and manifestations of the *rappel à l'ordre* in France varied, it was widely and authoritatively presented as a rejection of individual self-expression in favor of a return to national tradition, values inimical to Bloomsbury.[2] This difference is clear in Fry's response to Lhote's columns when translations appeared in the *Athenaeum* in 1919. Fry regretted what he called Lhote's "outburst of impatience with the whole modern movement," and condemned his French counterpart's admiration for Jacques Louis David's "cold and chauvinist rhetoric." The terms of Fry's critique—"it's no longer the passion for order but the love of authority"— became the basis of Clive Bell's essay, "Order and Authority," which appeared as a rebuttal to Lhote in the *Athenaeum* late in 1919.[3] This essay (discussed in the Introduction) contests the nationalist basis of Lhote's claims for the *rappel à l'ordre* by associating "order" with self-motivated individual sensibility in contrast to the submission of artists to exterior "authority."

Despite Bloomsbury's dissent from Lhote's interpretation of art's return to tradition, Fry and his colleagues were intrigued by French artists' re-engagement with pre-modern styles. Like many French critics, Lhote identified Picasso as a bellwether of the change, citing "the speculations of a more immediate realism towards which the prince of Cubism seems, more and more, to tend."[4] Lhote alluded here to

Facing page:
Detail of fig. 190.

what by 1919 was well known: Picasso's renewed interest in stylistic and icono-graphic precedents from eighteenth- and nineteenth-century French artists, espe-cially Jean-Auguste Dominique Ingres.[5] Bloomsbury's painters were probably the first in England to recognize Picasso's new direction, however. Following a short visit to Paris in 1916 (some months after Bell and Grant began copying proto-Renaissance paintings at Wissett), Fry reported to Bell that he had found Picasso "a little *dérouté* [thrown off course] for the moment but doing some splendid things all the same—among others an Ingres-like realistic drawing. . . ."[6] Although Bloomsbury was not immediately inspired by Picasso's example to revisit Ingres in particular, knowing that "the prince of Cubism" had returned to pre-twentieth-century styles can only have encouraged the group's experiments in historical quo-tation.[7]

Nor was Picasso alone among the French artists Bloomsbury admired in rethink-ing the implications of art history at this era. Matisse during the war also reversed his evolving abstraction to re-examine late nineteenth-century conventions of style (brushy variations on Impressionism) and motif (especially harem images and domestic interiors). Matisse's *rappel* is exemplified by his 1917 *Music Lesson*, which, it has been noted, copies the basic composition of his *Piano Lesson* from the year before, revising the image to add elements from the traditional iconography of domestic genre painting rendered in more realistic detail.[8] Matisse's revisionism compares to Grant's 1918 transformation of an earlier abstraction into a still life (discussed in Chapter 9).

The three chapters in this final section examine Bloomsbury's decorative designs of the Twenties and thirties, which developed in the context of the French *rappel à l'ordre* and parallel trends in Britain, where nationalist claims animated critical rhet-oric. Announcements of a return to national tradition had animated British critical rhetoric throughout the war years and by 1921, when several journals ventured overviews of post-war art, were accepted as fact.[9] A review in *Colour* began from the premise that "there is no real break between the past and present in art" and went on to praise the recent recovery of English art from the "rather too sentimental" excesses of the nineteenth century and the subsequent over-correction in which "art became too theoretical, too diagrammatic": "What seems to be happening now, is that our younger painters"—among whom Fry and Grant (aged fifty-four and thirty-five respectively) were listed—"with a full sense of the importance of design, are finding its elements in natural forms and colours instead of in geometrical sym-bols" with the happy result that nothing in exhibitions of recent art "should be unintelligible to the ordinary person."[10] The art critic Frank Rutter, who (as noted in Chapter 3) had titled his 1910 paean to Post-Impressionism *Revolution in Art* and dedicated it to "rebels . . . fighting for freedom of any kind," in 1921 under the title "Extremes of Modern Painting" condescended to both Picasso's cubist "puzzle-pictures" and a pre-war British avant-garde that "imitated the defects of painters whose excellences they did not understand." Rutter concluded:

> Since 1918 there has been a general return to realism, but the experiments of the extremists are not valueless. They have widened the horizon of painting and opened the road to a new realism in which the firm structure and rigid design of the Cubists will be combined with a truth and beauty of colour derived from the Impressionists. But the wisest artists of all will be those who . . . follow the advice of Van Gogh and pay heed "not so much to the teaching of painters as to the teaching of nature."[11]

Such quotations exemplify the assertions of consolidation and consensus that characterized not only art criticism, but British post-war culture in general, a con-nection implicit in the language of *The Nation*'s report that "our artistic hierar-chies" intended to "strike a truce (on the 'forget and forgive' basis) with what passes for 'modern' painting."[12] More subtly than in 1910, when Post-Impressionism was attacked as a manifestation of anarchism, aesthetics and politics were linked in rhetorics that absorbed pre-war modernism into the reigning consensus. Bloomsbury's artists confronted such claims not just as general proposals, but specifically directed at their own practice, as critics welcomed their return to the fold, always on the condition that abstraction be abandoned. The *Athenaeum* in 1920, for instance, praised Fry's portraits as "an expression of interest, not in significant form, but in that particular person," recommending that he "forget all about … significant form."[13] Also in 1920, Claude Phillips in the *Daily Telegraph*, after characterizing Grant as "one of the most brilliant post-impressionists or extremists" who "challenged the unhappy citizen to face a show of the most defiant modernity," asserted that "when he is not painting opaque green, black-shadowed flesh [he] is a striking and original colourist" and advised Grant to "put from him the hideous trivialities imposed by the opinion and example of a limited clique."[14]

Such calls for "extremists" to disband and to re-integrate with tradition found echoes within Bloomsbury. By 1927, Fry's *Cézanne* described both Impressionism and cubism as "loop[s] in the curve of pictorial tradition," useful for bringing "back certain valuable material into the main current," but finally rejoining the flow, each movement having "abandoned a great deal of what at the time seemed of great importance to its exponents."[15] The effects of such ideas on Bloomsbury's easel painting can be debated. Careful scrutiny of Grant's paintings of the Twenties, for instance, might nuance subsequent sweeping critical generalizations that Grant "leaned more and more on comfortable formulae" in his post-war art, doing "less than justice to his abilities since those heady days of 1914" by retreating "to a surprisingly tame form of naturalism."[16] Nevertheless and despite certain exceptions, it is true that Bloomsbury's post-war paintings shied away from experimentation with abstraction, often repeated compositional patterns, and toned down their color.

The same is not true of Bloomsbury's decorative work. Though certainly different from their pre-war designs, the Bloomsbury artists' domestic decorations of the Twenties and Thirties display a wide range of stylistic reference, facture, and scale. This distinction has been noted by more astute critics, among them Simon Watney, who blamed Fry's participation in the *rappel à l'ordre* for pushing Bell and Grant into narrow practices of fine art, so that "from 1919 onwards the wit and inventiveness which had so brilliantly informed their Post-Impressionist careers was almost exclusively reserved for their careers as interior decorators."[17] Fry's writings on Grant and Bell at this period do—rather ironically in view of the Bloomsbury critics' professed belief in self-discovered "order"—urge the artists to discipline themselves, especially in relation to Grant's instincts toward seductive sensuality. Reviewing an exhibition of Grant's in 1920, Fry warned against the dangers associated with his "gift of spontaneous and inevitable self-revelation": "there is a great temptation to the artist to rest satisfied with the exploitation of his spontaneous and instinctive reactions. . . . Such an artist, gifted in the special ways I have described, must have a tough intellect and a solid *morale* not to fall into the trap which Nature and the public have combined to lay so cunningly."[18] A 1922 review of Bell notes that "she has worked much with Duncan Gant, who is distinguished for the charm and elegance of 'handwriting,' " then commends her facture, in contrast, as "slower, more deliberate, less exhilarating." Praising Bell's art as "almost austerely simple and direct, with a keen sense of the underlying architectural framework," Fry urges her to resist "the influence of Duncan Grant's more playful and flexible spirit."[19] In response to this article, Bell wrote, "you know I care more for your opinion than for anyone else's."[20] The result, as Watney suggests, was a widening gap in Grant's and Bell's practice, between their tightly controlled (and increasingly repetitious) easel paintings and their more innovative decorative work, which evolved under the looser supervision of both the critics and the artists themselves, who absorbed the dictum, as Grant put it, that "decoration ought to be devoid of intention."[21]

For Watney, it is not just the diminishing interest of the easel paintings, but Bell's and Grant's "tragic relapse from their previous and intensely serious questioning of the whole Fine-v-Applied Art distinction" that is to be regretted.[22] In light of this split between Bloomsbury's easel painting and decoration, this section focuses on the latter. Unlike their easel paintings, which for the most part conformed to the general trend to re-investigate nineteenth-century *plein-air* precedents, the interiors Bell and Grant created after World War I indulge a deeper and more eclectic range of historical reference, stretching from the proto-Renaissance to include eighteenth-century painting and ceramics as well as nineteenth-century Aestheticism. This range, combined with techniques of facture and deployments of scale that emphasize qualities of pastiche, defies injunctions to discipline, both national and personal. Though this quality of playfulness was accepted as modern in the twenties and remains an unmistakably twentieth-century style, its deviation from another authoritative form of discipline—the functionalist evolutionary logic claimed by champions of the International Style—has excluded it from the historical canons of modernism. Nevertheless—and this will be the central argument of this final section—this work is modern: deeply implicated in developments that historians focusing on economics, literature, sexuality, and mass-culture have identified as definitive of modernity. Ultimately, what an analysis of Bloomsbury's later interiors reveals are the limitations that continue to bind art history to heroic narratives of modernism that were deployed in the thirties as part of ideological debates of that era (these will be discussed in the final chapter). The Bloomsbury artists' re-imagination of domesticity in the post-war era proposes very different meanings for the conditions of modernity.

Public Figures' Private Spaces
King's College, Cambridge, and 52 Tavistock Square (1920–24)

Although World War I officially ended on November 11, 1918, the announcement of the Armistice occasioned mixed reactions at Charleston, beset by the privations caused by the war. Vanessa Bell, heavily pregnant, stayed at home, cautiously measuring the effects of her alienation from the broader culture against her identification with her countrymen's joy. "It's extraordinary to feel that fighting is at an end," she wrote. "I can't quite make out why it makes so much difference to one, for one wouldn't have thought, at least I personally shouldn't, that one minded so very much what was happening to one's fellow creatures. But I think the relief now is simply in thinking that that horror has stopped, for nothing else is different from what it has been for some time." In this mood, Bell found David Garnett's euphoria "rather trying and it was a relief when his emotions carried him off to London for the night to join the rejoicings of the crowd." Duncan Grant, caught between the conflicting emotions of his two companions, announced a quick trip into the nearby town of Brighton in search of local celebration, then accompanied Garnett to London.[1]

The discontinuity among Charleston's residents on the night of the Armistice reflected growing divisions in the household and foreshadowed changes to come. Garnett, feeling increasingly trapped in the country, had developed a physical revulsion to smells associated with livestock and begun a series of affairs with women, the latter arousing Grant's frantic distress. It was, once again, Bell who held the household together, lecturing Grant and Garnett on jealousy, which she compared to a toothache as a pain one must learn to accept without wrath or moral approbation.[2] Bell's report to Fry articulated her attitude for his benefit:

> I can say it from my own experience . . . that there's no good in trying to force oneself to feel more than one feels or even to show more than one feels inclined at the moment to show, but one can force oneself not to expect or even want much more than is freely given, and I think any good relationship depends in the end upon the one person being able to do that. At least I have found that that is what I have to do and it seems to me probably always the case.[3]

Grant, in a journal he kept briefly at this troubled period, recorded his reactions to Bell's arguments:

> I was hurt slightly by her saying she got no more from me than a brotherly affection. . . . I am so uncertain of my real feeling to V[anessa] that I am utterly unable to feign more than I feel when called upon to feel much, with consequence that I seem to feel less than I do. I suppose the only thing lacking in my feeling to her is

passion. What of that there might be seems crushed out of me by a bewildering suffering expectation of it (hardly conscious) by her. I think I feel that if I showed any, it would be met by such an avalanche that I should be crushed. All I feel I can do in this case is to build slowly for her a completely strong affection on which she can lean her weary self.[40]

It was during this period of emotional turmoil in the spring of 1918 that Grant and Bell initiated the sexual relationship that resulted in her pregnancy, an outcome both welcomed.[5] Nevertheless, this climate of hurt feelings and stifled expectations at Charleston contrasts starkly with Bloomsbury's earlier enthusiasm for erotic and emotional experimentation.

This climate exerted an inhibiting effect on an artistic practice conceived as the free play of intuitive emotional expression. Bell's *Tub* and Grant's *Kitchen*, both discussed (in Chapter 12) as earlier manifestos for the modernist domesticity enacted at Charleston, contrast strongly with another mural-scale (approximately 5½ feet square) painting created at this period, Grant's *Interior* (fig. 161). Composed from sketches, Grant's image balances the figures of Bell and Garnett in Charleston's dining room, the artist's viewpoint—significantly—between them. Grant's journal records that on the morning he began the painting he "couldn't bear anyone being in the room even Nessa."[6] Although Bell was encouraging—"it's lovely colour of course and I think should be a very interesting space," she reported to Fry—and some historians have praised the picture's complex organization, its overriding effect is emptiness, with voids both down the central vertical axis and across the top half of the composition, which the still-life elements sprinkled around the periphery do little to fill.[7] Even more telling than the void at the artist's location is the suppression of the exuberant handling and rich color that had characterized Grant's earlier domestic depictions. Here a drab palette of greens and grays applied, to take the most optimistic view, with "more deliberation and solidity than is usual," looks to other commentators "so dense that it had perhaps become an unconscious expression of the emotional claustrophobia" at Charleston.[8]

The emotional pressures at Charleston were compounded by physical privations, which, despite the Armistice, worsened in the winter months, when both food and heating fuel were in short supply. Bell's daughter was born early Christmas morning, but five years later, her memory of "hearing the farm-men come up to work singing carols" after the delivery was overshadowed by "the horrors afterwards, when [the baby] nearly died through the doctor's idiocy and every possible domestic disaster seemed to happen" so that "I rather forgot the happy part of it."[9] A new doctor, a young woman who, Bell noted with pride, "patronizes the Omega," was summoned and saved the baby, but Bell reported to Keynes, "Such pandemonium as has reigned here for the last month must I think have equaled that at the Peace Conference."[10] Months later, Bell remained depressed and anxious over her responsibility for three children in a disintegrating household with straitened finances, and more than a year later she still vividly recalled "the horrors of that winter" of 1918, with "no coal, hardly any coke or wood, me upstairs with no nurse, Duncan cold and depressed downstairs and Bunny for some reason cheerful."[11]

Ultimately it was Keynes who came to the rescue. At Grant's behest, he took over the daily expenses and management of Charleston when he moved in for the summer of 1919 to finish *The Economic Consequences of the Peace*. More important, Keynes early in 1920 began successfully investing in international currency markets, first with his own money, then for Grant and Bell. By March of 1920, the return of Bell's confidence in Bloomsbury's claims for individual emotions over authoritative standards is marked in her vehement response to a relative who had sanctimoniously inquired about the paternity of her new daughter. About her relationship to Clive, Vanessa wrote:

we neither of us think much of the world's will or opinion, or that a "conventional home" is necessarily a happy or good one. . . . Perhaps the peace and strength you talk of can come in other ways than by yielding to the will of the world. It seems to me at any rate rash to assume that it can't, or in fact that there

161. Duncan Grant, *Interior*, 1918.
Oil on canvas, 163 × 174.8 cm. Ulster
Museum, Belfast.

is ever any reason to think that those who force themselves to lead lives according to convention or the will of others are more likely to be "good" (by which I mean to have good or noble feelings) than those who decide to live as seems to them best regardless of other standards.

Now claiming courage from her experiences during the war, Bell concluded, "Surely everyone who can think at all must have had to come to some conclusion as to what they value most during the last 5 years. It hasn't been possible not to face the question."[12]

Contributing to Bell's rediscovered confidence were the opportunities Keynes's investments allowed. In March 1920, the Charleston principals—Grant, Bell, and Keynes (Garnett having left the previous January)—set off, passing though Paris, for a six-week holiday in Italy. For Bell and Grant, this trip marked the end of the privations associated with the war and its aftermath. "So many things that have to be repressed in one seem to expand and develop when one gets to France again," Bell exclaimed in a letter describing the first days of their trip. From Italy, she reported: "the buildings are all so beautiful. We are overcome by the modern church decorations, sham marblings, flowers, vases, etc."[13] "After six years of England I often find it almost incredible that here one is in Italy again and think it will all vanish suddenly and I shall find myself back at Charleston or Gordon Square," Bell confessed; "One had got to think it impossible the war would ever come to an end or that one would ever get abroad again."[14] With their investments rising and the Italian currency plummeting, Keynes encouraged his companions to buy furniture and pottery, joking that it was their duty to prevent Italy's financial collapse.

Although a few weeks after their return to England in April, Keynes's investments failed, evaporating their gains along with their original capital, the pleasure of the trip sustained a bond among the voyagers. Bell told Keynes, "I don't think I've ever enjoyed anything so much for a long time, and it still makes me very happy to think of it."[15] Grant, back in England, advocated permanent expatriation, complaining to Bell, "I do seriously think one ought to go and live in Italy. Why should one waste the best years of one's life in this place if one is a painter?"[16] Bell's revived spirits, however, infused her perceptions of home with hopes of regaining what the war had destroyed. Writing from Charleston in August 1920, she exclaimed: "It's extraordinarily nice here. Not having spent the whole year here, for the first time I can feel as if it were a holiday to be here. It's almost like pre-war days at Asheham."[17] The fusion of these two impulses animated Grant's and Bell's first domestic commission of the 1920s: the redecoration of Keynes's Cambridge rooms to evoke what these British modernists most valued in Italy.

The new decorations in Keynes's Cambridge quarters updated Grant's 1910 mural of grape harvesters and dancers, which (as discussed in Chapter 3; see fig. 28) proposed an earlier version of a modern sensibility rooted in Italian tradition. The provocative sensuality of this bacchanal may have grown inappropriate to the economist's new-found public stature, however. Even before he became internationally renowned, Keynes's affairs with men opened him to blackmail threats from a landlady, and by 1919 gossip about his love life was troubling Treasury officials in the paranoid climate created by the right-wing press's claims that Germany held a "Black Book" with 47,000 names of influential Englishmen who could be blackmailed over their "sexual perversions."[18] It was at this period that Keynes—though he did not give up boyfriends—initiated a series of heterosexual flirtations, culminating in his engagement to Lydia Lopokova in 1923. Whatever Keynes's motivations, his new décor replaced the first mural's energetic eroticism with a setting suited in both style and subject to a public figure who might be expected to receive dignitaries and reporters. Keynes was actively involved in planning his new decorations, for he was living at Charleston during the summer of 1920 when Grant and Bell began painting the eight allegorical figures—four by each artist—for his sitting-room (figs 162, 163, 164). Supposedly representative of various academic disciplines, the figures' symbolism is uncertain. Noting the contrast between the females in their variously colored gowns and the males who are "nude mostly," Bell reported, "they are supposed to represent law, science, history, etc. though you mightn't think it—in fact we're always changing their arts and their sciences."[19] Though such high spirits moderated impulses toward seriousness in Keynes's new decorations, the figures, nevertheless, supplanted an iconography of uninhibited private sensuality with subjects more in keeping with the discipline(s) of an academic institution.

The changes effected in Keynes's redecoration are all the more striking in that they were worked out in relation to many of the same historical precedents invoked by Grant's earlier mural. Various sources have been suggested for the style and poses of the figures in the new decorations, including Piero della Francesca, Luca Signorelli, Bono de Ferrara, and Andrea del Castagno, all of whom—and many others—were fresh in the artists' minds following their trip to Italy.[20] Grant and Bell did not recreate any particular precedent, however, but invoked proto-Renaissance art more generally: the females echo the sibyls in Castagno's procession of famous

people at the Villa Carducci (now in the Uffizi), while the sinuous male nudes recall illustrations of panels by Ferrara in a recent issue of *The Burlington*. The effect of the decorations was to evoke in Keynes's Cambridge rooms the aesthetic—down to the modern painted marbling Bell noted in the churches—the three travelers believed they had found in Italy untouched by the war. This emphasis on historical stability marks an important shift in the meanings of Italian precedents since Grant's invocation of Piero in Keynes's first mural. Then, Italian sources justified a modernism that rejected Victorian norms in favor of "primitive" sensuality. Now the graceful figures, each poised in its own niche and emblematic of an academic discipline, proposed a modernism that, rooted in the static compositions of the

162 and 163. Duncan Grant and Vanessa Bell, Arts and Sciences decorations for John Maynard Keynes, King's College, Cambridge, 1920–22 as illustrated in *Vogue*, early March 1925.

164. Duncan Grant and Vanessa Bell, detail from Arts and Sciences decorations for John Maynard Keynes.

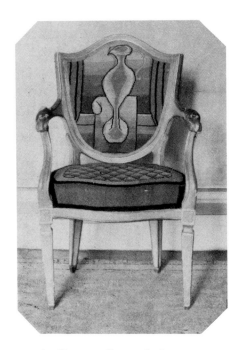

165. Duncan Grant, designer, embroidered chair back for John Maynard Keynes, worked by Marie Moralt, *c.*1920, as illustrated in *Vogue*, early November 1924.

proto-Renaissance, could transcend chaos and destruction. This shift is also reflected in the disciplined facture of the panels, so different from the exuberant brush that sketched the ring of dancers in Grant's first mural for Keynes.

The changing meaning of proto-Renaissance precedent is clear in the critical theory coming from Bloomsbury at the time. In a 1919 review for the *Athenaeum*, Fry used a domestic metaphor to compare a visit to the re-opened National Gallery to "the peculiar pleasure which one gets on turning out a long-locked drawer and discovering its half forgotten treasures." About these once-familiar paintings, Fry reported, "we really can look at them again," and their new setting "reveals entirely new aspects." Focusing his review on "the most convinced and intransigent artists of the early Quattrocento in Florence," what Fry now emphasizes is not the emotional self-expression he had claimed as a precedent for Post-Impressionism, but that "they could build figures—everything they did had something of architectural symmetry—of overpowering majesty without straining a gracious suavity of rhythm. They could convey the idea of pure simplicity with the assurance of perfect science."[21] Writing just a few months later in *The Burlington* about another quattrocento painter, Fry reiterated the value of order over passion: "The fact is Fra Angelico was, for all the fervour of his religious emotion, a fiercely intellectual artist, one whose immense sensibility was always under the control of an almost mathematically precise mind."[22]

Associations of modern painting with order and intellect have not worn well. Like the art of the *rappel à l'ordre* in France, the Bloomsbury artists' post-war search for a more disciplined modernism finds little favor with recent critics, who have characterized the figures in the Keynes decorations as "rather melancholy," "austere," so "dignified and sombre," "stiff and unaccented," that their "vitality . . . seems lost."[23] In their immediate post-war context, however, the decorations' bid to recapture lost ideals was welcomed. A feature on Keynes's rooms in *Vogue* began by characterizing the artists' "gift, nowadays so rare, for decorative work on a large scale," and joined this suggestion of old-fashioned artistry with praise for Keynes as an old-fashioned patron: "By combining exact scholarship with an interest in contemporary art, Mr. Keynes may be said to have restored a tradition that has been lost to our Universities since the Renaissance."[24]

When they installed their panels—the first four in 1920 and the rest in 1922—Bell and Grant also painted Keynes's rooms, highlighting architectural details to emphasize the figures' stately rhythm and embellishing the fireplace with modernist "marbling".[25] Bell completed the ensemble with dramatic appliqué curtains suggesting symmetrical urns in a garden, and Keynes installed the antique furniture he had purchased in Rome, including an armchair re-upholstered with a needlework back designed by Grant and worked by Marie Moralt, the young doctor interested in modern design who had saved Bell's baby eighteen months before (fig. 165). Grant's design for the chairback centers on a stylized gray-green ewer and pear similar to the still-life elements he had earlier superimposed on an abstract painting to mark his return to figuration (as discussed in Chapter 9, see fig. 121).[26] This jug-and-fruit motif became something of a signature for Grant in this period—this is especially clear in his 1920 *Venus and Adonis*, where an incongruously small jug with fruit takes the conventional place of the signature in the lower right corner (fig. 166). In this sense, the chair signs Grant's contributions to Keynes's renovated Cambridge rooms, marking the decoration not just as (in part) his design, but, more specifically, as the work of an artist who has foresworn the Post-Impressionist experimentation inaugurated by the room's earlier, now obliterated, décor for a more historically disciplined version of modernism.

Visiting Cambridge in 1923, Virginia Woolf noted in her diary that Keynes had "the pleasantest sitting room I have ever been in, owing to the colours & paintings, curtains & decorations of Bell & Grant."[27] Other visitors, however, were shocked at what was still a very unconventional environment. The memoirs of a secretary Keynes hired at this era describe "startling wall paintings of Duncan Grant . . . where a nude negress . . . alongside a cardinal in scarlet . . . proclaimed the free individualism which Keynes's literary style had led me to expect."[28] Though the

Re-Imagining Modernism

166. Duncan Grant, *Venus and Adonis*, *c.*1919. Oil on canvas, 63.5 × 94 cm. Tate Britain.

conspicuous absence of both nude negresses and scarlet cardinals in the décor demonstrates the potential for factual error in period accounts, this memoir registers how even this more disciplined post-war domestic environment served as a visual manifesto for forms of modernism beyond the visual. For both Keynes and Woolf, unconventional domestic settings were backdrops for celebrity in other forms of "modern" accomplishment. Where before the war, Bloomsbury's reputation was as an art-world contingent identified in the press by reference to Fry, the Omega, or Post-Impressionism, in the post-war years, Virginia Woolf's fiction, Leonard Woolf's journalism, and the Woolfs' joint efforts as publishers—combined with Strachey's *Eminent Victorians* and Keynes's *Economic Consequences of the Peace*—created a broader identity for the group, contextualizing its artists' output within broader challenges to prevailing norms of interest to a wide public. When, therefore, in 1923, with Leonard committed to more editorial work at *The Nation*'s London office and Virginia feeling increasingly trapped in suburban Richmond, the Woolfs decided to return to the neighborhood that gave Bloomsbury its name, their sitting-room (fig. 167) became another semi-public domestic space: a place for meetings, receptions, and dinners; a background for celebrity portraits; and—like Keynes's rooms–the subject of journalistic interest as the setting of an exemplary form of modernism.

The symbolic importance of these rooms begins with Virginia Woolf's diaries. The entry of 9 January 1924 opens with self-conscious portent: "At this very moment, or fifteen minutes ago, to be precise, I bought the ten years lease of 52 Tavistock Square London W.C. 1—I like writing Tavistock." Here, the Woolfs made their living quarters in the top two floors (the lower two being occupied by solicitors' offices) and installed the machinery and offices of the Hogarth Press in the old kitchens in the basement. The implications of this move were profound for Virginia, whom Leonard had brought to suburban Richmond ten years before after her nervous breakdown and suicide attempt. Now she could write to Vanessa, comparing her return to Bloomsbury to the sisters' first move from Kensington: "I feel as if I were going on with a story which I began in the year 1904: then a little insanity, and so back."[29] In her diary, Woolf lovingly listed the pleasures she associated with her return to London: "music, talk, friendship, city views, books, publishing, something central & inexplicable, all this is now within my reach, as it hasn't been since August 1913."[30]

The importance of Woolf's new environment was marked by her decision—for the only time in her life—to commission murals from Bell and Grant for her new

167. Duncan Grant and Vanessa Bell, decorated sitting room for Leonard and Virginia Woolf at 52 Tavistock Square, London, 1924, as illustrated in *Vogue*, early November 1924.

living quarters. Unlike both the Omega-era decorations and the interiors Grant and Bell designed for Charleston and for other Bloomsbury houses around 1924 (discussed in the following chapter), both Keynes's and the Woolfs' decorations use rigid framing elements to subject the gestural signifiers of modernist self-expression to an architectural order. At the Woolfs', each panel comprised an oval still life isolated on a white field, itself contained within rigid bands of crosshatching inside a solid frame for a ordered effect emphasized by *Vogue*'s photographs of the room, for which much of the furniture and all of the clutter of books and papers visible in more casual images were removed.[31] Gisèle Freund's celebrity photographs of the Woolfs seated before their decorations (fig. 168) suggest that, unlike the brilliant hues of Keynes's mural, the colors at Tavistock Square were muted, correlating with *Vogue*'s descriptions of the still-lifes as "painted in umbers, browns, and white, with touches of lettuce green" against grounds that alternated pale pink (as seen in the photograph) or yellow. These restrained tones, according to a photo caption, were separated from walls of "pale dove grey" by "tomato-red borders" (this last term, judging by its use elsewhere in this article to describe similar framing elements in an extant cabinet, connoted a more muted rusty color than might be associated with tomatoes today).[32] More evocative is Woolf's description of painted dots on the mantel: "a tender blue, like the blue of a chalk hill blue, or the sea at a distance, with chalk cliffs in the foreground."[33] Juxtaposed to these ordered panels, but sequestered above eye level, was a frieze-like strip of wallpaper energetically scrawled and spattered, according to *Vogue*, in "subdued violet on white and lemon yellow."[34] This element at Tavistock Square—like the patches of marbling behind the figures and bounded within geometrical shapes on the fireplace in Keynes's decorations—contrasts with the representational elements in the décor as if to demonstrate how the abstract colors and forms associated with modernist painting have been disciplined both within architectural boundaries and in relation to figuration. Just as Keynes's new decorations created a setting appropriate to his status as prominent scholar and patron, the disciplined modernism of the Woolfs' London sitting room, two flights up from their publishing firm, suited a couple ambitiously engaged in the art and business of modern literature. *Vogue* characterized the Woolfs' décor as "a very cool, restful, and at the same time lively scheme," while one visitor's memoirs describe the murals' "contribution to the unsolemn atmosphere of a room not like any other."[35] Both phrases register an effect of

Re-Imagining Modernism

balance (the term "unsolemn" is poised between solemnity and its antithesis) in this modernist environment.

And it is modernist, this despite the persistence of art historians in dismissing British art and design of this era as the detritus of a culture "opting for an evasion of its own modernity."[36] During the Twenties, even the unsubtle analysis of popular pictorial magazines recognized Grant's and Bell's interiors as modern alternatives to the standard " 'period' room . . . in the style of any stipulated monarch," which "can be bought wholesale"—as, indeed, is demonstrated by these journals' full-page advertisements for firms like Harrods.[37] Recent studies of the period, however, continue to condemn Bloomsbury's aesthetic as evidence of impulses toward "retreat, evasion, and concealment of modernity's impact" that negated "any real engagement with modernity" at this era. This dismissal of Bloomsbury's "private and quietist 'modernism' " narrows the definition of modernism to art picturing "the idioms and categories of industrialization," especially "urban culture [as] a principal expression of the technological genius of modernisation," with the goal of confronting "the systems of developed capitalism [to] mount an oppositional and critically evaluative account of its society against the dominant discourse."[38] To restrict modernism to critiques of industrial capitalism is acknowledged to exclude virtually all British art of the 1920s; in this view, therefore, Wyndham Lewis becomes the paradigmatic modernist because he gave up art-making altogether at this era, turning his attention to novels satirizing the failed avant-garde.[39] Lewis's satires—which

168. Gisèle Freund, Leonard and Virginia Woolf, 1939. Color photographic print, 30.1 × 20.1 cm. National Portrait Gallery, London.

tirelessly rehearse Jewishness, homosexuality, transgression of gender norms, and the class pretensions of the *nouveaux riches* as signifiers of the avant-garde's corruption—and his alternative ideal of a single genius/leader who would re-impose stability on the flux of post-war culture undoubtedly exemplify one characteristic attitude of the Twenties.[40] Though articulate and erudite, however, the extent to which his stance of perpetual resentment qualifies as "oppositional and critically evaluative" is debatable. Lewis's intellectual trajectory is acknowledged, even by sympathetic commentators, to end in a "private, textual, and ultimately fantastic world" bitterly antagonistic to both avant-garde and popular culture.[41] Ultimately, Lewis's ideal of a heroic leader who could end modern culture's "eternal mongrel itch to *mix*" led him to promote fascism in general and Hitler in particular.[42]

Lewis's career, happily, was not modernism's only legitimate course, aesthetically or politically. Politically, Bloomsbury believed that the principles of humanistic individualism that had sustained its pacifist subculture during the war could, in the post-war era, ground challenges to the ideologies of competitive *laissez-faire* capitalism and nationalist militarism. Keynes's economics and Leonard Woolf's advocacy for the League of Nations, for example, are not evasions of modernity, though their hopes that their activism would prevent another European war were to be unrealized, at least in the short run (one might argue that their potential was better realized in the second half of the twentieth century). Even in the context of the Twenties, however, Bloomsbury's ideas were central to efforts to define modernism, not as a denial of the economic and social conditions of the twentieth century, but as a rationale for managing modernity so as to achieve an unprecedented realization of the ideals of humanistic individualism. The rooms Bloomsbury's artists designed for their eminent colleagues at this period might be seen, respectively, to engage each of the terms in the concept of humanistic individualism. Keynes's Italianate personifications of academic disciplines clearly address the first, while the Woolfs' still lifes suggests a series of vignettes that speak to the latter. On a basic level, both the formal arrangement of each still life and its hand-made rendering reveal an individual sensibility—richly informed by a humanistic history of art.

Even if one accepts the premise that modernist individualism must engage with urban conditions, however, it would be wrong to rule the decorations for the Woolfs' sitting-room outside that definition. Both in subject and composition, the Woolfs' murals are, read rightly, testaments to the city as site of modern individuality. In Virginia Woolf's first diary entry about the Tavistock Square house, her enumeration of urban pleasures—"music, talk, friendship, city views, books, publishing"— is immediately preceded by a description of what could be seen from her new rooms: "the view of the square in front & the desolated buildings behind."[43] This juxtaposition corresponds to what would have been the experience of the decorations *in situ*, where the two series of three porthole-like still-life panels echoed the three windows that afforded the views Woolf described. The iconography of the still lifes includes elements from Woolf's list of urban pleasures—musical instruments, open books, writing materials—and the framed still-life format itself alludes to the museums and galleries that were central to Woolf's experience of London. Even the images that are not obviously urban Woolf perceived as city scenes. A letter describing her new home reports, "My rooms are all vast panels of moonrises and prima donna's bouquets—the work of Vanessa and Duncan Grant"; here even floral imagery is cast into the urban context of the curtain call.[44]

Even the most overtly bucolic image, the large central panel depicting a two-handled vase in a window overlooking a Mediterranean mountain village, can be seen as reflecting Bloomsbury's perception of post-war urbanism. The importance of Mediterranean tourism to Keynes's definition of modernism was linked to Grant's and Bell's 1918 decorations for his London house (discussed in Chapter 12), and it was from the city's railway stations that tourists—Woolf among them—departed for Europe. E. M. Forster's *Howards End* cited such associations with railway stations as a definitive aspect of urban identity. Describing London's stations as "our gates to the glorious and the unknown," Forster says that those "who have lived long in a great capital" have "strong feelings about the various railway termini," so

169. Duncan Grant and Vanessa Bell, panels from sitting room for Leonard and Virginia Woolf at 52 Tavistock Square, London, 1924, as illustrated in *Vogue*, early November 1924.

Italians in Berlin "call the Anhalt Bahnhof the Stazione d'Italia, because by it they must return to their homes." He concludes: "he is a chilly Londoner who does not endow his stations with some personality and extend to them, however shyly, the emotions of fear and love."[45] A crucial part of London's identity, therefore, was its status as a portal to the Mediterranean.

Iconographic references to city life were matched, in the Tavistock Square decorations, with allusions to the Woolfs' urban existence as authors and publishers of modernist texts. A still life of stringed instruments on the panel over the fireplace at Tavistock Square (fig. 172) echoes Bell's woodcut illustration for Woolf's short story "The String Quartet" (fig. 173) in the 1921 volume *Monday or Tuesday*, for which Bell also provided a cover that anticipates the decorations' format of a tondo in a rectangular frame (fig. 174). Dust jackets for books were themselves a modern innovation, and Bell's design for the 1922 *Jacob's Room*—an urn of flowers seen through a curtained window executed in rusty "tomato-red"—had established the distinctive style for Hogarth Press editions, which was now reiterated in the Woolfs' domestic decorations (fig. 175). Emphasizing the modernism of this aesthetic, Leonard Woolf described how book dealers objected to a cover that did not "represent a desirable female or even Jacob in his room," matching the consensus of "the literary 'establishment' " that the text was "unintelligible and absurd."[46] Bell's dust jacket for *Mrs Dalloway*, which Woolf completed at Tavistock Square late in 1924, compares even more closely to the murals (fig. 170). Here, in yellow and black, a fan and a bouquet—reversed, as they would be in a print made from the corresponding still-life in the decorations—sit on a window-sill before a view of a bridge over a river, which, given *Mrs Dalloway*'s famous vignettes of London, must be the Thames.[47] The look of the decorations in the Woolfs' London house, in short, reflected what was rapidly becoming the house-style of their press, asserting continuities between Bloomsbury's productions of art and literature that cannot be ignored in assessments of the group's place in the history of modernism.

The many claims that have been made for the modernism of Virginia Woolf's literature would comprise a book—at least—in itself. To apply just one modernist characteristic of Woolf's fiction from the Twenties to Bloomsbury's contemporaneous art—and to the decoration of Tavistock Square, in particular—consider her focus on the place of individual experiences and perceptions within the patterns of modern life. The first two novels Woolf completed at Tavistock Square, *Mrs Dalloway* and *To the Lighthouse*, take up this issue in explicit relation to the war, tracing its consequences in the experience of the survivors. Diametrically opposed to Wyndham Lewis's fantasy of a single hero with the authority to analyze and order

170. Vanessa Bell, cover for Virginia Woolf, *Mrs Dalloway*, London: Hogarth Press, 1925.

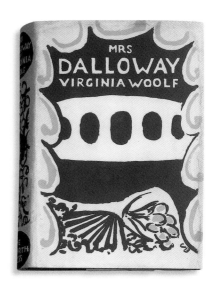

171. Embroidered firescreen for Leonard and Virginia Woolf, designed by Grant and worked by his mother, 1924, Monk's House.

172. Duncan Grant and Vanessa Bell, painted fireplace and overmantel in sitting room for Leonard and Virginia Woolf at 52 Tavistock Square, London, 1924.

173. Vanessa Bell, woodcut illustration for "The String Quartet," in Virginia Woolf, *Monday or Tuesday*, London: Hogarth Press, 1921.

post-war conditions, Woolf's fiction compares the perceptions of individuals who differ in respect to gender, class, age, and politics, juxtaposing what she called their "moments of being" to create the patterns she associated with "reality."[48] This aspect of Woolf's novels compares with the decorations Grant and Bell created as a setting for her London life: a series of still lifes balancing views out windows to suggest associative meanings for the city, none dominating the others, each with its own claims to formal significance, and all proposing various perspectives and scales (a piano is represented as congruent with objects on a table top, while vases and pitchers loom much larger than life over Virginia's head in Freund's photographs).

To dismiss such imagery as an evasion of modernity because it does not depict a skyscraper or a machine is to misunderstand the nature of both urbanism and modernity. The city is not, as is asserted in critiques of Bloomsbury, "the representative experience of modernity" simply because it is bad: the locus where "the insecurity and unreadability of modernisation press hardest. . . . the place of regimentation, and of the discipline of the machine, the hardening of economic and class distinctions, and the proliferation of the bureaucracies of modernity."[49] Such generalizations rehearse Romantic binaries, originated within an urban bourgeoisie for whom the countryside is a site of leisure, and ignore the changing structures of regimentation in rural life, its disciplines, its hierarchies—issues that are carefully elucidated in novels like *Howards End*. Obscured by this ideology, moreover, is the aspect of the modern city as a site of social and aesthetic innovation. Recent feminist theory has described the liberatory potential of the city's social and aesthetic "inexhaustibility," which constantly evades ambitions to totalize or force conformity.[50] It might be argued that this is the central theme of *Mrs Dalloway*, which opens by invoking the city as a place where, on an errand to buy bouquets—" 'I love walking in London,' said Mrs. Dalloway. 'Really it's better than walking in the country' "—a middle-aged woman's thoughts range from memories of garden parties before the war to reports of military carnage, while the urban spectacle reminds her that after her own death, "somehow in the streets of London, on the ebb and

Re-Imagining Modernism

flow of things, here, there, she survived." Though Woolf undoubtedly violates Lewis's prescriptions against temporal flux, *Mrs Dalloway* is far from evading modernity. On the contrary, the novel confronts what Bloomsbury believed to be the fundamental social and aesthetic challenge following a war that had shown how easily and sordidly lives and liberties could be sacrificed for authoritative abstractions. Just as Keynes's economics and Leonard Woolf's politics sought to undermine authoritarianism by expanding the ranks of a middle class with experience of individual autonomy, Virginia Woolf allied herself with Bloomsbury's artists and art theorists by developing forms of modernist expression that nurtured a diversity of individual subjectivities. Against an opposing modernist ideal invested in the authority of the heroic artist, or designer, or politician, Woolf saw herself as describing patterns—social and aesthetic—in which, as Leonard Woolf, borrowing from Marx, repeatedly put it, "the free development of each is the condition of the free development of all and in which the existence of every individual is widened, enriched, and promoted."[51]

As discussed in the introduction, this ideal led Bloomsbury to valorize domesticity as a primary arena of individual subjectivity. It is, therefore, appropriate that the decorations of the Woolfs' London sitting room should represent a sequence of still-lifes, several including a bouquet of flowers—the object of the urban quest that begins *Mrs Dalloway*—among other talismans of aesthetic creativity, each representing an episode of ordered individual subjectivity, a "moment of being." This vision of modernism challenged—and continues to challenge—more conventional

174. Vanessa Bell, cover for Virginia Woolf, *Monday or Tuesday*, London: Hogarth Press, 1921.

175. Vanessa Bell, cover for Virginia Woolf, *Jacob's Room*, London: Hogarth Press, 1922.

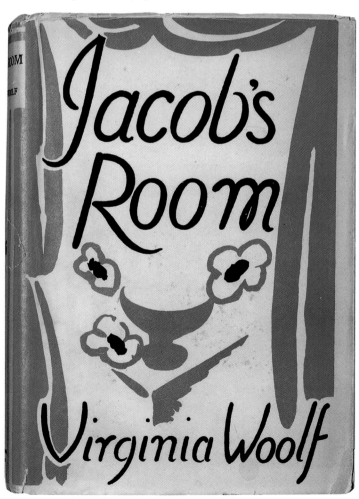

ideas of picture-making, like those of the book-dealers who demanded an image of Jacob in his room to illustrate a modern man in his modern place. The decorations' associations with domesticity and individualism will not, moreover, satisfy those whose ideals for modernism are heroic: isolated, austere, alienated. These rooms, which were the settings for Bloomsbury's increasingly prominent intellectuals of the 1920s, gave visual form to a different aspiration for modernism as a projection of a humanism with deep historical roots into an age when new conditions afforded opportunities for an unprecedented extension of humanistic values, which might challenge impulses toward regimentation and destruction.

Signifying Subculture
Gordon Square Houses and Charleston (1924–28)

The disciplined reassertion of humanistic individualism proposed by the interiors Grant and Bell created for their most prominent Bloomsbury colleagues (as discussed in the preceding chapter) offered one ideal of modern domesticity. But this was not the only aspect of Bloomsbury's post-war design. As the group reassembled in London and its circles of association widened to include a younger generation, other rooms in the subdivided town houses of Bloomsbury began to display a different kind of modern aesthetic. Illustrated in magazines as, for example, "A Bachelor Flat in Bloomsbury" or "a small house in Bloomsbury," these rooms were associated less with specific patrons than with the group as a whole. They, therefore, shift our attention to Bloomsbury's place in broader cultural changes taking place in England during the twenties, in particular the evolution of sexual subculture.[1] Not surprisingly, a key figure in this history was Duncan Grant, whose participation in post-war gay networks and production of explicitly homo-erotic imagery have been frankly discussed in recent books.[2] Grant, who was somewhat younger than his Bloomsbury colleagues, was a crucial link between what Virginia Woolf called "Old Bloomsbury" and the next generation.[3] Less predictably, another key figure in this history was Woolf herself. This history has been largely ignored, even in revisionist studies of Woolf and Bloomsbury, with scholars often simply amplifying complaints articulated by some of Bloomsbury's older members about the disruption of established patterns of affection and intimacy caused by the intrusion of outsiders into the group.[4] This chapter rejects such impulses to normalize Bloomsbury according to an ideal of stable heterosexual coupledom. As in the earlier stages of Bloomsbury's development, the group's participation in the burgeoning sexual subcultures of the Twenties was registered in the look of domestic space.

The continuing importance of domesticity for Bloomsbury may be most obvious in the determination with which the group, after the war, re-established homes in its eponymous London district, especially around Gordon Square.[5] Grant came first; immediately upon release from agricultural service, he regained a London base with Keynes at Number 46 and shortly thereafter rented Walter Sickert's former studio in nearby Fitzroy Street. Starting in 1920, the Bells sublet two floors of 50 Gordon Square from Vanessa's brother Adrian, who had taken over the lease from the Army and shared the lower floors with his wife and their two daughters. In 1922 Vanessa ceded her space at Number 50 to Clive, returning to attic rooms at Number 46 until 1925, when she and Grant set up in two floors of Number 37. The Stracheys, meanwhile, left Durbins in 1919 for 51 Gordon Square, which Lady Strachey shared with her unmarried daughters, Marjorie and Pippa, keeping rooms for visits from her other children. Two other Strachey sons, James and Oliver, also had flats in the square, and from 1924 Leonard and Virginia Woolf lived in nearby Tavistock Square. "I foresee that the whole square will become a sort of college," Lytton wrote Virginia in 1919, adding, with feigned horror, "the rencontres in the garden I shudder to think of."[6] Strachey's humor emphasizes his delight in Bloomsbury's return to its origins (as discussed in Chapter 1) as a community of sexual outsiders modeled on the social forms of a college.

As in a residential college, proximity helped sustain emotional and intellectual relationships among Bloomsbury's members. It also facilitated child care, which was a constant criterion in the group's negotiations of living quarters in Gordon Square. Most importantly, the cluster of dwellings around the square reaffirmed Bloomsbury's identity as a group, which had been weakened by the dislocations of the war and the post-war influx of new people with their own claims for attention. The founding in 1920 of a "Memoir Club" to reunite Bloomsbury's original members at one another's homes to hear recollections of the participants' pre-war history attests, as Keynes's biographer notes, "to the breakdown of the spontaneous sense of community."[7] One sign of the competing definitions of Bloomsbury, however, was the emergence of a rival to the Memoir Club: the larger and all-male Cranium Club, organized by David Garnett with some of the younger men on Bloomsbury's periphery, whose monthly meetings at a local restaurant were not dedicated to nostalgia.[8]

Like Bloomsbury's original members, this younger generation shared an interest in avant-garde art and literature and an antipathy to conventional norms of gender and sexual propriety, even in relation to the looser standards of dress and deportment of the twenties. Published memoirs from this generation dwell on raucous parties characterized by the talismans of modernity: cocktails, jazz, and what Frances Marshall Partridge described as "continuous passionate dancing, dancing of a high standard, whether Blues, Charleston or Black Bottom."[9] Bloomsbury gatherings had long been characterized by costumed performances, and these continued, now often in Grant's large studio in Fitzroy Street. The group's new members, however, were also part of wider networks of those the newspapers called "Bright Young People," whose extravagant fancy-dress parties, chronicled with alarmed fascination in the gossip columns, gave old Bloomsbury rituals new currency.[10] By the early 1930s, Vanessa Bell, writing to her twentyish son, reported on Bloomsbury parties where Virginia Woolf dressed as Sappho and described another evening at Edward Sackville-West's as "one of those parties where the ladies dress as men and vice versa," light-heartedly recounting how she was ardently pursued by a man who took her for another man in drag. "I realised the other night what it must be like to be you!" she concluded.[11]

Bloomsbury's older members worried over their new celebrity, deliberating in print over the pleasures and perils of what they called "snobbism," a "useful word" Fry called "the interest which we have received on lending the word 'snob' to the French." Fry's 1926 "Culture and Snobbism" describes snobs, though "capricious and uncertain," as the artist's "most potent ally" because their desire to be "in the swim" counters both the indifferent general public and the conservative guardians of high culture.[12] Fry's grudging acceptance of the "snobs" he distinguished sharply from true artists contrasts with the less cautious enthusiasm of others in Bloomsbury, especially Clive Bell, whom Vanessa—allied with Fry on this issue—dismissed as himself a "lady of fashion."[13] Among the most interesting documents in this debate is a paper Virginia Woolf read for the Memoir Club in 1936 on the topic "Am I a Snob?" Flouting this Old-Bloomsbury club's confidence in its elite status and its requirement that papers indulge in self-regarding nostalgia, Woolf humorously—but forcefully—challenged her audience's attitudes toward those they called snobs by narrating her relationship to society hostess Sybil Colefax so as to emphasize their similarities. Casting herself as "not only a coronet snob; but also a lit up drawing room snob; a social festivity snob," Woolf proudly claimed; "If you ask me would I rather meet Einstein or the Prince of Wales, I plump for the Prince without hesitation."[14]

Tensions within Old Bloomsbury over the emergence of suddenly sympathetic society hostesses characterized, as well, the group's relationship with that paradigmatic contingent of the post-war avant-garde, the Sitwells. Edith, Osbert, and Sacheverell Sitwell were the children of wealthy parents whose notorious public brawls climaxed with their mother's imprisonment in 1915. By 1923, the siblings had attracted so much attention that Noël Coward made them the butt of burlesque in his popular *London Calling!*, which exaggerated the bawdiness of Edith's poetry and the androgynous eccentricity of her bachelor brothers. Bloomsbury was simultaneously intrigued and intimidated by these sibling leaders of the younger generation, who seemed to replicate the group's own hitherto unique amalgam of family ties, dedication to the practice and promotion of modernist aesthetics, and attention-getting irreverence for social convention.

"It's strange how whole groups of people suddenly swim complete into one's life," Virginia Woolf remarked when she first met the Sitwells in 1918, but intimidation trumped intrigue in Grant's and Bell's first encounters.[15] Grant reported to Bell after a luncheon, "My word it's difficult to keep up with the Sitwells and only Roger could," while Bell, complaining how "huge and crowded and tiring" London seemed "nowadays," said of a Sitwell party, "Osbert is the worst possible host. He introduces you to a new person without telling you their name every two minutes."[16] Nevertheless, the connections between Bloomsbury and the Sitwells deepened. Fry painted Edith's portrait in 1918 and was enlisted by Osbert the following year to help decorate the brothers' new house in Chelsea, providing a colorful Omega table and screen, and painting the sitting room ceiling himself.[17] Osbert visited Charleston in 1919, while Fry and Clive Bell warmly reviewed—and, in Bell's case, hotly defended—the brothers' exhibition of recent French art at the Mansard Galleries.[18] The Sitwells' 1919 show built upon the precedent of Fry's *The New Movement in Art*, staged at the Mansard in 1917, and Fry's review emphasized Bloomsbury's relevance by comparing the style of the modern French painters to Virginia Woolf's prose. Woolf herself, after a dinner party with the Sitwells, ruminated in her diary over the difference between the Sitwells' reputation and their effect in person, concentrating on Edith:

> Edith is an old maid. I had never conceived this. I thought she was severe, implacable & tremendous; rigid in her own conception. Not a bit of it. She is, I guess, a little fussy, very kind, beautifully mannered. . . . She is elderly too, almost my age & timid, & admiring & easy & poor, & I liked her more than admired or was frightened of her. Nevertheless, I do admire her work, & thats what I say of hardly anyone.[19]

In 1925, the Hogarth Press published Edith's pamphlet, *Poetry and Criticism*, and it was she who convinced the Woolfs to produce Gertrude Stein's *Composition as Explanation*, which appeared in 1926. In 1927, Clive and Vanessa Bell were invited to the premier of the Sitwell brothers' play *All at Sea*. Underlying clichés of avant-garde rivalry—present in the Sitwells' later memoirs and emphasized by subsequent commentators—lies, therefore, a complicated history of professional and personal connection between Bloomsbury and these younger aspirants to London's avant-garde.

Another historical cliché that needs undoing is the presentation of this era as a meaningless round of cocktail parties and costume balls. This caricature obscures important developments in the history of sexual subculture in England, as, during the Twenties, substantial numbers of young, well educated men and women—personified by, but hardly limited to, the Sitwells—followed in Bloomsbury's footsteps by linking "modern" social and aesthetic reforms, to create complex networks of feminists, artists, flappers, and dandies.[20] When Wyndham Lewis's *Apes of God* was published in 1930, this lengthy satire of the Sitwellian avant-garde began from the premise that so many of the sexually transgressive, imitative, would-be artists he called "Apes" had "come onto the scene" that Bloomsbury had lost its "unique position"; of Bloomsbury, Lewis's guide to the avant-garde said, "I think you can disregard them. . . . the bloom is gone."[21]

Though Lewis's description of a Bloomsbury submerged in the forms of modernism it pioneered may have rung true for some, for the young men Frances Partridge called "fringe-Bloomsburies," the group was a crucial inspiration and refuge.[22] Despite the much-touted frankness within Bloomsbury, the sexual aspect of this history was expurgated from the group's multi-volume memoirs prepared for publication at mid-century.[23] That Bloomsbury's acceptance of homosexuality was what initially won the devotion of Partridge's "fringe," however, is implicit in circumspect short memoirs by George Rylands and Raymond Mortimer, who allude to their attraction to the group's freedom of conversation.[24] The importance of sexuality is clear in less guarded letters and memoirs not prepared for publication. One such memoir casually describes Bloomsbury at this era as "mainly homosexual," making this the premise to an anecdote about a hostess trying to find "a bevy of beauties" in Bloomsbury to attend a lecture—ultimately only Frances Partridge (then Marshall) and two Strachey nieces turned up, and the audience consisted, the narrator concludes, of "startlingly handsome young men. It was they rather who made up a bevy."[25] Other records reveal Lytton Strachey planning, with Mortimer and some of the other young men in Partridge's fringe, a same-sex "Lovers Through the Ages" costume party.[26] A series of letters Virginia Woolf wrote to amuse a friend isolated by illness in France describes the changes Bloomsbury was seeing in the mid-twenties, dwelling on the influx of "young men" who "tend to the pretty and ladylike, for some reason, at the moment. They paint and powder, which wasn't the style in our day at Cambridge." "Have you any views on loving one's own sex?" she asks; "All the young men are so inclined."[27]

The arch tone of Woolf's letters, intended to amuse an insider, belies her frank enjoyment of the "pretty and ladylike" youths Bloomsbury attracted, many of whom worked at the Hogarth Press. George "Dadie" Rylands, like other young Cambridge men, entered Bloomsbury by way of Keynes and Strachey, who continued a tradition of homoerotic mentorship at King's College (discussed in Chapter 3).[28] Rylands worked for the Woolfs at the Press in 1924, the year he also posed for the first photograph then-undergraduate Cecil Beaton published in *Vogue*, dressed as the Duchess of Malfi and, the photographer recalled, "standing in the subaqueous light outside the men's lavatory of the ADC Theatre at Cambridge."[29] Woolf's diaries record in fascinated detail how Mortimer was attracted and rebuffed by Rylands, whom she described in her letters as, "a very charming spoilt boy . . . all young and oldish men . . . fall in love with him, and he dines out every night, and treats his lovers abominably."[30]

Rylands's successors at the Press also came from circles of homoerotically inclined young men at Cambridge. One was Angus Davidson, who cited as his introduction to Bloomsbury Keynes's "rooms in King's, where he was generous and charming in his entertaining of undergraduates." There he was impressed by "splendid panels by Vanessa Bell and Duncan Grant" and "first met these two painters, who were afterwards to be numbered among my dearest friends."[31] The power of Bloomsbury's influence on this generation at Cambridge remains recorded on the walls of Rylands's sitting room, where he commissioned Dora Carrington and Angus's brother, Douglas Davidson, to paint decorations in what Vanessa Bell belittled as an "old-maidish" variation on Bloomsbury's style.[32] Again, Woolf manifested a fonder appreciation. Her letters describe Angus as "gentle, considerate, cautious, kind, with a mind smooth and sensitive as the thickest cream," and his dismissal from the Press for failing to satisfy Leonard's standards of punctuality and accuracy was noted with regret.[33] He was suceeded by John Lehmann, another protégé of Rylands, who recalled Woolf pumping him for sexual gossip: "Was X having a Lesbian affair with Y? Did I know anything about the latest young man Lytton Strachey was interested in?"[34]

Woolf's fascination with homosexuality and gender-crossing emerged publicly only with her 1928 *Orlando*, an illustrated romp through four centuries of history by the sex-switching title character inspired by the androgynous Vita Sackville-West. Woolf's letters describing her new London life in the winter of 1924–25, however, cite "my aristocrat," the "violently Sapphic" cousin of Edward Sackville-West, and confess "secret" plans to incite her "to elope with me next."[35] Tantalized by her discovery of a network of women comparable to that of the homoerotically inclined men of her circle, Virginia in 1925 recorded in her diary an ecstatic description of Vita, beginning, "These Sapphists *love* women; friendship is never untinged with amorosity."[36] Woolf's own impulses toward such a community are suggested by an episode when she, at a party given by Edith Sitwell for Gertrude Stein, "proposed, wildly, fantastically," as she wrote in her diary, that the Hogarth Press commission a memoir from Dorothy Todd, editor of British *Vogue* between 1923 and 1926.[37] When Woolf made this offer, Todd had just been fired by Condé Nast, who, to Bloomsbury's outrage, blackmailed her to accept this breach of contract by threatening to publicize her sexual relationship with *Vogue*'s glamorous fashion editor, Madge Garland.[38] With the banning of Radclyffe Hall's fictional *Well of Lonliness* two years in the future, no account of a real-life network of women "tinged with amorosity" for other women could possibly have been published at the time. Woolf's impulsive gesture of solidarity—and Todd's acceptance—went no further than this gathering of women that seemed, for a moment, to rival the community of amorous men to which Woolf was such a rapt spectator.

Although Woolf's aspirations to homoerotic community remained focused on her relationship with Sackville-West, the young men drawn to Bloomsbury sustained their social network over their often very long lives. Apart from Woolf's interest and modest remuneration from the Hogarth Press, what bound these young men to Bloomsbury was Duncan Grant. The Davidson brothers took turns as Grant's boyfriend—Douglas in 1921, Angus in 1922—followed in 1926 by Eddy Sackville-West, and all remained, along with Raymond Mortimer, part of his circle of friends. Their participation in Grant's life is recorded in accounts of trips taken together, letters exchanged, photographs and paintings (including some nudes), and even the roster of mourners at Grant's burial in 1978.[39] True to Bloomsbury's domestic focus, these relationships were also registered in the decoration of two dwellings in the group's London neighborhood. The first of these was at 3 Heathcote Street off Mecklenburgh Square, where from 1923 Angus Davidson shared a house with, at various times, his brother Douglas, Dadie Rylands, and John Lehmann.[40] The second was Raymond Mortimer's flat at 6 Gordon Place, adjacent to Gordon Square. During 1924, both of these domestic establishments were decorated in ways that announced—to both visitors and readers of *Vogue*, where they were illustrated—their inhabitants' allegiance to the Bloomsbury group. These rooms contribute, as well, to the visual history of sexual subculture, extending the project initiated by Grant in Keynes's first Cambridge rooms to create domestic settings appropriate to the lives and loves of the men who inhabited them.

Mortimer recalled that his motive in moving to Gordon Place was to join his new friends in Old Bloomsbury, who—among other virtues—"laughed a lot about the sexual life of their friends, in a way that was thought shocking in that still unpermissive age."[41] His fascination with Bloomsbury is recorded in Woolf's diary, which describes with some bemusement how, during Mortimer's first visit to her house in Sussex, he responded to remarks about her ancestors with a wistful "I wish I had distinguished Aunts" and announced, "I have a culte for Bloomsbury."[42] Mortimer's ambitions to participate in the community he idealized were realized, first in his relocation to Gordon Place, and then in his commission of Grant and Bell to decorate the sitting-room of his small flat. The resulting design spilled beyond the frames that disciplined the decorations for Keynes and the Woolfs, creating a tapestry of paintings that stretched from floor to ceiling and transformed the room into a formal garden, complete with fountain, manicured hedges, musical instruments, and urns of flowers and fruit (fig. 176). The effect is of a stage set for a *fête champêtre* after Giorgione, whose painting on this theme at the Louvre was sketched by both Grant and Bell at this period.[43] As in Keynes's rooms, the woodwork was embellished with circles and rectangles of daubed-on modernist "marbling," which tied these physical features of the room to the facture of the rectilinear hedges in the fictive garden. This modern Cytherea created an appropriate setting for someone wittily described by Virginia Woolf as a man whose "modernity . . . seems to me

176. Duncan Grant and Vanessa Bell, mural for Raymond Mortimer at 6 Gordon Place, London, 1924, as illustrated in Dorothy Todd and Raymond Mortimer, *The New Interior Design*, 1929.

177. Duncan Grant, painted overmantel for Angus Davidson at 3 Heathcote Street, London, 1923–24, as illustrated in *Architectural Review*, May 1930.

miraculous, as if he had already been to a lunch party which has not yet been given."[44] The nature of the guests Mortimer invited to populate his *al-fresco* stage may be inferred from Clive Bell's description of a party in this flat as "a regular bugger gathering with a smattering of English . . . girls and a few American Sapphists" that he fled upon the arrival of "a party of boxers."[45]

Grant's decorations for Davidson, likewise, exceeded the boundaries that ordered the interiors of Bloomsbury's more eminent members (fig. 177). Here, dripped and daubed wallpapers burst the restraints of color and form imposed by the narrow band of delicately colored "écriture" for the Woolfs, spreading over a chimney breast covered with mottled daubs of grey and white against pale green pilasters, and filling floor-to-ceiling alcoves with splashy brush strokes, one area, according to design magazines, of "deep blue and pale grey, bespattered with red spots," another "maroon, grey, white, and black with a border of maroon and mustard green"[46] (fig. 178). In the dining-room, this background set off Grant's painted sideboard and a corner cabinet decorated with a serenade scene evocative of opera, the singer on the lower door and his listener on the upper (figs. 179, 182). In the sitting room, above a fireplace framed by Grant's hand-painted tiles, a fresco exploded with an over-scale arrangement of arum lilies springing green and yellow from a white jardiniere on a crimson ground (fig. 180). The wall around this design, *Vogue* reported, was "French grey, with a broad band of yellow ochre at each side. The rest of the walls are a pale, rather bluish pink."[47]

The effect of these Bloomsbury environments can be compared to the Sitwell brothers' well known house, where Osbert mixed extravagant examples of Baroque and Victorian furniture with modern pieces—including Fry's Omega table—to create what one memoir described as "a temple of a now-forgotten style called the 'amusing.'"[48] Other writers searching for vocabulary to signify an aesthetic known in its own era simply as "modern," but so different from what was later sanctioned as modernism, also settled on the term "amusing." Paul Nash in 1932 recalled the already-vanished post-war era when "the adjective 'amusing' started on its endless flight from lip to lip." His description captured the style's transgression of national and sexual boundaries, as "charming young men and formidable ladies were hopping backwards and forwards between England and the Continent," importing "a piece of stuff from Paris, a German lamp, a steel chair, or just a headful of other people's ideas."[49] For the Sitwells, the transgressions associated with the new style

178. Duncan Grant, hand-painted papers for Angus Davidson at 3 Heathcote Street, London, 1923–24, as illustrated in *Architectural Review*, May 1930.

179. Duncan Grant, painted sideboard in alcove with hand-painted papers for Angus Davidson at 3 Heathcote Street, London, 1923–24, as illustrated in *Vogue*, early November 1924.

also included historical boundaries. Osbert described a "modern" sensibility as one that made new meanings from old modes, using, for example, "Victorian objects displayed for qualities other than those which the Victorians themselves admired in them."[50] Bloomsbury's decorations for the young men in its circle are very much a part of this trend, which, with the authorization of these period memoirs, I will call the Amusing Style.[51]

Although Grant never caught the Sitwells' passion for Victorian bibelots of shell and wax, his impulses toward "amusing" historical revisionism startled his Old-Bloomsbury colleagues, most notably over his infatuation with a pair of elaborately gilded and embroidered Victorian chairs he acquired at this time. Several of Grant's still lifes of this period are set on these chairs, as if to insist that modern perceptions could redeem objects pre-war Bloomsbury would have rejected as evidence of an earlier generation's aesthetic corruption (fig. 181). Grant's Old-Bloomsbury colleagues were clearly troubled by what they recognized as these trends in both Grant's art and the culture at large. Quentin Bell recalled that his father's denunciation of the chairs' "vulgarity" led to teasing about Grant's deep-seated "penchant for the really impossible work of art," while Fry was provoked enough to respond

180. Duncan Grant, painted overmantel for Angus Davidson at 3 Heathcote Street, London, 1923–24, as illustrated in *Vogue,* early November 1924.

181. One of a pair of chairs, nineteenth century, purchased by Duncan Grant, Charleston.

with two articles in the *Athenaeum* in which he attempted to discover formalist principles in modern artists' rehabilitation of Victoriana.[52]

The Victorian references in Grant's and Bell's Amusing designs had less to do with finding overlooked significant form, however, than with juxtaposing quotations from late-nineteenth-century avant-garde art clearly presented as such. Their symmetrical garden for Raymond Mortimer, for instance, updates the symmetrical motif of Roger Fry's 1894 mural at C. R. Ashbee's 37 Cheyne Walk (discussed in Chapter 2), while Grant's bouquets of lilies on embroidered chairs and over Davidson's fireplace revive a well known emblem of the Wildean Aesthete.[53] Overtly generic composition, incongruous scale, and patches of abstract "écriture" or "marbling" emphasize their status as quotations of earlier images, an effect registered in *Vogue*'s caption under a photograph of the cabinet Grant painted for Davidson's dining room (fig. 182), which spins out a series of received ideas to support the claim that, "Mr. Duncan Grant has restored fantasy to furniture":

> What—one immediately wonders—does this corner-cupboard contain? Raisins and oranges, wines from Xeres and Oporto? Or music, and the manuscripts of unforgotten songs? Or love-letters, perhaps—for the cupboard has a key?. . . . Mr. Grant has turned a cupboard into a romance. He has transformed this Cinderella of furniture among furniture into poetic loveliness.[54]

This pastiche of references does not describe the specific iconography of Grant's design. Rather, it playfully—amusingly—rehearses a range of plots historically associated with love and eroticism, asserting a kind of equivalence to a cupboard

Re-Imagining Modernism

182. Duncan Grant, painted cupboard
for Angus Davidson, 1923–24.
Oil on wood, 186 × 93 × 46 cm.
City of Portsmouth Museum and
Art Gallery.

that has been turned into a "romance". The allusions are not to a specific coupling, but to a genre recognized as such by the sophisticated modern viewer who can—like jazz musicians or stream-of-consciousness novelists—riff through variations on a familiar theme for the formal pleasure that allows.[55] In this sense, Bloomsbury's decorative work in the Twenties relates closely—more than does the easel painting, and more, perhaps, than the artists themselves realized—to concurrent developments in formalist theories of literature, which emphasized the free play of connotation and allusion.[56]

If this kind of pleasure in quotation and association is one mark of a modern aesthetic, the particular genre invoked here had more specific resonance. The restaging

183. Duncan Grant, Harlequin screen, 1924. Private collection, as illustrated in *Vogue*, early January 1924.

of old romances is a staple of opera, ballet, and theater—all forms of culture that, like interior decoration, were associated with femininity and, therefore, under the influence of medical theories of sexual type, linked to male homosexuality by the early twentieth century.[57] In both this cupboard and the Mortimer murals, allusions to theater are reinforced by depicted curtains, pulled back as if on a stage. Similar curtains also appear in many of Grant's paintings at this period, images that restage romances from the repertory of classical myth—always with an emphasis on the stage. Grant's *Venus and Adonis*, for instance, already cited (in Chapter 13) as paradigmatic of his post-war painting (fig. 166), anticipates both the stage-like composition and—with its references to artistic precedents from Piero di Cosimo through Titian and Giorgione to Poussin—the pastiched quality of his Davidson and Mortimer decorations.[58] Grant imbued his own rooms with an aura of theatricality at this era, creating a large three-fold screen that dominated a succession of his London flats with the image of Harlequin and Columbine dancing to the accompaniment of a violin-playing Pierrot (fig. 183). That this scene is performed as theater is clear from the presence of an audience personified by what look to be three women in modern dress; Grant's claim that these females were actually modeled by the Davidson brothers only reinforces the associations of the stage with sexual subculture.[59]

The *commedia dell'arte* iconography in the screen Grant designed for himself asserts an ambition to participate in the modernism of the Sitwells and *Vogue*. The Sitwells had made Harlequin their mascot, invoked in the titles and illustrations of several publications as well as in the frescos of *commedia dell'arte* figures they commissioned from Gino Severini for their father's castle in Tuscany, which were illustrated in *Vogue* late in 1922.[60] The rapid reappearance of this imagery in Grant's London rooms reflects his eager response to younger modernists who seemed to accord the provocative fancy-dress Bloomsbury had long enjoyed the imprimatur of journalistic significance as "fashion," rather than the "scandal" attending such

Re-Imagining Modernism

Bloomsbury costume capers as the "Dreadnaught Hoax" (discussed in Chapter 5). If the iconography of Grant's screen proclaimed his alliance with the youthful modernists of the Twenties, however, his composition also asserted Bloomsbury's prior claims to forms now made fashionable. Grant harks back to memories of the pre-war Ballets Russes, in particular their *Petrouchka*, premiered in London in 1913, in which the title character, a sad white-coated clown, was locked in a booth like that in which Grant depicts his Pierrot, while his lady-love danced with the more flamboyantly attractive Moor. Like that ballet, which was praised as both "supremely modern, and supremely baroque," Grant's screen was heralded in *Vogue* as a fusion of old and new: "very modern and poetic in feeling but . . . as decorative as the beautiful screens of the 18th century."[61] When *Vogue*, just a few months after its feature on Severini's Sitwell murals, ran its first profile on Grant, his associations with the ballet were suggested by illustrations of his costume designs for Léonide Massine's and Lydia Lopokova's dances in the review *You'd be Surprised* at Covent Garden.[62]

Theatricality, gender-transgression, historical pastiche: these qualities, especially taken together, suggest the celebratory form of artifice known as "camp," associated by the 1920s with homosexuality.[63] An updated form of Aestheticism, camp's knowing, often exaggerated, rehearsal of Wildean tastes and styles uses the act of quotation to assert an ironic distance that allows for connotative meanings other than—even diametrically opposed to—denotative content. As such, camp is often correlated to the situation of homosexuality in the first half (at least) of the twentieth century, which relied on forms of signification carefully calibrated to be recognizable to some, but not all. Not only an attribute of dress and deportment, camp was also associated with "the elements of visual decor."[64] To describe the interiors for Mortimer and Davidson as camp, therefore, is not simply to label an aesthetic quality, but to assert the meaning of that look in relation to subcultural practices staged in and around those spaces.

Grant's investment in camp is clear. A letter written to Vanessa Bell during a trip with one of his boyfriends, for example, finds Grant delighting in the Theatre Royal of Lynn: "the prettiest little theatre I ever did see. It must have been built I should think in the [18]40 or 50s and it's perfect, a real horseshoe with just the right amount of trashy rococo ornament everywhere. . . . It somehow suggests visits from great stars and their traveling companions in the past and sure enough in the foyer I found signed photos of Irving, Macready, and to me unknown but impressive ladies dressed up as Cleopatra."[65] Grant's pleasure in reading fanciful romances of "great stars and their traveling companions" in outdated architectural ornament and old photographs is pure camp, a sensibility also indulged and refined in Bloomsbury's famous party-performances that pillaged history and current events to retell stories in ways that exaggerated incongruity, extravagance, and artifice. Virginia Woolf's *Freshwater* (discussed in Chapter 1) was staged at one such gathering. At another in 1924, recent news accounts of sexual impropriety between a wealthy Sussex landowner and his kennel maids was transformed into a musical in which Vanessa Bell—head of another Sussex country house—was seduced in exchange for paintings by Cézanne and Giotto. In this drama, Grant played a wolfhound attended by a trio of kennel maids in evening gowns with pearl chokers, a chorus played *en travastie* by the fringe: Dadie Rylands, Douglas and Angus Davidson—or as Virginia Woolf described them, "the Davidsons, three of them, hung with chandeliers and stately as caryatids."[66]

Men who seem to be women and an audience transformed into actors—the campy elements of Bloomsbury's parties—are exactly those reproduced on Grant's Harlequin screen, reflecting the links between Bloomsbury, the Bright Young People, and the Amusing Style settings for sexual deviance in the Twenties. Subsequent commentary has reflected a later era's faith in the explanatory truth of biological categories like homosexual and heterosexual by passing quickly over Bloomsbury's love of transvestism and bawdy farce as an irrelevant—even embarrassing—distraction from the group's intellectual history.[67] The recent reorientation of linguistic and anthropological theories of sexuality away from essentialist categories of sexual orientation and toward more fluid notions of performance has the ironic effect of returning self-styled postmodernists to interests that character-ized "modern" sexuality in the Twenties, among them the play with gendered roles and costumes to create forms of outsider identity that allow for a wide range of unconventional romantic and erotic relationships. From this perspective, the culture of *Vogue* and the Sitwells, costume parties and camp, re-emerges as crucial to the history, not just of Bloomsbury and modernist aesthetics, but of sexuality.

To take seriously Bloomsbury's involvement in this culture may resolve issues that have troubled commentators since the Twenties, among them Virginia Woolf's uncharacteristic decisions to publish in and be photographed—in Victorian cos-tume, no less—for *Vogue* (as discussed in Chapter 1) while it was under Todd's edi-torship.[68] *Vogue*'s unprecedented blurring of the boundaries between art and fashion, avant-garde and mass culture, embodied the experimental ethos of the twenties. More specifically, with Dorothy Todd as general editor, her lover Madge Garland as fashion editor, Raymond Mortimer in charge of book and theater reviews, and Dadie Rylands writing copy, the staff of London *Vogue* seemed—briefly—to exemplify the new culture of sexual nonconformity.[69] The style of this subculture was androgynous in both the extravagant fancy-dress of its parties and its everyday mode of unisex woolen "jumpers" and short hair, a style Woolf adopted at this time.[70] The strength of Woolf's identification with *Vogue* is clearest in her reaction to Logan Pearsall Smith, Fry's friend and a founding member of the Society for Pure English, who complained to her of seeing "Bloomsbury descend from the heights and scatter its pearls in Mayfair" by publishing in a fashion maga-zine.[71] Recounting their exchange, Woolf commented: "Bunkum. Ladies clothes and aristocrats playing golf don't affect my style; and they would do his a world of good."[72] More politely—but just as firmly—she answered Smith with two points: "the young would say, Todd lets you write what you like" and "Duncan says he is perfectly ready to paint covers for her. . . . Duncan's argument is that if Bloomsbury has real pearls, they can be scattered anywhere without harm."[73] Woolf's twinned points of reference here—"the young" and Duncan—reflect the terms of her iden-tification with the modernity exemplified by *Vogue*.

It was not just Woolf, but Bloomsbury as a whole that Smith charged with slouch-ing toward fashionable Mayfair, however. The regular appearance of Bloomsbury members in *Vogue*—as both the topics and the authors of articles, and as the sub-jects and makers of images—identified the group with broad challenges to conven-tions of sexuality and gender being mounted in the name of modernity. Virtually every *Vogue* article on any subject announced its concern with what is "modern," "contemporary," or characteristic of "today," and with so many articles proposing Bloomsbury interiors as appropriate settings for "those who enjoy living in the pres-ent," it is worth considering how *Vogue*'s presentation of Bell's and Grant's domes-tic designs fit with its gender-blurring modernity.[74] *Vogue*'s first feature on Grant, as already noted, linked his domestic designs to his ballet costumes. Associations of Grant's aesthetic with a feminized (and thus, increasingly, homosexualized) theatri-cality were emphasized in subsequent articles on Grant's applied and fine art, cate-gories that the magazine consistently blurred. An article on Grant's paintings, for instance, after noting that one water-color was a study for the backdrop to a ballet, speculated: "how admirable it would be reproduced upon material for curtains; they would by themselves make one of the most beautiful rooms imaginable."[75] Associations with theater, performance, and fancy dress are emphasized in *Vogue*'s descriptions of the "curious fancifulness" of Grant's aesthetic, and of the artist as a "*fantaisiste*" and "a most fanciful, poetic and individual painter."[76]

This language—probably Mortimer's—echoes characterizations of Grant's work by Roger Fry and Clive Bell. Fry in 1920 had described Grant's *Venus and Adonis* as a "strikingly original and poetical" invention that displayed "the individual and per-sonal quality of his vision" in a way that "belongs entirely to our own age and coun-try." Such allusions to Grant's modern and individual form of poetic fancy were attached, by both Fry and Bell, to the twinned historical precedents of the Greeks and certain seventeenth-century British poets as signifiers of erotic transgression. For Fry, Grant's art "has that 'Doric delicacy' " scholars found in Milton's *Comus* (a

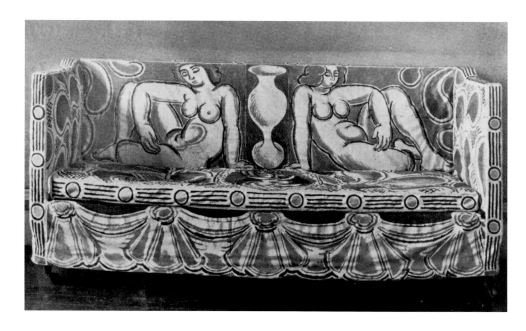

184. Duncan Grant, painted sofa cover, 1923. Present location unknown, as illustrated in *Vogue*, early January 1924.

poem known for its bacchic eroticism).[77] For Bell, also writing in 1920, "there is something Greek about" Grant: "not the archeological Greece of Germany, nor yet the Graeco-Roman academicism of France, but rather the romantic, sensuous Hellenism of the English literary tradition." Grant's art, Bell goes on, "reminds one unmistakably of the Elizabethan poets, something fantastic and whimsical and at the same time intensely lyrical."[78] Bell's specification of the exact kind of Greekness Grant's art embodies—neither archeologically accurate nor the neo-classicism of state-sanctioned academies, but romantic, sensual, and carried forward by Elizabethan poets—accumulates signifiers of homoeroticism indebted to Wilde, with the implications of sensuality heightened by his description of "the quality of his paint" as "charming as a kiss."[79] Wilde's "Portrait of Mr. W. H." had analyzed sonnets by Shakespeare and some of his Elizabethan contemporaries to argue that homoerotic passion was both a motivating force for Shakespeare and a manifestation of his inheritance from the Greeks. Shakespeare's sonnets, Wilde argued, "revealed to us . . . the soul, as well as the language of neo-Platonism," for his era "touched Hellenism at so many points," catching its "inner meaning" and "divining its secret" so that Greek love replaced biblical fear as the basis of knowledge, and "friendship" was restored to "the high dignity of the antique ideal."[80] More colloquially, as the young Lytton Strachey put it in 1896, "I may be sinning, but I am doing so in the company of Shakespeare and Greece."[81] Comparisons with the Greeks and Elizabethan poets clearly situated Grant's art in a homoerotic context, implications that linger in *Vogue*'s repeated allusions to Grant as poetic and fanciful.

This rhetoric complemented *Vogue*'s illustrations of Bloomsbury design. Coverage of a small exhibit of Bloomsbury's domestic work organized by Vanessa Bell at 46 Gordon Square, for instance, began with photographs of the Harlequin screen and a canvas sofa-cover painted by Grant with reclining female nudes reminiscent of Michelangelo's androgynous figures of Night and Day in the Medici chapel (fig. 184).[82] These generic classical figures take their place in the crowd of mythological couples—Venus and Adonis, Cupid and Psyche, Apollo and Daphne, various nymphs and satyrs—that sprang from Grant's brush at this period. His apparently boneless bodies, decorated with button-like nipples or squiggly penises, curl and stretch in sensual spirals, with roles and poses assigned to the two genders interchangeably, so that, for instance, a rather grown-up Cupid (fig. 185; framed, once again by theatrical curtains) in a watercolor mirrors Venus's pose of erotic availability in the contemporary *Venus and Adonis*.[83] In this way, even the gendered nude body becomes a form of costume, easily donned or doffed in the interest of particular performances, just as cross-gender nudity was enacted at the Bloomsbury

185. Duncan Grant, *Cupid and Psyche*, c. 1920. Watercolor on paper, 36.5 × 37.5 cm. Private collection.

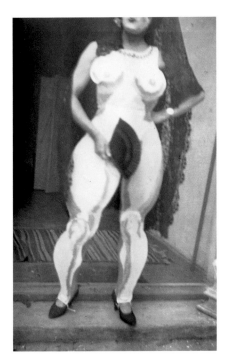

186. Photograph of Duncan Grant as a Spanish dancer in a performance in the garden at Charleston.

187. Duncan Grant, hearth decorations, Charleston studio, photographed *c.* 1934 by Barbara Bagenal.

Facing page: 188. Duncan Grant, hearth decorations, Charleston studio, originally painted *c.* 1925, lower half repainted *c.* 1932. Charleston Trust.

parties recorded in period photographs (including an image of Grant as a topless female dancer; fig. 186) and letters (such as Virginia Woolf's description of a party where John Sheppard, Keynes's former housemate at 46 Gordon Square, appeared "half naked, tightly swathed in red silk, shingled as to his head, with colored garters" impersonating a "Miss T."—perhaps Dorothy Todd—"to perfection"[84]).

The play with gender in the culture of Bloomsbury and *Vogue* suggests that the common critical practice of reading Grant's mythological images as allegories of his relationship with Vanessa Bell may be over-specific. Without treating his paintings as *romans à clef*, however, we may see his repeated return to certain myths as an affirmation of eroticism expressed in motifs of amorous chase, capture, and escape, which parallel his own habits of arousing and being aroused by new partners while evading coupled stasis. Simon Watney has cited Grant's "awareness of the passion and transience of sexual pleasure, as well as its delights" in analyzing his mythical subjects as allusions to the idea that "one is subject to one's fate in certain areas, that one does not choose to fall in love, or to be attracted to certain types of people, that desire will likely lead to pain as well as pleasure, and that the goal of pleasure is thus all the more precious."[85] Watney's observation that Grant's mythical imagery is primarily associated with his decorative work (including water-color sketches for unrealized projects) reinforces its status as an expression of a way of life.

This visual rhetoric found its most complete expression, appropriately enough, at Charleston, Grant's and Bell's own home, where around 1925, having negotiated a longer lease, they embarked on an ambitious plan of expansion and redecoration.[86] Small changes enlivened almost every room. Bell painted the woodwork around a downstairs fireplace with her characteristic circles and cross-hatchings, and Fry helped reopen the massive hearth in the dining room. The most dramatic change, however, was a spacious studio addition designed by Fry to use walls of the existing sheds and privy. "The great object is to have as much room and spend as little money as possible. That, of course, appeals to my avaricious nature, which is almost as much gratified by saving other people's money as my own," Fry explained, going on to reiterate the architectural principles that had governed his design for Durbins: "if we can keep the builder from putting in knick-knacks and mouldings, why it may be respectable."[87] Not withstanding such proclamations of parsimony, Charleston's new studio—like Durbins's "house-place"—offered a generously scaled, double-height, light-filled space. Also at this period, Grant and Bell carried out in the new studio and a nearby sitting room some of the major decorative schemes for which Charleston is best known today.

Like the house-place at Durbins, the studio at Charleston was painted grey and overlooked by Fry's Wei-dynasty bodhisattva (one of two casts commissioned from the original, which Fry sold in 1925 to pay for an exhibition of his paintings in New York). Over the mantel, Grant painted a *trompe-l'œil* niche for this Chinese figure, bracketed by simple floral still lifes (figs 186 and 187).[88] This solemn, altar-like overmantel contrasts with the decorations around the hearth below: a bowl of goldfish—Matissian symbols of the good life—flanked by two androgynous male nudes rendered in the roiling curves typical of Grant's figures at this period, who appear to balance the mantel on elbows upraised in a voluptuous gesture evocative of Michelangelo's most erotically charged sculptures.[89] The male nudes in the new studio were complemented by a pair of female nudes above the fireplace in the sitting room nearby (fig. 189). Painted as if crouching on the mantel, these figures—descendants of Ingres's bathers—present an oval frame that held a mirror until the heat of an oil lamp (Charleston was not electrified until 1933) cracked the glass and it was replaced by paintings, first a yachting scene, later the current floral still life.

The pastiche of references—to Durbins, Michelangelo, and Ingres—in the redecoration of Charleston was intensified by Grant's purchase, from a defunct art school in Lewes, of plaster casts of famous sculptures: heads from the Apollo Belvedere and the Hermes of Praxiteles, a torso of Venus, a full-size Antinous, and more. The result, Clive Bell complained, turned a walk in the garden into an assault by familiar quotations.[90] But this, it seems, was just the effect Charleston's artists intended. In their paintings Charleston appears as a fabric of quotations: images of

Re-Imagining Modernism

190. Duncan Grant, *The Mantel at Charleston*. Private collection.

images, interiors that look like pictures, casual accumulations of domestic objects that become still lifes. Bell included the plaster casts in a number of still lifes and garden scenes set at Charleston.[91] Grant, too, in paintings like *Still Life with Portrait of Nijinsky* (discussed in Chapter 6) cropped and combined elements from Charleston's interiors to create vignettes that encapsulate the house's aesthetic. In his *Mantel at Charleston* (fig. 190), the feet of the bodhisattva and the painted gold-fish from the studio fireplace create a vertical armature across which runs the mantel supporting a horizontal string of smaller images and objects, each itself a brief quotation evoking its own range of associations.[92] Paintings of Charleston by both artists repeat the motif of windows or open doors that look like framed pictures, placing even the natural environment in artful quotation marks. In both Bell's 1926 *The Open Door* (fig. 191) and Grant's 1929 *The Doorway* (fig. 192), frames within frames and repetitions of color and line present the garden as a picture in a picture, while floral interior elements—a bouquet or flowered upholstery—seem to take on a witty, *trompe-l'oeil* quality of sham authenticity.

Charleston's artful blend of old and new—epigrammatic quotations and histori-cal allusions presented with the facture of modernist individualism—offers the strongest evidence of the Bloomsbury painters' place in the modernism of the gen-eration personified by the Sitwells. In 1924, Sacheverell Sitwell had published a book of essays celebrating the fanciful art and architecture of Baroque Italy, Spain, and Mexico. Sitwell presented his passion for the "self-confidence and fluency" of the Baroque as modern, an avant-garde affront to "elderly critics . . . bred to hate these manifestations." His ornate prose style might itself be described as a pastiche of the genres of history, memoir, aesthetic analysis, and fantasy. Sitwell's lightly ironic encomiums to the anthropomorphic decorations produced in an era when "the architecture of private houses was inquired into, dissected, and re-formulated" are of a piece with the brushy allusions to figurative architectural features—cary-atids and the like—in the redecoration of Charleston.[93] Bloomsbury's embrace of Sitwellian enthusiasms is registered in a letter Fry wrote from Mantua in 1932, in which his pre-war contempt for post-Renaissance Italian art gives way to pleasure in the "rich and Baroque" frescos at the Palazzo del Te by "that extremely tiresome painter Giulio Romano—but what an architect! and what a decorator!" (fig. 193). The palazzo, with its murals of distorted architectural figures and pastiched per-spectives, Fry told Bell, "was a mine of ideas for house decoration and . . . you and D[uncan] ought to go and bag from them."[94]

Today, the sleek, mechanical aesthetics of Art Deco and the International Style have eclipsed Amusing Style enthusiasm for historical quotation in histories of design between the wars. A recent exhibition catalog on British design in the 1930s dismisses both the "ornamental atavism" of revival styles and Bloomsbury's "dis-tinctly fusty" eclecticism in order to trace a single "Modern line" associated with Gropius and Le Corbusier.[95] This restrictive definition of modernist design simply rehearses the terms in which the victors of the ideological battles of the Thirties (discussed in the following chapter) described their suppression of the Amusing Style, and with it the experimentation with modes of performance that challenged conventions of sexuality and gender associated with the Bright Young People. In the

Facing page: 189. Duncan Grant, overmantel decorations, Charleston garden room, *c.* 1928. Charleston Trust.

191. Vanessa Bell, *The Open Door*, 1926.
Oil on board, 75 × 62.3 cm. Bolton
Museum and Art Gallery.

192. Duncan Grant, *The Doorway*,
1929. Oil on canvas, 88 × 77.5 cm.
Arts Council Collection, Hayward
Art Gallery.

193. Giulio Romano, frescoes at Palazzo del Te, Mantua, 1526–34.

Twenties, however, Bloomsbury's domestic aesthetic was read, at least by sub-scribers to *Vogue*, as paradigmatic of modernism. And we can read both the art and the *Vogue* coverage as manifestations of burgeoning sexual subcultures that came to play a definitive role in shaping later twentieth-century art and society—and that, therefore, must factor into viable definitions of modernity and modernism. Neither reading, however, redeems Bloomsbury's Twenties decorative work for heroic narra-tives of modernism, which continually rehearse the triumph of heteronormative masculinity metaphorized in the submission of the ambiguities of the past to the scale, speed, force, and look of industrial machines. In contrast to this heroic ideal, Bloomsbury, including—or especially—those on and closest to its Twenties "fringe," conceived the work of modernism to include the reconception of gender and sexuality. Like Woolf's *Orlando* or Sitwell's *Southern Baroque*, and like the cos-tumed performances and parties of which the group was so fond, the rooms dis-cussed in this chapter, with their campy allusions to Aestheticism and quotations of *fêtes champêtres* and Baroque villas, are modern in the way they stage (with all the associations of theatricality that term implies) forms of domesticity appropriate to sexual subculture.

Re-Imagining Modernism

The End of Amusing
Interiors and Commissions (1927–36)

This book began by wondering over the two voices—each with its own idea of modernism—in Dorothy Todd's and Raymond Mortimer's 1929 book, *The New Interior Decoration*. The fourteen intervening chapters have sought to interest readers in a now-neglected form of modernism that in 1929 seemed a viable alternative to Art Deco and the International Style. This chapter, by way of conclusion, returns to issues raised in the introduction concerning the relationship between Bloomsbury's domestic style and what, during the 1930s, became mainstream modern design. Historians of modern design often present the Thirties as a point of origin: the first chapter in the heroic narrative of the rise of the International Style in Britain. This tale of modernist pioneers has transformed recently, under the pressure of postmodernism, into a bitter story of confusion and timidity in the British reception of Continental modernism, as historians still focused on the International Style try to explain the collapse of credibility in its ideals.[1] This chapter turns away from the conventional emphasis on the International Style, analyzing contests over the meaning of modern design around 1930 with an eye not to what began, but to what ended. The rise of the International Style during the Thirties meant the end of what I have called the Amusing Style. Starting from Roger Fry's critical response to the theoretical premises of designers like Le Corbusier, this chapter examines debates over modernism at the period in order to understand how the same forces that occasioned the most elaborate decorative commissions from the Bloomsbury artists ultimately subsumed their aesthetic.

Conventional histories of design present the 1925 *Exposition des Arts Décoratifs* in Paris, for which the Art Deco style is named, as a Rubicon that left all who passed through converted to streamlined contours and smooth surfaces. But this overstates both the immediacy and singularity of the exhibition's effect. It would be more accurate to say that the *Exposition* cast British designers into a state of turmoil where wildly varying self-styled "modern" design philosophies competed to resolve what was widely seen as a crisis of purpose in the profession. The astonishment registered by the London architecture journals' coverage of the Paris exhibition marks the gulf between Continental and British design before 1925. Recognizing that something different was happening in Europe, journalists announced that "a modern expression has arrived," embodied in "French furniture and painting," specifically in the anti-eclecticism that reflected "the French instinct to concentrate upon the *ensemble*" and subordinate every detail "to the needs of the room itself."[2] Contrasted to the "tendency which English people have of rather overcrowding with odds and ends, of multiplying angles, changes of direction, detail in general," the modern "*ensemblier*" was unequivocally French, so much so that the *Architectural Review* worried over how to "translate this last-born of French technical terms. An 'all-togetherist'—how cumbersome!"[3]

Very quickly, the architecture press focused on Le Corbusier, whose model *Pavillon de L'Esprit Nouveau* seemed to push the cohesiveness of the Art Deco *ensemble* to its furthest extreme. Initially, however, British journalists interpreted the starkness of Le Corbusier's décor as an eccentricity analogous to the Amusing mannerisms of Sitwellian modernism, and susceptible to similar purple-prosed exegesis. The *Architectural Review* described Le Corbusier's unembellished rooms as decorated by "the greatest of all artists, Nature herself," asking:

> Is not every wall patterned by sunlight and shadow, is not the whole filled with a fanciful reality? Ghostly grey at dawn, changing with every fleeting iridescent colour of the sunrise, blatantly, cruelly brilliant at high noon, soothing with restful and deepening tones at the close of day, who is there to say that this room is not decorated?[4]

Such perceptions were overturned by the publication of Frederick Etchells's translation of Le Corbusier's *Vers une architecture* in 1927. With an introduction stressing functionality and an English title emphasizing novelty, *Towards a New Architecture* shifted discussions of Corbusian design to the architect's now-familiar claims to embody logic, health, economy, technological sophistication, and a renunciation of the past. By 1928, the *Architectural Review* praised the "fundamental sanity" of Le Corbusier's ideas and endorsed his claims that efficient design will "develop in mind and heart a cleanliness, a probity of thought, a self-reliance, nay, more, a passion for vigorous social and aesthetic equipment of so unequivocal a quality that the miserable kind of make-beliefs, for so long the basis of most of our architecture as it is of most of our social life, must, in time, be weakened by such efforts, and the way be made clear for a new individual and corporate renaissance."[5]

From today's perspective, Le Corbusier's claims for heroic progress clearly differ from Bloomsbury modernism. In the Twenties, however, Fry's and Le Corbusier's shared antagonism toward the historical styles still favored for prestigious public and private buildings prompted the *Architectural Review* to treat both authors as twin manifestations of one "modern" sensibility. In 1928, the next issue of the *Architectural Review* after the one praising *Towards a New Architecture* carried an equally enthusiastic essay on Fry's pamphlet, *Architectural Heresies of a Painter*, published seven years earlier. Summarizing Fry's rejection of "fine allusions" and "historical associations" in favor of "formal arrangements that have integrity and significance," the *Review* presented his architectural ideas as, like Le Corbusier's, evidence of a "clear-sighted" new generation's "disgust" over the "licence" displayed by its elders' "architectural orgies."[6] But although journalists paired Fry and Le Corbusier, Fry's reaction to *The New Interior Decoration* confirms Bloomsbury's antagonism toward Corbusian modernism. Writing to Bell about the book, Fry reported, "you and D[uncan] provide almost the only pleasure for I find most of this modern stuff incredibly German even when the French do it. It's desperately theoretical and doctrinaire. It's not quite so simple to be simple as they think."[7]

Clearly troubled by the new direction of modernist design, Fry developed his arguments against Corbusian modernism in subsequent lectures.[8] Distinguishing between designs that are simply "bare" and those that are truly "simple," Fry argued that simplicity "is not by any means a simple matter . . . it cannot be attained by merely suppressing things." Noting that the streamlining of ships and other "machines which move rapidly or against a resisting medium" loses any claim to functionality when applied to a house, Fry characterized Le Corbusier's interiors as "what I call the gadgett style." Corbusian interiors, Fry claimed, were not actually functional, but simply illustrated the "magic words," "simplicity" and "functionalism," much as Victorian decorators had used floral imagery to illustrate their ideal of "natural" design.

Having relegated Corbusian functionalism to the status of illustration, Fry returned to the formalist distinction between necessarily artificial mimesis and the reality of aesthetic emotion to uphold, instead, an aesthetic criterion of "ease," which he defined as "the ease of apprehension, the evidence throughout of a simple controlling idea." This argument renames the basic formalist principle of "unity" that Fry articulated in his 1909 "Essay on Aesthetics," reiterating his definition of the "specific pleasure which we call aesthetic" as the apprehension of "a single idea informing every part of a whole" so that "we feel that the whole has an organic and vital unity." Where in 1909 Fry contrasted formalist aesthetics with literature, however, now he compared architecture to written language. "Just as in a long sentence the mind can grasp an extremely complicated sense if all the subordinate clauses are properly related to the main clause, so in a well articulated design the mind can grasp the significance of the whole at once even though it may be extremely complicated in detail." As an example, Fry compared a passage by John Milton to an elaborate Queen Anne interior; in both, he said, "we recognize a number of distinct clauses all related together." He continued:

> Supposing some owner of such a room in his zeal for simplicity was to take offence at that carving on the chimney breast and over the door and was to say, "Away with such frivolities and excrescences—let us be simple." He would in fact immensely impair the aesthetic simplicity of the design, for these carvings are no longer merely decorative, they have an important function in the whole design, they punctuate certain clauses so to speak and thereby increase very greatly the clarity and perspicuity of the whole statement of the idea.

Rejecting Corbusian minimalism as the paradigm of modernism, Fry turned instead to Virginia Woolf, quoting from *Mrs Dalloway* to demonstrate modern "prose with its success of more or less equally potent phrases." The conclusions he draws from this comparison reveal his distance from what became the modernist canon.

For Fry, the linguistic model explained his aesthetic dissatisfaction with Le Corbusier's style, in which:

> there is no attempt to direct my gaze, no help to me to concentrate on one thing rather than another. The relations of the parts to one another are quite vague and problematical. If I describe my impressions I have to say a flat surface, and another flat surface at right angles to it and another flat surface at right angles to both. I can hardly say a wall and a ceiling for there is nothing but their position to differentiate them. Whereas in the [Queen Anne] interior the mouldings at the base and top of the wall were equivalent to saying a wall *which* rises from the ground and *which* supports the ceiling. The mouldings give us the power of using a relative clause whereas in the modern interior we are reduced to a kind of pidgin English with no possibility of syntax.

In contrast, Fry cast his lot with the Sitwells, upholding the Mexican Baroque as meeting the criteria of modernist aesthetics. "I will not be so paradoxical as to call it simple," Fry said of a Mexican church interior, "but I consider it far more organic, more easily grasped and apprehended as a unity than many efforts of the modern style. Indeed it is astonishing to see what a pandemonium of riotous forms can be more or less harmonized and orchestrated as it were by a sufficiently powerful grouping under headings." Finally—and most surprisingly, given Fry's connections to Woolf—Fry compares her prose to Jacobean interiors as similar manifestations of the "weak unity and low organization" of simple additive construction, like "an earthworm from which a piece can be cut without impairing too much its efficiency." Although successful on its own terms, a modernism that limited itself to such plain speaking, whether verbal or visual, Fry argues, limited the potential for "aesthetic pleasure" inherent in more complex forms and hand-made surfaces expressive of "the sensibility of the artist-craftsman." Bloomsbury's interiors of the late Twenties and Thirties display a continuing commitment to this model, in which complex aesthetic pleasure derives from self-expression enabled by the deployment—not the suppression—of a vocabulary of forms and styles inherited from the past.

The fundamental compatibility of Bloomsbury and the Sitwells was recognized by friends and foes alike. Among the former, Boris Anrep united Bloomsbury with the Sitwells in his Amusing Style mosaics in the main entrance of the National Gallery, completed between 1930 and 1933. In this project, described by Frances Partridge as "a kind of artistic cocktail party with a classical theme; the guests attired as Gods and Muses," Clive Bell appeared as Bacchus and Virginia Woolf as Clio, the Muse of History, while Osbert Sitwell personified Poetry in a company that also included such elders of the Bright Young People as Mary Hutchinson (personifying Erotic Poetry) and Lydia Keynes (as Song and Dance), along with the film star Greta Garbo (as Melpomene, the Muse of Tragedy).[9] The flip side of the same coin was Wyndham Lewis's satiric 1930 novel *The Apes of God*, which skewered Bloomsbury and the Sitwells (Osbert satirized as "Lord Osmund") as sequential generations of a nugatory avant-garde. Mocking the eclecticism that was the hallmark of Amusing decoration, Lewis described Lord Osmund's art collection as a "strange embrace of Past and Present of so casual a nature as to produce nothing but an effect of bastardy."[10] Blinkered by his fixation on his London rivals, however, Lewis's amusing satire of the Amusing Style marks him—albeit unwittingly—as part of this milieu, so much so that his lengthy catalog of the decadent subgroups of the late-Twenties avant-garde fails to register the looming challenge posed by Corbusian contingents.

Lewis's generational linkage of Bloomsbury with the Sitwells echoed these groups' self-perception, as evidenced by both Bloomsbury's attitude of paternalistic indulgence toward the Sitwells and the Sitwells' competitiveness with their Bloomsbury elders. Whether condescending or rivalrous, both groups let their fundamental aesthetic and social compatibility lull them into a misplaced confidence that Britain's avant-garde had achieved consensus on the meaning of the modern. When Clive Bell reviewed Osbert Sitwell's and Nina Hamnett's collaborative 1928 *People's Album of London Statues*, a whimsical tour of Victorian public sculpture, he hailed Sitwell as a colleague in the minority that "wages ceaseless and quite unavailing war on stupidity and vulgarity" and praised the book for giving "pleasure to intelligent people," comments that reflected a naive confidence in an intelligentsia united against an agreed-upon adversary.[11] Minor differences between the Sitwells and Bloomsbury allowed each group to imagine itself on the cutting edge of this unified avant-garde, obscuring challenges from the Continent. For the Sitwells, the increasing age and acclaim of Bloomsbury's members reinforced their self-perception as irreverent champions of the young, while for Bloomsbury the Sitwell brothers' conspicuous affluence confirmed the older group's self-image as the most avant-garde. Meeting Osbert by chance in Sicily in 1927, Virginia reported, he "was very friendly, but he is lodged in a grand hotel outside the town, whereas we lodge in a cheap Italian inn, where no one speaks English . . . —so I don't suppose we shall see Osbert."[12] Nevertheless, Woolf remained indulgent. In 1934, Woolf's diary records her impression of Osbert's "childish vanity . . . so easily touched by praise, so eager," but concludes, "Still I like him—why I don't know"; a few years later, she concluded a joking anecdote at the Sitwells' expense with the acknowledgment, "fond as I am of parts of them."[13]

194. Rex Whistler, murals in the refectory at the Tate Gallery, 1925–27, as illustrated in *Architectural Review*, July 1928.

The extent to which competition with Bloomsbury also obscured the Sitwells' perception of Continental trends is clear in Osbert's writings. When in 1928, for instance, the Tate—in a manifestation of the ubiquity of the Amusing Style—unveiled Rex Whistler's massive (1300 square feet) new murals in its restaurant, Sitwell, in the *Architectural Review*, praised this cheerful pastiche of travelers in costumes of various eras progressing through a landscape punctuated with monuments of eighteenth-century English architecture, calling it a "deft and lighthearted . . . criterion of our changed taste" (fig. 194). Despite the *Review*'s recent coverage of the Art Deco show and related Continental design, Sitwell contrasted Whistler's aesthetic not with streamlined modernism, but with Bloomsbury. Dismissing "all the talk that goes on about 'pure painting' " in order to uphold Rex Whistler's place in "the old Italian-English school, without any tincture of French influence," Sitwell speculated that "the only lack of enthusiasm [for the murals] was probably among that section of the public who regretted that these walls had not been "'*Cézanned*,' served up *à la Provençal*."[14]

Especially after Fry's death in 1934, Osbert Sitwell exaggerated both the single-mindedness of Bloomsbury's commitment to abstraction and his own role in introducing Continental modernist art to England.[15] This competitive sniping has

Re-Imagining Modernism

195. Vanessa Bell and Duncan Grant, decorated rooms for Mary and St John Hutchinson at 3 Albert Gate, London, 1926, as illustrated in *Vogue*, late August 1926.

196. Vanessa Bell, painted panels inspired by Italian sequin pictures, part of decorated rooms for Mary and St John Hutchinson at 3 Albert Gate, London, 1926, as illustrated in *Vogue*, late August 1926.

blinded historians to the similarities between Sitwell and Fry in the Twenties. Far from disdaining the legacy of British art, Fry, in his introduction to a 1929 book on Georgian art and design, marveled over the profusion of "great names of English painting" during a period when "the stream of Renaissance tradition which had arrived so late in England . . . [was] mingling in that jumble of exotic and picturesque stylistic fashions with which we have struggled so uneasily ever since." Duncan Grant, responding to one of Fry's lectures at this period, thanked him for his "hymn of praise for Gainsborough," confiding that "only two painters have ever reduced me to tears—though Watteau sometimes brings a lump to my throat—and those two are Giorgione and Gainsborough."[16] Bloomsbury's sympathy with Sitwell's "old Italian-English school" ideal was matched by a shared rhetoric of avant-garde superciliousness. Fry's introduction to the book on Georgian art claimed that the British had killed the only two kings prior to George IV who were interested in art, concluding, "George IV, living in less brutal times, only had the windows of his state coach broken by an infuriated mob. A taste for art is clearly dangerous for a wearer of the British crown."[17] His dandyish tone echoes Sitwell's encomium to Whistler's Tate mural, which noted the recent flooding of the cafeteria with the comment that "one can quite see that . . . art would be as unpopular with the English climate as with the English people."[18]

If reading Sitwell and Fry side by side suggests their fundamental compatibility, a look at Bloomsbury's late-Twenties interiors reinforces the theoretical coherence of these avant-garde contingents. When in 1926 the Hutchinsons (whose earlier commissions are discussed in Chapter 12) moved from River House to new quarters

198. Vanessa Bell
and Duncan
Grant,
mural at the Château
d'Auppegard, 1927.

overlooking Regent's Park and again asked Bell and Grant to decorate, *Vogue* praised the resulting blend of figurative panels inspired by "old Italian sequin pictures" and "delicate" still lifes that displayed "a classical feeling befitting the period of the house"[19] (figs 195 and 196). A pair of painted panels representing female figures with baskets of fruit on their heads—a throwback to Grant's pre-war iconography (discussed in Chapter 3)—was also a part of this commission, augmenting what Sitwell might have called its "old Italian-English" effect (fig. 197).[20] The following year, Bell and Grant created murals with tondos showing landscapes and the labors of the seasons for the Château d'Auppegard, the seventeenth-century French country house of the painters Nan Hudson and Ethel Sands (fig. 198). Vita Sackville-West raved over these "six scenes of rustic employments—vintage, haymaking, harvest, and so on—in a manner mixed between idyllic-pastoral and romantic—and very modern; the result is absolutely enchanting."[21] Like Sitwell, Sackville-West welcomed as "modern" such playfully historicist pastorales.

Bell's and Grant's most elaborate exercise in this kind of decoration was the dining room they created in 1929 for the country house of the poet Dorothy Wellesley, a cousin by marriage to the Sitwells and a close friend of Sackville-West, whose taste for Baroque painting, honed through long residence in Rome, allied her with others in the British avant-garde of the twenties (figs 199, 200 and 201).[22] Quite compatible with the Sitwells' eclecticism, this room blended simple furniture with mural-scale panels depicting quasi-baroque gods and putti. Bell and Grant designed the furniture, painted and tiled with simple patterns in cool colors, to contrast with the murals' warmer flesh tones, loosely brushed and stippled with sponges. Electric sconces below octagonal mirrors echoed the octagonal table and reflected the painted decorations. Bell added curtains described as "pale mauve silk appliqué with yellow and orange and studded with patches of sequins" and concluded, "I must say the whole effect is very luminous and atmospheric, with the six mirrors and curtains glittering with silk and sequins, and the electric light arrangements are I think very good."[23] Grant concurred, noting how "the mirrors make it look much larger and brighter."[24] In retrospect, he judged the dining room "the best thing we did really—wonderful at night with the lights and pictures reflected in the looking glasses."[25] Madge Garland, writing in *The Studio*, praised the "general effect" of "iridescence" in this room, the Bloomsbury artists' first complete design in the manner of the French *ensemblier*.[26]

Left and facing page:
197. Vanessa Bell and Duncan Grant, painted panels, part of decorated rooms for Mary and St John Hutchinson at 3 Albert Gate, London, 1926, as illustrated in *Vogue*, late February 1926.

Re-Imagining Modernism

Behind the room's shimmering fantasy lay a careful consideration of its constituent elements. On the most basic level, here, as at the Château d'Auppegard, the careful framing of the representational elements provided the architectural vocabulary Fry demanded as the grammar of apprehensible design. What makes this project modern, in Bloomsbury's terms, is that these elements are not real moldings, panels, niches, or frames, nor do they make any claims to *trompe l'œil* or historical accuracy. Instead, they foreground their handmade facture as an expression of their makers' individual sensibilities. This distinction between modern and revival styles is implied in Fry's response to Bell's description of revisions she and Grant were making as they worked on the frescos at the Château d'Auppegard. Endorsing their new ideas, Fry contrasted them with the preliminary sketches, which he described as "a little too literal in their dix-huitièmerie."[27] More explicit articulation of Bloomsbury's decorative aesthetic at this period appears in Bell's letters. Complaining about how much work was involved in Wellesley's decorations, Bell reported that Grant had to scrap one panel because he had made "the figures rather solidly modeled and relieved in their spaces," making it "into too much of a picture." Grant was starting over "using very few colours and keeping more of the outlines and of the ground," and Bell describes herself "trying to reduce my seven foot panel to something in the nature of a drawing again."[28] These comments confirm what the look of these projects suggests: an ideal of modernism as a personal, expressive re-interpretation—a shimmering sketch, rather than a slavish re-creation—of a wide range of historical precedents. This ambition to update and personalize the past is literalized in one of Bell's panels, where the figure of Bacchus rising over his celebrants quotes one of her own photographs of her son Quentin romping naked in the garden at Bosham in 1915, blending art-historical reference with personal memory (fig. 202).[29]

In mainstream histories of modern design, Bell's and Grant's idea of modernism as a clever recycling of personal memory and historical precedent cannot rival the Corbusian modernism of streamlined functionalism. Yet—to reiterate my Introduction's discussion of the 1929 *New Interior Decoration*—this was not the perception before the Thirties: Madge Garland's report on the Wellesley commission was published in a *Studio* feature on "The 1930 Look," sandwiched between neo-Corbusian furniture designed by the young Francis Bacon and sleek Art Deco interiors available from the firm of Waring and Gillow. But this multiplicity of modernisms could not last. During the Thirties, deviations from functionalist modernism were suppressed with increasing vehemence by taste-makers, using rhetorics of crisis borrowed from Le Corbusier. The architect Trystan Edwards noted this trend in 1929 in the last article skeptical of Le Corbusier published in the *Architectural Review*. Writing under the headline "The Dead City," Edwards condemned the inflexible standardization advocated in Le Corbusier's *Urbanisme* (translated by Etchells as *The City of Tomorrow*), citing the book as "of great interest" only for the "methods of his propaganda" that

> are gradually being adopted by the whole Modernist School. First the "reformer" refers to some admitted and obvious defect in a building or buildings of the past, and suggests that the defect is common to all the buildings admired by those who belong to the opposite school of architectural opinion; and then by loud and reiterated clamour, he frightens the reader into supposing that there is only one way of dealing with the evil in question, and that is by accepting his own remedy.[30]

Edwards does not say so, but his critique of rhetorics where diagnoses of crisis create the premise for drastic and authoritative reform applied also to the *Architectural Review*, which by 1929 was sounding increasingly shrill alarms over British design. An editorial in the April issue solicited endorsements from literary luminaries Arnold Bennett, H. G. Wells, and George Bernard Shaw in order to berate major British retailers—especially Harrods, the most prominent—for ignoring British artists and designers in favor of old-fashioned revival styles and a modernism consisting of "French cretonnes, German carpets, fancies from the hand of

199–201. Vanessa Bell and Duncan Grant, dining room at Penns-in-the-Rocks, 1929. Destroyed, as illustrated in *The Studio*, August 1930.

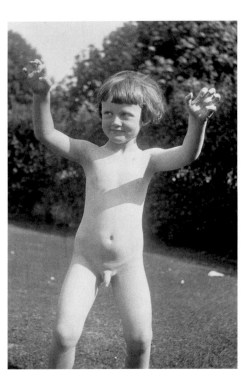

202. Quentin Bell photographed *c.* 1915 by Vanessa Bell. Tate Gallery Archive.

a ghost in the drafting-room of a manufacturer, and anonymous productions from the 'studio' of the store itself."[31] Ratcheting up the rhetoric two issues later, an editorial savaged a rebuttal from Harrods's "wily" chief designer as the "wisdom of the serpent" and attacked England's "Kings of Commerce" for turning a "frozen shoulder" to artists: "The French know better, and so do the Germans and the Swedes."[32]

The threat of foreign domination here is coupled with the weakness of modern British design, which the *Review* blamed on the anonymous "draughtsmen, and pretty poor draughtsmen too" employed by manufacturers. John Gloag, writing in the *Review*, traced the sorry state of modern British design to what he called (in reference to a manufacturing district in London) Shoreditch's "largely Semitic attempt to imitate the confident creative work of French designers," adding "the voluptuous embellishment that expresses the Oriental soul." Such manifestations of foreignness could not be countered by Britain's indigenous amateurs, "a regrettable

Re-Imagining Modernism

host of arty-crafty experimentalists who are so earnest and vocal that people are apt to recall their antics and their incredible clothes whenever modern furniture is mentioned." To redress this crisis of feeble Britishness overcome by foreign-influenced mass culture, the *Review* proposed the promotion of individual British modernists–even if their points of reference were Continental. "Some day it will be discovered that there may be money in putting names to designs—the names of the men who originated them," Gloag predicted, and a *Review* editorial urged the stores to follow the example of French dealers in Lalique glass who "make it their business to see that the NAMES of these artists are in the forefront of the battle."[33]

Whatever its logical flaws, this strategy of countering perceived foreign influences by branding international modernism with the names of individual British authorities reflected broad cultural trends of the early 1930s. Echoing Gloag's diagnosis of the crisis in British design, the quarterly journal *Scrutiny* rose to prominence in this era with a rhetoric of Britain besieged by the "international" aesthetics of jazz and film, in the face of which British "amateurs," unlike American and French intellectuals, were failing to protect their national culture. "In literature the advertisement-writer and crime-novel type of mind has forced the academic citadel and is doing very well," warned *Scrutiny*, while in music, jazz "has the same level of appeal as the popular press and film."[34] Casting themselves as the authorities who would defend England from international commercial culture, *Scrutiny*'s writers traded in what Gloag capitalized, "NAMES," gaining personal recognition for *ad hominem* attacks on others in the intelligentsia who, as a review of Rudolf Arnheim's book, *Film*, complained, threw a "psychological smoke-screen" of sophistication over their "own surrender to the onanistic flesh-and-underclothing motifs" of popular entertainment.[35]

The Sitwells and Bloomsbury were consistent targets of *Scrutiny*. In 1933, the magazine diagnosed the "formula" of Lytton Strachey's writing as "the familiar Metro-Goldwyn-Mayer heart-throb and mirthquake one," calculated to appeal to a " 'middlebrow' public" used to "commercial fiction" and now piqued by Strachey's "Freudian and free-thinking seasoning." This review concludes, "Though Sitwellianism is no longer *chic*, Strachey is an influence in life as well as letters; he set a tone which still dominates certain areas of the highbrow world, e.g. that part of Bloomsbury which has a well known annex in Cambridge. The deterioration and collapse represented by Mrs Woolf's latest phase"—here *Orlando* is cited as the first of her bad books—"is one of the most pernicious effects of this environment." That what was condemned was the literary manifestation of the Amusing Style is implied by the disparagement of Strachey's "style" as "a mere tasteful (or tasty) pastiche."[36] The implication becomes explicit in a 1936 essay on E. M. Forster, which was paired with the Strachey review in an early anthology of *Scrutiny* articles selected by the journal's lead editor, F. R. Leavis. Here, Q. D. Leavis—the editor's wife—blamed Strachey and Woolf for undermining their colleague's "natural endowments as a critic, so that you do get the impression that Mr Forster is disinclined to risk being thought too serious, he takes so much care to elicit the 'How amusing' response."[37] *Scrutiny*'s strongest attack on Bloomsbury came in a lengthy review of Woolf's *Three Guineas*, which, though it was authored by Q. D. Leavis, deploys enough barbed witticisms attributed to her colleagues to qualify as a group manifesto. Condemning the educational reforms Woolf advocated, Leavis complained, "She wants to penalize specialists in the interests of amateurs, and so her university . . . could only be a breeding-ground for boudoir scholarship (a term I once heard applied to the learning of one of Mrs Woolf's group)." The review concludes, "there is no longer any use in this field of speculation for the non-specialist like Mrs Woolf."[38]

Against the "boudoir" amateurism of the Amusing Style, *Scrutiny* proposed a critical mission characterized—like Corbusian design—as the practice of experts exercising moral probity and a quasi-scientific objectivity and discipline. The ironies attending *Scrutiny*'s rise to fame as a journal that exploited the attributes of celebrity culture and commercial entertainment—name recognition and a swash-buckling prose in the service of heroic narratives of good against evil—have been well explicated by historians sensitive to the broad cultural trends of the Thirties.[39] Such analyses should counter the tendency of design history to accept at face value rhetorics of a "crisis" in British design caused by competition from Continental manufacturers around 1930. Campaigns for reform in domestic design were part of a broader pattern of alarms being sounded over national identity in response to the international popular culture associated with the modern tastes of the Bright Young People.

The British Broadcasting Corporation was deeply involved in campaigns over the meaning of the modern. Counterintuitive as it may seem for an aural medium, interior design was a central concern of B.B.C. programmers, another self-described contingent of experts dedicated to the defense of national identity. When the B.B.C. was reorganized as a corporation in 1927, its status as a government monopoly was justified as a response to the penetration into England of foreign radio signals carrying the popular dance music loosely characterized as "jazz."[40] Against the threat of jazz—doubly foreign in that it was American mass culture transmitted from continental Europe—the B.B.C. mounted a campaign to inculcate an appreciation of classical music as a characteristic of modern Britishness. Despite its impressive commitment to young British composers (connoisseurs marveled at nationwide broadcasts of concerts so rarefied they attracted just four or five listeners in London), most of the classical music the B.B.C. deployed as an antidote to jazz was neither modern nor British. Bach, Mozart, and Beethoven were cast into the service of British modernity in what the B.B.C.'s Director-General promoted as a "policy of broadcasting carefully and persistently on the basis of giving people what one believes they should like *and will come to like*," a project that has been ably analyzed as promulgating a conception of modern Britishness defined as "an idealized version . . . of middle class identity."[41] Other B.B.C. policies, such as its announcers' uniform Oxbridge accent and now-notorious requirement (eventually abandoned) that presenters wear full evening dress, underlined the identification of modern Britishness with the expertise of the educated upper middle class.

The B.B.C.'s musical pedagogy was closely paralleled by its design programming starting in 1930, when an initiative to encourage what it called "intelligent listening" began supplementing broadcasts with pamphlets, discussion groups, and articles in its new magazine, *The Listener*.[42] Anxious to embody the values it promoted, the BBC made its new London headquarters, Broadcasting House, a paradigm of modernist style. In an echo of the B.B.C.'s sartorial policies, the look of the studios was promoted as essential to the quality of radio broadcasts. As the *B.B.C. Year Book* for 1933 explained, religious performances were recorded "in a temple-like structure elaborately unsectarian" (though the illustration reveals it to have been dominated, in High Church fashion, by a huge crucifix), literary discussions were staged in a library with false books but Arnold Bennett's real chair, and discussions of current events emanated from a functionalist studio.[43] The *Architectural Review* devoted much of two issues to what it called "The New Tower of London," when it opened in 1932. Ignoring the revival-style library, the *Review* saluted the B.B.C.'s modernist patronage of British firms, which had resulted in "a few of the more advanced manufacturers . . . undertaking the construction of articles comparable in quality and design with the best goods of foreign design." Although the "inspiration is necessarily to some extent Continental, the materials used are all of British, or at least imperial, origin," the *Review* announced.[44]

Presented as "men who are experts," the designers responsible for Broadcasting House were featured in B.B.C. broadcasts and publications, where they exhorted the public to apply modernist principles at home.[45] The architect–author of a typical *Listener* article erased all debate over varieties of modernism by describing " 'scientific architecture' (or 'modern' or 'functionalist', whichever word you like to use)" as a single practice, "which is the result of intense reasoning." Readers were instructed, "The question we must always ask is not whether these buildings appear beautiful, but whether they are fit for their function," and dissent from this standard was condemned as a failure "to grasp the reality of new conditions." Perfectly enacting the B.B.C.'s confidence that it understood its listeners' tastes better than they did themselves, this author asserted, "the great mass of English people are suffering from this time-lag between what they really need and what they 'feel' they like."[46] Recent claims that "Modernist design propaganda broadcast on the B.B.C." at this era was concerned "with what was variously termed social, workers', or mass housing" is contradicted by the frankly middle-class perspective consistently articulated by these men.[47] In a typical discussion, printed in *The Listener* under the title "Modern Dwellings for Modern Needs," Wells Coates, who designed the news and drama studios for Broadcasting House, spoke for a "we" with a family history of home ownership and the habits of playing golf, driving motor cars, and enjoying the leisure in which to "read, write, play the piano or listen to the gramophone or wireless," but now challenged by keeping house with fewer servants. Asserting that the first "demand" of modern life is that we "get rid of some of the many personal effects we carry about" and treat houses like cars with built-in furniture, Coates instructed listeners that "our *real* possessions" are "good manners" and "good taste." Householders who tried to follow Coates's exhortations to refuse "to put up with the shoddy pretences to beauty at second hand" and demand instead the work of "the modern architect" might be forgiven some confusion over his confident but contradictory pronouncements—in the same paragraph—that "for economy's sake" bathrooms "should be no larger than they need be for use" and that the requirements of good health dictate "the bathroom . . . ought to be as large as available money can make it . . . and give access to a protected balcony or terrace, for athletics and sun-bathing exercises."[48]

If specifics of the modernist ideal were ambiguous, however, the threats to it were not. Nostalgia and fancy were both anathema. The B.B.C. staged design debates as a two-sided battle between Corbusian functionalism and the revival styles advocated by academic and Arts and Crafts architects, such as Reginald Blomfield and M. H. Baillie Scott.[49] The Amusing Style, as an alternative form of modernism, was consigned to a silence broken only by brief allusions to "merely childish" furniture that looked like something it was not. Moral opprobrium was attached to deviations from the standard of functional efficiency, which were denounced—illogically, given that efficiency was constantly justified as labor saving—as evidence of "laziness" in both the designer and the buyer. This language was picked up by Paul Nash's influential *Room and Book*, which condemned the "craze" for antique furniture, acknowledged to be "the favorite flavour of eighty per cent of the population," as a symptom of "lazy mindedness" and "sentimental nostalgia."[50] Such moralism is clearest in a commentary by Frank Pick, President of the Design and Industries Association, who wrote in *The Listener* that the standard of "fitness for purpose must transcend the merely practical and serve a moral and spiritual order as well." Asserting that "there is only one right solution" to most issues of design, Pick blamed "perverse" consumers for forcing "the wretched designer" away from functional domestic design and toward the aesthetics of fashion, where "the length of a skirt" is allowed a "variety of solution." Exemplifying the experts' tendency to derogate mass culture by its association with women, Pick described the heroic designer forced by the "devils of fashion" into perversions stigmatized as feminine—or effeminate.[51] This essay was among those reprinted in 1934 in John Gloag's influential *Design in Modern Life*, an anthology culled from B.B.C. broadcasts and publications.

The dynamics implicit in the B.B.C.'s promotion of modernism for a general audience are more blatant in the design periodicals addressed to a readership of experts. Writing in the *Architectural Review* in 1930, Gloag belittled the "poor, dear public," which, though "it may have antipathies" and "dim traditional preferences," shows by the look of its "homes in the suburbs of London or any big city" that its decorating has "no will to get anything in particular."[52] The following issue of the *Review* announced a campaign—coincident with the B.B.C.'s first series of programs on design—to promote British artists as designers, led by a special double issue of the magazine devoted to "Modern English Interior Decoration." John Betjeman's often-cited survey of the history of British interior design, which appeared in this special issue of the *Review*, pushed the paradoxical logic—as well the class and gender biases—of the discourse of Britishness and expertise to an extreme. From opening lines that invoke a "British public" summoned by dinner gongs (those who ring the gong were not included), Betjeman went on to condemn the fruits of "COMMERCE," identified as "Comfort and Ignorant Wealth," which "account for the permission that was given to Germany to thicken English design." For Betjeman, Britain's salvation from threats foreign and commercial would be "intelligent designers," disciplined enough to eschew "the 'awf'lly modern' " style (pronounced as no B.B.C. presenter would intone it). This ersatz modernism, characterized by "cushions, whose colours resemble the allied flags," Betjeman said, "started in 1920 and [is] known as 'jazz.' " The culprits behind this undisciplined internationalism were young women "in simple frocks" who, failing to understand that decoration is not Britain's "strong point," amateurishly paint furniture and create needlework, metalwork, " 'lampshade-work' and any other kind of 'work' that can be devised. The harm they have done is terrific, for now the truly simple efforts of Le Corbusier and Dufy are hardly appreciated." This muddled nationalist rhetoric, which made British women working in the Arts and Crafts tradition into a foreign threat to a Britishness embodied by Continental designers, culminates in Betjeman's conclusion worrying over the challenge from "French, German, and Swedish" manufacturers who, by following Le Corbusier, have appropriated a truly British legacy, "when we bear in mind the axioms of Soane in that their simplicity is the result not of whim but of logic."[53]

Analogies to jazz as a corruptor—popular and feminine—of British modernism also characterize the best known text from the *Architectural Review*'s design campaign: the manifesto on "Modern English Furnishing" published by Paul Nash in the January 1930 issue, which became the opening essay in his *Room and Book* of 1932. Where Betjeman invoked John Soane to cast Corbusian aesthetics as British, Nash cited the Adam brothers as the last designers to have extracted "from foreign material" a personal style "in keeping with the almost indefinable spirit of the English tradition." To define the "almost indefinable," Nash urged readers to compare the "refinement" of an Adam house with the "vulgarity" of anonymous designs, quoting Robert Adam's denunciation of "the race of those reptile artisans who have crawled about and infested this country for many years." Applying this principle to the present, Nash concluded "the 'commercial modern' is the worst enemy to progress that the movement has to face."[54] Nash did not identify exemplary modernists by name in this essay, though to understand "the essential ideas of the new aesthetic," he guided readers to Le Corbusier, and the first five illustrations in the article showed glass and steel furniture by Denham Maclaren (far from actually being functional, these were so complex, and photographed so confusingly, that a reader wrote to ask if the table was pictured from the top or the side). When Nash reprinted this article under the title "The Modern Aesthetic" in *Room and Book*, however, he followed it with an historical survey of "Modern English Furniture" that borrowed freely from Betjeman. Here Nash dealt quickly with the "sad story" of the Omega as a "temporary phase which was not altogether happy in its after effects," when "vulgar adaptations" engulfed "the charming inventions of the Omega . . . in the new vogue of Jazz which lingers in Suburbia to this day." Insisting, "We do not any longer cover walls and wood with painted patterns," Nash commended a number of modernist designers, among them Wells Coates, but above all Frederick Etchells for translating Le Corbusier.[55] Praising *Room and Book* in the *Architectural Review*, R. H. Wilenski quoted Wyndam Lewis on the "*queerer*" qualities of the "*amusing*" fondness for "stuffed birds, wax flowers, and so forth," going on to emphasize the need for "creative professional designers" to counter the "parlour pastimes" of the "dilettantish activities of the Bloomsbury School of Interior Decorators which began with the Omega workshops."[56]

Despite his disparagement of the axis of influence from Omega to "Jazz," Nash in *Room and Book* praised Bell and Grant for their modern fabrics, and elsewhere commended Omega embroideries as the origin of "the modern movement in textile design."[57] Thus, the Bloomsbury artists—and the Amusing Style in general—were not immediately or completely excluded from the project to redefine modernist domesticity in the 1930s. The Amusing Style was, rather, relegated to the feminized

204. Paul Nash, entry for *Architectural Review* competition, 1930, as illustrated in *Architectural Review*, November 1930, pl. 8.

203. Raymond McGrath, entry for *Architectural Review* competition, 1930, as illustrated in *Architectural Review*, November 1930, pl. 1.

margins of modernist practice—to textiles and experiments with color—where it occupied as a no man's land between modern and popular taste, a reminder to more heroically minded modernists of the risks attending deviation from the standards of science and technology. This dynamic is made vividly clear by a competition the *Architectural Review* sponsored in 1930 to promote British designers. An editorial in the May double issue on interior design asserted the magazine's neutrality in the contest among self-proclaimed modern styles, declaring, "There is no need to be bound to any school of thought—mechanist, Tottenham Court Hotspur, or Mr. Raymond Mortimer's *école des Cocottes*."[58] Indeed, francophile coquettishness was given visual pride of place with a full-page illustration of Grant's Amusing Style serenader cabinet (discussed in Chapter 14) opposite this text. A hierarchy was nevertheless evident in the results of the competition judged by the *Review*'s editor. Despite his claim that modernism "cannot be defined positively as metal furniture and the Corbusier aesthetic," first and second place went to designers favoring glass and tubular steel furniture.[59] A project of murals submitted by Vanessa Bell (with Grant's collaboration) was awarded a grudging third place as the best of a bad lot of similarly misguided designs.

It is worth dwelling briefly on this *Architectural Review* competition, for it encapsulates many of the principles and the paradoxes that characterized the redefinition of modernism taking place in Britain in 1930. Paradox was built into the competitors' guidelines, which established the exemplary "intelligent client" as Lord Benbow, a knighted industrialist, "now the owner of a large racing stable and stud-farm." Benbow sought a "distinguished modern treatment in the decoration of his apartments" tempered by his "invincible loathing of abstract patterns, which he has never been able to understand" and preference for sporting subjects. Both the first and second prize plans (figs 203 and 204) responded to this call for a masculine modernism (a domestic commission untroubled by the femininity of a female client)

The End of Amusing

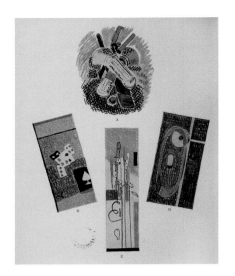

Above right, 205. Vanessa Bell (with Duncan Grant), entry for *Architectural Review* competition, 1930, as illustrated in *Architectural Review*, December 1930, pl. 2.

Above, 206. Details of murals by Vanessa Bell and Duncan Grant for *Architectural Review* competition, 1930, as illustrated in *Architectural Review*, December 1930, pl. 1.

207. Details of rugs and murals by Vanessa Bell and Duncan Grant for *Architectural Review* competition, 1930, as illustrated in *Architectural Review*, December 1930, pl. 3.

with fabrics designed by Nash, who, therefore, would seem to emerge as the leader of the new modernism, were it not that the *Review*'s editor sternly criticized his second-place entry for compromising its "subtle fugue-like organization" of formal elements by indulging temptations to amusement. Condemning as "faintly ridiculous" Nash's rug imitating a tennis court and cocktail bar "constructed on lines of a grand-stand surmounted by a pennant of Lord Benbow's racing colours," the editor complained that "the artist either misunderstood the purport of the remarks regarding Lord Benbow's sporting tastes, or deliberately surrendered to his sense of humor." Some capriciousness over what constituted "ridiculous" interior design is evident in the *Review*'s unblinking acceptance of a massive alabaster yacht, curtains with hurdling and golf motifs, and wallpaper displaying "an abstract design of seagulls, harbour-buoys and yacht slips" in the first-place entry, submitted by Raymond McGrath, the first Cambridge-trained expert in architecture, described in the *Review* as the "chief specialist" who had overseen the interior of Broadcasting House.[60]

The end of the Amusing Style was heralded by more than the *Review* editor's gratuitous standards of appropriate iconography, however. His relegation to inglorious third place of the proposal submitted by Bell and Grant (figs 205–7) hinged on his assessment that, despite a "very beautiful" color scheme, their murals (brushy still lifes of hunting and horse-racing accouterments), carpets, and painted furniture were applied to rather than derived from the space. Complaining that "the same scheme could be carried out in almost any kind of room," the editor asserted the logical-sounding criterion of "Modern" interior design as "involving, first and foremost, the imaginative exploitation of the plan conceived three-dimensionally." Bell's error in ignoring this precept was not unique. The *Review* cited hers as typical of a "large number" of submitted designs "which bear no relation at all to the peculiar character of Lord Benbow's apartments." Preserving some discretion, the *Review* mentioned only one losing competitor by name: Mary Adshead—significantly another female muralist associated with the Amusing Style—who, displaying "a gusto which one admires but cannot approve," wrapped "a design which would have been most impressive had it been designed for a pure rectangle" around the bay "without regard to classic symmetry."[61] The illustrations of the winning designs in the *Architectural Review* suggest that the injunction to exploit the plan meant little beyond filling the space to the corners; Nash's second-place design blithely altered the shape of the one bay it pictures to match the rectilinear furniture.[62]

Re-Imagining Modernism

Nevertheless, this criterion strikes at the heart of the Amusing Style's delight in quotation and pastiche, where (as argued in the previous chapter) these were signified by incongruous scale and juxtapositions that flouted the visual norms other modernists promoted as morally wholesome. Whether expressed as an ideal of truth to materials or of form following function, the insistence that modern design be whatever it is through and through (the chair as a tool for sitting, with all its constituent elements clearly displayed in their unvarnished materiality) is diametrically opposed to the campy pastiche of the Amusing Style (a cupboard conceived as a "romance," to take an example from the previous chapter).

Bloomsbury's artists responded ambivalently to being catapulted into these debates over modern domestic design. Their letters from the opening months of 1930 ricochet from resolutions to abandon design and concentrate on "painting pictures" to reports on schemes to interest stores in "employing artists in decorative work," and even to speculations about restarting the Omega.[63] Although this last idea was not realized, campaigns to promote British artists as designers resulted in commissions for Bell and Grant to design dishware and textiles. The ceramics commissions extended the commercial reach of work Grant and Bell had carried on throughout the Twenties, when they painted tiles for stoves, fireplaces, and table tops with an Amusing blend of historical and topical motifs: frolicking goddesses, the accoutrements of *fêtes champêtres*, modern women smoking cigarettes, and Lytton Strachey as an odalisque.[64] Two prominent patrons' commissions for hand-decorated dinnerware reveal the persistence of a taste for the gender-bending historical pastiche of the Amusing Style. In 1928, David Eccles, later knighted for his promotion of British crafts, commissioned from Grant and Bell twelve dessert plates decorated with scenes chosen by Virginia Woolf from *Orlando*, her playful new novel of gender crossing.[65] Four years later, Kenneth Clark commissioned a massive dinner service—about 140 pieces—featuring fifty plates adorned with what Vanessa Bell described as "portraits of celebrated females—it ought to please the feminists—of all times": "12 queens . . . 12 actresses or dancers, 12 Beauties and 12 writers" complemented by serving dishes decorated with nude goddesses (fig. 208).[66] Two more plates displayed self-portraits, incorporating Grant within this party of famous women.

Like Eccles, Clark was an influential taste-maker (he was offered the directorship of the National Gallery in 1933), whose commission was a significant imprimatur of official favor. Although Clark's memoirs attempt retroactively to distance him from the Amusing Style, the record of ongoing guidance from his circle tells another story.[67] A collector of Far Eastern ceramics told by the Clarks of their commission sent Bell and Grant what might be described as a manifesto for the Amusing Style. Announcing that "the vast repertoires of traditional art [may] be ransacked for every emblem that may enliven dinner table discussion," he asserted, "one is pleased at meals by the familiar, the friendly even the facetious."[68] By this standard, Bell and Grant could not fail to satisfy. Familiar and facetious faces from the past— including the overlapping histories of Bloomsbury painting and costume parties— thronged the all-female party, among them the Queen of Sheba and the Empress Theodora, whose visages had inspired pre-war experiments in Post-Impressionism (discussed in Chapter 5), and the actress Ellen Terry, who had figured prominently in the Stephen sisters' matriarchal heritage and, therefore, in Bloomsbury's amateur theatrics (discussed in Chapter 1). More facetiously perhaps, Queen Victoria appeared twice, once in youth and once in formidable old age, and the "Beauties" were as up to date as could be, with images of Greta Garbo and "Miss 1933". The advice Grant and Bell received for their commission registers not only the approbation for the Amusing Style in Clark's circle, but also its discouragement of what was, at the time, functionalist modernism's complement: the craft revival in ceramics associated with Bernard Leach.[69] Clark's adviser discouraged Bell and Grant from "designing original pottery" after their simple, heavy Omega-ware, advocating, instead, their use of commercially produced blanks; to this end, he arranged the artists' meeting with a Wedgwood agent in London.[70] When Bell, who always retained a preference for the chunky Omega plates—"for tableware one can't have

208. Duncan Grant and Vanessa Bell, Famous Women plates, hand painted on Wedgewood blanks, 1933. Private collection.

anything better"—rejected Wedgwood's modern forms and glazes, the firm invited the artists to its headquarters to choose from older models.[71] Ultimately, the artists settled on what Bell described as "an original Josiah Wedgwood shape . . . not at all unlike the Omega shape with a concave rim" and a "glaze which gives rather a lovely cool white very like Delft."[72] The result is consummately Amusing: sophisticated historical allusions rendered with an exuberant, self-conscious simplicity evocative of the amateur theatrics of costume parties.

Elements of the Amusing Style also animated more commercial commissions that were the direct outcome of the campaigns to induce manufacturers to employ artists as designers. Bell and Grant were included, with other modern artists, in a 1933 project by two commercial potteries, Foley and Wilkinson, to produce "limited edition" dishware sold under the signatures of the artist-designers. Both Bell and Grant produced tea sets that jazzed up conventional floral patterns with larger scale, brighter colors, and freer handling —one of Grant's patterns was whimsically titled "Old English Rose"[73] (fig. 209). The following year, Bell and Grant were commissioned to design larger sets of dinnerware, which were hand-painted by Clarice Cliff and her staff for the Wilkinson company, and also marketed with facsimile signatures of the artists.[74] These designs, too, centered on simplified and magnified floral motifs, which were rimmed around with patterns of circles enlivened, in Grant's design (fig. 210), by dots and swags, and in Bell's by cross-hatching. Raymond Mortimer's review of an exhibition of artist-designed tableware at Harrods in 1934 singled out Bell's and Grant's ceramics as "ravishing in colour and sensitive in drawing. . . . If a tea cup or a soup plate could be said to sing, these services could be called musical." This accolade, with its emphasis on sensuality and embrace of metaphor, implied an aesthetic at odds with the new rhetoric of technology and

Re-Imagining Modernism

210. Duncan Grant, Clarice Cliff dish, 1934. Charleston Trust.

209. Duncan Grant, Foley tea set, 1933. Private collection.

function, and Mortimer made this antagonism explicit in the introduction to his review, where he claimed as both leftist and modernist a philosophy at odds with functionalism. Challenging those who would dismiss his ideas as "bourgeois fantasy," Mortimer invoked William Morris to argue for the salutary effect of good design, not in terms of functional efficiency, but because "the material objects most closely connected with us. . . . complement and as it were continue our bodies," and, therefore, "excite in most men and women an affection which . . . is ultimately erotic rather than aesthetic."[75] Mortimer's celebration of the sensual, even erotic, aspect of domestic design stakes out a clear opposition to the Corbusian house-machine promoted by more influential modernists (discussed in the Introduction) as a prophylactic against bodily traces.

The sensuality Mortimer detected in Grant's and Bell's ceramic services is clearly visible in Grant's commercial textiles commissioned at this period by Alan Walton for his family's textile printing firm.[76] Grant, despite an initial reluctance to participate, ultimately designed nine fabrics for Walton, featuring his familiar repertoire of accessories from a *fête champêtre*: flowers, bunches of grapes, and garden urns.[77] Most Amusing among Grant's designs were his 1931 "Winds" (fig. 211) and 1935–36 "Apollo and Daphne" (fig. 212) patterns; both depict a flirtatious chase of a nude goddess (far from resisting Apollo, the fleeing Daphne turns to pelt him with flowers from her bouquet). Although modernist design histories disparage Grant's fanciful textiles in contrast to the "straightforward but effective geometric designs" (among them Bell's subdued pattern of circles and squares) Walton solicited from other artists, Grant's fabrics were well received at exhibitions in 1931 and '32, and the "Apollo and Daphne" pattern won a prize at a design exhibition in Paris in 1937. Even the terms of commendation for Grant's designs, however, reveal that functionalism had become the modernist standard, for his Amusing patterns were welcomed as amiably eccentric vestiges of the past. Paul Nash, writing in *The Listener*, described Grant's "idea of a curtain design" as "entirely his own and as contradictory as possible" to those of other modernists, before saluting his textiles as evidence of "artistic individuality."[78] Cyril Connolly, in the *Architectural Review*, upheld Bell's "circles and squares" as his "favorite" of Walton's artist-designed fabrics, then praised Grant's fabrics in terms that might serve as an elegy for the Amusing Style as a whole. Crediting Grant for breaking "from the other staid and inoffensive hues into something like gaiety," Connolly read this exuberance as old-fashioned, remarking that his fabric "looks its best with Chippendale." This leads to the conclusion:

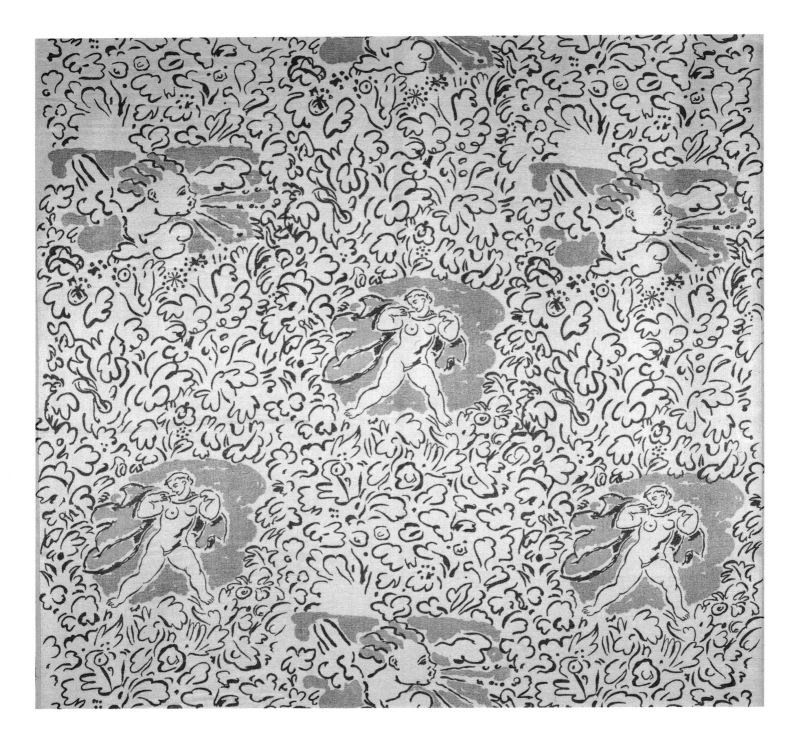

211. Duncan Grant, fabric, "The
Winds," 1931, for Allan Walton.
Victoria and Albert Museum,
London.

The exhibition is a noble and successful experiment, but not a daring one; there is
even something depressing and defeatist about it. "Life is a terrible thing," [the
displays] seem to say, "but a few discriminating people can have some rather
charming chintzes, or one or two amusing pots in their rooms; if they care to."[79]

The pleasures of Amusement were, thus, marginalized as a nostalgic reprieve from
the grim rigors of modern life.

Grant's and Bell's distance from the modernist mainstream may be clearest in
their most concerted project to capitalize on new initiatives for artist-designed
domestic furnishings: a music room created in 1932 for display in the London
gallery of Alex Reid and Lefevre (fig. 213). This ensemble was conceived to recapture the *élan* of the Omega, with Virginia Woolf inviting Ottoline Morrell to what
she conspiratorially assured her would be "a quite ghastly party" for the November

Re-Imagining Modernism

212. Duncan Grant, fabric, "Apollo and Daphne," 1935–36, for Allan Walton. Victoria and Albert Museum, London.

opening, "a purely commercial (don't whisper it) affair, to induce the rich to buy furniture, and so employ a swarm of poor scarecrows who are languishing in Fitzroy Street."[80] Woolf funded the party as a Christmas present to her sister, gloating afterwards about "us two hussies entertaining the peerage" with "boys in white jackets handing blue green and yellow drinks."[81] She also subsidized two-thirds of the cost of the display, partially repaid with a carpet designed for her by Grant. Woolf's carpet—a handsome composition with stylized bouquets of flat leaves and blossoms hovering above silhouetted vessels, to which Grant at the last minute incongruously added fish—produced a giddy encomium from its owner (fig. 214). The rug, Woolf said, was "a triumphant and superb work of art," which "produces in me the sensation of being a tropical fish afloat in warm waves over submerged forests of emerald and ruby. You may well ask what sort of forest that is—I reply it

is the sort of fish I am." Anticipating the effect of her new carpet on her own writing, Woolf, drawing a contrast that would have confirmed *Scrutiny*'s deepest suspicions, concluded that, "thank God," she had recently finished an article on her father.[82]

Woolf's subsidy of the music room ultimately earned her several of its parts: a set of caned side chairs with embroidered panels, a cabinet, a mirror in a painted frame, and a three-paneled screen painted by Vanessa Bell with music-making female nudes.[83] In addition to the pieces acquired by Woolf, the music room displayed hand-painted ceramic tiles and vases, a gramophone painted by Bell, and a piano and stool painted by Grant (with a cushion embroidered by his mother). Chairs and a sofa were upholstered in a yellow version of Walton's "Grapes" pattern by Grant, who also designed two carpets and a valance printed—Amusingly—with a sketchy rendition of elaborate swags. Painted swags also surrounded the six large floral still lifes, each, according to Grant, evocative of a famous composer. With the same insouciance that characterized their shifting attributions of the liberal arts and sciences to the figures in Keynes's Cambridge sitting room, however, Bell confided to Fry, "I can't see that one's more suitable than another. What sort of design would you give to Bach and what to Chopin?"[84] With Mozart, Debussy, and Stravinsky among the other composers Grant later recalled as his inspiration, the designs claimed references to the classical music that taste-makers were promoting as the antidote to jazz. Visually, however, the room flaunted its Amusing disdain for the rigors of high modernism with its cheerful pastiche and quotation. The ubiquitous images of swags flouted injunctions to truth to materials, and the other motifs indulged in jazzy play with themes and variations (three musical nudes, six symbolic

The End of Amusing

bouquets) emphasized by leaps of scale (the bouquets on the wall are larger than the nudes on Bell's painted screen, while the leafy motifs Grant painted on the piano magnify aspects of his designs for the rugs and textiles). As in Dorothy Wellesley's dining room, numerous small mirrors multiplied the effect with their fragmented reflections.

Again, the terms of Cyril Connolly's approbation signal the end of the Amusing era. Praising what he called Grant's and Bell's new-found "riotous sense of colour" and "romantic splendor," and displaying his own facility with Amusing metaphor, Connolly described the music room as "a great canvas of autumn: not the usual drooling sickbed of the countryside, but those conjunctions of sun and wind that suddenly illuminate gardens and beech woods." That this eccentric vision of the English landscape was a form of foreignness became explicit in Connolly's report on the opening party, where "the room vibrated to a Debussy solo on the harp," the music blending "with the surrounding patterns of flowers and falling leaves in a rare union of intellect and imagination, colour and sound, which produced in the listener a momentary apprehension of the life of the spirit, that lovely and un-English credo." In this formulation, the attraction of the Amusing Style depends on its transience, as the future of British modernism is ceded to other aesthetics. Emphasizing these implications, Connolly's review brackets praise for the music room between assertions that its success marks an exception that proves a very different rule. He opens by distinguishing Grant and Bell from "the defeatist, the rather *triste* good taste of their younger imitators," and ends with the decidedly backhanded compliment that the room "is a fine sight for the connoisseur who enjoys discriminating between the work of the two painters, one so much better than the other, down to the lover of beauty, whose love is now consistently unrequited."[85] Between the self-defeating oxymoron of "*triste*" Amusing Style followers and the assertion of a contemporary moment marked by something other than "beauty," the stopgap of a two-person aesthetic in which one of the artists is so inferior to the other (but which?) casts the pleasures of the music room as a form of nostalgia for a transient pleasure already fleeting in the face of British modernity.

If reviews of the music room were mixed, the commercial verdict was unambiguous. No sales resulted from the display. Most of the furniture ended up at the Woolfs' Sussex house or at nearby Charleston, and this project intended to inaugurate a new round of decorative commissions instead became the last domestic interior Grant and Bell designed.[86] In hindsight, the music room's failure was over-determined. Economic anxiety stunted the market for large-scale interior design, and the room's Amusing aesthetic might have been better marketed to the adult children of the eminent personages of her own generation whom Woolf took such pleasure in entertaining.[87] An analogous mismatch of Amusing informality with staid convention marked the look of the room as it was installed in an upscale gallery. Forbidden to mar the wall, the artists incorporated its flat beige color into the smaller pieces of furniture and the framing elements of their painted panels, deadening these elements, which then jarred with the far more brilliant textiles and embroideries. Overriding these particular shortcomings, however, was the collapse of the Amusing Style in the face of the rhetorics of logic and efficiency associated with what was rapidly becoming definitive "modern" design.

Like the failure of the Lefevre Gallery music room, the success of Corbusian modernism was over-determined. As its name implies, the International Style was implicated in global social and aesthetic forces beyond the scope of this book. Indeed, there is some irony in British experts' strenuous deployment of nationalist rhetorics to promote Le Corbusier's Continental aesthetic, inspired by American commercial construction, over the Amusing Style, which was firmly rooted in the British legacy of Aestheticism. The language of nationalism, however, as this chapter has argued, masked deeper anxieties over challenges from within Britain to middle-class norms of gender, sexuality, self-discipline, and expressiveness. Bloomsbury's long association with those challenges made its domestic aesthetic anathema to the culture of experts, so that, during the 1930s, Bloomsbury was pushed ever farther toward the margins of the modern.

215. Duncan Grant, design for "The Sheaf," decoration for the *Queen Mary*, 1936. Oil on board, 235 × 137.5 cm. Wolfsonian Museum of Florida International University.

This marginalization was dramatically demonstrated in 1936 when the Cunard White Star lines rejected three large decorative panels it had commissioned from Duncan Grant for the ocean liner the *Queen Mary* (figs. 215, 216). Grant was one of several artists involved in this project, another outcome of the campaigns to use artists as designers. His commission—two overmantels and a twenty-two-foot high vertical panel, as well as carpets and textiles (fig. 217) for a large saloon—was among the largest and most prominent, however, and, although several other artists' contracts were also cancelled, his attracted the most attention.[88] Attempting to explain the cancellation, Cunard's representatives hinted to Grant at "the influence of Buckingham Palace" over the ship bearing the name of the reigning queen.[89] Officially, Cunard offered the explanation that "too high a proportion of the murals would appeal to a limited coterie interested in the development of modern painting," a rationale vague enough to allow commentators at the time and since to cast the controversy into the familiar narrative of the avant-garde artist held back by the retrograde patron.[90] But Grant's panels were not stylistically radical. As one reviewer described them, "the young men and women who pluck flowers or dance or play guitars among the flower-decked fields in them are nice, well made creatures who suffer no anatomical distortions in the interest of aesthetics."[91] A closer look at

216. Duncan Grant, "Seguidilla," decoration for the *Queen Mary*. Private collection.

Cunard's letter specifies the problem with Grant's work as its association with a "limited coterie" identified with "painting." Given the slick, Art Deco aesthetic adopted for the liner, this language suggests a disciplinary distinction to the contrast between a "coterie" taste for painting's handmade facture and the shiny, machined surfaces of, for example, Maurice Lambert's metal reliefs teeming with female figures, which were accepted for the room. By late 1935, when Grant's panels were under debate, newspaper publicity for Cunard promised "modern but restrained decoration" for the *Queen Mary*, reinforcing the sense that the directors were choosing one kind of modernism over another.[92] Once again, the factual errors of Kenneth Clark's memoirs from the 1970s impose the revealing clarity of retrospect over the muddled cross-currents of the period. Although it is not true that the wife of Cunard's chairman rejected Grant's panels in favor of the quintessentially Art Deco motifs of deer and gazelles, as Clark claims, his anecdote encapsulates the conflict between the handmade whimsys of the Amusing Style and the machined aesthetic the *Queen Mary* helped enshrine as the look of the modern (the ship is today preserved as an Art Deco period piece).[93]

Grant began his *Queen Mary* decorations very much in the spirit of the Amusing Style. A letter to Bell at the start of the project exults over the smaller commission for a painted panel, doors, and textiles he secured for her, citing "the amusing shape of the room" and describing the work as "amusing to do."[94] And reviewers praised Grant's panels in Amusing terms. *The Times* admired their "light-hearted swing" and "freshness," while the *Guardian* found them "bright in colour and cheerful in mood" and "bound together by a swinging rhythm." Like Cunard's letter, the

Re-Imagining Modernism

Guardian's review hints at a contest between modernisms, citing Grant as "alone" among British artists in maintaining what it calls an English "charm . . . informed by the breath of life," despite his embrace of francophile formalism that treats "picture-making as a science."[95] By the mid-thirties, however, the tide was shifting definitively in favor of the rhetorics of rationalism. The light-hearted charms of the Amusing Style easily became epithets of abuse, as Clive Bell—always quick to pick up rhetorical fashions—demonstrated in an attack on the *Queen Mary*'s decoration in *The Listener*. Bell's jibes at the "ignorant business man" willing to sacrifice the "beautiful" for things that "look expensive" to flatter "the frivolous the frightened attitude toward art of rich people who are not sure of themselves," strike a more anti-authoritarian tone than most essays published by the BBC. Nevertheless, Bell echoed the rhetoric of seriousness claimed by the new generation of design experts in condemning as "artistico-comical" the "titterings in paint, wood, glass, plaster, and metal" inside the *Queen Mary*: "Nothing is suffered to be merely good-looking; it must be funny as well; which means hardly anything is good-looking and that almost everything is vulgar," he complained. "The whole boat giggles from stem to stern."[96] Bell's vehemence in recanting his earlier praise for Grant's "fantastic and whimsical" aesthetic so muddied the terms of debate that Kenneth Clark dropped his campaign to pressure Cunard to install Grant's panels.[97] After their exhibition in 1937 elicited commentary critical of Cunard's rejection, the company refused to allow the panels to be shown in the British Pavilion of the 1939 World's Fair in New York, and they remained in storage for most of the next thirty-five years.[98]

Grant's friends report that he was "personally devastated" by the debacle over the *Queen Mary*.[99] Although he and Bell continued to paint furniture and pottery for friends, their era of ambitious, well publicized interiors ended as modern design shifted decisively to other ideals. Bitterly assessing the demise of the Amusing Style in his memoirs, Osbert Sitwell mourned its replacement by "the word *Austerity*," with its "new sub-fusc and squalid twist of meaning."[100] Whether belittled as austere or celebrated as simple, the machined surfaces and streamlined forms of Art Deco and the International Style supplanted the handmade facture and whimsical subject matter that had characterized the Amusing Style. A concomitant rhetorical victory of the "expert" over the "amateur"—to this day characteristic of academic commentary on design in general, and Bloomsbury in particular—substituted institutionally credentialed authorities with claims to universal knowledge for the intellectually and sensually promiscuous iconoclasm Bloomsbury had imagined to be the hallmark of modernism.

In the terms of my Introduction, this history marks the victory of heroic utopians over subcultural housekeepers. And, indeed, after the 1930s Grant and Bell turned increasingly inward, as their lives and their art focused ever more intensely on familiar spaces and faces. Their isolation strained relations with those in Bloomsbury whose careers remained more public. Socially, Charleston drew away from Keynes, and it was at this era that Virginia Woolf complained of Grant and Bell, "There they sit, looking at pinks and yellows, and when Europe blazes all they do is to screw up their eyes and complain of a temporary glare in the foreground. Unfortunately politics get between one and fiction."[101] Yet, especially in the last decade of Grant's life, Charleston—as it had in the Twenties—overlapped with the re-emerging sexual subcultures. Pioneering feminist scholars like Carolyn Heilbrun visited, and Grant forged lasting friendships with young men like Simon Watney, who has written movingly of his relationship with an octogenarian fascinated by "the contemporary social life of the still swinging Sixties. He was ever eager to hear of one's amours, keen to meet friends and lovers, especially if they could be pressed into service as sitters."[102] Though by no means all of the young men Grant entertained and painted were part of the art world, his sketch of the artist couple Gilbert and George, who visited Charleston in the early 1970s, attests to his curiosity about a younger generation of gay British artists.[103] As with so many other aspects of Bloomsbury, these connections might tempt us to valorize the group and its aesthetic as prescient of what has come to be called postmodernism, and certainly the group has been a useful precedent for some influential shapers of the feminist and queer identities often associated

with postmodernity, Heilbrun and Watney among them.[104] But even more usefully, perhaps, the Bloomsbury artists' thirty-year project to make modern rooms to suit their ideals for modern life attests to the persistence within modernism of subcurrents associated with the suppressed categories in the "cascade of oppositions" that (as discussed in the Introduction) defined the mainstream: decoration, leisure, pleasure, femininity, sensuality. Forgoing temptations to heroicize Bloomsbury by claiming its accomplishment as paradigmatic for more recent developments in art and culture, I have attempted to historicize the group as evidence of the social and aesthetic potential—long overlooked and often denied—of subculture. Starting at home, Bloomsbury's artists imagined and created modes of modernism that sustained them and their community throughout most of the twentieth century. More than the specifics of their ideologies or styles, it may be their recognition of the importance of domestic space—space that is neither the depersonalized totality of hegemonic utopias nor the isolated manifestation of individual consciousness associated with objects of fine art—that today arouses our interest in Bloomsbury's artists.

Facing page:
217. Duncan Grant, fabric designed for the *Queen Mary*, 1936. Victoria and Albert Museum.

The End of Amusing

Introduction: Heroism and Housework: Competing Ideas of the Modern

1 Todd translated Le Corbusier's *The Four Routes* and is further discussed in Chapter 14.

2 D. Todd and R. Mortimer, *The New Interior Decoration*, 2, 7, 14–17, 19–20, 28, 39; captions to plates 2, 4.

3 See H.-R. Hitchcock and P. Johnson, *The International Style*, and T. Riley, *The International Style*.

4 P. Greenhalgh, *Modernism in Design*, 2–5.

5 Originally produced for the cover of the catalog, *Cubism and Abstract Art*, MoMA's chart is widely reproduced.

6 Lawrence Gowing characterizes Grant and Bell as "premature post-Modernists" ("Remembering Duncan and Vanessa," in H. Lee, ed., *A Cézanne in the Hedge*, 33). For a very cogent discussion of these terms, see A. Jones, *Postmodernism and the En-Gendering of Marcel Duchamp*, 1–28.

7 R. Venturi, *Learning from Las Vegas*, 87–104.

8 P. Wollen, "Fashion/Orientalism/The Body," 29, ellipses in original.

9 See P. Bürger, *The Theory of the Avant-Garde*; L. Nochlin, "The Invention of the Avant-Garde, France, 1830–80," in T. B. Hess and John Ashbury, eds., *The Avant-Garde*, 11–18; R. Poggioli, *The Theory of the Avant-Garde*.

10 Le Corbusier, *Towards a New Architecture*, *passim.*, but especially 18–23. J. Guiton, *The Ideas of Le Corbusier*, 67, 86. This argument is developed in more detail in C. Reed, ed., *Not at Home*, 7–17.

11 C. Greenberg, "The Avant-Garde and Kitsch," *Art and Culture*, 3–21.

12 C. Greenberg, *Collected Essays*, vol. 2, 242, 136.

13 C. Greenberg, "Cézanne," *Art and Culture*, 58.

14 C. Greenberg, "Feeling is All," *Collected Essays*, vol. 3, 100–1.

15 A. Gibson, *Theory Undeclared*, 200–23.

16 Adolph Gottlieb and Mark Rothko, letter to The *New York Times*, 1943, in E. H. Johnson, ed., *American Artists on Art from 1940 to 1980*, 10–14.

17 Robert Motherwell, in Max Kozloff, "An Interview with Robert Motherwell," 37.

Motherwell deployed similar rhetoric in other interviews, for instance describing the move to the large format as evidence of "a *heroic* impulse as compared with the intimacy of a French painting" (in de Antonio and Tuchman, *Painters Painting*, 65, emphasis in original).

18 On Monet, see S. Levine, "Décor/Decorative/Decoration in Claude Monet's Art." On the Nabis, see G. Groom, ed., *Beyond the Easel*.

19 M. Denis, "De Gauguin et de Van Gogh au classicisme," *Théories*, 270–1, my translation.

20 In R. L. Herbert, ed., *Modern Artists on Art*, 5. Despite this theoretical contempt for the "decorative," the Cubist contingent associated with Gleizes and Metzinger experimented with domestic design (discussed in Chapter 7), only to be marginalized by the more consistently anti-domestic cubism of Braque and Picasso.

21 Jenny Anger, "Forgotten Ties: The Suppression of the Decorative in German Art and Theory, 1900–1915," in C. Reed, ed., *Not at Home*, 130–46.

22 Historians have exaggerated the differences between Aestheticism and the Arts and Crafts Movement, but many guilds straddled both camps and Wilde often cited Morris and Ruskin in his lectures promoting Aestheticism ("The English Renaissance," "House Decoration," and "Art and the Handicraftsman," in *Miscellanies, The Complete Works of Oscar Wilde*, 243–308; four of his articles promoting the Arts and Crafts Exhibition of 1888 are also in this volume, 93–109).

23 See R. Fry, *A Roger Fry Reader*, 167–91. Bloomsbury's links to the Victorian avant-garde are further discussed in Chapters 2, 7, and 8.

24 This history gives the lie to the oft-rehearsed complaint that Bloomsbury made British art dependent on continental European models. Unflattering as it may be to nationalist pride, all the contenders for avant-garde status in pre-War Britain looked to the Continent—Sickert's Camden Town group to the Impressionists (as discussed in Chapter 1), the Rhythm group to the Fauves, the Vorticists to the Futurists, and Bloomsbury through Maurice Denis to Cézanne—and all accused each other of embodying a typically British insular provincialism.

25 On Lewis and gender, see L. Tickner, *Modern Life and Modern Subjects*, 79–115.

26 W. Lewis, open letter, in Q. Bell and S. Chaplin, "The Ideal Home Rumpus" ("greenery-yallery" is a quote from *Patience*, Gilbert and Sullivan's parody of Oscar Wilde and the Aesthetes).

27 W. Lewis, in M. M. B., "Rebel Art in Modern Life."

28 V. Woolf, *Moments of Being*, 58, 110.

29 V. Woolf, speech before the London/National Society for Women's Service, 21 January 1931, in *Pargiters*, xxxix, xliv.

30 V. Bell to V. Woolf, 31 July 1907, *Selected Letters*, 52.

31 H. Kramer, "The Essential Cubism in London," *New Criterion*, June 1983, rpt. *Revenge of the Philistines*, 77.

32 M. Foucault, *Madness and Civilization, Discipline and Punish*, and *The History of Sexuality*.

33 L. Strachey to D. Grant, 23 August 1909, British Library.

34 L. Strachey to L. Woolf, in M. Holroyd, *Lytton Strachey*, 271.

35 E. M. Forster, *Marianne Thornton*, 188; unpublished memoir, in J. Colmer, *E. M. Forster*, 3.

36 E. M. Forster, *Howards End*, 336. On the autobiographical aspects of this novel, see P. N. Furbank, *E. M. Forster*, 16.

37 I frankly confess to having failed to discover a noun that conveys Bloomsbury's sense of its members' sexual identity. Bloomsbury refused the medicalizing terminology of nineteenth-century science ("homosexual," "homophile," "invert," etc.) by affirmatively redeploying epithets (primarily "bugger" or "sodomite"), but these terms sit awkwardly in academic prose. Although the recent reappropriation of the term "queer" may be the nearest approximation of Bloomsbury's vocabulary, its gender neutrality is not faithful to Bloomsbury's terms, which distinguished between male and female same-sex attraction (for the latter they generally used "Sapphist").

38 S. K. Tillyard's *The Impact of Modernism* ignores Bloomsbury biography and misrepresents the group's relationship to its Victorian antecedents in order to mischaracterize the group's engagement with domesticity as a cunning effort to "engage, court and secure that audience with more

understanding, sophistication, and dexterity than anybody else" (250); for a more detailed critique, see my review.

39 To cite a few specific examples of political activity by Bloomsbury's authors and artists: Lytton Strachey, writing under the imprimatur of the National Council Against Conscription, like Bell, produced a controversial pacifist pamphlet (M. Holroyd, *Lytton Strachey*, 614–15); Roger Fry helped refugees with agricultural reclamation on the French front during World War I; Duncan Grant volunteered time to suffrage groups and designed a poster (color plate 1 in L. Tickner, *Spectacle of Women*); Virginia Woolf, in addition to her well known writing feminist writings, helped with Labour Party political organizing, ran meetings of the Women's Cooperative Guild in her home, and served on numerous left-leaning committees; Vanessa Bell, at the onset of the first World War, volunteered at the National Council for Civil Liberties (as discussed in Chapter 10).

40 On Woolf's politics, see A. Zwerdling, *Virginia Woolf and the Real World*. On Julian Bell, see his edited volume, *Reminiscences of War Resisters in World War 1*, and P. Stansky and W. Abrahams, *Journey to the Frontier*. On Fry, see E. Jones, *Margery Fry*.

41 C. Bell, *Civilization*, 19, 120, 92. The first passage repeats an argument first made in Bell's *Peace At Once*, 9–11, 19–20. Compare E. M. Forster, "Tolerance," in *Two Cheers for Democracy*.

42 L. Woolf, *Barbarians at the Gate*, 52, 57. The passage from Pericles is translated slightly differently: "In everyday life we are not suspicious or angry if our neighbour follows his own bent."

43 L. Woolf, *Quack, Quack*, 108–93.

44 W. Lewis. *The Art of Being Ruled* and *Hitler*.

45 This is the logic of Nikolaus Pevsner's influential 1936 *Pioneers of Modern Design from William Morris to Walter Gropius*. See also H.-R. Hitchcock and P. Johnson, *The International Style*, 36; or Charles Harrison's gratuitous connection of the centenary of Ruskin's birth to the founding of the Bauhaus in 1919 (*English Art and Modernism*, 368 n. 13). Such claims to match the minimalist aesthetic of the International style with the rhetoric of simplicity in Ruskin and Morris misread the English sources, for both Ruskin and Morris explicitly rejected the look of mechanized functionality and fought social trends toward standardization, denouncing systems that treated workers like technology, in Ruskin's words, "counted off into a heap of mechanism," (*Stones of Venice*, vol. 2, chapter 6, section 15, in *Works of Ruskin*, vol. 10, 195; compare W. Morris, "Art and the Beauty of the Earth," *Collected Works*, vol. 22, 166–7).

46 In Chapter 3 of *The Optical Unconscious*, Rosalind E. Krauss yokes Duchamp and Fry in a brilliant critique of the modernist belief in an "autonomous realm of the visual." Krauss presumes a continuity between Fry and her mentor, "Clem" Greenberg, but I suggest that it is Fry's deviation from what she calls "mainstream modernism" (128) that makes his career such a rich field for the analysis of the contradictions and inconsistencies within modernist aesthetics. Fry's 1917 "Art and Life," in *Vision and Design*, for instance, while it asserts the formalist isolation of the aesthetic sphere, both articulates an aversion to purely optical theories of art associated with Impressionism and insists on the importance of what Fry calls "instinct" over rationality, both positions Krauss associates with Duchamp and contrasts to modernism.

47 R. Fry, *Vision and Design*, 9.

48 V. Woolf, *Roger Fry*, 214–15.

49 R. Fry, *Vision and Design*, 47. The argument here is rehearsed using other examples of Fry's writings in my "Roger Fry: Art and Life."

50 See for example R. Fry, *Vision and Design*, 77; this issue is discussed in greater detail in reference to the craftsmanship of Omega furnishings in Chapter 7.

51 C. Bell, *Art*, 8.

52 C. Bell, *Art*, 8.

53 R. Fry, *A Roger Fry Reader*, 161.

54 R. Fry, *The New Movement in Art*, 6.

55 R. Fry, "The Present Situation," unpublished lecture, 1924, King's. On the consistency of Fry's commitment to these values, compare his *Reflections on British Painting*, 18; this text delights in iconoclastic evaluations of, for example, the respected eighteenth-century painter Richard Wilson, whose "feeling for interval" is assessed as inferior, not only to Seurat's, but to an anonymous staff photographer for *The Times* (47).

56 V. Bell to D. Grant, 5 March 1914, *Selected Letters*, 158.

57 C. Bell, *Peace at Once*, 19–20.

58 C. Bell, *Since Cézanne*, 123–4 (on the context of this essay, see Section v introduction). Throughout *Since Cézanne* Bell's arguments for the subjective basis of art criticism reject a wide range of claims to authority, governmental, patriarchal, and even revolutionary:

> It would, of course, be much nicer to think that the essential part of the critic's work was the discovery and glorification of absolute beauty: only, unluckily, it is far from certain that absolute beauty exists, and most unlikely, if it does, that any human being can distinguish it from what is relative. The wiser course, therefore, is to ask of critics no more than sincerity, and to leave divine certitude to superior beings—magistrates, for instance, and fathers of large families, and Mr. Bernard Shaw (171).

59 Grafton Galleries, *Second Post-Impressionist Exhibition*, 9.

60 C. Bell, *Art*, 28, 51.

61 R. Fry, unpublished lecture, *c.* 1928, King's (1/124).

62 Cheryl Mares, "Reading Proust: Woolf and the Painter's Perspective," in D. Gillespie, *The Multiple Muses of Virginia Woolf*, 58–89.

63 V. Woolf, "Mr. Bennett and Mrs. Brown," *Collected Essays*, vol. 1, 324; "Modern Fiction," *Collected Essays*, vol. 2, 106. For a more detailed discussion of Woolf's relation to Bloomsbury's formalist aesthetics, see my "Through Formalism."

64 L. Woolf, *Beginning Again*, 36–7.

65 R. Fry, notes for lecture, "Applied Art and the New Movement," King's. Lisa Tickner analyzes how modernist rhetorics of "authenticity, significant form and expressive intensity . . . accessible to an audience unschooled in the symbolic and idealising aspects of representational painting" were applied in the 1914 Whitechapel Art Gallery exhibition of modern British painting (*Modern Life and Modern Subjects*, 6).

66 R. Fry, *Vision and Design*, 292.

67 L. Woolf, *Sowing*, 153.

68 J. M. Keynes, "My Early Beliefs," in S. P. Rosenbaum, *The Bloomsbury Group*, 61.

69 E. M. Forster, *Two Cheers for Democracy*, 68.

70 V. Woolf to B. Nicolson, 13 August 1940, *Letters*, vol. 6, 414.

71 J. M. Keynes, "My Early Beliefs," in S. P. Rosenbaum, *The Bloomsbury Group*, 58. Le Corbusier, *Towards a New Architecture*, 126. Bloomsbury might not have unanimously accepted Keynes's characterization of Freud and Marx. The

Woolfs' Hogarth Press published the first English translations of Freud, and Leonard's *Barbarians at the Gate* defined civilization, in a paraphrase of Marx, as "a society in which the free development of each is the condition of the free development of all and in which the existence of every individual is widened, enriched, and promoted" (123 and throughout). Acknowledging his debt to Marx's *Communist Manifesto*, Woolf argues strenuously (including relevant passages from Engels as an appendix) that it is reductionist to see Marx as concerned only with economic systems and values.

72 Benjamin's overlapping drafts, repeating many of the same phrases, are quoted here from "Louis-Philippe or the Interior," in *Charles Baudelaire*, 167; and "Erfahrung und Armut," *Gesammelte Schriften*, vol. 2, part 1, 217–18 (my translation). Benjamin elsewhere describes Le Corbusier's architecture as marking "the terminus of the mythological figuration 'house'" (*Arcades Project*, 407; this text also offers another translation of "Louis Philippe," 8–9).

73 On Le Corbusier's political alliances with various governments, see Mark Antliff, "La Cité française: Georges Valois, Le Corbusier, and Fascist Theories of Urbanism," in M. Affron and M. Antliff, *Fascist Visions*, 134–70; and Robert Fishman, "From the Radiant City to Vichy: Le Corbusier's Plans and Politics, 1928–1942," in R. Walden, *The Open Hand*, 244–83.

74 R. Fry, "Pictures and the Modern Home."

75 On partisan attacks on Bloomsbury, see my "Bloomsbury Bashing" and "A Tale of Two Countries."

76 R. Williams, "The Significance of 'Bloomsbury' as a Social and Cultural Group," in D. Crabtree and A. P. Thirlwall, eds, *Keynes and the Bloomsbury Group*, 62–3. Williams's brief and brilliant analysis of the way "class-fractions" are both produced and absorbed by the bourgeoisie offers a much needed corrective to the exaggerated claims for the radicalism of certain contingents of the avant-garde made in supposedly revisionist histories of British modernism, claims that inevitably fall back on the depiction of industrial— that is undomestic—subject matter as the criterion of radical purpose and effect (for example, C. Harrison, *English Art and Modernism*, and D. P. Corbett, *The Modernity of English Art*, as discussed in Chapter 14).

77 Alberto Melucci's influential definition of the "new social movements" emphasizes their difference from the "grandiose social visions of the future" that animated Marxist and Freudian theory. The first three of Melucci's "four novel structural characteristics" of current social movements overlap with Bloomsbury's definitive features: emphasis on control of information and "symbolic resources," instead of "material goods and resources"; a sense of group identity and "participation as an end in itself"; and the integration of "private life and public life" within an activist agenda (the applicability of the fourth characteristic, truly global rather than merely internationalist consciousness, relates to some— Leonard Woolf, E. M. Forster, or Julian Bell—in Bloomsbury, but was not a defining characteristic of the group). Melucci briefly acknowledges "historical continuities" between these new movements and the nineteenth century, but this is not his interest (*Nomads of the Present*, passim, quotations from 205–6, 214).

78 Modernist ambitions for universality, and corollary indifference to subcultural politics, resulted in Wilde's political ideas being ignored until the first histories of gay subculture; pioneering studies include J. Weeks, *Coming Out*, and M. Bronski, *Culture Clash*, 58–63. In contrast,

paradigm-setting work on subculture, such as Dick Hebdige's 1979 *Subculture: The Meaning of Style*, was compromised by a blindness to sexuality as a determining force in subcultural formation. Although Jean Genet—reiterating many of Wilde's most characteristic notions—is Hebdige's "model for the construction of style in subculture" (138), he ignores sexuality even in the case of David Bowie's "alleged 'emasculation' of the Underground tradition" (60–1). Failing to recognize what Roland Barthes and Genet have in common, Hebdige is stymied by the similarity of their readings of the dominant culture (137–8).

79 O. Wilde, *The Soul of Man Under Socialism* (volume in *The Complete Works of Oscar Wilde*), 22, 10, 4, 52.

80 Fry's essay, originally titled "The Artist in the Great State," was commissioned for H. G. Wells's 1912 *Socialism and the Great State* and expanded in 1920 for *Vision and Design*, 55–78 (quotations, 65, 77).

81 R. Fry to H. Anrep, 1927, *Letters of Roger Fry*, 601. On Bloomsbury's links to Wilde, see my "Making History," 197–216.

82 There is an enormous literature on the invention of sexual identity, largely expanding on M. Foucault's *The History of Sexuality*. On its British manifestations in particular, see L. Bland and L. Doan, eds, *Sexology in Culture*; S. Rowbotham and J. Weeks, *Socialism and the New Life*; and J. Weeks, *Coming Out*.

83 E. Carpenter, *The Commonweal*, 4 May 1889, in W. H. G. Armytage, *Heavens Below*, 300.

84 V. Woolf, *Roger Fry*, 232.

85 R. Fry to M. Mauron, 17 May 1921, *Letters of Roger Fry*, 508–9. R. Fry to M. Fry, 2 August 1933, King's. Compare Leonard Woolf's *Barbarians at the Gate*, which concludes: "though we may have learnt the logic of facts in private life, it is the rarest thing in the world for us to recognize it in communal life" (154).

86 Wilde allies individuality and criminality in "Pen, Pencil, and Poison," though the criminals here are also artists (*Intentions*, 57–92). He contradicts this position in *The Soul of Man under Socialism*, arguing that, "Crime, which, under certain conditions, may seem to have created individualism, must take cognizance of other people and interfere with them," so it is not truly individualistic (29). On Fry and criminality, see V. Woolf, *Roger Fry*, 235.

87 O. Wilde, *Soul of Man Under Socialism*, 29.

88 R. Fry, *Vision and Design*, 256.

89 C. Bell, *Old Friends*, 130. Compare Vanessa Bell to Clive Bell, 14 June 1931, *Selected Letters*, 364.

90 L. Woolf, *Beginning Again*, 25–6.

91 R. Williams, "The Significance of 'Bloomsbury' as a Social and Cultural Group," in D. Crabtree and A. P. Thirlwall, eds, *Keynes and the Bloomsbury Group*, 66–67.

92 E. K. Sedgwick, *Between Men*, 173. On this misunderstanding of Wilde, see A. Gopnik, "The Invention of Oscar Wilde." Bloomsbury's rejection of Wilde's status as an isolated dissenter is clear in Fry's treatment of another iconoclast, the painter James Abbot McNeill Whistler; see *A Roger Fry Reader*, 8–10, 21–38.

93 D. Todd and R. Mortimer, *The New Interior Decoration*, 2, 29.

94 V. Woolf, "Great Men's Houses," *The London Scene*, 23.

95 R. Fry, "Cézanne", *Vision and Design*, 256–65.

96 C. Bell, "Criticism," *Since Cézanne*, 178.

97 V. Woolf, *A Room of One's Own*, 47

Section I: Rooms of One's Own: Three Early Domestic Environments

1 L. Strachey, "Lancaster Gate," *Lytton Strachey by Himself*, 16.

2 S. P. Rosenbaum, *Victorian Bloomsbury*, 262.

3 V. Woolf, *Moments of Being*, 164–5. Both Strachey's and Woolf's essays anticipate the form of E. M. Forster's life of his aunt, Marianne Thornton, which begins with a description of the family house and is subtitled *A Domestic Biography*.

4 L. Strachey, "Lancaster Gate," *Lytton Strachey by Himself*, 19.

5 L. Strachey, "Lancaster Gate," *Lytton Strachey by Himself*, 16.

6 Despite the Bells' often-cited claim that Molly MacCarthy coined the term "Bloomsbury" to describe the group, its first documented use is in Lytton Strachey's diary of 1910 (S. P. Rosenbaum, *The Bloomsbury Group*, 4; cf. 78, 86).

Chapter 1: Vanessa Bell and 46 Gordon Square (1904–12)

1 V. Bell to C. Bell, 24 December 1912, Tate. V. Bell, memoir, in F. Spalding, *Vanessa Bell*, 43.

2 V. Woolf, *Moments of Being*, 184.

3 V. Woolf, *Moments of Being*, 144.

4 V. Bell, *Sketches in Pen and Ink*, 99.

5 V. Woolf, *Moments of Being*, 182, 185, 148.

6 V. Woolf, *Complete Shorter Fiction*, 27–43.

7 V. Bell to V. Woolf, 2 August 1907, 26 December 1909, *Selected Letters*, 72; compare 25 August 1908, Berg.

8 V. Woolf, *Moments of Being*, 184.

9 V. Woolf, *Diary*, vol. 3, 255.

10 V. Woolf, *Moments of Being*, 163.

11 V. Bell, memoir, in F. Spalding, *Vanessa Bell*, 49.

12 M. R. Anand, *Conversations in Bloomsbury*, 72, double ellipses in original; compare L. Strachey, *Eminent Victorians*, 207–41; L. Woolf, *Sowing*, 78–94; V. Woolf, *Roger Fry*, 32–5, 38–9, and *The Pargiters*, xxxi–xxxiii.

13 L. Woolf, *Sowing*, 103, 151–2.

14 V. Woolf to T. Stephen, May 1903, *Letters*, vol. 1, 77. Compare Woolf's unfinished essay of 1906 on "that respectable custom which allows the daughter to educate herself at home, while the son is educated by others abroad" (Appendix C in Q. Bell, *Virginia Woolf*, vol. 1).

15 V. Woolf, *Moments of Being*, 190, 192.

16 V. Woolf, *Moments of Being*, 191.

17 L. Woolf, *Beginning Again*, 33, 35.

18 V. Bell, *Sketches in Pen and Ink*, 105.

19 V. Bell to C. Bell, 31 December 1909, Tate.

20 L. Strachey to D. Grant, 2 June 1907, British Library; the Bells' drawing room had a sofa incorporating parts of an antique French bedstead (V. Bell to R. Fry, 23 November 1911, Tate).

21 V. Bell, *Sketches in Pen and Ink*, 102, 98.

22 V. Bell to V. Woolf, 29 October 1904, Berg.

23 V. Woolf, *Moments of Being*, 122. V. Bell to V. Woolf, 24 October 1904, Berg.

24 V. Bell to V. Woolf, 25 November 1904, Berg.

25 L. Strachey to D. Grant, 2 June 1907, British Library.

26 Q. Bell, "The Omega Revisited."

27 V. Woolf, *Three Guineas*, 61–2.

28 V. Bell to V. Woolf, 1 November 1904, Berg. At least some of the photographs remained at 46 Gordon Square twenty years later (V. Woolf to V. Sackville-West, 6 March 1923, *Letters*, vol. 3, 18–19).

29 V. Woolf, *Three Guineas*, 113. In an echo of Bell's gesture, the Strachey sisters later hung their hall at nearby 51 Gordon Square with photographs of the their relatives, whom aspiring scholars were asked to identify (E. F. Boyd, *Bloomsbury Heritage*, 4–5).

30 V. Woolf, "Julia Margaret Cameron," V. Woolf and R. Fry, *Victorian Photographs of Famous Men and Fair Women*, 13.

31 V. Bell to V. Woolf, 23 April 1927, *Selected Letters*, 313. The Pattle sisters' mother was Adeline de l'Etang by birth.

32 V. Woolf, "Julia Margaret Cameron," V. Woolf and R. Fry, *Victorian Photographs of Famous Men and Fair Women*, 14.

33 V. Woolf, *Moments of Being*, 88; compare V. Woolf, "The Angel of the House," *Pargiters*, xxix–xxxi.

34 L. Stephen, ed., *Dictionary of National Biography*, vol. 8, 300.

35 V. Woolf, *Diary*, vol. 1, 237.

36 V. Woolf *Freshwater*, 83.

37 V. Woolf, "Julia Margaret Cameron," V. Woolf and R. Fry, *Victorian Photographs of Famous Men and Fair Women*, 18.

38 Woolf was included in *Vogue*'s occasional "We nominate for the Hall of Fame" feature (late May 1924, 49). Two published versions of this photograph are listed in E. Richardson's *Bloomsbury Iconography* (which also includes a survey of Julia Margaret Cameron's pictures of Julia Jackson Duckworth Stephen [Table A1]). A subsequent *Vogue* photo session, in which Woolf wore up-to-date clothes, is noted in V. Woolf, *Diary*, vol. 3, 12.

41 V. Woolf to V. Bell, 2 June 1926, *Letters* 3, 271. A 1921 letter from Bell asks Grant to bring "Aunt Julia's portrait," apparently to paint from (*Selected Letters*, 254). In 1975, the Gallery Edward Harvane exhibited an undated Bell oil of her mother with the note "This is one of several versions taken from a photograph" (*Homage to Duncan Grant* no. 25).

40 Based on the photograph reproduced in V. Woolf and R. Fry, *Victorian Photographs of Famous Men and Fair Women*, plate 19, (omitted from 2nd edn), *The Red Dress* has been dated on the basis of Bell's correspondence to c.1929 and was no. 8 in Alex. Reid & Lefevre's 1934 *Recent Paintings by Vanessa Bell*. Grant's letters also document him copying from Cameron's photographs (D. Grant to V. Bell, 18 February 1930, Tate).

41 Bell's photography has also been seen in relation to Cameron's precedent by Val Williams, who describes Bell's snapshots as rejecting Cameron's "extroversion" and making a "burlesque [of]" those whom Cameron might well have revered" (*Women Photographers*, 82).

42 V. Woolf, *Moments of Being*, 185.

43 V. Bell, *Selected Letters*, 29.

44 V. Bell, *Selected Letters*, 11, 30.

45 When Furse died, Sargent offered to complete his unfinished commissions, and the catalog to Furse's memorial exhibition begins with his essay praising Whistler (Burlington Fine Arts Club, *An Exhibition of Pictures and Sketches by Charles Wellington Furse*).

46 Furse's portrait, exhibited at the New English Art Club in 1902, was destroyed in Bell's London studio during an air-raid in 1940 (R. Shone, *Art of Bloomsbury*, 226).

47 V. Bell, *Sketches in Pen and Ink*, 81. Unlike Bell, Furse's wife regretted the passing of the Victorian aesthetic, which she associated with the avant-garde of the generation of her father, John Addington Symonds (K. Furse, *Hearts and Pomegranates*, 8–9, 205–6). The language Furse uses to describe her family (41) parallels very closely Bloomsbury's later self-descriptions.

48   V. Bell to V. Woolf, 5 April 1905, *Selected Letters*, 30.

49   Q. Bell, *Virginia Woolf*, 96.

50   V. Woolf, *Moments of Being*, 195.

51   The determination to join the avant-garde, evident in Bell's painting, is exemplified also by her founding in 1905 of the "Friday Club," a discussion and exhibition society for modernist painters (see R. Shone, "The Friday Club").

52   On the artist as *flâneur*, see R. L. Herbert, *Impressionism*, 33–40. Not only Degas, but also Whistler, Sickert's other influential teacher, figures prominently in the history of the artist-*flâneur* (T. Reff, *Degas*, 15–36, 232–4). For Sickert's embodiment of the *flâneur* persona, see C. Bell, *Old Friends*, 13–24, and W. Baron's "Sickert's Attitude to his Subject Matter" (*Sickert*, 181–9); the latter outlines a near blueprint of the *flâneur*, without acknowledging its status as a convention of French modernism. Ignorance of the *flâneur* convention has allowed misplaced claims for Sickert as a champion of the working classes he depicted (see my "Bloomsbury Bashing" and *Roger Fry Reader*, 119–21).

53   *Apples* has been variously dated between 1908 and 1910. I favor the earlier date on stylistic grounds; the later date rests on this work's tentative identification with the *London Morning Bell* exhibited in the summer of 1910 (Arts Council, *Vanessa Bell*, no. 5). A close comparison in Sickert's oeuvre is *La Seine du Balcon*, first exhibited in Paris in 1909 (W. Baron, *Sickert*, catalog no. 285).

54   W. Sickert, "The Study of Drawing."

55   W. Sickert, "A Critical Calendar."

56   C. Baudelaire, "The Painter of Modern Life," *"The Painter of Modern Life" and Other Essays*, 1–18.

57   Despite arguments for certain partial exceptions (see especially S. Fillen-Yeh, ed., *Dandies*), the fundamental incompatibility of femininity and the *flâneur*, influentially analyzed in Janet Wolff's "The Invisible *Flâneuse*" is not in doubt (*Feminine Sentences*, 34–50).

58   V. Woolf, *Room of One's Own*, 50.

59   W. Sickert to N. Hudson and E. Sands, Spring 1911, in W. Baron, *Camden Town*, 34. On Sickert's assumption of authority over women artists see W. Baron, *Sickert*, 131; on his relations with women in general, see 118–19, 188 n. 5.

60   W. Sickert to E. Sands, in W. Baron, *Sickert*, 181; emphasis in original. The French phrase translates as, "talking of oneself is what is least powerful."

61   D. Grant interview in S. Watney, *Art of Duncan Grant*, 85, emphasis in original. Tellingly, Sickert's 1914 commission to decorate Ethel Sands's dining room remained unfinished until Grant and Bell were called in to complete the work in 1929 (W. Baron, *Miss Ethel Sands*, 120–3, 204).

62   W. Sickert, "Idealism."

63   V. Woolf, "Modern Fiction," *Collected Essays*, vol. 2, 106. This is not to imply that Woolf disparaged Sickert.; her admiration for his narrative art is clear in her "Walter Sickert," *Collected Essays*, vol. 2, 233–44.

64   V. Woolf, *Moments of Being*, 184.

65   A. John, *Chiaroscuro*, 67.

66   G. Greer, *The Obstacle Race*, 52–4.

67   M. Holroyd, *Augustus John*, 59, 107–252.

68   M. Holroyd, *Augustus John*, 285.

69   D. Grant to L. Strachey, 7 April 1907, British Library.

70   J. M. Keynes, in M. Holroyd, *Augustus John*, 302.

71   C. Bell, *Pot Boilers*, 212–13. R. Fry, "The Artist and Psychoanalysis," *A Roger Fry Reader*, 358.

72   D. Grant, "Virginia Woolf," in S. P. Rosenbaum, ed., *The Bloomsbury Group*, 67.

73   Lisa Tickner notes the stance of the figures in these images in connection with her argument that *Studland Beach* depicts "a domestic space" ("Vanessa Bell," 72).

74   F. Spalding, *Vanessa Bell*, 124.

75   Dating these two works is inexact because of their interchangeable subject matter and scale, combined with Bell's habit of dating letters only with the month and day. Letters referring to progress on a "nativity" have been assigned to three different years (V. Bell to R. Fry, 10 October 1911, 17 October 1912, 24 October 1913, Tate). The second painting was exhibited in the second Grafton Group show, January 1914, when it was cataloged as *Women and Baby*, but also referred to as *Nativity* (G. R. H., "The Grafton Group at the Alpine Gallery"); it was exhibited in 1916 and published in 1926 under the title *A Nativity* (J. Collins, *Omega Workshops*, 125; R. Fry, "Vanessa Bell," 33).

76   On Gauguin, see A. Solomon-Godeau, "Going Native."

77   G. R. H., "The Grafton Group at the Alpine Gallery."

78   V. Bell to R. Fry, 23 November 1911, *Selected Letters* 112; which John painting she refers to is unclear. Bell's unchallenged assessment calls into question Michael Holroyd's claim (*Augustus John*, 366) that Fry's disapproval of John's art began in 1917.

79   V. Bell to C. Bell, 15 August 1912, *Selected Letters*, 123.

Chapter 2: Roger Fry and Durbins (1909–19)

1   R. Fry to C. R. Ashbee, 21 November 1887, *Letters of Roger Fry*, 118; compare R. Fry to G. B. Shaw, *c*.1928, 633.

2   R. Fry to G. L. Dickinson, 24 January 1889, *Letters of Roger Fry*, 122.

3   The Frys' correspondence is at King's. On Helen Fry's dementia, see V. Woolf, *Roger Fry*, 146–7, and F. Spalding, *Roger Fry*, 66 [Spalding's 1999 revised edition suggests Helen Fry suffered from schizophrenia and inherited syphillis (264)].

4   R. Fry to M. Fry, 28 March 1913, *Letters of Roger Fry*, 366. R. Fry to V. Bell, 10 February 1918, Tate.

5   J. Ruskin, *Stones of Venice*, vol. 2, chapter 6, section 13, *Works of Ruskin*, vol. 10, 193.

6   J. Ruskin, *Mornings in Florence*, chapter 2, section 36, *Works of Ruskin*, vol. 23, 331–33. Compare the opening passages of Fry's 1901 essay on Giotto (*Vision and Design*, 131–77).

7   On Ruskin's guild, see C. W. Morley, *John Ruskin*.

8   R. Fry to A. Anrep, 31 August 1929, *Letters of Roger Fry*, 640.

9   C. R. Ashbee to R. Fry, 23 April 1888, King's.

10   "The New 'Magpie and Stump.'" On the mural, see A. Crawford, *C. R. Ashbee*, 72–3, 238, 297–304.

11   R. Fry to R. C. Trevelyan, 15 March 1896, *Letters of Roger Fry*, 165; see also D. Crackenthorpe, *Hubert Crackenthorpe*, 122.

12   F. Spalding, *Roger Fry*, 10, 55–6. Fry later decorated the Cambridge rooms of G. L. Dickinson (E. M. Forster, *Goldsworthy Lowes Dickinson*, 195).

13   *Letters of Roger Fry*, 177; A. Crawford, *C. R. Ashbee*, 303.

14   F. Spalding, *Roger Fry*, 129–30.

15   N. Pevsner, "Omega." For the comparison with Le Corbusier, see A. Powers, "Roger Fry and the Making of Durbins," 22; for the comparison with Loos see I. Nairn and N. Pevsner, *Surrey*, 289 (this account is riddled with factual errors).

16   R. Fry to W. Rothenstein, 2 January 1910, *Letters of Roger Fry*, 327.

17   R. Fry, "A Possible Domestic Architecture" *Vogue* [London], late March 1918, rpt. *Vision and Design*, 272–8.

18   V. Woolf, *Roger Fry*, 163–4.

19   "G." "The Revival of English Domestic Architecture," 25, emphasis in original. Compare M. H. Baillie Scott, *Houses and Gardens*.

20   F. Spalding, *Roger Fry*, 8.

21   V. Woolf, *Roger Fry*, 25. On Woolf's ambivalent relationship to her father, see S. P. Rosenbaum, *Victorian Bloomsbury*, 85–90.

22   A close comparison to the north facade is Voysey's 1896 Annesly Lodge, which stood in Hampstead only a few blocks from the house Fry occupied before moving to Guildford.

23   Comparisons include Edgar Wood's Wesleyan school in Manchester; Charles Holden's 1905 library in Bristol with its pilasters, blank walls, and bold panels of checkerboard tiling; C. R. Mackintosh's contemporary library wing on the Glasgow School of Art with its industrial-scale windows; Ashbee and Holden's unrealized Danvers Tower project of studios and apartments, especially in an early version by Ashbee featuring a roof line of squared-off pilasters (at the British Architectural Library Drawings Collection, London); and various "rationalized" Edwardian factories discussed in A. Service, *Edwardian Architecture*, 128–39.

24   The woodwork of the gallery and triple vaulted entrance hall reflect—albeit on a smaller scale—Voysey's interiors illustrated in *The Studio* 21, January 1901.

25   M. H. Baillie Scott, "An Ideal Suburban House" and "A Country Cottage." See also J. D. Kornwolf, *M. H. Baillie-Scott*, 128. Compare William Morris's historical case for the central hall in "Art and Socialism," *Collected Works*, vol. 23, 199–200.

26   W. Gill to D. Grant, 6 April 1966, Tate.

27   C. F. A. Voysey, "Remarks on Domestic Entrance Halls." R. Fry, *Vision and Design*, 276; compare Fry's "Architectural Heresies of a Painter," *Roger Fry Reader*, 217.

28   M. H. Baillie Scott, *Houses and Gardens*, 14–15, 66–8. R. Fry, *Vision and Design*, 275, 277. Compare W. Morris, "Making the Best of It," *Collected Works*, vol. 22, 92–3.

29   Charles Dowdeswell, unpublished memoir, in S. Weintraub, *Whistler*, 227.

30   Photo caption in "A Possible Domestic Architecture," quoted in J. Collins, *Omega Workshops*, 90. Fry's daughter records that the screen was later reattributed to nineteenth-century Japan (M. Chamot, et al., *Tate Gallery Catalogues*, vol. 1, 195). The Peacock Room is now at the Freer Gallery, Washington D.C.

31   F. Spalding, *Roger Fry*, 57–9; on the circumstances of the harpsichord's commission, see P. Stansky, *Redesigning the World*, 113. The instrument is illustrated with Renaissance prototypes in a 1900 "Studio Talk" column of *The Studio*.

32   On Fry's contributions to the management of the Burlington, see Denys Sutton's introduction to *Letters of Roger Fry*, 13; and F. Spalding, *Roger Fry*, 78–80.

33   S. E., "The Modern House and the Modern Picture."

34   Mackmurdo's house is extant at 25 Cadogan Gardens. Mackmurdo's window treatment does not

correspond to any double-height interior spaces, but merely sets panes of traditional scale in oversized, recessed panels.

35 "Century Guild Design" (there are slight variations between these renderings and the house as built); R. Fry, *Vision and Design*, 278. Mackmurdo's house, extant at 8 Private Road, Enfield, is discussed as an example of pioneering modernism in domestic architecture in N. Pevsner, *Studies in Art, Architecture and Design*, 134.

36 F. Spalding, *Roger Fry*, 61.

37 This house is extant at 22 Willow Road.

38 Pamela Diamand, "Durbins," in H. Lee, *A Cézanne in the Hedge*, 52.

39 V. Bell, *Sketches in Pen and Ink*, 123.

40 R. Fry, *Vision and Design*, 275.

41 V. Bell, *Sketches in Pen and Ink*, 122.

42 D. Grant to J. M. Keynes, 29 November 1910, British Library; V. Bell to C. Bell, Summer 1911, Tate.

43 J. Ruskin, *Sesame and Lilies*, Lecture 3, Sections 117–18, *Works of Ruskin*, vol. 18, 163–5; *Praeterita*, vol. 1, ch. 2, section 39; vol. 2, ch. 4, section 80, *Works of Ruskin*, vol. 35, 34, 318.

44 Quoted in V. Woolf, *Roger Fry*, 15.

45 A plan of the garden sketched by Fry's daughter is in the archives at King's.

46 Fry's *The Artist's Garden at Durbins* has been dated to *c*.1915. It is shown, however, in progress on the easel in Fry's studio in photographs of Durbins's interior taken late in 1917 for *Vogue*, and a date of 1917–18 is more compatible with its style. The effect of enclosure in Fry's painting is all the more pronounced in comparison with Vanessa Bell's *Hog's Back from Durbins* (private collection), a sketch of the same scene from the higher perspective of Fry's studio window; in Bell's version, the bottom of the garden opens onto the broad expanse of the river below and the bare crest of the distant hill seems readily accessible.

47 R. Fry to O. Morrell, 23 November 1910, Texas. On the importance of Fry's encouragement, see E. Gill, *Autobiography*, 163.

48 R. Fry, *Letters of Roger Fry*, 31. Gill completed at least three similar cupids in 1910, one in white marble now at the University of Texas at Austin, the others apparently lost (all illustrated in J. Collins, *Eric Gill: The Sculpture*, 65, 69). It is not clear which—if any—was Fry's.

49 On this commission, see J. Collins, *Eric Gill: The Sculpture*, 72–5. The first version is now at the University of California at Los Angeles, and the second in the Dutch Garden at Holland Park, London. Two preparatory sketches dated July 1911 show the second version and are inscribed, in clear reference to Durbins, "There is a hillside at Guildford from which there is a jolly fine view: The statue should echo the slope of the hill and 'appreciate' the view," (Anthony d'Offay Gallery, *Eric Gill*, 24); the maquette is illustrated in J. Collins, *Eric Gill: Sculpture*, 34. Gill may have been surprised by Fry's reaction to his first sculpture, in which the figure touches her breasts and crotch in a variation on the conventional pose of the Venus Pudica, for Fry had praised an earlier relief showing a man and woman having sex. Though he acknowledged "the pornographic side of the thing," Fry praised the figures, saying "The more I look at them the more I like it," and concluded, "It ought to be put up in a public place. It can't be till we're much more civilized in the real sense" (R. Fry to E. Gill, 15 February 1911, quoted in R. Speaight, *Eric Gill*, 53; Speaight misidentifies this work as a piece made for Fry, but the date of the letter suggests the reference is to Gill's provocatively titled *Votes for Women*, which was available for view to insiders in a

closet at the Chenil Gallery, as discussed in J. Collins, *Eric Gill: The sculpture*, 70). Subsequent critics have approvingly quoted Gill's snide response to Fry's worries over his first version's impact on "strawberries and cream and tea on the lawn" (R. Cork, "From Art Quake to 'Pure Visual Music,'" in C. Green, *Art Made Modern* 64), but this remark, which Gill actually attributes to his brother, should be read in the context of his correspondent, William Rothenstein, who had fallen out with Fry over the first Post-Impressionist exhibition.

50 D. Sutton, introduction to *Letters of Roger Fry*, 31, 56, ill. 79; J. Collins, *Omega Workshops*, 73–4. In 1991 Gaudier's maquette was sized up and cast in an edition of three; see S. P. Rosenbaum, "Gaudier-Brzeska's Posthumous Sculpture for Roger Fry."

51 R. Fry, "An English Sculptor," *Nation*, 28 January 1911, rpt. *A Roger Fry Reader*, 133–5.

52 R. Fry, "Gaudier-Brzeska."

53 V. Bell, *Sketches in Pen and Ink*, 123.

54 V. Bell to R. Fry, 23 November 1911, *Selected Letters*, 112–13.

55 V. Woolf, *Roger Fry*, 163.

56 See texts and commentary in *A Roger Fry Reader*, Chapter 2.

57 C. Bell, "The Art of Brancusi." For details on the art Fry owned, see my "The Roger Fry Collection." The bodhisattva is now at the Worcester [Massachusetts] Museum of Fine Arts. Fry's daughter recalls the Brancusi head as a version of *Melle. Pogany*, but this memory is unconfirmed by the photographs taken in 1917, when this piece, identified as "Portrait: Head (Bronze)," was on loan to the exhibition *The New Movment in Art*, and an Oriental vase was in its place.

58 Grant's portrait is at the Courtauld Institute Galleries; Fry's is at the University of Leeds.

59 On the dress and fabric, see Crafts Council, *Omega Workshops*, 59–60, 90.

60 R. Fry to V. Bell, summer 1917, Tate; compare *Letters of Roger Fry*, 416.

61 V. Bell, *Sketches in Pen and Ink*, 127. Compare V. Bell, *Selected Letters*, 130.

62 R. Fry to V. Bell, *c*.1911, Tate.

63 R. Fry to V. Bell, 11 May 1917, Tate.

64 J. Collins, *Omega Workshops*, 16, ill. 3; this drawing has also been described as a preliminary design for Bell's mural in her own studio at 46 Gordon Square (Spink, *Duncan Grant and Vanessa Bell*, 8).

65 R. Fry to V. Bell, 29 April 1916, Tate.

66 R. Fry to R. Vildrac, 17 February 1916, King's. On the Stracheys and Durbins, see M. Holroyd, *Lytton Strachey*, 631, 661, 695.

67 R. Fry, *Vision and Design*, 238–9, 274, 277. On "plastic," see *A Roger Fry Reader*, 118–18, 121–4.

68 R. Fry, "Architectural Heresies of a Painter," *Roger Fry Reader*, 212–28; Le Corbusier, *Towards a New Architecture*, 7. On the beauty of engineering, compare C. Bell, *Art*, 221.

69 Fry in 1912 defended John James Burnet's stark Kodak building ("The Regent-Street Quadrant," *The Times*, 3 October 1912, *Roger Fry Reader*, 195), while Clive Bell's *Art* praised London's factories, bridges, and iron-framed structures (221, 264–5).

70 R. Fry, *Vision and Design*, 277. Fry returned to this argument in 1932, specifically in response to the modernist rhetoric of "functionalism" in his "Sensibility versus Mechanism" and an untitled lecture on architecture and design (King's 1/129), discussed in Chapters 14 and 15.

71 Le Corbusier, *Towards a New Architecture*, 211.

72 R. Fry, *Vision and Design*, 274.

73 Le Corbusier, *Towards a New Architecture*, 83. R. Fry, *Vision and Design*, 278.

Chapter 3: Duncan Grant and King's College, Cambridge (1910)

1 V. Woolf, *Moments of Being*, 195–6.

2 V. Bell to D. Carrington, 25 January, 1932, *Selected Letters*, 371.

3 V. Bell to V. Woolf, 3 October 1910, Berg.

4 L. Strachey to L. Woolf, 6 Feburary 1908, in S. P. Rosenbaum, *Edwardian Bloomsbury*, 220.

5 V. Bell to J. M. Keynes, 19 April 1914, *Selected Letters*, 163.

6 V. Woolf, *Moments of Being*, 196. V. Bell, *Sketches in Pen and Ink*, 106. On homophobic reactions to the Bloomsbury women's attitudes, see my "Bloomsbury Bashing."

7 Grant's faster acceptance into Bloomsbury is explained by his more frequent presence in Fitzroy Square (Keynes was often at Cambridge), his easy-going personality, and the Bells' admiration for his art; also working to Keynes' disadvantage was Strachey's jealousy of his relationship with Grant.

8 D. Grant to J. M. Keynes, 10 November, 17 November 1909, British Library.

9 V. Bell to C. Bell, 2 October 1914, Tate.

10 The chairs are discussed in D. Grant to J. M. Keynes, 7, 13, and 19 October 1910, 3 March 1911, British Library.

11 For an overview, see S. P. Rosenbaum, *Victorian Bloomsbury*; on Moore, see T. Regan, *Bloomsbury Prophet*.

12 G. L. Dickinson, *Autobiography*, 64.

13 H. and M. Cecil, *Clever Hearts*, 38.

14 P. Wilkinson, *A Century of Kings*, in R. Skidelsky, *Hopes Betrayed*, 235; on Browning's influence on Keynes, see 108–10. For an overview of Browning's career, see I. Anstruther, *Oscar Browning*, which attributes to him a pamphlet on Greek love, including a passionate defense of male–male kissing (59–60).

15 C. R. Ashbee, journal, 14 December 1886, King's.

16 J. M. Keynes to D. Grant, 25 October 1908, British Library. Perceptions of Cambridge as a haven for homosexuality pepper Keynes's letters to Grant at this period: "practically everybody in Cambridge, except me, is an open and avowed sodomite" (28 July 1908, King's); "Even the womanisers pretend to be sods, lest they shouldn't be thought respectable" (11 February 1909, in R. Skidelsky, *Hopes Betrayed*, 234).

17 D. Grant to J. M. Keynes, 26 October 1910, British Library.

18 Byrne R. S. Fone, "This Other Eden: Arcadia and the Homosexual Imagination," in S. Kellogg, *Essays on Gay Literature*, 14–16. See also M. Bronski, *Culture Clash*, 53–5.

19 J. A. Symonds, *Studies of the Greek Poets*, Chapter 12, rpt. in *Male Love*, 128, 130, 142–5.

20 G. L. Dickinson, *The Greek View of Life*, 134.

21 Noel Annan, quoted in J. Weeks, *Coming Out*, 253 n. 5.

22 G. L. Dickinson, *Autobiography*, 90.

23 G. L. Dickinson, *Autobiography*, 138.

24 V. Bell to V. Woolf, 20 May 1912, Berg.

25 E. M. Forster, *Maurice*, 211. In a true-to-life version of this scenario, one of the Stephen sisters' relations had been forced to flee to Italy, when his mother-in-law, Virginia (one of the Pattle

sisters) publicized his homosexual infidelities (Q. Bell, *Virginia Woolf*, 14–15).

26 For an overview of homoerotic English writings on Italy, see R. Aldrich, *The Seduction of the Mediterranean*, 69–100.

27 D. Grant to J. M. Keynes, 10 June 1910, British Library. These photographs are mentioned in letters, D. Grant to J. M. Keynes, 18 May, 2 June 1910, British Library. Other nude photographs of Grant in classical poses, which may be from this era or earlier, are reproduced in D. Turnbaugh, *Duncan Grant*, ills. 3, 4.

28 D. Grant to L. Strachey, 16 June 1907, British Library. On Louisa Ewbank, a cousin of Grant's mother whom he visited more than once in Florence, see F. Spalding, *Duncan Grant*, 32.

29 On Grant's many early copies of Piero, see S. Scrase and P. Croft, *Maynard Keynes*, 26; F. Spalding, *Duncan Grant*, 33; S. Watney, *Art of Duncan Grant*, 27.

30 D. Grant to J. M. Keynes, 13 October 1910, British Library.

31 In addition to *The Lemon Gatherers*, discussed here, examples of this motif in Grant's work include the library door at Charleston (fig. 131; *c.*1917–18); decorative panels worked with Vanessa Bell for Mary Hutchinson (discussed in Chapter 14; fig. 197); and a tile table representing the Queen of Diamonds (in Christie's London, *British and Irish Modernist and Contemporary Paintings, Drawings and Sculpture*, 11 November 1988, lot 372). A panel by Vanessa Bell dated to 1913 (now at Charleston) uses the same motif.

32 L. Strachey (pseud: Ignotus), "The Sicilians." On Strachey's work for the *Spectator*, see S. P. Rosenbaum, *Edwardian Bloomsbury*, 285–310. On this source for *The Lemon Gatherers*, see Tate Gallery, *Duncan Grant*, no. 12.

33 L. Strachey to D. Grant, 1 March 1908, British Library.

34 T. Smith, *Love in Earnest*, 62–4; Grant's von Gloeden photograph is illustrated in my "Making History." On van Gloeden, see R. Aldrich, *The Seduction of the Mediterranean*, 143–52.

35 Misrepresentations of this phrase appear in R. Deacon, *The Cambridge Apostles*, 65; and G. Himmelfarb, *Marriage and Morals*, 45.

36 J. M. Keynes to L. Strachey, 2 April 1906, in R. Skidelsky, *Hopes Betrayed*, 171. See also L. Strachey, in C. Hession, *John Maynard Keynes*, 46. Geoffrey Scott went on to have affairs with a number of prominent women, including Vita Sackville-West (V. Glendenning, *Vita*, 132–8). On the Oxford/Cambridge distinction, see also a letter in which Grant analyzed for Strachey another of their cousins:

> Ian is ridiculously nice but so polite . . . that I feel it would be absurd even to try to become intimate with him. And then with his thick veneer of Oxford conservatism it would be *quite* impossible to let him know what one was like. There is, however, a mysteriously beautiful and haunting expression which occasionally appears in his eyes which rather baffles me. Perhaps if he had gone to Cambridge. (D. Grant to L. Strachey, 23 January 1907, 10 August 1907, British Library).

37 L. Strachey to D. Grant, 7 April 1906, British Library.

38 L. Strachey to D. Grant, 11 March 1906, British Library.

39 L. Strachey to D. Grant, 20 February 1907, British Library.

40 Grant later repainted the basket as a turban (Crafts Council, *Omega Workshops*, 8, 93).

41 L. Strachey to L. Woolf, in M. Holroyd, *Lytton Strachey*, 282. On Keynes's earlier rooms, see R. Skidelsky, *Hopes Betrayed*, 124.

42 D. Grant, in I. Dunlop, *Shock of the New*, 158.

43 V. Bell, *Sketches in Pen and Ink*, 129–30.

44 Preface, *Manet and the Post-Impressionists* (1910), *A Roger Fry Reader*, 81–2, 84.

45 R. Fry, "The Grafton Gallery—I" (1910), *A Roger Fry Reader*, 87–8. A crucial difference between Grant's citations of Italian art and the formalist privileging of proto-Renaissance precedent is the evaluation of Michelangelo, whom Fry disparaged. As late as 1920, Grant still defended Michelangelo's accomplishment to a skeptical Vanessa Bell and Roger Fry (V. Bell to R. Fry, 29 April 1920, Tate).

46 R. Fry to D. Grant, 9 November 1910, *Selected Letters*, 337–8. Grant had shown watercolors with the New English, but his oil paintings had been rejected (F. Spalding, *Duncan Grant*, 84).

47 D. Grant to J. M. Keynes, 29 November 1910, British Library.

48 R. Shone and D. Grant, "The Picture Collector," in M. Keynes, ed., *Essays on John Maynard Keynes*, 286.

49 Among the paintings in the first Post-Impressionist exhibition, Jules Flandrin's *La danse des vendanges* was closest in theme to Grant's mural, but offers only a very loose visual precedent (see illustration in Jacqueline Marval, "Les Danseurs de Flandrin"). Nor do the examples of Cézanne's bathers in the exhibition—*Les Ondines* (Venturi 538, Orienti 239) and *Baigneurs* (Venturi 273, Orienti 288)—provide formal sources for Grant. Although Grant's dancers seem to echo André Derain's nudes of 1905–07, the three Derains in the show were landscapes. There are striking similarities between Grant's Cambridge mural and the orchard scenes of Hans von Marées's Neapolitan frescoes, but Grant had not been to Naples at this point, and he was not in Paris for the von Marées retrospective in October of 1909. While Grant might have been interested in the pastoralized masculine eroticism of von Marées's other murals, which were published in London and Paris—see Julius Meier-Graefe, *Modern Art*, vol. 2, 116–25, and the same author's "Hans von Marées," both of which reproduce triptychs in the Schleissheim Gallery—the Naples murals remained unpublished in the English and French journals with which Grant was familiar.

50 R. Fry, "The Post-Impressionists—II" (1910), rpt. *A Roger Fry Reader*, 90. The paintings were *Trees near Melun*, lent by Bernard Berenson, now at the Belgrade Museum of Art and Archeology; *Collioure*, lent by Leo Stein, now at the Barnes Foundation; and *La Femme aux yeux verts*, 1909, lent by Harriet Levy, now at the San Francisco Museum of Modern Art (A. G. Robins, *Modern Art in Britain*, 188).

51 Conflicting versions of Grant's visit to Stein and Matisse are presented in J. Rothenstein, *Modern English Painters*, vol. 1, 243; R. Shone, *Bloomsbury Portraits*, 57–61; and S. Watney, *Duncan Grant*, 26–7, 82. Picassos in the Stein collection have also been suggested as sources for the Keynes mural (R. Shone, *Artists of Bloomsbury*, 69). The connection to *Le Dos* is suggested in J. Collins, *Omega Workshops*, 280, n. 26.

52 Frances Spalding casts doubt on Grant's memory of visiting the Steins before 1913 (*Duncan Grant* 129–30) and places his first meeting with Matisse in 1911 (*Duncan Grant*, 107–8). Late in life, Grant declined to lecture on Matisse, saying, "I think I only saw him three times in my life and

all at very long intervals (D. Grant to M. Hutchinson, 31 February 1955, Texas).

53 Grant lists Matisse, along with Gauguin and Cézanne, as artists he noticed at the Brighton show (D. Grant to J. M. Keynes, 18 August 1910, British Library); on this show, see J. B. Bullen, *Post-Impressionists in England*, 77–92. Fry's "The Autumn Salon" describes the exhibition as "a salon of decorators," focusing on schemes by Matisse, Denis, and Bonnard. While praising the "linear rhythm" of Matisse's *Music* and *Dance*, Fry criticized their "extremely crude" color.

54 Documentation is incomplete for this project, a collaboration between the ceramist André Metthey and the dealer Ambroise Vollard; for the most thorough account see *La Céramique Fauve*, 50–2, 105–7. In 1909, Vollard enlisted the help of Eugène Druet in selling these pieces, and the catalog to *Manet and the Post-Impressionists* confirms that they were lent by the Galeries E. Druet.

55 *A Roger Fry Reader*, 94, 105.

56 On Matisse's ceramics, see J. Neff, *Matisse and Decoration*, and *La Céramique Fauve* 77–87. The Steins' vase (no. 15 in Neff's catalog) is illustrated in Museum of Modern Art, *Four Americans in Paris*, no. 11.

57 W. Wees, *Vorticism*, 17, 25–6. A few years later, a cartoon titled "Futurist Fashions for 1913" in the society journal *The Bystander* showed "A Post-Impressionist Costume/Garnished with White Green and Purple Fumes" worn by a caricatured suffragette (1 January 1913, 13). An unfinished satirical novel by Lytton Strachey, written at this period, described upper-crust women at a tea party dismissing the suffragettes and Post-Impressionism (see S. P. Rosenbaum, *Edwardian Bloomsbury*, 305).

58 "Manet and the Post-Impressionists," 598.

59 Christina Walsh, *Daily Herald*, in P. Stansky, *On or About December 1910*, 7. For the suffragette Mary Lowndes's admiration of the exhibition, see I. Dunlop, *Shock of the New*, 146.

60 J. J. Woods, "The Post-Impressionists," *Art Chronicle*, 19 November 1910, in S. Tillyard, *Impact of Modernism*, 120.

61 W. B. Richmond, "Post-Impressionists," *Morning Post*, 16 November 1910, rpt. in J. B. Bullen, ed., *Post-Impressionists in England*, 114–17. On the counter-decadents, see R. Gagnier, *Idylls of the Marketplace*, 149–55.

62 W. Blunt, *My Diaries*, 15 November 1910. D. MacCarthy, "The Art Quake of 1910," 124.

63 R. Ross, "Post-Impressionists at the Grafton: The Twilight of the Idols," *Morning Post*, 7 November 1910, rpt. J. B. Bullen, ed., *Post-Impressionists in England*, 100–4.

64 I. Dunlop, *The Shock of the New*, 120.

65 V. Woolf, "Mr. Bennett and Mrs. Brown," *Collected Essays*, vol. 1, 320.

Section II: Sailing to Byzantium: Post-Impressionist Primitivism

1 John Singer Sargent, "Post-Impressioism," *Nation*, 7 January 1911, rpt. J. B. Bullen, *Post-Impressionists in England*, 152–3.

2 W. Sickert, "Post-Impressionists," *Fortnightly Review*, January 1911, rpt. J. B. Bullen, *Post-Impressionists in England*, 154–66. On Sickert's relationship to Post-Impressionism, see *A Roger Fry Reader*, 119–21.

3 M. Holroyd, *Augustus John*, 355, 361–2.

4 E. Gill to W. Rothenstein, in W. Rothenstein, *Men and Memories*, vol. 2, 213–14.

5 W. Rothenstein to R. Fry, 19 March 1911, King's. Rothenstein maintained this opinion, belittling the Post-Impressionist exhibitions, casually combined in his memory into one, in his memoir *Men and Memories*, vol. 2, 212–20; on his conflict with Fry, see *Letters of Roger Fry*, 344–7.

6 R. Fry to E. Fry, 24 November 1910, *Letters of Roger Fry*, 338. R. Fry to M. Fry, in V. Woolf, *Roger Fry*, 157.

7 S. K. Tillyard's *The Impact of Modernism* (92–131) argues that reviews of the show were almost equally divided pro and con, although she assesses satires as neutral, and reviews like Sickert's are counted as supportive simply because they accept some of the works on display while still criticizing Fry. However the reviews are now read, the overriding fact demonstrated by Fry's letters at the time and subsequent accounts of the exhibition by Bloomsbury's members is that Fry and his colleagues felt attacked because of the exhibition, and their defensive cohesion was instrumental in forming Bloomsbury and initiating its future aesthetic projects.

8 C. J. Weld-Blundell, "Manet and the Post-Impressionists." R. Ross, "The Post-Impressionists at the Grafton" *Morning Post*, 7 November 1910, rpt. J. B. Bullen, ed., *Post-Impressionists in England*, 101. For other personal attacks on Fry, see I. Dunlop, *The Shock of the New*, 143.

9 As a partner at the Carfax Gallery, Ross mounted a successful show of Fry's watercolors in 1903, and they corresponded amicably until the first Post-Impressionist exhibit.

10 R. Fry, "Post-Impressionism," *Fortnightly Review*, 1 May 1911, rpt. *Roger Fry Reader*, 99. The published version of the lecture by T. B. Hyslop, Physician Superintendent to the Royal Hospitals of Bridewell and Bedlam, did not mention Fry by name, but ends with a discussion of insanity among art critics ("Post-Illusionism and the Art of the Insane"). Imputations of insanity run through many of the other attacks on the exhibition, and are made personal to Fry in Royal Academician W. B. Richmond's letter to the *Morning Post* ("Post-Impressionists"). Despite the attacks on Fry by the medical establishment at this point, the aesthetic theories he proposed in the 1909 "An Essay in Aesthetics" (*Vision and Design*, 16–38) were quickly appropriated by psychologists. Edward Bullough's 1912 article "Psychical Distance," rehearses Fry's theories as original research and is credited with these ideas in such authoritative texts as Ernst Kris' *Psychoanalytic Explorations in Art*, which at the same time perpetuates Hyslop's argument that abstract art is pathological (97).

11 R. Fry to G. L. Dickinson, 15 October 1910, *Letters of Roger Fry*, 337.

12 R. Fry, *Vision and Design*, 291.

13 R. Fry to M. Fry, 28 March 1913, *Letters of Roger Fry*, 366.

14 W. Rothenstein to R. Fry, 17 April 1911, *Letters of Roger Fry*, 41–2; see also 344–7. For another view of the dispute, see M. Holroyd, *Augustus John*, 371–2.

15 V. Woolf, *Roger Fry*, 162.

16 C. Bell, *Old Friends*, 80.

17 D. Grant to J. M. Keynes, 28 February 1910, British Library. This was the first Friday Club meeting Grant attended.

18 V. Bell to R. Fry, August 1911, Tate.

19 V. Bell to R. Fry, 9 August 1911, Tate.

Chapter 4: Greek Loves: Mediterranean Modernism and the Borough Polytechnic Murals (1911)

1 R. Fry, "Post Impressionism," *Fortnightly Review*, 1 May 1911, rpt. *Roger Fry Reader*, 107.

2 R. Fry to M. Fry, 6 March 1911, *Letters of Roger Fry*, 342. The commission came through Basil Williams, one of Fry's circle of activist college friends, who served on the Polytechnic's overseeing committee.

3 J. Ruskin, *A Joy Forever*, Lecture 2, Section 104, *Works of Ruskin*, vol. 16, 88–9. On earlier school murals, see C. Willsdon, *Mural Painting in Britain*, 255–83.

4 The wax ground Fry prescribed for the Borough Polytechnic murals was a technique he learned from Ashbee during his 1893 work on a Guild of Handicraft showplace discussed in Chapter 2 (J. Collins, *Omega Workshops*, 14).

5 The most obvious comparison is the Austrian modernist Gustav Klimt, who, like other members of the Viennese Secession, made extravagant use of Byzantine models in creating a modernism very different—both visually and ideologically—from Fry's (C. Schorske, *Fin-de-Siècle Vienna*, 208–78) and apparently unknown to Bloomsbury.

6 R. Fry, letter in *The Burlington Magazine* March 1908, rpt. *Roger Fry Reader*, 72–5. Fry repeats this argument in a letter to G. L. Dickinson (31 May 1913, *Letters*, 369) and Clive Bell repeats it in *Art* (94).

7 R. Fry, introduction to M. Denis, "Cézanne," *Burlington*, January 1910, rpt. *Roger Fry Reader*, 78.

8 R. Fry to O. Morrell, 16 April 1911, Texas. Compare *Letters of Roger Fry*, 347–8.

9 R. Ross, *Morning Post*, 4 January 1912, in J. Collins, *Omega Workshops*, 19.

10 On the relative isolation of Tunis from the English, see J. Pemble, *Mediterranean Passion*, 50.

11 Bloomsbury's association of Islam with challenges to Christian dogma clearly participates in the "Orientalism" influentially critiqued by Edward Said, though he is not concerned with Europeans who used Islam to criticize their own culture and shies away from issues of sexuality (*Orientalism*, see especially 167, 188, 190); for a critique of Said on sexuality, see T. Hastings, "Said's *Orientalism* and the Discourse of (Hetero)sexuality." Steven Marcus's description of the early Victorian pornographic novel, *The Lustful Turk*, is more useful for suggesting the sexual license the British associated with Mediterranean culture, from Turkey and Tunis to Algeria and even Italy, where Catholic abbots procure British maidens for Arab clients (*The Other Victorians*, 197–203); compare the last two stories in Lytton Strachey's *The Really Interesting Question*, both with Islamic settings.

12 E. Carpenter, *Ioläus*, 99–110. R. Burton, *Book of the Thousand Nights*, vol. 10, 206–7. See also L. Crompton, *Byron and Greek Love*, 111–18.

13 D. Grant to J. M. Keynes, 20 January 1911, British Library.

14 J. M. Keynes to L. Strachey, in R. Skidelsky, *Hopes Betrayed*, 258. Such reports underlie Strachey's facetious request, a few years later, that Grant paint him "a little Tunisian view that I should really like, with a chocolate-coloured male bum in the foreground" (L. Strachey to D. Grant, 6 February 1914, British Library).

15 J. M. Keynes, in R. Skidelsky, *Hopes Betrayed*, 258.

16 In V. Woolf, *Roger Fry*, 98.

17 R. Fry to G. L. Dickinson, 28 May 1891, King's.

18 R. Fry, "Artlessness." On Fry's inversion of nationalist rhetorics at this era, see *A Roger Fry Reader*, 118–19.

19 Vanessa Bell, following her miscarriage in Turkey, was too weak to contribute to the Borough Polytechnic project. "What wouldn't I give to be helping you to decorate some room," she wrote to Fry, adding her suggestions on his work: "I like your sketch of the elephant very much. You might paint the great big wrinkles it has in its skin with some of what you call my slithery strokes" (V. Bell to R. Fry, 16 August 1911, Tate). Fry reassured her with the promise that they would "design great walls to be done when you're well again" (R. Fry to V. Bell, c.1911, Tate).

20 B. Adeney to Tate Gallery, 31 December 1953, Tate.

21 J. B., "The Amusements of London." Compare Ruskin's vague definition of the Byzantine to include Greek, Roman, "then Arabian—Persian—Phoenician—Indian—all you can think of, in art of hot countries up to the year 1200." Although Ruskin disparaged those he called "foolish modern critics" who see "nothing in the Byzantine school but a barbarism to be conquered and forgotten," he nevertheless valued it only for its contributions to Gothic art (J. Ruskin, *Ariadne Florentina*, *Works of Ruskin*, vol. 22, 343). His admiration for the Byzantine St. Mark's in Venice is discussed in the introduction to his *Works*, vol. 10, l-li.

22 "Interesting Experiment."

23 R. Ross, "New Art in the Borough." Ross's favorable reaction was conditioned by his long-standing acquaintance with Fry's comparison of modern art to Byzantine precedent. In Ross's "Post-Impressionists at the Grafton," the favorable discussion of Gauguin, incongruously bracketed by his vindictive introductory and concluding remarks about the show, invokes Egyptian fresco, saying, "Here is Byzantinism vindicated."

24 J. B., "Amusements of London."

25 "Interesting Experiment."

26 W. Morris, *News From Nowhere*, Chapter 2, *Collected Works*, vol. 16, 7.

27 S. S. Saale, "Sonnet," *The Artist*, 1 September 1890, quoted in B. Reade, *Sexual Heretics*, 228; many similar examples are anthologized in this text. Symonds's description of the "living echo" of Greek sculpture in "the fields where boys bathe in early morning" is also an apt precedent (*The Greek Poets*, quoted in Chapter 3, n. 19).

28 W. Pater, *The Renaissance*, 75–6. Michelangelo's *Battle of Cascina* was widely known through both the copy in the collection of the Earl of Leicester and prints that isolated particular figures; any of these sources could have facilitated Grant's appropriation of Michelangelo's leftmost figure.

29 R. Fry to G. L. Dickinson, 17 May 1891, *Letters of Roger Fry*, 144.

30 R. Fry to G. L. Dickinson, 28 May 1891, King's (also quoted n. 17).

31 V. Woolf, *Moments of Being*, 198.

32 I. Anstruther, *Oscar Browning*, see especially Chapter 8; J. A. Symonds, *Memoirs*, 265–67.

33 E. Carpenter, "Homogenic Love," in B. R. S. Fone, *Hidden Heritage*, 246–7.

34 R. Fry, in V. Woolf, *Roger Fry*, 47. On Carpenter, see S. Rowbotham and J. Weeks, *Socialism and the New Life*, 27–138.

35 R. Fry to E. Carpenter, 22 August 1890, in F. Spalding, *Roger Fry*, 24. On the sandals, see F. MacCarthy, *The Simple Life*, 18. More concrete evidence of Fry's admiration is his 1894 portrait of Carpenter wearing what Fry called his "very anarchist overcoat" (R. Fry to M. Fry, 14 January

1894, *Letters of Roger Fry*, 156. See also F. Spalding, *Portraits by Roger Fry*, 7, 17). Fry's portrait (now at the National Portrait Gallery) monumentalizes Carpenter, contrasting his elongated figure (a full six heads high in contrast to the physical standard of five) to low studio furniture to create an effect of great stature.

36   See G. L. Dickinson, *The Greek View of Life*. Dickinson's memorial essay on Carpenter records his admiration for Carpenter's courage in publishing early defenses of homosexuality, especially as this did not, "as is sometimes the case, make him an enemy of women" ("Edward Carpenter as a Friend," in G. Beith, *Edward Carpenter*, 37). On Dickinson's work for the League, see E. M. Forster, *Goldsworthy Lowes Dickinson*, 163–73, 184–9; on his other pacifist writings, see 173–6.

37   C. R. Ashbee, *An Endeavor*, 39.

38   E. M. Forster, terminal note to *Maurice*, 249.

39   J. M. Keynes to D. Grant, 24 December 1910, 11 September 1913, in R. Skidelsky, *Hopes Betrayed*, 257, 280.

40   D. Grant to J.M. Keynes, 3 February 1911, British Library; Compare E. Carpenter, *Love's Coming of Age*, 38.

41   W. Whitman, *Complete Poetry*, 65, 26–7.

42   C. R. Ashbee, journal, Easter 1907, in F. MacCarthy, *The Simple Life*, 165.

43   E. Carpenter, *Angels' Wings*, 79–80.

44   C. Lewis Hind, "Fine Art in the Borough," clipping in Grant's scrapbook, Tate. D. MacCarthy, "Post-Impressionist Frescoes," 661.

45   "The Decorations at the Borough Polytechnic."

46   A Post-Impressionist Scribbler, "Pictorial Art in South London."

47   S. K. Tillyard notes this development in relation to reviews of the second Post-Impressionist exhibition in 1912 (*The Impact of Modernism*, 190), but responses to the Borough Polytechnic project show Fry's ideas permeating British art criticism by 1911.

48   A. Crawford, *C. R. Ashbee*, 24.

49   "Decorations at the Borough Polytechnic."

50   J. B., "The Amusements of London."

51   R. Fry to M. Fry, *Letters of Roger Fry*, 353.

52   Obituary of Fry, King's College Annual Report of the Council, 17 November 1934, in F. Spalding, *Roger Fry*, 149. Richard Cork's *Art Beyond the Gallery* exaggerates the specifics of what is known about this occasion (120).

53   C. Willsdon, *Mural Painting in Britain*, 287.

54   R. Fry, Omega Workshops fundraising letter, 11 December 1912, rpt. *Roger Fry Reader*, 196.

55   R. Fry, in [Anon.] "Post-Impressionism in the Home."

56   J. Collins, *Omega Workshops*, 15–16.

Chapter 5: Forging a Feminist Primitivism: Byzantine Women by Duncan Grant and Vanessa Bell (1912)

1   F. Spalding, *Duncan Grant*, 19–20; and L. Tickner, *The Spectacle of Women*, fig. 4 and color plate 1.

2   J. E. Harrison to J. M. Keynes, 12 or 14 February 1912, British Library. See also interview with Grant, in S. Watney, *The Art of Duncan Grant*, 84–5, and R. Shone, *Artists of Bloomsbury*, 83. This documentation refutes Judith Collins's doubts about the existence of a Newnham College commission (*Omega Workshops*, 23). On Harrison's acquaintance with Fry, see V. Woolf, *Roger Fry*, 92.

3   A second design by Mrs. Bernard Darwin, though commended by Henry Tonks in remarks to the Newnham College Council, was also unrealized (cited in C. Willsdon, *Mural Painting in Britain*, 283, n. 101).

4   First Kings, Chapter 10. Frances Spalding suggests that Grant's rendition of the story is based on the version in the Koran (*Duncan Grant*, 121), but that text does not support this claim.

5   Tate, *Duncan Grant, Birthday*, no. 8. The queen's face is also similar to the figure in profile in Michelangelo's *Entombment* at the National Gallery, which Grant copied in 1910 (see Chapter 3; fig. 30). Lytton and Philippa Strachey are reported to have posed for the Newnham picture (F. Spalding, *Duncan Grant*, 121).

6   Q. Bell, *Virginia Woolf*, 157–61. V. Woolf, *Three Guineas*, 36–62.

7   E. Lauter, *Women as Mythmakers*.

8   L. Strachey to D. Grant, 26 March 1906, British Library. As discussed in Chapter 3, "the O. B." refers to Oscar Browning. On Strachey's fanciful retellings of history as a form of "camp" specific to Bloomsbury, see George Piggford, "Camp Sites: Forster and the Biographies of Queer Bloomsbury," in R. K. Martin and G. Piggford, *Queer Forster*, 95–102.

9   R. Shone, *Bloomsbury Portraits*, 80.

10   P. G. Konody. "English Post-Impressionists."

11   V. Bell to R. Fry, Spring/Summer 1912, Tate.

12   V. Bell to R. Fry, 6 June 1912, Tate.

13   V. Bell to C. Bell, 16 January 1912, Tate. This work is no. 2 in Anthony d'Offay Gallery, *The Omega Workshops*.

14   C. Bell, *Art*, 128–30. Bell here recapitulates not just the broad outlines of Fry's ideas, but specific examples from his letters; see R. Fry to G. L. Dickinson, 31 May 1913, *Letters of Roger Fry*, 369.

15   V. Bell to R. Fry, 5 July 1911, Tate.

16   V. Bell to R. Fry, 2 March 1922, Tate.

17   My analysis takes issue with Judith Collins who dates Bloomsbury's "interest in Byzantine art" to April or May of 1913, dismissing, in a distinction that is not self-evident, the two versions of the Empress Theodora as "Byzantinism of a superficial sort" (*Omega Workshops*, 65). From Fry's 1908 letter to the *Burlington* (quoted in Chapter 4 at note 6), Fry made Byzantine precedent central to his defense of Post-Impressionism. By 1912, all the artists of Bloomsbury were well acquainted with Byzantine mosaics. In 1926, Bell and Grant returned to Ravenna, and in 1933, Theodora appeared, along with the Queen of Sheba, on their hand-painted plates (discussed in Chapter 15, fig. 208). Grant is quoted, late in his life, citing the Ravenna mosaics as the "greatest decorations" he had ever seen, in Richard Shone, "Duncan Grant: Designer and Decorator," in T. Bradshaw, ed., *A Bloomsbury Canvas*, 24.

18   The stylistic rivalry evident in Grant's and Bell's Theodora images also characterizes their portraits from this period of the painter Henri Doucet, whose status as an exemplary French Post-Impressionist is discussed in Chapter 7. A similar comparison is evident between Bell's portraits of painters in her circle and Grant's 1913 *Group at Asheham* (Hirschl & Adler, *British Modernist Art*, no. 128).

19   V. Bell to R. Fry, 11 September 1912, Tate.

20   V. Bell to R. Fry, Spring/Summer 1912, Tate.

21   Bell's self-portrait was exhibited as Fry's work in F. Spalding, *Portraits by Roger Fry*, no. 7.

Chapter 6: Country and City: Asheham and Brunswick Square (1911–12)

1   Matisse's pastoral appeal to urban patrons is analyzed in Joyce Henri Robinson, "Hi Honey, I'm Home: Weary (Neurasthenic) Businessmen and the Formulation of a Serenely Modern Aesthetic," in C. Reed, *Not at Home*, 98–112.

2   R. Fry, "The Grafton Gallery—I," *Nation*, 19 November 1910, rpt. *Roger Fry Reader*, 88.

3   V. Woolf to L. Woolf, 31 August 1911, *Letters*, vol. 1, 476.

4   V. Bell to C. Bell, February 1911, Tate.

5   R. Fry, "The Grafton Gallery—I," *Nation*, 19 November 1910, rpt. *Roger Fry Reader*, 86.

6   V. Woolf to M. MacCarthy, April 1911, *Letters*, vol. 1, 456.

7   L. Woolf, *Beginning Again*, 56.

8   V. Bell to V. Woolf, 19 August 1912, Berg. Compare V. Bell to C. Bell, 20 August 1912, Tate.

9   A related image of domestic conviviality in the same arm chairs is the 1911 *Conversation Piece* (University of Hull), long known as *Conversation at Asheham*, though recent research suggests it was painted at Little Talland House (R. Shone, "Getting it Together," 44).

10   R. Shone, *Art of Bloomsbury*, 88.

11   V. Bell to V. Woolf, 22 August 1915, *Selected Letters*, 186.

12   V. Woolf, "A Haunted House," *Complete Shorter Fiction*, 165–7. Compare L. Woolf, *Beginning Again*, 56–61.

13   Bell's letters before this date mention sketching in Scotland and at Durbins and Studland Bay; no finished paintings correspond to references to the first two sites, and the Studland Bay paintings focus on figures by the sea (these are insightfully analyzed in L. Tickner, *Modern Life and Modern Subjects*, 117–41).

14   V. Bell to R. Fry, 4 September 1912, Tate.

15   L. Woolf, *Beginning Again*, 21. This group constituted the original residential unit at Brunswick Square. After the Woolfs married and moved out, Gerald Shove (after July 1912) lived in Virginia's former second-floor rooms and Geoffrey Keynes in Leonard's attic (after October 1912); Harry Norton, who had accompanied the Bells to Turkey in 1911 (see Chapter 4), later replaced Shove.

16   V. Woolf, *Letters*, vol. 1, xvii, Q. Bell, *Virginia Woolf*, vol. 1, 116–17, 175. Bell analyzes Virginia's flirtation with Clive and brief engagement to Strachey as manifestations of her domestic unhappiness (134, 141). Compare V. Woolf, *Letters*, vol. 3, 261.

17   V. Woolf, *Moments of Being*, 185 (discussed in Chapter 1). V. Woolf to O. Morrell, 9 November 1911, *Letters*, vol. 1, 480.

18   V. Woolf, *Moments of Being*, 201.

19   V. Woolf to V. Bell, 25? July 1911, *Letters*, vol. 1, 472.

20   V. Woolf to L. Woolf, 2 December 1911, *Letters*, vol. 1, 484. L. Woolf, *Beginning Again*, 50–2. Q. Bell, *Virginia Woolf*, 186. Virginia was writing *The Voyage Out* and Leonard was working on *The Village in the Jungle* at this time. When Virginia Woolf left Brunswick Square to set up housekeeping with Leonard, her call for a new tenant estimated the year's expenses at 150 pounds (V. Woolf to V. Dickinson, 29? October 1912, *Letters*, vol. 2, 12).

21   J. M. Keynes to F. Keynes, 23 December 1911, in R. Skidelsky, *Hopes Betrayed*, 271.

22   V. Bell, *Sketches in Pen and Ink*, 110.

23   Leonard Woolf, *Beginning Again*, 52.

24   V. Woolf to M. Vaughan, June 1912, *Letters*, vol. 1, 503.

25 D. Grant, transcript of 1972 interview by D. Brown, Tate. Photographs of models in the studio reveal panels of what could be stenciling or fabric with a design of circles and squares.

26 Measurements estimated by Judith Collins (*Omega Workshops*, 24).

27 J. M. Keynes to F. Keynes, 23 December 1911, in R. Skidelsky, *Hopes Betrayed*, 270–1.

28 On the exaggeration of the differences between Bloomsbury and the Camden Town artists, see my "Bloomsbury Bashing."

29 W. Baron, *The Camden Town Group*, 26, 40, 218.

30 Grant's participation in the second Camden Town show was somewhat half-hearted. His still life, *Parrot Tulips* (now in the Southampton City Art Gallery)—a sole submission to an exhibition that allowed each painter to show four works—deviated from the urban themes of the other artists.

31 R. Shone, *Bloomsbury Portraits*, 74, n. 16. On Waddington, see F. Spalding, *Duncan Grant*, 83.

32 D. Grant, quoted in R. Cork, *Art Beyond the Gallery*, 121.

33 Examples of Etchells's painting from this period include his *Entry into Jerusalem*, and *From an English Sporting Print*, both c.1912, now at Charleston.

34 V. Bell to R. Fry, 6 June 1912, Tate. This letter is misdated, and so misread as referring to the Borough Polytechnic panels in R. Shone, *Bloomsbury Portraits*, 68.

35 D. Grant to J. M. Keynes, 18 September 1912, British Library.

36 Grant's four other paintings in the show were *The Dancers*, now at the Tate; *Pamela*, now at the Yale Center for British Art; a portrait of Henri Doucet, probably the one illustrated as no. 59 in *Letters of Roger Fry*; and *Seated Woman*, later hung at Durbins and now at the Courtauld Institute Galleries.

37 Matisse's *Dance II* is at the Hermitage Museum in St. Petersburg.

38 R. Holt, *Sport and the British*, 126.

39 V. Bell memoirs, in F. Spalding, *Vanessa Bell*, 27–8; V. Woolf, *Moments of Being*, 155–6, 171–2.

40 P. Cunnington and A. Mansfield, *English Costume for English Sports and Recreation*, 81–97. The reading of this figure as a woman in a skirt is confirmed by the description of the mural in David Garnett's memoir, *The Golden Echo*, 251.

41 In L. Kirstein, *Nijinsky Dancing*, 137–8. George Bernard Shaw's 1910 *Misalliance* also used a crashing airplane to signify modernity "dropping in" on the complacent British bourgeoisie. A Russian comparison is provided by Mikhail Matiushin's futurist opera, *Victory of the Sun*, of 1913, in which sportsmen and airplanes feature as signs of modernity, and the sun is captured and rolled about on stage like a ball. In the original Saint Petersburg production, Kazimir Malevich designed the sets and costumes.

42 In D. Chadd and J. Gage, *The Diaghilev Ballet in England*, 20.

43 R. Nijinsky, *Nijinsky*, 200.

44 In L. Kirstein, *Nijinsky Dancing*, 137.

45 The quotation is attributed in various accounts to both Bakst and Nijinsky. See O. Morrell, *Memoirs*, 216; R. Buckle, *Diaghilev*, 233–4; R. Buckle, *Nijinsky*, 259; D. Turnbaugh, *Duncan Grant*, 48.

46 L. Woolf, *Beginning Again*, 37.

47 L. Woolf, *Beginning Again*, 49. P. Wollen, "Fashion/Orientalism/the Body."

48 On Bloomsbury and Tolstoy, see my "Making History," 196–7. On the Hogarth Press's

Russian authors, see J. H. Willis, *Leonard and Virginia Woolf as Publishers*, especially Chapter 3.

49 R. Fry, Introduction to *The Second Post-Impressionist Exhibition*, 7.

50 B. Anrep, "The Russian Group," *The Second Post-Impressionist Exhibition*, rpt. J. B. Bullen, *Post-Impressionists in England*, 356–8. When the paintings Anrep selected arrived from Russia, they did not live up to Fry's expectations. He complained to Duncan Grant, "they're rather pretty and romantic—well, I daresay it's as well that the British Public should have something it'll like" (R. Fry to D. Grant, Autumn 1912, *Letters of Roger Fry*, 360).

51 Claims that *Le Dieu Bleu* was not performed in London are corrected by Nesta MacDonald (*Diaghilev Observed*, 74) and S. L. Grigoriev (*The Diaghilev Ballet*, 90).

52 L. Woolf, *Beginning Again*, 49.

53 R. Skidelsky, *Hopes Betrayed*, 284–5.

54 E. Marsh to R. Brooke, June 1913, in C. Hassall, *Edward Marsh*, 231–2.

55 J. Cocteau, in *Comoedia Illustré*, 15 June 1911, in R. Buckle, *Diaghilev*, 199.

56 C. Ricketts, *Self-Portrait*, 179.

57 *Daily News*, 22 June 1911, in R. Buckle, *Diaghilev*, 205. For comparable views of Parisian ballet, see R. Herbert, *Impressionism*, 102–7.

58 A. Benois, *Reminiscences of the Russian Ballet*, 316.

59 Michel Fokine, *Memoirs of a Ballet Master*, 155–6.

60 "Nijinsky Puts New Life into Ballet Russe [*sic*]," *New York Times*, 13 April 1916, in N. Macdonald, *Diaghilev Observed*, 173–4.

61 R. Buckle, *Diaghilev*, 248.

62 P. Lieven, *The Birth of the Ballets-Russes*, 262–3. Alexandre Benois's 1941 *Reminiscences of the Russian Ballet* also openly acknowledged Diaghilev's homosexuality.

63 *Pall-Mall Gazette*, 13 June 1912; *Times*, 10 July 1912; both quoted in R. Buckle, *Diaghilev*, 230, 232; Richard Cappell, *Daily Mail*, 1 July 1913, in N. Macdonald, *Diaghilev Observed*, 95. See also R. Buckle, *Diaghilev*, 37–8.

64 J. M. Keynes to L. Strachey, 17 July 1911, in R. Skidelsky, *Hopes Betrayed*, 259; see also 352–3. Keynes's marriage is also discussed in Chapter 13.

65 M. Holroyd, *Lytton Strachey*, 543–4.

66 R. Buckle, *Diaghilev*, 234.

67 D. Turnbaugh, *Private*, 66–7.

68 R. Shone, *Bloomsbury Portraits*, 72.

69 Crafts Council, *Omega Workshops*, 81.

70 O. Sitwell, *Great Morning!*, 258. Sitwell exaggerates his role in introducing Bloomsbury to the Russian Ballet as late as 1918 (270).

71 The impact of the Ballets Russes on English art has been noted, not only in such obvious contexts as Gaudier-Brzeska's sculptural homage to the dancers of *L'Oiseau de Feu*, but as the inspiration for Spencer Gore's brilliant cabaret decorations of 1912 and David Bomberg's paintings on dance themes, begun in 1913 (see R. Cork, *Art Beyond the Gallery*, 72; *Vorticism*, 393).

Section III: On to Omega: The Workshops' Origins and Objects

1 Transcript of conversation with Simon Watney, 26 July 1976, courtesy of Watney.

2 V. Bell to C. Bell, 27 December 1912, *Selected Letters*, 131–32.

3 R. Fry to M. Fry, 28 June 1912, *Letters of Roger Fry*, 359.

4 L. Woolf, *Beginning Again*, 94.

5 Grafton Gallery, *Second Post-Impressionist Exhibition*, 12.

6 R. Fry, "The Grafton Gallery: An Apologia," *Nation*, 9 November 1912, rpt. *Roger Fry Reader*, 112.

7 R. Fry, "Introduction" and "The French Group" in Grafton Galleries, *The Second Post-Impressionist Exhibition*, 7, 17 ("The French Group rpt. as "French Post-Impressionists," *Vision and Design*, 237–43).

8 R. Fry, untitled lecture manuscript, undated [1920s], King's 1/133.

Chapter 7: The Origins of the Omega

1 R. Fry, "The Present Situation," unpublished lecture, 1924, King's 1/111.

2 R. Fry, "Sensibility *versus* Mechanism," 497. Fry here responds to J. E. Barton's B.B.C. lectures on modern art, but he might just as easily be referring to any of the advocates of modernist design then being promoted by the *Architectural Review* and the B.B.C. (discussed in Chapter 15). Paul Nash's manifestos on modern design—"Modern English Furnishing" in the *Architectural Review* in 1930 and "The Artist and the House" in *The Listener* in 1932—call for the establishment of Omega-like institutions without mentioning the precedent of the Omega (Nash's 1932 *Room and Book*, did cite the Omega, but derogatorily as a late echo of the "Morris movement" with the "melancholy difference" that its members were painters, rather than craftsmen so that "just as in the middle of the nineteenth century heavy ornament had spread until it eclipsed the whole room, so now painting invaded not only the furniture but the walls and even ceilings of the house" [24]). John Betjeman's "1830–1930—Still Going Strong," in the *Architectural Review* complimented Fry's fabrics and ceramics, but misdated them to the year before the Omega opened and ignored their connection to the workshops (233).

3 N. Pevsner, "Omega," 48.

4 Quotations from transcript of B.B.C. discussion of the exhibition, "The Omega Workshops, 1913–1920," curated by Carol Hogben at the Victoria and Albert Museum over the winter 1963–64 (Victoria and Albert Archives); there was no catalog to the show. For Quentin Bell's riposte to this broadcast, see his "The Omega Revisited." The linear historical narrative assumed by the commentators is that outlined in Nikolaus Pevsner's influential *Pioneers of the Modern Movement*.

5 W. Januszczak, "Fry's French delights". Januszczak's attitude is cogently criticized in S. Watney, "Critics and Cults."

6 Isabel Anscombe's *Omega and After* asserts, "The Omega Workshops have been described as a last outpost of the Arts and Crafts Movement, but this was never so," then claims Fry was "uninterested" in continental designers (31). S. K. Tillyard's *The Impact of Modernism* offers a partial corrective to the first claim, tracing the Bloomsbury critics' use of an Arts and Crafts vocabulary. Ignoring—even obscuring—Fry's experience in various Arts and Crafts institutions (as described in Chapter 2), however, Tillyard perpetuates the tendency to see Bloomsbury as unconnected to its English forerunners (see my review). Tillyard also rejects the relevance of any French connection, asserting that the Omega's apparent links to France were just Fry's attempts to create a "fashionable yardstick by which to measure British efforts" (66).

7   As a young man, Morris eschewed politics, writing in 1856: "I can't enter into politico-social subjects with an interest, for on the whole I see that things are in a muddle, and I have no power or vocation to set them right in ever so little a degree. My work is the embodiment of dreams in one form or another (W. Morris to C. Price, July 1856, *Collected Letters*, vol. 1, 28). By his own account, it was his discovery, in the course of furnishing Red House around 1859, "that all the minor arts were in a state of complete degradation" so that, "with the conceited courage of a young man I set myself to reforming all that" ("My Very Uneventful Life," *Selected Writings*, 30) that led to his political career, as, "little by little I was driven to the conclusion that all . . . uglinesses are but the outward expression of the innate moral baseness into which we are forced by our present form of society, and that it is futile to attempt to deal with them from the outside" (preface to *Signs of Change, Collected Works*, vol. 23, 2).

8   W. Morris, "Making the Best of It," *Collected Works*, vol. 22, 86.

9   R. Fry, Omega Workshops prospectus, rpt. *Roger Fry Reader*, 198.

10   R. Fry, *Vision and Design*, 77, and "What to Do with Our Artists."

11   J. Ruskin, *Two Paths*, Lecture 3, Section 95, *Works of Ruskin*, vol. 16, 342. The Omega's work with refugees is discussed in the introduction to Section IV.

12   J. Ruskin, *Stones of Venice*, vol. 2, chapter 6, Sections 14, 15, 19, *Works of Ruskin*, vol. 10, 193–4, 199. R. Fry, preface to the Omega Workshops Catalog, rpt. *Roger Fry Reader*, 201; on the Omega's links to Ruskin, see 167–77.

13   Victor Plarr, *Ernest Dowson*, in P. Stansky, *Redesigning the World*, 103–4. Plarr's evocation of "Fitzroy institutions," including "what was known as 'Fitzroy silence' at our austere dinners and lunches," presages Virginia Woolf's description of "the "silence [that] was difficult not dull" that characterized Bloomsbury's gatherings (*Moments of Being*, 189). Compare W. Rothenstein, *Men and Memories*, 332.

14   J. Ruskin, *Stones of Venice*, vol. 1, chapter 2, Section 17, in *Works of Ruskin*, vol. 9, 72. The Omega peacock scarf and table are illustrated in J. Collins, *Omega Workshops*, nos. 39, 41. On Ashbee's use of the peacock, see A. Crawford, *C. R. Ashbee*, 229–230. Grant's 1915 Omega signboard replaced the sign bearing an "emaciated Byzantine youth," discussed at the end of this chapter.

15   R. Fry, prospectus for the Omega Workshops, rpt. *Roger Fry Reader*, 199.

16   R. Fry, "A Modern Jeweler."

17   W. Morris quoted in E. P. Thompson, *William Morris*, 105. Morris reiterates this defense in his letters (see W. Morris to G. Burne-Jones, 1 June 1884, *Collected Letters*, vol. 2, 283–7). On Morris's business practices, see C. Harvey and J. Press, *William Morris*, which defends his refusal to accept profit sharing or any other challenge to his status as "master" of his employees. See also P. Floud, "The Inconsistencies of William Morris."

18   R. Fry, "The Present Outlook in Painting and Applied Art," unpublished lecture, King's 1/113.

19   P. Greenhalgh, "Art, Politics and Society at the Franco–British Exhibition of 1908," 445.

20   E. Gill, "The Failure of the Arts and Crafts Movement," 297. Gill reiterates this critique in his *Autobiography*, 268–70.

21   C. R. Ashbee, *Craftsmanship in Competitive Industry*, 17.

22   P. Stansky, *Redesigning the World*, 10.

23   C. R. Ashbee, journal, July 1913, King's.

24   J. Ashbee to C. R. Ashbee, August 1913, King's.

25   J. Collins, *Omega Workshops*, 139–40.

26   W. Gill to D. Grant, 4 July 1966, Tate.

27   W. R. Lethaby, "Town Tidying," *Form in Civilization*, in Peter Fuller, "William Lethaby, Keeping art ship-shape," S. Backmeyer and T. Gronberg, eds, *W. R. Lethaby*, 32. Contrast Fry's ideals for art education (*Roger Fry Reader*, 240–5, 266–77).

28   Richard Shone suggests *Pots et Citron* was bought before the first Post-Impressionist exhibition, making it the first Picasso in any English collection ("Pictures at Charleston," in H. Lee, ed., *A Cézanne in the Hedge*, 151). A letter from Bell to her sister describing the purchase, however, is dated to 19 October 1911 (Berg).

29   Crafts Council, *Omega Workshops*, 45.

30   V. Bell to D. Grant, 25 March 1914, *Selected Letters*, 160. Fry acquired Picasso's *Tête d'homme* from the gallery of Daniel-Henri Kahnwieler in October of 1913. On this piece, see C. Poggi, *In Defiance of Painting*, 79–81, 88–9.

31   P. G. Konody, *Observer*, 4 July 1915, in J. Collins, *Omega Workshops*, 111. See also R. Shone, *Bloomsbury Portraits*, 104.

32   "Grafton Group at the Alpine Club Gallery." As late as 1916, a review of an art exhibition at the Omega reproved Duncan Grant for being "lamentably indifferent to quality" as evidenced by the shaky "edges" in his paintings (O. R. D. "Decoration: Plain or Artistic").

33   V. Woolf, *Roger Fry*, 160. Memoir of an unidentified Slade student in G. Gerzina, *Carrington*, 25. Tonks's satirical watercolors were exhibited in 1923.

34   Osbert Sitwell, quoted in M. Webb, "A Last Flourish of Aestheticism," 17. See also R. Shone, *Bloomsbury Portraits*, 108. This dynamic is evident from the Omega's opening, with a supportive *Times* reviewer insisting in two 1913 reviews that the look of Omega work belies the skill of its artists: "the simplicity of the designs, and their lack of illusive representation, may lead the public to believe that any one could do them. That is not so, for the best of them are controlled by a clear and certain purpose" ("A New Venture in Art"); "Much of this decoration looks as if it were very easy to do; but there is the artist's certainty of intention" ("The Omega Workshops"). As late as 1984, Roy Strong in the *Financial Times* attacked the Omega as a "monument to amateurism and muddle" demonstrating "that deadly lack of seriousness and professionalism that has been the ruin of so much in this country" ("Why Omega is the Last Word").

35   V. Woolf, *Roger Fry*, 196.

36   Roger Fry, in M. M. B., "Post-Impressionist Furniture." Fry reiterated this point in other Omega promotions (J. Collins, *Omega Workshops*, 51).

37   V. Bell to R. Fry, Spring 1914, in I. Anscombe, *Omega and After*, 39. Perpetuating this perspective, Duncan Grant cheerfully told an interviewer in 1970 that "all the Omega stuff has gone to pieces," a claim the next decade's spate of Omega shows belied (C. Mason, *Duncan Grant at Charleston*).

38   Georges Desvallières, "Présentation de *Notes d'un peintre*," (1908), rpt. in H. Matisse, *Ecrits et propos sur l'art*, 39. Claims that Matisse looked to "image-makers of the Middle Ages, ingenuous as well as ingenious, and farther in the past, to Hindu and Persian art" reappear in a 1909 account of an interview with the artist (J. Flam, ed., *Matisse on Art*, 49). On this point, see R. Shiff, *Cézanne and the End of Impressionism*, 58.

39   H. Matisse, "Notes of a Painter," rpt. *Matisse on Art*, 38–9.

40   R. Fry, "Grafton Gallery—I," *Nation*, 19 November 1910, rpt. *Roger Fry Reader*, 89.

41   R. Fry, *Last Lectures*, 39–40.

42   J. Rothenstein, *Modern English Painters*, 242.

43   R. Fry, undated lecture manuscript, King's 1/163. The catalog for *Manet and the Post-Impressionists* records three painted vases by Vlaminck, two by P. Girieud, and one each by Matisse and Othon Friesz (Matisse's piece is fig. 35). Also around 1907, Matisse was commissioned by Karl-Ernst Osthaus to paint a triptych of ceramic tiles for his country house in Westphalia (J. Neff, "An Early Ceramic Triptych by Henri Matisse"), though it is unlikely that Fry knew this work.

44   R. Fry, Omega Workshops fund raising letter, rpt. *Roger Fry Reader*, 196. A less upbeat characterization of Poiret's reaction to the Omega appears in Fry's "What to do with our Artists": "I was warned by M. Poiret . . . that England was the most hopeless of all countries, the one least open to new ideas, the most satisfied with pastiche and superficial charm."

45   On Omega textile designs, see Crafts Council, *Omega Workshops* 52, 59–60. These anticipate the look of textiles Dufy designed for Poiret during and after 1918 (see Arts Council, *Raoul Dufy*).

46   X. M. Boulestin, *Myself, My Two Countries*, 155. Boulestin sold Poiret's wares in London for nine months before the outbreak of World War I. Poiret cast his lot firmly with Boulestin, visiting him in London, selling his collections through him, and planning with him to open a Maison Poiret in London—this last project, scheduled for October of 1914, was precluded by the War (Poiret finally opened a London shop in 1921). After the Armistice, Boulestin returned to London and made a career as a chef. For an example of Boulestin's cartoons, see *The Bystander* 15 January 1913, 134. For Virginia Woolf's unwitting role in making Boulestin a restauranteur, see J. Noble, ed., *Recollections of Virginia Woolf*, 175.

47   P. White, *Poiret*, 117–34. Sarah Bowman's *A Fashion for Extravagance* details the career of one Martine girl, a concièrge's daughter whose chalked sidewalk drawings recommended her to Poiret's attention (27–8).

48   S. K. Tillyard dismisses the Omega's French sources by asserting that the Ecole Martine was so dependent on English precedent that any influence it had on Fry was "simply reimporting" English ideas (*The Impact of Modernism*, 66).

49   "Ces enfants, livrées à elles-mêmes, oubliaient en peu de temps les préceptes faux et empiriques qu'elles avaient reçus, à l'école, pour retrouver toute la spontanéité et toute la fraîcheur de leur nature" (P. Poiret, *En Habillant l'époque*, 147).

50   "De jeunes Parisiennes de 13 à 17 ans s'y livrent avec fougue aux fantaisies décoratives de leur fraîche imagination. Et nous en avons un art charmant, éclatant, un peu faisandé" (F. Roches, "Le Salon d'automne de 1912," 308–9).

51   C. Bell, *Art*, 289. Bell's lack of support for the Omega is clear from remarks in several letters. Fry complained to him, "I've been absorbed into the Omega and at moments feeling towards it almost as you do" (R. Fry to C. Bell, 16 September 1913, Tate), while Vanessa Bell reported to Fry that Clive "has taken a great dislike" to her new Omega chair covers: "He says that though I am 'a good painter' I have no talent for designing such things, which is rather depressing" (22 October 1913, Tate).

52   R. Fry, Preface to the Omega Workshops catalog, rpt. *Roger Fry Reader*, 201.

53   R. Fry, "The Present Outlook in Painting and Applied Art," unpublished lecture, 1924,

King's. As discussed in Chapter 4, Fry overestimated the Borough Polytechnic artists' anonymity.

54 R. Fry, in "Post-Impressionism in the Home."

55 W. Morris, "The Gothic Revival II," *Unpublished Lectures*, 90. Such rhetoric was echoed by Fry in a 1912 essay claiming, "what the history of art definitely elucidates is that greatest art has always been communal, the expression . . . of common aspirations and ideals" (*Vision and Design*, 62).

56 Stefan Muthesius, in "'We Do Not Understand What is Meant by a "Company" Designing,'" 117. S. K. Tillyard, *The Impact of Modernism*, 10.

57 The French avant-garde's fixation on individualism goes well back into the nineteenth century, setting it apart from contemporary developments in England (see E. Herbert, *The Artist and Social Reform*, 82–5). Another aspect of European indifference to anonymity is suggested by Debora Silverman's comparison between Ruskin's ideas and those of his nearest French counterparts, the Goncourt brothers, whose promotion of a craft revival in the 1870s–80s, far from contributing to any egalitarian social reforms modeled on the Middle Ages, embraced a nostalgia for the eighteenth-century aristocracy ("The Brothers de Goncourts' Maison d'un Artiste").

58 Significant European interest in the English Arts and Crafts Movement began only in the 1890s. At this point, some of Morris's political writings did appear in anarchist and socialist magazines, such as *Les temps nouveaux* in 1892 and *La Société nouvelle* in 1894 (E. Herbert *The Artist and Social Reform*, 16, 198–9; D. Silverman, *Art Nouveau in Fin-de-Siècle France*, 345, n. 20). Their failure to take hold, however, is evident in the records of an 1897 international conference in Geneva to address Morris's influence on "the new decorative art." The keynote speaker, Jean Lahor, outlined Morris's social ideals and saluted the radical who "dreamed and desired that which we should all dream and desire: that the lot of the factory worker should change, that the worker should again become more like the craftsmen he used to be, and free himself from the automation forced on him by the machine, and that as much as possible and as often as possible he should make works of art." But his speech then shifted from collective social change to individual aesthetic innovation, concluding with the hope that a European artist might achieve what Morris had not: finding a style, "an aesthetic formula that would be new, and that would through the elements of its novelty—simplicity, sincerity, and logic—be suitable for all homes" (J. Lahor, *William Morris*, 8–10 [my translation]).

59 Didier Grumbach, introduction to Y. Deslandres and D. Lalanne, *Poiret*, 13–14.

60 "J'aime la Bretagne, j'y trouve le sauvage, le primitif. Quand mes sabots résonnent sur ce sol de granit, j'entends le ton sourd, mat et puissant que je cherche en peinture" (V. Merlhès, ed., *Correspondance de Paul Gauguin*, 172). Fred Orton and Griselda Pollock have shown how the Parisian artists' primitivizing vision misrepresented the economic and social situation of Brittany ("Les Données Bretonnantes," *Avant-Gardes and Partisans Reviewed*, 53–88).

61 Among the most overtly Bretonist works in the first Post-Impressionist show were Gauguin's *Two Breton Peasants*, *Groupe de Bretonnes*, two images of Pont Aven in Brittany, and two canvases titled *Paysage Breton* and *Paysage Bretonne* [sic]. Denis's *St. Georges* depicted the saint fighting a dragon in front of a well known rock formation at Ploumanach on the Breton coast. On the term "cloisonnism," see B. Welsh-Ovcharov, *Vincent Van Gogh and the Birth of Cloisonnism*.

62 A decorative arts instructor for the municipal schools of Paris, Gabriel-Claude recruited at least some of the girls from among her students when she set up the Ecole Martine. After she married Paul Sérusier a few months later and left the school, she was not replaced, and the girls worked on their own under the supervision of a monitor.

63 These modernist tenets remained current through the 1984 Museum of Modern Art exhibition, *"Primitivism" in Twentieth Century Art*. Curator William Rubin asserted in the catalog to that show that, "Tribal art expresses a collective rather than individual sentiment" (36). Anthropologists lent their authority to this view, claiming that the art of "preliterate cultures" "isn't personal. It doesn't reflect a private point of view. . . . It's a corporate statement by a group" (Edmund Carpenter, in T. McEvilley, "Doctor Lawyer Indian Chief," 59). Part of the postmodern challenge to modernism has been to challenge this version of primitivism; revisionary anthropologists warn against generalizing over the enormous range of cultures covered under such vague terms as "tribal" or "preliterate" and argue the absence of terms associated with Enlightenment ideas of aesthetics may be evidence of different—rather than absent—concepts of quality and individual expressiveness (for an overview, see C. Geertz, *Local Knowledge*, 94–120).

64 Obviously the Douanier Rousseau is not anonymous, but—like "Grandma Moses" later—the nickname identifying social status makes the individual into a generic marker for a class of people not usually imagined to be artists.

65 P. Poiret, *En habillant l'époque*, 148. Fernand Roches, "Le Salon d'automne de 1912," reports of the Martine exhibit: "Quelqu'un disait: 'Ces enfants-là ont dû avoir des nourrices russes.—Oui, Nijinski'" (309).

66 P. Wollen, "Fashion/Orientalism/the Body." X. M. Boulestin, *Myself, My Two Countries*, 154.

67 Fry's early primitivist writings include his "Oriental Art" and "Bushman Paintings," both of 1910 (the latter rpt. as "The Art of the Bushman," *Vision and Design*, 85–98). For references to the barbaric and to children's art in Fry's defenses of the first Post-Impressionist exhibition, see *Roger Fry Reader*, 84, 86, 95.

68 Before the war closed down trade routes, the Omega sold North African ceramics and textiles as well beads and fabrics from the Middle East (W. Gill to D. Grant, 12 September 1966, Tate; R. Shone, *Bloomsbury Portraits*, 109). Vanessa Bell's letters refer to purchases of "large quantities of crockery, stuffs, etc." in Ravenna, "mostly to be sold at Fitzroy Sq." (V. Bell to V. Woolf, 3 May 1913, *Letters*, 138). On children's drawings at the Omega, see *Roger Fry Reader*, 239–43. The Omega apparently also marketed trays painted by children, such as the one illustrated in Q. Bell, "The Omega Revisited."

69 Modernist primitivism has been often and ably criticized for the way its homogenizing tendencies reflect racist attitudes about the mystical, childlike simplicity of non-European peoples. Less often articulated, but equally important, are its more positive attributes, enumerated by Guy Brett as "the desire to escape the restrictions of one's inherited and localized worldview, of ethnocentrism; to challenge official academic culture and bourgeois values; to look critically at spiritual needs in a corporate, technological civilization; to seek a kind of psychological renewal in the primary energies of materials, colours, forms, and so on." Such attractions, Brett argues, were more pronounced "before 'modernism' became part of official culture and power" ("Unofficial Versions," in S. Hiller, ed., *The Myth of Primitivism*, 113–14, 124). On debates over Fry's primitivism, see *Roger Fry Reader*, 247, n. 24.

70 *The Times*, 16 May 1908, quoted in P. Greenhalgh, "Art, Politics and Society at the Franco–British Exhibition of 1908," 449–50. The much publicized argument among Vlaminck, Derain, and Picasso in 1906 over whether an African sculpture was "almost as beautiful," "as beautiful" or "even *more* beautiful" than the Venus de Milo is resumed by Jack Flam, "Matisse and the Fauves," in W. Rubin, *"Primitivism" in Twentieth Century Art*, 214.

71 *The Times*, 12 June 1908, quoted in A. Coombs, "For God and England."

72 H. Tonks to R. Ross, 15 May 1910, in *Robbie Ross: Friend of Friends*, 181.

73 Many critics have analyzed this definitive feature of modernism; among the most influential, see J. Baudrillard, *For a Critique of the Political Economy of the Sign*, 102–12. It is worth noting, in relation to Baudrillard's linkage of the rise of the signature with the demise of copying that the Omega also encouraged its artists to copy—sometimes in modernist style—from the canons of art history. An exhibition of this work at the Omega is discussed in Chapter 10.

74 *Tzanck Check* was published under the title *Dada Drawing* in Picabia's Dada journal *Cannibale* in 1920. See Peter Read, "The *Tzanck Check* and related works by Marcel Duchamp," in R. Kuenzli and F. Naumann, eds, *Marcel Duchamp*, 95–105.

75 Lewis's "Round Robin" letter, with its references to "mid-Victorian languish of the neck", is discussed in the Introduction. On his resentment of the Omega's commitment to anonymity, see R. Shone, *Bloomsbury Portraits*, 114–15.

76 V. Woolf, *Diary*, vol. 1, 228. Compare R. Fry to V. Bell, 1 June 1917, Tate; the commission to decorate two rooms came from Mary Hutchinson.

77 The catalog to the Crafts Council exhibition, *The Omega Workshops*, attributes many Omega designs and objects to individual makers and includes short biographies of the participating artists. My own work on the Fry Collection, funded by a grant for connoisseurship and published as "The Roger Fry Collection at the Courtauld Galleries," made attributions (in consultation with scholars and dealers) of designs not included in the Crafts Council exhibition.

78 R. Fry, Omega Workshops fund raising letter, rpt. *Roger Fry Reader*, 196.

79 Fry invited Vildrac to London to lecture on modern poetry during the second Post-Impressionist exhibition and they planned a one-man show for Fry at the Galérie Vildrac in 1912. Neither of these schemes was realized, but in 1913 Vildrac organized the French component of Fry's second Grafton Group exhibition.

80 On the Abbaye see G. Duhamel, *Le temps de la recherche*; C. Sénéchal, *L'Abbaye de Créteil*; and D. Robbins, "From Symbolism to Cubism." David Cottington's *Cubism and the Politics of Culture in France* contests Robbins' depiction of the Abbaye as a radical political enterprise, characterizing it instead as simply an attempt by the artists to reduce the time they spent earning a living (84–5).

81 R. Fry, "What to do with our Artists." Grant recalled that "the original idea was a place where you could go and work if you were hard-up" (in S. Watney, *The Art of Duncan Grant*, 85). Many

memoirs locate the origin of the Omega in an incident when Grant could not afford the train fare to Durbins (W. Gill to D. Grant, June 1966, Tate Gallery Archives; P. Diamand, in Anthony d'Offay Gallery, *The Omega Workshops* n.p. and in Beaverbrook Art Gallery, *Bloomsbury Painters*, 18), though Frances Spalding casts reasonable doubt on Grant's veracity in his excuse, pointing out the far more extensive excursions he undertook at this period (*Duncan Grant*, 113).

82 Abigail Frost's "Omega Anonymous" provides the comparative salaries. Fiona McCarthy observes that the Omega's willingness to pay artists for time spent making things "not necessarily required, or even saleable" contributed to its financial collapse (Crafts Council, *Omega Workshops*, 20). Not all those who worked at the Omega were paid the "artist" salary, however; Vanessa Bell's letters refer to "apprentice" members and differences in wages even within Bloomsbury's ranks (V. Bell to R. Fry, 14 October 1913, *Letters*, 149).

83 Funded by art patrons Paul and Jean Alexandre, the artists' residence was run by Doucet and the sculptor Maurice Drouard (P. Sichel, *Modigliani*, 140–1). The bonds of affection between Doucet and the Bloomsbury artists—especially Fry—are clear in letters reacting to news of his death in battle in 1915. Fry wrote, "My dear Doucet is killed. It's a terrible loss to me. I have so few artist friends who are like him. I worked better with him than anyone else" (R. Fry to Princess Lichnowsky, April 1915, *Letters*, 384). Bell wrote, "One can't say anything but can only think how terrible a waste that such a charming gentle creature should be killed (V. Bell to R. Fry, April 1915, Tate; compare V. Bell, *Selected Letters* 178).

84 On Doucet's wall painting, see W. Gill to D. Grant, June 1966, Tate. Also attributed to Doucet are a set of unrealized designs for bird-shaped pots (J. Collins, *Omega Workshops*, 49–50; Crafts Council, *Omega Workshops*, 82).

85 In addition to the oil version of *The Studio*, Bell painted a watercolor study, now titled *Henri Doucet and Duncan Grant at Asheham* (in Sotheby's London, *Modern British and Irish Paintings, Drawings and Sculpture*, 10 May 1989, no. 66) and a portrait (Hirshl & Adler, *British Modernist Art*, no. 102; this source also reproduces Grant's *Group at Asheham*, no. 128). Grant's portrait of Doucet, which was owned by Vildrac, is illustrated in *Letters of Roger Fry* (no. 59). Bloomsbury welcomed Doucet less for his art than for his potential to inspire them with his example of his practice: "it certainly does do one good I think to work with him whatever one may think of his art," Bell commented (V. Bell to R. Fry, September 1913, Tate). Two years later, Bell called his death "the worst thing that has happened" to date in the war; "even if he wasn't a great artist it was so important that he should work in the way that he did and live that kind of life and be happy in that sort of way" (V. Bell to R. Fry, 2 May 1915, *Selected Letters*, 178).

86 Fry's translation of Jouve's war poem *Vous êtes hommes* was titled *Men of Europe*. The Abbaye published Jouve's *Artificiel*. On the Omega books, see J. Collins, *Omega Workshops*, 115–20.

87 On Omega performances, see I. Anscombe, *Omega and After*, 60–1; J. Collins, *Omega Workshops*, 102–4; *Roger Fry Reader*, 280. On comparative Abbaye performances, see C. Sénéchal, *L'Abbaye de Créteil*, 52–6.

88 The conventional forms of the furniture at the Maison Cubiste aroused criticism at the time, with one reviewer complaining, "Color seems to be, in effect, a decorative element very much in the

modern taste. But the furnishings of Monsieur Mare decidedly recall too much those of our grand-parents" (F. Roches, "Le Salon d'automne de 1912," 307 [my translation]). Far more daring than the interiors, however, the Maison Cubiste's exterior facade designed by the sculptor Raymond Duchamp-Villon, won praise for its cubist forms. On the Maison Cubiste, see N. Troy, *Modernism and the Decorative Arts in France*, 79–92.

89 Fry, in M. M. B., "Post-Impressionist Furniture." Despite the popularity of the cat design, no embroidered versions of this pattern survive. A preliminary sketch at Charleston, however, augments the Courtauld Gallery's more finished design. Also at the Courtauld is a related circular design of a giraffe. On Duchamp-Villon's tondos, see G. H. Hamilton and W. C. Agee, *Raymond Duchamp-Villon*, 72–5.

90 "The Omega Workshops: Decorative Form and Colour."

91 "The Grafton Group," *Pall-Mall Gazette*.

92 R. Fry, in M. M. B., "Post-Impressionist Furniture." See also J. Collins, *Omega Workshops*, 42.

93 Judith Collins convincingly attributes the window, now at the Victoria and Albert Museum, to Fry, and proposes as its source Cézanne's *Les Moissonneurs* of 1876, which was in the second Post-Impressionist show (*Omega Workshops*, 88). The motif is general enough however to relate to any number of Cézanne's paintings. On the textile, see Collins, 45; R. Cork, *Art Beyond the Gallery*, 142; Crafts Council, *Omega Workshops*, 60; R. Shone, *Bloomsbury Portraits*, 118.

94 J. Collins, *Omega Workshops*, 285, n. 51.

95 M. M. B. "Post-Impressionist Furniture."

96 *Daily Mirror*, 8 November 1913, in R. Cork, *Art Beyond the Gallery*, 154.

97 *The Bystander*, 31 December 1913, 748.

98 V. Woolf, *Roger Fry*, 190. Bell's futurist style may account for Grant's later misattribution of the work to Wyndham Lewis (see J. Collins, *Omega Workshops*, 66–7).

99 P. G. Konody, *Observer*, 14 December 1913, in J. Collins, *Omega Workshops*, 66; compare his "Post-Impressionists at the Grafton Gallery." S. K. Tillyard puts Konody's anti-German stance in the context of the *Observer*'s overall editorial preoccupation "with threats to the British Empire and constitution" (*The Impact of Modernism*, 96–7).

100 V. Bell to R. Fry, 17 September 1913, Tate.

101 V. Bell to R. Fry, c. September 1913, Tate; 18 September 1913, *Letters*, 144 (which also reproduces her sketch of her panel).

102 G. B. Shaw to R. Fry, 22 May 1914, in F. Spalding, *Roger Fry*, 190.

103 For different versions of this anecdote, see Q. Bell, "Omega Revisited," 200, and F. Spalding, *Duncan Grant*, 137.

Chapter 8: A Modern Eden (1913–14)

1 J. Ruskin, *Works of Ruskin*, vol. 7, 13, in J. Spear, *Dreams of an English Eden*, 2. On Edenic rhetoric in the writings of other prominent Victorians and Bloomsbury's response, see C. D. Goodwin, "Economic Man in the Garden of Eden."

2 See for instance, J. Ruskin, *Sesame and Lilies*, lecture 3, *Works of Ruskin*, vol. 18.

3 A. Vallance, *The Art of William Morris*, 38, 58. Although Rossetti's Red House panels depicting the meeting of Beatrice and Dante on earth and again in paradise are among the most celebrated of his works today, the Adam and Eve composition is lost without visual record.

4 Pamela Diamand's unpublished memoir, "Recollections of Roger Fry and the Omega Workshops," records this technique, quoting Duncan Grant much later calling this work "the first action painting" (King's 13/22).

5 M. M. B. "Post-Impressionist Furniture." Authorship of this mural has been credited to Bell, aided by Grant and Doucet (J. Collins, *Omega Workshops*, 286, n. 69).

6 P. G. Konody, "Post-Impressionism in the Home." Bell's remark that her nursery presented "a most truthful portrait of Indian and African animal life" (V. Bell to V. Woolf, 17 August 1913, Berg), often quoted as referring to the Omega nursery, in fact refers to the nursery she painted at Gordon Square. The specific iconography of the nursery may also have been influenced by the fact that Fry's eleven-year-old son, Julian, had been inspired by his visit to the second Post-Impressionist exhibition to paint an elephant on his nursery wall at Durbins (P. Diamand, "Durbins," in H. Lee, ed., *A Cézanne in the Hedge*, 57).

7 P. G. Konody, "Post-Impressionism in the Home."

8 Two embroidered versions of this screen are discussed and illustrated in R. Shone, *Art of Bloomsbury*, 144–5. Three versions of Grant's designs on paper are extant, two in private collections and one in the Omega design files at the Courtauld Institute Galleries. The screen in the photograph of the antechamber—apparently identical to that in front of the mountainscape mural in press photos of the Omega showrooms—appears to be painted, perhaps because no embroidered version was ready by the workshops' opening. The likelihood of this scenario is strengthened by Vanessa Bell's report, in the same letter that describes her work on the exterior signs for the Omega, that, though work on an embroidered screen was going quickly, "I certainly shan't have it done in time" (V. Bell to R. Fry, 18 September 1913, *Selected Letters* 143–4). This passage is cited (though the letter is misdated to 15 September) in discussions of this screen (see R. Shone, *Duncan Grant Designer*, 12; and D. Scrase and P. Croft, *Maynard Keynes*, 62–3), where it is assumed Bell refers to the opening of the Ideal Home Exhibition on 9 October 1913, but the rest of the letter deals with preparations for the Omega's fall opening (technically a re-opening, since the showroom was temporarily opened in July).

9 J. Collins, *Omega Workshops*, 84.

10 C. Bell, *Art*, 128; this passage is discussed in Chapter 5.

11 D. Grant to J. M. Keynes, 30 April 1913, British Library.

12 V. Bell to V. Woolf, 3 May 1913, *Selected Letters*, 138–9. The folk-art figures—painted on cut-out flats, with something of the static solmnity of the mosaics—remained with Grant throughout his lifetime. They flank the door in a c.1930 photograph of his studio (in J. Lehman, *Virginia Woolf and her World*, 39), appear as the backdrop in a 1930s home-made production of Shakespeare's *Anthony and Cleopatra* (R. Shone, *Artists of Bloomsbury*, 28), and remain at Charleston today. One also dominates Grant's painting, *The Kitchen*, discussed in Chapter 11.

13 Twenty years later, the Museum of Modern Art would enact a similar dynamic, buttressing its presentation of modernism with exhibitions of "primitive" art, not only from Africa and Latin America (the *American Sources of Modern Art* and *African Negro Art* shows of 1933 and 1935), but also with "folk art" of the United States (*American Folk Art*, 1932).

14 R. Fry to G. L. Dickinson, 31 May 1913, *Letters of Roger Fry*, 369.

15 Edenic references were not unique to Bloomsbury among British modernists. In 1911, the first issue of *Rhythm*, the magazine of the British Fauves, carried an image of Eve on its cover (Sheila McGregor, "J. D. Fergusson and the Periodical 'Rhythm,'" in Scottish Arts Council, *Colour Rhythm and Dance*, 14). Around 1912, Wyndham Lewis painted two versions of *The Creation*, one of which is illustrated in the catalog to the second Post-Impressionist exhibition. In 1913 Edward Wadsworth showed a painting (lost without visual record) on this theme at the Dore Galleries' Post-Impressionist and Futurist exhibition (R. Cork, *Vorticism*, 105).

16 M. M. B., "Post-Impressionist Furniture." For attribution to Doucet, see F. Spalding, *Roger Fry*, 178; for at least partial attribution to Grant, see J. Collins, *Omega Workshops*, 51. Buttressing the case for Doucet's role is Fry's daughter's recollection of the Omega's opening, where "I watched [Doucet] painting a dress-length of crêpe-de-chine in liquid dyes with a motif, which like most of his work contained figures against a dense background of purples, blues, and peacock colours" (P. Diamand, "Recollections of Roger Fry and the Omega Workshops," unpublished ms., King's 13/22).

17 L. Strachey, "Christ and Caliban," in M. Holroyd, *Lytton Strachey*, 187.

18 L. Woolf, *Downhill All the Way*, 235.

19 A. Bennett, *The Pretty Lady*, 169–70; this connection is noted in R. Shone, *Bloomsbury Portraits*, 97.

20 Quoted in R. Shone, *Bloomsbury Portraits*, 99. *Pretty Lady*'s allusions to the Omega are strengthened by comparison with Bennett's journal recording how Fry's explanations sparked his appreciation for the Omega's work, "especially the stuffs"; the novel describes the "grey-haired, slouch hatted" "creative leader of the newest development in internal decoration," who "amused and stimulated" the narrator with his argument that "the only inspiring productions are the coloured cotton stuffs designed for the African native market" (169). Fabrics for African export were sold at the Omega.

21 N. Troy, *Modernism and the Decorative Arts in France*, 85–90.

22 "'Futurist' Woolwork."

23 C. L. Hind, "New Art and Newer Literature."

24 R. Fry, "What to do with our Artists."

25 M. Dickinson to J. Ashbee, 28 March 1920, King's. Janet Ashbee's negative assessment of the Omega is quoted in Chapter 7 at note 25.

26 Alpine Club Gallery, *Grafton Group*. An unexplained exception was made for the work of the two non-English painters included in the show, Wassily Kandinsky and Max Weber; viewers could learn the authorship of specific pieces by asking the exhibition secretary.

27 C. Bell, *Art*, 79; this comparison is drawn by J. Collins, *Omega Workshops*, 39.

28 C. Bell, *Art*, 81.

29 *Daily Telegraph*, 22 March 1913, in J. Collins, *Omega Workshops*, 40. No visual records remain of Lewis's *Three Women*.

30 "Picture Shocks." Grant recalled the dimensions of the work in a 1972 interview with David Brown (Tate). On the history of Grant's *Construction*, see J. Collins, *Omega Workshops*, 284, n. 28.

31 "The Grafton Group at the Alpine Gallery"; "The Grafton Group," *The Times*.

32 "'Futurist' Woolwork"; "The Grafton Group," *The Times*.

33 "Picture Shocks." *The Times* also described Grant's figure as "a man, who at first sight might be taken for a gorilla" ("The Grafton Group").

34 D. Garnett, *Flowers of the Forest*, 34. Garnett's characterization comes in an anecdote from 1915. That Grant reworked the painting in 1914 is documented in a letter, though this identifies the subject less specifically as "man and a church" (V. Bell to C. Bell, April 1914, Tate).

35 C. R. Ashbee, *Socialism and Politics*, 53.

36 C. R. Ashbee, *An Endeavor*, 38.

37 A. Service, *Edwardian Architecture*, 60.

38 C. M. "A Folk Art Revival."

39 C. L. Hind, "New Art and Newer Literature."

40 T. E. Hulme, "Modern Art," 342.

41 This was the occasion on which critics condemned the workmanship of Picasso's assemblages, as discussed in Chapter 7. Vildrac also sent works by Auguste Chabaud and Charles Vilette.

42 "Je constate cette fois pour la première fois que les tableaux français ne detonent pas sur nos toiles. C'est à dire que je crois que nous avons tellement profité par votre entente que maintenant nous commencons à batir de vraies toiles. J'en suis très fier" (R. Fry to C. Vildrac, 1 January 1914, King's). Sutton's translation downplays the force of Fry's language (*Letters of Roger Fry*, 377).

43 R. Fry to V. Bell, 7 May 1928, Tate. For this retrospective of artists associated with the London Group, the painting was, as Fry reports in this letter, "in some idiotic way . . . entitled 'The Leg,' which I can only suppose is someone's joke about the size of Eve's thigh." On the show, see D. Wilcox, *The London Group*, 22–3, which also reprints Fry's introduction to the catalog, where he regretted the loss of the "adventurous courage of the early years" manifest in the fact that "large-scale compositions have given place to works more suitable to the exiguity of modern apartments" (249).

44 Especially in the breasts and shoulders, Grant's Eve might be compared to Matisse's 1907 *Blue Nude* (Baltimore Museum of Art). As with Bell's nursery, however, Grant's experimentation with Matisse's stylistic mannerisms anticipates aspects of Matisse's later work. The rigid figures and stylized foliage of his 1913 *Adam and Eve* find their closest parallel in Matisse's 1916 *Bathers by a River* (Art Institute of Chicago), while his rotund Eve anticipates Matisse's nudes from the 1920s. A far earlier precedent for Grant's Eve might be Pontormo's mannerist *Leda*, which Grant would have seen in the Uffizi Gallery in Florence. On the sources and history of Grant's *Adam and Eve*, see Tate Gallery, *Illustrated Catalog of Acquisitions*, 157).

45 "Post Impressionism: The Grafton Group."

46 "The Normal and the Abnormal."

47 G. R. H., "The Grafton Group at the Alpine Gallery."

48 G. R. H., "The Grafton Group at the Alpine Gallery."

49 D. Grant to G. Mallory, 19 February 1914, in R. Shone, *Bloomsbury Portraits*, 2nd edn, 124.

50 "Post-Impressionism." Untitled clipping, *Daily Chronicle*, 11 January 1914, in D. Grant's scrapbook, Tate.

51 R. Davies, "The Grafton Group," 436.

52 A wide body of literature examines the sexual dynamics of Matisse and Picasso's early work. For pioneering studies, see C. Duncan, "Virility and Domination", and L. Steinberg, *Other Criteria*.

53 The accuracy of the study as a guide to the final image is suggested by several reviews that, not withstanding their overall disapproval, praised what the *Glasgow Daily Herald* called the "rainbow color" of *Adam and Eve* ("Post Impressionism: The Grafton Group").

54 S. Watney, *The Art of Duncan Grant*, 35. Strengthening the case for this identification is Eve's resemblance to the solitary female figure in Grant's 1912 *Tub* (Tate Gallery), a painting on a theme that in his later works clearly refers to Bell (as discussed in Chapter 11).

55 V. Bell to D. Grant, 14 January 1914, *Selected Letters*, 153–4.

56 R. Fry, in M. M. B., "Post-Impressionist Furniture."

57 R. Fry, "What to do with our Artists."

58 Preface to the Omega Workshops Catalog, rpt. *Roger Fry Reader*, 201.

59 Claims for the complexity of formal emotions in painting are consistent from Fry's 1909 "Essay in Aesthetics" (*Vision and Design*, 16–38) to his 1926 "Some Questions in Esthetics" (*Transformations*, 1–57).

60 R. Fry to D. Grant, 1914, *Letters of Roger Fry*, 377–8.

61 V. Bell to D. Grant, 25 March 1914, *Selected Letters*, 162.

62 V. Bell to C. Bell, 2 April 1913, Tate. Fiona MacCarthy intelligently explores the tension between the theory of joyful craftwork and its repetitive practice, noting that the most routine work was not carried out by the principal artists (Crafts Council, *Omega Workshops*, 13–18).

63 V. Bell to R. Fry, 6 February 1913, *Selected Letters*, 135. This idea updates marketing strategies of Sickert's Camden Town artists, whose "tradition of Saturday afternoon receptions at which the aristocracy might be lured, perhaps, into buying a picture by a promise of a glimpse of the Vie de Bohème" is described by participating artist Walter Bayes as relying on conversational references to such sexual indiscretions as female models cohabiting with male artists (in S. Watney, *English Post-Impressionism*, 35).

64 P. G. Konody, "Post-Impressionism in the Home."

65 R. Strong, "Why Omega is the last word."

66 R. Cork, *Art Beyond the Gallery*, 159; see also 149.

67 M. Amaya, "Omega's Dauby Doodles," 35.

68 V. Bell to R. Fry, 2 November 1912, Tate.

69 D. Grant, quoted in F. Spalding, *Duncan Grant*, 218.

Chapter 9: Abstraction and Design (1914–15)

1 R. Fry, unpublished lecture, 1926, King's 1/163.

2 "The Father of Post-Impressionism."

3 R. Fry, *Vision and Design*, 32. See also Fry's last defense of *Manet and the Post-Impressionists*, which asserts "a certain amount of naturalism, of likeness to the actual appearances of things is necessary, in order to evoke in the spectator's mind the appropriate associated ideas" ("Post-Impressionism," *Fortnightly Review*, 1 May 1911, rpt. *Roger Fry Reader*, 103).

4 R. Fry, *Vision and Design*, 239–40. Compare reiterations of this position in Fry's "The Grafton Gallery: An Apologia," *Nation*, 9 November 1912, rpt. *Roger Fry Reader*, 116.

5 R. Fry, "The Allied Artists," *Nation*, 2 August 1913, rpt. *Roger Fry Reader*, 151–3. Kandinsky had shown in previous Allied Artists exhibitions, but in these sprawling, unjuried, annual shows it was easy to overlook particular pieces. Fry seems to have first noticed Kandinsky in January of 1913, when he visited the collection of Michael Sadler, from whom he borrowed two Kandinsky watercolors, both called *Composition*, for the first Grafton Group show in March. On

Sadler's Kandinskys, see M. Sadleir, *Michael Ernest Sadler*, 237–40.

6   Michael Sadleir, son of the collector Michael Sadler, published two important defenses of Kandinsky in 1912, the first in *Art News* and the second in the journal *Rhythm*. While praising Kandinsky's theories of abstract art as the expression of the "common soul of man and nature," Sadleir also quotes the artist warning of a "double-danger": "Anti-naturalism may become pure pattern making, and form and colour mere symbols" ("After Gauguin," *Rhythm*, Spring 1912, rpt. J. B. Bullen, *Post-Impressionists in England*, 285–9).

7   There is no Omega box in Vanessa Bell's much more volumetric rendition of the same scene, now called *Still Life On the Corner of a Mantelpiece*, also at the Tate. The Omega flowers are described in W. Gill to D. Grant, 28 September 1967, Tate. Still lifes with Omega flowers by the Bloomsbury artists are illustrated and discussed in R. Shone, *Art of Bloomsbury*, 119–23, 131–5.

8   None of the central objects in this display is known to be extant. Omega marquetry was carried out by John Joseph Kallenborn's nearby firm (J. Collins, *Omega Workshops*, 59), and not all the pieces designed by the Bloomsbury artists were abstract: Collins illustrates a tray decorated with an elephant and a cabinet sporting giraffes (pl. VI, VII). The tray and dressing table illustrated here, along with an inlaid end table (Crafts Council, *Omega Workshops* no. F8), were among the first Omega furnishings decorated with abstract motifs.

9   Judith Collins notes one such comparison of a drawing called a rug design with Grant's 1915 painting *In Memoriam: Rupert Brooke* (*Omega Workshops*, 113).

10   S. Watney, *English Post-Impressionism*, 82. These ideas were also developed by Lisa Tickner in a lecture at the Tate Gallery, 23 January 2000. On Sickert's series, see W. Baron, *Sickert*, 108–9, 348–9.

11   J. Dunn, *A Very Close Conspiracy*, 243. Waldemar Januszczak reads the "snaky eyes and clumsy lips" of the portrait as "genuinely inventive pictorial invective" ("A lot of fuss"). In fact, all evidence of antagonism between the two women—which was never bad enough to preclude Hutchinson from buying and commissioning Bell's art—dates to after World War I. In 1915, Hutchinson's help finding housing outside London at a time when Bell's pacifism had ruptured other friendships (see Chapter 10) brought the two women into close and congenial contact. It is not clear that either of the 1915 portraits was the one that apparently distressed Hutchinson when it was displayed in 1917 (see R. Shone, *Art of Bloomsbury*, 105).

12   That Grant's images of the same sitters and poses show Bell to have been far more interested in creating rectilinear settings is shown by comparisons with Grant's portrait of Mary Hutchinson (private collection, illustrated in R. Shone, *Art of Bloomsbury*, fig. 106), and between Grant's and Bell's Iris Tree portraits (private collections, illustrated in G. Naylor, *Bloomsbury*, 228–9); and between his portrait of Bell and her self-portrait, discussed in Chapter 10.

13   A related argument could be made comparing Bell and Grant's simultaneously painted portraits of David Garnett, made at Eleanor (see Chapter 10) in the spring of 1915, though the issues and images are somewhat different. Garnett, Grant's lover, was a young man, and Bell's ambitions to integrate him into her modernist household were ambivalent. The background of her portrait of him is less like her rectilinear

abstractions than are her portraits of women, but, as in her images of women, she pulls colors from the background into the figure's eye and hair, creating a much more stylized—that is, self-consciously modernist—effect than Grant's depiction. Bell's portrait is at the National Portrait Gallery; Grant's is in a private collection.

14   V. Bell to V. Woolf, 17 August 1913, Berg. In one letter Bell discusses the level of detail in the work, saying "if I started to do much more to any one bit I should have to carry it all much farther," a remark more likely to apply to painting than to collage (V. Bell to C. Bell, mid-August 1913 Tate). A later letter from Clive Bell asks her not to "paint out the nursery," a remark, that, again seems more appropriate to painted murals than to collaged elements, which would be scraped off (C. Bell to V. Bell, early 1917, Tate). Other painted murals at Gordon Square are discussed later in this chapter.

15   This comparison was first noted by Judith Collins (*Omega Workshops*, 128). Other extant examples of Bell's abstract paintings do not seem to allude to landscape; in addition to my illustrations see two paintings, both called *Abstract Composition*, in private collections, illustrated in Anthony d'Offay Galleries, *Omega Workshops*, nos. 13, 14).

16   R. Shone, *Bloomsbury Portraits*, 84.

17   Apparently one of three works Fry exhibited under this title in 1915, the version in the Tate is the only one still extant (J. Collins, *Omega Workshops*, 120). Although the visual connections are not as clear, Grant said that copying Picasso's *Tête d'homme* prompted him to create the collaged version of *Interior at Gordon Square*, discussed below (F. Spalding, *Duncan Grant*, 172).

18   W. Sickert, "Monthly Chronicle," 118. As late as 1931, reviews still caustically recalled how Fry "ridiculously employed segments of omnibus tickets and rags in emulation of the Parisian 'farceurs'" ("The Art of Roger Fry").

19   It is not clear if the work now in the Courtauld Galleries is a finished painting or a preliminary sketch. Although its high degree of finish and size comparable to the *Essay in Abstract Design* suggest the former, photographic evidence remains of a different version (R. Shone, *Bloomsbury Portraits*, 143), and Fry used the verso of the extant work to plan decorations for his painted harpsichord (fig. 80). On Fry's fondness for one-point perspective—and his insistence on three-dimensionality in general—see my "The Fry Collection," 767–8, and *A Roger Fry Reader*, 121–4. One of Fry's now-lost abstractions exhibited in 1915 may have more closely resembled Grant's abstract paintings like the one analyzed later in this section, since Sickert's review describes it as using "patches of paper that have a mechanical pattern of marbling and such like ready printed on them" ("Monthly Chronicle," 118).

20   This work is dated by letters describing Grant at work on the scroll (V. Bell to R. Fry, 24 August 1914, *Selected Letters*, 169). The nature of the musical accompaniment he intended for his piece is debatable. In 1974, with Grant's agreement, the Tate filmed the scroll unwinding horizontally to the adagio movement from J. S. Bach's first Brandenburg Concerto. Grant's musical tastes in 1914 were more avant-garde, however, and he reported being influenced by a newspaper report of a concert of Alexander Scriabin's music performed with an accompaniment of colored lights (R. Shone, *Bloomsbury Portraits*, 142–3).

21   The connection to Apollinaire's journal—the issue of 15 March 1914—is made in Simon

Watney's definitive analysis of this piece (*Art of Duncan Grant*, 39–41). Buffet had published an essay on "Impressionisme musicale" in the journal *La Section d'Or*, which was published to coincide with the exposition by that name in Paris in 1912. Other comparisons have been made between Grant's scroll and Blaise Cendrars's and Sonia Delaunay's 1913 *La Prose du Transibérien et de la Petite Jehanne de France* (S. Watney, *English Post-Impressionism*, 98), a scroll combining poetry with abstract forms similar in concept to Grant's, but different in style. Grant denied knowledge of this precedent (interview with D. Brown, 1936).

22   W. Pater, *The Renaissance*, 135. For Fry, see *Roger Fry Reader*, 98, 100–1, 105, 116.

23   S. Watney, *Art of Duncan Grant*, 41.

24   The house-like form is central also to a collage by Grant owned by Simon Watney and to an anonymous collage featuring marbled and textured papers among the Omega designs at the Courtauld Institute Galleries.

25   All discussions of this work report Grant's much later statement that he intended to memorialize, as well, Rupert's brother Alfred, who was killed a month later.

26   On Kupka's metaphysical motivations, see Margit Rowell, "Frantisek Kupka: A Metaphysics of Abstraction" (Guggenheim Museum, *Frantisek Kupka*, 47–80). Kupka's influence on Bloomsbury has been asserted based on visual comparisons of his sparer paintings with Bloomsbury's abstraction and the fact that the Bloomsbury artists might have seen one example—his *Vertical Planes III*—at the Salon des Indépendants exhibition in Paris in 1913 (this idea is advanced tentatively in J. Collins, *Omega Workshops*, 114, and repeated with greater certainty in R. Cork, *Art Beyond the Gallery*, 172). There is some doubt that this painting was in the 1913 Indépendents show, however, and no evidence that anyone in Bloomsbury saw the show. No mention of Kupka appears in the artists' writings. Within Kupka's career, moreover, the spare abstractions were subsidiary to more curvilinear and crystalline styles of abstraction. *Vertical Planes III* was not exhibited again until 1926 and received no critical attention until it was shown at Museum of Modern Art in 1936. While comparisons between Kupka and Bloomsbury may help establish the group's place in the pre-war European avant-garde, the relationship seems to be one of coincidental affinity rather than direct influence or even common attitudes.

27   V. Bell to V. Woolf, 17 August 1913, Berg. Brooke was not on this trip, and Bell's interest was aroused primarily by the female Neo-Pagans. In another letter about the same trip, she remarked, "I wish we were all healthy young women like the Oliviers" (V. Bell to C. Bell, 12 August 1913, *Selected Letters*, 140).

28   V. Woolf to K. Cox, 13 August 1918, *Letters*, vol. 2, 267–8.

29   V. Woolf, "The Collected Poems of Rupert Brooke," *Times Literary Supplement*, 8 August 1918, rpt. as "Rupert Brooke," *Books and Portraits*, 85–9. The assessment of Brooke's poetry came from Frances Darwin Cornford.

30   The allusion to Greek funeral monuments is noted in S. Watney, *The Art of Duncan Grant*, 42.

31   S. Watney, *The Art of Duncan Grant*, 43. The foil is no longer in place on the painting. Richard Shone asserts it was added some years after the painting was first painted (*Bloomsbury Portraits*, 144), but Grant's interest in collage peaked in 1915, and Watney treats the foil as integral to the piece, concluding that its removal was "a regrettable over-restoration of the picture after the artist's death" (*Art of Duncan Grant*, 91).

Both Watney and Shone knew Grant in his later years and draw on their memories of his often conflicting accounts of his early work. Grant's use of the foil reflection contrasts with Woolf's memory of Brooke trying to find a poetic metaphor to suggest "the brightest thing in nature" and choosing "a leaf in the sun" (*Books and Portraits*, 88). The comparison points up the fact that Brooke was a more conventional artist and person than Bloomsbury recognized (on Brooke and his circle, see P. Delany, *The Neo-Pagans,* and M. Green, *Children of the Sun*).

32 Doucet died 5 March 1915; see notes 83 and 85 in Chapter 7. Gaudier died 5 June 1915; see Fry's obituary, R. Fry, "Gaudier-Brzeska."

33 R. Fry to M. Fry, 11 October 1915, in J. Collins, *Omega Workshops*, 124.

34 R. Fry to N. Wedd, 28 July 1915, King's. On the embroideries, see J. Collins, *Omega Workshops*, 105–6. Fry's "The Friend's Work for War Victims in France," is one of several essays (others at King's) on his experience for which he could not find a publisher in the pro-war periodicals of the era.

35 F. Spalding, *Roger Fry*, 199. Fragmentary versions of this anecdote are recorded in C. R. Ashbee's journal (14 November 1916, King's) and in R. Cork, *A Bitter Truth*, 80, which also illustrates the source photo. Fry attributed a favorable review in the *Daily Telegraph* to its reviewer having "found a moral unintended by me in the Kaiser picture" (in V. Woolf, *Roger Fry*, 203); compare *Letters of Roger Fry*, 390–1.

36 V. Bell to R. Fry, Summer 1916, Tate. This connection was made in F. Spalding, *Portraits by Roger Fry*, 11.

37 At an exhibition of Mark Gertler's work later in 1915, a viewer pasted a label reading "Made in Germany" onto a painting of Eve (F. Spalding, *Duncan Grant*, 166). For a discussion of this trend in relation to Vorticism, see R. Cork, *Vorticism and Abstract Art*, vol. 1, 269–70. For the comparative French phenomenon, see K. Silver, *Esprit de Corps*, 8–12.

38 D. Grant to O. Morrell, Autumn 1915, Texas. In addition to himself and Bell, Grant refers here to Robert Trevelyan and Harry J. T. Norton.

39 On Keynes, see V. Bell to C. Bell, 2 October 1914, Tate (quoted in Chapter 3, at n. 9).

40 D. Grant to O. Morrell, 14 May 1915, Texas. Although Bell decided to do the house up for let in 1915 (V. Bell to R. Fry, April 1915, Tate), it was not taken until 1916, and then by Keynes, who preserved it as the center of Bloomsbury's London operations (as discussed in Chapter 12).

41 R. Fry to V. Bell, 15 June 1916, *Letters of Roger Fry*, 398.

42 V. Bell to R. Fry, 22 June 1916, Tate.

43 R. Fry to V. Bell, 1 June 1917, Tate. The painting described here is probably the *Irises* illustrated in the catalog of Sotheby's London sale, *Modern British Irish Paintings, Drawings and Sculpture*, 10 May 1989, no. 63.

44 R. Fry to V. Bell, 6 April 1919, *Letters of Roger Fry*, 449. This abstraction was later destroyed in a fire without photographic record.

45 Duncan Grant, interviewed by Michael Shepherd, *Sunday Telegram*, 19 January 1975, quotation courtesy of Simon Watney.

46 F. Spalding, *Roger Fry*, 168.

47 J. Collins, *Omega Workshops*, 111.

48 D. Garnett, *Flowers of the Forest*, 34–5.

49 D. H. Lawrence to O. Morrell, 27 January 1915, *Letters of D. H. Lawrence*, vol. 2, 263.

50 S. Watney, *Art of Duncan Grant*, 43.

Section IV: An Aesthetic of Conscientious Objection: Bloomsbury's Wartime Environments

1 Bloomsbury was far from unique in experiencing World War I as a devastating historical rupture. C. F. G. Masterman's *England After the War* attests to the ubiquity of this sensation; see especially his chapter "The Plight of the Middle Class." For Bloomsbury, however, the war brought a special and acute sense of alienation borne of their lonely and difficult opposition to the conflict that created such profound change.

2 L. Woolf, *Beginning Again*, 197. Compare C. Bell, *Old Friends*, 80.

3 V. Woolf, "The Leaning Tower," *Collected Essays*, vol. 2, 162–81.

4 V. Bell, *Sketches in Pen and Ink*, 111–13.

5 Clive Bell, "Before the War," *Potboilers*, 247, 256.

6 V. Woolf, *Roger Fry*, 238.

7 R. Fry to R. Vildrac, 14 August 1914, *Letters of Roger Fry*, 380.

8 On the Debussy, see Chapter 7, n. 87. On Dickinson, see E. M. Forster, *Goldsworthy Lowes Dickinson*, 178–80. Fry also lodged an impoverished Belgian painter and his family, who "nearly wrecked the household," at Durbins (V. Woolf, *Roger Fry*, 201–2).

9 R. Fry to N. Wedd, 28 July 1915, King's.

10 V. Bell, *Sketches in Pen and Ink*, 112. Grant's recollection of the Omega's "short period," which "came to an undue, early end, mostly I think due to the war" (in S. Watney, *The Art of Duncan Grant*, 85) echoes Bell's focus on their abbreviated time in its history.

11 V. Bell to R. Fry, 25, 26 June 1915, Tate.

12 N. Hamnett, *Laughing Torso*, 81, 43. Winifred Gill later recalled, "When I remember Nina Hamnett at work it is always a candlestick she has in her hand" (W. Gill to D. Grant, 4 July 1966, Victoria and Albert).

13 R. Fry to V. Bell, 15 June 1916, *Letters of Roger Fry*, 398; see also D. Hooker, *Nina Hamnett*, 23, 96.

14 V. Bell to R. Fry, Summer 1916, Tate.

15 J. Collins, *Omega Workshops*, 133.

16 L. Gordon-Stables, "On Painting and Decorative Painting." A painted screen depicting a crowded carrousel and owned by the Sitwells is attributed to the Omega in S. Bradford, et al., *The Sitwells*, 55, though the discussion of its possible artists ranges incongruously beyond those associated with Omega. Richard Shone's suggestion of Dolores Courtney or Nina Hamnett is far more plausible ("The Sitwells and the Art of the 1920s and 1930s," 16).

17 R. Fry to V. Bell, 29 April 1916, Tate.

18 M. Troly-Curtin, "Phrynette's Letters."

19 V. Bell to R. Fry, early Spring 1916, Tate.

20 R. Fry to V. Bell, 29 April 1916, Tate. Fry's estrangement from Bell and Grant is discussed further in Chapter 12.

21 R. Fry to V. Bell, 9 July 1916; V. Bell to R. Fry, 17 August 1916, Tate.

22 R. Fry to V. Bell, late May 1917, Tate.

Chapter 10: Outposts of Peace: Eleanor and Wissett (1915–16)

1 C. Bell, *Peace at Once*, 13.

2 V. Bell to C. Bell, 17 June 1915, Tate.

3 The much misunderstood circumstances of this legal action are clarified in J. Beechey, "Clive Bell." Despite this censorship, Bell reiterated the main points of *Peace at Once* in "Art and War,"

published in 1915 in the *International Journal of Ethics* and anthologized in *Pot Boilers*, 231–46.

4 V. Bell to R. Fry, 16 August 1914, Tate.

5 V. Bell to R. Fry, 28 August 1914, Tate; V. Bell to V. Woolf, 22 August 1915, *Selected Letters*, 187.

6 V. Bell to R. Fry, 28 August 1914, Tate. On Stephen's and Grant's prevarications over military service, see J. MacGibbon, *There's the Lighthouse*, 89–90, 102; and F. Spalding, *Duncan Grant*, 157; a letter from Grant to Ottoline Morrell (7 September 1914, Texas) reiterates his intention to join the National Reserve.

7 V. Bell to R. Fry, 24 August 1914, Tate.

8 V. Bell to R. Fry September/October 1914, Tate.

9 This title, applied to the work some time after its initial sale as *Bottles*, seems confusingly to refer to the journalistic shorthand for an 1882 treaty between Germany, Italy, and Austria–Hungary. The title is first documented in a letter Fry wrote about seeing this piece in a private collection (R. Fry to V. Bell, 14 February 1923, *Letters of Roger Fry*, 532); at that remove he may have misremembered the phrase "Triple Entente," the term used for the treaty secretly negotiated between Britain, France, and Russia at the outset of World War I, which, to the dismay of pacifists, committed Britain to Germany's defeat without public debate. Frances Spalding suggests that the phrase "triple alliance" might also be drawn from news accounts about potential coalitions of striking workers in the news at the time (*Duncan Grant*, 151). The simplest explanation is that "triple alliance" was a phrase used casually at the period by many, Bell among them, to describe unions of three (see for example, V. Bell to R. Fry, Summer 1915, Tate).

10 R. Shone, *Artists of Bloomsbury*, 124.

11 V. Bell to R. Fry, 21 and 27 May 1915, Tate.

12 V. Bell to R. Fry, May 1915, Tate.

13 V. Bell to H. Young, 15 April 1915, *Selected Letters*, 175–6.

14 V. Bell to R. Fry, April 1915, Tate.

15 V. Bell to C. Bell, May 1915, Tate.

16 V. Bell to C. Bell, May 1915, Tate; V. Bell to D. Garnett, 12 April 1915, in F. Spalding, *Vanessa Bell*, 139.

17 V. Bell to D. Garnett, 22 September 1915, in F. Spalding, *Vanessa Bell*, 147.

18 V. Bell to R. Fry, 2 May 1915, *Selected Letters*, 177–8.

19 R. Fry to C. Bell, 9 May 1915, *Letters of Roger Fry*, 385.

20 V. Bell to R. Fry, 15 April 1915, Tate.

21 V. Bell to R. Fry, 14 June 1915, Tate.

22 R. Fry to V. Bell, 1911?, *Letters of Roger Fry*, 349.

23 V. Bell to R. Fry, 9? April 1915, *Selected Letters*, 174.

24 D. Grant to M. Hutchinson, 19 February 1915, Texas. V. Bell to R. Fry, May 1915, Tate.

25 V. Bell to V. Woolf, April 1915, Berg.

26 V. Bell to C. Bell, May 1915, Tate.

27 F. Spalding, *Vanessa Bell*, 146; *Duncan Grant*, 177.

28 V. Bell to V. Woolf, 31 August 1915, *Selected Letters*, 188.

29 Regulation 13 of the Defense of Realm Act is cited and discussed in F. W. Hirst, *The Consequences of the War to Great Britain*, 106–7.

30 J. MacGibbon, *There's the Lighthouse*, 102–3. M. Holroyd, *Lytton Strachey*, 615.

31 On the legal history of conscription, see R. C. Lambert, *Parliamentary History of Conscription in Great Britain*; on the resistance, see J. W. Graham, *Conscription and Conscience*.

32   V. Bell to Ottoline Morrell, 23 February 1916, Texas.

33   V. Bell to R. Fry, 1 January 1916, Tate.

34   D. Garnett, *Flowers of the Forest*, 123.

35   D. Grant to B. Grant, Spring 1916, in R. Skidelsky, *Hopes Betrayed*, 326.

36   V. Bell to O. Morrell, 21 February 1916, Texas.

37   V. Bell to R. Fry, 6 July 1916, Tate.

38   V. Bell to J. M. Keynes, 20 April 1916, *Selected Letters*, 193–4.

39   V. Bell to C. Bell, April 1916, Tate.

40   V. Bell to R. Fry, 27 April 1916, Tate.

41   V. Bell to R. Fry, Spring 1916, Tate.

42   V. Bell to R. Fry, 10 May 1916, Tate.

43   Q. Bell, "Omega Revisited," 201. The spattered wall papers Grant provided for Mary Hutchinson's River House (discussed in Chapter 12) suggest another version of this technique. See also Chapter 8, note 4.

44   D. Garnett, *Flowers of the Forest*, 114–15.

45   V. Bell to R. Fry, 26 June 1916, Tate. Strachey's essay "Monday June 26th 1916" catalogs his emotions during one day of his visit with Proustian detail (*The Shorter Strachey*, 21–37).

46   V. Bell to L. Strachey, 27 April 1916, *Selected Letters*, 194–5.

47   V. Bell to R. Fry, early Spring 1916, Tate.

48   D. Grant to V. Bell, 15 May 1916, Tate.

49   D. Grant to R. Fry, Spring 1916, Tate.

50   Exemplifying his much-rehearsed indifference to discussions of all but the formal aspects of his painting, Grant at various times placed the setting of this painting at Wissett, Charleston, and Gordon Square. The last claim has been rightly ruled improbable, based on the date of the painting (R. Shone, *Art of Bloomsbury*, 192), and the figs suggest Wissett.

51   V. Bell to R. Fry, 10 May 1916, Tate.

52   R. Fry to V. Bell, 7 June 1916, *Letters of Roger Fry*, 397.

53   V. Bell to R. Fry, August 1916, Tate.

54   V. Bell to R. Fry, 10 May 1916, Tate. The subject of Grant's copy, which Bell's letter acknowledges to be barely begun and unlikely to be finished, is unknown.

55   The difficulty of securing new art at this time is clear from the 1917 exhibition, *The New Movement in Art*, which Fry curated for the Royal Birmingham Society of Artists (a modified version of the show then traveled to the new Mansard Gallery on the top floor of Heal's, a fashionable housewares retailer near the Omega). Much of the show consisted of pre-war paintings by English and Continental artists drawn from Fry's collection.

56   R. Fry, "Children's Drawings," *Burlington*, June 1917, rpt. *Roger Fry Reader*, 266–7.

57   R. Fry to V. Bell, 7 March 1917, Tate.

58   R. Fry, preface, *Exhibition of Omega Copies and Translations*.

59   R. Fry to M. Fry, 2 May 1917, *Letters of Roger Fry*, 410.

60   R. Fry to V. Bell, 8 September 1916, *Letters of Roger Fry*, 402. This fresco in the upper church at Assisi, attributed to Buonamico Christofani Buffalmacco in Fry's day, is now given to the Master of the St. Cecilia altarpiece (see Q. Bell, *et al.*, *Charleston*, 56).

61   R. Fry to V. Bell, 6 April 17, *Letters of Roger Fry*, 408. For her part, Bell found photographs of Giottos Fry sent her "astonishing," with one "rather like a Matisse" (V. Bell to R. Fry, 6 July 1916, Tate).

62   R. Fry to M. Fry, 2 May 1917, *Letters of Roger Fry*, 410.

63   Not all the works exhibited in *Copies and Translations* are identifiable today (those in public

collections are indicated here). Bell sent five copies: two Giottos from Assisi, including *Saint Francis dividing his cloak with the beggar*; a Sassoferrato *Madonna* at the National Gallery; a Bronzino; and a 13th-century Persian miniature. Grant sent four copies: two of Piero della Francesca, the portrait of *Federigo da Montefeltro* (now at Charleston) and a detail of Mary and Joseph from the *Nativity* at the National Gallery (King's College, Cambridge), both copied around 1905–06; and two recent copies, one of a Sassetta, probably *The Mystic marriage of St. Francis* (King's); and one of Antonio Pollaiuolo's *Apollo and Daphne* at the National Gallery. Fry contributed eight copies: the St. Francis from Cimabue's Assisi frescoes, and the *Healing of Wounded Man of Lerida*, also from Assisi; a Raphael *Madonna*; the same Sassoferrato *Madonna* painted by Bell; a Ludger Tom Ring; a Byzantine enamel; and his own copy of Grant's *Ass*, itself based on a Persian miniature.

64   Fry filled gaps in the exhibition with three old copies by his wife and two by his fifteen-year-old daughter. On the exhibition, see J. Collins, *Omega Workshops*, 147–50.

65   R. Fry to V. Bell, 18 May 1917, Tate.

66   R. Fry to V. Bell, 17 June 1917, *Letters of Roger Fry*, 412–13.

67   R. Fry, *The New Movement in Art*, 5.

68   C. Bell, *Pot-Boilers*, 254–5. "Before the War" first appeared in the *Cambridge Magazine*, May 1917.

69   V. Bell to R. Fry, 5 May 1916, Tate.

70   D. Grant to V. Bell, 1 September 1916, Tate.

71   D. Garnett to L. Strachey, September 1916, British Library.

Chapter 11: Making Charleston (1916–17)

1   L. Woolf, *Beginning Again*, 178–9; compare V. Woolf to K. Cox, 25 June 1916, *Letters*, vol. 2, 102. J. MacGibbon, *There's the Lighthouse*, 105–7.

2   V. Woolf to V. Bell, 14 May 1916, *Letters*, vol. 2, 95.

3   V. Bell to D. Grant, late September 1916, in F. Spalding, *Duncan Grant*, 190–1.

4   M. Panter-Downes, "Charleston, Sussex," 60. Jill Johnston incorrectly reported, "During the war, half the year was spent at Charleston, the other half at Gordon Square in London" (*Secret Lives in Art*, 75); compare Gertrude Himmelfarb: "Charleston became the wartime center of the clan—'Bloomsbury by the Sea'" (*Marriage and Morals Among the Victorians*, 38).

5   D. Garnett, *Flowers of the Forest*, 130–41.

6   L. Woolf, *Beginning Again*, 60.

7   V. Woolf to V. Bell, 14 May 1916, *Letters*, vol. 2, 95; compare Q. Bell, *Elders and Betters*, 5.

8   C. Bell to V. Bell, winter 1916 and October 1916, Tate. Compare V. Woolf to V. Bell 22 January 1917, *Letters*, vol. 2, 137. The Bells sold one of Thackeray's manuscripts, which Vanessa had inherited from her father, to pay for the move to Charleston.

9   R. Shone, *Bloomsbury Portraits*, 164.

10   D. Garnett to D. Grant, September/October 1916, in F. Spalding, *Duncan Grant*, 191–2.

11   V. Bell to D. Grant, September 1916, in F. Spalding, *Duncan Grant*, 190–1. V. Bell to R. Fry, October/November 1916, Tate.

12   V. Woolf to M. Llewelyn Davies, 29 December 1916, *Letters*, vol. 3, 133. Grant's 1917 still life, *Paper Flowers*, depicting a corner of the mantel in the sitting room at Charleston, also records this brilliant wall color (R. Shone, *Artists of Bloomsbury*, 131–2).

13   Q. Bell and V. Nicholson, *Charleston*, 24.

14   Italian wallpapers were later collaged into this composition, which is documented in its first state in a photograph.

15   R. Fry, "The Artist as Decorator," *Colour*, April 1917 rpt. *Roger Fry Reader*, 208–9. An example of this Omega work is on the wall behind the bed commissioned by Lalla Vandervelde in 1916 (fig. 149).

16   Crafts Council, *Omega Workshops*, 48.

17   V. Bell to R. Fry, 3 August 1917, Tate. A subsequent letter from Fry refers to this as "D's mosaic," suggesting that Grant was primarily responsible. This is not the same patio as the "piazza," designed by Quentin Bell in 1946 and also decorated with bits of broken china and glass, in Charleston's garden today.

18   Simon Watney's *Duncan Grant* is especially eloquent on this point (51–4).

19   Grant's *Through a Window* is no. 35 in D. Scrase and P. Croft, *Maynard Keynes*. Keynes also bought *The Kitchen*, another image evocative of Charleston, discussed later in this chapter.

20   No visual record remains of the decoration on the lower panel of the door, which was accidentally broken in 1918; its current decoration dates from 1958 (Q. Bell and V. Nicholson, *Charleston* 23, 29). Grant's still life is similar to Bell's *Charleston Pond* (fig. 156), in which an Omega vase and a painted box, probably from the Omega, share colors with the pond seen through the window.

21   V. Bell to R. Fry, Winter 1917, Tate. Bell here calls this room "the studio," a purpose it served only briefly (see her *Selected Letters*, 200–1).

22   V. Bell to R. Fry, 22 February 1917, in Q. Bell and V. Nicholson, *Charleston*, 112.

23   V. Bell to R. Fry, July 1915, in R. Tranter, *Vanessa Bell*, 17.

24   In Q. Bell and V. Nicholson, *Charleston*, 96.

25   D. Garnett, *Flowers of the Forest*, 175.

26   The bench, much weathered in existing photographs, is no longer extant, but a pen sketch of the figures remains in a private collection. My thanks to Simon Watney for bringing this to my attention.

27   S. Watney, *Art of Duncan Grant*, 47; Crafts Council, *Omega Workshops*, 47.

28   This oil on board painting is now in the collection of Wolfgang Kuhl, London.

29   D. Garnett, *Flowers of the Forest*, 125.

30   V. Bell to R. Fry, June/July 1916; 26 July 1916, Tate.

31   D. Grant to V. Woolf, March 1917, in S. Watney, *The Art of Duncan Grant*, 46. The facetious tone of this anecdote is reinforced by Grant's claim that Bell was knitting stockings "(a thing she has never done before) and reading at the same time *Framely Parsonage* [a Trollope novel] through a pair of horn spectacles." The flamingos anecdote nevertheless, has been reported as fact in several accounts of Bloomsbury.

32   D. Garnett, *Flowers of the Forest*, 109.

33   V. Woolf, *Diary*, vol. 1, 78.

34   O. Morrell, *Memoirs*, vol. 2, 123. Several months after Morrell's visit to Wissett, Keynes reported to Bell, "Ott thought Wissett very nice and you all 'such darlings,' but couldn't help feeling that you would really be much happier if you were here at Garsington instead" (J. M. Keynes to V. Bell, 25 August 16, Northwestern).

35   V. Bell, *Selected Letters*, 182.

36   D. Grant to V. Bell, Spring 1916, Tate.

37   D. Garnett, *Flowers of the Forest*, 110–11. In this telling, Morrell's tastelessness is emphasized by Garnett's claim that the supposed Grant was largely his own work.

38 R. Fry, "The Artist's Vision," *Vision and Design*, 47–54.

39 V. Bell to R. Fry, June/July 1916, Tate.

40 V. Bell to D. Grant, 3 August 1921, *Selected Letters* 253. Bell's failure to sympathize with Vita Sackville-West's love of her ancestral castle, Knole, reflects the persistence of these values (V. Bell to V. Woolf, 2 February 1928, Berg).

41 V. Woolf to V. Dickinson, 10 April 1917; V. Woolf to Lady Robert Cecil 14 April 1917, *Letters*, vol. 2, 147–9,

42 D. Garnett, *The Flowers of the Forest*, 177.

43 A. Garnett in Q. Bell, et al., *Charleston*, 104–5.

44 A. Garnett, *Deceived with Kindness*, 35.

45 V. Bell to S. Sydney-Turner, 19 January 1917, *Selected Letters*, 202–3.

46 V. Bell to R. Fry, January 1918, *Selected Letters*, 209.

47 V. Bell to R. Fry, *c.* May 1917, Tate.

48 V. Bell to R. Fry, January 1918, *Selected Letters*, 209.

49 Comparisons to specific Matisse paintings are offered in F. Spalding, *Vanessa Bell*, 170–1; and in Susan Casteras, "Of Granite and Rainbow," Vassar College Art Museum, *Vanessa Bell*, 22.

50 V. Bell to R. Fry, 23 April 1917, Tate. This interpretation of *The Tub* as an assertion of order challenges common presentations of it as anguished autobiography. I endorse Mary Ann Caws's argument that other commentators' experiences of this painting are inflected by their own anxieties over Bell's unconventional romantic and sexual decisions, making *The Tub* "one of those test case pictures, about our own relation to our bodies . . . or, perhaps, our own pasts" (*Women of Bloomsbury* 171). Pessimistic interpretations of the painting are contradicted by the record in Bell's letters of this period of her sympathy with Hutchinson's emotions and her excitement about the picture (see V. Bell to R. Fry, January 1918, *Selected Letters*, 209).

51 Both Grant and Bell produced woodcut versions of their bathing images for the Omega's 1918 book, *Original Woodcuts by Various Artists*. The importance of Grant's painting, as well as an idea of its color, may be gleaned from the existence of a copy, painted around 1940, now in the Wolfgang Kuhle collection.

52 That this painting was begun in 1914 is suggested by its style and confirmed by both Grant's recollection and a preparatory sketch in a notebook dated 1914 (D. Scrase and P. Croft, *Maynard Keynes*, 27). A pencil sketch for the nude youth was owned by Fry and illustrated in a 1918 essay on drawing ("Line as Means of Expression in Modern Art," *Roger Fry Reader*, 327). The final version of *The Kitchen* was exhibited at the Omega late in 1917 (J. Collins, *Omega Workshops*, 155).

53 Bell is identified in Crafts Council, *Omega Workshops*, 88; the male figure is called a self-portrait in S. Watney, *Art of Duncan Grant*, 45; Douglas Turnbaugh identifies it as Julian Bell (*Duncan Grant*, caption to ill. 35).

54 I am not proposing the kind of specific source others have looked for in Bell's invocation of Matisse. Although Fry noted Bonnard's domestic commissions exhibited in Paris in 1910 ("The Autumn Salon") and praised him as an exemplary French formalist in 1911 ("Plastic Design," rpt. *Roger Fry Reader*, 139), Bonnard, unlike Matisse, was little noticed by Bloomsbury's critics until after World War I. Clive Bell claimed that "Duncan Grant, at the time when he was painting pictures which appear to have certain affinities with those of Bonnard, was wholly unacquainted with the work of that master" (*Since Cézanne*, 23; see also 107). Grant's correspondence with Keynes suggests that

he remained unaware of similarities between their work before 1919 (J. M. Keynes to G. Grant, 14 May 1919, in R. Skidelsky, *Hopes Betrayed*, 372). Rather than constructing a case for specific visual sources, I would emphasize that Bloomsbury's wartime art was dedicated to sustaining initiatives the group associated with French modernism in general.

55 "Advanced Pictures."

56 S. Watney, *Art of Duncan Grant*, 45.

57 O. Morrell, *Memoirs*, 230. Virtually all memoirs of Grant mention the charm of his childish manner (e.g. Q. Bell, *Elders and Betters*, 60–1.) A representative sampling of such sentiments expressed during or about this period would include Virginia Woolf's 1919 description of "that adorable man" wearing "an astonishing mixture of red waistcoats and jerseys, all so loose that they had to be hitched together by a woolen belt, and braces looping down somewhere quite useless. . . . a wonderful creature, you must admit, though how he ever gets through life—but as a matter of fact he gets through it better than any of us" (W. Woolf to V. Bell, 16 February 1919, *Letters*, vol. 2, 331). Woolf's diary records how in conversation Grant "stumbled along until, by means which he only knows the secret of, he had us all laughing until the tears came" (*Diary*, vol. 1, 198). Praising Grant's "genius" as a painter, Clive Bell described his art as "something fantastic and whimsical" (*Since Cézanne*, 111). Fry more completely merged the personality of the man with the qualities of his art, claiming the "happy dispositions of his nature reveal themselves in his work," noting, in particular, his *Woman in the Tub*, with its "odd and unexpectedly happy use of the accessories of the toilet as elements of the design" (*Duncan Grant*, v–ix).

58 L. Woolf, *Beginning Again*, 27. Grant noted this "very good description of Nessa" (D. Grant to A. Garnett, 19 May 1964, King's). Compare Julian Bell's poem about his mother—"such calm of mind"—and Virginia's Woolf's essay on Bell's "uncompromising" art: "No stories are told; no insinuations are made," her painting "would never mix itself up with the loquacities and trivialities of daily life. It would go on saying something of its own imperturbably" (both in S. P. Rosenbaum, ed., *The Bloomsbury Group*, 169–73; compare also Angelica Garnett in this source, 173–7).

59 V. Woolf to J. Bell, 20 June 1936, in D. Gillespie, *The Sisters' Arts*, 47.

60 J. Lehmann, *In My Own Time*, 95.

Chapter 12: Urban Outposts: River House and 46 Gordon Square (1916–19)

1 C. Bell, "Before the War," *Pot Boilers*, 253–6.

2 V. Bell to R. Fry, 17 August 1916, Tate. Fry in J. Collins, *The Omega Workshops*, 152.

3 D. Grant to B. Grant, Spring 1916, in R. Skidelsky, *Hopes Betrayed*, 326; this passage is discussed in Chapter 10.

4 "A Harmony of the Furnishing of Two Centuries," 41.

5 V. Bell to R. Fry, 2 August 1916, Tate.

6 V. Bell to St. J. Hutchinson, 24 August 1916, Texas.

7 This bed has been lost, but the study for the nude juxtaposes flat forms of a bright pink body and red flowers against a blue ground in ways that resemble Matisse's nudes in the 1930s (for example, his *Pink Nude* at the Baltimore Museum of Art). Though the black-and-white photograph of Mary Hutchinson's bedroom published in *Vogue* shows the finished bed to have corresponded very closely with the composition of the study, the

caption describes it as a "yellow bed" ("A Harmony of the Furnishings of Two Centuries," 41). This may refer to the frame into which the image was set, or might suggest that Bell switched to a different color scheme from the study; in either case, the inference of high-key Post-Impressionist color remains.

8 Fry's responsibility for the design of Vandervelde's bed—one of thirteen pieces of painted furniture still extant from her commission—is suggested by a page in the Omega files at the Courtauld Institute Galleries, which bears pencil drawings of the reclining nude in two styles, the second made by tracing the outlines of the first, and annotated "design for bedstead by Roger Fry (acc. Duncan Grant)." The sheer quantity of work involved in this commission, however, has aroused speculation that the actual painting was carried out by others working at the Omega (J. Collins, *Omega Workshops*, 142). If so, part of Fry's interest in this project may have been to show the effect of different hands executing the same composition in different styles, an issue that was always important for the Omega because of its policy of allowing many artists to work from common designs. The still life composition from the footboard, in fact, was reused with slight variations in handling on a toybox apparently unrelated to the Vandervelde commission (Anthony d'Offay, *Omega Workshops* no. 119).

9 "A Harmony of the Furnishing of Two Centuries," 40.

10 "Modern English Decoration," 44.

11 Cited in Chapter 7, n. 96; introduction to Section III, n. 1.

12 This design may replicate the drip-work "marbling" Quentin Bell remembered at Wissett (described in Chapter 10). Richard Shone claims the River House decoration depicts a volcano—the flying lava presumably—perhaps appropriate to a fireplace (*Art of Bloomsbury*, 147).

13 "The Chimney Piece," 39.

14 The date of this work is documented in a letter from Bell to Fry, reporting that "Duncan and I spent 3 or 4 days finishing Mary's room, the back part which we had always promised to do as soon as we could. I did a panel on the door and he one over the mantelpiece" (30 November 1919, Tate). *Vogue* illustrated Bell's door and referred to Grant's "fruit growing out of mantelpieces" in a way that linked this motif to her "flowers blossoming on doors" ("Modern English Decoration, 44).

15 C. Bell to V. Bell, 9 August 1916, Tate.

16 In the autumn of 1916, Keynes moved in with John Shepperd, a Cambridge classicist who was working as a translator in the War Office, and in March 1917 they were joined by Harry Norton, who had lived at Brunswick Square. The redecoration was carried out between August and September of 1918.

17 Keynes's motives in joining the Charleston household are sensitively analyzed by his biographer (R. Skidelsky, *Hopes Betrayed*, 332).

18 J. M. Keynes to D. Grant, 14 January 1917, British Library.

19 L. Woolf, *Beginning Again*, 241; *Downhill all the Way*, 59–60. On Bell's illustrations for Woolf, see D. F. Gillespie, *The Sisters' Arts*, 118–23. The Hogarth Press in 1927 produced a far more elaborate edition of *Kew Gardens*, with Bell's woodcuts merging with Woolf's prose on each page.

20 R. Fry to V. Bell, 7 January, 23 March 1917, Tate.

21 V. Bell to R. Fry, *c.* July 1918, Tate.

22 Fry's letters explain that he had to choose

between keeping Durbins or the Omega (R. Fry to R. Vildrac, 17 February 1916, King's).

23 R. Fry to V. Bell, 11 June 1917, *Letters* 411–12.

24 Both the painted and the collaged versions of Grant's *Interior at 46 Gordon Square* (figs. 117, 118) show red walls in this room, and red is also the background for Bell's and Grant's simultaneous portraits of Iris Tree, painted in 1915, probably in this space.

25 The pose is exactly that of a pastel by Grant, attributed to 1916 in the records of the Anthony d'Offay Gallery. Bell's letters from Charleston refer to her sharing the commission for the doors with Grant, reporting "we are doing them now and when Duncan gets a holiday we shall go to Gordon Square and put them up there and paint the doors around them" (V. Bell to R. Fry, 20 August 1918, Tate). Grant's biography reports that Bell's pregnancy prevented her from doing more than supervising the decorations from the sofa, and that the young painter Edward Wolfe assisted Grant at that stage (F. Spalding, *Duncan Grant*, 211). Since the images seem to have been painted during the summer at Charleston (whether on canvas later adhered to the door or on the doors themselves is unclear), *Vogue*'s attribution of the doors to Grant alone is in error ("The Art of Duncan Grant").

26 The window shown in *Charleston Pond* is sometimes misidentified as that of the downstairs sitting room, because the curtains are the same as in Grant's 1917 portrait of Bell (National Portrait Gallery), which is set in that space. But the wall colors are not the same and the vista is clearly from the upstairs room, which was Vanessa's studio at the time this was painted and later became Clive's bedroom. Bell and Grant around 1926 created a similar decoration for Clive Bell, another part-time Charleston resident, in his study at Number 50 Gordon Square. Once again, the top panel of a cupboard door shows the pond at Charleston as seen through a window with a still-life element on the sill, though here Keynes's simple jug has grown into an elaborate display of fruit around a formal compotier.

27 J. M. Keynes to F. A. Keynes, 21 September 1918, in R. F. Harrod, *Life of John Maynard Keynes*, 227.

28 R. F. Harrod, *Life of John Maynard Keynes*, 318.

29 These have been described as dining room doors (Crafts Council, *Omega Workshops*, 41) and given the later date of *c*.1921 (D. Scrase and P. Croft, *Maynard Keynes*, 28). There is no evidence for the later date, however, and their size and hardware accord with the caption accompanying *Vogue*'s 1923 illustrations of the doors in situ, which refers to them as "cupboard doors in a bedroom at Mr. J. M. Keynes's house in Gordon Square" ("The Art of Duncan Grant," 51); this article attributes the London and Rome scenes to Grant, and Paris and Istanbul to Bell.

30 On associations between stylistic conservativism and nationalist, pro-war subjects—especially in government commissions—see R. Cork, *A Bitter Truth* (especially 10, 73–81, 131–9, 167–70, 194–203). Even Grant, when conscientious objector exemptions to military service were canceled in April 1918, attempted to secure service with the Ministry of Information as a War Artist. This plan was thwarted by his refusal to apply for the required commission as a Major in the Army, forcing the Ministry to apply for Grant's time to the tribunal regulating conscientious objectors, a request that was rejected. Despite the delicacy of these negotiations, Grant could not bring himself to accept the Ministry's first proffered subject,

gangs of German prisoners doing farm work under supervision of a guard (F. Spalding, *Duncan Grant*, 206–7; Grant's letter refusing the prisoner subject is in R. Ross, *Robert Ross*, 328).

31 C. Bell, *Potboilers*, 239–40.

32 R. Fry, *Vision and Design*, 9. Grant cited at note 3.

33 J. M. Keynes, *Economic Consequences of the Peace, Collected Writings*, vol. 2, 6–7, 20, 158 n. 1, 169–70.

34 J. M. Keynes, *Economic Consequences of the Peace, Collected Writings*, vol. 2, 181–2.

35 V. Woolf to K. Cox, 12 February 1916, *Letters*, vol. 2, 77–8.

36 This transition is discussed in my "Through formalism."

37 Fry did hand print wallpapers for the London house that, after selling Durbins in 1919, he shared with his sister Margery, at this time a leader in penal reform. Perhaps in part because of the house's unfashionable location in Camden Town "close to Holloway prison—where no one else would dream of living," according to May Dickinson, Fry's ad hoc decorations, unlike schemes by Grant and Bell, were not seen as worthy of journalistic coverage, and, therefore, not recorded apart from descriptions by Fry's daughter. She recalled vibrant wallpapers installed "as panels to give height and shape and contrast to the rooms and to outdo any existing paint" (in R. Fry, *Letters of Roger Fry*, 59–60; Fry describes his printing process in R. Fry to V. Bell, 22 February 1919, Tate). By his own admission, Fry had to "everywhere do without repainting the hideous paint which is in horribly good condition. It was too expensive. I'm nearly ruined by the Omega" (R. Fry to V. Bell, 11 March 1919, Tate).

Section V: Re-Imagining Modernism

1 Lhote first used the phrase to describe Picasso's and Braque's recent painting (Nathalie Reymond, "Le rappel à l'ordre de André Lhote," in Université de Saint-Etienne, *Le Retour á l'ordre*, 222). Lhote, who was among the artists in the gallery of Fry's friend Charles Vildrac, was well known to Bloomsbury: twelve of his paintings were included in the second Post-Impressionist exhibition, from which Fry bought one for himself, and Fry's correspondence with Vildrac reveals that two plates by Lhote were consigned for sale at the Omega (R. Fry to R. Vildrac, 17 February 1916, King's—this tantalizing fragmentary reference to French modernist ceramics sold at the Omega offers no details). Lhote's phrase became popular enough that Jean Cocteau used it to title a collection of essays in 1926.

2 K. Silver, *Esprit de Corps*, 197–200.

3 R. Fry to J. Marchand, 8 September 1919, *Letters of Roger Fry*, 455–6. Clive Bell's "Order and Authority" appeared in the *Athenaeum* of 7 and 14 November (rpt. *Since Cézanne*, 122–38).

4 A. Lhote, "Cubism and the Modern Artistic Sensibility."

5 On Picasso's historical references see Chapter 6 of K. Silver, *Esprit de Corps*, and Alexandra Parigoris, "Pastiche and the Use of Tradition, 1917–1922," in E. Cowling and J. Mundy, eds, *On Classic Ground*, 296–308.

6 R. Fry to V. Bell, 3 July 1916, *Letters of Roger Fry*, 399–400. On how the drawing Fry cites "became known throughout the Parisian art scene and . . . taken as a sign of changing times," see K. Silver, *Esprit de Corps*, 69–73. Notes—probably from one of Fry's lectures—in one of Grant's undated sketchbooks refer to Picasso's mixture of "abstract work" with "his simultaneous production

of purely 'volumic' Ingresesque drawings" (reference courtesy of Simon Watney).

7 References to Ingres in Bloomsbury design would wait until the mid-Twenties and the over-mantel at Charleston (fig. 189). At that period, Grant also painted female musicians on small cabinet doors on a bookcase (now at Charleston) for Clive Bell's London flat in a style that might be described as an hommage to Picasso's hommage to Ingres.

8 K. Silver, *Esprit de Corps*, 200–3.

9 The *Studio*'s June 1918 review of the annual Royal Academy exhibition, for instance, praised the way that "since the war began British art has appreciably gained in stability and in steadfastness of purpose," concluding that this "strengthening of the artistic sentiment implies a development in the character of the nation, and a hardening in the popular resolve to fight things out to the end" ("The Royal Academy Exhibition"). See also Chapter 12, n. 30.

10 C. M. "Notes of the Month," xvi–xviii.

11 F. Rutter, "Extremes of Modern Painting," 311, 313, 314–15.

12 J. M. Murry, "English Painting and French Influence," 600.

13 A. Clutton-Brock, "Mr. Roger Fry."

14 C. Phillips, "Paterson Gallery."

15 R. Fry, *Cézanne*, 31. Fry echoes influential French texts, including Le Corbusier's and Amédée Ozanfant's co-authored *Après le cubisme* of 1918, and Blaise Cendrar's 1919 "Pourquoi le 'Cube' s'effrite," as discussed in K. Silver, *Esprit de Corps* 227–34, 321–2. Fry's changing attitudes are manifest much earlier in his letters (R. Fry to V. Bell, 6 April 1919, *Letters*, 449, discussed in Chapter 9).

16 R. Cork, "Richard Cork's London Art Review."

17 S. Watney, *English Post-Impressionism*, 116; see also 107. Compare R. Mortimer, *Duncan Grant*, 12.

18 R. Fry, "Mr. Duncan Grant's Pictures," 587.

19 R. Fry, "Vanessa Bell and Othon Friesz," *New Statesman*, 3 June 1922, rpt. *Roger Fry Reader*, 348–9. I have argued that Fry's reading of Bell's art is deeply inflected by his sense of her personality (*Roger Fry Reader*, 311) and, though Fry would have denied it, one might see his claims as reflecting his continuing jealousy over her intimacy with Grant.

20 V. Bell to R. Fry, June 1922, *Selected Letters*, 267–8.

21 Transcript of conversation with Simon Watney, 26 July 1976, courtesy of Watney.

22 S. Watney, *English Post-Impressionism*, 116.

Chapter 13: Public Figures' Private Spaces: King's College, Cambridge and 52 Tavistock Square (1920–4)

1 Bell reported Grant's departure for Brighton (V. Bell to R. Fry, 11 November 1918, *Selected Letters*, 216), but several accounts place him in London, among them D. Garnett, *Flowers of the Forest*, 189–93; and D. Carrington to N. Carrington, quoted in M. Holroyd, *Lytton Strachey*, 749.

2 F. Spalding, *Duncan Grant*, 200.

3 V. Bell to R. Fry, *c.* July 1918, Tate.

4 D. Grant, unpublished journal, in F. Spalding, *Duncan Grant*, 201.

5 On Grant's desire for children, see F. Spalding, *Duncan Grant*, 200. Both Vanessa and Clive Bell also welcomed the baby (F. Spalding, *Vanessa Bell*, 175–6).

6 D. Grant, unpublished journal, in F. Spalding, *Duncan Grant*, 200.

7 V. Bell to R. Fry, 22 February 1918, in R. Shone, *Bloomsbury Portraits*, 179, which offers a favorable analysis of the picture.

8 R. Shone, *Bloomsbury Portraits*, 179; F. Spalding, *Duncan Grant*, 200.

9 V. Bell to M. Snowden, 25 December 1923, in A. Garnett, *Deceived with Kindness*, 40. Compare V. Bell, *Selected Letters*, 253.

10 V. Bell to R. Fry, 6 February 1919, *Selected Letters*, 230; V. Bell to J. M. Keynes, 30 January 1919, in F. Spalding, *Duncan Grant*, 215.

11 V. Bell to R. Fry, 15 August 1920, Tate.

12 V. Bell to M. Vaughan, 16 March 1920, *Selected Letters*, 237. Madge Vaughan, daughter of John Addington Symonds and sister of Katharine Furse (whose house and its influence on Bell is discussed in Chapter 1), had married a Stephen cousin.

13 V. Bell to R. Fry, 24 March 1920, Tate (an abridged version is in *Selected Letters*, 238–9).

14 V. Bell to R. Fry, 11 April 1920, Tate.

15 V. Bell to J. M. Keynes, 15 May 1920, in F. Spalding, *Duncan Grant*, 227. On Keynes's investments, see R. Skidelsky, *Economist as Savior*, 41–3.

16 D. Grant to V. Bell, late August 1920, Tate.

17 V. Bell to R. Fry, 15 August 1920, Tate.

18 R. Skidelsky, *Hopes Betrayed*, 301; Skidelsky argues that "by writing [*The Economic Consequences of the Peace*] he renounced the privacy which he had always valued so highly" (400). As early as 1906, a letter to Mary Berenson warned her away from Keynes as "a disciple of the deplorable practices of Oscar Wilde" (in C. Hession, *John Maynard Keynes*, 58), and a letter from Grant to Vanessa Bell refers to "the scandal about Maynard that has reached the 'upper ten'" (early 1919, Tate). On the paranoia over homosexuality at the period, see P. Hoare, *Wilde's Last Stand*, and Lucy Bland, "Trial by Sexology?: Maud Allan, *Salome*, and the 'Cult of the Clitoris' Case," in L. Bland and L. Doan, eds, *Sexology in Culture*, 183–98.

19 V. Bell to R. Fry, 26 August 1920, Tate.

20 Dennis Proctor assumes Signorelli is the model (*Autobiography of G. Lowes Dickinson*, 10), while Simon Watney proposes Piero and Castagno (*Art of Duncan Grant*, 51). The case for Ferrara (illustrated in the November 1919 *The Burlington*) is convincingly made in Hirschl & Adler Galleries, *British Modernist Art*, which also makes a garbled case for Castagno, misidentifying the location of the relevant frescos (136). Bell's letters from Italy specifically mention the artists' excitement over Signorelli, Piero, and Castagno (V. Bell to R. Fry, 27 April 1920, *Selected Letters*, 242). Such proto-Renaissance precedents are sufficient to explain any similarity to Burne-Jones's 1882 music panels, a comparison made by Richard Morphet to argue for Bloomsbury's place in a specifically English art history (in R. Shone, *Art of Bloomsbury*, 26).

21 R. Fry, "Explorations at Trafalgar Square," 211. Such comments do not flatly contradict his earlier readings—in Fry's 1910 "The Post-Impressionists—II" he cited "the great monumental quality of early art, of Piero della Francesca" (*Roger Fry Reader*, 91)—but the new valorization of their "science" differs from Fry's earlier emphasis on proto-Renaissance self-expression in contrast to "representative science" (see, for example, *Roger Fry Reader*, 95).

22 R. Fry, "Notes on the Exhibition of Florentine Painting," 4.

23 R. Shone, *Bloomsbury Portraits*, 234–5.

24 "An Economist and Modern Art," 46–7.

25 The fireplace is illustrated in "The Chimney Piece."

26 The chair is illustrated in "Modern Embroidery" and "Modern English Decoration," and discussed in R. Shone, *Duncan Grant: designer*, no. 30.

27 V. Woolf, *Diary*, vol. 2, 231.

28 In R. Skidelsky, *Economist as Savior*, 37; on the unreliability of this memoir, see 52–3, 55.

29 V. Woolf to V. Bell, 27 April 1924, *Letters*, vol. 3, 104.

30 V. Woolf, *Diary*, vol. 2, 283.

31 For comparisons, see Bell's 1934 paintings of Woolf in front of one panel of the decoration; the oil version is in a private collection (illustrated in R. Shone, *Art of Bloomsbury*, 224), the looser watercolor Bell gave to Leonard Woolf is at Monk's House. Blurry casual photographs (in the Tate Gallery Archives) also document the room's greater variety and density of furnishings, as well as bookish clutter. Although this project has been misunderstood as comprising just three panels (H. Lee, *Virginia Woolf*, 562; F. Spalding, *Duncan Grant*, 265), photographs reveal two sets of three figurative panels, a seventh figurative panel over the fireplace, and an undetermined number of smaller blank panels with crosshatched frames.

32 The framing elements in an extant cabinet for Angus Davidson (discussed in Chapter 14) are compared to Woolf's decorations as "again, in tomato red" ("Modern English Decorations," 106).

33 V. Woolf to V. Bell, 7 April 1929, *Letters*, vol. 4, 37.

34 "Modern English Decoration," 43.

35 "Modern English Decoration," 45; W. Plomer, *Autobiography*, 249.

36 D. P. Corbett, *The Modernity of English Art*, 58.

37 "The Contemporary Style in Decoration." The *Vogue* article featuring the Woolfs' sitting room reiterates this comparison ("Modern English Decoration"). Roger Fry's unpublished 1924 lecture "The Present outlook: painting and applied art" also contrasts Bloomsbury modernism to revival styles (King's 1/113).

38 D. P. Corbett, *The Modernity of English Art*; such phrases permeate this text, with these quotations taken from 1, 58, 2, 100, 7. Complaining that Bloomsbury defined modernism "as a practice in which modernity was addressed through formal significance and the cultivation and refinement of the individual sensibility," Corbett concludes: "In fact, modernity as a subject was not explicitly addressed at all" (77). Although Corbett lists "the reconfiguration of social and gender roles" among the "events of modernisation" (11), his fixation on images of industry forecloses consideration of such issues, which (in an argument developed through this and the following chapter) I see as central to any understanding of Bloomsbury's modernism in the twenties.

39 Following his opening postulation of a single "experience of a modern culture," D. P. Corbett argues that, following World War I, the "direct registration of the modern seemed for over a decade to be all but impossible in English painting" (*The Modernity of English Art*, 1; see also Chapter 4, "The End of Painting: Wyndham Lewis").

40 See especially Lewis's 1930 *Apes of God*, which turns on his former patrons, the Sitwells. Lewis's 1926 *The Art of Being Ruled* presents much of its argument for authoritarian government as a response to the shifting sex/gender norms characterized by, in the title of one chapter, "The 'Homo' The Child of the 'Suffragette.'" Lewis's fixation on the ideal of a single leader helps explain

his inability to sustain collaborative endeavors. After angrily withdrawing from the Omega Workshops during its first year of operation (as discussed in the Introduction) Lewis established his own competing Rebel Art Centre nearby, which produced curtains, scarves, fans, and painted furniture. It collapsed after only four months over the same issue that led Lewis to break with the Omega: the contributing artists' resentment of anonymous production, which effectively assigned all credit for the institution and its works to the organizer (R. Cork, *Vorticism*, 159). Lewis blamed his subsequent professional setbacks on persecution by Fry; his charges, made in John Rothenstein's *Modern English Painters* (207–8), are perpetuated and exaggerated throughout J. Meyers *The Enemy*. But after Lewis broke with the Omega, Fry invited him to continue to exhibit with the Grafton Group (J. Collins, *Omega Workshops*, 69). This pattern was repeated after the war in relation to the Russian Ballet. Lewis first tried to design for the ballet, then when these plans fell through, attacked on the ballet in his 1927 *Time and Western Man*, a "rewriting of history" in which, as Corbett puts it, "Lewis's marginality takes on a heroic cast" (142). Corbett's claim that Lewis's "embittered and paranoid" texts are indicative of the structural condition of post-war culture ignores examples of this pattern in his pre-war behavior.

41 D. P. Corbett, *The Modernity of English Art*, 146.

42 W. Lewis, *Time and Western Man*, quoted in D. P. Corbett, *The Modernity of English Art*, 144. Lewis called for "some modified form of fascism" as the best government for "anglo-saxon countries as they are constituted today" in his 1926 *Art of Being Ruled* (369); his sympathetic *Hitler* appeared in 1931.

43 V. Woolf, *Diary*, vol. 2, 283.

44 V. Woolf to J. Case, 12 April 1924, *Letters*, vol. 3, 97; this letter has been misunderstood as referring to panels in Woolf's bedroom (H. Lee, *Virginia Woolf*, 562).

45 E. M. Forster, *Howards End*, 12.

46 L. Woolf, *Downhill all the Way*, 76.

47 Bell's sketch for the cover shows longer, flatter bridges that more clearly evoke those of London (illustrated in J. Lehmann, *Virginia Woolf and her World*, 50).

48 On the phrase "moments of being," see V. Woolf, *Moments of Being*, 70. Lewis repeatedly attacked the disorder of stream-of-conscious fiction as represented by James Joyce and Ezra Pound—two more former colleagues he renounced—in *Time and Western Man*.

49 D. P. Corbett, *The Modernity of English Art*, 101. As with his treatment of "gender roles," Corbett initially acknowledges the city's associations with the "freedoms and opportunities of modernity" but then ignores this aspect of urban culture in his focus on industrial regimentation.

50 Recent feminist analysis of the richness of urbanism may be traced to Jane Jacob's influential *The Death and Life of Great American Cities*; the term "inexhaustibility" is taken from a particularly thoughtful example of this genre: Iris Marion Young's "The Ideal of Community and the Politics of Difference," in L. Nicholson, ed., *Feminism/Postmodernism* (see especially 318–19).

51 L. Woolf, *Barbarians at the Gate*, 123 (this passage is discussed in the Introduction). On Virginia Woolf's relationship to Bloomsbury's visual aesthetics in the Twenties, see my "Through Formalism."

1 "A Bachelor Flat in Bloomsbury." "Modern English Decoration," 45.

2 See D. Turnbaugh, *Duncan Grant and the Bloomsbury Group*, and *Private*.

3 Woolf coined "Old Bloomsbury" to introduce an autobiographical essay written in the early 1920s and posthumously published under that title (*Moments of Being*, 181–201). Clive Bell used the phrase in his 1954 essay, "Bloomsbury" (*Old Friends*, 130).

4 The popular deployment of Woolf's name and image as an icon of "high culture" in the "timeless pantheon of British 'greatness'" has been remarked by many feminist scholars; see, for example, Jane Garrity, *Virginia Woolf in the Age of Mechanical Reproduction*, 185–7). On the tendency of even feminist scholarship to normalize Woolf, see my "Bloomsbury Bashing", and R. Marler, *Bloomsbury Pie*, 184–7.

5 In addition to the commissions discussed in this chapter, Grant and Bell oversaw the painting of Adrian and Karin Stephen's rooms at 50 Gordon Square and the entrance hall and five-story stairwell at the Stracheys' Number 51. These projects, completed in the early twenties and poorly documented, seem to have consisted of carefully chosen colors applied with the irregular handling that Fry's essays on interior design describe as significant of artistic sensibility (see Chapter 11). Grant's assistant for the latter project, the young artist Robert Medley, recalled "a complicated mixture of powder colours, whitening and size prescribed by Duncan and resembling 'French grey,' . . . which I had to brew up over a gas ring in the dining room" (*Drawn from the Life*, 53).

6 L. Strachey to V. Woolf, 28 September 1918, in M. Holroyd, *Lytton Strachey*, 784. On Strachey's role in bringing women and gay men together in Bloomsbury, see Chapter 3; on the ideal of the city as a college, see Chapter 1.

7 R. Skidelsky, *Economist as Savior*, 12. The first meeting of the Memoir Club is described in Virginia Woolf's *Diary* on 6 March 1920 (vol. 2, 23).

8 The founding members of the Cranium Club in 1924 are listed in R. Skidelsky, *Economist as Savior*, 13.

9 F. Partridge, *Memories*, 90–1; compare D. Garnett, *The Familiar Faces*, 11–12. On the modernity of cocktails and dancing, see R. Graves and A. Hodge, *The Long Week-End*, 38, 42.

10 M. Green, *Children of the Sun*, 209–10; D. Goldring, *Odd Man Out*, 226–8.

11 V. Bell to Q. Bell, 26 January 1932, 22 June 1930, *Selected Letters*, 357, 354.

12 R. Fry, *Transformations*, 80, 85; this essay incorporates remarks about "snobbism" that appeared in many of Fry's lectures beginning around 1924.

13 V. Bell to V. Woolf, 9 March 1928, Berg. With characteristically vehement inconsistency, Clive Bell's 1921 "Plus de Jazz" (*Since Cézanne*, 213–30) denounces the influence of the café culture of which he, by his own admission, was a part.

14 V. Woolf, *Moments of Being*, 210.

15 V. Woolf, *Diary*, vol. 2, 202.

16 D. Grant to V. Bell, 7 July 1919; V. Bell to R. Fry, 15 October 1919, Tate.

17 O. Sitwell, *Laughter in the Next Room*, 179. Fry's portrait of Edith Sitwell (Sheffield City Galleries), the brothers' sitting room, and the Omega screen are illustrated in S. Bradford, et al., *The Sitwells*, 55, 56, 64.

18 R. Fry, "Modern French Art at the Mansard Gallery," *Athenaeum*, 8 August 1919, rpt., *Roger Fry Reader*, 339–42. C. Bell, "The French Pictures at Heal's"; Bell engaged a lively exchange of letters following his review (*Nation*, 6 September 1919, 672; 27 September 1919, 766).

19 V. Woolf, *Diary*, vol. 3, 24; see also 132–3, *Diary*, vol. 4, 332, and *Letters*, vol. 3, 352, on Woolf's lifelong admiration for Edith Sitwell. Woolf was five years older than Edith Sitwell, but the Sitwells' reputation as leaders of the younger generation is registered in her surprise at the closeness in their ages.

20 These networks extended far beyond Bloomsbury and deserve their own study. On this era, see R. Graves and A. Hodge, *The Long Week-End*, especially the chapters on "Women" and "Sex". Martin Green's *Children of the Sun* offers the most thorough examination of sexual subculture in Britain in the twenties, though its focus on Brian Howard and Harold Acton is acknowledged to be tangential to the young men closest to Bloomsbury (69). Nerina Shute's marvellously titled memoir, *We Mixed our Drinks*, charts, albeit condescendingly, one journalist's coming-to-terms with the increasingly visible communities of "pansy boys" and lesbians (see especially 23, 76, 82–4).

21 W. Lewis, *Apes of God*, 132. Where the Sitwellian figures Lewis focuses on are given satirical names, Bloomsbury—like Gertrude Stein—is named simply as context.

22 F. Partridge, *Memories*, 90.

23 Autobiographies by David Garnett, Leonard Woolf, and John Lehmann exemplify this. On Garnett's shifting standards of candor, see R. Marler, *Bloomsbury Pie*, 80–3. Lehmann's reticence about the importance of homosexuality in his autobiography is particularly striking in contrast to his thinly fictionalized novel, *In the Purely Pagan Sense*.

24 Both in J. Nobel, ed., *Recollections of Virginia Woolf*, 142, 169; see also R. Mortimer, "Lively Portraits." Even in the relatively open environment of the avant-garde in the twenties, pressures to be "cured" of homosexuality prompted Edward Sackville-West and "several other wretched undergraduates" to enroll in a psychiatric clinic in Germany (L. Strachey to D. Carrington, 3 June 1923, in H. Holroyd, *Lytton Strachey*, 856–7).

25 Clare Balfour Sheppard, unpublished memoir, in H. and M. Cecil, *Clever Hearts*, 219.

26 M. Green, *Children of the Sun*, 210.

27 V. Woolf to J. Raverat, 24 January 1925, *Letters*, vol. 3, 155. Bloomsbury parties, Woolf reported a few weeks later, were now attended by "40 young men; all from Oxford too, and three girls, who are admitted on condition that they either dress exquisitely, or are some man's mistress, or love each other. . . . Lytton gravitated to the 40 young men, and was heard booming and humming from flower to flower" (V. Woolf to J. Raverat, 5 February 1925, *Letters*, vol. 3, 164).

28 M. Holroyd, *Lytton Strachey*, 829. R. Skidelsky, *Economist as Saviour*, 92. The climate at Cambridge is suggested by Duncan Grant's comparison, in a 1924 latter from Berlin, of "the homosexual cafés that are so famous here" to a "Cambridge party at a rather shabby undergraduate's rooms" (D. Grant to V. Bell, 16 June 1924, Tate).

29 Cecil Beaton, in J. Ross, *Beaton in VOGUE*, 7.

30 V. Woolf, *Diary*, vol. 2, 266. V. Woolf to J. Raverat, 9 November 1924, *Letters*, vol. 3, 145.

31 Angus Davidson in J. Noble, ed., *Recollections of Virginia Woolf*, 53.

32 F. Spalding, *Vanessa Bell*, 227. Other painted doors and a painted screen by Davidson were featured in *Vogue* (early July 1926, 66; late August 1926, 30); *Creative Arts* featured a room decorated by Davidson in August 1928; his painted furniture and *écriture* overmantel are illustrated in D. Todd and R. Mortimer, *New Interior Design*, pl. 74, 80, 82; his painted record cabinet for Mortimer is visible in photographs of Grant's and Bell's mural, and a rug he designed is visible in an illustration of the painted serenade cabinet (both discussed later in this chapter) when the latter was reproduced in the *Architectural Review*, May 1930, 222. Douglas also designed a rug at Charleston, and embroidered some chair seats to Grant's design (V. Woolf, *Letters*, vol. 3, 150).

33 V. Woolf to J. Raverat, 26 December 1924, *Letters*, vol. 3, 150.

34 John Lehmann, in J. Noble, ed., *Recollections of Virginia Woolf*, 30. Lehmann's own fondness for this kind of gossip is clear in another memoir, which recalls how, conversing with Lytton Strachey, he "egged him on to tell me many fond and malicious stories of Leonard, one of his oldest Cambridge friends" (*Whispering Gallery*, 186).

35 V. Woolf to J. Raverat, 24 January 1925, *Letters*, vol. 3, 155–6.

36 V. Woolf, *Diary*, vol. 3, 51.

37 V. Woolf, *Diary*, vol. 3, 89. In addition to recording her impulse in her diary, Woolf tested the response of her inner circle in a letter to Bell, reporting cautiously, "I have asked her to write her life, but I gather that there are passages of an inconceivable squalor" (V. Woolf to V. Bell, 2 June 1926, *Letters*, vol. 3, 270)—the connotations of "squalor" are suggested in a contemporary letter from Vita Sackville-West describing a Bloomsbury party in Gordon Square that she attended with Woolf: "The conversation became personal and squalid. I was amused" (V. Sackville-West to H. Nicholson, 1 July 1926, in *Vita and Harold*, 152).

38 Vita Sackville-West reported this episode to her husband, Harold Nicolson, commenting: "So poor Todd is silenced since her morals are of the classic rather than the conventional order. . . . The affair has assumed in Bloomsbury the proportions of a political rupture" (in L. Cohen, "Virginia Woolf, Fashion, and British *Vogue*," 10).

39 Extant is at least one portrait, *Edward Sackville-West at the Piano* (private collection). In addition to the images of Angus Davidson recorded in Elizabeth Richardson's *A Bloomsbury Iconography*, a 1923 portrait was included in the Christie's sale of 21 March 1996, and a reclining nude for which he was the model is in the Wolfgang Kuhle collection; Grant also used a photograph of Davidson (reproduced in D. Turnbaugh, *Duncan Grant* no. 18, identification from Tate Gallery Archives) as the basis for a figure in paintings of male bathers, the composition of which is repeated in at least two versions (one in a private collection; the other at the National Gallery of Victoria, Melbourne). Davidson was among the mourners at Grant's burial (D. Turnbaugh, *Duncan Grant*, 106).

40 Lehmann records that when he took over Rylands's rooms in 1931, this house was shared by the Davidson brothers (*Whispering Gallery*, 166). Rylands and Douglas Davidson had in 1925 sublet rooms from Vanessa Bell in Gordon Square (J. Noble, ed., *Recollections of Virginia Woolf*, 141).

41 Interview in J. Noble, ed., *Recollections of Virginia Woolf*, 169; listing Bloomsbury's members around Gordon Square, Mortimer recalled, "I went to live there chiefly for that reason" (167).

42 V. Woolf, *Diary*, vol. 2, 264.

43 This design was adapted from decorations Grant had painted on the concrete wall of a porch (since destroyed) for the painter Peter Harrison at Moon Hall in Surrey (V. Bell, *Selected Letters*, 283; R. Shone, *Bloomsbury Portraits*, 235). On Grant's and Bells' copies of Giorgione, see S. Watney, *The Art of Duncan Grant*, 60.

44 V. Woolf to L. Strachey, 3 September 1927, *Letters*, vol. 3, 419.

45 C. Bell to V. Bell, 9 June 1930, Tate.

46 "Modern English Decoration," 45. J. Betjeman, "1830–1930," 241, 292.

47 "Modern English Decoration," 66. The wall around the flower piece was later also ornamented, as seen in fig. 2 of R. Shone, *Duncan Grant designer*.

48 Alan Pryce-Jones, in J. Pearson, *The Sitwells*, 154. Osbert Sitwell's proud identification with this style of decoration is exemplified in his essay "Moving House" (in *Queen Mary and Others*).

49 P. Nash, *Room and Book*, in *Paul Nash: Writings*, 90. Laurence Whistler also cites the use of the term "amusing" as characteristic of the period (*The Laughter and the Urn*, 97).

50 O. Sitwell, *Nobel Essences*, 63. Memoirs from outside the avant-garde record the slow spread of the "neo-Victorian fashion" for "gay little drawing-rooms furnished with an amusing chaise-longue" and "madly funny statue" through the middle class into the early 1930s, always associated with the Sitwells' influence (N. Shute, *We Mixed our Drinks*, 76).

51 No phenomenon better exemplifies the Amusing ideal of blending Victorian and vanguard aesthetics than in the now-forgotten vogue for modernist embroidery. Design publications promoted this work as "modern" both because its format suited the smaller scale of new dwellings and because the motifs reflected their makers experience of "abstract designing" associated with "Cubism and the like." (M. Hogarth, *Modern Embroidery*, 10; R. R. Tatlock, "Modern Designs in Needlework," 209. The former draws from a 1932 exhibition at the Victoria and Albert, the latter reviews an exhibition at the Independent Gallery in 1925; both illustrate Bloomsbury needlework, which—like Grant's embroidered chair for Keynes (fig. 165)—tends to replicate on a smaller scale the iconography of lilies and *fêtes champêtres* of their mural decorations. The Davidson brothers were part of this vogue: Douglas designed a rug now at Charleston and Angus embroidered chair seats to Grant's design (cited in V. Woolf, *Letters*, vol. 3, 150).

52 Quentin Bell in "Charleston on *Kaleidoscope*," 48. R. Fry, "The Ottoman and the Whatnot," and "The Artist's Vision," both in *Vision and Design*, 39–54; although Fry does not mention Grant specifically, his letter to Bell about these articles regrets that "I couldn't get in your chairs" (R. Fry to V. Bell, 22 June 1919, Tate). Grant bought the chairs in 1918; they appear in his *Still Life with Prie-Dieu* (private collection, illustrated in S. Watney, *Art of Duncan Grant*, pl. 36), and *Hollyhocks on a Prie-Dieu at Charleston* (private collection, illustrated in Spink Gallery, *Duncan Grant and Vanessa Bell*, no. 46).

53 That Ruskin's commendation of the "useless" lily (as discussed in Chapter 7) evolved into a primary symbol of the Aesthete is evident in Gilbert and Sullivan's *Patience*, a satire of Wilde in which lilies are repeatedly invoked: Bunthorne, the impostor Aesthete, advises men, "you will rank as an apostle in the high aesthetic band/ If you walk down Piccadilly with a poppy or a lily in your medieval hand;" he confesses his actual un-Aesthetic attitude to the audience with, "A languid love for lilies does not blight me;" and is forced in

the finale to remain "contented/ With a tulip or lily."

54 "Modern English Decoration," 44. The serenade motif echoes a painting in the same room of a woman at a balcony, visible in the photograph of the sideboard.

55 Compare Virginia Woolf's narration of Mrs. Ramsay's rumination over a dish of fruit on the table in the famous dinner-party scene in *To the Lighthouse*: "Rose's arrangement of the grapes and pears, of the horny pink-lined shell, of the bananas, made her think of a trophy fetched from the bottom of the sea, of Neptune's banquet, of the bunch that hangs with vine leaves over the shoulder of Bacchus (in some picture), among the leopard skins and the torches lolloping red and gold. . . . [I]t seemed possessed of great size and depth, was like a world in which one could take one's staff and climb up hills, she thought, and go down into valleys. . . ." (150–1).

56 On the development of Bloomsbury's formalist theory in relationship to literature in the 1920s, see my "Through Formalism."

57 On the theater's links to femininity and homosexuality, see M. Green, *Children of the Sun*; on interior decoration, see P. McNeil, "Designing Women."

58 Specific precedents are suggested by Richard Shone (*Art of Bloomsbury*, 196), and Simon Watney (*Art of Duncan Grant*, 47).

59 A preliminary sketch for this screen is illustrated in S. Watney, *Art of Duncan Grant*, 36, which also records Grant's claim about the models; two pastel and gouache color studies are illustrated in Spink, *Duncan Grant and Vanessa Bell*, 29–30.

60 "A Modern Fresco Painter." Severini's illustrations of harlequins and pierrots also appeared in the Sitwells' publications (see S. Bradford, et al., *The Sitwells*, 91, 95), and the Sitwells evoked harlequin in such titles as Edith and Osbert's 1916 *Twentieth Century Harlequinade and other Poems*, and Sacheverell's 1922 *The Hundred and One Harlequins*. On the use of *commedia dell'arte* figures in post-war Continental art, see E. Cowling and J. Mundy, eds, *On Classic Ground*, 14.

61 *Observer* [London], 2 September 1913, in N. Macdonald, *Diaghilev Observed*, 76. "The Contemporary Style in Decoration," 50. Grant's screen is linked to *Petrouchka* in S. Watney, *Art of Duncan Grant*, 36; it has also been tied to the Russian Ballet's *Carnaval* (R. Shone, *Duncan Grant designer*, 25).

62 "The Art of Duncan Grant."

63 The term "camp," in circulation in England by the late nineteenth century, first appeared in dictionaries of slang in 1909, defined as "actions and gestures of exaggerated emphasis. . . . Used chiefly of persons of exceptional want of character, e.g. 'How very camp he is'" (in Mark Booth, "*Campe-toi!*: On the Origins and Definitions of Camp," in F. Cleto, ed., *Camp*, 75). Jean Cocteau is said to have introduced the term to a mass audience in *Vanity Fair* in 1922 (Philip Core, from *Camp: The Lie that Tells the Truth*, in Cleto, 81); see other references from the 1920s and before in Cleto (459). On the historical roots of camp, see also Thomas A. King, "Performing 'Akimbo'" (M. Meyer, ed., *The Politics and Poetics of Camp*, 23–50).

64 Susan Sontag, "Notes on Camp," 1964, rpt. F. Cleto, *Camp*, 55. The theoretical literature on camp is enormous, but from the first efforts at definition, commentators address the characteristics described here. Sontag's famous summary of camp qualities is dedicated to Wilde, and defines camp as "a certain mode of Aestheticism" that "sees everything in quotation

marks." Jack Babuscio's often-anthologized 1977 "The Cinema of Camp" defines the four definitive aspects of camp as irony, aestheticism, theatricality, and humor. Both discuss camp's relationship to homosexuality (in Cleto, 53–64, 117–35). Philip Core's 1984 *Camp: The Lie that Tells the Truth* asserts that camp "originated as a Masonic gesture by which homosexuals could make themselves known to each other. . . . and remains the way in which homosexuals and other groups of people with double lives can find a *lingua franca*" (in Cleto, 82). On Wilde and camp, see Gregory W. Bredbeck, "Narcissus in the Wilde" (in M. Meyer, ed., *Politics and Poetics of Camp*, 51–74).

65 D. Grant to V. Bell, 31 July 1932, Tate. The references are to Victorian actors Henry Irving and William Charles Macready. See also Chapter 5, n.8

66 V. Woolf to M. Joad, 20? July 1924, *Letters*, vol. 3, 120. This party is also remembered by Frances Partridge (*Memories*, 92) and described—misdated to 1926—in H. and M. Cecil, *Clever Hearts*, 215–16.

67 The application of these categories to individuals in Bloomsbury is transformed from unhappy anachronism to pernicious misrepresentation by Phyllis Rose's citation of heterosexual activity by men like Grant and Keynes to prove that they were not really homosexual (*Woman of Letters*, 77; on the persistent homophobia of this text, see my "Bloomsbury Bashing").

68 Woolf abandoned *Vogue* when Todd was fired, placing her article, "Cinema," already underway, with another periodical (L. Brosnan, *Reading Virginia Woolf's Essays and Journalism*, 50). This ended Bloomsbury's longstanding relationship with *Vogue*, begun under the previous editor Elspeth Champcommunal, war-widow of a French painter, who encouraged the Omega and befriended Fry and Bell, sharing their unconventional attitudes toward child-rearing and sexual propriety (see R. Fry to V. Bell, 11 August 1921, Tate).

69 This aspect of *Vogue*'s history deserves further study. Among other gay contributers to the magazine at this period was the American designer Robert Locher (B. Fahlman, "Modern as Metal and Mirror," 109–12).

70 Cecil Beaton's upside-down, heads-only photographs of groups of stylish young women and men including the Sitwells, published in *Vogue* in 1927 and 1929, exaggerate the androgynous effect of their hair-styles (in J. Ross, *Beaton in Vogue*, 102, and G. Howell, *In Vogue*, 47). On "jumpers," see R. Graves and A. Hodge, *The Long Week-End*, 41–2.

71 L. P. Smith to V. Woolf, quoted in L. Brosnan, *Reading Virginia Woolf's Essays and Journalism*, 56.

72 V. Woolf to J. Raverat, 24 January 1925, *Letters*, vol. 3, 154.

73 V. Woolf to L. P. Smith, 28 January 1925, *Letters*, vol. 3, 158. Such confident assertions are ignored in Jane Garrity's "Virginia Woolf, Intellectual Harlotry, and 1920s British *Vogue*," which fails to register Woolf's powerful—if ambivalent—attraction to Todd's lesbianism. Garrity grimly misreads Woolf's anxieties about shopping with Todd, her characterizations of Todd as an animal, and metaphors of prostitution in her descriptions of her relationship with Todd as unambiguously condescending and pejorative, when this language might be profitably compared to Woolf's epistolary rhetorics of affection and flirtation, which regularly assign animal identities to her intimates and construe sexual meanings from ordinary social interactions (in P. Caughie, ed., *Virginia Woolf in the Age of Mechanical Reproduction*, 185–218).

74 "The Contemporary Style in Decoration," 74.

75 R. M[ortimer], "Duncan Grant at the Independent Gallery," 57. "The Contemporary Style in Decoration," cites Grant's designs for *Twelfth Night* at the Théatre du Vieux Colombier, crediting them with contributing "largely to the success of this production, a success greater than that of any play which has been produced at this remarkable theatre" (74).

76 "The Art of Duncan Grant," 51; R. M[ortimer], "Duncan Grant at the Independent Gallery," 57.

77 R. Fry, "Mr. Duncan Grant's Pictures," 587. That Milton's poem signified erotic high-jinks is evident from Lytton Strachey's casual invocation of the term "Comus uproar" to describe a Bloomsbury party at which, he claimed, "the nudity reached a pitch—Duncan in bathing-drawers, and Marjorie with nothing on but a miniature of the Prince Consort" (L. Strachey to C. Lamb, 23 June 1913, in M. Holroyd, *Lytton Strachey*, 538).

78 C. Bell, *Since Cézanne*, 106, 111. Consistent with their attitudes about the fashionable culture of the twenties in general and about Grant's relationship with Vanessa Bell, Clive Bell's deployment of this rhetoric is more enthusiastic than Fry's anxious plea that the artists resist the facile charms of Grant's "poetic" sensibility.

79 C. Bell, *Since Cézanne*, 109.

80 O. Wilde, "The Portrait of Mr. W. H." [because the revised and definitive version of this 1889 text was not published until 1920, it is not in the multi-volume *Complete Works of Oscar Wilde* to which other writings of Wilde's are cited; this quotation comes from the misleadingly titled one-volume *Complete Works of Oscar Wilde* (London: William Collins, 1996), 1174.] Shakespeare was also among the authors anthologized in Edward Carpenter's *Ioläus*, a compendium of homoerotic texts published in 1902.

81 L. Strachey, *Lytton Strachey by Himself*, 82. Strachey's fascination—even identification—with the androgynous Elizabeth I culminated in his popular *Elizabeth and Essex* of 1928, a book that itself became part of the twenties' culture of androgyny; on Strachey and Elizabeth, as well as on the twinning of Shakespeare and Plato as icons of homoeroticism, see B. Fassler, "Theories of Homosexuality as Sources of Bloomsbury's Androgyny," 238, 243, 251.

82 "The Contemporary Style in Decoration," 51.

83 By the same token, the juxtaposition of three Grant paintings illustrated in R. Shone, *Bloomsbury Portraits*, 2nd ed., 196–7, shows the same pose used for a male nude in the *c.1921 The Bathers* (owned by Keynes and now by King's College) and for the nymph in a *c.1926 Nymph and Satyr* (owned by Raymond Mortimer, now in a private collection), and its reverse view in a 1921 reclining male nude.

84 V. Woolf to L. Strachey, 3 September 1927, *Letters*, vol. 3, 418. The caption under a photograph of Grant "disguised rather than dressed as a Spanish dancer" records that "Duncan's modest pose before the photographer gives but little notion of his scandalously indecent appearance when he was on stage, with the gramophone playing Spanish music" (Q. Bell and A. Garnett, *Vanessa Bell's Family Album*, 127).

85 S. Watney, *Art of Duncan Grant*, 50.

86 The lease on Charleston remained far from secure, as the Bells' correspondence reveals (V. Bell to C. Bell, 29 February 1928, Tate).

87 R. Fry to H. Anrep, 18 April 1925, *Letters of Roger Fry*, 564.

88 R. Fry to M. Mauron, 14 April 1925, *Letters of Roger Fry*, 563.

89 The upraised elbow pose recalls Michelangelo's famous *Dying Slave*, and might be seen as responding to Boris Anrep's mosaic on Lytton Strachey's mantel of the well-known Hellenistic marble the *Sleeping Hermaphrodite*. Grant's pleasure in his design is suggested by the fact that, around 1932 when the plaster on which the figures were painted deteriorated, he eschewed his usual instinct to revise, copying the figures onto the new plywood facing of the hearth (details of the deteriorated figures are illustrated in Q. Bell and V. Nicholson, *Charleston*, 72). The overmantel floral still lifes were also repainted in a somewhat simplified style at a later date (the originals are visible in fig. 187 from the mid-1930s).

90 Q. Bell, et al., *Charleston*, 100; see also "Charleston on *Kaleidoscope*," 48.

91 Bell's views of the garden statuary include the *c.1935, The Garden at Charleston*, and 1956 *Statue Reflected in the Pond, Charleston* (both in private collections). Her still lifes with statuary include the 1947 *Still Life with Bust and Flowers* (Charleston), 1949, *Still Life with White Roses* (private collection), and *c.1950 Still Life with Bust by Studio Window* (City of Aberdeen Art Gallery and Museums); the first and last are illustrated in R. Shone, *Art of Bloomsbury*, 233.

92 Grant's painting is probably contemporary with his 1972 *The Mantelpiece at Charleston*, illustrated in R. Shone, *The Art of Bloomsbury*, 241. Comparable paintings by Bell that seem to quote vignettes at Charleston include her *c.1947 Autumn Flowers on the Studio Mantelpiece*, *c.1948 Flowers on the Studio Mantelpiece*, *c.1950 Flowers in a Painted Vase* (also set on the studio mantel), and *c.1957 Poppies in the Garden Room* (all in private collections).

93 S. Sitwell, *Southern Baroque*, 7–8, 27.

94 R. Fry to V. Bell, 25 May 1932, Tate.

95 Arts Council, *Thirties*, 84.

Chapter 15: The End of Amusing: Interiors and Commissions (1927–36)

1 In November 1979, a special issue of the *Architectural Review* on the 1930s presented the decade as "the period when a pioneering few" pushed "the steady advance of the Modern Movement" (note the singular construction) by "the discarding of historic styles" in favor of a functional approach to "clients' needs and an acceptance of modern materials and techniques." This "unassuming and straightforward" modernism was favorably contrasted to a emerging post-modernism defined simply as "stuck-on historic ornament or symbolism" (photo captions, 274). By 1990, the lead author of this issue, Tim Benton, in "The Myth of Function" was dissecting "the collapse of Modernism" in Britain, placing the blame on faulty early theorization of functionalism. Also in 1990, Julian Holder's "'Design in Everyday Things': Promoting Modernism in Britain" attacked "the British establishment" for its "serious misreadings–which reduce Modernism to a style and which continue to our own day," though his acknowledgment of successful working-class housing projects built in Britain during the 1920s and '30s in non-Modernist (usually Neo-Georgian) styles undermines his claim that the International Style was alone "'honest' and appropriate" for mass housing (both in P. Greenhalgh, ed., *Modernism in Design*, 41–52, 123–43).

2 H. de C., "Paris 1925," 14; V. Blake, "Modern Decorative Art," 24.

3 V. Blake, "Modern Decorative Art—II," 181; "Modern Decorative Art," 24. Three years later, the *Architectural Review*, attempting to stimulate British responses to Continental design, claimed, "the idea of the *ensemblier* is English, but, like other English inventions of the nineteenth century, it was exploited abroad" ("Arnold Bennett, H. G. Wells, Bernard Shaw, and Harrods," 164).

4 Silhouette, "The Modern Movement in Continental Decoration," 123.

5 G. H. G. Holt, "The Merit of Le Corbusier." *The Architect's Journal* also favorably reviewed *Towards a New Architecture* in its 21 September 1927 issue. On Le Corbusier's importance to discourses of modernist functionality in Britain, see Tim Benton, "The Myth of Function" in P. Greenhalgh, ed., *Modernism in Design*, 43–9.

6 H. de C. "The Heresies of a Painter," 186–7; this author's longstanding familiarity with Bloomsbury's aesthetic theories is suggested by the language of his coverage of the Art Deco show, where he described "new expressive forms taking over the emotional intention of old" and praised the "nervous insistence upon the significance of form" in French design ("Paris 1925," 14). The parallels between Fry's *Heresies* and Le Corbusier's writings are discussed in Chapter 2.

7 R. Fry to V. Bell, 16 May 1929, Tate. Bloomsbury's antagonism toward both the new avant-garde and the forces of convention is exemplified by this letter's report of Fry's London landlord forbidding him to paint his front door the color he had chosen.

8 R. Fry, untitled manuscript, c. 1932, King's, 1/129 (my dating of this document rests on its reference to a radio broadcast that is almost certainly Fry's 1932 "Sensibility *versus* Mechanism"). This draft overlaps with another (King's 1/150), which shares the same topic and some pagination, suggesting the presentation of this material in numerous lectures. Fry rehearsed his argument again in a memorandum he insisted upon adding to the official report, issued in 1932, by the Committee on Art and Industry appointed by the Board of Trade under the leadership of Lord Gorell, to promote the exhibition of "articles of everyday use and good design." The quotations in my synopsis of Fry's argument against Corbusian modernism are from the two lecture manuscripts; his exact visual references are unclear from the slide cues, which refer to "Corbusier interior," "Queen Anne interior," "Corbusier wall," etc.

9 F. Partridge, "Sitwells and Bloomsberries," 27. Anrep's links to Bloomsbury date back to 1912, when he organized the Russian section of the Second Post-Impressionist Exhibition, and in 1925 he created a mosaic mantelpiece for Lytton Strachey featuring a reclining nude in the pose of a Hellenistic sleeping hermaphrodite, whose face resembled Strachey's companion Dora Carrington. Anrep's participation in the "Amusing Style" is epitomized in his 1922 mosaic in the London home of Mr. and Mrs. William Jowitt titled *Various Moments in the Life of a Lady of Fashion*, which Fry praised for its "completely modern theme" rendered "in a manner which belongs to the artistic vision of to-day and to no other period in this history of Art" (R. Fry, "Modern Mosaic and Mr. Boris Anrep," 277).

10 W. Lewis, *Apes of God*, 512. Lewis's satires of the avant-garde rely on associating it with—in addition to sexual and gender deviance—Jewishness and new money. Despite occasional flashes of wit, Lewis's satire is most notable today for its anticipation of the rhetorical strategies of fascist anti-intellectualism.

11 C. Bell, "Our Stone Population."

12 V. Woolf to V. Bell, 14 April 1927, *Letters*, vol. 3, 362; compare *Letters*, vol. 4, 108.

13 V. Woolf, *Diary*, vol. 4, 225; V. Woolf to E. Smyth, 8 January 1935, *Letters*, vol. 5, 362.

14 O. Sitwell, "This Strange Country," 11–13. Years later, Sitwell's elegy to Whistler, who died in World War II, continued to assert the modernism of his historical quotation, claiming that his art "could have existed in no other age save that in which it flowered, and yet it was almost wholly dependent on the past for its inspiration" (*Noble Essences*, 303).

15 Despite the rather Bloomsburyish caryatids and canephoroe on the dust-jackets of four of the five volumes of Osbert's autobiographical essays (reproduced in S. Bradford, et al., *The Sitwells*, 181; compare especially the cover of Fry's 1927 *Flemish Art*), his text repeatedly distinguishes him from "those who were led by the late Mr. Roger Fry," whose "enthusiasm for pure painting, and its progress, induced in him a rather contemptuous attitude towards survivors from other epochs" (*Left Hand Right Hand*, 246; see also 269), and exaggerate his claims to avant-garde leadership, asserting, for instance, that "the advanced painters of England" were unaware of the Russian Ballet before World War I (*Great Morning!* 270; on Bloomsbury's pre-War relationship to the Russian Ballet, see Chapter 3). Sitwell acknowledges Bloomsbury's influence before 1918, only to date "its so rapid decline" to the beginning of his own career (*Laughter in the Next Room*, 20–1). Throughout his late writings, Sitwell casts himself as forward-looking and Continental by contrasting Fry as old-fashioned and English. Sitwell, for instance, cites Fry inaccurately as a "fervent admirer and disciple of Alma-Tadema's genius" (*Left Hand Right Hand*, 251; see also *Noble Essences*, 186) and as someone who knew nothing about European cuisine and ate only tinned food (*Noble Essences*, 193; *Laughter in the Next Room*, 46–7); although Fry did not live as luxuriously as Sitwell, his *boeuf en daube* was immortalized by Virginia Woolf in *To the Lighthouse*.

16 D. Grant to R. Fry, 1929?, Tate.

17 R. Fry, "Introduction," *Georgian Art*, 3, 7, 9.

18 O. Sitwell, "This Strange Country," 11.

19 "The Work of Some Modern Decorative Artists," 29, 30. This commission was finished by 1926 as indicated by a letter (V. Woolf to V. Bell, 19 May 1926, *Letters*, vol. 3, 264), which is misdated to 1927 in R. Shone, *Bloomsbury Portraits*, 235.

20 Illustrated in *Vogue* in 1926 as "big cartoons for a decoration by Duncan Grant and Vanessa Bell" (C. Bell, "The London Group and Sargent," 54), these are almost certainly the "sketches for the panel[s] in Mary's room" that Grant said he would send to the London Group exhibition (D. Grant to V. Bell, 26 December 1925, Tate).

21 V. Sackville-West to Harold Nicolson, 2 October 1928, *Vita and Harold*, 204.

22 D. Wellesley, *Far Have I Traveled*, 162. Though this project is dated to 1930 in some secondary literature, Vanessa Bell's letters from the summer of 1929 describe their work on the paintings (V. Bell to C. Bell, 9 July, 3 August 1929; V. Bell to R. Fry, 29 July 1929, Tate), which were installed in November (V. Bell to Q. Bell, 27 November 1929, *Selected Letters*, 345–6). They continued adding furniture and carpets to the room into 1932.

23 A. and C. Scott, "Sad Day at Penns-in-the-Rocks"; V. Bell to Q. Bell, 27 November 1929, *Selected Letters*, 346. Bells' and Grant's simple furniture is quite compatible with the modern dining set by the Parisian designer Eyre de Lanux

featured in the *Studio* in April 1930 (M. Garland, "Interiors by Eyre de Lanux," 263).

24 D. Grant to E. Grant, November 1929, in F. Spalding, *Duncan Grant*, 313.

25 Quoted in R. Shone, *Duncan Grant designer*, 23.

26 M. Garland, "A Room Decorated by Duncan Grant and Vanessa Bell," 142.

27 R. Fry to V. Bell, 24 June 1927, Tate. For the letter Fry is responding to, see V. Bell, *Selected Letters*, 320–1.

28 V. Bell to R. Fry, 13 July 1929, Tate.

29 Q. Bell and A. Garnett, *Vanessa Bell's Family Album*, 47.

30 A. T. Edwards, "The Dead City," 138. Edwards's critique of Le Corbusier's *The City of Tomorrow* as "an over-simplification of the city, whereas what we require is not simplicity, but order" (138) anticipates Fry's contrast of Corbusian "simplicity" with formalist order in his 1932 lecture (King's 1/129; cited at note 8). That Edwards was a student of Reginald Blomfield, the historicist architect whose attack on Fry's *Heresies of a Painter* was quoted as publicity on the cover of the published version of this talk (*A Roger Fry Reader*, 171) suggests the muddled lines of antagonism and allegiance in British reception of the International Style.

31 "Arnold Bennett, H. G. Wells, Bernard Shaw, and Harrods," 163.

32 "Harrods—and Sweden," 313–14.

33 J. Gloag, "Prophets and Profits." "Give the Public What it Wants," 224–5. Writing in the *Architectural Review* two years later, John Gloag also urged "those who distribute the goods produced by makers of furniture and textiles and wallpapers . . . to end the reign of anonymity" (R. H. Wilenski and J. Gloag, "Two Points of View," 150).

34 B. Pattison, "Music in Decline," 204. Andrew Stephenson over-simplifies the rise in the rhetoric of the "professional" expert against the Bloomsbury "amateur" in art criticism at this period as a result of competitive pressures caused by the economic crisis of the Thirties. Though not wrong, Stephenson fails to contextualize this rhetorical shift in art criticism within widespread critical assertions of expert authority against the threat of working-class tastes and popular culture. This context complicates Stephenson's association of "professionals" with workers against the bogey of bourgeois amateurism. As with Sickert's competition with Fry (discussed in Chapter 1), a contest between factions of the bourgeois avant-garde is here misrecognized as a challenge to the bourgeoisie.

35 W. Hunter, "*Film* by Rudolf Arnheim," 211.

36 T. R. Barnes, "*Characters and Commentaries*, by Lytton Strachey," *Scrutiny*, vol. 1, 1933, rpt. F. R. Leavis, ed., *A Selection from Scrunity*, vol. 1, 139–40. On citations of Bloomsbury and comparisons with French and American culture in *Scrutiny*, see F. Mulhern, *The Moment of "Scrutiny"*, 122–7.

37 Q. D. Leavis, "*Abinger Harvest*, by E. M. Forster," *Scrutiny*, vol. 5, 1936, rpt. in F. R. Leavis, ed., *A Selection from Scrunity*, vol. 1, 135–6.

38 Q. D. Leavis, "Caterpillars of the Commonwealth Unite!" 208, 214.

39 D. LeMahieu, *A Culture for Democracy*, 294–304.

40 Disparagement of "jazz" influences in various art forms might be traced to Clive Bell's "Plus de Jazz," originally published in the *New Republic*, 21 September 1921 (rpt. *Since Cézanne*, 213–30). Bell's defense of the seriousness of high modernism, however, differs from later critiques of jazz in crucial ways: unconcerned about popular

culture *per se*, he uses the idea of jazz to draw distinctions within the European avant-garde. The avant-garde, therefore, is not seen as a solution to the problem of popular culture, and Bell's attitude, although undoubtedly racist, is not xenophobic (to the contrary, he treats the francophone and anglophone avant-gardes as one entity). On the context of this essay in post-war debates about modernism, see M. North, *Reading 1922*, 143–7.

41 J. C. W. Reith quoted in D. LeMahieu, *A Culture for Democracy*, 146; LeMahieu, 188 (my discussion draws heavily on 90–8, 141–54, 179–90, 276–80). Despite the similarity of their rhetoric, the B.B.C. got no credit from *Scrutiny*, which condemned the taste of its musical programmers and disparaged the idea of radio broadcasts of music as a threat to indigenous English traditions (B. Pattison, "Music in Decline" and "Music and the Community").

42 Nikolaus Pevsner's generally disparaging *Enquiry into Industrial Art in England* praised the B.B.C.'s "propaganda . . . for the promotion of better design. As in so many other respects, the B.B.C. have been among the first to show themselves sensitive of an imminent change for the better" (175).

43 Arts Council, *Thirties*, 205.

44 Broadcasting House is extensively featured in the *Architectural Review*, July and August 1932; quotations from V. H. Goldsmith, "The Studio Interiors," 56, and R. Byron, "Broadcasting House," 49.

45 Edward Halliday and Gordon Russell, "The Living Room and Furniture," *The Listener*, 3 May 1933, rpt. C. Benton, ed., *Documents*, 70.

46 Frederic Towndrow, in "Is Modern Architecture on the Right Track?" *The Listener*, 26 July 1933, rpt. C. Benton, ed., *Documents*, 84.

47 Julian Holder, "'Design in Everyday Things': Promoting Modernism in Britain," in P. Greenhalgh, ed., *Modernism in Design*, 123–43. Compounding this essay's contradictions between argument and evidence discussed in note 1, Holder asserts "British Modernists'" concern with mass housing as "axiomatic" (126), but his own examples suggest that programs addressed to this topic began only in 1937 (135)—seven years into B.B.C. programming on modern design. By this time, the B.B.C.'s antagonism to popular culture was being modified in response to audience surveys and journalists' attacks on programming for "pseudo-highbrows" (LeMahieu, 275–91, quoting Collie Knox in the *Daily Mail* [275]). In the culture of rigidifying gender roles after World War II, Modernist claims for the International Style appropriateness for mass housing or public space were largely devoid of objective criteria, simply accepting the look of technology as the guarantee of efficiency and relying substantially on pejorative contrasts between the masculine professionalization of the architect/planner with the female customer/patron or interior designer in order to brand dissenters by implication as inefficient, amateur, effete, and feminine.

48 Geoffrey Boumphrey and Wells Coates, "Modern Dwellings for Modern Needs," *The Listener* 24 May 1933, rpt. C. Benton, ed., *Documents*, 72–5. Compare the very similar terms of E. Halliday and G. Russell, "The Living Room and Furniture," also in Benton, 67–71.

49 Baillie Scott and Blomfield were among the respondents to a questionnaire in the feature "Is Modern Architecture on the Right Track?" in *The Listener* of 26 July 1933, and Blomfield debated a modernist architect in *The Listener* of 28 November 1934 (both rpt. C. Benton, ed., *Documents*, 79–88, 90–4). Fry's difference from

Baillie Scott is discussed in Chapter 2; on Blomfield's antagonism to Fry, see note 31 in this chapter. Neither of these figures was associated in any way with the Amusing Style. Fry's brief attempt, on the authority of his Omega work, to stake out dissenting ground within modernism in *The Listener* in 1932 debated the equation of functionalism with beauty ("Sensibility *versus* Mechanism"). Perhaps because B.B.C. broadcasts and publications had positioned him as an "expert" in art history, however, Fry drew his examples of successful design mainly from painting and drawing, and all from before the twentieth century (Fry praised the almost completed Cathedral of Westminster, but it was a late-nineteenth-century design).

50 E. Halliday and G. Russell, "The Living Room and Furniture," *The Listener*, 3 May 1933, rpt. C. Benton, ed., *Documents*, 69, 70. P. Nash, *Room and Book*, 35.

51 Frank Pick, "Meaning and Purpose of Design," *The Listener*, 28 June 1933, rpt. C. Benton, ed., *Documents*, 78. This trend in modernism has been influentially analyzed by Andreas Huyssen in "Mass Culture as Woman," *After the Great Divide*, 44–62. On the rhetoric of "fitness for purpose" as a counter to Bloomsbury formalism, see M. Saler, *The Avant-Garde in Interwar England*, 72–8.

52 J. Gloag, "Prophets and Profits."

53 J. Betjeman, "1830–1930," 231, 240. On this article's influence, see Andrew Causey's Introduction in P. Nash, *Writings on Art*, 17; Causey identifies Betjeman "as a counterweight to the rigorously modernist side of the *Review*" during the 1930s (21).

54 P. Nash, "Modern English Furnishing, *Architectural Review*, January 1930, 43–8, rpt. as "The Modern Aesthetic," *Room and Book*, 3–15. On the reception of *Room and Book*, see P. Nash, *Writings on Art*, 16.

55 P. Nash, *Room and Book*, 25, 27–8, 31. The reader's letter about the cocktail table is in *Architectural Review*, vol. 67, March 1930, 165, followed by the obscurantist editorial response, "For a precise description of its intricacies, he should apply to Mr. Denham Maclaren . . . we can do nothing to explain what would require the gift of tongues to elucidate." Nash's antagonism toward the Amusing Style intensified through his subsequent writings. A 1932 article in *The Listener* began from the premise that "interior building and decoration is now a scientific matter," and concludes: "it should be made clear that I am not advocating that the artist should be turned loose with his eternal brushes and paint; rather he should be relieved of them by the manservant in the hall, along with his coat and hat. It is not intended that the artist should be encouraged to paint 'frescoes' or panels, or be allowed, for one moment, to contemplate applying his colours to any of the furniture or knick-knacks." Truly modern artists, Nash insisted, would work with building materials from stone to "synthetic and artificial patent compositions" to design truly modern rooms ("The Artist in the House," *The Listener* 16 March 1932, rpt. *Paul Nash: Writings on Art*, 72–3).

56 R. H. Wilenski, "Two Points of View," 149, italics in original. Wilenski's influence on Nash is discussed by Andrew Causey in P. Nash, *Writings on Art*, 9.

57 P. Nash, "Modern English Textiles," *Artwork*, January–March 1926, rpt. in *Paul Nash: Writings on Art*, 49–50; compare Nash's *Room and Book*, 26, 31. Focusing on embroidery, Nash overlooks the commercially produced Omega textiles that are the closest precedent to his own practice.

58 "Give the Public What it Wants," 225. Although in this context the Cocotte style associated with Mortimer seems to refer to the Amusing designs illustrated, Mortimer also used this term disparagingly in reference to what would today be called Art Deco (R. Mortimer and D. Todd, *The New Interior Decoration*, 22–3; R. Mortimer, "Modern Furniture and Decoration," 253).

59 "Lord Benbow's Apartments," 202.

60 "Lord Benbow's Apartments," 201–4. On McGrath, see V. H. Goldsmith, "The Studio Interiors," 53, and R. Byron, "Broadcasting House," 49.

61 "Lord Benbow's Apartments," 203, 242.

62 Nash's commitment to design with modern materials, which led to his election as head of the Society of Industrial Artists shortly after it was founded in 1930 and his appointment to oversee the design courses at the Royal College of Art, was more rhetorical than practical. Manufacturers complained that under his direction the R.C.A.'s design graduates lacked basic skills needed for industrial production (M. Saler, *The Avant-Garde in Interwar England*, 64, 71).

63 D. Grant to V. Bell, 9 January 1930; V. Bell to C. Bell, 28 January, 7 February 1930; R. Fry to V. Bell, 7 March, 30 March 1930, Tate. Discussions to restart the Omega are also recalled in F. Partridge, *Memories*, 176.

64 Tiles for the playwright Beatrice Mayor, including one with a cigarette-smoking woman, are illustrated in "Modern English Decoration," 44; see also R. Mortimer and D. Todd, *New Interior Decoration*, pl. 92. The two-tile "Lytton Strachey in Repose," a title said to have been invented later, was commissioned in 1925, as were tiles for a small stove by Margaret Bulley, a writer on art education who lived in Gordon Square; both are now at the Victoria and Albert (R. Shone, *Duncan Grant designer*, 31; Crafts Council, *Omega Workshops*, 69).

65 Eccles's recollection that this commission to Grant and Bell celebrated his 1928 marriage (P. Dormer, "History Man," 16) corrects the date and attribution to Bell alone in Crafts Council, *Omega Workshops*, 69. Bell and Grant painted a similar set of octagonal plates with images of frolicking female nudes for Woolf (at Monk's House).

66 V. Bell to R. Fry, 2 October 1932, Tate.

67 Clark's presentation of this commission as his effort to "revive" Grant's "interest in decorative art" has been doubted by historians given Grant's and Bell's active involvement in domestic design throughout this period (K. Clark, *Another Part of the Wood*, 248, as discussed in R. Shone, *Duncan Grant designer*, 26, and F. Spalding, *Duncan Grant*, 321.) Clark's rhetoric of aesthetic purpose lost and regained (under the direction of experts like himself), which by the 1970s permeated histories of British high culture, seems an attempt to gloss over his association with the discredited Amusing Style.

68 W. W. Winkworth to V. Bell, 3 March 1932, King's.

69 Tanya Harrod argues that modernists like Herbert Read and Paul Nash saw British crafts as complementing the machine aesthetic in the late twenties, though by the mid-thirties they rejected hand-made goods by their countrymen, restricting their appreciation of "primitive" crafts to those of non-European manufacture ("House-Trained Objects," in C. Painter, ed., *Contemporary Art and the Home*, 64).

70 W. W. Winkworth to V. Bell, 3 March 1932, King's; on Winkworth's advocacy of Wedgwood, see F. Spalding, *Vanessa Bell*, 258.

71 V. Bell to R. Fry, 7 August 1934 (probably misdated for 1933), Tate.

72 V. Bell to R. Fry, 12 June 1932, Tate. Around this time, Bell also decorated other Wedgwood pieces in a floral pattern unrelated to the Clark commission (Crafts Council, *Omega Workshops*, 68–9).

73 Bell also created designs in cut glass probably for a related project by Stuart & Sons (as described in Arts Council, *Thirties*, 95), but there is no evidence these were carried out (V. Bell to R. Fry, 7 August 1934, Tate). Larger coffee cups in the "Old English Rose" pattern exist at Charleston, but there is no evidence that these were marketed (I am grateful to Tony Bradshaw for this information). Richard Shone also cites a second tea set pattern by Grant (*Duncan Grant designer*, 32). There is disagreement over whether the limited edition ceramics were a "considerable commercial success," (Crafts Council, *Omega Workshops*, 68) or "commercially . . . a flop" (F. Spalding, *Vanessa Bell*, 259).

74 About the first project, Bell reported that Foley's art director was "wildly enthusiastic" about their designs and "insists upon their being carried out as well as possible. We are to go on having proofs until they're as good as we think they can be" (V. Bell to R. Fry, 7 August 1934, Tate). A similar attitude seems to have guided the second project too, for variations on Bell's pattern exist, some (for example a plate at the Milwaukee Museum of Art) quite different from Wilkinson's "Vanessa" pattern, which, facilitated by hand-painting, itself included a some variations in the basic motif of two blossoms on three circles. Although Bell hoped their designs could be used on Omega molds, the commercial firms used them on lighter more generic plates and serving dishes (V. Bell to R. Fry, 7 August 1934; D. Grant to V. Bell, 1 May 1935, Tate).

75 R. Mortimer, "Saucers and Socialism."

76 Examples of Walton's own painted furniture and rug designs were illustrated alongside Bell's and Grant's in *Vogue*'s feature "The Work of Some Modern Decorative Artists."

77 In a moment of exasperation with decorative work, Grant first reacted to Walton's requests for designs with, "I can't feel I want to make many stuffs but I wish him success" (D. Grant to V. Bell, 10 December 1930, Tate). He relented, however, for Richard Shone lists nine designs by Grant (*Duncan Grant designer*, 28); another is illustrated and cataloged (as 4.7) in Arts Council, *Thirties*, 143).

78 P. Nash, "Modern English Textiles I," *The Listener*, 27 April 1932, in *Paul Nash: Writings on Art*, 73.

79 C. Connolly, "Genuine Arts and Crafts."

80 V. Woolf to O. Morrell 25? November 1932, *Letters*, vol. 5, 130.

81 V. Woolf, *Diary*, vol. 4, 131; see also *Letters*, vol. 5, 136.

82 V. Woolf to D. Grant, 24 November 1932, *Letters*, vol. 5, 129. Woolf's letter confirms the late addition of the fish to Grant's design, illustrated in R. Shone, *Duncan Grant designer*, 24. Leslie Stephen was among the Victorian critics upheld in *Scrutiny* in contrast to the corruption of contemporary values.

83 The chairs and cabinet are now at Monk's House. That repayment was to be in unsold elements from the display is suggested by Woolf's joking worry a few days after the party that "I may be landed with four great panels" (*Diary*, vol. 4, 131). Ultimately, so little sold that Woolf had ample choices. Woolf later purchased Bell's painted screen from the display; it is now at the Portsmouth Museum and Art Gallery (F. Spalding, *Duncan Grant*, 324).

84   V. Bell to R. Fry, 9 September 1933, Tate. See also R. Shone, *Duncan Grant designer*, 20.

85   C. Connolly, "A Music Room," 75. Richard Shone reports that this review, unsurprisingly, strained relations between Connolly and Bloomsbury's artists (*Bloomsbury Portraits*, 239).

86   Although sales records are incomplete, a letter from Virginia Woolf suggests that no furniture had sold by the second week in December, and betrays some anxiety that, at her sister's discounted prices, she will end up owning the entire display (V. Woolf to V. Bell, 12 December 1932, *Letters*, vol. 5, 136). Richard Shone describes the music room as "Grant and Vanessa Bell's last 'domestic' interior" (*Duncan Grant designer*, 20).

87   Woolf's misperception that a shared taste for the Amusing linked her to the aristocracy marks her light-hearted diary entry celebrating her acquisition of Grant's carpet as a sign that, "we have risen socially to the rank of the younger sons of baronets—it is like being real gentry, sitting with our feet embedded in pile" (*Diary*, vol. 4, 131).

88   Bell reported that "most" of the commissions to artists "are being stopped or interfered with" as the Cunard executives "are doing their best to get rid of all the artists" (V. Bell to J. Bell, 24 September 1935, *Selected Letters*, 399). Stanley Spencer was among those whose murals were refused (C. Willsdon, *Mural Painting in Britain*, 7).

89   D. Grant to V. Bell, 24 September 1935, Tate; this letter also reports that Cunard's representatives blamed the influence of the Catholic Church, "in the hands of the Irish," for changes to Bell's commission, which was to have graced the lounge outside the Catholic chapel. Whatever the merits of the latter claim, censorious influence from Buckingham Palace is documented in Cunard's correspondence files, as quoted in F.

Spalding, *Duncan Grant*, 339.

90   Letter to Grant 21 September 1935, in F. Spalding, *Duncan Grant*, 337.

91   "N." "A Duncan Grant Exhibition."

92   New York *Herald Tribune*, 1 December 1935, in F. Spalding, *Duncan Grant*, 529 n. 23. Between September 1935 and February 1936, when his final work was rejected, Grant negotiated with Cunard over details of his panels, reducing the size of the figures and changing the size of the panels to meet his patron's changing demands, which helps account for the nebulous relationship of the figures to one another and to the ground.

93   K. Clark, *Another Part of the Wood*, 248; the archival research presented in Frances Spalding's *Duncan Grant* (336–44) reveals that Clark erred in claiming that Grant worked for a small sum, that the panels were ever installed, and that Percy Bates's wife played any role in the controversy. A far more likely influence was the launch of the rival ship *Normandie* in 1935, which was celebrated for its stylish Art Deco interiors. The *Queen Mary* is permanently docked in Long Beach, California, where it continues to operate as a luxury hotel.

94   D. Grant to V. Bell, 1 June 1935, Tate. Bell described her image as a couple strolling in the Borghese gardens, concluding, "I hope it's the kind of subject millionaires will like" (V. Bell to J. Bell, 1 November 1935, *Selected Letters*, 402). Despite some disagreements with Cunard over her panel and the firm's refusal of her textile designs, Bell's panel was accepted, though she felt it was installed in too small a room (*Selected Letters*, 397; F. Spalding, *Vanessa Bell*, 284).

95   Eric Newton, quoted in F. Spalding, *Duncan Grant*, 343; "N." "A Duncan Grant Exhibition."

96   C. Bell, "Inside the Queen Mary," 658, 660.

97   C. Bell, "Duncan Grant" (1920), rpt. *Since*

Cézanne, 111. In contrast, a 1934 review claims that Grant's new art shows his "native lyricism and sensibility directed and conditioned by hard thinking" as he "has deliberately called the intellect into play" (C. Bell, "Duncan Grant," 763, 764).

98   F. Spalding, *Duncan Grant*, 343–4. In 1974, Grant's panels were purchased by Kenneth Clark's son; they are now dispersed in private collections.

99   S. Watney, *Art of Duncan Grant*, 63.

100   O. Sitwell, *Noble Essences*, 303. Laurence Whistler contrasts "Amusing" with "disturbing" as the adjective of the 1980s (*Laughter and the Urn*, 97).

101   V. Woolf to J. Bell, 20 June 1936, in D. Gillespie, *The Sisters' Arts*, 47. Woolf to some extent matched her tone to her correspondent, whose passion for forceful political action shortly afterwards led to his death.

102   S. Watney, *Art of Duncan Grant*, 14; Grant's letters to Watney brim with fond gay innuendo.

103   Grant's sketch of Gilbert and George is reproduced in R. Shone, *Art of Bloomsbury*, 286. On Grant's community of young men making their way in the art world, see R. Marler, *Bloomsbury Pie* 61–4; note the nude man, coyly ignored in the caption of a photograph of Grant's bedroom around 1980 (*Art of Bloomsbury*, 10). On the less artistically inclined of Grant's models, see D. Turnbaugh, *Duncan Grant*, 98.

104   Heilbrun's 1964 *Toward a Recognition of Androgyny*, which deals extensively with Bloomsbury, was a foundational second-wave feminist text, and Watney's *Policing Desire* was at least as important in shaping gay identity in relation to AIDS in the 1980s. Identities based on gender and sexuality are posited as basic characteristics of postmodernism by such influential theorists as Andreas Huyssen ("Mapping the Post-Modern," in *After the Great Divide*, 178–221).

Works Cited

Public collections of letters and manuscripts are cited as follows:

Berg   Berg Collection, New York Public Library
British Library   Department of Manuscripts, British Library
King's   King's College Archives, Cambridge University
Northwestern   Special Collections, Northwestern University Library
Tate   Charleston Papers, Tate Gallery Archives
Texas   Ransom Humanities Research Center, University of Texas at Austin

A Post-Impressionist Scribbler, "Pictorial Art in South London." *National Review* 58, December 1911.

"Advanced Pictures." *The Times* [London], 20 November 1917, 11.

Affron, Matthew and Mark Antliff, eds., *Fascist Visions: Art and Ideology in France and Italy*. Princeton: Princeton University Press, 1997.

Alex, Reid and Lefevre, *Recent Paintings by Vanessa Bell*. London: 1934.

Aldrich, Robert, *The Seduction of the Mediterranean: Writing, Art, and Homosexual Fantasy*. New York: Routledge, 1993.

Alpine Club Gallery, *The Grafton Group*. London: 1913.

Amaya, Mario, "Omega's Dauby Doodles." *Studio International*, vol. 196, no. 1004, 1984, 33–5.

Anand, Mulk Raj, *Conversations in Bloomsbury*. London: Wildwood House, 1981.

Anscombe, Isabelle, *Omega and After*. London: Thames & Hudson, 1981.

Anstruther, Ian, *Oscar Browning: A Biography*. London: John Murray, 1983.

Anthony d'Offay Gallery, *Eric Gill, 1882–1940: Drawings and Carvings, A Centenary Exhibition*. London: 1982.

Anthony d'Offay Gallery, *The Omega Workshops: Alliance and Emnity in English Art, 1911–1920*. London: 1984.

Anthony d'Offay Gallery, *Vanessa Bell: Paintings from Charleston*. London: 1979.

De Antonio, Emile and Mitch Tuchman, *Painters Painting: A Candid History of the Modern Art Scene*. New York: Abbeville Press, 1984.

Armytage, W. H. G., *Heavens Below: Utopian Experiments in England, 1560–1960*. Toronto: University of Toronto Press, 1961.

"Arnold Bennett, H. G. Wells, Bernard Shaw, and Harrods," *Architectural Review*, vol. 55, April 1929, 163–4.

"The Art of Duncan Grant," *Vogue* [London], late February 1923, 50–1, 70.

"The Art of Roger Fry," *Morning Post*, 13 February 1931.

Arts Council, *Raoul Dufy*. London: 1983.

Arts Council, *Thirties: British art and design before the War*. London: 1980.

Arts Council, *Vanessa Bell 1879–1961: A Memorial Exhibition of Paintings*. London: 1964.

Ashbee, C[harles]. R[obert], *Craftsmanship in Competitive Industry*. 1908, rpt. New York: Garland Publishing, 1977.

——, *An Endeavor Towards the Teaching of John Ruskin and William Morris*. 1901, rpt. n.p. Folcroft Library Editions, 1973.

——, *Socialism and Politics: A Study in the Readjustment of the Values of Life*. London: Brimley Johnson and Ince, Ltd., 1906.

J. B., "The Amusements of London." *The Spectator*, 11 November 1911, 795–6.

M. M. B., "Post-Impressionist Furniture." *Daily News and Leader*, 7 August 1913, 10.

——, "Rebel Art in Modern Life." *Daily News and Leader*, 7 April 1914.

"A Bachelor Flat in Bloomsbury," *Vogue* [London], late April 1925, 44–5.

Backemeyer, Sylvia and Theresa Gronberg, eds., *W. R. Lethaby, 1857–1931: Architecture, Design, and Education*. London: Lund Humphries, 1984.

Baillie Scott, M[ackay] H[ugh], "A Country Cottage," *The Studio*, no. 108, March 1902, 86–95.

——, *Houses and Gardens*. London: G. Newnes, 1906.

——, "An Ideal Suburban House," *The Studio*, no. 22, January 1895, 127–32.

Baron, Wendy, *The Camden Town Group*. London: Scolar Press, 1979.

——, *Miss Ethel Sands and Her Circle*. London: Peter Owen, 1977.

——, *Sickert*. London: Phaidon Press, 1973.

Baudelaire, Charles, *"The Painter of Modern Life" and Other Essays*, Jonathan Mayne trans. London: Phaidon, 1964.

Baudrillard, Jean, *For a Critique of the Political Economy of the Sign*. Charles Levin, trans. St Louis: Telos, 1981.

Beaverbrook Art Gallery, *Bloomsbury Painters and their Circle*. Fredericton, New Brunswick: 1976.

Beechey, James, "Clive Bell: Pacifism and Politics." *Charleston*, 14, Autumn/Winter 1996, 5–13.

Beith, Gilbert, ed., *Edward Carpenter: In Appreciation*. London: George Allen and Unwin, Ltd., 1931.

Bell, Clive. *An Account of French Painting*. London: Chatto and Windus, 1932.

——, *Art*. New York: Frederick A. Stokes, 1914.

——, "The Art of Brancusi." *Vogue* [London], 66, late December 1925, 43–5.

——, *Civilization* London: Chatto and Windus, 1928.

——, "Duncan Grant." *New Statesman and Athenaeum*, 19 May 1934, 763–64.

——, "The French Pictures at Heal's." *Nation*, 16 August 1919, 586–88.

——, "Inside the Queen Mary," *The Listener*, 8 April 1936, 658–60.

——, "The London Group and Sargent." *Vogue* [London], late February 1926, 54–5, 80.

——, *Old Friends: Personal Recollections*. 1956, rpt. London: Cassell Publishers, 1988.

——, "Our Stone Population." *Nation and Athenaeum*, 8 December 1928, 360.

——, *Peace At Once*. London: The National Labour Press, Ltd., 1915.

——, *Pot-Boilers*. London: Chatto and Windus, 1918.

——, *Since Cézanne*. London: Chatto and Windus, 1922.

Bell, Julian, ed., *Reminiscences of War Resisters in World War I*. 1935, rpt. New York: Garland, 1972.

Bell, Quentin. *Bad Art*. London: Chatto and Windus, 1989.

——, *Bloomsbury*. London: Weidenfeld and Nicolson, 1968, rpt. 1986.

——, "Bloomsbury and 'the Vulgar Passions.'" *Critical Inquiry*, vol. 6, no. 2, Winter 1979, 239–56.

——, *Elders and Betters*. London: John Murray, 1995.

——, "The Omega Revisited." *The Listener*, 30 January 1964, 200–1.

——, *Ruskin*. 1963, rpt. New York: George Braziller, 1978.

——, *Virginia Woolf: A Biography*, 2 vols. New York: Harcourt Brace Jovanovich, 1972.

——, and Stephen Chaplin, "The Ideal Home Rumpus." *Apollo*, October, 1964, 284–91.

——, and Angelica Garnett, *Vanessa Bell's Family Album*. London: Jill Norman and Hobhouse, 1981.

——, and Virginia Nicholson, *Charleston: A Bloomsbury House and Garden*. New York: Henry Holt, 1997.

Bell, Vanessa, *Selected Letters of Vanessa Bell*. Regina Marler, ed., New York: Pantheon, 1993.

——, *Sketches in Pen and Ink: A Bloomsbury Notebook*. Lia Giachero, ed. London: Hogarth Press, 1997.

Benjamin, Walter, *Arcades Project*. Howard Eiland aand Kevin McLaughlin, trans. Cambridge, Mass.: Harvard University Press, 1999.

——, *Charles Baudelaire: A Lyric Poet in the Era of High Capitalism*. Harry Zohn, trans. London: NLB, 1973.

——, *Gesammelte Schriften*. Rolf Tiedemann and Hermann Schweppenhäuser, eds. Frankfurt am Main: Suhrkamp Verlag, 1977.

Bennett, Arnold, *The Pretty Lady*. London: Cassell, 1918.

Benois, Alexandre, *Reminiscences of the Russian Ballet*. Mary Britnieva, trans. London: Putnam, 1941.

Benton, Charlotte, ed., *Documents: A collection of source material on the Modern Movement*. Milton Keynes: Open University Press, 1975.

Betjeman, John, "1830–1930—Still Going Strong: A Guide to the Recent History of Interior Decoration." *Architectural Review*, vol. 67, May 1930, 231–40.

Beurdley, Cecile, *L'Amour Bleu*. Michael Taylor, trans. New York: Rizzoli, 1978.

Blake, Vernon, "Modern Decorative Art." *Architectural Review*, vol. 58, July 1925, 24–33.

——, "Modern Decorative Art–II." *Architectural Review*, vol. 58, November 1925, 181–6.

——, "Morris, Munich, and Cézanne." *Architectural Review*, vol. 65, April 1929, 207–8.

Bland, Lucy and Laura Doan, eds., *Sexology in Culture: Labeling Bodies and Desires*. Chicago: University of Chicago Press, 1998.

Blunt, Wilfred, *My Diaries*. London: Martin Secker, 1920.

Boulestin, X[avier] Marcel, *Myself, My Two Countries . . .* London: Cassell, 1936 [also translated as *Ease and Endurance*. Robin Adair, trans. London: Home and Van Thal, 1948].

Bowman, Sarah and Michel Molinare, *A Fashion for Extravagance: Art Deco Fabrics and Fashions*. New York: E. P. Dutton, 1985.

Boyd, Elizabeth French, *Bloomsbury Heritage: Their Mothers and Their Aunts*. London: Taplinger Publishing Co., 1976.

Bradford, Sarah, Honor Clerk, Jonathan Fryer, Robin Gibson, John Pearson, *The Sitwells and the Arts of the 1920s and 1930s*. London: National Portrait Gallery, 1994.

Bronski, Michael, *Culture Clash: The Making of Gay Sensibility*. Boston: South End Press, 1984.

Brooke, Rupert, "The Post-Impressionist Exhibition at the Grafton Galleries." *Cambridge Magazine*, 23 November 1912.

Buckle, Richard, *Diaghilev*. New York: Atheneum, 1979.

——, *Nijinsky*. London: Weidenfeld, 1971.

Bullen, J. B., ed., *Post-Impressionists in England*. New York: Routledge, 1988.

Bullough, Edward, "Psychical Distance." *British Journal of Psychology*, 5 June 1912, 87–117.

Burlington Fine Arts Club, *Exhibition of Pictures and Sketches by Charles Wellington Furse, A.R.A.* London: 1906.

Burton, Richard F., *The Book of the Thousand Nights and a Night*, 17 vols. n.p.: Burton Club, n.d.

Byron, Robert. "Broadcasting House." *Architectural Review*, vol. 72, August 1932, 47–9.

H. de C. [de Cronin Hastings]. "The Heresies of a Painter; or The Architecture of Roger Fry." *Architectural Review*, vol. 63, May 1928, 184–7.

——, "Paris 1925: A General View." *Architectural Review*, vol. 58, July 1925, 8–14.

Carpenter, Edward. *Angels' Wings*. London: Swan Sonnenschein and Co., 1898.

——, *Civilisation: Its Cause and Cure, and other essays by Edward Carpenter*. London: S. Sonnenschein and Co., 1889.

——, *My Days and Dreams: Being Autobiographical Notes*. London: George Allen and Unwin, 1916.

——, *Iöläus: an anthology of friendship*. Manchester: S. Clarke, 1902.

——, *Love's Coming of Age*. 1896, rpt. New York: Boni and Liveright, 1911.

——, *Towards Democracy*. 1883, rpt. London: Swan Sonnenschein and Co., 1907.

Caughie, Pamela, ed., *Virginia Woolf in the Age of Mechanical Reproduction*. New York: Garland, 2000.

Caws, Mary Ann, *Women of Bloomsbury: Virginia, Vanessa, and Carrington*. New York: Routledge, 1990.

Cecil, Hugh and Mirabel, *Clever Hearts: Desmond and Molly MacCarthy*. London: Victor Gollancz, 1990.

Cendrars, Blaise and Sonia Delaunay, *La Prose du Transibérien et de la Petite Jehanne de France*, 1913, rpt. as *Archives des lettres modernes*, 224, Antoine Sidoti, ed. Paris: Lettres Modernes, 1987.

"Century Guild Design," *The Hobby Horse* 2, 1887, 161–3.

La Céramique Fauve: André Metthey et les peintres. Nice: Musée Matisse and Réunion des musées nationaux, 1996.

Chadd, David and John Gage, *The Diaghilev Ballet in England*. Norwich: 45th Norfolk and Borwich Triennial Festival of Music and the Arts, 1979.

Chamot, Mary, Dennis Farr, and Martin Butlin, *Tate Gallery Catalogues: The Modern British Paintings, Drawings, and Sculpture*. London: Oldbourne Press, 1964.

"Charleston on *Kaleidoscope*" [discussion with Michael Holroyd, Richard Shone, Frances Partridge, John Jacob, Quentin Bell, Noel Annan. BBC, 26 May 1986], *Charleston Newsletter* 15, June 1986, 44–52.

"The Chimney Piece from One Generation to Another," *Vogue* [London], early January 1925, 38–9.

Clark, Kenneth, *Another Part of the Wood: A Self-Portrait*. New York: Harper and Row, 1974.

Cleto, Fabio, ed., *Camp: Queer Aesthetics and the Performing Subject*. Ann Arbor: University of Michigan Press, 1999.

Clutton-Brock, Alan, "Mr. Roger Fry." *Athenaeum*, 18 June 1920, 805–6.

Cohen, Lisa, "Virginia Woolf, Fashion, and British *Vogue*." *Charleston* 18, Summer/Winter 1998, 5–12.

Collins, Judith, *Eric Gill: Sculpture*. London: Lund Humphries, 1992.

——, *The Omega Workshops*. Chicago: University of Chicago Press, 1984.

Colmer, John, *E.M. Forster: The Personal Voice*. London: Routledge & Kegan Paul, 1975.

Connolly, Cyril, "Genuine Arts and Crafts." *Architectural Review*, vol. 71, January 1932, 23.

——, "A Music Room decorated, furnished and painted by Vanessa Bell and Duncan Grant." *Architectural Review*, vol. 73, February 1933, 74–5.

"The Contemporary Style of Decoration," *Vogue* [London], early January 1924, 50–1, 74.

Coombes, Annie E. S., "For God and England: Contributions to an Image of Africa in the First Decade of the Twentieth Century." *Art History*, vol. 8, no. 4, December 1985, 453–66.

Corbett, David Peters, *The Modernity of English Art*. Manchester: Manchester University Press, 1997.

Cork, Richard, *Art Beyond the Gallery in Early Twentieth-Century England*. New Haven: Yale University Press, 1985.

——, *A Bitter Truth: Avant-Garde Art and the Great War*. New Haven: Yale University Press, 1994.

——, "Richard Cork's London Art Review." *Evening Standard*, 13 August 1975.

——, *Vorticism and Abstract Art in the First Machine Age*, 2 vols. London: Gordon Fraser, 1975, 1976.

Cottington, David, *Cubism and the Politics of Culture in France, 1905–14*. Ph.D. diss: University of London, 1985.

Cowling, Elizabeth and Jennifer Mundy, eds., *On Classic Ground: Picasso, Léger, de Chirico and the New Classicism, 1910–1930*. London: Tate Gallery, 1990.

Crabtree, Derek and A. P. Thirlwall, eds., *Keynes and the Bloomsbury Group*. London: Macmillan, 1980.

Crackenthorpe, David, *Hubert Crackenthorpe and English Realism in the 1890's*. Columbia: University of Missouri Press, 1977.

Crafts Council. *The Omega Workshops 1913–19*, London: Crafts Council, 1984.

Crawford, Alan, *C. R. Ashbee: Architect, Designer and Romantic Socialist*. New Haven: Yale University Press, 1985.

Crompton, Louis, *Byron and Greek Love*. Berkeley: University of California Press, 1985.

Cunnington, Phillis and Alan Mansfield, *English Costume for Sports and Outdoor Recreation from the Sixteenth to the Nineteenth Centuries*. London: Adam and Charles Black, 1969.

O. R. D., "Decoration: Plain or Artistic." *Westminster Gazette*, 17 November 1916.

Davies, Randall, "The Grafton Group." *New Statesman*, 10 January 1914, 436–7.

Deacon, Richard, *The Cambridge Apostles*. New York: Farrar, Straus & Giroux, 1985.

"Decorations at the Borough Polytechnic," *Athenaeum*, 23 September 1911, 366.

Delany, Paul, *The Neo-Pagans: Friendship and Love in the Rupert Brooke Circle*. London: Macmillan, 1987.

Denis, Maurice, *Théories, 1890–1910*. Paris: L. Rouart et J. Watelin, 1920.

Deslandres, Yvonne and Dorothée Lalanne, *Poiret: Paul Poiret, 1879–1944*. Paula Clifford, trans. London: Thames and Hudson, 1987.

Dickinson, G[oldsworthy] Lowes, *The Autobiography of G. Lowes Dickinson*. Dennis Proctor, ed. London: Gerald Duckworth & Co., 1973.

——, *The Greek View of Life*. London: Methuen and Co., 1896.

Dormer, Peter. "History Man" [interview with Lord Eccles]. *Crafts*, vol. 53, November/December 1981, 16–18.

Duhamel, Georges, *Le temps de la recherche*. Paris: Paul Hartmann, 1947.

Duncan, Carol, "Virility and Domination in Early Twentieth-Century Vanguard Painting." 1973, rpt. in Norma Broude and Mary D. Garrard, eds. *Feminism and Art History*. New York: Harper and Row, 1982, 292–313.

Dunlop, Ian, *The Shock of the New: Seven Historic Exhibitions of Modern Art*. New York: American Heritage Press, 1972.

Dunn, Jane, *A Very Close Conspiracy: Vaness Bell and Virginia Woolf*. Boston: Little, Brown and Co., 1990.

"S. E.," "The Modern House and the Modern Picture." *Burlington*, vol. 10, no. 47, February 1907, 293–6.

"An Economist and Modern Art," *Vogue* [London], early March 1925, 46–7.

Edwards, A. Trystan, "The Dead City." *Architectural Review*, vol. 66, September 1929, 135–8.

Fahlman, Betsy, "Modern as Metal and Mirror: The Work of Robert Evans Locher." *Arts*, vol. 59 no. 8, April 1985, 108–13.

Fassler, Barbara, "Theories of Homosexuality as Sources for Bloomsbury's Androgyny." *Signs* vol. 3 no. 2, 1979, 237–51.

"The Father of Post-Impressionism." *Pall-Mall Gazette*, 4 October 1912.

Fillen-Yeh, Susan, ed., *Dandies: Fashion and Finesse in Art and Culture*. New York: New York University Press, 2001.

Floud, Peter, "The Inconsistencies of William Morris." *The Listener*, 14 October 1954, 615–17.

Fokine, Michel, *Fokine: Memoirs of a Ballet Master*. Vitale Fokine, trans. Boston: Little, Brown and Co., 1961.

Fone, Byrne R. S., ed., *Hidden Heritage: History and the Gay Imagination, An Anthology*. New York: Avocation Publishers, 1980.

Forster, E[dward] M[organ], *Goldsworthy Lowes Dickinson*. London: Edward Arnold, 1934.

——, *Howards End*. London: Edward Arnold, 1910.

——, *Marianne Thornton* London: Edward Arnold, 1956.

——, *Maurice*. New York: W. W. Norton, 1971.

——, *Two Cheers for Democracy*. New York: Harcourt, Brace and Company, 1938.

Foucault, Michel, *Discipline and Punish: The Birth of the Prison*. Alan Sheridan, trans. New York: Random House, 1977.

——, *The History of Sexuality, Volume I: An Introduction*. Robert Hurley, trans. New York: Random House, 1978.

——, *Madness and Civilization*. Richard Howard, trans. New York: Random House, 1965.

Frost, Abigail, "Omega Anonymous." *Crafts*, vol. 66, Jan/Feb. 1984, 40–4.

Fry, Roger, "Artlessness." *Nation*, 20 May 1911, 287.

——, "The Autumn Salon." *Nation*, 29 October 1910, 194–5.

——, "Bushman Paintings." *Burlington*, vol. 16, March 1910, 334–8.

——, *Catalogue of an Exhibition of Works Representative of the New Movement in Art Selected and Arranged by Mr. Roger Fry*. London: Mansard Galleries n.d. [1917].

——, *Cézanne*. 1927, rpt. Chicago: University of Chicago Press, 1989.

——, *Characteristics of French Art*. London: Chatto & Windus, 1932.

——, "Children's Drawings at the County Hall." *New Statesman and Nation*, vol. 5, no. 122 (new series), 24 June 1933, 844–5.

——, *Duncan Grant*. London: Hogarth Press, 1923.

——, *Exhibition of Omega Copies and Translations*. London: Omega Workshops, 1917.

——, "Explorations at Trafalgar Square." *Athenaeum*, 18 April 1919, 211–12.

——, *Flemish Art*. London: Chatto and Windus, 1927.

——, "The Friends' Work for War Victims in France." *Charleston*, 12, Autumn/Winter 1995, 22–4.

——, "Gaudier-Brzeska." *Burlington*, vol. 29, August 1916, 209–10.

——, "The International Society's Exhibition." *Athenaeum*, 2 November 1901, 601–2.

——, *Last Lectures*. Cambridge: Cambridge University Press, 1939.

——, *Letters of Roger Fry*. 2 vols, Denys Sutton, ed. London: Chatto and Windus, 1972.

——, "A Modern Jeweler." *Burlington*, vol. 17, June 1910, 169–74.

——, "Modern Mosaic and Mr. Boris Anrep" *Burlington*, vol. 42, June 1923, 272, 277–8.

——, "Mr. Duncan Grant's Pictures at Patterson's Gallery." *New Statesman*, 21 February 1920, 586–7.

——, "Notes on the Exhibition of Florentine Painting at the Burlington Fine Arts Club." *Burlington*, vol. 35, no. 196, July 1919, 3–12.

——, "Oriental Art." *Quarterly Review*, 212, January 1910, 225–39.

——, "Pictures and the Modern Home." Unpublished MS for *Vanity Fair* [New York]. King's 1/46.

——, *Reflections on British Painting*. 1934, rpt. Freeport, N.Y.: Books for Libraries Press, 1969.

——, *A Roger Fry Reader*. Christopher Reed, ed. Chicago: University of Chicago Press, 1996.

——, "Sensibility *versus* Mechanism." *The Listener*, 6 April 1932, 497–9.

——, *Transformations: Critical and Speculative Essays on Art*. London: Chatto and Windus, 1926.

——, "Vanessa Bell." *Vogue* [London], early February 1926, 33–5, 78.

——, *Vision and Design*. London: Chatto and Windus, 1920.

——, "What to do with Our Artists." *The Bystander*, 10 December 1913, 608.

——, "A Whistler Nocturne." *Athenaeum*, 29 July 1905, 153–4.

Fry, Roger, et al., *Georgian Art (1760–1820): An introductory review of English Painting, Architecture, Sculpture, Ceramics, Glass, Metalwork, Furniture, Textiles, and other arts during the reign of George III*, Burlington Magazine Monograph—III. London: B. T. Batsford, 1929.

Furbank, P. N., *E.M. Forster: A Life*. New York: Harvest/HBJ, 1978.

Furse, Katharine, *Hearts and Pomegranets: The Story of Forty-Five Years, 1875–1920*. London: Peter Davies, 1940.

"'Futurist' Woolwork: Samples of Weird Art at a Picture Show," *Daily Express*, 18 March 1913, 2.

"G.," "The Revival of English Domestic Architecture, VI: The Work of Mr C. F. A. Voysey." *Studio* 11 June 1897, 16–25.

Gagnier, Regenia, *Idylls of the Marketplace: Oscar Wilde and the Victorian Public*. Stanford: Stanford University Press, 1986.

Gallery Edward Harvane, *A Homage to Duncan Grant*. London: 1975.

Garland, Madge, "Interiors by Eyre de Lanux." *The Studio*, vol. 99, no. 445, April 1930, 263–5.

——, "A Room Decorated by Duncan Grant and Vanessa Bell." *The Studio*, vol. 100, no. 449, August 1930, 142–3.

Garnett, Angelica, *Deceived with Kindness*. London: Hogarth Press-Chatto and Windus, 1984.

Garnett, David, *The Familiar Faces*. London: Chatto and Windus, 1962.

——, *The Flowers of the Forest*. London: Chatto and Windus, 1955.

——, *The Golden Echo*. London: Chatto and Windus, 1953.

Geertz, Clifford, *Local Knowledge*. New York: Basic, 1983.

Gernsheim, Helmut, *Julia Margaret Cameron: Her Life and Photographic Work*. 2nd edn New York: Aperture Foundation, 1975.

Gerzina, Gretchen Holbrook, *Carrington: A Life*. New York: W. W. Norton, 1989.

Gibson, Ann, *Theory Undeclared: Avant-Garde Magazines as a Guide to Abstract Expressionist Images and Ideas*. Diss. University of Delaware 1984.

Gill, Eric, *Autobiography*. 1940, rpt. London: Lund Humphries, 1992.

——, "The Failure of the Arts and Crafts Movement." *Socialist Review*, vol. 4, no. 22, December 1909, 289–300.

——, *Letters of Eric Gill*. Walter Shewring, ed. New York: Devin-Adair, 1948.

Gillespie, Diane, *The Sisters' Arts: The Writing and Painting of Virginia Woolf and Vanessa Bell*. Syracuse, New York: Syracuse University Press, 1988.

"Give the Public What it Wants," *Architectural Review*, vol. 67, May 1930, 223–5.

Glendenning, Victoria, *Vita: A Biography of Vita Sackville West*. New York: Alfred A. Knopf, 1983.

Gloag, John, "Prophets and Profits." *Architectural Review*, vol. 67, April 1930, 215–16.

Goldring, Douglas, *Odd Man Out: The Autobiography of a "Propaganda Novelist"*. London: Chapman and Hall, 1935.

Goldsmith, V. H., "The Studio Interiors." *Architectural Review*, vol. 72, August 1932, 53–6.

Goodwin, Craufurd D., "Economic Man in the Garden of Eden." *Journal of the History of Economic Thought*, Fall 2000, 405–32.

Gopnik, Adam, "The Invention of Oscar Wilde." *New Yorker*, 18 May 1998, 78–88.

Gordon-Stables, Louise, "On Painting and Decorative Painting." *Colour*, June 1916, 187–8.

Grafton Galleries, *Manet and the Post-Impressionists*. London: 1910.

——, *Second Post-Impressionist Exhibition*. London: Ballantyne and Company, 1912.

"The Grafton Group," [London] *The Times*, 20 March 1913, 4.

"The Grafton Group," *Pall-Mall Gazette*, 27 March 1913, 4.

"The Grafton Group at the Alpine Club Gallery," *Athenaeum*, 10 January 1914, 70.

Graham, John W., *Conscription and Conscience: a history 1916–19*. London: George Allen & Unwin, 1922.

Graves, Robert and Alan Hodge, *The Long Week-End: A Social History of Great Britain 1918–1939*. 1940, rpt. New York: W. W. Norton, 1963.

Green, Christopher, ed., *Art Made Modern: Roger Fry's Vision of Art*. London: Merrell Holberton, 1999.

Green, Martin, *Children of the Sun: A Narrative of 'Decadence' in England After 1918*. New York: Basic, 1976.

Greenberg, Clement, *Art and Culture: Critical Essays*. Boston: Beacon Press, 1961.

——, *The Collected Essays and Criticism*, 4 vols. John O'Brian, ed. Chicago: University of Chicago Press, 1986–93.

Greenhalgh, Paul, "Art, Politics and Society at the Franco-British Exhibition of 1908." *Art History*, vol. 8 no. 4, December 1985, 434–52.

——, ed., *Modernism in Design*. London: Reaktion Books, 1990.

Greer, Germaine, *The Obstacle Race: The Fortunes of Women Painters and their Work*. New York: Farrar Straus Giroux, 1979.

Grigoriev, Serge L. *The Diaghilev Ballet, 1909–1929*. London: Constable, n.d.

Groom, Gloria, ed., *Beyond the Easel: Decorative Painting by Bonnard, Vuillard, Denis, and Roussel, 1890–1930*. New Haven: Yale University Press, 2001.

Guggenheim Museum, *Frantisek Kupka, 1871–1957: A Retrospective*. New York: Solomon R. Guggenheim Museum, 1975.

G. R. H., "The Grafton Group at the Alpine Gallery." *Pall Mall Gazette*, 8 January 1914, 5.

Hamilton, George Heard and William C. Agee, *Raymond Duchamp-Villon*. New York: Walker, 1967.

Hamnett, Nina, *Laughing Torso*. 1932, rpt. London: Virago Press, 1984.

"A Harmony of the Furnishing of Two Centuries at River House," *Vogue* [London], early February 1919, 40–1.

Harrison, Charles, *English Art and Modernism 1900–1939*. Bloomington: Indiana University Press, 1981.

Harrod, R. F., *The Life of John Maynard Keynes*. London: Macmillan, 1952.

"Harrods—and Sweden," *Architectural Review*, June 1929, 313–16.

Harvey, Charles and Jon Press, *William Morris: Design and Enterprise in Victorian Britain*. Manchester: Manchester University Press, 1991.

Hassall, Christopher, *Edward Marsh: Patron of the Arts*. London: Longmans, 1959.

Hastings, Tom, "Said's *Orientalism* and the Discourse of (Hetero)sexuality." *Canadian Review of American Studies*, vol. 23 no. 1, Fall 1992, 139–46.

Hebdige, Dick, *Subculture: The Meaning of Style*. London: Methuen, 1979.

Heilbrun, Carolyn, *Toward a Recognition of Androgyny*. New York: Alfred A. Knopf, 1964.

Henderson, Philip, *William Morris: His Life, Work and Friends*. 1967, rpt. London: André Deutsch, 1977.

Herbert, Eugenia, *The Artist and Social Reform: France and Belgium, 1885–1898*. New Haven: Yale University Press, 1961.

Herbert, Robert L., *Impressionism: Art, Leisure, and Parisian Society*. New Haven: Yale University Press, 1988.

——, ed., *Modern Artists on Art: Ten Unabridged Essays*. Englewood Cliffs, N. J.: Prentice-Hall, 1964.

Hess, Thomas B. and John Ashbury, eds., *The Avant-Garde* (*Art News Annual* 34). New York: Newsweek, 1968.

Hession, Charles H., *John Maynard Keynes: A Personal Biography of the Man Who Revolutionized Capitalism and the Way we Live*. New York: Macmillan, 1984.

Hiller, Susan, ed., *The Myth of Primitivism: Perspectives on Art*. London: Routledge, 1991.

Himmelfarb, Gertrude, *Marriage and Morals Among the Victorians*. New York: Alfred A. Knopf, 1986.

Hind, C. Lewis, "New Art and Newer Literature." *Daily Chronicle*, 24 March 1913, 4.

Hirschl and Adler, *British Modernist Art, 1905–1930*. New York: 1987.

Hirst, Francis W., *The Consequences of the War to Great Britain*. London: Humphrey Milford, 1934.

Hitchcock, Henry-Russell and Philip Johnson, *The International Style: Architecture Since 1922*. 1932, rpt. New York: W. W. Norton and Company, 1966.

Hoare, Philip, *Wilde's Last Stand: Decadence, Conspiracy and the First World War*. London: Duckworth, 1997.

Hogarth, Mary, *Modern Embroidery*. London: The Studio, 1933.

Holroyd, Michael, *Augustus John*. New York: Holt, Rinehart and Winston, 1975.

——, *Lytton Strachey: A Biography*. New York: Holt, Rinehart and Winston, 1971.

Holt, Gordon H. G., "The Merit of Le Corbusier." *Architectural Review*, vol. 63, April 1928, 124.

Holt, Richard, *Sport and the British: A Modern History*. Oxford: Clarendon Press, 1989.

Hooker, Denise, *Nina Hamnett: Queen of Bohemia*. London: Constable, 1986.

Howell, Georgina, *In Vogue: Seventy-five years of Style*. London: Condé Nast, 1991.

Hulme, T. E., "Modern Art—I: The Grafton Group." *The New Age*, 15 January 1914, 341–2.

Hunter, William, "*Film* by Rudolf Arnheim." *Scrutiny*, vol. 2, no. 3. September 1933, 211–12.

Huyssen, Andreas, *After the Great Divide: Modernism, Mass Culture, Postmodernism*. Bloomington: Indiana University Press, 1986.

Hyslop, T. B., "Post-Illusionism and the Art of the Insane." *Nineteenth Century*, February 1911, 270–81.

"Interesting Experiment," *The Times*, 19 September 1911.

Jacobs, Jane, *The Death and Life of Great American Cities*. New York: Random House, 1961.

Januszczak, Waldemar, "Fry's French delights." *Guardian*, 18 January 1984, 9.

John, Augustus, *Chiaroscuro: Fragments of Autobiography*. London: Arrow Books, 1952.

Johnson, Ellen H., ed., *American Artists on Art from 1940 to 1980*. New York: Harper and Row, 1982.

Johnston, Jill, *Secret Lives in Art: Essays on Art, Literature, Performance*. Chicago: Chicago Review Press, 1994.

Jones, Amelia, *Postmodernism and the En-Gendering of Marcel Duchamp*. Cambridge: Cambridge University Press, 1994.

Jones, Enid Huws, *Margery Fry: The Essential Amateur*. Oxford: Oxford University Press, 1966.

Kellogg, Stuart, ed., *Essays on Gay Literature*. New York: Harrington Park Press, 1985.

Keynes, John Maynard, *The Collected Writings of John Maynard Keynes*, 29 vols. London: Macmillan, St. Martin's Press for the Royal Economic Society, 1971–1983.

Keynes, Milo, ed., *Essays on John Maynard Keynes*. Cambridge: Cambridge University Press, 1975.

Kirstein, Lincoln, *Nijinsky Dancing*. New York: Alfred A. Knopf, 1975.

Konody, P. G., "Post-Impressionism in the Home." *Observer*, 14 December 1913, 8.

——, "Post-Impressionists at the Grafton Galleries." *Observer*, 13 November 1910, 9.

Kornwolf, James D., *M. H. Baillie Scott and the Arts and Crafts Movement*. Baltimore: Johns Hopkins Press, 1972.

Kozloff, Max, "An Interview with Robert Motherwell." *Artforum*, September 1965, 33–7.

Kramer, Hilton, *Revenge of the Philistines: Art and Culture 1972–1984*. New York: Free Press, 1985.

Krauss, Rosalind E., *The Optical Unconscious*. Cambridge, Mass.: MIT Press, 1993.

Kris, Ernst, *Psychoanalytic Explorations in Art*. New York: International Universities Press, 1952.

Kuenzli, Rudolf and Francis M. Naumann,

eds., *Marcel Duchamp: Artist of the Century*. Cambridge: MIT Press, 1989.

Lahor, Jean [pseud. for Henri Cazalis], *William Morris et le mouvement nouveau de l'art decoratif*. Geneva: Eggimann, 1897.

Laing, Donald A., *Roger Fry: An Annotated Bibliography of the Published Writings*. New York: Garland Publishing, Inc., 1979.

Lambert, R. C., *Parliamentary History of Conscription in Great Britain*. London: Allen & Unwin, 1917.

Lauter, Estella, *Women as Mythmakers: Poetry and Visual Art by Twentieth-Century Women*. Bloomington: Indiana University Press, 1984.

Lawrence, D. H., *Letters of D. H. Lawrence*, 7 vols. George J. Zytarck and James T. Bouton, eds. Cambridge: Cambridge University Press, 1979–93.

Le Corbusier, *The Four Routes*. Dorothy Todd, trans. London: Dennis Dobson Ltd., 1947.

——, *Towards a New Architecture*. Frederick Etchells, trans. New York: Holt, Rinehart & Winston, n.d.

Leavis, Q. D., "Caterpillars of the Commonwealth Unite!" *Scrutiny*, vol. 7, no. 2, September 1938, 203–14.

Lee, Hermione, *Virginia Woolf*. London: Chatto and Windus, 1996.

Lee, Hugh, ed., *A Cézanne in the Hedge and other memories of Charleston and Bloomsbury*. London: Collins and Brown, 1992.

Lehmann, John, *In My Own Time: Memoirs of a Literary Life*. 1955, rpt. Boston: Little, Brown and Co., 1969.

——, *In the Purely Pagan Sense*. London: Blond and Briggs, 1976.

——, *Virginia Woolf and her World*. New York: Harcourt Brace Jovanovich, 1975.

——, *The Whispering Gallery: Autobiography I*. London: Longman, Green, 1955.

LeMahieu, D. L., *A Culture for Democracy: Mass Communiciation and the Cultivated Mind in Britain Between the Wars*. Oxford: Clarendon, 1988.

Levine, Steven Z., "Décor/Decorative/Decoration in Claude Monet's Art." *Arts*, vol. 51, no. 6, February 1977, 136–9.

Lewis, Wyndham, *Apes of God*. London: Arthur Press, 1930.

——, *The Art of Being Ruled*. London: Chatto & Windus, 1926.

——, *Hitler*. London: Chatto and Windus, 1931.

——, *Wyndham Lewis on Art: Collected Writings, 1913–1956*. Walter Michel and C. J. Fox, eds. New York: Funk and Wagnalls, 1969.

Lhote, André, "A first visit to the Louvre." *Athenaeum*, 22 August 1919, 787–8.

——, "Cubism and the Modern Artistic Sensibility." *Athenaeum*, 19 September 1919, 914–15.

Lieven, Prince Peter, *The Birth of the Ballets-Russes*. L. Zarine, trans. 1936, rpt. New York: Dover Publications, Inc., 1973.

"Lord Benbow's Apartments, The Architecural Review Competition: Assessor's Report and Awards," *Architectural Review*, vol. 68, November and December 1930, 201–4, 242.

C. M., "Notes of the Month." *Colour*, March 1921, xiv–xx.

MacCarthy, Desmond, "The Art-Quake of 1910." *The Listener*, February 1945, 123–4, 129, rpt. *Memories*. London: MacGibbon and Kee, 1953, 178–85.

——, *Portraits*. London: MacGibbon & Kee, 1949.

——, "Post-Impressionist Frescoes." *The Eye-Witness*, vol. 1, no. 21, 9 November 1911, 661–2.

MacCarthy, Fiona, *The Simple Life: C. R. Ashbee in the Cotswolds*. Berkeley: University of California Press, 1981.

Macdonald, Nesta, *Diaghilev Observed by Critics in England and the United States, 1911–29*. New York: Dance Horizons, 1975.

MacGibbon, Jean, *There's the Lighthouse: A Biography of Adrian Stephen*. London: James and James, 1997.

"Manet and the Post-Impressionists," *Athenaeum*, 12 November 1910, 598–99.

Marcus, Steven, *The Other Victorians: A Study of Sexuality and Pornography in Mid-Nineteenth-Century England*. New York, Basic Books, Inc., 1966.

C. M. [Charles Marriott], "A Folk-Art Revival." *Evening Standard* [London], 25 March 1913.

Marsh, Edward, *A Number of People: A Book of Reminiscences*. London: William Heinemann, 1939.

Martin, Robert K. and George Piggford, eds., *Queer Forster*. Chicago: University of Chicago Press, 1997.

Marval, Jacqueline, "Les Danseurs de Flandrin." *L'Art Decoratif*, vol. 29, April 1913, 165–76.

Mason, Christopher, *Duncan Grant at Charleston* [film], 1970.

Masterman, C. F. G., *England After War*. London: Hodder and Stoughton, 1922.

Matisse, Henri, *Ecrits et propos sur l'art*. Dominique Fourcade, ed. Paris: Collection Savoir Hermann, 1972.

——, *Matisse on Art*. Jack D. Flam, ed. New York: Dutton, 1973.

McEvilley, Thomas, "Doctor Lawyer Indian Chief: '"Primitivism"' in 20th Century Art' at the Museum of Modern Art in 1984." *Artforum*, vol. 23, November 1984, 54–61.

McNeil, Peter, "Designing Women: Gender, Sexuality and the Interior Decorator, *c.*1890–1940." *Art History*, vol. 17, no. 4, December 1994, 631–57.

Medley, Robert, *Drawn from the Life: A Memoir*. London: Faber and Faber, 1983.

Meier-Graefe, Julius, "Hans von Marées." *Gazette des Beaux Arts*, vol. 51, 1909, 286–300.

——, *Modern Art*. 2 vols. Florence Simmonds and George W. Chrystal, trans. London: Heineman, 1908.

Melucci, Alberto, *Nomads of the Present: Social Movements and Individual Needs in Contemporary Society*. John Keane and Paul Mier, eds. Philadelphia: Temple University Press, 1989.

Merlhès, Victor, ed., *Correspondance de Paul Gauguin*. Paris: Fondation Singer-Polignac, 1984.

Meyer, Moe, ed., *The Politics and Poetics of Camp*. London: Routledge, 1994.

Meyers, Jeffrey, *The Enemy: A Biography of Wyndham Lewis*. Boston: Routledge and Kegan Paul, 1980.

The Minories, *The Eccentric A.H. Mackmurdo*. Colchester: 1979.

"Modern Embroidery," *Vogue* [London], late October 1923, 66–7, 78.

"Modern English Decoration," *Vogue* [London], early November 1924, 43–5, 106.

"A Modern Fresco Painter," *Vogue* [London], early September 1922, 66–7, 92.

Moore, G. E., *Principia Ethica*. 1903, rpt. Cambridge: University Press, 1966.

Morley, Catherine W., *John Ruskin: Late Work 1870–1890, The Museum and Guild of St. George: An Educational Experiment*. New York: Garland, 1984.

Morrell, Ottoline, *The Memoirs of Lady Ottoline Morrell: A Study in Friendship 1873–1915*. Robert Gathorne-Hardy, ed. New York: Knopf, 1964.

Morris, William, *The Collected Letters of William Morris*. 3 vols. Norman Kelvin, ed. Princeton: Princeton University Press, 1984.

——, *Collected Works of William Morris*. 24 vols. May Morris, ed. London: Longmans Green and Company, 1910–15.

——, *Selected Writings and Designs*. Asa Briggs, ed. London: Penguin, 1962.

——, *The Unpublished Lectures of William Morris*. Eugene D. Lemire, ed. Detroit: Wayne State University Press, 1969.

Mortimer, Raymond, *Duncan Grant*. Harmondsworth: Penguin, 1944.

——, "Saucers and Socialism." *New Statesman and Nation*, 27 October 1934, 585–6.

——, "Duncan Grant at the Independent Gallery." *Vogue* [London], late June 1923, 56–7.

——, "Lively Portraits: The Bloomsbury Set from the Inside." *Sunday Times* [London], 11 November 1956, 4.

——, "Modern Furniture and Decoration." *Architectural Review*, December 1930, 252–3.

"Mural Decoration: A Slade Experiment in Shadwell," *The Times* [London], 24 September 1924.

Murry, J. Middleton, "English Painting and French Influence." *Nation* [London], 31 January 1920, 600–01.

Museum of Modern Art, *Four Americans in Paris: The Collections of Gertrude Stein and her Family*. New York: 1970.

Muthesius, Stefan, "'We Do Not Understand What is Meant by a "Company" Designing': Design versus Commerce in Late-Nineteenth Century English Furnishing." *Journal of Design History*, vol. 5, no. 2, 1992, 113–19.

N., "A Duncan Grant Exhibition." *Manchester Guardian*, 9 November 1937, 12.

Nairn, Ian and Nikolaus Pevsner, *Surrey, The Buildings of England*, 2nd edn London: Penguin: 1970.

Nash, Paul, *Room and Book*. New York: Scribner's, 1932.

——, *Writings on Art*. Andrew Causey, ed. Oxford: Oxford University Press, 2000.

Naylor, Gillian, ed., *Bloomsbury: Its Artists, Authors and Designers*. Boston: Little, Brown and Company, 1990.

Neff, John Hallmark, "An Early Ceramic Triptych by Henri Matisse." *Burlington*, vol. 114, no. 837, December 1972, 848–53.

"The New Magpie and Stump—A Successful Experiment in Domestic Architecture," *Studio*, vol. 5, 1895, 67–74.

"A New Venture in Art: Exhibition at the Omega Workshops," *The Times* [London], 9 July 1913, 4.

Nicholson, Linda J., ed., *Feminism/Postmodernism*. New York: Routledge, 1990.

Nicolson, Benedict, "Post-Impressionism and Roger Fry," *Burlington*, vol. 93, January 1951, 10–15.

Nicolson, Nigel, ed., *Vita and Harold: The Letters of Vita Sackville-West and Harold Nicolson*. London: Weidenfeld and Nicolson, 1992.

Nijinsky, Romola, *Nijinsky*. New York: Simon and Schuster, 1934.

Noble, Jane Russell, ed., *Recollections of Virginia Woolf*. New York: William Morrow, 1972.

"The Normal and the Abnormal," *Morning Post*, 3 January 1914.

North, Michael, *Reading 1922*. Oxford: Oxford University Press, 1999.

"The Omega Workshops: Decorative Form and Colour," *The Times* [London], 10 December 1913, 13.

Orton, Fred and Griselda Pollock, *Avant-Gardes and Partisans Reviewed*. Manchester: Manchester University Press, 1996.

"The Painted Door," *Vogue* [London], early July 1926, 66.

Painter, Colin, ed., *Contemporary Art and the Home*. Oxford: Berg, 2002.

Panter-Downes, Mollie, "Charleston, Sussex." *New Yorker*, 18 August 1986, 61–7.

Partridge, Frances, *Memories*. London: Victor Gollancz, Ltd, 1981.

——, "Sitwells and Bloomsberries." *Charleston* 11, Spring/Summer 1995, 25–27.

Pater, Walter, *The Renaissance: Studies in Art and Poetry*. London: Macmillan, 1914 [first edition published as *Studies in the History of the Renaissance*. London: 1873].

Pattison, Bruce, "Music and the Community." *Scrutiny*, vol. 2, no. 4, March 1934, 399–404.

——, "Music in Decline." *Scrutiny*, vol. 3, no. 2, September 1934, 198–205.

Pemble, John, *The Mediterranean Passion: Victorians and Edwardians in the South*. Oxford: Oxford University Press, 1987.

Pevsner, Nikolaus, "Arthur H. Mackmurdo." *Architectural Review* 1938, rpt. *Studies in Art, Architecture, and Design*. London: Thames and Hudson, 1968, 132–9.

——, *An Enquiry into Industrial Art in England*. Cambridge: Cambridge University Press, 1937.

——, "Omega," *Architectural Review* 90. August 1941, 45–48.

——, *Pioneers of the Modern Movement*. London: Faber and Faber, 1936. Revised as *Pioneers of Modern Design from William Morris to Walter Gropius*. Harmondsworth: Penguin, 1964.

Phillips, Claude, "Paterson Gallery," *Daily Telegraph*, 16 February 1920.

Pierson, Stanley, *British Socialists: The Journey from Fantasy to Politics*. Cambridge, Mass.: Harvard University Press, 1979.

Plomer, William, *The Autobiography of William Plomer*. London: Cape, 1975.

"Picture Shocks: Originality at a Super-Post-Impressionist Exhibition," *Star* [London], 29 February 1913.

Poggi, Christine, *In Defiance of Painting: Cubism, Futurism, and the Invention of Collage*. New Haven: Yale University Press, 1992.

Poggioli, Renato, *The Theory of the Avant-Garde*. Gerald Fitzgerald, trans. Cambridge, Mass.: Harvard University Press, 1962.

Poiret, Paul, *En habillant l'époque*. Paris: Bernard Grasset, 1930.

Pollock, Griselda, *Vision and Difference: Femininity, Feminism, and Histories of Art*. London: Routledge, 1987.

"Post-Impressionism," *Nottingham Daily Guardian*, 8 January 1914.

"Post Impressionism: The Grafton Group," *Glasgow Daily Herald*, 8 January 1914.

"Post-Impressionism in the Home," *Pall Mall Gazette*, 11 April 1913, 3.

A Post-Impressionist Scribbler, "Pictorial Art in South London." *National Review* 58, December 1911, 648–56.

Powers, Alan, "Roger Fry and the Making of Durbins." *Charleston* 13, Spring/Summer 1996, 14–22.

Reade, Brian, ed., *Sexual Heretics: Male Homosexuality in English Literature from 1850 to 1900*. New York: Coward-McCann, Inc., 1970.

Reed, Christopher, "Bloomsbury Bashing: Homophobia and the Politics of Criticism in the Eighties." *Genders* 11, Fall 1991, 58–80.

——, "Durbins." *Charleston Newsletter* 21, June 1988, 23–6.

——, "Making History: The Bloomsbury Group's Construction of Aesthetic and Sexual Identity." *Gay and Lesbian Studies in Art History*, Whitney Davis, ed. New York: Haworth Press, 1994

Works Cited

(simultaneously released as *Journal of Homosexuality*, vol. 27, no. 1–2, 1994), 189–224.

——, ed., *Not At Home: The Suppression of Domesticity in Modern Art and Architecture*. London: Thames and Hudson, 1996.

——, Review: "The Impact of Modernism." *Charleston Newsletter* 22, December 1988, 43–5.

——, "Roger Fry: Art and Life." *Charleston* 20, Autumn/Winter 1999, 10–17.

——, "The Roger Fry Collection at the Courtauld Institute Galleries." *Burlington*, vol. 132, November 1990, 766–72.

——, "A Tale of Two Countries." *Charleston* 22, Autumn/Winter 2000, 35–9.

——, "Through Formalism: Feminism and Virginia Woolf's Relation to Bloomsbury Aesthetics." *Twentieth Century Literature*, vol. 38 no. 1, Spring 1992, 20–43, rpt. *The Multiple Muses of Virginia Woolf*, Diane F. Gillespie, ed. Columbia: University of Missouri Press, 1993, 11–35.

Reff, Theodore, *Degas: The Artist's Mind*. New York: Harper & Row, 1976.

Regan, Tom, *Bloomsbury's Prophet: G.E. Moore and the Development of his Moral Philosophy*. Philadelphia: Temple University Press, 1987.

Richardson, Elizabeth, *A Bloomsbury Iconography*. Winchester: St. Paul's Bibliographies, 1989.

Ricketts, Charles, *Self-Portrait*. Cecil Lewis, ed. London: Peter Davies, 1939.

Richmond, William Blake, "Post-Impressionists." *Morning Post*, 16 November 1910, 5.

Robbins, Daniel, "From Symbolism to Cubism: The Abbaye of Créteil." *Art Journal*, vol. 23, no. 2, Winter 1963–4, 111–15.

Robins, Anna Gruetzner, *Modern Art in Britain, 1910–1914*. London: Merrell Holberton, 1997.

Roches, Fernand, "Le Salon d'automne de 1912." *L'Art Décoratif*, vol. 28, November 1912, 281–28.

Rose, Phyllis, *Woman of Letters: A Life of Virginia Woolf*. London: Pandora, 1978.

Rosenbaum, S. P., ed., *The Bloomsbury Group: A Collection of Memoirs, Commentary and Criticism*. Toronto: University of Toronto Press, 1975.

——, *Edwardian Bloomsbury: The Early Literary History of the Bloomsbury Group*. New York: St. Martin's Press. 1994.

——, "Gaudier-Brzeska's Posthumous Sculpture for Roger Fry." *Charleston* 15, Spring/Summer 1997, 22–4.

——, *Victorian Bloomsbury: The Early Literary History of the Bloomsbury Group*. New York: St. Martin's Press, 1987.

Ross, Josephine, *Beaton in Vogue*. London: Condé Nast Publications, 1986.

Ross, Robert, "New Art in the Borough." *Morning Post*, 19 September 1911, 5.

——, *Robert Ross, Friend of Friends: Letters to Robert Ross, Art Critic and Writer, together with extracts from his published articles*. Ross, Margery, ed. London: Jonathan Cape, 1952.

Rothenstein, John, *Modern English Painters*, 3 vols. 1952, rpt. London: Macdonald & Co., 1984.

Rothenstein, William, *Men and Memories: A History of the Arts, 1872–1922*. New York: Tudor Publishing, n.d.

Rowbotham, Sheila and Jeffrey Weeks, *Socialism and the New Life: The Personal and Sexual Politics of Edward Carpenter and Havelock Ellis*. London: Pluto Press, 1977.

"The Royal Academy Exhibition," *Studio*, vol. 74, no. 303, June 1918, 12.

Rubin, William, ed., *"Primitivism" in Twentieth Century Art: Affinity of the Tribal and the Modern*. 2 vols. New York: Museum of Modern Art, 1984.

Ruskin, John., *The Works of Ruskin*. 39 vols. E. T. Cook and Alexander Wedderburn, eds. London: George Allen, 1905.

Rutter, Frank, "Extremes of Modern Painting." *Edinburgh Review*, April 1921, 298–315.

——, *Revolution in Art: An introduction to the study of Cezanne, Gauguin, Van Gogh, and other modern painters*. London: Art News Press, 1910.

Sadleir, Michael, *Michael Ernest Sadler*. London: Constable, 1949.

Said, Edward W., *Orientalism*. New York: Random House, 1978.

Saler, Michael T., *The Avant-Garde in Interwar England: Medieval Modernism and the London Underground*. Oxford: Oxford University Press, 1999.

Scheerbart, Paul, *Glasarchitektur*. Berlin: Verlag der Sturm, 1914.

Schorske, Carl, *Fin-de-Siècle Vienna*. New York: Knopf, 1980.

Scott, Amoret and Christopher. "A Sad Day at Penns-in-the-Rocks." *The Lady*, 28 February 1957.

Scottish Arts Council, *Colour Rhythm and Dance: Paintings and Drawings by J. D. Fergusson and his Circle in Paris*. Edinburgh: 1985.

Scrase, David and Peter Croft, *Maynard Keynes: Collector of pictures, books, and manuscripts*. Cambridge: Fitzwilliam Museum, 1983.

Sedgwick, Eve Kosofsky, *Between Men: English Literature and Male Homosocial Desire*. New York: Columbia University Press, 1985.

Sénéchal, Christian, *L'Abbaye de Créteil*. Paris: Librairie Andre Delpeuch, 1930.

Service, Alistair, *Edwardian Architecture*. London: Thames and Hudson, 1977.

Shiff, Richard, *Cézanne and the End of Impressionism: A Study of the Theory, Technique, and Critical Evaluation of Modern Art*. Chicago: University of Chicago Press, 1984.

Shone, Richard, *The Art of Bloomsbury: Roger Fry, Vanessa Bell and Duncan Grant*. London: Tate Gallery, 1999.

——, *Bloomsbury Portraits: Vanessa Bell, Duncan Grant, and Their Circle*. Oxford: Phaidon, 1976.

——, *Duncan Grant designer*. Liverpool: Bluecoat Gallery. 1980.

——, "The Friday Club." *Burlington*, vol. 117, May 1975, 279–84.

——, "Getting it Together: *The Art of Bloomsbury* at the Tate Gallery." *Charleston Magazine* 20, Fall/Winter 1999, 42–44.

——, "'Group' (1913): a sculpture by Roger Fry." *Burlington*, vol. 130, December 1988, 924–7.

——, "The Sitwells and the Art of the 1920s and 1930s." *Charleston* 11, Spring/Summer 1995, 15–17.

Shute, Nerina, *We Mixed Our Drinks: The Story of a Generation*. London: Jarrolds, n.d.

Sichel, Pierre, *Modigliani: A Biography of Amedeo Modigliani*. New York: E. P. Dutton, 1967.

Sickert, Walter, "A Critical Calendar." *English Review*, March 1912, 713–20.

——, "Idealism." *Art News* [London], 12 May 1910.

——, [unsigned], "A Monthly Chronicle: Roger Fry." *Burlington*, December 1915, 117–18.

——, "The Study of Drawing." *The New Age*, vol. 8 no. 7, 16 June 1910, 156–7.

Silhouette, "The Modern Movement in Continental Decoration. IV.—The Living-Room." *Architectural Review*, vol. 60, September 1926, 120.

Silver, Kenneth, *Esprit de Corps: The Art of the Parisian Avant-Garde and the First World War, 1914–1925*. Princeton: Princeton University Press, 1989.

Silverman, Debora L., *Art Nouveau in Fin-de-Siecle France: Politics, Psychology, and Style* Berkeley: University of California Press, 1989.

——, "The Brothers de Goncourts' Maison d'un Artiste." *Arts*, vol. 59 no. 9, May 1985, 119–29.

Sitwell, Edith and Osbert, *Twentieth Century Harlequinade and other Poems*. Oxford: B. H. Blackwell, 1916.

Sitwell, Osbert, *Great Morning!* Boston: Little, Brown and Company, 1947.

——, *Laughter in the Next Room*. Boston: Little, Brown and Company, 1948.

——, *Left Hand, Right Hand*. Boston: Little, Brown and Company, 1943.

——, *Noble Essences*. Boston: Little, Brown and Company, 1950.

——, *Queen Mary and Others*. New York: John Day, 1975.

——, "This Strange Country." *Architectural Review*, vol. 64, July 1928, 11–13.

Sitwell, Sacheverell, *The Hundred and One Harlequins*. London: Grant Richards, 1922.

——, *Southern Baroque Art: A Study of Painting, Architecture and Music in Italy and Spain of the 17th and 18th Centuries*. 1924, 3rd edn, London: Duckworth's Georgian Library, 1931.

——, *Laughter in the Next Room*, Boston: Little, Brown and Company, 1948.

Skidelsky, Robert, *John Maynard Keynes: The Economist as Savior, 1920–1937*. New York: Allen Lane, 1994.

——, *John Maynard Keynes: Hopes Betrayed, 1883–1920*. New York: Viking, 1983.

Smith, Timothy d'Arch, *Love in Earnest: Some Notes of the Lives and Writings of English 'Uranian' Poets from 1889 to 1950*. London: Routledge & Kegan Paul, 1970.

Solomon-Godeau, Abigail, "Going Native." *Art in America*, July 1989, 119–27, 161.

Spalding, Frances, *Duncan Grant: A Biography*. London: Chatto and Windus, 1997.

——, *Roger Fry: Art and Life*. New York: Granada, 1980.

——, *Portraits by Roger Fry*. London: Courtauld Institute Galleries, 1976.

——, *Vanessa Bell*. London: Weidenfeld & Nicolson, 1983.

Speaight, Robert, *The Life of Eric Gill*. New York: P. J. Kenedy and Sons, 1966.

Spear, Jeffrey L., *Dreams of an English Eden: Ruskin and His Tradition in Social Criticism*. New York: Columbia University Press, 1984.

Spink [Gallery], *Duncan Grant and Vanessa Bell: Design and Decoration 1910–1960*. London: 1991.

Stansky, Peter, *On or About December 1910: Early Bloomsbury and its Intimate World*. Cambridge, Mass.: Harvard University Press, 1996.

——, *Redesigning the World: William Morris, the 1880s and the Arts and Crafts*. Princeton: Princeton University Press, 1985.

—— and William Abrahams, *Journey to the Frontier, Julian Bell and John Cornford: Their Lives and the 1930s*. London: Constable, 1966.

Steinberg, Leo, *Other Criteria: Confrontations with Twentieth-Century Art*. New York: Oxford University Press, 1972.

Stephen, Leslie, ed., *Dictionary of National Biography*. London: Smith, Elder, and Co., 1886.

Stephenson, Andrew, "Strategies of Situation: British Modernism and the Slump, c. 1929–34." *Oxford Art Journal*, vol. 14, no. 2, 1991, 30–51.

Strachey, Barbara and Jayne Samuels, eds., *Mary Berenson: A Self Portrait from Her Diaries and Letters*. New York: W. W. Norton, 1983.

Strachey, Lytton, *Eminent Victorians*. New York: Harcourt Brace, 1918.

Works Cited

——, *Lytton Strachey by Himself: a Self-Portrait.* Michael Holroyd, ed. London: Heinemann, 1971.

——, *Queen Victoria.* New York: Harcourt, Brace, 1921.

——, *The Really Interesting Question and Other Papers.* Paul Levy, ed. London: George Weidenfeld and Nicholson, 1972, rpt. New York: Capricorn Books, 1974.

——, *The Shorter Strachey.* Michael Holroyd, ed. Oxford: Oxford University Press, 1980.

——, [pseud: Ignotus]. "The Sicilians." *Spectator* 100, 29 February 1908, 336–7.

Strong, Roy, "Why Omega is the last word." *Financial Times*, 26 January 1984, 19.

"Studio Talk," *Studio*, vol. 19, 1900, 192–4.

Symonds, John Addington. *Male Love: A Problem in Greek Ethics and Other Writings.* John Lauritsen, ed. New York: Pagan Press, 1983.

——, *The Memoirs of John Addington Symonds.* Phyllis Grosskurth, ed. New York: Random House, 1984.

——, *Studies of the Greek Poets*, 2 vols. 3rd edn London: Adam and Charles Black, 1893.

Tate Gallery. *Duncan Grant.* London: 1959.

——, *Illustrated Catalog of Acquisitions 1984–86.* London: Tate Gallery, 1986.

——, *Duncan Grant: A display to celebrate his 90th birthday.* London: 1975.

R[obert] R[attray] T[atlock], "Modern Designs in Needlework." *Burlington*, October 1925, 209–10.

Thompson, E. P., *William Morris: From Romantic to Revolutionary.* 2nd edn. London: Merlin Press, 1971.

Tickner, Lisa, *Modern Life and Modern Subjects: British Art in the Early Twentieth Century.* London: Yale University Press, 2000.

——, *The Spectacle of Women: Imagery of the Suffrage Campaign, 1907–14.* Chicago: University of Chicago Press, 1988.

——, "Vanessa Bell: Studland Beach, Domesticity, and 'Significant Form.'" *Representations* 65, Winter 1999, 63–92.

Tillyard, S. K., *The Impact of Modernism, 1900–1920.* New York: Routledge, 1988.

Todd, Dorothy and Raymond Mortimer, *The New Interior Decoration.* London: B. T. Batsford, 1929.

Todd, Pamela, *Bloomsbury at Home.* London: Pavilion, 1999.

Torgovnick, Marianna, *Gone Primitive: Savage Intellects, Modern Lives.* Chicago: University of Chicago Press, 1990.

Tranter, Rachel, *Vanessa Bell: A Life of Painting.* London: Cecil Woolf, 1998.

Troly-Curtin, Marthe, "Phyrnette's Letters to Lonely Soldiers." *Sketch*, 4 October 1916, 4.

Troy, Nancy, *Modernism and the Decorative Arts in France: Art Nouveau to Le Corbusier.* New Haven: Yale University Press, 1991.

Turnbaugh, Douglas Blair, *Duncan Grant and the Bloomsbury Group.* Secaucus, N.J.: Lyle Stuart, 1987.

——, *Private: The Erotic Art of Duncan Grant, 1885–1978.* London: Gay Men's Press, 1989.

Université de Saint-Etienne, *Le Retour á l'ordre dans les arts plastiques et l'architecture, 1919–1925.* Centre Interdisciplinaire d'Etudes et de Recherche sur l'Expressions Contemporaine, 1974.

Vallance, Aymer, *The Art of William Morris.* London: George Bell & Sons, 1897.

Vassar College Art Museum, *Vanessa Bell.* Poughkeepsie: 1984.

Venturi, Robert, Denise Scott Brown, and Steven Isenour, *Learning from Las Vegas*, 2nd edn. Cambridge, Mass.: MIT Press, 1977.

Voysey, C. F. A., "Remarks on Domestic Entrance Halls." *Studio*, vol. 21, January 1901.

Walden, Russell, ed., *The Open Hand: Essays on Le Corbusier.* Cambridge, Mass.: MIT Press, 1977.

Watkins, Nicholas, *Matisse.* New York: Oxford University Press, 1985.

Watney, Simon, *The Art of Duncan Grant.* London: John Murray, 1990.

——, "Critics and Cults." *Charleston Newsletter* 17, December 1986, 25–9.

——, *English Post-Impressionism.* London: Studio Vista, 1980.

——, *Policing Desire: Pornography, AIDS, and the Media.* London: Methuen, 1987.

Webb, Michael, "A Last Flourish of Aestheticism." *Country Life*, 2 January 1964, 16–17.

Weeks, Jeffrey, *Coming Out: Homosexual Politics in Britian from the Nineteenth Century to the Present.* London: Quartet Books, 1977.

Wees, William C., *Vorticism and the English Avant-Garde.* Toronto: University of Toronto Press, 1972.

Weintraub, Stanley, *Whistler: A Biography.* New York: Weybright & Talley, 1974.

Weld-Blundell, C. J., "Manet and the Post-Impressionists." *The Times* [London], 7 November 1910, 11–12.

Wellesley, Dorothy, *Far Have I Travelled.* London: James Barrie, 1952.

Wells, H. G., ed., *Socialism and the Great State: Essays in Construction.* New York: Harper & Brothers, 1912.

Welsh-Ovcharov, Bogomila, *Vincent Van Gogh and the Birth of Cloisonism.* Toronto: Art Gallery of Ontario, 1981.

Whistler, Laurence, *The Laughter and the Urn: The Life of Rex Whistler.* London: Weidenfeld and Nicolson, 1985.

White, Palmer, *Poiret.* London: Studio Vista, 1973.

Whitman, Walt, *Complete Poetry and Selected Prose.* James E. Miller, ed. Boston: Houghton Mifflin Co., 1959.

Wilcox, Denys J., *The London Group, 1913–39.* Aldershot, U.K.: Scolar Press, 1995.

Wilde, Oscar, *The Complete Works of Oscar Wilde.* 10 vols [not numbered]. Robert Ross, ed. Boston: Wyman-Fogg, Co., n.d.

Wilenski, R. H. and John Gloag, "Two Points of View." *Architectural Review*, vol. 71, April 1932, 149.

Williams, Val, *Women Photographers: The Other Observers 1900 to the Present.* London: Virago, 1986.

Willsdon, Clare A. P., *Mural Painting in Britain 1840–1940: Image and Meaning.* Cambridge: Cambridge University Press, 2000.

Wolff, Janet, *Feminine Sentences: Essays on Women and Culture.* Berkeley: University of California Press, 1990.

Wollen, Peter, "Fashion/Orientalism/The Body." *New Formations* 1, Spring 1987, 5–33. Rpt. *Raiding the Icebox.* Bloomington: Indiana University Press, 1993, 1–34.

Woolf, Leonard, *Barbarians at the Gate.* London: V. Gollancz, Ltd, 1939 [American edition titled *Barbarians Within and Without.* New York: Harcourt, Brace, 1939].

——, *Beginning Again: An Autobiography of the Years 1911–1918.* London: Hogarth Press, 1963.

——, *Downhill all the Way: An Autobiography of the Years 1919 to 1939.* London: Hogarth Press, 1967.

——, *Sowing: An Autobiography, 1880–1904.* London: Hogarth Press, 1960.

——, *Quack, Quack.* London: Hogarth Press, 1935.

Woolf, Virginia. *Books and Portraits: Some further selection from the literary and biographical writings of Virginia Woolf.* Mary Lyon, ed. New York: Harcourt Brace Jovanovich, 1977.

——, *Collected Essays.* 4 vols. London: Hogarth Press, 1966–7.

——, *The Complete Shorter Fiction.* Susan Dick, ed. London: Triad Grafton Books, 1985.

——, *The Diary of Virginia Woolf.* 5 vols. Anne Olivier Bell and Andrew McNeillie, eds. New York: Harcourt Brace Jovanovich, 1977–1984.

——, *Freshwater: a comedy.* Lucio P. Ruotolo, ed. New York: Harvest/HBJ, 1976.

——, *The Letters of Virginia Woolf.* 6 vols. Nigel Nicolson and Joanne Trautmnn, eds. New York: Harcourt Brace Jovanovich, 1975–1981.

——, *The London Scene: Five Essays by Virginia Woolf.* New York: Frank Hallman, 1975.

——, *Moments of Being*, 2nd edn. Jeanne Schulkind, ed. New York: Harvest/HBJ, 1985.

——, *The Pargiters.* Mitchell A. Leaska, ed. London: Hogarth Press, 1978.

——, *Roger Fry.*1940, rpt. New York: Harcourt Brace Jovanovich, 1968.

——, *A Room of One's Own.* 1929, rpt. New York: Harcourt Brace Jovanovich, 1957.

——, *Three Guineas.* London: Hogarth Press, 1938.

——, *To the Lighthouse.* London: Hogarth Press, 1927.

——, *Walter Sickert: a Conversation.* London: Hogarth Press, 1934.

——, and Roger Fry, *Victorian Photographs of Famous Men and Fair Women by Julia Margaret Cameron.* London: Hogarth Press, 1926, rpt. [with more and different illustrations] Boston: David R. Godine, 1973.

"The Work of Some Modern Decorative Artists," *Vogue* [London], late August 1926, 27–31, 68.

Workman, Gillian, "Leonard Woolf and Imperialism." *Ariel*, vol. 6 no. 2, 1975, 1–21.

Zwerdling, Alex, *Virginia Woolf and the Real World.* Berkeley: University of California Press, 1986.

Works Cited

Index

Photographic Acknowledgements